UPPER FALLS, RUMFORD.

THE

WATER-POWER OF MAINE,

BY

WALTER WELLS,

SUPERINTENDENT

HYDROGRAPHIC SURVEY OF MAINE.

AUGUSTA:
SPRAGUE, OWEN & NASH, PRINTERS TO THE STATE.
1869.

PREFACE.

In accordance with the recommendation of Gov. Chamberlain, an exploration of the water-power of the State was ordered by the Legislature of 1867, and was entered upon under the general supervision of a Commission, consisting of Hons. John A. Poor, A. D. Lockwood and Hannibal Hamlin. The Commissioners, having conducted the enterprise through its preliminary stage, retired at the close of 1867, and should not, accordingly, be held responsible for any shortcomings of this Report.

In regard to the *arrangement* of the water-powers, (in Part III,) it need only be explained that such powers as are located in *townships without proper names*, will be found under the letter T. All others appear under the names of the towns, townships, etc., in the appropriate alphabetical place.

In the selection of water-falls for *pictorial illustration*, no regard was had to picturesque effects, but simply to the value of the privileges for manufacturing purposes. So many powers of equal value remain unrepresented, that each of those shown may be regarded as the type of a class. Multitudes of cascades in the mountainous parts of the State present extraordinary attractions to the artist and tourist, but less to the manufacturer, and could not be exhibited in a work of this strictly economical character. Nearly all the sketches and drawings for the engravings were made by Mr. George F. Morse, Superintendent of the Portland Company's Locomotive and Machine Works, Portland.

A proper *Water-Power Map* of the State was intended, giving the location and height of each fall and rapid, the areas and storage of the lakes and ponds, the sites of artificial reservoirs, etc. It was found impracticable, however, to collect the necessary data in season for this Report. The Map given, shows the position, form, and relative size of the several river-basins, the courses and principal affluents of the streams, their chief lake connections, and the lines of railroad.

An *Index* to Parts I and II, and to the first Division of Part III, is appended to the Report. The second Division of Part III, constituting much the larger part of the whole volume, needs no index, or no other index than is involved in the alphabetical arrangement of the towns.

TABLE OF CONTENTS.

PART I.

MAINE AS A WATER-POWER DISTRICT.

DIVISION I.

GEOGRAPHICAL, TOPOGRAPHICAL AND RELATED CONDITIONS.

DIVISION II.

METEOROLOGICAL CONDITIONS.

DIVISION III.

MISCELLANEOUS MATTER.

PART II.

THE PRINCIPAL RIVER SYSTEMS OF MAINE.

DIVISION I.

THE PRIMARY OR INTERIOR SYSTEMS.

DIVISION II.

THE SECONDARY OR SEABOARD SYSTEMS.

PART III.

THE WATER-POWERS OF MAINE.

DIVISION I.

MISCELLANEOUS AND GENERAL VIEWS OF THE WATER-POWERS.

DIVISION II.

STATISTICAL AND DESCRIPTIVE VIEWS OF THE WATER-POWERS.

ILLUSTRATIONS.

ERRATA.

Please make the following corrections before reading :

Page 21, second paragraph, seventh line, insert "to" between "however" and "the."

Page 72, Chapter XV., second line, "southeast," should be "southwest."

Page 92, seventh line, "feet" should follow "cubic."

Page 111, last two lines should be interchanged.

Page 181, about middle of page, "Holbrook" should be "Hotbrook" in both cases.

MEMORANDA.

Information respecting the *volume of water* on the Penobscot river, will be found in the Appendix, the same having been communicated too late for insertion in Chapter XVIII. Will the reader please make a note of this on page 105.

Under the heading "Orono," page 383, please mark [See also "Bradley and Orono," in Appendix] the matter given in the Appendix came too late for insertion in the proper place.

Also under the heading "Oldtown," page 382, please mark [See also "Bradley and Oldtown," in Appendix.]

Under "Milford," page 360, mark [See also "Milford and Oldtown," in Appendix.]

PART I.

Maine as a Water-Power District.

DIVISION I.

Geographical, Topographical and Related Conditions.

CHAPTER I.

GEOGRAPHICAL AND CONTINENTAL POSITION.

Section 1.—Geographical Position.

Maine lies between 43° 6′ and 47° 27′ 33″ N. lat.; between 66° 56′ 48″ and 71° 6′ 41″ W. lon. The 45th parallel crosses the State within thirty miles of its geographical centre. This position, almost precisely equidistant betwixt the equator and the pole, influences the water-power of the State in an important degree, and chiefly through its *meteorological* conditions.

In the mid latitudes.

In consequence of this position the rainfall of the State is drawn upon for only the proportion of evaporation due to a *moderate temperature*, is neither burned away in long-sustained and excessive heat, nor converted *wholly* and for months into snow and ice, in either of which events the sources of constant water-supply would be cut off, and water-power as an economical motor be put out of the question.

Consequent temperature and the effects thereof.

In further consequence of this position the *winds* of Maine are *variable*, not constant like those of the tropics, nor periodical like those of the Indian peninsulas. They prevail during the year for a longer or shorter time from every quarter of the compass, and bring therefrom every variety of heat and cold, of moisture and dryness, in succession. The draft rarely prevails from any one compass point for more than two or three days successively, so that the various climatic phases attendant upon change of wind follow one another in rapid succession.

Consequent character of the winds.

Consequent character of the rains.

It further results from the geographic position of the State that the *precipitation of moisture* in Maine is *non-periodic*. It takes place in the form of either rain or snow, at all seasons of the year, and tends therefore to furnish water-power at all seasons of the year. Its fall is gentle, occupies not unfrequently several days for the deposition of a single inch of water. It therefore rarely impairs the availability of our water-power with sudden and great inundations. It is generally associated with a more or less protracted continuance of cloud, or fog, or mist, which lessens evaporation, and by consequence augments the volume of the rivers.

Sum of effect.

In short, it is only in the mid latitudes that water-power can, in general, be counted upon as an available motor, and the position of Maine is such as to command this advantage at its maximum.

Section 2.—Continental Position.

Under the lee of the continent.

The first point to be remarked under this head is the location of Maine on the *leeward side of the continent* in the latitude of prevalent westerly winds. By prevalent, is meant predominating over any other single system of winds from any other quarter of the compass; and not predominating over all the others in combination. By westerly, are particularly specified the winds between south of west and north of northwest. The winds referred to are emphatically continental winds. They are arid at all seasons. At all seasons they tend to reduce the volume of rainfall and to absorb it, when precipitated, in thirsty evaporations. Their influence, therefore, is not favorable to either the volume or constancy of our water-power.

In the rain draft from the Gulf of Mexico.

The second feature in the continental position of Maine is its location in the draft of the *southwest winds from the Gulf of Mexico*. This great mediterranean sea is remarkable for its singular elevation of temperature, by which it is constituted an evaporating caldron, 800,000 square miles in area. The prevalent winds from and over this heated sea are southwest—the southwest *return-trades* of the north-temperate zone. Maine lies directly in the track of this great humid draft; and it is in fact, though not so in appearance, the vapor of this wind that is precipitated upon us in our so-called northeasterly storms, the rain being furnished in large measure by an upper current whose movement is opposite to the northeast drift beneath. The deposition is relatively more abundant in Maine than further south, by reason of the low temperature of the State, to be noticed subsequently.

On the seaboard.

In the third place *Maine is situated upon the coast.* It is not an inland but a maritime region. Whatever favorable conditions as respects rainfall, abated summer heat, humid atmosphere, and surplus moisture for water-power, attach to this position, Maine enjoys in equal measure with any of the Atlantic seaboard States.

Projected from the U. S. coast line.

In the fourth place Maine projects to the eastward from the general coast line of the United States, so that south, southeast, and in part southwest winds reach its shores *directly from the ocean,* charged with oceanic influences. So that in addition to a substantially equal ocean exposure on the east, it enjoys one to the south. South winds are quite prevalent in Maine through the summer for a part of the day, blowing with very considerable power as a diurnal sea breeze. These winds are moist and cool, and so in such degree as quite seriously to affect the process of hay-making and grain-curing. They therefore check evaporation, and thus exercise an important influence upon the volume of the rivers.

In short, the position of Maine is such that from the west of south to the north of east through east, the winds are *oceanic,* and from the north of east to west of north are sufficiently recent from the passage over watery areas to be marine in character. In other words, the winds from the direction of Cape Cod Bay round by Newfoundland to Hudson's Bay, or from two-thirds of the compass, taken as a whole, are *maritime* winds.

Situated at the northeast corner of the grand division.

The last feature to be remarked in the continental position of Maine is its location so *near the northeast angle of the continent.* As is well known, the entire circulation of the Arctic ocean—including all the waters originally drawn into it via Behring's Straits and the great current on the north of Europe—after having been reduced to icy temperature by long exposure in the polar basin and become loaded with enormous masses of ice, is poured in a constant and voluminous stream down by the east coast of Greenland, by Baffin's Bay and the channels of the archipelago north of Hudson's Bay, directly upon our northeastern continental frontier. These frigid waters fill up Hudson's Bay, the Gulf of St. Lawrence, and their outlying appendages, and are carried as an inshore drift of somewhat abated temperature off our coast.*

Hence our winds from the north, northeast and east, are at all seasons of a marked low temperature, and their effect is at all seasons to abate evaporation and increase the discharge of the rivers.

Gulf-Stream vapors.

Still further, by another remarkable geographical arrangement, enormous volumes of water of almost tropical temperature are borne in an extensive ocean current from the southwest, and, a few hundred miles east of our domain, or off Newfoundland, are brought into sudden contact with the polar drift before remarked. The atmosphere overhanging the warm current—the Gulf Stream—is charged with immense quantities of moisture. Upon contact with the cold atmosphere incumbent upon the polar drift, the moisture is condensed, covering thousands of square miles with thick and comparatively constant fogs, burying up the Grand Banks, the Gulf of St. Lawrence, and the adjacent ocean and land in their dense volumes, and giving to the whole region an inglorious celebrity in the annals and estimation of seamen.

These vapors are brought in by east and northeast winds, and sometimes involve a considerable part of the State for days, and with some interludes, for weeks together, especially during the latter part of summer. The cool fogs of the Dog days, a most grateful feature of our climate in contrast with the sultry heats experienced at that season in the interior, are derived from the source in question. Not wholly, however, as an important portion of our summer fog comes from the southward, consisting of the warm humidity of a lower section of the Gulf Stream condensed by passage over the cold drift along our coast. The effect of the fog is, as observed at Bowdoin College, to reduce the temperature in summer, 6°·5 below the normal.

Practical effect thereof.

The obvious effect of the atmospheric condition thus induced, which exhibits itself in various forms, misty, foggy, hazy, vaporous, is, greatly to abate the evaporating intensity of the sun and to reserve a large proportion of the rainfall for removal by rivers. This effect is the more influential, because, as just observed, it is exerted with the most energy in the mid and late heats of summer, when the streams tend to run lowest. It

* The *Clione limacina*, a marine animal strictly Arctic in habits and associations, has been observed in vast numbers in Portland harbor.

contributes also essentially to the sum of water precipitated, though the amount of this as defined from that furnished by the rain-bearing southwest winds, cannot probably be determined.

Sum of the effect of continental position.

The practical effects of the continental position of Maine, as exerted upon the matter in hand, may be summed up as follows:—As inducing a rainfall materially above that due to astronomic position, as diminishing evaporation very considerably below the normal; as therefore necessitating an unusual volume in the rivers, an unusual constancy of the volume, and by consequence and in the last result, further necessitating uncommon resources of water-power, so far as this is dependent upon a copious flow in the streams.

CHAPTER II.

HORIZONTAL AND VERTICAL DIMENSIONS.

Section 1.—Horizontal Dimensions.

Details of.

Maine extends through 302 statute miles in latitude and 288 statute miles in longitude. The general periphery of the State, measured as nearly as practicable in a right line, is about 875 miles. Measured with allowance for the principal flexures it is somewhat over 1,000 miles; but including the sinuosities of the shore, of boundary river courses and highland ridges, it is estimated not less than 3,700 miles, of which from 2,000 to 3,000 are coast. The length of the shore line in a nearly direct course is about 226 miles. The territorial area of the State is about 31,500 square miles, or 1,200 square miles less than all the rest of New England combined.

Annual receipt of moisture determined by.

The annual rainfall upon this breadth of country, assumed at 42 inches, if accumulated to the depth of Lake Erie, would cover 871 square miles; and if to the depth of the German Ocean, would still constitute a lake of 170 square miles' extent. Its total measure is about 3,073,000,000,000, or not far from three trillion cubic feet. Upon supposition that 40 per cent. of the whole rainfall is removed by drainage, the annual discharge from our surface by rivers would amount to 1,229,200,000,000, or nearly one and a quarter trillion cubic feet, equal to 3,368,000,000 cubic feet per day. These figures, therefore, represent approximately our annual and diurnal sum of water-power material, as determined by our yearly rainfall, by evaporation, and our horizontal dimensions.

Section 2.—General Elevation.

Estimated figure of the elevation of Maine.

The mean elevation of a country is one of the most difficult of its physical conditions to ascertain, and is generally one of the last to be ascertained. After exploring all sources of information within reach, as the surveys of the British and our own government, made in connection with the N. E. Boundary controversy, surveys for railroads, surveys for canals, and private explorations in special localities, the observations involved being several hundred in number,* I have fixed upon the figure 600 feet as very nearly expressing the mean height of the surface of our State above the level of the sea.

Resultant theoretical or gross water-power.

The 1,229,200,000,000 cubic feet, more or less, of water annually delivered by our rivers, fall therefore on their passage to the sea through the mean distance of 600 feet, and in their descent yield a gross power of 4,429 horse for each foot of fall. This being multiplied by the total average fall in feet, gives 2,656,200 horse-powers gross, which are equivalent to the working energy of over 34,000,000 men, laboring without intermission from year's end to year's end.

The power, if its efficiencies were concentrated into the ordinary working hours in manufactories, namely, eleven, for 312 days per annum, would be equal to 6,623,100 horse.

Not all susceptible of improvement.

Of course a very considerable fraction of the force alluded to, exists where circumstances prevent it from being of present economical value, some of it where it can never be made of account as a source of power; much of it is consumed in overcoming the friction and resistance encountered by the waters on their passage to the tide, and much of it enters the ocean in the form of the *velocity* of rivers. But there still remains an enormous sum of power that can be made available for use at low cost, as is demonstrated in Part III. of this Report. As to the actual amount that can be brought into use for the usual working hours of the year, with an expenditure that would be deemed reasonable at now existing prices of mechanical power, it is a sufficiently close approximation to assign a figure between one and two millions of horse-powers.

* A portion of these will be found in Part II., in connection with other *details*.

Subsection A.—THE ELEVATION AS DISPOSED IN SLOPES. The state surface as disposed in its different parts with respect to height above sea level, exhibits the following grand features: First, an acclivity or ascending slope from the shore line 140 miles into the interior. Secondly, from the divide or water-shed ridge there reached, a counter slope or declivity extending 78 miles in the widest part to the northern boundary. Thirdly, a general falling off of the surface from west to east, the altitudes above the sea being less as the distances from the White-Mountain highland are greater.

The slopes.

The divide separating the first two slopes has a height above sea level varying from 1,800 feet in the west to 600 in the east, 1,085 feet on the average.* The crest of elevation bounding the third slope on the west, is for a long distance elevated not far from 2,000 feet, and determines the flow of waters from the adjacent State into our own.

Their boundary and dividing ridges.

The three grand features of surface conformation specified, account for and determine the directions of our rivers, which being reduced to a mean for all the streams, are south-southeast in the southern portion of the State, and east-northeast in the northern.

General movement of our fluviatile waters.

The territory north of the cross ridge is called the *Northern Slope*, south of it, the *Southern Slope*. The area of the former is 7,400 square miles, of the latter 24,100 square miles.

Names and areas of the slopes.

Subsection B.—CHARACTERISTICS OF THE SLOPES. The Northern Slope is marked by a *comparative uniformity of elevation* over its different parts. The descent from the water-shed ridge on the south to the St. John on the north, is not sufficient to give more than a slow movement to the streams; and the depression of the whole basin to the eastward is so slight that the current of the St. John itself is moderate. The Aroostook leaves the State at the elevation of 345 feet, and the St. John, of 419 feet above tide, and that amount of fall is accordingly lost to the State —not gained, however, it may be added, with two or three important exceptions, to the adjacent province for the purposes of *power*, for there is comparatively little available power upon them beyond State. Such is the general levelness of the surface of the Northern Slope that quite extensive districts are permanently

Of the Northern Slope.

* *Ex-parte* N. E. Boundary Survey.

swampy; rapids and falls are much less numerous and less strongly marked than upon the Southern Slope, and the rivers of the region are, therefore, as a whole, of somewhat inferior consequence as tributary to the water-power of the State—inferior as compared with those of the southern section.

Features of the Southern Slope. Its pitch seaward.

The features of the Southern Slope affecting its water-power are of a most decided character. First, its *general pitch seaward*—which as defined by a total mean descent of 1,085 feet in a mean distance of about 140 miles, corresponds to an angular depression of 5′, circular measurement, per mile—is sufficient to constitute the region proper water-power country; sufficient to carry off the surplus waters without protracted exposure and waste; not sufficient to hurry them off in unmanageble volumes to be succeeded by dearth, and sufficient to secure a great number of privileges upon which the waters can be used over and over again. The slope is most rapid in the western part of the State, and, by consequence, in that part, other things being equal, water-power is most abundant.

Uniform distribution of its declivity.

Secondly, the declivity of the Southern Slope is to an unusual degree *distributed uniformly from its upper or interior limit to the ocean.* Many water-sheds use up the greater part of their fall near their upper or interior limit, where the streams are yet too small and inconstant for water-power, so that through the lower part of their course the rivers move upon almost a level, and however valuable for the purposes of navigation afford no facilities for manufacturing. Our Southern water-shed on the contrary descends with comparative uniformity to the sea, the last steps being taken in numerous instances close on the coast line, as at Kennebunk, Saco, Falmouth, Brunswick, Warren, Ellsworth, Cherryfield, Columbia Falls, Machias, Dennysville, etc. Water-power, accordingly, so far as dependent upon the general descent of the water-shed, may be expected to be found across the entire breadth of the Slope from the interior to the sea, and it is so found.

Other features.

Other features of the Slope favorably affecting its relations to water-power, as its brokenness of surface, the hardness of its rocks and their arrangement, the feasibility of natural and artificial reservoirs, etc., will be considered hereinafter, under the appropriate heads.

Section 3.—MOUNTAINS.

The mountains of Maine are characterized by the following features: First, in a geographical comparison their *size and height are insignificant.* Their loftiest peak stands in the sixth rank on the scale of elevation, it being less than one mile high. Secondly, they consist not of *ridges,* which formation is impressed upon the Appalachian Chain in the middle and southern parts, but of *peaks,* generally more or less conical in form, standing sometimes in isolation, sometimes in clusters, sometimes in short ranges of greater or less continuity. Thirdly, they are comparatively *bare of dirt,* especially about their summits,—they are out-croppings of bald rock and not immense swells of land. Fourthly, about their bases they are *heavily wooded.*

Their leading features.

Consider the bearing of these several characteristics upon the water-power of the State. Streams from and among mountains of great height are worthless for power purposes, being alternately overwhelming torrents and attenuated rills. Thus the Ardèche in France, an Alpine stream, with a catchment basin of about 925 square miles, a little larger than that of the East and West Machias, sometimes rises sixty feet in the lower part of its course, and its volume sometimes goes up from a few score to 8,845 cubic yards per second, or more than the mean delivery of the Nile, whose basin is nearly a thousand times larger. Some of our mountain streams, as the Wild river, Swift river, Ellis river, and others, specified in Part III., fluctuate considerably, and are of comparatively little value on this account as working streams, but they do not vary enough or are not large enough to affect seriously the rivers into which they empty.

Their effect as regards the uniformity of river volumes.

The conical form and dispersed arrangement of our mountains result in the expression of less moisture from the clouds upon their windward slopes than would occur upon continuous ridges, and by consequence in a more *equal diffusion* of rainfall in all parts. There is a somewhat heavier downfall upon one slope of our mountains than upon the other according to the direction of the rain wind. Thus the Saco rises very rapidly in south and southeast storms, the upper Androscoggin in northeast storms, owing to the unequal deposition upon the opposite slopes of the White Mountains. The Willey family perished in a southeast rain.

As regards the diffusion of rainfall.

As our mountains thus exercise some influence upon the distribution of rainfall, so they doubtless exercise

As regards the amount of rainfall.

some influence upon the *amount of rainfall*, increasing it in a degree. The amount, however, is not great, but there are no data for determining definitely how great. The Saco and Androscoggin rivers are the principal gainers by whatever it may be.

As regards the retention of snow.

Our mountains are not sufficiently high to *preserve snow all the year*; of course, therefore, they fail to contribute to the volume and constancy of the streams from this source for the whole year. They do, however, conserve the accumulations of winter until the last of June in their ravines and forests, and through these add to the volume of the rivers. The White Hills do not lose their snow wholly during the year, and the resulting gain is to a large extent ultimately ours, by reason of the diversion of the Saco and Androscoggin into our domain.

Effect of the nakedness of our mountain summits.

The comparative nakedness or denudation of soil of our mountain summits, tends to the sudden precipitation of water into the drainage channels. This tendency is however checked by the mass of spongy vegetable deposit in the forests about the bases of the mountains, which not unfrequently holds in its interstices a weight of water twice greater than its own. It is further abated by the comparatively moderate size and height of the elevations themselves.

Sum of effect.

On the whole, therefore, the influence of the mountains of Maine upon its water-power, in respect at least to the volume and constancy of motor material, is small. This is great gain, for the utmost that water-power can hope from mountainous districts, in the particulars in question, is not to be damaged greatly. In this statement no reference is had to the office of mountains in contributing to the required *slope of watersheds* or to the *brokenness of surface* indispensable to waterfalls, circumstances which in so far as considered at all in this Report, are considered elsewhere.

Subsection A.—DISTRIBUTION OF THE MOUNTAINS. The principal summits of the State are included in a district, approximately triangular in form, the vertices of which fall respectively near Fryeburg, the Bald Mountain Ridge, and Mars Hill, the sides being respectively 125, 135 and 240 miles long, and the area of the whole about 6,600 square miles.

Its important features noted.

The features of this distribution, important in their bearings upon our water-power, are, first, the location of the principal mountain district on the Southern Slope of the State; secondly, its horizontal expansion in the western part, to which may be added its higher general altitude in the same part. These conditions, taken together, indicate clearly in what portion of the State, other circumstances being equal, the streams will be affected with the greatest variations of volume at different seasons, and their currents most broken with rapids and falls. The loftiest single summit in Maine, Katahdin, 5,385 feet, stands about midway the system, or east thereof, but as a whole the mountain district is much more elevated in the west, and in the west therefore its influences are most marked and powerful.

Section 4.—VALLEYS.

Defined. By valleys are here meant those depressions in the general surface of the State which, whether more or less extended and profound, suffice to accumulate the surplus waters of adjacent districts ultimately into a single drainage channel. The number of these, large and small, is of course indefinitely great, but of none will any detailed description be given in this connection, a very general view sufficing our present purposes.

Their character. Our valleys partake of the plain rather than of the ravine character. They consist mainly of broad tracts of country depressed along their central axis and separated one from another by wide low swells instead of steep escarps and abrupt mountain chains or ridges. Their surface is variously broken and diversified with local elevations and depressions, which however do not materially affect their general form.

Effect thereof. The general form referred to is of high importance as regards water-power, since the descent of the watersheds to the streams determined by it is so gradual as to throw off the surplus volumes of the rains or of snow-meltings with moderate rapidity, and so as consequently to reduce the liability to destructive freshets. It is further of importance, since it affords room for the formation of *large* lakes and ponds; and still further of importance in that, as it discourages the sudden discharge of surplus waters into the streams, so in the same act it conserves them against the season of drouth and low water.

Lowness of the water divides. The crests of the water-sheds of these valleys are in many localities so low relatively to the adjacent parts of the basins, as barely to determine the flow of the waters in one direction rather than another, and this is especially the case in the vicinity of the ridge dividing the Northern and Southern Slopes.

The waters of the St. John Southwest Branch and of the Penobscot Northwest Branch are drawn in part from the same swamps, the Kennebec and Penobscot are separated at points by only a mile or two of very low country; the head waters of the Penobscot in freshets actually become commingled with those of the Allaguash, Aroostook, and St. Croix. So that the geographical marvel is many times repeated within our limits, of rivers interlocking at their sources and flowing off in different directions upon different slopes; a circumstance that in the case of a common canal betwixt the Orinoco and the Amazon has been thought worthy of elaborate discussion by the pen of Humboldt.

Valleys of the Southern Slope. The valleys of the southern part of the State, in contrast with that of the northern, are not determined in their line of length by the trend of the Appalachian ridges, their axis being in almost every case disposed with reference to those ridges at a very large angle, almost a right angle in several cases. They assume, therefore, the appearance of channels worn or of passages forced, from the interior to the ocean, in some sort contrary to, and in spite of the opposition of, the great geological tendencies of the region as exhibited in the Appalachian chain. The rivers likewise in the tortuosity of their courses, their abrupt turns, their circuitous detours around obstructing hills, their numerous rips and rapids, with reaches of still water above and below, their multitude of pitches and falls, with now and then a proper cataract—afford constant and striking evidence of the imparallelism of their lines of motion with that of any settled regular lines of geological depression or fracture. They force their way to the ocean amongst the hills as best they can. Hence, in part, their extraordinary amount of water-power.

Valleys and railroad construction. The valleys of the State are of great importance in that, leading as they do into its interior by the immediate side of and enclosing the waterfalls, they afford comparatively uniform planes upon which roads and railroads can be constructed at moderate cost. For in consequence of this the extraordinary facilities of approach to our water-power, afforded by our numerous and excellent harbors and the navigable portion of our streams, can be still further carried out to any required extent. The advantage referred to has already in the southern part of the State been turned to some account; though as yet there is not a single railroad that follows the lines of our river valleys one-fourth the distance from the ocean to the northern boundary. The railway that now terminates at Skowhegan can be extended the whole distance to the St. John river, via the Kennebec, West Penobscot and Allaguash valleys, without any serious natural obstacle. The same holds true of the Penobscot, Mattagamon (East Branch), Aroostook and Fish River valleys. The importance of this is not easily realized at the present time, but it will be in the course of years.

CHAPTER III.

GEOLOGICAL RELATIONS.

Hardness of the rocks of Maine.

The most important of those features in the geological condition of Maine, which obviously influence its water-power, is, the *remarkable induration of the rocks.* This character results from or is associated with (under the general geological law) their extreme antiquity; very much the larger portion having taken form and coherence as rocks, at a period antedating the introduction of life upon the globe, or at least at so early a period that subsequent exposures and internal changes have obliterated every trace of organized life.

Consequent unevenness of the river beds.

The attribute in question is of the highest consequence as regards water-power, in various respects. It is only rocks of extreme hardness, that can, as a general statement, be counted upon to *retain the roughness and brokenness* of form impressed upon them by geological forces either primordially or in later periods; and by consequence upon such rocks only that the uneven condition of river beds so indispensable to water-power can be secured, and be maintained indefinitely. Accordingly, streams in our State are found to be still broken with very numerous falls and abrupt rapids, the abrading action of the waters having failed to impair the precipitousness of their descent, or to make any profound impression upon the surrounding strata.

As regards canons.

In further consequence of this feature of our underlying strata, the *cañon form of ravage* upon river beds is, except locally, unknown in our state. Were the conditions predisposing to water-power with us in all other respects the same as at present, with the exception that our rivers should cut their channels to enormous depths, as in Arkansas, Texas, Kansas, etc., miles in length and hundreds of feet deep, thus separating the country by enormous chasms, and grading off the courses of the streams to uniform planes of descent—water-power in our limits would be an impossibilty, it could not exist. There are a few ravines or gorges traversed by the rivers of the State which for a short distance approximate the cañon, as for example the "Gorge" of the Seboois, and the "Rapids" below Indian Pond on the Kennebec, but even these are not so pronounced in their features as to forbid entirely the use of the water-power.

As regards waste of water by percolation. In further consequence of this feature, our rocks are comparatively *proof to the circulation of water in their structure*, which in certain formations is conducted so freely as quite materially to affect the proportion of water flowing upon the surface of the land, and hence into the channels of the rivers. This is especially the case with the softer limestones, which are apt to be hollowed into conduits and even caverns by the solvent power of carbonic and perhaps other acids derived from vegetable decomposition, held in solution in the percolating waters. Such caverns often run great distances under ground, and become the water-way of considerable streams and even rivers, as in the caverns of the Peak and Castleton in Derbyshire, England, and in that of the Nicajack Cave in Georgia, where a waterfall occurs three miles under ground. In the limestone districts of Carniola and Illyria, "almost every lake and river has a subterranean source and subterraneous exit." The caves and underground streams of Kentucky are doubtless referable to the agency in question. It is safe to assert that, comparatively speaking, next to none of the rainfall of Maine is disposed of in this summary manner, and thereby lost to the rivers.

Vast quantities of water, likewise, are absorbed in the crevices and fissures abundant in limestone and other soft rocks, which in the season of drouth is lifted to their surface and burned away by evaporation. This elevating process may go on hundreds of feet above the water line in the earth and above the level of the sea, it being dependent upon capillary forces and therefore quite irresponsible to ordinary gravitating agencies. It is evident that the water thus circulating, as it were in an independent system of conduits, will not add materially to the sum of water-power in the rivers. This process of absorption into and evaporation from the rocks, goes on of course with us, as everywhere, but far less freely than in districts whose geological formations are of more recent date.

Water-tight reservoirs.

The character of our rocks, now remarked, is of peculiar importance in connection with the *water-retaining capacity of our lakes,* these being in the large majority of cases in consequence of it, underlaid and walled in with imporous material. A leaky lake or pond will hold water no better than a leaky cistern. It is important also as rendering water-retaining *artificial* reservoirs feasible to a remarkable extent, everywhere, in fact, where the lay of the land favors, or admits of, their construction and of the necessary convergence of the streams.

Rocks allied to granite in their water-power reaction.

As a particular phase of the first geological characteristic already noticed, should be instanced the relatively enormous development of *rocks allied to granite in their water-power reaction,* including true granite, syenite, gneiss, and the schists which in thickness and solidity of layers approach gneiss.

There are about 13,500* square miles of the State surface occupied with the rocks referred to. The whole region west of the Kennebec is given up to their occupancy, 3,400 square miles of which are almost exclusively underlaid with granite. A belt of the same family of rocks extends along the sea coast through its whole extent.

The rocks specified, more especially granite and gneiss, are characterized by irregular forms in eminent degree, the natural result of their endurance under wear. Above all other rocks they break up the surface of water-sheds and the channels of streams, and thus at once produce waterfalls and maintain them against impairment by natural forces.

Their favorable location.

The rocks are so *located* as to exert the most favorable influence upon our water-power. As extended along the coast they produce a large number of powers in close proximity to navigable waters. As thus situated, also, they have in ages past checked the wear of our river valleys and the cutting backward of our river channels, processes which of necessity begin at the mouths of streams and retrocede as the softness of the surrounding materials allows, and which are attended with the impairment or total obliteration of water-power.

The rocks in question are accumulated upon the Southern Slope of the State, and in particular and in their most characteristic forms, upon the western part thereof, and there conspire with high

* Estimated from Hitchcock's Geological Map of Maine and the accompanying Report.

elevation and favorable planes of descent, to produce the largest possible amount of power. Hence in the region of the Salmon Falls, Saco, Presumpscot and Androscoggin rivers, an amount of manufacturing power is found, quite in excess of that due to the areas of the basins.

The stratified rocks. The 13,500 square miles of rocks referred to in the foregoing paragraphs being excluded, there remain 18,000 square miles of the more definitely stratified masses, in which the schistose character is conspicuously exhibited. As found with us they are chiefly clay slate and mica schist.

The grand circumstance to be noticed respecting these rocks, is, (as is true indeed of all the stratified rocks in the State,) that the lines of stratification are *right-angled to the courses of the principal rivers*, and of all our chief rapidly sloping rivers. As thus disposed the out-cropping ridges of the strata, as a general rule, run across the streams, and so produce pitches and sudden descents, which according to their steepness, brokenness, and the associated volume of water, take the form of rapids, rips, falls, or cataracts. There are very many water-powers in the State referable to this origin.

It may be added respecting these rocks that as found with us they are of exceptional solidity, and accordingly, save in the limited districts where lime enters as an important ingredient into their constitution, as on the Aroostook, they are found upon streams resisting water wear, not unfrequently with almost the pertinacity of granite.

Exposure of the rock. Lastly, the pulverized material constituting soil, is in Maine as indeed throughout New England, shallow in depth. By consequence the *rock is to an unusual extent exposed.* Especially is this true in and upon the water courses. Some of our rivers and very many of our smaller streams run in channels of stone, and the sides and bed of nearly all, especially on a Southern Slope, are rock-set and rock-bound, though at the surface locally covered with earth.

The importance thereof. The practical importance of this fact is great. Those riparian ravages and vagrant diversions of river courses which in alluvial districts are productive of so much inconvenience and occasionally of serious loss of property are with us substantially unknown. Canals and raceways can be constructed in the native rock, and once completed need no repairs. Mills and appurtenant structures can be planted upon ledge bottom and so made proof at once against the corrosion of under currents and the momentum of freshets.

In particular, as the result of the fact that our streams are thus carried in rock-bound conduits, dams are susceptible of location at almost any point where the slope of the stream is sufficient to form a rapid, and upon improvement to constitute a water-power. So that, dam succeeding dam, the whole descent of the streams is capable of being utilized for power purposes, the loss from flowage and from the degradation and erosion of the banks upon elevation of the water surface, being as a general statement, very small.

Building material.

From the statements already made it is easy to infer that stone of suitable quality for construction purposes is in nearly all parts of the State comparatively abundant and cheaply procurable. The granite quarries of the coast in particular are unrivalled for the excellence of the stone and the facility with which enormous masses are transferred direct from the native bed to the decks of ships.

CHAPTER IV.

CONDITIONS OF SURFACE.

The conditions of surface which in any region exercise a marked influence upon its water-power, are three—namely, surface aspect, surface materials, and vegetation.

Section 1.—SURFACE ASPECT.

Hilliness of Maine.

By far the most important and characteristic feature of the topography or surface forms of Maine is its *hilliness*. The grade of unevenness intended to be specified is above the undulating and below the mountainous, approaching the former more nearly than the latter. In other words, Maine as a whole is *moderately hilly*.

Its effect.

In consequence of the unevenness of the State surface, the surplus of the rainfall is gathered into the streams with less waste by the atmosphere and by infiltration, than is associated with flat water-sheds, and the volume of the streams is accordingly more copious. The surface being only *moderately* broken, the waters are not hurried into the rivers in torrents,—torrents which cannot be used in passing and leave nothing to be used when passed. The hilliness in question tends, therefore, to secure a moderate supply of water to the drainage channels, and to secure it all the year, avoiding alike the evaporation and infiltration waste of the level water-shed and the torrent waste of the mountainous. So that, as a whole, the surface forms of the State reäct most favorably upon the constancy of the water-power, and therefore upon its economical value.

Section 2.—Surface Materials.

Effect of soils upon the escape of water.

From a drainage area of bare rock, water would pour off, as from the pavements of a city into the gutters, with great rapidity, would presently disappear entirely, and the streams would dry up. Soil, on the other hand, dams the water back by its particles and detains it by adhesive attraction; the water finds by consequence slow passage through the millions of channels opened for it amongst the grains of the dirt, and continues therefore to feed for a long time the associated streams.

Thus in the dry deserts of the low latitudes, where as in western Sahara, or Australia, rain sometimes intermits for two years, the springs at the bottom of the *waddies* or valleys, yield without cessation their treasures of water, and as it were from inexhaustible subterranean fountains. One of the names given to the Sahara, in the poetical language of the Arabs, is the "Desert of the Hidden Sea." So that the waters received in the occasional bursts of rain is thus demonstrably held, even for years, in the surface matters of the basin, all the while slowly working passage to the points of discharge.

Bulk of the surface materials of Maine.

Where surface material are accumulated in immense mass, as upon the large *alluvions*, the surplus of the rains in considerable measure penetrates below the streams and works off into the ocean by constant and diffused flowage through the whole body of the ground. Hence the fact that the soil of Maine is shallow, as it unquestionably and obviously is, as compared with the formation referred to, reacts favorably upon the volume of the rivers. A shallow depth is sufficient since our rains are uniformly distributed, are rarely for a long time intermittent, and are never very heavy, sufficient to absorb the water against evaporation, and not sufficient to sqander it in or through the lower depths of the ground.

The physical *quality* of soils with respect to the absorption and transmission of water is of not less consequence than their quantity. Gravels and sands absorb water with great freedom, but being unable to retain it, affect streams running through them with marked fluctuations of volume, so at least unless their mass is great. Clays although a little tardy in the reception of water are extremely retentive of it, and thus on the whole equalize the flow of streams. Loams, i. e., mingled sand and clay, as also vegetable mould, are both retentive of water and freely receptive of it, and accordingly impart to streams great regularity of volume—not passing it too rapidly as do sands, and not suddenly shedding it as do clays in a degree.

The *quality* of soils as affecting the disposal of water.

It is undoubtedly true in Maine, as indeed nearly all the world over, that sand, i. e., rock broken into fine grains but not powdered, is more abundant than those exceedingly minutely divided soils which are as respects their reäction upon water, clayey in quality. A very large proportion of our subsoil appears to be *pan*, that is, sand consolidating or cementing into ledge. Relatively, however, the ordinary proportion of granulated and of powdered surface materials, the soil of Maine is believed to be more than ordinarily clayey.

The prevalent soil of Maine.

In response to inquiries sent into every town and plantation in the State, the prevailing surface materials have been represented as follows:

RIVER BASINS.	Gravel.	Sand.	Sandy Loam.	Loam.	Clay Loam.	Clay.
Saco,	2	3	2	4	1	2
Androscoggin,	8	3	3	5	1	3
Kennebec,	6	6	1	14	4	7
Penobscot,	16	7	3	15	5	16
St. John,	......	1	......	5	......	2
Presumpscot,	3	6	2	3	1	5
Sheepscot,	2	......	......	2	2	3
Narraguagus,	3	3	......	2	......	5
Denny's,	2	......	......	2	2	2
	42	29	11	52	16	45

The loams and clays are represented in 113 units and the sandy soils in 82 units. The testimony in many cases refers to the existence of "clayey subsoils" where sand is abundant at the surface, which make their appearance only in cuttings, excavations for wells, cellars, in river beds, etc. Not improbably returns from the interior and mountainous portions of the State will show a larger proportion of loose soils.

Consistently with the facts reported is that prime necessity of successful tillage with us, which is insisted upon first and last in our agricultural journals and in the invaluable reports of the Secretary of the Board of Agriculture, namely, underdraining.

Effect of the sands and gravels in Maine. The sand and gravel, or *drift* materials found upon our surfaces, exert an influence upon water-power much less marked and detrimental than would be exercised were our rainfall less uniformly distributed through the year. Sands and gravels cannot hold water long, and in our State they are not required to hold it long, one downfall succeeding another at not remote intervals, and supplying the loss of percolation and evaporation.

Section 3.—VEGETATION.

Under this head forests alone will be referred to. This form of vegetation far exceeding any other in its area of occupancy of the State surface, and from its bulk and large development exercising the most powerful influence upon water disposal.

Forests and rainfall. As to whether forests materially increase the *sum of water precipitated*, there is, notwithstanding the various facts and incidents alleged, no evidence on a sufficiently broad scale and sufficiently unequivocal to be at all decisive of the question. It is however quite certain that their influence in this regard is of far less consequence than as exercised upon the ultimate disposal of the water after it has once reached the earth. This latter will now be considered.

The living tree and water waste. The *living tree* may be regarded as an evaporating machine, exposing as it does a surface of transpiration far greater than the area of ground covered by its mass. A single black birch has been estimated to run sixty barrels of sap from one tap in the Spring. The experiments of Williams went to show that trees in their full vigor evaporate a proportion of water greater by one-third than a water surface equal in extent to the breadth of ground covered by the trees. Whether this estimate be greatly or slightly excessive, there is no question that as living organisms trees waste the supply of river material, and thus reäct unfavorably upon water-power. With us however trees operate thus for less than one-third of the year, the actual period of growth falling below four months.

Regarded as *masses of matter* trees have an effect quite to the contrary. First, *they shade the ground,* and thus prevent the sun from parching away the water contained in the ground, which accordingly stands its chance of ultimately reaching mill wheels. Our forests being for the greater part evergreen, shade the ground *at all seasons.* They check therefore the waste of winter snow as well as the waste of summer rain. Nothing is more common than for patches of ice formed of solidified snow, to be found lying here and there in the defiles and ravines of our woods as late as early June, saturating the ground about them in their melting, and sending off streamlets to the nearest brook, lake or river.

Forests shade the ground.

Forests *check the movement of the atmosphere,* both the horizontal and the vertical, one or the other of which is always in circulation, and thus prevent or diminish the removal of moisture from their area of occupation by the convective power of the winds. This is a circumstance of great importance, as may be inferred from the rapidity with which roads dry up, or clothes from the laundry dry off, during the prevalence of wind. Our woods being so largely evergreen check the movement of the winds at all seasons, and abate evaporation therefore at all seasons, a matter of some consequence since vaporization goes on from snow and ice, and from water at all temperatures, and is accelerated by wind from four to ten fold, as experiments show, and according to circumstances, whatever the temperature may be.

Obstruct the atmospheric currents.

In the fourth place, forests roughen and break up the ground through which their roots force passage, so that water can penetrate it; and so that in innumerable depressions and sinks formed by the heaving ground over the roots, its volume when in surplus can be husbanded against too sudden removal. This is especially important upon hilly and mountainous water-sheds, contributing to their uniformity of discharge.

Roughen the ground.

Lastly, as was observed in the section on mountains, forests cover the ground beneath them with *masses of vegetable matter* which holds water like a sponge, and thus favor the uniformity of the volume of the connected rivers.

Accumulate water-holding matter.

The combined and last result of all these influences is to *increase the amount* of water that shall, other conditions favoring, be available for manufacturing. The further result is to *regulate the supply or delivery* of the water, in which respect the function of forests is probably of not less importance

Sum of the effect of forests.

than in regard to the volume of water. In one word, forests contribute in a very important measure to the two prime essentials of water-power, namely, its volume and constancy, their influence in this respect being exceeded by only that of lakes and surface materials.

Subsection A.—EXTENT OF THE FOREST SURFACES OF MAINE. The following table probably gives a tolerably close approximation:

Area of the State,	31,500	square	miles.
Approximate area of lakes, ponds, and river surfaces,	3,200	"	"
Total land surface,	28,300	"	"
In farms,	9,000	"	"
In the wilderness state, therefore,	19,300	"	"
Of the farm lands there are tilled,	4,200	"	"
Leaving in pastures, woodlots, etc.,	4,800	"	"
Of this one-half (?) woods,	2,400	"	"
Total woods, 19,300 + 2,490 — 500,	21,200	"	"

The 500 square miles subtracted are by way of allowance for bare spots, mountain tops and slopes, ledges, heaths, and tracts too barren to support trees. We have therefore a sum total of forest surface, in farm and out, of about 21,000 square miles, and of this not far from 15,000 square miles in the northern and southeastern districts, are to only a limited extent entrenched upon by clearings.

The primeval woods of Maine, accordingly, still cover an extent seven times that of the famous "Black Forest" of Germany at its largest expanse in modern times. The States of Rhode Island Connecticut, and Delaware, could be lost together in our northern forests, and still have about each a margin of wilderness sufficiently wide to make its exploration without a compass a work of desperate adventure.

Favorable location of the forests. The forests are to an important extent so located as to exercise their characteristic influence upon water-power to the best advantage, namely, within and upon the mountain region of the State. So situated, their special efficiency will be readily understood and appreciated in view of statements already made.

Their prospective permanence. Thus located, much of the forest, that upon the mountains themselves, inaccessible from their situation and form, bids fair to be as permanent as the rocky elevations upon which it is planted. For a long time the woods about the head waters of our rivers will remain substantially as they now are, deprived indeed of their heavier timber, but still woods, and dense woods. So that the influence of forests upon water supply with us, as it is unquestionably important, so does it in considerable measure bid fair to be permanent.

Effect of the removal of the forests.

The cutting-off of our forests, even if quite thoroughly effected, would have a far less detrimental influence upon the delivery of our rivers in point of both annual sum and volume at different seasons, than would be experienced in lower latitudes, hotter climates, and districts affected by periodical rains, or in districts excessively mountainous, as amongst the Alps, and visited by rains of great violence and volume. Because the Azores, the Madeira islands, Palestine, the piedmontane districts of the Alps, etc., have suffered variously from water dearth, or inundation, or both, in consequence of the removal of forests, it by no means follows that Maine will suffer in the particulars referred to, in equal degree or even seriously.

Maine having a cool climate, non-periodic rains, an exposure oceanic on the south, maritime on the east, northeast, and southeast, being swept by Gulf-Stream vapors, and being furnished with enormous natural reservoirs, can be shorn of its woods with comparative impunity, so far at least as respects the flow of the rivers, and without reference to agricultural or other reäctions. In other words, the circumstance of less or more vegetation upon its surfaces becomes comparatively unimportant in a district whose general geographic conditions and exposures are such, and are such as to exercise an influence so pronounced and commanding upon both the precipitation and removal of water. On this same principle, the northwest coasts of North America, all northwestern Europe, the British Isles, China, (proper), and many other regions are and will remain heavily watered countries whether their woods are cut off or not.

In particular, the natural reservoirs of the rivers of Maine are of such capacity, that were the forests wholly cut away, the low-run volume of the streams, or of nearly all, could still, by the use of the reservoirs, be raised to and maintained at a figure greatly in excess of the *natural* or present summer run. Of this we have demonstration in the fact that the streams which are the most constant in their supply of water, as at present used, are on the coast, and in particular in the southwest part of the State, the Mousam, Presumpscot, Salmon Falls, etc., from whose drainage territory the greater part of the forest has been removed, but whose storage basins have been brought into use, and which realize hundreds per cent. more power than when the forests were comparatively intact, and the reservoirs unimproved.

Effect of forest removal as exerted upon agriculture.

It may be proper to add that the reasons for preserving forests are much more urgent with reference to agriculture than water-power. So, first, because trees operate in favor of cultivated plants, as shelters, etc., in modes which are quite inoperative as regards water-power; and so, secondly, because streams being fed by under-ground storage, suffer far less in dry times, especially the larger streams, than cultivated plants, because they draw water supplies from much greater depths and masses of earth. The retention of vast bodies of forest is quite a different matter from preserving tracts and belts of moderate size scattered over the general face of the country, though too frequently confounded with it in discussions upon the topic.

CHAPTER V.

LAKES.

Section 1.—INFLUENCE OF LAKES UPON WATER-POWER.

Importance of lakes with reference to water-power.

There is no other physical feature of a country that, under the control of man, can be made to contribute to the constancy of water-power in equal measure with lakes. The importance of this will appear when it is remembered that water-power, only in proportion as it is constant, becomes suitable for extensive manufacturing, where large amounts of capital are invested in stock and materials. It may be profitably employed for local conveniences and in small establishments, even though it be variable at different seasons, and at some parts of the year reduced to almost nothing. But under such conditions only can highly variable water-power be advantageously employed, as against steam in connection with which intermissions of efficiency can be guarded against by proper precautions, and flood and drouth alike are shorn of their power. Some of the more important modes will now be specified in which lakes exert a favorable influence upon water-power.

They store up the surplus of heavy rains and of snow-meltings, and so provide power material in the season of excess against the season of dearth. They are therefore natural *reservoirs*, oftentimes of a capacity which man would not presume to emulate by artificial constructions, provided, too, almost free of cost, and capable of being put to actual use with insignificant outlay.

Lakes as storage basins.

Lakes with us and *in our climate* serve a double use as reservoirs, namely, against both the drouth of summer and the drouth of winter. During our mid winter, precipitation takes place largely in the form of snow. Moreover the water upon the surface of the ground is to a considerable extent turned to ice and immovably fixed, and the ground itself in all its upper stratum, saturated with wet, is frozen solid, and yields no contributions to the streams. Accordingly such streams as are unprovided with reservoirs run low in winter, though rarely, if ever, so low as in mid-summer. Those on the contrary fed by lakes and ponds continue to yield approximately their usual supply, the great body of the water being protected against congelation by the sheet of ice and snow incumbent upon the surface of the reservoirs.

Lakes contribute to *lessen the frequency and violence of freshets*. In the act of storing up water in floods and snow-meltings, they reduce the pressure upon the discharge capacity of the streams, thereby enabling them to pass off the surplus volumes with a comparatively moderate rise of surface. Upon rivers subject to excessive floods manufacturing works have to be constructed of great strength to withstand, and with extreme nicety to exclude, the water; and most generally if so built as to be safe against the overflow of one season, are high and dry at the low water of another.

Lakes diminish freshets.

Lakes give opportunity for the *formation of far less ice* than would be made out of an equal quantity of water dispersed in streams and upon the general surface of the land, the great body of the water being protected from the action of the cold by the non-conducting covering of ice and snow incumbent upon it. Lake ice before "going out" becomes rotten, breaks up and separates into a mere sludge of crystals, incapable of harm, whereas the ice of streams is torn from its resting-place by the strong traction of the current, while yet it has cohesiveness enough to cling together in large masses and to deal very heavy blows.

Lakes and the formation of ice.

The water of lakes warm in winter.

The water of lakes and ponds is *warm* so that mills near them and fed by them experience no trouble from the forming of ice about their wheels in even the coldest weather.

Lakes and the *annual amount* of river discharge.

Lakes *add to the annual amount of river discharge* by accumulating the water from a wide land surface into a limited receptacle whose surface alone is exposed to the sun and winds, and whose great body is sheltered against waste. Water when in the mass of the ground is most tenaciously held against evaporation, but when the ground will hold no more and a residue must be disposed of, that is far better conserved in a lake than when dispersed upon a land surface.

Intercept the circulating waters of the lower ground.

Lakes operate to the same result by dividing with their deep concavities the strata of the ground, and thus receiving a larger share of that volume of water which circulates in the earth, below the streams, and which otherwise would work off into the ocean by diffused flowage through subterranean channels. Hence it is that many of our lakes, as, conspicuously, the Schoodic chain and Sebago, discharge far more water than they visibly receive from the inflow of tributary streams.

Section 2.—THE LAKE SYSTEM OF MAINE.

Number and area of the lakes in Maine.

The first feature of the lacustrine system of the State to be noticed, is the extraordinary *number and size of the component lakes*. Maine in fact constitutes the southeastern extreme of the Great North American Lake System, which extends hence westward to the Great Lakes inclusive, and thence to the Arctic sea. There are but three or four districts on the globe, not more extensive than Maine and equally habitable in other respects, upon which an equal number of receptacles for impounding rainfall of not inferior capacity and surface is to be found. The total count of those represented upon the maps, as connected with our rivers both within and beyond the State, not including the multitudes of small ponds scattered about the State in such profusion that almost every neighborhood and school district has one, and not including the great number of small ponds in the wilderness districts which are not represented upon any map—is not less than one thousand six hundred and twenty. In fact the Kennebec river has more lakes connected with it than the gigantic Orinoco, and the Penobscot than the Amazon, or than all the rivers in Africa so far as known!

The lakes referred to and defined above possess at the lowest estimate deducible from the various state and county maps and the "plans" of the State Land-Office, a combined area of 2,300 square miles. The estimates returned in response to inquiries touching the extent of lakes and ponds, have in the large majority of cases overrun the figures deduced from the maps. In the construction of town plans, etc., there is in general no disposition to exaggerate the water surfaces, as this would involve the diminution of land and lumber tracts.

Area of the lakes of Maine.

To the above figures should be added 900 square miles, more or less, on conjecture, of river and stream surface, giving a grand total of 3,200 square miles of inland water. Maine contains more lake surface than a million square miles of the United States, situated in the central and west-central districts and south of the lake belt, not including the lagoons and bayous connected with some of the rivers, which are not proper lakes.

TABLE OF LAKE SYSTEMS.

Systems.	No. of Lakes.	Aggregate area.	Ratio of lake to basin surface.	Average area of the Lakes.
Saco,	109	84 square miles.	1 : 16.6	0.75 square miles.
Androscoggin,	148	313 " "	1 : 17	1.43 " "
Kennebec,	311	450 " "	1 : 12.9	1.44 " "
Penobscot,	467	585 " "	1 : 14	1.25 " "
St. Croix,	61	150 " "	1 : 6.5	2.95 " "
St. John,	206	350 " "	1 : 21.1	1·75 " "
Denny's etc.,	22	38 " "	1 : 9.8	1.72 " "
Machias, East and West,	56	68 " "	1 : 11.7	1.20 " "
Narraguagus, etc.,	38	25 " "	1 : 22	0.65 " "
Union, (not including islands)	43	60 " "	1 : 8	1.39 " "
St. George, Sheepscot, etc.,	72	50 " "	1 : 16	0.70 " "
Presumpscot,	45	97 " "	1 : 5.3	2.10 " "
Royal, etc.,	6	4 " "	1 : 42	0.66 " "
Mousam, etc.,	14	10 " "	1 : 26	0.71 " "
Piscataqua,	22	16 " "	1 : 34	0.72 " "
	1,620	2,300 square miles.	-	-

Of the above lakes 1,568 are located within the State boundaries, and 2,200 square miles of the total surface likewise. There are in the State one lake to each twenty square miles of territory, and one square mile of lake to each 14.3 square miles of territorial area.

The second feature of the lacustrine system of Maine, and which for our purposes gives the first marked significance and importance, is the almost universal *connection of the lakes with the rivers*. The *Androscoggin Lake System*, the *Kenne-*

Lakes connected with the rivers.

bec Lake System, the *Penobscot Lake System*, etc., receive their titles, respectively, not from the mere contiguity of the lakes to the streams, but from the fact of actual connection, from the fact that the lakes and the rivers constitute, in each case, a single organism of aqueous circulation, and operate together for the fulfilment of a common function.

The practical result is, that whereas in many regions lakes are merely inert volumes of water, with us they are by the fortunate circumstance referred to transformed to receptacles of manufacturing power, and may upon proper improvement contribute greatly to the wealth and population of the State.

The lakes situated at the head of the rivers.

The third feature of note in the inland water system of Maine, is the establishment of so many of the lakes at and about the *head of the rivers*. The Umbagog series at the source of the Androscoggin, Moosehead serving as the fountain of the Kennebec, the double St. Croix series, Sebago and its outlying appendages at the head of the Presumpscot, the Allaguash chain, the Fish river lakes, the reservoirs about the head waters of the Penobscot, the Machias lakes, the Union lakes, etc., are striking illustrations of the law; and thus situated are obviously located at the point of greatest conservation of force.

Upon and above the mountain district.

In the fourth place, the lakes of Maine to an important extent are situated either *above or upon the mountain region* of the State, and are obliged to seek passage for their waters over its broken surface, or through its rugged ravines, over rough and impeded channels, and are thus made to nourish a considerably larger number of powers than under other circumstances could reasonably be looked for, and in particular, multitudes of smaller powers upon the lesser streams, in addition to the larger upon the main rivers nearer to the sea.

High elevation of the lakes.

Fifthly, the *high elevation above tide* at which many of the largest lakes are held, is a circumstance of first-rate importance as regards water-power. The table subjoined gives a few facts in illustration, the figures denoting the height of the lacustrine surfaces above sea level in feet.

ELEVATION OF A FEW OF THE LARGER LAKES.

Lake	Elevation	Lake	Elevation
Moosehead,	1,023	Richardson,	1,456
Wood,	1,094	Mooseluomaguntic,	1,486
Attean,	1,094	Rangeley,	1,511
Long pond,	1,094	Mattagamon, (about)	850
Schoodic, (about)	300	Chamberlain,	926
Sebec, (about)	375	Pomgocwahem and Churchill,	914
Baskahegan, (about)	400	Allaguash (about)	950
Pamedumcook, the Twins, and Milinoket, (about)	500	Eagle,	579
Ripogenus,	878	Square and Cross,	587
Chesuncook,	900	Long,	603
Cauquomgomoc, (about)	930	Portage, (about)	625
Squawpan, (about)	580	Fish River (about)	660
Sebago,	247	Chiputneticook,	382
Umbagog,	1,256	" Grand,	449

Now Lake Itasca at the extreme head waters of the Mississippi river is elevated only 1,575 feet, or but little above the height of Rangely lake. Lake Superior, of the Great Lakes, at the source of the St. Lawrence 1,800 miles by the river from the ocean, is elevated only 630 feet, or about two-thirds the height of Moosehead. Lake Winnepiseogee in New Hampshire is but 501 feet above tide, or four to five hundred feet below the large lakes at the head of the Penobscot,—Chesuncook, Chamberlain, etc. So that our lakes hold their waters, as just observed, in a state of great and unusual reserved power—power that is given forth as the waters fall to the sea along the courses of our rivers.

The lakes and ponds of Minnesota are as a whole elevated higher above sea level than the lakes of Maine; but the fall of their surplus waters to the tide is not effected within her limits, nor indeed in less than thousands of miles of horizontal run, and accordingly is comparatively unproductive of power available for use.

Convertibility into storage basins.

Lastly. The tables given in Part II. of this Report show the lakes and ponds of Maine to be susceptible in remarkable degree of conversion into storage basins, and indeed to be already very generally converted into such for log-driving purposes. The average depth of reserve that can be held upon their surfaces is certainly not below eight feet, and the increase of the natural low run of the streams that can be commanded by their use is confidently believed to be much in excess of one hundred per cent.

Examples of increase of power by reservoirs.

The statistics of Part III. give striking examples of the increase of power realized upon appropriation of reservoirs. These are the most remarkable as exhibited upon small streams, which if unfurnished with storage basins would be entirely worthless for manufacturing purposes. Thus the Megunticook stream at Camden, though only 3.5 miles long, nevertheless being fed by several ponds, yields an annual product of several hundred thousand dollars in manufactured goods, and yet its available power is by no means wholly employed. In like manner a mere brook in Bridgton manufactures $600,000 of goods yearly, its power being far from wholly used. Dexter stream, which without the reservoir pond at its head, would be substantially dry in summer, realizes by the use of the pond, constant power on the Dexter Falls alone of 360 horse, with machinery only moderately economical of water. The Sabattus stream, fed by the Sabattus pond, yields at lowest run a power of 500 horse on a fall of only thirty feet in Lisbon; without the pond its power in a drouth would scarcely be worth the using.

On the larger streams also results sufficiently striking have been reached by the means in reference, though not in equal degree, on account of the almost universally inadequate and partial use of the available reservoirs. Thus the power of the Salmon-Falls river has been increased one hundred per cent. by the use of about six square miles of ponds. At Mechanic Falls on the Little Androscoggin, a constant power of 1,053 horse is secured on a fall of 37 feet, by the use of the great natural storage basins tributary to the river, and much more can be had when required. Other examples to the same effect are given in Part III. of the Report.

The resulting superiority of our water-power.

It is easy to see, therefore, how great an advantage our water-power has over that situated further South, in Virginia, the Carolinas, Georgia, and Alabama, which is obliged to rely upon the natural flow of the streams for its supplies, or if furnished with reservoirs at all, has to depend upon artificial constructions of comparatively great cost and limited capacity. For this reason, if for no other, that power can never compete on equal terms with the water-power of Maine.

Why *rivers* are not discussed at this point.

If the matter under discussion were the general physical geography of the State, a view of its *Rivers* would be in order at this point. But the special objects had in view, require such prominence to be given to these, as necessitates their treatment in an independent PART of the discussion.

CHAPTER VI.

THE TIDAL WATER-POWER OF MAINE.

The value of tidal water-power.

The tides upon the coast of Maine are so remarkable for volume as to require special notice in the discussion of its water-power. Tidal force is not considered available for ordinary manufacturing purposes in which large numbers of hands are employed, because of the unseasonable and constantly changing hours in which it is necessarily used: this at least without considerable expense in the way of supplementary basins for the reception of the mill discharge during the time of high tide, by the use of which the season of work can be regulated to convenience. But on the other hand for certain forms of manufacturing, as sawing lumber, grinding grain, grinding slate for paint or plaster of Paris, sawing marble, etc., in which large amounts of power are used and only a few attendants are required, it is of decided value. The flow of the tide is so great on our coast, that with suitable wheels it can be operated to advantage sixteen hours out of the twenty-four. The supply of water of course never fails, and the extreme fluctuations of volume are very small as compared with those experienced upon even the most constant of fresh water privileges. There is less trouble from ice, and the privileges are obviously accessible to market by the cheapest form of transportation.

The coast of Maine is in nearly all parts iron-bound, so that dams and mill structures can be planted upon firm foundations. Upon the vast reaches of sandy and swampy coast south of us, the tide, however great might be its rise and fall, would be unavailable for power to any considerable extent, except at great cost, on account of the impossibility of securing solid basis for superstructures.

The following table exhibits the *mean* range from low to high water at various points upon the coast:

MEAN HEIGHT OF THE TIDE ON THE COAST OF MAINE.

Localities.	Feet.	Localities.	Feet.
Eastport,	18.1	Castine,	12.0
Machias,	13.0	Camden,	9.8
Machiasport,	16.0	Thomaston,	9.4
Jonesport,	15.0	Damariscotta,	8.1
Columbia Falls,	14.0	Wiscasset,	9.4
Steuben,	13.0	Harpswell, (Basin)	9.0
Winter Harbor,	10.5	Portland,	8.9
Cold Harbor, Swan's Island,	12.0	Saco,	8.5

Mean, 11.6 feet.

MEAN TIDE BEYOND STATE ON THE ATLANTIC COAST.

Localities	Feet.	Localities.	Feet.
Portsmouth, N. H.,	8 6	Brunswick, Ga.,	6.8
Boston, Mass.,	10.0	Fernandina, Fla.,	5.9
Nantucket,	3.2	Charlotte, Fla.,	1.1
Providence, R. I.,	5.1	Mouth Mississippi,	1.3
New York, N. Y.,	4.8		

Mean, 5.2 feet.

Effect of the broken shore line.

The value of this form of power in its sum for the State is indefinitely increased by the great length and broken outline of our shore, which, as before remarked, is extended to the estimated length of 2,000 to 3,000 miles in a direct horizontal distance of 226 miles. The contour of the coast is such, that coves, inlets, and reëntering arms of the sea in great numbers and of large size, are susceptible of inexpensive improvement as storage basins and reservoirs of power.

Prospective employment of tide power.

For many years, doubtless, and until our fresh-water power is measurably put to use, salt-water power will be employed only in small amount, and only where insignificant outlay will be required. But it is in nowise improbable that in time the large sites will be utilized, works constructed on a great scale, and enormous amounts of labor accomplished by this great natural motor. If anywhere in the world it can be done to advantage, it is here, by reason of favoring physical conditions, and to all the higher advantage in connection with the great manufacturing system to be established on our rivers.

DIVISION II.

METEOROLOGICAL CONDITIONS.

In this division of the subject, two fundamental properties of our climate—namely, *temperature* and *rain*, will be considered, in so far as they directly affect our water-power, and *no farther*.

What will be considered in Division II. of Part I.

CHAPTER VII.

TEMPERATURE.

Section 1.—Mean Annual Temperature.

The mean temperature of the State for the year is exhibited in the records, the results of which are subjoined, covering a long period of years, and representing as nearly as possible the different parts of our domain.

TABLE OF MEAN ANNUAL TEMPERATURE IN MAINE.

Localities.	Mean Temperature.	Years registered.
Fort Kent,..	37°.04	4
Hancock Barracks,................................	40.50	17
Fort Fairfield, ...	38 11	–
Eastport,..	43.02	25
Steuben, ...	42.37	13
Castine,...	43.40	40
Portland,..	43.14	10
Portland Observatory,............................	42.90	31
Williamsburg, ...	41.50	6
Brunswick,.......................................	44.50	50
Cornish,...	42.85	7
Gardiner, ...	43.94	66
Bath,..	44.50	10

The mean of the first three points, 38°.55, represents (nearly) the temperature of the northern third of the State. The mean of the remaining points, 43°.21, represents approximately the temperature of the southern two-thirds. Hence the average temperature of the whole State is 41°.65.

The significance of this figure will appear, when it is recollected that in no other part of the northern hemisphere, except northeast China, does the isotherm of 41°.65 sink so near the equator, as in Maine and the adjacent districts on the east and west.

Mean temperature relatively low.

The mean temperature of the State is, therefore, for a region situated upon the 45th parallel, unusually low. That is to say *relatively* low, low for the latitude. Abyssinia and southern Hindoostan are cold countries for the latitude, on account of their high elevation. The coast of California also is cold for the latitude, on account of the cold marine under current upheaved upon its shores. Yet the former two countries are hot, and the latter is warm, to live in, though all are *relatively* cold. Correspondently Maine is not declared to be cold with reference to comfortable habitableness or capacity of vegetable production, since maize ripens every year, but cold in the relative sense, and for a country no further removed toward the poles.

In consequence of what.

The low temperature, though referable in part to other causes, is due mainly to the cold ocean current off the northeast shores of the continent, before referred to. The effect of this is exerted on so grand a scale, that all the northeast portion of the grand division is constituted a geographical region of relatively deficient heat. The focus of this district, is situated at the northeast corner of Hudson's Bay, its annual defect of heat being 13°. In all the adjacent regions the temperature is lower than is due to the latitude, in proportion to their proximity to the focus. Thus at Quebec the deficiency is nearly 7°, at New York 4°, throughout Maine is not far from 5°.5. In other words our mean annual temperature is what might be looked for were our geographical centre as near the fiftieth parallel as it now is the forty-fifth.

Its effect upon water waste.

The low temperature in question, without impairing the habitability of the State in other respects, *contributes essentially to its water-power.* So, first, by condensing a large share of moisture from the warm south, southeast, and southwest winds, and thus inducing a more copious rainfall than could be looked for from our location on the mid parallel and upon the lee side of the continent. So, secondly, by *diminishing the waste of water by evaporation*, and preserving therefore a larger proportion for removal by rivers.

Section 2.—SEASON TEMPERATURES.

The temperatures of only the summer and winter seasons need be considered in this Report, they exerting upon the water-power of the State the most characteristic and powerful influence.

Subsection A.—SUMMER TEMPERATURE. The table annexed represents the mean summer heat at points widely dispersed over our territory.

TABLE OF SUMMER TEMPERATURE IN MAINE.

LOCALITIES.	Latitude.	Temperature.
Fort Kent,	47°- 15	61°.68
Fort Fairfield,	46—46	61.58
Houlton,	46—7	63.33
Eastport,	44—15	60.50
Castine,	44—23	62.00
Williamsburg,	45—21	59.10
Brunswick,	43—53	59.90
Bath,	43—53	64.80
Gardiner,	44—10	66.80
	45°- 03′	

The mean of the first three or northern stations being allowed to represent the temperature of one-third of the State; and the mean of the remainder to represent the temperature of two-thirds, we obtain as the average summer temperature, 62°.43.

For the purpose of comparison the table of summer temperatures is given below for the district of country extending *west*. Comparison with districts west.

TABLE OF SUMMER TEMPERATURE IN DISTRICTS WEST.

LOCALITIES.	Latitude.	Temperature.
Andover, Mass.,	42°- 40′	68°.70
Troy, N. Y.,	42—43	70.00
Salem, N. Y.,	43—15	68.26
Green Bay, Wis.,	44—30	68.50
Fort Crawford, Wis.,	43—05	72.28
Fort Atkinson, Iowa,	43—00	68.00
Fort Snelling, Minn.,	44—53	70.64
Fort Ridgely, Minn.,	44—15	70.00
Pembina,	48—56	70.00
Fort Randall, Da.,	43—01	75.40
Mean,	44°.01	70°.17

Upon comparison with the Maine stations there will be seen to be a difference of 1°-2′ in the mean latitude, and of 7°.74 in the mean temperature. It appears therefore that the summer temperature of Maine is lower than of the interior districts in substantially the same latitude, by over twenty per cent. of their temperature reckoning from the freezing point of water.* Stated otherwise, the chances of water dearth arising from summer heat are diminished over twenty in the hundred with us, as compared with the most favored and valuable water-power region in the country, removed from the seaboard. In this remark special reference is had to Wisconsin, Iowa, and Minnesota, the only States possessed of water-power adapted to *extensive* manufacturing west of the Alleghany Mountains.

Comparison with districts south.

If the comparison be further extended so as to cover the water-power country adjacent to the Appalachian highland south of us, and which with the western district specified comprehends all the water-power of the country suited to extensive manufactures, results equally suggestive are reached.

TABLE OF SUMMER TEMPERATURE IN DISTRICTS SOUTH.

LOCALITIES.	Latitude.	Temperature.
Newark, N. J.,	40°-45	71°.25
Fort Delaware,	39—25	75.90
Richmond, Va.,	37—20	77.90
Murfreesborough, N. C.,	36—30	78.00
Charleston, S. C.,	32—45	80.59
Savannah, Ga.,	32—05	80.70
Mean,	36°-28′	77°.05

As compared with the Maine stations here is an excess in temperature of 14°.62. In other words the summer heat of Maine is less than of the districts compared, by about thirty-two per cent. of their temperature, reckoning from congelation point.

Effect of the low summer temperature upon water waste.

The great importance of the low summer temperature thus exhibited, as regards the matter in hand, namely, the conservation of water for power purposes, may be inferred from the following facts:—

EVAPORATION AT DIFFERENT SEASONS OF THE YEAR.

LOCALITIES.	Summer.	Winter.	Ratio.
Near London, Eng.,	July, 3.75 inches.	January, 0.50	750 : 1
Near Montreal, Ca.,	June, 3.72 "	January, inappre-	–
	July, 3.78 "	ciable.	–
Melbourne, Australia,	Dec. 11.01 "	May, 1.97	6 : 1
	Jan. 11.23 "	June, 1.50	7 : 1
	Feb. 8.14 "	August, 2.57	3 : 1

From which it appears that the draft upon rainfall by evaporation is far greater in summer than in winter, and by consequence

* Evaporation is comparatively unimportant below this point.

that a reduction of a few degrees in summer heat must result in a very important abatement of water waste.

Its effect as regards manufacturing labor.

It well known that at the large majority of manufacturing labors the burden of the day's work is felt by the operative to be much heavier in summer than in winter. The cold of the latter season can be so guarded against and mollified, that throughout the whole establishment precisely or very nearly that temperature can be secured which is most contributive to vigorous exertion. But the heat of summer pervading and penetrating everything, and brought in at every open window with the necessary supplies of fresh air, cannot be shut out. It cannot be qualified. It oppresses the worker with a languor rarely experienced in out-of-door avocations, and renders it impossible for him to do so much or do so well as he can easily do in cool weather. Accordingly, the evidence is that in Maine, where the summer temperature is low, where it rises above the point of *comfort* for but a few days for the whole season, operatives, circumstanced equally in every other respect, accomplish more than in the interior and more southern States by the truly remarkable fraction of *Ten* per cent.

It is not necessary to expatiate upon the importance of this fact since it really covers a very considerable part of the whole ground betwixt manufacturing simply without loss and manufacturing with liberal profit,—profit and loss both for the operative and for the whole State. It is more essential to insist upon the view that as the fact is a fact now, so will it, being founded upon the unchangable conditions of nature, remain a fact for all coming time; and that by consequence for all coming time, other things being equal, the State will be able to reap from the labors of its citizens employed in manufacturing, a proportion of advantage greater than can be acquired by other States from the labors of an equal number of their citizens similarly employed. This is the uniform judgment and testimony of the superintendents of factories, who have had the opportunity of comparing the efficiency of labor here and labor elsewhere, and is most positively insisted upon by those who have had the largest and most varied experience in this and other States.

Apparently rebutting facts stated.

These views may seem to conflict with certain facts brought out in the census for 1860, from which it appears, first, that the number of pounds of cotton manufactured yearly to each spindle, for the decade 1850–60, was—

In the United States,	72.2
In the New England States,	61
In the Middle States,	88.26
In Maine,	78

And appears further that the value of the product of each spindle, was—

In the United States,	$22.86
In the New England States,	20.30
In the Middle States,	30.48
In Maine,	22.12

From which it is evident that in pounds of cotton consumed per spindle and in the value of the annual product, Maine falls behind the Middle States by an important per centage.

The explanation of the facts. The explanation of this is to be found in the circumstance, first, that the yarns for the Middle State goods are largely spun in New England and elsewhere, and accordingly the manufactories of those States receive their material already half wrought, and of course appear to advantage when estimated by the relation which the value of the finished goods holds to the number of spindles in their own works. The explanation is found, secondly, in the circumstance that the goods produced in the Middle States are not fine goods, but are of the classes medium to coarse. They therefore require comparatively large amounts of raw material by which their cost and value as finished goods are raised to a relatively high figure, as above indicated. But when employed on the same grade of goods, and performing each, all or an equal number of the processes of manufacture, the factory operative in Maine can and does accomplish more than the operative in the Middle, Interior, or Southern States, by a per cent. not less at least than that before specified.

Why winter temperature is specially considered. Subsection B.—WINTER TEMPERATURE. The consideration of the temperature of winter is next in consequence to that of summer, because the winter of Maine is extremely pronounced in character and exercises no inconsiderable influence upon the volume of the streams, especially the smaller.

The table annexed exhibits the temperatures observed for the three winter months at the places specified, the figures being respectively, in the larger number of cases, the mean of several or many years' record:

TABLE OF WINTER TEMPERATURE IN MAINE.

Localities.	Temperature.
Fort Kent,	11°.36
Fort Fairfield,	14.28
Houlton,	16.41
Eastport,	23.90
Fort Preble,	24.70
Bath,	24.00
Gardiner,	19.01
Mean,	19°.09

Material for comparison is afforded in the table following, which shows the winter temperature at points westward, situate in substantially the same latitude:

Comparison with districts west.

TABLE OF WINTER TEMPERATURE IN DISTRICTS WEST.

Localities.	Temperature.
Burlington, Vt.,	21°.60
Plattsburgh, N. Y.,	20.22
Ogdensburgh, N. Y.,	22.60
Fort Mackinac, Mich.,	20.00
Saut St. Marie, Mich.,	18.30
Marquette, Lake Superior,	17.53
Green Bay, Wis.,	19.92
Fort Atkinson, Iowa,	20.62
Fort Snelling, Minn.,	16.07
Fort Ridgely, Minn.,	17.00
Fort Ripley, Minn.,	10.00
Mean,	18°.53

The winter of Maine, therefore, is not so severe as is experienced in the correspondent latitudes in the interior. This is due to the mollifying influences of the surrounding sea, the effect of which though it be (in this latitude) to lower the mean for the year, raises it for the winter.

Whether, however, our winter be warmer or colder than other districts experience and their populations are obliged to endure, is for our purposes only an incidental consideration. The main point to be observed, is, that the winter temperature of the State is below the freezing point of water, and very considerably below—12°.91 below.

The winter temperature below the freezing point.

It follows from this, first, that the surface ground with its contained water tends to freeze solid and to a very considerable depth, and thereby to refuse admission to any rainfall received, or to supply the streams from its own previous accumulations. It follows, secondly, that the surface water upon the drainage sheds tends throughout the season in question to turn

The practical effects of this.

to ice wholly, especially when dispersed in shallow depths, in brooks, shoal ponds, swamps, etc. It follows, thirdly, that precipitation inclines to be very largely in the solid form, chiefly snow. From these circumstances combined the streams tend to run low. They do run low usually, particularly the smaller, whose supplies are furnished mainly by merely surface drainage.

Modifications.

Fortunately, however, these three circumstances do not practically combine their efficiencies to reduce river supply. For when precipitation comes in the form of snow the ground does not freeze, or freeze much, and continues therefore to supply the rivers with the reserved abundance of the autumn rains, a supply but little diminished by evaporation and accordingly surprisingly durable. When the snow falls to the depth of several feet, as it does nearly every winter, the ground, if frozen, thaws out, the lower stratum of the snow melts, and charges the earth, which in turn feeds the streams.

The severity of temperature scarcely ever fails to relax for brief periods during the winter, so as to admit of rains and of the melting of part of the accumulated snow, by which the lakes and reservoirs are filled. So that while the streams run low they do not run dry, or hardly ever so low as in the ordinary reduced summer supply. In other words, the water-power of the State suffers next to no inconvenience from deficiency of water consequent upon and produced by the cold of winter. Further remarks upon the effects of the deep snows will be offered in a subsequent chapter.

The making of thick ice upon lakes and streams.

Two special circumstances of some practical consequence attend the protracted low temperature of our winter, namely, the formation of ice of great solidity and thickness upon lakes and rivers, and the liability to ice accumulations about the water gearing of mills and factories. As respects the first-mentioned circumstance, it carries for practical purposes its own correction with it; for the brief thaws and short rains experienced in our winters do not, except at extremely wide intervals, suffice to break up the ice upon the rivers and never upon the lakes, which therefore remains unbroken until spring and, as before noticed, until it has become, under the action of the hot sun and long days, comparatively incapable of harm, brittle and ready to shatter to pieces upon a slight blow. South and west of us, on the contrary, where the winter cold is less protracted and intense, and longer, heavier, and more frequent rains are interspersed with snows, the ice is almost always broken up during the winter, and carried from the tributaries into the main streams, is piled up in large masses twelve or fifteen feet in thickness, which subsequently freeze together and thus become really dangerous and destructive, when finally set in motion in early spring. This is the case on the Connecticut river where a thaw and partial breaking-up of the ice may be looked for with almost absolute assurance during January and February of each year.* So that practically no river in Maine requires greater precautions to be taken against ice, by way of extra strength in bridges, mill foundations, etc., than are indispensible upon the above-mentioned and other streams west and south of us.

The formation of ice about mill works.

As respects the second circumstance mentioned above, the gathering of ice about the machinery of mills, no practical difficulty of a serious nature is experienced, or at least none such as cannot be readily obviated by a little precaution in the construction of works with reference to the exclusion of cold.

Conclusion.

In conclusion it appears that the thermal condition of the State, on the whole, influences very favorably both the volume and constancy of the rivers. The temperature for the year is low, and evaporation for the year, as affected by temperature, is therefore of necessity comparatively small. The temperature of summer, in particular, is by various circumstances abated, and the evaporating waste of water, by consequence, correspondently abated. The severity of the winter though minatory of water dearth, is nevertheless so broken by relaxations of cold, by occasional rains, and above all so counteracted by the deep ground-covering of snow, as practically to be shorn of its threatened injurious effects.

---

* James B. Francis.

CHAPTER VIII.

RAINFALL OF MAINE.

Section 1.—ANNUAL RAINFALL.

The yearly receipt of moisture in Maine, including both rain and snow, is exhibited in the following table, which is digested from the records of the Smithsonian Institution expressly for this Report, and furnished by courtesy of the Regent, Prof. Joseph Henry:

TABLE OF ANNUAL RAINFALL IN MAINE.

LOCALITIES.	Latitude.	Depth in inches.	Years.
Bath,	43°-55′	37.08	9
Biddeford,	43—30	49.75	4
Brunswick,	43—54	44.68	32
Bucksport,	44—34	44.36	4
Cornish,	43—40	47.85	11
Dexter,	44—55	38.72	4
Eastport,	44—54	40.09	2
Fort Kent,	47—15	36.45	1
Fort Preble,	43—39	45.14	8
Fort Sullivan,	44—54	39.41	8
Fryeburg,	44—03	45.11	5
Gardiner,	44—10	42.09	26
Hancock Barracks,	46—07	36.97	9
Kennebec Arsenal,	44—19	34.81	1
Lee,	45—25	46.30	2
Lisbon,	44—00	46.00	7
Perry,	45—00	50.29	9
Portland,	43—38	48.63	3
Saco,	43—31	45.11	8
Standish,	43—45	39.42	1
Steuben,	44—31	53.26	12
Twenty-one Stations,	Mean Lat., 44°-27	Mean depth, 43.24	Total yrs. 166

The stations for the southern half of the State being in large numerical excess, some deduction from the figures expressing the average depth above reached, should be made for the whole State. The yearly fall for the State is unquestionably as high as forty-two (42) inches.

Comparison with districts west.

The table annexed shows the annual fall at points in the belt of country extending west along the parallels substantially correspondent, to the interior of the national domain.

TABLE OF ANNUAL RAIN IN DISTRICTS WEST.

LOCALITIES.	Latitude.	Depth in inches.	Years.
Burlington, Vt., ...	44°-30′	33.90	21
Plattsburg, N. Y., ...	44—41	33.39	10
Fort Niagara, N. Y., ...	43—18	31.77	5
Fort Brady, Mich., ...	46—30	31.35	16
Detroit Barracks, Mich., ...	42—20	30.07	12
Fort Gratiot, Mich., ...	42—35	32.62	11
Fort Mackinac, Mich., ...	45—51	23.87	10
Fort Howard, Wis., ...	44—30	34.65	7
Fort Winnebago, Wis., ...	43—31	27.49	9
Milwaukie, Wis., ...	43—04	27.20	7
Muscatine, Ia., ...	41—28	44.33	10
Fort Madison, Ia., ...	40—38	50.04	4
Fort Ridgely, Minn ,..........	44—15	25.52	2
Fort Ripley, Minn., ...	46—19	29.48	6
Fort Snelling, Minn., ...	44—53	25.43	19
Fifteen Stations, ...	Mean Lat., 43°-52	Mean depth, 32.06	Total yrs. 149

It will be seen, therefore, that the points beyond State have a mean latitude 35′ lower than the Maine stations, yet their rainfall is 11.18 inches less! In other words, the rainfall of Maine as compared with the districts west in the same latitude, is about thirty-five per cent. [of their rainfall] in excess.

Comparison with districts south.

With a view to further comparison a synopsis is presented hereunder of the yearly rainfall at points south of us on the Atlantic coast:

TABLE OF ANNUAL RAIN IN DISTRICTS SOUTH.

LOCALITIES.	Latitude.	Depth in inches.	Years.
Portsmouth, N. H., ...	43°-04	35.57	13
Cambridge Observatory, Mass., .	42—23	44.48	12
New Bedford, Mass., ...	41—42	41.03	42
Providence, R. I., ...	41—49	40.05	23
Fort Hamilton, N. Y. Harbor, ..	40—37	43.65	14
Philadelphia, Pa., ...	39—57	43.56	19
Germantown, Pa., ...	40—03	38.10	8
Baltimore, Md., ...	49—17	42.00	19
Washington, D. C., ...	38—53	41.00	4
Alexandria, Va., ...	38—49	36.30	3
Fort Monroe, Va., ...	37—00	45.18	19
Fort Johnston, N. C., ...	34—00	46.00	
Charleston, S. C., ...	32—46	48.29	15
Fort Moultrie, S. C., ...	32—45	44.92	12
Whilemarsh Island, Ga., ...	32—20	39.03	4
Savannah, Ga., ...	32—06	48.66	19
Athens, Ga., ...	33—58	36.54	4
St. Augustine, Fla., ...	29—48	31.80	3
Oglethorpe Barracks, Fla., ...	32—05	53.33	
Nineteen Stations, ...	Mean Lat., 36°-50	Mean depth, 42.02	Total yrs. 239

The extraordinary result is reached that whereas the points are on the average 7°-37′ lower in latitude, and are therefore on general principles entitled to a very considerably larger annual fall of rain, their actual fall is 1.22 inches less than at the Maine stations.

The local causes of our rainfall.

This remarkable deviation from the ordinary law of rain distribution becomes perfectly intelligible when the *local* conditions of our State are taken into account, those that have been already referred to, chiefly its exposure to cold surrounding seas, with consequent low temperature and further consequent copious precipitation.

Their permanence.

But though local, the conditions are not impermanent. We shall continue to have the ocean south of us as well as east; we shall continue to have the humid airs of Newfoundland close upon our eastern frontier and swept over us by summer drafts; we shall continue to have the vapor-condensing northeast winds from Labrador and the cold seas beyond, wringing out the clouds upon our mountains and valleys, and so long as these continue we shall not lack for water-power material.

The rainfall of Maine and that of various river basins.

The annual receipt of moisture in Maine, is, in the table following, compared with that of several great river basins:

RAINFALL UPON RIVER BASINS BEYOND STATE.

RIVER BASINS.	Inches.	Deficiency as compared with Maine.
Ohio river basin, ...	41.50	0.50 inches.
Upper Mississippi basin, i. e., all above St. Louis, ...	35.20	6.80 "
Red river basin, ...	39.00	3.00 "
Arkansas river basin, ...	29.00	13.00 "
Missouri river basin, ...	20.90	21.10 "
Entire Mississippi basin, ...	30.00	12.00 "

This shows that no one of the districts can compare with Maine upon equal terms, and with the exception of the Ohio basin, only upon terms of marked inferiority, as regards the annual access of water-power material.

Section 2.—SEASON RAIN.

Under this head the precipitation of only summer and winter will receive particular attention.

Subsection A.—SUMMER RAIN. The following table, digested from material furnished by Prof. Henry of the Smithsonian Institute, exhibits our condition as regards this highly important climatic feature:

SUMMER RAIN IN MAINE.

LOCALITIES.	Depth in inches.	LOCALITIES.	Depth in inches.
Bethel,	10.30	Fryeburg,	11.05
Biddeford,	11.14	Gardiner,	10.46
Brunswick,	11 71	Hampden,	11.92
Bucksport,	9.76	Kennebec Arsenal,	10.80
Cornish,	12 48	Lisbon,	10.38
Dexter,	8.66	Monson,	12.25
Eastport,	12.52	Perry,	11.01
Fort Kent,	11.65	Portland,	12.97
Fort Preble,	10.28	Saco,	11.02
Fort Sullivan,	10.6	Steuben,	10.83
Foxcroft,	13.52		
Twenty-one stations,		Mean depth, 11.13 inches.	

For comparison the following record is given for various points over the country: Comparison with extra-state districts.

SUMMER RAIN BEYOND STATE.

LOCALITIES.	Depth in inches.	LOCALITIES.	Depth in inches.
Portsmouth, N. H.,	9.21	Detroit, Mich.,	9.29
Cambridge, Mass.,	11.17	Fort Gratiot, Mich.,	9.99
New York, N. Y.,	11.48	Fort Mackinac, Mich.,	8.88
Philadelphia, Pa.,	11.93	Fort Winnebago, Wis.,	11.46
Baltimore, Md.,	11.04	Milwaukie, Wis.,	9.70
Washington, D. C.,	10.43	Athens, Ill.,	13.30
Fort Monroe, Va.,	15.08	Fort Ridgely, Minn.,	9.29
Fort Johnston, N. C.,	16.32	Fort Snelling, Minn.,	10.92
New Orleans, La.,	17.28	Fort Ripley, Minn.,	12.64
Germantown, O.,	10.03	Fort Riley, Kan.,	7.15
Marietta, O.,	12.78	Jefferson Barracks, Mo.,	12.88
Muscatine, Ia.,	15.08	Fort Belnap, Tex.,	6.31
New Harmony, Ind.,	12.79	Fort Worth, Tex,,	8.80
Memphis, Tenn.,	7.80	San Francisco, Cal.,	0.09
Nashville, Tenn.,	14.00	Sacramento, Cal.,	0.00
Thirty Stations,		Mean depth, 10.60.	

Excess of the Maine Stations, 0.53 inches.

When now it is considered that in the districts compared with Maine, or the greater part of them, the actual summer,—the season of high heat and rapid evaporation—is much longer than in Maine, well nigh twice longer at the southern stations, and that at nearly all, the summer temperature is considerably higher than with us, our advantage with respect to the conservation of water-power material and its resultant available sum, will be seen to be great. The actual summer with us is only about three months and fifteen days long, from May 31st to September 14th, exemption from frost being counted upon only within these dates.

Subsection B.—WINTER RAIN. The word rain, as here used, comprehends aqueous downfall in all its forms—snow, sleet, rain, etc.

WINTER RAIN IN MAINE.

LOCALITIES.	Depth in inches.	LOCALITIES.	Depth in inches.
Bath,	11.40	Gardiner,	10.27
Belfast,	8.85	Houlton,	7.48
Bethel,	8.99	Augusta,	10.10
Biddeford,	12.47	Lee,	11.74
Brunswick,	9.84	Lisbon,	9.54
Bucksport,	8.63	Monson,	8.85
Cornish,	11.17	Oak Grove Seminary,	9.45
Dexter,	9.17	Perry,	10.86
Eastport,	6.12	Portland,	12.17
Fort Kent,	9.71	Saco,	11.82
Fort Preble,	10.82	Standish,	9.10
Fort Sullivan,	10.62	Steuben,	14.30
Fryeburg,	10.04	West Waterville,	9.83
Twenty-six stations,		Mean depth, 10.13.	

Proportion of winter moisture received in snow.

A considerable proportion of the precipitation during four months and a half takes place in the form of snow. The table following shows the depth received :

ANNUAL DEPTH OF SNOW IN MAINE.

LOCALITIES.	Depth in inches.	Years.	LOCALITIES.	Depth in inches.	Years.
Gardiner,	83,50	24	Bath,	83.00	7
Brunswick,	66.00	44	Steuben,	102.00	7
Portland,	60.54	4	Cornish,	96.00	7
"Oxford County,"*	90.00	12			
Stations,			Mean depth, 83.02 inches.		

Eighty-three and two-hundredths inches of new-fallen snow correspond to 6.91 inches of water. The *total* downfall for the four months and a half during which snow falls is about 15.62 inches, 6.91 of which, as just shown, come in snow. Accordingly about 44 per cent. of the total downfall during the four and a half months of actual winter in Maine, is snow. The per cent. during the three months of nominal winter is of course greater.

* Blodgett's Climatology of the United States.

ANNUAL DEPTH OF SNOW BEYOND STATE.

LOCALITIES.	Depth in inches.	Years.	LOCALITIES.	Depth in inches.	Years.
Dover, N. H., ...	68.60	10	Hartford, Ct., ...	43 00	24
Montreal, Can., ...	67.00	10	Lambertville, N. J., .	25.50	8
Worcester, Mass., ...	55.00	12	Cincinnati, O., ...	19.00	4
Amherst, Mass., ...	54.00	7	Beloit, Wis., ...	25.00	3
Eight stations, ...			Mean depth, 44.63 inches.		

Excess at the Maine stations, 38.39 inches, or 86 per cent.

Practical effects of the amount of snow.

It has already been noticed in the section upon *Winter Temperature,* that in consequence of so large a proportion of moisture falling in the form of snow, the streams in Maine *run low in winter;* but observed further that they never run so low as in summer. Accordingly, manufacturing, being limited by the *lowest* run, may justly be declared to suffer nothing in the way of water dearth, in consequence of the profuse snowfall of the State. Nor does it suffer in the season of snow-melting, and for the reasons following. The snow solidifies during the winter into a mass of icy or semi-icy consistency, and in this form dissolves but slowly before the advancing heat of the year. The spring winds are cold and retard the process of liquefaction; especially is this the case in the evergreen forests, which preserve the snow in the northern part of the State in favorable localities to early summer. The ground—which, as before noticed, even if frozen before snowfall, usually thaws out during the winter beneath the protecting mass—has time as the melting proceeds, to charge itself to the full, thus retarding the discharge into the rivers. Accordingly the accumulations of the winter go off with far less swelling of the streams than is experienced further south and in the interior, where the depth of snow is much less, but where the spring heats come on suddenly and are untempered by cold sea winds.

Section 3.—Uniform Distribution of Rain.

Rain is distributed to Maine with remarkable uniformity at different seasons of the year. Thus the summer fall at twenty-one stations has been shown to be 11.13 inches; the winter fall at twenty-six stations, 10.13 inches. The receipt for spring and autumn are nearly equal, and are each about 10.50 inches.

Consequent uniformity of the rivers.

The practical consequence of this, taken in connection with other climatic features before noticed, is, that

4

the rivers of the State to a remarkable extent enjoy immunity from those ruinous drawbacks to water-power manufacturing, *water-dearth and freshet.* Such a phenomenon is never seen in Maine, (which is almost every summer seen in the interior and western parts of the country) as rivers draining hundreds of square miles of territory, drying up into half-stagnant tarns and chains of pools, their beds converted into wastes of fissured, sun-baked mud, strewn with stumps and the debris of freshets, leaving bridges hundreds of feet in length standing *upon dry land,* and with no water in sight, where at other seasons a torrent twenty feet deep fills the entire channel.

On the contrary we find the larger streams of Maine, with their storage basins almost entirely unused for summer reserve, nevertheless yielding for the ordinary manufacturing hours of the day, at their lowest sites, and at strictly low summer run, the Androscoggin 125,000 cubic feet per minute, the Kennebec 170,000, the Penobscot 318,000, and others in proportion. This, be it observed, is the run determined by nature and comparatively unaffected by human interference. As such, it is capable of increase upon the streams referred to by more than one hundred per cent. by the use of reservoirs, and upon other rivers in equal and upon many in much higher proportion.

As our streams suffer comparatively little from dearth of water so do they suffer little from excess of water. Our freshets, which rarely carry off so much as a bridge, and never one properly established, and are destructive to only insufficiently secured lumber, never approximate in volume those experienced further south and in the interior, where the rains are more violent and the snow-melting, as before noticed, more rapid. Not *one* of our larger rivers is subject to such rises, as compel the construction of mill works above the level of advantageous use of the ordinarily low summer water.

The range from low to high water upon the chief rivers of the State, will be given in Part II., with other details.

The heaviest rainfall upon the Southern Slope.

The statement that the precipitation of moisture throughout the State is uniform requires to be modified in one regard. The sum of rainfall on the Southern Slope is somewhat heavier than on the Northern, as appears from the table annexed.

DISTRIBUTION OF RAIN TO THE NORTHERN AND SOUTHERN SLOPES.

	Localities.	Annual rain.
Northern Slope.........	Fort Kent, ...	36.46 inches.
	Hancock Barracks,.....................	36.97 "
	Mean,.........................36.71	
Southern Slope.........	Fort Sullivan, ...	39.39 inches.
	Fort Preble,.........................	45.25 "
	Gardiner, ...	44.36 "
	Waterville,..........................	42.91 "
	Saco, ...	45.90 "
	Mean,.........................43.56	

This shows that upon the Southern, the *water-power* Slope, about eighteen per cent. more rain is received than upon the Northern; and that accordingly our water-power is in receipt of an annual sum of motive material larger than would result from perfectly uniform distribution.

CHAPTER IX.

EVAPORATION IN MAINE.

What proportion of the total annual rainfall is wasted by the atmosphere may be ascertained either by direct observations upon evaporation or by measurement of the discharge of streams. In either case the experiments require to be conducted with care, throughout the year, and indeed for a series of years. By neither of the methods has the yearly sum of evaporation in our State been determined; and of the data necessary for determination only a few elements, as the maximum and minimum delivery of a few of the rivers, are at command.

The per centum of annual water-waste can however be arrived at with tolerable accuracy, by reference to the statistics of evaporation in other districts, with suitable allowance for difference in latitude, temperature, winds, ocean exposure, etc.

The following table shows the proportions of downfall, drainage and evaporation in districts beyond State, as observed under con ditions favorable for accurate results.

DOWNFALL, DRAINAGE, AND EVAPORATION BEYOND STATE.

LOCALITIES.	Downfall.	Drainage.		Evaporation.	
	Inches.	Inches.	Ratio.	Inches.	Ratio.
Long Pond, Boston Water Works,....	40	18	0.45	22	0.55
Schuylkill Naval Reservoirs,........	36	18	0.50	18	0.50
Rivington Pike,....................	55	24	0.44	31	0.56
West-Fork Reservoirs,..............	36	14	0.39	22	0.61
England and Ireland,...............	36	12	0.33	24	0.67
Ohio river basin,..................	41.5	9.9	0.24	31.6	0.76
Upper Mississippi basin,...........	35.2	8.4	0.24	26.8	0.76
Missouri basin,....................	20.9	3.	0.15	17.9	0.85
Arkansas basin,....................	29.3	4.3	0.15	25.0	0.85
Red river basin,...................	39+	8+	0.20	31.0	0.80
Entire Mississippi valley,..........	30+	8+	0.25	22.0	0.75

Evaporation from the reservoir basins.

It will be noticed, first, that in the case of the various *reservoirs*, etc., the per cent. of evaporation is very low, sinking to 0.50 of the total downfall in one instance. The slopes of the catchment basin of these water receptacles, as compared with large hydrographic areas, converge directly and abruptly to a single point, so that the surplus water is gathered speedily and with little waste into the holding basins. Moreover the surface of the slopes is smoothed, and its natural channels kept clear, so as to facilitate the passage of the water to the reservoirs. Accordingly less water will in general be wasted from the receiving surfaces of water works than from extensive water-sheds in the same region. Accordingly we are not at liberty to infer that 45 per cent. of our annual downfall is secured to the rivers, because that proportion is netted from the water-shed of the Boston Water Works.

Evaporation west of the Mississippi river.

It will be noticed in the second place, that the proportion of evaporation in the geographical districts lying west of the Mississippi river is high, rising to four-fifths of the total downfall at the least, and to eighty-five per cent. over by far the larger part of the region. This is due to their mid-continental position with its associated atmospheric aridity, to their location under the lee of lofty mountains, and to the deficiency of forests, which amounts indeed to total deprivation over the larger part of the whole territory. Unquestionably, then, evaporation in Maine is much less than in the region in question.

The Ohio and upper Mississippi basins.

In the Ohio and upper Mississippi basins, the general conditions affecting water-waste, namely, the humidity of the atmosphere, forests, the number of rainy and cloudy days, the duration and severity of winter, bear, as a whole, a closer relation to the corresponding conditions in our State. In the former, however, the summers are longer and hotter and the mean temperature of the year higher; in the latter the summers are hotter and the air dryer throughout the year; so that in each the proportion of evaporation is greater than with us.

The British Isles.

In the case of the British Isles, the main points to be noted, are, that our mean annual temperature is 7°.25 lower than theirs—48°.90,* and our winter temperature 20° below theirs—39°; further, much the larger proportion of our surface is covered with forests. On the other hand, their summer temperature is 2.43 lower than ours; and the winds the most prevalent with them, the west and southwest, are oceanic. Their winters are open, ours are sealed against evaporation by frost for months. On the whole, our yearly temperature being so much below theirs, our winters frost-bound, our surfaces forest-clad, and our winds as a whole maritime, the percentage of evaporation must be judged decidedly less with us than in the insular districts in question.

Inferred or estimated proportion of evaporation in Maine.

On the whole, it would seem safe to assign as a figure very closely approximating our actual annual evaporation, 0.60 of the yearly downfall. In other words, of the 42 inches of rain received yearly, 25.20 are reabsorbed by the atmosphere, and 16.18 pass off by the rivers to the sea.

Views of Prof. Henry.

In this conclusion I am confirmed by the judgment of two eminent physicists of our country, and the two perhaps the best competent to give intelligent judgment on such questions. Says Professor Henry, "If it has been found by careful observation that evaporation from the surface of the Boston Water Works, is fifty-five per cent. of the quantity of water received, I would infer that sixty or sixty-five per cent. would be a sufficient average allowance for Maine."

Views of Gen. Humphreys.

Major General A. A. Humphreys, Chief of Engineers, U. S. A., whose work upon the Physics and Hydraulics of the Mississippi river, is an honor to the scholarship not of this country alone but of modern times, in a letter to the writer remarks: "From the various facts which you mention I should incline to the opinion that 70 per cent. is too large a fraction of evaporation for Maine. The hot suns of summer and the dry westerly winds would tend to make the per centage large, but the

* Mean of thirty-five stations.

vast and dense forests, the humid winds of the other seasons, the cold of the long winters, must tend to make the proportion of evaporation small."

Overcast and stormy days.

The rapidity of evaporation in any district will be influenced powerfully, it is evident, by the number of cloudy, rainy, and snowy days occurring during the year. The following table represents all the facts that have come to hand touching this meteorological feature of the State:

WEATHER AT PORTLAND.

Year.	Clear.	Cloudy.	Variable.	Rain or Snow.
1856,	21	55	290	140
1857,	-	-	-	157
1858,	17	65	283	136
1859.	17	65	-	138

WEATHER AT STEUBEN.

Mean Cloudiness.		Mean Cloudiness.	
1854,	6.10	1857,	6.16
1855,	6.18	1858,	5.62
1856,	6.12	1859,	5.86

Humidity of the climate evidenced by vegetation.

The humidity of the climate of Maine claimed to be so marked for a district situate on the lee of a land breadth of thousands of miles, is in a manner demonstrated by the persistence and vigor of its grass and forest vegetation. In the condition of nature the whole surface of the State, from the froth rim of the spring tides to the top of the tallest mountains, a few only excepted, was and would be completely buried in dense and humid woods. Wherever the labor of man has made a *clearing,* immediately unless prevented by stub-scythe, fire, and the ploughshare, innumerable shrubs and treelets swarm into its occupancy, almost strangling one another with their numbers, and in a few years forests again are waving on the recent scene of unaccustomed sunshine. If the clearing be prosecuted to the thoroughness of *subduing,* grasses crowd in, a dense and beautiful turf, which happily adds to an emerald verdure the substantial quality of most excellent nourishment for all cattle. Even when the fertile surface of the ground is flayed off, and only lean gravel, or hard clay, or intractable pan, is opened to the elements, as in railway cuttings and embankments, canal excavations, brickyards, etc., soon, if not disturbed, a myriad army of grass spires, fed by the rains and moist winds, takes possession of the vacant space, and in a few years more the rail car or the canal boat moves through an avenue of young and thriving woods. Even our mountains when by accident burned over, and burned it may be to the very bone, soon gather greenness in their seams and furrows, which gradually spreads and climbs in altitude, so that the next generation beholds green woods covering close the stained and fire-blistered rocks.

In all this we are reminded not of arid continental interiors or of prairies, savannahs, llanos and pampas, treeless plains, but rather of wet coast regions and wooded lands, the forest coasts of Norway drenched with abundant rain and crowned with lofty pines, the *Selvas* of the Amazon, and the ancient great woods of Ireland and England, long since disappeared. It is not necessary to say that such determined persistence and vigor of grass and forest life are never exhibited except in climates characterized by comparative humidity.

DIVISION III.

MISCELLANEOUS MATTER.

CHAPTER X.

HEALTHINESS OF THE CLIMATE OF MAINE.

The two grand forms or families of diseases which may be regarded as in a manner characteristic of the easterly half and interior of the United States, and which chiefly affect the desirableness of the region as a field for immigration, are *Malarious* diseases and *Respiratory* diseases.

Malarious diseases.

The malarious diseases here referred to, embrace the various forms of intermittent, remittent and autumnal fevers, and those febrile ailments which are usually referred to a miasmatic origin. Distempers of this character prevail in districts at once moist and hot, especially where fertility of soil is associated. "The Mississippi Valley has been preëminent as the theatre of malarious fevers which have been the scourge of immigrants from nearly all parts of the world. To the natives of the north of Europe and the British Isles in particular, the change has been extremely trying, and prostration by some one of its forms mild or severe has been almost certain to attend the new-comer. India itself has not been more certain to break the health of the emigrant than the Mississippi Valley, though the American forms of disease were always attended with a much smaller ratio of mortality."* It suffices our purposes to say that this class of diseases are *unknown in Maine*. In the early settlement of other parts of New England and in New York they have in time past had foothold, but in no part of our State do they now exist, or have they at any time existed. We have sufficient humidity, and

* Blodgett's Climatology of the United States.

in parts sufficient accumulation of vegetable matter in the soil to give origin to the affections referred to, but the low temperature of our summer and the influences of the sea, forbid their generation.

Respiratory diseases.

Diseases of the respiratory organs, which are always and everywhere the characteristic forms of unhealth prevailing in countries at once *moist* and *cool*, are the most fatal, and contribute more largely to the annual mortality in our State. Not however in an exceptional degree, as appears from the following statistics:

TABLE OF PULMONARY DISEASES.

	Per cent. of entire mortality.
England and Wales, last half of 1838,	26.60
Hasting's District in England, mean of 20 years,	35.06
Maine, year closing July 1, 1850,	27.35
Vermont, year closing July 1, 1850,	28.24
Massachusetts, mean of 12 years,	27.94
Rhode Island,	25.52

As to the fatality of the diseases in question upon a *manufacturing* population, the citations from our State and Vermont as compared with Massachusetts, would hardly seem to justify the popular impression of their unusual malignancy. The large per cent. of mortality from these diseases in England and Wales, whose climate is mild and equable, is possibly, however, referable to confinement in workshops, the breathing of air variously contaminated, etc., measurably inseparable from manufacturing labor.

It is certain that immigrants from northwestern Europe, the British Isles, all Germany, Holland, Belgium, Norway and Sweden, incur far less risk to their health upon removal to a climate like that of Maine, which is in many important respects like their own, than to the interior and southern portions of the country. With the people of Southern Europe the liabilities might be reversed.

Epidemics and infections.

As regards epidemics and infections, among the more terrible but obscure forms of which are the *plagues* of the Old World, and of which with us the *yellow fever* and the *cholera* are the most malignant types, *none of these have ever prevailed in Maine*, except that sporadic cases of the cholera have occurred. The yellow fever has come several times as far east as Portsmouth, and has been fairly epidemic in New York, New Haven, Providence, etc., but has not come within our limits unless it may possibly be in isolated cases by direct importation. Both of these forms of disease, and indeed the whole class, seem to be dependent in general upon a high temperature, calms, great moisture, and a stagnant condition of the atmosphere, for their generation and spread. Thus the deaths from cholera in the United States in 1850 were 18,243 in summer to 1,427 in winter. The yellow fever nearly always ceases with the first hard frost. The conditions referred to as essential to the diseases specified, do not exist with us, except rarely and for a day at a time, and hence our entire exemption.

Evidence of the U. S. military records.

The records of mortality at the United States military stations of the New England States and of Maine in particular, indicate a high general salubrity of climate. The interior and northern portion of Maine is especially instanced as free from tendencies to respiratory disorders, the resident population being declared to an unusual degree exempt from their ravages, and new comers, soldiers, settlers and others, already affected, deriving immediate and marked benefit.

The climate and manufacturing labor.

The favorable character of the climate of Maine as regards manufacturing labor has already been noticed in Chapter VIII.

CHAPTER XI.

COMPARATIVE COST OF WATER-POWER AND STEAM-POWER.

Section 1.—Cost of Steam-power and Water-power Equipment.

Upon this topic a few estimates are submitted.

Cost of steam-power equipment.

At Fall River, a leading manufacturer estimates the cost of steam-power equipment, including engines, boilers and connecting apparatus, but not foundations or engine-houses, from $100 to $115 per horse-power.

Nelson Curtis, Esq., agent of the Atlantic Works, Boston, Mass., in response to inquiry estimates "in round numbers the cost of engines complete with boilers and equipment, including foundations and masonry, of 300 horse-power and upwards, but not including the engine-house, at $115 per nominal horse-power."

George F. Morse, Esq., Superintendent of the Portland Company's Works, Portland, Me., estimates that "the total equipment for steam-power, including chimney, buildings, boilers, engines, and all connections, ready for starting, for a power of 300 horses, can be furnished at the rate of $100 per horse."

The *actual cost* of steam equipment, as employed in the water department of various cities, has, so far as facts have come to hand, outrun these estimates from fifty to a hundred and fifty-per cent., varying from $150 to $300 per horse-power.

The cost of water-power equipment.

Mr. Francis estimates the cost of the development of the water-power at Lowell for canals and dams, as about $1,000,000, or $100 per horse-power; the cost of wheels and other arrangements for using the power as about $1,000,000, or $100 per horse-power, making a total of $200 per horse-power. The cost of wheels and accessory arrangements Mr. F. judges to have been quite "*twice the average*," as, the great object having been to procure the utmost effect from the power, no expense has been spared, and numerous changes made. Moreover, the main canal as originally constructed proved inadequate, and a second canal had to be made at large expense. The development of the power at this place, being almost the first on so large a scale, was in a manner experimental, and naturally therefore not conducted to the best advantage in all respects.

In regard to the cost of the development of the Saco Falls, J. G. Garland, Esq., of Biddeford, makes the following statement:

The banks of the river adjoining the falls were originally exceedingly rugged, rough, and high; were formed of solid trap ledge, extremely difficult and expensive to excavate, thereby necessitating very unusual outlay for mill sites, canals, raceways, wheelpits, etc. From 1750 to about 1830 the power was employed almost exclusively for saw mills, the mills being located where the power could be cheaply applied to the simple "*tub*" wheels operating under low heads of six to ten feet, the whole fall of 40 feet being divided by dams into three falls, respectively 8, 16 and 16 feet high.

If the improvement of the fall had been delayed until the introduction of turbine wheels admitting of high heads, and until its development could have been carried out to the best advantage for the whole fall, the expense would have been much less than that really incurred, viz., $170 per effective horse-power. This covers the cost of excavations, foundations, dams, canals, flumes, raceways, wheelpits and wheels.

It appears therefore that the preparatory equipment of water-power, even when got ready for use under circumstances necessitating quite unusual expenditure, when carried out in the most durable manner, the dams of split stone laid in cement, the wheels of the most expensive patterns, and the appurtenant constructions of the most solid and enduring forms, and so carried out as to realize the utmost effect from the power possible under the circumstances—nevertheless costs not over $200 per horse power.

This of course greatly exceeds the cost under ordinary circumstances, where everything is taken at the best advantage. Hiram F. Mills, C. E., in his Memorial to the Legislature of Maine, estimates that on the Penobscot river, within twelve miles of Bangor and its excellent harbor, stone dams could be built with necessary canals, wheel-pits, and wheels set ready for the main shafting, at a cost not exceeding $4,500,000, the power being, as he estimates, 40,000 gross, and the cost per horse power therefore $112.50.

This figure is much in excess, under ordinary and favorable conditions, of the expense of wooden dams, lower grade wheels, and constructions of less permanent character. Improvements of this sort can be got ready for use on ordinary sites for $50 per horse power, and will outlast the most durable steam apparatus.

In fact, at sites naturally favorable and possessed of power in excess of demands upon it, power can be brought into use for a small part of even this outlay for preparatory equipment.

Section 2.—Comparative cost of operating Machinery by Steam and by Water.

The cost of raising water at the Philadelphia Water Works for the year 1867 by water-power as contrasted with steam-power, is shown by the following statistics abstracted from the Report of the Chief Engineer, Frederick Graff, Esq.:

COST OF WATER-POWER AND STEAM-POWER AT THE PHILADELPHIA WATER WORKS.

	Form of power used.	Cost of raising each million gallons one foot.
Fairmount Works,	Water-power,	$0.02 1-4
Schuylkill Works,	Steam-power,	0.11 1-10
Delaware Works,	" "	0.29 2-10
Twenty-Fourth Ward Works,	" "	0.08 3-10
Germantown Works,	" "	0 19 1-10

Mean cost per steam, $0.16 9-10.

This shows that the cost of raising water by steam-power, coal being $5.50 per ton, exceeded the cost by water-power on the average seven-fold.

From the annual report of Moses Lane, Esq., Chief Engineer of the Brooklyn Water-Works, for the year 1867, the following instructive facts are gathered.

The cost per million gallons (128,000 cubic feet) for pumping at the said works, has been for a series of years as follows, the water being raised 163 feet vertical:

COST OF STEAM-POWER AT THE BROOKLYN WATER WORKS.

	1862.	1863.	1864.	1865.	1866.	1867.
Labor, superintendence, repairs, etc., ...	$12.22	13.50	16.89	18.74	19.84	18.20
Interest on cost of works, etc., ...	$9 04	7.23	5.90	5.14	4.33	3.85
	$21.26	20.73	22.79	23.88	24.17	22.05

Showing an average of $22.48. Hence the average cost of raising a million gallons *one foot* has been thirteen cents and a fraction over, or nearly six times the cost at the Philadelphia water-wheels. The cost of coal at the engine house of the Brooklyn Water Works, 1867, was $7.11 per gross ton. The cost for steam-power at these works varies from $72 to $100 per horse-power per annum.

Messrs. Charles Staples & Son, machinists, of Portland, estimate the cost per annum of steam-power in their works, with the best equipment, for fuel, attendance, etc., for a power of twenty horse, at $150 per horse-power, operating ten hours a day.

Again, the cost of operating the wheels of the Fairmount Water Works for the year 1852 by water-power, was 2¾ cents per day for each horse-power of work done. Whereas, the steam pumping engines of the water works of Hartford and Cambridge, coal being $6 per ton, were run at a mean expense of 22½ cents to each horse-power of work done.* This difference of 19¾ cents per day to each horse-power in favor of water-power, would in the case of the power at Lewiston involve a saving of $1,303 per day, over an equal power operated by steam, coal being $6 per ton; a saving of $1,382 per diem in case of the power on the Kennebec at Waterville, of $1,273 in case of the power on the Androscoggin at Brunswick, and of $3,135 in case of the power at Rumford, or $2,198,830 per annum for all combined.

* Annual Reports.

Now the total amount of cotton consumed in Massachusetts in the year 1860 was 63,333 tons. The cost of transporting this cotton 2,000 miles by sea, at the rate of four mills per ton per mile, would be $506,664. Its transportation 200 miles by rail at three cents per mile would be $379,998; total, $886,662. So that the net per annum advantage arising from the use of water-power to the amount of the foregoing four powers alone, over an equivalent amount of steam-power, would pay for the transportation specified two and a half times over; or otherwise, pay for it once, and leave a net profit of over $1,300,000. The net advantage accruing from the use of the 65,000 (net) horse-power on the Androscoggin river below Rumford falls, over an equivalent amount of steam-power, would pay for the moving of the above amount of material over 2,000 miles *by rail.*

William Fairbaim, Esq., one of the most eminent of the civil engineers of England, contrasting the cost of steam and water-power, refers to the Catrine Mills, the two hundred horse-power of water-power employed in connection with which cost the enormous sum of £18,000, the annual rental on which would be £1,260. He then shows that the rental of an equivalent amount of steam-power would be £1,500, *coal being only* $1.75 *per ton.*

CHAPTER XII.

ACCESSIBILITY OF THE WATER-POWER OF MAINE.

As regards trans-ocean transit.

The grand highway of ocean travel and of freight transportation connecting the great commercial centres of the old and new worlds, leads along the coast of Maine almost within sight of its headlands. Indeed the pathway of steam as well as sail communication widens up to and into the harbors of Maine, Portland being a point of departure for steamers to trans-ocean ports.

As regards trans-continental transit.

As respects railway transit it is conceded that any trunk line constructed with a view to best accommodate trans-continental communication and reduce ocean passages to the shortest possible length, must pass through Maine. So that as respects access to the *world at large* by the great inter-continental highway of traffic and travel on sea and land, the water-power manufacturers of Maine will be and are very favorably located.

Local facilities for navigation.

Further, as remarked before, the coast of the State is thickset with first-class harbors from end to end, scarcely any other seaboard of equal length on the globe affording the parallel of this feature. The great rise and fall of the tide coöperating with the prevalent off-shore northwest wind, keeps these harbors clear of ice for a much longer proportion of the year than could otherwise be looked for; several, as Portland, Dyer's bay, Musketoe, Cutler, Machiasport, Camden (outer), Eastport, Lubec and others, being unobstructed at all seasons. A large number can be kept open by the use of an ice boat, or common tug boat, for an hour or two a day for half a dozen days during the winter. Many of the largest water-powers are located close upon the coast, as before particularized; several of the largest though retired from the shore line are nevertheless upon navigable waters. A vast amount of power is thus brought within 12 to 30 hours of Boston and New York by coasters or steamers.

The water-power of the Carolinas and Georgia, on the contrary, is removed even at its lowest sites from 60 to 150 miles from the seaboard, access to which by the rivers is by impeded and intermittent navigation,—navigation not susceptible of substantial and permanent improvement, and which finds on the coast only few and inferior harbors.

Local facilities for land transport.

Railroads are already constructed parallel to the lower sections of the main water-power rivers, the Androscoggin, the Kennebec, the Penobscot, the St. Croix, and the Saco. As before noticed, the valleys of these rivers admit of the ready extension of railways far into the interior, and by consequence of the opening-up of the water-power to use. The water-power of even the St. Croix will upon the completion of the European and North American Railway be brought within sixteen hours of Boston. That of the Saco is now within four hours of the same point, of the Androscoggin within six, of the Kennebec within eight, of the Penobscot within twelve hours.

It is evident therefore that as regards *access to our own commercial centres* by rail, steamer, or coaster, the water-power manufacturers of this State are and will be advantageously located. Herein, *not in a location territorially central,* consists the real economical accessibility of power, and its value as affected by position.

The manufacturing system of Maine continuous with that of the rest of New England.

The manufacturing system of Maine will be in close proximity to those or rather that of New Hampshire, Massachusetts, Connecticut and Rhode Island. This in very important respects will prove of great advantage, especially in the earlier stages of our manufacturing development; economical connection with other series of establishments being highly promotive of manufacturing prosperity; and in all stages of development the relation in question will constitute an important advantage.

Summary statement.

In fine, there is no district in the country or in the world, possessed of any considerable amount of unimproved and available water-power, that can be for a moment compared with Maine in point of short and cheap access to the great centres of supply and demand. The remotest water-power upon the Southern Slope of the State is not half so far from first-class harbors as the city of Pittsburg, and not twice as far therefrom as the manufacturing towns of western Massachusetts are from Boston.

CHAPTER XIII.

CONCLUSION OF PART I.

Recapitulation of incidents favoring water-power.

The view hereinbefore given of the physical conditions of the State which more closely affect its water-power, general as it has necessarily been, is certainly such as would beforehand warrant the expectation of very unusual measures and unusual availability of manufacturing power within our limits. The location of the State amid surrounding seas; its extent of surface; the disposition of its slopes; its geological structure; its surface forms and extensive forests; its grand system of lakes, with their uniform connection with the rivers and susceptibility of reservoir improvement; the low annual temperature, and especially low summer temperature, which at once reduces evaporation and contributes to vigorous labor; the winds of the State, as a whole, maritime in character; the copious rainfall, with its uniform distribution throughout the year and diffusion over the whole State; the late lingering of the snow in Spring; the small per cent. of evaporation, resulting from the low temperature, from the number of rainy, snowy, and cloudy days; the consequent large residuum of water for removal by rivers, and which our favorable surface forms determine to be removed by rivers—taken together, constitute a sum of favorable conditions, which, it is confidently believed, no other equal area on the globe can surpass or indeed can so much as equal. Other districts may have and certainly do have some one or more of the advantageous features more decidedly developed than Maine, but none can parallel fully, as is believed, their combined series.

When to the foregoing the considerations are added of the high salubrity of the climate and its adaptedness to mauufacturing industry, of the superiority of water-power over steam-power in economy, and of the favorable situation of our power with reference to the commercial routes and centers of the world, the upbuilding of a great system of manufacturing in our midst would seem to be inevitable, a question only of time and of proper exhibition of our resources.

The great and natural business of Maine.

The view before given still further goes to show that no other avocation, which is of sufficient scope and permanence to afford basis for the employment of great populations, through which general and widely diffused opulence may be attained, flourishing cities and towns builded, not upon the coast merely or navigable rivers, but over a large portion of the State, and through which we can ever hope to take a stand side by side with the flourishing and weathy communities adjacent—is available to our hand at all commensurate in promise with, or so open to advantageous prosecution above all competitors as, manufacturing—manufacturing by water-power. It is true whatever facilities for commerce the mere circumstance of excellent harbors, and harbors in large numbers can furnish, we possess; but other States have harbors which if not equal to ours, are adequate to all required purposes, and are the seats already of extensive traffic—traffic that does not readily change its direction or its marts. Without derogating aught from our agricultural capabilities, it is sufficient to say that our attractions in that sphere are at present and bid fair to be for some time to come, unless assisted from extraneous sources, outweighed by those of the central districts of the country, a disability which all the New England States labor under in common, and that accordingly no considerable increase of our population and wealth is to be looked for from this source alone and by itself. Our stores of lumber are great but they are not exhaustless; no wealthy and stable communities are or ever can be created on the basis of this resource. Our minerals are, it is quite safe to assume, not of such sort as promise any large increase of wealth in and through their development. Shipbuilding, an important occupation, is in a measure precarious and is necessarily limited in its amount—limited, that is to say, as the employment of a whole State

Our own people necessitated to manufacturing.

It is important to notice, therefore, that to a large extent *our own population* can, when once a beginning is made, be counted upon for interest, investment, and service in manufacturing operations, the local temptations in other directions being not strong, and general employment for the *whole year*, and to the great majority of our workers not being afforded and not being susceptible of profitable prosecution, outside of manufacturing avocations. As compared with the occupants of States whose soil is more generally and exuberantly fertile and whose agricultural capacities are therefore naturally larger, or of States whose vast mineral treasures invite and command labor, we can, other things being equal, engage in manufacturing to decided advantage and as it were naturally, and can coöperate more zealously and with greater singleness of aim with the capitalist who comes amongst us to make use of our "hitherto neglected waters."

Our grand resources inexhaustible.

The people of the State may justly congratulate themselves upon the fact, and invite the attention of those living elsewhere to the fact, that our grand resource is of a kind that will never fail or become materially modified, because it is based upon the unchanging features and sustained by the perpetually recuperative processes of nature. It can never fail so long as the Gulf Stream flows, so long as the Mediterranean of Mexico exhales its vapors, so long as our interior districts are upheaved upon the shoulders of the White Mountain plateau, so long as the waters of Umbagog, Moosehead, Sebago, Chesuncook, and the Schoodic lakes, with hundreds more, fall through hundreds of feet, over hundreds of waterfalls, in iron-bound channels, and at last through magnificent harbors, to the sea.

This grand resource is *power*.

This grand resource is not mere inert material but is *power*, the swiftest creator of wealth, the most importunate demand of all active civilizations, power that once utilized may be made productive, in the long run of time, of greater opulence than can be gathered from any mines of iron or coal, or reservoirs of oil, or placers or lodes of precious metals, found in any equal area in this country, resources that ultimately fail, and many of them speedily fail. In the civilization of to-day mechanical power in an available shape at low cost is but another name and form for wealth.

It is productive power.

Hence it is that Lowell, operating 9,000 horse-powers of water-power, has already a population of 40,000; Fall River, operating 1,600 horse-powers of water and 4,300 of steam, has a population of 23,000, and a valuation of $16,300,000; Lawrence, with a power nearly equal to Lowell, has a population of about 30,000; Biddeford and Saco, with 3,750 gross horse-power, 150,000 spindles, show a population of 16,000. Forty-two hundred horse-powers in operation at Lewiston have already gathered a population of 22,000, and $8,000,000 valuation. And *in general*, it is found that for each 100,000 spindles a population can be counted upon of 10,000; or in other terms a population of 1,000 to each 166 horse-powers employed in cotton manufacture. This at least where the power is employed to good advantage and time is given for it to exert its full effect,—a longer period of years for the greater part than our American manufacturing towns have yet had.

Why our water-power has not been more improved.

The people of the State may with propriety account for and extenuate to the general public the past non-use of our water-power and our consequent inability to improve it so rapidly as is desirable, by reference to the disturbances connected with the "Northeastern Boundary," which for many years discouraged immigration and improvements; by reference also to the ignorant and bigoted State policy formerly for a long time in the ascendant, which virtually forbade such combinations of capital as alone could and can improve power of such magnitude; and by reference to the preposterous and guilty neglect of the State to ascertain and advertise its resources.

The policy of the State now highly favorable to manufacturing.

In contrast with that former ruinous legislation we are now able to show upon our statute books the most liberal provisions for the encouragement of manufacturing industry; first, in the matter of exemption of new manufacturing establishments from taxation; second, in the exceedingly favorable provisions relating to flowage; thirdly, in allowing towns to subscribe to the stock of manufacturing enterprises.

Public interest in and desire for manufactures.

Finally, in all parts of the State, and amongst all classes of our population, the utmost anxiety is felt that our abundant water-power shall be put to use. We feel that in a peculiar manner this is our grand resource, and that our prosperity is dependent upon its development. We are disposed by all means in our power,—by favoring legislation, both State and municipal, by local and substantial coöperation, and by friendly dispositions upon all hands, to make our State acceptable for residence and investment to the employers of water-power in any form.

PART II.

The Principal River Systems of Maine.

DIVISION I.

The Primary or Interior Systems.

CHAPTER XIV.

INTRODUCTORY OBSERVATIONS.

There are 5,151 streams in Maine represented upon the State map. These ramifying into innumerable branches thread the surface of the State with a fine network of brooks and rivulets, so that in all parts it seems alive and in motion with running waters—a distinctive and characteristic feature, which strikes the attention of the stranger and the traveller.

The streams of Maine.

As is remarked in PART I., the character of this Report requires the *rivers* of the State to be treated with more formality and at greater length than its other hydrographic features. Accordingly they are made the subject of distinct discussion in this the second PART of the Report.

The rivers treated by themselves.

A river system comprehends both the river and its basin—the drainage area and the drainage stream. There are, accordingly, as many river systems in the State as there are rivers. In a Report of this size only a few of these can be made subjects of particular consideration, and these in respect to only those features which bear most closely upon water-power.

Definition of the river system.

As regards the *river basins* the features referred to are as follows: Position; form; linear and square dimensions; elevation; disposition of slopes, both riverward and seaward; geological structure; surface aspect and materials, including vegetation; and the amount of rainfall.

Leading features of the river basins.

As respects the *rivers*, the features necessary to be put in relief are their course; magnitude, including length and volume; constancy of volume; reservoirs, both natural

Leading features of the rivers.

and artificial; slope or rapidity of descent seaward, especially in their water-power portion.

The water-powers treated elsewhere. The one feature of the rivers, however, which in an inquiry into their water-power stands first in the order of importance, namely—the number, location, size and character of their *falls and rapids*, is made the subject of a separate PART of the general discussion. The necessity of this will be evident, when it is considered that very many powers of importance are found upon streams that cannot receive attention in our necessarily brief review of the principal river systems.

CHAPTER XV.

THE SYSTEM OF THE SACO.

Section 1.—THE SACO BASIN.

Location. The drainage district of the Saco is situated in the southeast part of the State, covering the belt of country betwixt the White Mountains and their southwesterly extensions, and the sea. It is, therefore, in close proximity to the seaboard, and to the great manufacturing district of New England exterior to the State. The west and northwest portion of the basin is located in New Hampshire.

Form. [See Map.] Gradually widening from its southeast point interiorward for twenty miles, thence to its northern boundary of nearly uniform width, with the large proportion of the drainage territory on the right bank of the main stream.

Dimensions. Greatest length, which is on the line from the ocean to Mt. Washington, about 74 miles. Greatest breadth, across the head of the basin, about 30 miles. Area or square dimensions, 800 square miles in Maine, 600 square miles in New Hampshire; total, 1,400 square miles. Of this all but about ten square miles situated below the Saco falls, is tributary to the water-power of the main river.

Elevation. The height of the following points is given by Mr. John F. Anderson, Engineer of the Western Division of the Hydrographic Survey:

Authorities	Hall's Survey of Saco River Railroad marked H. Wadsworth's Survey of Saco River Railroad marked W. Anderson's Survey of Port. & Roch. Railroad marked A. Grant's Survey of Port. & Ogdensburg Railroad marked Gr. Guyot's Paper upon the Appalachian System marked G.	Feet above high tide.	
Miles.	Localities.	Surface of land.	Water.
	Initial point, the center of the Portland, Saco and Portsmouth Railroad track, 400 feet east of Saco Depot, assumed and computed height, (H.)	63	-
8 4-10	Saco river, about 400 feet above Salmon Falls, (H.)	-	109
9 6-10	Port. & Roch. Railroad crossing above Bar Mills, (A.)	-	137
14	Below Moderation Mills, (H.)	142	-
-	Above Moderation Mills, (H.)	160	-
16 7-10	Top of a "horseback" ridge,(H.)	270	-
20	Little Ossipee, (H.)	232	-
21 6-10	Half mile west of Steep Falls, (H.)	278	-
27 7-100	Saco river, quarter mile above Gould's Island, (H.)	-	252
30 22-100	Great Ossipee, (W.)	-	271
34	Foot of Great Falls, Saco river, (W.)	-	271
34 1-4	Head of Great Falls, Saco river, low water, (W.)	-	343
-	Head of Great Falls, Saco river, high water, (W.)	-	346
35	Saco river at Hiram bridge, low water, (W.)	-	344
-	Saco river, 400 feet above low water, (H.)	-	351
39	Ten Mile brook, (H.)	359	-
42	Shepard's river, near Brownfield Centre, (H.)	368	-
44 1-2	Fryeburg, on plains, (H.)	388	-
48	Fryeburg, near village, (H.)	414	-
-	South Conway post office, (G.)	450	-
56	North Conway,	-	-
62	Crossing of road junction of Ellis & Saco river (G.) water (Gr.)	576	543
62 3-4	Saco river, (Gr.)	-	555
63 1-2	" " "	-	571
65 1-4	" " "	-	605
66 16-100	" " "	-	618
67 9-10	" " "	-	653
68 89-100	" " "	-	700
70 1-10	" " "	-	755
70 94-100	Water in Saco river, (Gr.)	-	821
72 72-100	" " " "	-	887
74 12-100	Underpinning old Crawford house, (Gr.)	994	-
74 12-100	Old Crawford house or Davis tavern, (G.)	986	-
75 52-100	Water in Saco river, (Gr.)	-	1055
76 9-100	" " " "	-	1155
78 3-10	" " " "	-	1242
79 23-100	" " " "	-	1284
79 8-10	" " " "	-	1324
79 86-100	Underpinning of Willey House, (Gr.)	1340	-
-	Willey House, (G.)	1335	-
81 1-10	Water in Saco river, (Gr.)	-	1493
81 73-100	" " " "	-	1672
82 2-10	" " " "	-	1886
-	The Notch, (G.)	1904	-
82 72-100	Crawford House, (G.)	1920	-
-	Hollis Centre,	173	-
-	Weymouth's, near west line of Hollis,	277	-
-	Hanson's near Waterboro' Centre,	285	-

The *mean* elevation of the basin as a whole, is below that of the Androscoggin, but above that of any other river district of which a proportionally large part is situated so near the sea. Its upper section covers an important portion of the highest mass of land (the White-mountain plateau) of any considerable extent, east of the highlands of the Rocky mountains, with the exception of a limited tract in North Carolina.

Geological relations. The entire basin is occupied with granite, or gneiss scarcely distinguishable from granite, with patches of mica schist here and there. In all parts of the district stone of good quality for construction purposes is abundant. A quarry of excellent granite has been worked extensively at Biddeford.

Surface conditions. The district is in its northwest part exceedingly mountainous in its topographical features; thence southeastward it subsides successively into hilly, undulating, and finally quite level surfaces near the sea. The great body of pulverized material lying above the bed rock, is, as returns to interrogatories indicate, made up of sand and gravel with sandy and gravelly loams. The lower portion of the basin is quite thoroughly denuded of forests. The upper half is still heavily wooded, being cleared only upon the intervales of the streams and the more cultivable portions. "Probably full half of the entire district is still wilderness."*

Rainfall. Estimated from the average for the State, 135,000,000,000 cubic feet yearly. The downfall is probably somewhat in excess of the mean for the State, owing to the influence of the mountains and the lower latitude of the basin; but the amount of excess, if any, is not known, and is accordingly not represented in the figures.

Section 2.—The Saco River.

Course. The mean direction of the Saco is southeast. The chief deviation from this course occurs at Fryeburg, where it originally, and prior to the construction of a "cut" across an enclosed peninsula, traversed, and to this day in part traverses, an extensive loop or curve, and finally leaves the town only about four miles from the point of access. Otherwise, and excepting mere local sinuosities, it follows nearly the shortest line from the mountains to the sea.

---

* Hon. Joseph Hobson, Saco.

The principal affluents are the following:

	Name.	Where received.
From the right bank,	Little Ossipee,	Limington.
	Great Ossipee,	Cornish.
From the left bank,	Upper Kezar,	Fryeburg.
	Great Cold,	Stowe.

Name.	Basin.			Stream.	
	Length, miles.	Breadth, miles.	Area, sq. miles.	Length, miles.	Estimated discharge, cubic feet.
Little Ossipee,	17	16	182	30	7,100,000,000
Great Ossipee,	27	18	240	33	9,300,000,000
Upper Kezar,	12	8	62	14	2,400,000,000
Great Cold,	12	7	60	12	2,340,000,000

The length of the streams as given above does not include their local windings.

The Saco in its upper part is drawn around the southern slope of the White-mountain cluster in such a manner as to carry off a considerable part of the surplus waters that would otherwise be discharged by the Merrimac; this contributes largely to its annual delivery, but not to its uniformity of volume at different seasons.

Length.

Of the main river from its sources amongst the mountains to the sea, not including the minuter windings, about 95 miles, 25 miles of which, more or less, are in New Hampshire. The main water-power section of the river is about 35 miles long, from Hiram Falls to the tide. The stream is about 600 feet wide in the vicinity of Saco.

Volume.

The yearly discharge, estimated at 40 per cent. of the annual precipitation, is, from the entire basin both within and beyond State, about 54,000,000,000 cubic feet.

Variations of volume.

Excessive in the upper part, owing to the mountainous character of the country. The lower portion of the river likewise fluctuates widely in its mass of water at different seasons, though much less than the upper, owing, first, to the narrowness of the "Gates,"—the passage at Hiram Falls—which dams back the mountain water over extensive intervales and marshes above; owing, secondly, to the comparative levelness of the lower portion of the basin; and, thirdly, to the improvement of the lakes and ponds for storage.

In the drouth of summer nearly 40,000 cubic feet per minute for eleven hours a day are commanded at Saco, or 18,000 cubic feet per minute for the whole twenty-four hours. The low run continued day and night throughout the year would carry off over 9,000,000,000 cubic feet, or about one-sixth of the estimated delivery of the river for the year. The volume at low water can be increased two or three fold by the use of the reservoirs of the river.

The discharge of the river in ordinary freshets, eight feet on the middle dam at Saco, is about 1,950,000 cubic feet per minute. Ten feet are alleged to be found on the dam in extreme freshets.

The range from lowest to highest water at various points is as follows:

LOCALITIES.	Feet.	LOCALITIES.	Feet.
Saco falls,	8 to 10	Bonny Eagle falls,	6
Union falls,	7	Great falls, Hiram,	12
Salmon falls,	8	Fryeburg Centre,	14
Bar Mills falls,	6	Toll bridge, Fryeburg,	11.50

The range in feet above the Great falls is not a fair expression of the volume of the river in that section in time of flood, the water being diffused over an immense expanse of low land as before noticed, and of course proportionately reduced in elevation.

Slope. The descent of the river in Maine is moderately steep, being from the State line at Fryeburg, 67 miles to the tide at Biddeford, 450 feet, or about seven feet to the mile, which gives an average angular depression of 4′.3 per mile. The current is generally moderate, the greater part of the descent taking place in sudden breaks or falls. The level of tide is reached about four miles from the coast, at Biddeford, and there by a comparatively abrupt pitch of 40 feet.

The slope in the 35 miles constituting the principal water-power portion of the river, from Biddeford to Hiram Great Falls, is at the rate of 9.8 feet per mile, corresponding to an angular descent of 6′.8 per mile. In this portion it is a succession of rapids and falls, and offers numerous sites for manufacturing of the highest value.

Lakes. The total number of lakes in the portion of the Saco basin situated in Maine, and represented on the State map, is 75, or more than twice the number due to the average for the whole State. The small ponds are undoubtedly more fully represented on the map for the thickly settled than for the wilderness portions of the State. The lakes are small compared with the average for Maine, and there are none strictly first-class in size.

PRINCIPAL RESERVOIRS OF THE SACO AND ITS TRIBUTARIES.

Name.	Connected with	Approximate area in square miles.	Present storage in feet.	Additional storage feasible in feet.
Horne pond,	Little Ossipee riv.,	0.60	*	*
Long "	do do	0.75	–	–
Mudgett pond,	do do	0.60	–	–
Pearce "	do do	0.30	–	–
Poverty "	do do	0.45	–	10 to 20
Turner "	do do	0.60	–	–
Adams' "	do do	0.75	Dam.	–
Balch pond, with flowage,	do do	2.50	8	4
Little Ossipee pond,	do do	1.75	4	–
Nine ponds,	–	8.30	–	–

Name.	Connected with	Approximate area in square miles.	Present storage in feet.†	Additional storage feasible in feet †
Spectacle ponds,	Great Ossipee riv.,	0.30	8	3
Colcord's pond,	do do	0.80	10	6
Bickford "	do do	0.50	8	2
Spruce "	do do	0.40	6	4
Lord's "	do do	0.50	10 or 12	–
Province pond, [N. H.]	do do	1.75	–	–
Pine river " "	do do	–	12	–
Ossipee " "	do do	7.00	–	–
Various ponds tributary to Ossipee pond,	do do	4.00	–	–
Twelve ponds,	–	15.25	–	–

Name.	Connected with	Approximate area in square miles.	Present storage in feet.‡	Additional storage feasible in feet.‡
Barker pond, }	Saco river,	4.50	5	2
Great Hancock pond, }			4	2
Middle " " }			–	Could have dam.
Little " " }				Dam feasible.
Small ponds connected, }				All can be flowed.
Moose pond,	do do	4.50	Dam.	Several feet, with flowage.
Lovell "	do do	2.00	–	
Pleasant pond,	do do	1.00	–	–
Keyes' "	do do	0.50	Dam.	Several feet.
Lower Kezar pond,	do do	2 00	–	§
Upper Kezar "	do do	5.00	Dam.	8, with large flowage.
The Five Kezar ponds,	do do	0 50	Dam.	5
Kimball pond,	do do	1.75	–	–
Charles "	do do	1.00	–	Several feet with large flowage.
Bog "	do do	0.50	–	
Walker's " [N. H.]	do do	1.00	9-foot dam.	–
Twenty ponds or more,	–	24.25	–	–

* Blanks, as above, indicate that the storage has not been reported.

† Storage of the Great Ossippee, reported by Luther Edgecomb and E. S. Ridlon, Esqs., of Kezar Falls.

‡ Storage reported chiefly by E. C. Farrington, Esq., of Fryeburg.

§ Lower Kezar pond can be flowed six to twelve feet, covering six square miles of ponds and meadows. The cost for dams would not exceed $1,000.

The foregoing 41 ponds with their associated flowage sum 46.80 square miles of surface. It is obvious therefore that the low run of the river, and by consequence its manufacturing capacity, can be increased very greatly. The lowlands above the Great Falls could be converted into an enormous reservoir, though at considerable expense for damages.

The sum total of lake surface connected with the Saco, as computed from the State and county maps, is 55 square miles in Maine, 29 in New Hampshire, 84 in all, or one square mile to each 16.66 square miles of basin. The lakes average 0.75 of a square mile each in extent.

Forty hours are required for the passage of water from Ossipee pond to Saco in an ordinary stage of the river.

POWER ON THE LOWER SECTION OF THE SACO.

If the mean volume of water that, in the present condition of its reservoirs, can be commanded on the Saco river from Hiram Falls to the tide, be assumed to be 27,000 cubic feet per minute, for eleven hours a day, in the low run of summer, the gross power developed in the 343 feet of fall, is 17,493 horse-power for the hours specified, or 699,720 spindles. A large proportion of this power can be economically improved, the opportunities for dams, canals, and mills being unusually good. The judicious use of the reservoirs would undoubtedly increase this amount of power by two hundred per cent.

The Saco is crossed by two railroads in its lower section, connecting with Boston and Portland.

The river is navigable to the foot of the Saco falls, but is closed by ice about three and a half months yearly.

CHAPTER XVI.

THE SYSTEM OF THE ANDROSCOGGIN.

Section 1.—THE ANDROSCOGGIN BASIN.

Location. The drainage district of the Androscoggin occupies the region of country lying between the sea on the southeast, and the *northerly* outposts of the White Mountains on the northwest. It is in its southern part separated from the Saco basin by the hydrographic area of the Presumpscot and Royal, but in the northern is conterminous with it.

Form. [See Map.] Expanded laterally in the central portion and tapering to a point at each extreme. As a whole elongated, and with the head waters therefore at a considerable remove from the ocean.

Dimensions. Greatest length, from the ocean to the remotest sources of the river, 110 miles; greatest breadth, from Randolph, N. H., to Fayette, Me., 70 miles. Square dimensions, in Maine, about 2,750 square miles; in New Hampshire, about 850 square miles; total, 3,600 square miles. Of this nearly the whole is located above the lowest mill privilege, and contributes to the water-power of the main river.

Elevation. Considerably greater than of any other hydrographic district in the State, a large proportion of the northern part of the basin being uplifted upon the northerly offsets of the White mountains and their subjacent and outlying highlands.

The following points, it will be noticed, are situated mainly upon the river or upon railroads, and are therefore considerably below the level of the surrounding districts. The figures denote height above tide:

LOCALITIES	Feet.	LOCALITIES.	Feet.
Danville Junction,..............	180	Androscoggin river at Bethel,..	620
Auburn (station)	210	White's Corner,..............	659
Lewiston "	212	Mouth Pleasant river, about...	632
Leeds "	260	Gilead,....................	700
Mechanic Falls (station)	270	State line, (G. T. R. crossing)..	690
Oxford (station)................	310	Gorham station (N. H.)........	802
East Livermore (station)........	360	Head of Berlin Falls, (N. H.)..	1,048
South Paris "	370	Head of Androscoggin river,...	3,000
Lock's Mills "	710	N. E. head of Magalloway riv.,	2,640
Head of Rumford Falls, about...	600	N. W. " " "	2,917
Bethel (station)................	640	Umbagog Lakes,......1,256 to	1,511

The high general elevation of this district combined with its brokenness of surface, secures a very large amount of power upon the streams, in proportion to its extent and its volume of annual discharge.

Geological relations. Gneiss is prevalent at the outfall of the river; thence north to Jay mica schist, with abundant granite on the right bank. From Jay northward, granite and gneiss, with clay slate about the Umbagog lakes. Good building stone abundant in all parts of the basin, as detailed in Part III. of this Report.

Surface conditions, Surface aspect, hilly in the lower third; excessively broken and mountainous in the upper two-thirds, with narrow intervales and limited level tracts interspersed.

Surface materials, indicated as follows, in response to inquiries, some of the towns specifying two or more of the forms as abundant:

Gravel.	Sand.	Sandy Loam.	Loam.	Clay Loam.	Clay.
8	3	3	5	1	3

Showing a preponderance of coarse soil and one admitting the rapid absorption and transmission of water.

E. S. Coe, Esq., of Bangor, a most competent authority, judges 1,480 square miles of the basin lying north of the river and west of Rumford, in both Maine and New Hampshire, to be still covered with forests. This is considerably over one-third of the whole drainage territory, without any account of the large amount of forest below Rumford on both sides of the river. Undoubtedly considerably over half still remains in the wilderness state.

Rainfall. The yearly precipitation of moisture upon this basin, including both the Maine and New Hampshire portions thereof, is estimated as nearly 338,000,000,000 cubic feet. These figures are based upon an assumed average downfall of forty-two inches, the influence of the mountains being disregarded because not ascertained.

Section 2.—THE ANDROSCOGGIN RIVER.

Course. West of south in the northern part, east in the central, southeast in the lower, as a whole south-southeast.

The principal tributaries are as given below : Affluents.

	Name.	Where received.
From the right bank, ...	Little Androscoggin,....	Auburn.
	Twenty Mile,..........	Turner.
From the left bank,...............	Sabattus,..............	Lisbon.
	Dead,........	Leeds.
	Webb's,...............	Dixfield.
	Swift,................	Mexico.
	Ellis,.................	Rumford.

Name.	Basin.			Stream.	
	Length, miles.	Breadth, miles.	Area, sq. miles.	Length, miles.	Estimated discharge, cubic feet.
Little Androscoggin, ...	30	15	280	40	10,920,000,000
Twenty-Mile,................	19	13	150	25	5,850,000,000
Sabattus, ...	16	7	75	-	2,925,000,000
Dead, ...	22	5	85	28	3,300,000,000
Webb's,.....................	17	11	135	23	5,265,000,000
Swift, ...	22	8	133	24	5,187,000,000
Ellis,......................	18	13	150	25	5,850,000,000

The figures for the two streams which unite and form the Androscoggin are as follows, those for the Outlet Stream being for the whole Umbagog-lake system :

Name.	Basin.			Stream.	
	Length, miles.	Breadth, miles.	Area, sq. miles.	Length, miles.	Estimated discharge, cubic feet.
Magalloway, ...	37	18	400	50	15,600,000,000
Outlet Stream,..............	50	20	500	53	19,500,000,000

The Androscoggin takes its origin and is entitled to its name, only from the point of confluence of the Magalloway and Umbagog-lake waters. The number of streams in the system, represented on the State map, is 669, of which 543 are in Maine and 126 in New Hampshire.

Length. Of the Androscoggin proper, 157 miles; from the remotest sources of the Magalloway, 200 miles; 66 miles of its length are in New Hampshire. Its most valuable water-power section, from Rumford falls to the tide, is 75 miles long; but in fact it is a water-power river in its whole length from the lakes to Brunswick, 150 miles.

Volume. The estimated discharge from the basin for the year amounts to 135,000,000,000 cubic feet. Of this nearly the whole is tributary to the working power of the river, all in fact except a small quantity passed into it below the Brunswick falls.

6

Variations of volume.

This river, like the Saco, belongs to the class of variable rather than of constant rivers, as regards its mass of water at different seasons of the year. This is due to the excessively mountainous character of the upper portion of its catchment basin, together with the bareness of a considerable part of the mountain surfaces. Hence it rises rapidly, and falls away rapidly, runs high in spring freshets and low in summer drouths. This at least is naturally its character, and aside from modifications effected by artificial improvements, and especially its character above the Rumford falls.

Below the falls, however, it is materially altered. The channel at the pass of the falls is only ninety feet wide, and accordingly, like the "Gates" at Hiram falls on the Saco, dams back the volume of freshets, producing a great rise above, but equalizing the flow below. Hence the chief manufacturing portion of the river is in a manner protected against the chance of destructive rises of water.

The natural inconstancy of the river is already to a considerable extent overcome, and can be to a far higher degree, by the use of its great reservoirs for storage purposes, and this at little expense. Further remarks upon this will presently be made in another connection.

Mr. Lockwood reports the low run at Lewiston at 94,000 cubic feet per minute, for eleven hours a day, or 42,000 per minute for the twenty-four hours. The low run at Brunswick—to which over 400 square miles more of territory are tributary, and streams which are largely improved for manufacturing, and therefore comparatively furnished at low water—is not far from 125,000 cubic feet per minute, eleven hours a day, or 57,000 per minute for the whole twenty-four hours. The low run continued day and night throughout the year would carry off about 29.3 billions of cubic feet, or less than one-fourth of the estimated total annual discharge of the river. So favorable an exhibit is due in part to the reserve of water for manufacturing purposes.

The range from lowest to highest water at several points appears in the table annexed:

Localities.	Feet.	Localities.	Feet.
Brunswick falls,	10	Rumford falls,	20
Lewiston "	8	Bethel, (average)	22
Lisbon "	7	Bethel, (extreme)	28
Livermore "	8		

Slope.

From the point where the waters of the Magalloway and the Umbagog lakes coalesce and give origin to the Androscoggin, to the tide at Brunswick, is a distance of 150 miles, with a fall of 1,256 feet. The mean slope, therefore, is 8.33 feet to the mile, corresponding to an angular depression of 5′.5 circular measurement per mile. The current is generally swift, but like that of the Saco, is gentle or even languid in parts for considerable distances, as above Rumford falls, the greater proportion of the whole descent accomplishing itself in steep rapids and in numerous and comparatively profound falls.

The slope of the river in its main water-power section, from Rumford falls to the tide, a distance of 75 miles and a fall of 600 feet, is eight feet to the mile, or 5′.2 circular measurement.

Lakes.

As respects the *number* of lakes the Androscoggin system, as represented on the State map, falls somewhat below the average for the State, the enumeration for the Maine portion being 133, and for the New Hampshire portion 15, a total of 148; whereas the number proportioned to its area would be 195. A large number of small ponds scattered throughout the mountainous portion of the basin are not represented upon the map. These afford local power of value and contribute to the uniformity of the main stream, and will do so in still higher degree when put to use as reservoirs.

PRINCIPAL RESERVOIRS OF THE ANDROSCOGGIN AND ITS TRIBUTARIES.

Name.	Connected with		Approximate area in square miles.	Present storage in feet.*	Additional storage feasible in feet.*
Taylor pond,............	Little Andros'n riv.,		2.00	4	†
Upper Range pond,.......	do	do	0.85	4	-
Middle Range "	do	do	0.55	4	-
Lower Range "	do	do	0.50	4	-
Tripp "	do	do	1.25	No dam.	4
Thompson "	do	do	8.00	6	-
Hogan and Green ponds,..	do	do	1.40	Dam.	-
Saturday pond,..........	do	do	0.75	9	-
Moose "	do	do	0.80	No dam.	10
Matthews "	do	do	0.25	†	-
Great Pennessewassa pond,	do	do	2.50	12	[large flat.
North pond,.............	do	do	0.30	0	15, and on a
Little Pennessewassa pond,	do	do	0.30	No dam.	10
Sand pond,..............	do	do	0.30	15	-
Moose (Paris) pond,......	do	do	0.35	No dam.	Several feet.
Mud and Hicks ponds,....	do	do	0.55	No dam.	Several feet.
Bryant's pond,..........	do	do	0.60	Dam.	Might be im-
Indian "	do	do	0.30	Dam.	[proved.
Twitchell "	do	do	0.35	Dam.	-
Twenty-one ponds,......	-		21.90	-	-

* Storage of the Little Androscoggin river, reported by S. F. Waterman and Isaac Farrington, Esqs., of Mechanic Falls. Messrs. W. and F. judge the ponds connected with the river to sum 28 square miles of surface.

† Blanks, as above, indicate that the storage has not been reported.

PRINCIPAL RESERVOIRS OF THE ANDROSCOGGIN AND ITS TRIBUTARIES.

Name.	Connected with	Approximate area in square miles.	Present storage in feet.	Additional storage feasible in feet.
Pleasant pond, ...	Twenty Mile riv.,	0.60	*	*
Brettun's "	do do	0.30	Dam.	-
Bear "	do do	1.05	Dam.	-
South "	do do	0.55	-	-
North "	do do	0.75	-	-
Bungermuck pond, ...	do do	0.80	8	0
Labrador [2] ponds, ...	do do	0.35	4	0.70 sq. miles [can be flowed.
Pleasant (Sumner) pond, ..	do do	0.25	3	
Nine ponds, ...	-	4.65	-	-

Name.	Connected with	Approximate area in square miles.	Present storage in feet.	Additional storage feasible in feet.
Androscoggin pond, ...	Dead river,	5.75	0	6, with large damage.
Wing's pond, ...	do do	1.00	6 to 8	2 to 4, by cutting down outlet.
Lovejoy's pond, ...	do do	1.00	6 to 8	2 to 4, by cutting down outlet.
Pond above Lovejoy's, ...	do do	0.20	6 to 8	2 to 4, by cutting down outlet.
Crotched pond, ...	do do	2.25	4	Several feet.
Parker's "	do do	3.10	3	4
David's "	do do	0.80	Dam.	-
Tilton's "	do do	0.25	-	-
Flying "	do do	1.25	8	-
Kimball's "	do do	0.25	-	-
Mt. Vernon pond, ...	do do	0.35	Dam.	Several feet.
Eleven ponds, ...	-	16.20	-	-

Name.	Connected with	Approximate area in square miles.	Present storage in feet.	Additional storage feasible in feet.
Webb's pond, ...	Webb's river,	3.00	-	9
Swift-river ponds (three in township E,)	Swift do	2.25	-	-
Ellis pond, ...	Ellis do	1.25	Dam.	-
Little Ellis pond, ...	do do	0.85	Dam.	-
Six ponds, ...	-	7.35	-	-

* Blanks not reported.

PRINCIPAL RESERVOIRS OF THE ANDROSCOGGIN AND ITS TRIBUTARIES.

Name.	Connected with	Approximate area in square miles.	Present storage in feet.*	Additional storage feasible in feet.*
Sabattus pond,	Androsco'gin riv.,	4.00	Dam.	
Wilson "	do do	3.00	8	2 or 3
Little Wilson pond,	do do	0.20	Dam.	–
Bates pond,	do do	0.30	–	–
Long "	do do	0 35	4 to 5	2
Round "	do do	0.25	4 to 5	2
Moosehill pond,	do do	0.25	–	[by flowing.
Whitney "	do do	1.00	Dam.	Can be increased
Forest "	do do	0.25	Dam.	–
Worthley "	do do	2 00	3	5, by flowing.
Concord (2) ponds,	do do	0.65	–	Several feet.
North "	do do	0.85	–	4
South "	do do	0.80	–	–
Burnside " [N. H.].	do do	1.50	–	–
Umbagog,	do do	18.00 }	14	–
Welokenebacook and the pond below,†	do do	11.15 }	12	–
Molechunkemunk,†	do do	10.00 } 80	12	–
Mooselucmaguntic,	do do	21.00 }	14	–
Cupsuptic,	do do	3.00 }	14	–
Rangely lake,	do do	14.00 }	4	4
Quimby pond,	do do	0.40	–	4
Gull (2) ponds,	do do	0 80	–	–
Long pond,	do do	1.00	–	10
Various small ponds,	do do	1.00	–	–
Parmachene lake,	Magalloway river,	3.50	–	–
John's pond,	Kennebago do	1.50	–	–
Kennebago pond,	do do	4.00	–	Several feet.
Thirty-six ponds,	–	105.85	–	–

The foregoing 83 principal lakes and ponds sum 156.25 square miles in surface.

The aggregate of lake surface in the Androscoggin basin, estimated from the map, is 213 square miles; or one square mile to each seventeen square miles of basin. The average size of the lakes is 1.43 square miles, or nearly twice the average for the Saco basin.

The Umbagog reservoirs.

The Umbagog series, comprising four, or, as sometimes divided, six large lakes, have an area, as computed from the map, of seventy-seven square miles. The several lakes of the system are not upon the same level, as shown in the table annexed:

Name.	Distance from the preceding lake.	Height above tide in feet.	Difference of level in feet.
Umbagog,		1,256	–
Richardson,	5 miles,	1,456	200
Mooselucmaguntic,	1 mile,	1,486	30
Rangely,	2 miles,	1,511	25

* Storage of the upper portion of the Androscoggin reported by E. S. Coe, Abner Toothaker and others.

† Molechunkemunk and Welokenebacook are sometimes classed together as Richardson lake.

They have been converted into reservoirs under conditions as follows:

Name.	Height of dam.	Greatest head of water.
Umbagog, ...	Fourteen feet.	Fourteen feet.
Richardson, ...	Sixteen "	Twelve "
Mooselucmaguntic, ...	Twenty "	Fourteen "
Rangely, ...	Ten "	Four "

The lowest dam in the Umbagog series is at Errol, N. H., and is below the junction of the Magalloway and the Outlet stream. By its means the former is at high stages of water backed into Umbagog lake and thus made tributary to its storage. The area tributary to the whole system is about 900 square miles, including the Magalloway country, and the surface being mountainous and heavily wooded, its drainage is great.

The mean head raised upon the lakes by the present dams is eleven feet, which involves the storage of nearly 24,000,000,000 cubic feet of water. The lakes always fill to their utmost capacity in the spring, and in the fall usually rise about two feet, the gates of the dams being left open. The three principal dams have in addition to the gates, waterways averaging thirty feet wide by six feet deep.

The water reserved as above stated, if reduced one-fourth by evaporation and infiltration on its way to the tide, would yield in the total descent of 1,256 feet, a gross power of 200,000 horse, for eleven hours a day, 312 days a year. Upon the "Lewiston falls" alone it would yield about 9,000 horse-power for the same time, more than doubling the present power. But in fact the storage could be used in six months, if so required, the natural run of the river sufficing for the other six.

The "Black branch canal."

The Black branch of Ellis river approaches at its northwest extreme within a short distance of Richardson lake of the Umbagog series. A survey was made in the year 1866 by Noah Barker, Esq., late State Land Agent, with a view to determining the feasibility, at reasonable expense, of a cut from lake to branch, of such dimensions as to admit of the running of lumber, and the diversion of the waters of the upper five lakes, or a part thereof, from their natural discharge into Umbagog lake, directly into Black branch, and thence into Ellis river and the Androscoggin.

Mr. Barker reports the distance from the southeastern extremity of the lake to a point of equal elevation on the branch, 5,200 feet.

Maximum depth of excavation required, (the ordinary level of the lake being assumed as the datum-line,) 28.32 feet. Total amount of excavation, 151,255 cubic yards. Whether any part of the under-stratum is ledge was not ascertained.

At the low stage of the river, water from Umbagog lake reaches Lewiston in from thirty-six to forty-eight hours.* The time occupied varies with the lowness of the river and the volume liberated from the reservoir.

POWER ON THE LOWER SECTION OF THE ANDROSCOGGIN.

If the mean volume of water that can, in the present state of its reservoirs, be commanded on the river, in the low run of summer, from Rumford falls to the tide, be assumed to be 75,000 cubic feet per minute, for eleven hours a day, the total power of this section of the river is 85,200 horse-power, gross measurement, for the hours specified, or 3,747,600 spindles. What proportion of this power can be economically appropriated, it is not possible now to determine; the proportion is, however, unquestionably unusually large, owing to the favorable conditions of the bottom and banks, and the advantageous character of the falls and rapids with reference to improvement. Not an eighth part of it is now used.

The water-power of this river from the tide to Jay inclusive, is already furnished with excellent railroad communication close at hand, and from Bethel to the State line the Grand Trunk follows the immediate bank of the river. Indeed, no portion of the river below the State line is far removed from railroads. It is navigable to the foot of the lowest falls, for small craft, for about two-thirds the year.

---

*S. R. Bearce & Co.

CHAPTER XVII.

THE SYSTEM OF THE KENNEBEC.

Section 1.—THE KENNEBEC BASIN.

Location. The basin of the Kennebec lies next east of that of the Androscoggin, and extends from it nearly to the mid longitudes of the State, and from the highest latitude of Moosehead lake to the sea.

Form. [See Map.]

Dimensions. Length, 145 miles; breadth, 75 miles; area, 5,800 square miles. It lies wholly within the limits of the State. About 450 square miles are drained into the river below the Augusta falls.

Elevation. Less than that of the Androscoggin, owing to its further removal from the White-mountain highland. At the same time, midway the basin, north and south, there occur in isolated peaks, *Saddleback*, *Abraham*, *Bigelow*, etc., the loftiest elevations in Maine except Katahdin.

The following table indicates the general rise of the surface from the tide at Augusta to the head of the basin. The points designated are, however, lower than the districts by which they are respectively surrounded, since they are situated near or upon the river:

LOCALITIES.	Feet.	LOCALITIES.	Feet.
Foot of Ticonic bay,..........	36	Moosehead lake, (about)....	1,023
Ken'bec at Kendall's Mills dam,	76	Long pond, (Moose river), ..	1,094
Head of Kendall's Mills rips,..	91	Wood pond, ...	1,094
Waterville (station),..........	107	Attean pond, ...	1,094
Kendall's Mills (station),......	120	Parlin pond,...............	1,610
Skowhegan plain,............	220	Moose river, at mouth of N. W. branch,.............	1,244
Surface of Ken. riv. under Norridgewock bridge, June, '68,*	137.75	Valley of Sandy stream,....	1,210
Same point in freshet, 1832,*..	156.50	Source of Sandy stream, ...	1,868
Surface at top of dam at Madison bridge,*..............	233.20	Source of Wood stream,.....	2,089
		Height of Lake Emily, ...	1,950
Caratunk falls,* head of,......	316	S. W. head Moose river, ...	3,113

* E. S. Waters, Division Engineer, Somerset R. R., at the request of Col. A. W. Wildes, Chief Engineer.

In the following table, the elevation of places somewhat removed from the main river is given:

Localities.	Feet.	Localities.	Feet.
Monmouth (station), ...	270	Canaan village, ...	228
Winthrop "	213	Pittsfield (station), ...	202
Readfield "	320	Newport "	192
Belgrade "	260	East Newport, ...	251
West Waterville (station), ...	243	Dexter, ...	422
Clinton (station), ...	128	Thorndike, ...	496
Burnham "	158	Unity, ...	194
Farmington "	441	Morrison Corners, Clinton, ...	215

HEIGHTS OF THE SEBASTICOOK RIVER.*

Locality	Feet.	Locality	Feet.
At Hunter's mills, ...	118	Moose pond, ...	244
At Burnham, ...	134	Little pond above Moose pond,.	260
At Libby's mills, ...	213	One mile above, ...	301

HEIGHTS ON THE BELFAST AND MOOSEHEAD LAKE RAILWAY.†

Locality	Feet.	Locality	Feet.
Plymouth bog, ...	256	Boundary of Thorndike & Jackson, back of Peace hill, ...	518
Plymouth village, ...	275	Sparrow's ledge, Thorndike, ...	514
Me. Cen. R. R. in Plymouth vil.,	187	In the road E. of Harmon's Cor. (near Morton's), Thorndike,.	482
East Branch Sebasticook river in Detroit village, ...	159	Head of Parsons' valley, Thorndike, ...	410
Carleton's mill pond, Troy, ...	187	Coffin notch, Thorndike, ...	598
Green's Corners, ...	270		
Chase's Corners, near Unity vil.,.	207		
Abbott's summit, Knox, ...	523		

The prevailing rock from the mouth of the river to Gardiner upon both slopes is gneiss, mica schist occupying a considerable portion, however, of the right bank. From Gardiner northward, mica schist—running into clay slate in spots and elsewhere into gneiss, and broken by intrusions of granite, as at Hallowell and Augusta for example—prevails as far as Concord and Bingham, where clay slate is alone or chiefly exhibited. The slate occupies the north part of the basin, with the exception of a belt of sandstone west, and a district of granite east of Moosehead lake. In nearly all parts of the basin granite of sufficiently good quality for ordinary building purposes is to be had near at hand. The granite of Hallowell is one of the best building stones in the world, of great solidity, and almost marble-like in appearance when dressed.

Geological relations.

Hilly from the sea north 60 miles. In lower Somerset county the hills subside into low undulations. About the confluence of Dead river, mountains close in upon the river, and cover the whole breadth of the basin. In the vicinity of Moosehead lake the mountains recede or disappear, and the valley opens into a broad, plain country. The northeast part of

Surface conditions.

* From a survey for a proposed canal, by James Hall, C. E. Docs., 1837.
† Reported by A. L. Mortimer, C. E., from a Preliminary Survey by Col. A. W. Wildes, C. E.

the basin is very rough, being covered with the easterly offsets of the White Mountains. As a whole the topograhpical aspect of the district is broken and diversified.

Towns have reported their prevalent surface materials as follows:

Gravel.	Sand.	Sandy Loam.	Loam.	Clay Loam.	Clay.
6	6	1	14	4	7

Showing a marked preponderance of finely pulverized and water-retaining soil. Sands and gravels are probably more abundant in the northern and mountainous districts.

The proportion of forest-covered surfaces still remaining upon the basin is judged to be not less than 3,800 square miles, or two-thirds of its whole extent.*

Rainfall. The annual sum of rainfall due to the area of this hydrographic district, is 565,000,000,000 cubic feet.

Section 2.—THE KENNEBEC RIVER.

Course. South—diversified by a sweep to the west in the northern part, an abrupt diversion to the east in the central, and a gradual recovery of westing in the southern.

Affluents. The principal tributaries are the following:

	Name.	Where received.
From the right bank,	Cobbosseecontee,	Gardiner,
	Emerson,	Waterville,
	Sandy,	Starks,
	Carrabassett,	Anson,
	Dead,	Bowtown,
	Moose,	Moosehead lake,
From the left bank,	Sebasticook,	Winslow,
	Wesserunsett,	Skowhegan.

Name.	BASIN.			STREAM.	
	Length, miles.	Breadth, miles.	Area, sq. miles.	Length, miles.	Estimated discharge, cubic feet.
Cobbosseecontee,	25	15	195	36	7,700,000,000
Emerson,	20	15	185	42	7,300,000,000
Sandy,	40	23	510	60	19,890,000,000
Carrabassett,	36	24	290	43	11,310,000,000
Dead,	41	40	832	64	32,448,000,000
Moose,	48	24	650	70	25,350,000,000
Sebasticook,	50	27	710	59	27,690,000,000
Wesserunsett,	22	8	110	25	4,290,000,000

* J. M. Haynes, Esq.

As appears above, the Kennebec draws the far greater proportion of its waters from the west. The river is, in fact, a sort of catch-water conduit running across the outfalls of the drainage valleys leading to it from the White Mountain upland. There are 1,084 streams in the system, represented upon the State map. The Kennebec is entitled to its name from Moosehead lake to the sea. Moose river is rather a tributary than a continuation.

Length.

From Moosehead lake to the ocean, including the more considerable windings, 155 miles. From the source of Moose river to the sea, 227 miles. The grand water-power section of the river, from Moosehead to Augusta, is 112 miles long, in other words its whole length to the tide. The average width of the river at Augusta, mean of four points, is 750 feet.

Volume.

The estimated annual discharge of the river is, in cubic feet, 226,000,000,000. Of this about 26,000-000,000 cubic feet fall into the main river below the Augusta falls, and is productive of important power on its passage to the river, as on the Cobbosseecontee.

Variations of volume.

In the summer of 1866 Col. DeWitt found 130,000 cubic feet per minute passing Augusta at the time of lowest run, for the whole 24 hours.

The above figure is based upon measurements made in the summer of 1866 only. During that season the rainfall was considerably in excess of the ordinary *mean* for that part of the year. The following table furnished by R. H. Gardiner, Esq., gives the receipt of moisture at Gardiner for five months of 1866, and the mean moisture for the same months for 30 years :

1866.	Inches	Mean for 30 years, inches.
May,	4.968	4.107
June,	3.498	3.227
July,	3.012	3.441
August,	5.502	4.143
September,	5.664	3.218
	22.642	18.036

It appears therefore that the receipt of moisture at this point, and probably throughout the Kennebec basin, for the designated five months, exceeded the average by 4.6 inches, or by twenty-five per cent.

Taking account of July, August and September alone, the ordinary extreme dry months, the excess is about thirty-three per cent. It is reasonable to suppose, therefore, that the delivery of the Kennebec river for the ordinary dry months of that summer was greatly in excess of its delivery for the dry months of summer in the average of years. Yet in the severest drouths the ordinary feet flow at Augusta will probably be found to be 78,000 cubic per minute for the 24 hours, or 170,000 cubic feet per minute for 11 hours a day. The low run, at Augusta, continued throughout the year, would carry off nearly 40 billion cubic feet, or one-fifth of the estimated total annual flow at that point.

The mean flow for the whole summer season of 1866 was found to be 175,500 cubic feet per minute. This being for the whole summer season was not so much in excess of the average as was the extreme low run. It is a low estimate that the average will be found to be 122,350 cubic feet per minute for the twenty-four hours, or 293,640 cubic feet for 11 hours a day.

Col. DeWitt computes the volume of water passing the Augusta dam in time of freshet, as follows:

Depth on the dam.	Cubic feet per minute.
5 feet,	1,931,904
7 "	3,199,392

From five to seven feet on the dam are usually observed; ten feet are alleged to have been seen *once* during the past twenty years.

The average range from lowest to highest water at various points, is exhibited in the following table:

LOCALITIES	Feet.	LOCALITIES.	Feet.
Augusta dam,	7	Skowhegan, below the falls,	18
Waterville,	8	Norridgewock,	15 to 20
Somerset Mills,	8	Madison bridge,	
Kendall's Mills,	8	Carratunk falls,	
Skowhegan, above the falls,	12		

The absolute range is greater than upon the Saco and Androscoggin, as would be anticipated from the larger size of the river. It is greater in the upper section of the river than below; but it is at no point so suddenly reduced, as below Rumford falls on the Androscoggin, and Hiram falls on the Saco. As a whole, the river is moderately constant in its volume in its natural state, and is capable of being made by reservoir improvement practically uniform throughout the year, to the requirements at least of enormous manufacturing. This river, in common with the Saco and Androscoggin, is affected with its chief variations of volume, by and on account of the mountainous character of the upper portion of its tributary area. And, as on those rivers, the range of variation is reduced by the immense expanse of lake suriace connected with it, and the forests in possession of so considerable a part of the tributary country.

Slope.

The descent of the river from Moosehead lake to the tide is about 1,023 feet,* the distance being 112 miles. This gives a mean descent 9.1 feet to the mile, or 5′.9 circular measurement, throughout the water-power portion of the river, or its whole length to the tide. This is a greater fall than any other large river in the State has, concentrated into a proportionally short distance.

Whether the power due to this amount of fall is susceptible of economical improvement in equal measure with that of the Androscoggin and Saco, may perhaps be questioned. Five hundred feet of the fall, more or less, are distributed to the twenty-eight miles betwixt the Forks and the outlet dam of the lake. Accordingly the river for an important part of this distance is a *torrent*, walled in by steep precipices of rock from twenty to fifty feet in height, so that only a part of the power could be put to use without excessive outlay. The power below the Forks is unsurpassed as respects feasibility of improvement. The slope of the river from Wood pond on Moose river to tide water is about 6.5 feet to the mile.

Lakes.

The lacustrine system of the Kennebec, as exhibited on the State map, shows 311 lakes and ponds. The number due to the size of the basin, according to the mean distribution of lakes throughout the State, is 290, so that the numerical excess is about seven per cent.

---

* This figure is estimated from the height of Wood pond, as given upon Col. Graham's Map of the N. E. Boundary, viz., 1,094 feet.

PRINCIPAL RESERVOIRS OF THE KENNEBEC AND ITS TRIBUTARIES.

Name.	Connected with	Approximate area in square miles.	Present storage in feet.	Additional storage feasible in feet.
Snow pond,	Emerson st'm,	5.15	4 to 5	4, with large flow-
Long "	do do	4.85	1 to 2	[age.†
Great "	do do	9.00	Dam.	-
Richmond pond,	do do	0.85	*	-
McGrath "	do do	0.75	-	-
Little "	do do	0.35	-	-
East "	do do	2.50	8	-
North and Little ponds,	do do	4.00	-	-
Nine ponds,	-	27.45	-	-

Name.	Connected with	Approximate area in square miles.	Present storage in feet.	Additional storage feasible in feet.
Bog pond,	Sandy river.	1.00	-	-
Clear-Water pond,	do do	1.75	8	3
Norcross "	do do	0.35	-	[on four.
Chesterville, 6 small ponds,	do do	2.00	Dam.	4 or 5 can be had
Wilson's pond,	do do	1.25	7	Can raise 2 ft. and lower outlet 3 ft.
North "	do do	1.00	Dam.	Can raise dam and
Taylor "	do do	0.20	-	[lower outlet.
Sandy river, 4 ponds,	do do	1.00	2	Several feet.
Lufkin pond,	do do	1.25	0	5
Sylvester "	do do	0.30	Dam.	-
Eighteen ponds,	-	10.10	-	-

Name.	Connected with	Approximate area in square miles.	Present storage in feet.‡	Additional storage feasible in feet ‡
Fahi pond,	Carrabassett	0.60	4	4
Sandy "	do river,	0.40	-	-
Embden pond,	do do	3.50	4	12
Hancock "	do do	1.00	4	Several feet.
Spruce "	do do	0.35	-	-
Rowe, "	do do	0.70	-	8
Gilman's "	do do	0.50	Dam.	-
Judkins "	do do	0.75	-	-
Butler "	do do	0.40	-	-
Porter's "	do do	1.00	Dam.	4 [eral feet.
Tufts "	do do	0.50	-	Can be raised sev-
Dutton "	do do	0.20	8	Several feet.
Jerusalem "	do do	0.30	Dam.	Several feet.
Middle Carrying-place, pond,	do do	0.30	Dam.	Several feet.
Fourteen ponds,	-	10.20	-	-

* Storage of Emerson stream reported by John Ayer, Esq.
† Blanks, storage not reported.
‡ Storage of the Carrabassett reported by Columbus Steward, Esq.

PRINCIPAL RESERVOIRS OF THE KENNEBEC AND ITS TRIBUTARIES.

Name.	Connected with.	Approximate area in square miles.	Present storage in feet.*	Additional storage feasible in feet.*
Spencer pond,	Dead river.	5.00	8	4
No. 5, R. 7, pond,	do do	0.50	-	6
Great "	do do	4.00	-	Considerable.
"King and Bartlett" pond,	do do	1.00	-	-
Long pond,	do do	2.00	-	5
Flag-Staff pond,	do do	3.00	5 to 6	More feasible.
Carrying Place, the largest pond,	do do	2.00	-	5
"Jim," No. 1, R. V, F. Co pond,	do do	1.00	8	2
Timbrook, No. 2, R. 4, pond,	do do	1.25	9	- [all.
Chain, 3 ponds,	do do	5.00	8	2; one dam flows
Twelve ponds,	-	24.75	-	-

Name.	Connected with.	Approximate area in square miles.	Present storage in feet.*	Additional storage feasible in feet.*
Brassua lake,	Moose river,	6.00	No dam.	5
Misery, No. 2, R. 7., pond,	do do	1 50	2 or more.	Can be raised.
Parlin pond,	do do	2.75	5, formerly.	3
Long‡ "	do do	8.00	No dam.	8, with ease.
Wood "	do do	3.00	No dam.	8, by dam at out-
"Little Big Wood" pond,	do do	1.35	7	[let of Long pd.
Attean pond,	do do	5.00	No dam.	8, by dam at outlet of Long pd.
Holeb "	do do	3.00	No dam.	Can be raised by a dam at Holeb fls.
Thorndike, 2 ponds,	do do	1.00	One, 6 feet.	The other can be raised 6 feet.
Eleven ponds,	-	31.60	-	-

Name.	Connected with.	Approximate area in square miles.	Present storage in feet.	Additional storage feasible in feet.
China pond,	Sebasticook	6.30	6	-
Patte's, "	do river,	0.85	-	-
Lovejoy's pond,	do do	0 70	-	-
Sandy "	do do	0 95	6	- [let.
Twenty-Five Mile pond,	do do	4.25	2	2, by lowering out-
Carlton Bog,	do do	1.75	-	4, on 3.50 square
Plymouth pond, with flowage,	do do	3.00	10	[miles. -
Skinner's pond,	do do	0.70	-	-
Stetson "	do do	2.50	-	Several feet.
Newport "	do do	7.50	4	4
Corinna "	do do	0.60	-	-
Dexter "	do do	3.00	8	-

* Storage of Moose and Dead rivers reported chiefly by Ex-Governor Coburn.

‡ The dam formerly one and a half miles below the outlet of this pond, flowed Long, Wood, and Attean ponds 4 feet.

PRINCIPAL RESERVOIRS OF THE KENNEBEC AND ITS TRIBUTARIES.

Name.	Connected with	Approximate area in square miles.	Present storage in feet.	Additional storage feasible in feet.
Palmyra, 2 ponds,........	Sebasticook	0.60	-	-
Stuart's pond,............	[river.	0.80	-	-
Indian, with flowage,.....	do do	2.50	Dam.	-
Little Indian pond,.......	do do	0.35	-	-
Weymouth "	do do	0.40	-	- [dam.
Rogers' "	do do	0.90	-	Can have a high
Mill "	do do	1.10	-	[more.
Moose "	do do	*9.50	4	Several feet, 10 or
Stafford "	do do	0.35	-	-
Starbird "	do do	0.35	-	-
Barker's "	do do	0.35	-	-
Twenty-four ponds,...	-	48.30	-	-

Name.	Connected with	Approximate area in square miles.	Present storage in feet.†	Additional storage feasible in feet.†
Madison pond,...........	Wesserunsett	3.00	7	3
Wentworth pond, }	do river,	1.00	No dam.	10
Baker's " }			No dam.	Can be made a good reservoir.
Wyman, "	do do	0.75	No dam.	9
Weeks' "	do do	0.60	6	
Five ponds,..........	-	5.35	-	-

Name.	Connected with.	Approximate area in square miles.	Present storage in feet.	Additional storage feasible in feet.
Webber pond,...........	Kennebec	2 10	6	-
Three-mile pond,........	do river,	2.00	8	-
Sibley and Morrill pond,..	do do	2.00	-	10, on Morrill.
Long pond,...............	do do	0.95	-	-
Austin, 5 ponds,.........	do do	3.20	-	All can have dams.
Robinson's pond,.........	do do	0.75	-	-
Pleasant "	do do	3.15	4	8
Mores Bog Stream pond, Carratunk,............				
Otter, 2 ponds,..........	do do	0.50	-	-
Chase, 3 ponds,..........	do do	1 00	-	-
Mosquito pond, in Forks pl.	do do	1.00	-	12
Moxie, "	do do	7.00	6	3
Lower Baker pond,.......	do do	1.00	-	-
Black-Stream, lower pond,.	do do	1 25	8	2
Black-Stream, upper "	do do	0.50	7	2
Pierce pond,.............	do do	3.50	10	-
Lower Carrying-place, ...	do do	1.00	0	High dam.
Cold-Stream pond,........	do do	1.25	-	12
Chase's-Stream pond, ...	do do	0.60	-	-
Indian pond,.............	do do	6.00	12	[outlet.
Moosehead lake, ...	do do	120.00	8	4, by cutting down

* The Selectmen of Hartland report the area at twelve square miles, and that the surface can be raised 20 feet without changing the channel of discharge.

† Storage reported by Wm. H. McLaughlin, Esq.

PRINCIPAL RESERVOIRS OF THE KENNEBEC AND ITS TRIBUTARIES.

Name.	Connected with	Approximate area in square miles.	Present storage in feet.	Additional storage feasible in feet.
Lower Roach pond,.......	Kennebec	5.00	8	4
Middle " "	[river,	2.50	0	0
Upper " "	do do	3.00	Poor dam.	-
Tomhegan "	do do	0.75	No dam.	6
Spencer "	do do	1.50	4	-
Western Outlet, 3 ponds,..	do do	1.25	Dam feasible.	-
Thirty-six ponds,.....	-	173.25	-	-

The following lakes and ponds are discharged into the tide waters of the Kennebec below Augusta. The Cobbosseecontee series, support water-powers of unsurpassed excellence, as at Gardiner and Winthrop:

Name.	Connected with.	Approximate area in square miles.	Present storage in feet.*	Additional storage feasible in feet.*
Pleasant pond,..........	Cobbosseecon- [tee river,	1.50	4	3, by higher dams & 3 by cutting down the "Rips" and "Hazards" ledge.
1st Purgatory pond,......	do do	0.70	3	The three Purgatory ponds can be raised 8 feet and drawn down 4 feet.
2d " "	do do	0.50	Dam.	
3d " "	do do	0.20	-	
Cochnewagan "	do do	1.00	7	0
Wilson's "	do do	0.90	4	0 (?)
Cobbosseecontee Gt. pond,.	do do	8.00	4	Can draw down and [add six feet.
Narrows pond,...........	do do	0.90	-	
South "	do do	1.95	3	3
North, "	do do	3.00	-	-
Carleton "	do do	0.40	-	-
Greely "	do do	0.85	-	-
Sanborn's "	do do	0.30	0	Can be flowed.
Desert "	do do	0 30	-	-
Jimmy's "	do do	0.30	-	-
Fifteen ponds,.......	-	20.90	-	-
Nequosset pond,..........	Kennebec riv.	0.80	-	-
Worromontogus pond,.....	do do	1.75	Dam.	10
Small ponds in Augusta,...	do do	1.50	-	-
Great Swamp in Dresden,..	do do	0.90	-	-
Eight ponds,.........	-	4.95	-	-

The foregoing 152 principal reservoirs of the Kennebec and tributaries sum 357.15 square miles. The total lake and pond surface contained in the Kennebec basin is about 450 square miles, or one square mile to each 12.9 square miles of tributary country. The lakes average 1.44 square miles each in extent.

* Storage of the Cobbosseecontee reported by R. H. Gardiner, Esq.

Moosehead lake. Moosehead lake is 35 × 12 miles, and covers 120 square miles. It is of such depth as to be crossed by steamboats from end to end. The inflow in the spring alone is usually about seven feet. The dam now commands a head of eight feet over the entire surface, and by cutting down the channel, ten or twelve feet can be had. This head, it is estimated, the 1,000 square miles of tributary country will yield nearly or quite every year. The reserve is now used for only log-driving purposes, as there is no demand for it for manufacturing uses. It is a reservoir of remarkable character, situated at the head of a great river, profusely supplied, held at a great elevation above tide, and commanded by a comparatively inexpensive dam. At the lowest estimate it will add two hundred per cent. to the low-run power of the Kennebec river. Lake Winnepiseogee in New Hampshire, the grand feeder of the Merrimac, holds a storage of 40 inches upon 72 square miles of water surface.

The Penobscot river off the *northwest* angle of the lake is somewhat higher than the surface of the latter. It has been proposed (and a charter for the purpose was sought from the Legislature in 1839) to cut a canal so as to unite the waters, for the purpose, as was then contemplated, of running timber into the Kennebec waters, and thereby avoiding the "long, difficult and expensive driving" down the Penobscot. This canal was to be called the *Seeboomook Sluiceway*. The distance from Meadow pond, which is connected and lies on the same level with the river, to a stream emptying into the lake, is 4,210 feet. The lake is 11.36 feet below the pond. The deepest part of the cut would be 58.70 feet, the land being in general very favorable for excavation. The charter was not granted on account of opposition from the Penobscot region.

It is evident that advantage of the peculiar conditions referred to, might be taken for other and far more important purposes than those had in view in 1839. The waters of the Penobscot might be turned into the lake in flood time, and in time of drouth drawn off into the Penobscot again by a canal from the *northeast* angle of the lake which is several feet higher than the river off against it, from which it is separated by only three miles of low land. To what extent Moosehead could be made a reservoir to a greater depth than 12 feet without dykes to prevent overflow, I am not able to learn.

At the season of low water it requires from 12 to 18 hours for the swell consequent upon hoisting the gates at the outlet of Indian pond (an expansion of the river below Moosehead) to reach Skowhegan.* In July, 1867, the gates being opened at 2 o'clock A. M., the wave reached that point, in general, from 3 to 4 o'clock P. M.; the rise was eight to twelve inches. J. M. Haynes, Esq., Treasurer Kennebec Land and Lumber Company, states the time required for the wave to reach Augusta from the dam at the lake (not Indian pond) to be 40 hours; that the time varies three hours according as the wind (if strong) is favorable or adverse, and five hours according as the river is high or low. The wave is nine hours in passing from the lake dam to Indian-pond dam, the expansion of the pond surface necessitating a larger time for perceptible rise.

Power on the Lower Section of the Kennebec.

If the mean volume of water that can be commanded upon the river from Carratunk falls to Augusta be assumed to be forty per cent. less than at Augusta, or 170,000 cubic feet per minute for 11 hours a day, for the low summer run, the gross power upon this portion of the river, for the hours specified, is 101,000 horse, or 4,040,000 spindles. An utterly insignificant part of the power is now used, and at no point are works now constructed of sufficient magnitude to hold back any considerable amount of water in the hours of non-use.

Railroads are already in operation as far north as Skowhegan and are being constructed to Carratunk falls, with a view to continuation to Moosehead lake.

The river is navigable to Augusta for small vessels, and above to Waterville, by lighters, these being "locked" over the Augusta fall. The records of Hon. R. H. Gardiner show that from 1789 to 1865 the river opened to navigation twenty-one times in March and fifty-five times in April, the mean period of opening being April 6, and of closing December 12.

* William Philbrick, Esq., Skowhegan.

CHAPTER XVIII.

THE SYSTEM OF THE PENOBSCOT.

Section 1.—The Penobscot Basin.

Location. The hydrographic district of the Penobscot lies next east of that of the Kennebec, and is expanded over and contained within the east-central and northern portions of the great Southern Slope. No part of the basin extends beyond the boundaries of the State.

Form. The Penobscot is the only great fluviatile district in Maine, which illustrates in its actual configuration the geographical ideal of the river basin—appearing as a mere point at the mouth of the stream, thence, interior-ward, expanding symmetrically upon both sides of the central channel, presently embranching into subordinate basins, themselves disposed likewise symmetrically about tributary streams, and themselves yet further breaking up into still smaller basins located upon still smaller tributaries, until the whole takes on the similitude of a mighty tree, that from one trunk ramifies into innumerable branches, and from one grand aorta divaricates into numberless arteries and veins, by which, upon occasion, its entire volume of fluids in conducted to and poured into a common channel of circulation and discharge.

Dimensions. Greatest length, from north to south, 160 miles; greatest breadth, 115 miles; area 8,200 square miles, —considerably the largest river district contained wholly in the State. Eight hundred square miles discharge their surplus water into the main river below its lowest water-power, at Bangor.

Elevation. The Penobscot country is less elevated above the sea than the Kennebec, and considerably less than the Androscoggin, as results from the subsidence of the whole State surface from west to east, before remarked. The northern portion is however quite elevated, the divide having a mean height of 1,085 feet. The loftiest portion of the basin is at the head waters of the main river (west branch)—from 1,600 to 2,000 feet.

In the table following, the height above tide of points either immediately adjacent to the river, or on the river itself, is given:

LOCALITIES.	Feet.	LOCALITIES.	Feet.
Foot of Corporation dam, Veazie,	5.4	Winn (small stream at R. R. crossing), ...	210
Top " " "	20.8	Mattawamkeag river, ...	190
Foot of Ayer's falls, Orono, ...	27.2	Pamedumcook and the Twin lakes, about, ...	500
Head " " "	35.4	Three miles below Ripogenus lake, ...	663
Stillwater, in Orono village, ...	37.5	Mattagamon lake, about	850
Foot of falls at Great Works, Oldtown, ...	57.5	Ripogenus lake, ...	878
Head of falls at Great Works, Oldtown, ...	68.6	Chesuncook lake, ...	900
Foot of falls at Dwinal's mills, Oldtown, ...	71.8	Penobscot, off northeast angle of Moosehead lake, ...	1,000
Head of falls at Dwinal's mills, Oldtown, ...	78.3	Penobscot, off northwest angle of Moosehead lake, ...	1,034
Foot of falls at Dwinal's mills, Milford, ...	80.7	Penobscot in Sand bay, 1612 to	2,100
Head of falls at Dwinal's mills, Milford, ...	92.3	Penobscot head, No. 5, R. 19,	1,808
Passadumkeag river, ...	106	" " No. 6, R. 18,	1,742
Mattanawcook stream, ...	172	" lake, head of S. W. branch, ...	1,509

Heights on European & North American Railway at crossings, as specified below:

LOCALITIES.	Feet.	LOCALITIES.	Feet.
Mattakeunk stream, ...	199	Hot brook, ...	417
Gordon brook, ...	231	Baskahegan stream five miles below the lake, ...	370
Mattagordus stream, ...	301	Forks of Crooked brook, ...	366
Mud Point "	310	Calais and Houlton road, ...	412
Divide between Mattawamkeag and Baskahegan waters, ...	616		

Heights on the Maine Central Railroad.		Heights on a trial route from Waterville to Bangor, via Dexter.	
LOCALITIES.	Feet.	LOCALITIES.	Feet.
Hermon station, ...	140	West Garland, ...	350
Carmel "	149	East of North branch, ...	201
Etna "	250	Levant, ...	132
		Kenduskeag stream, ...	110

HEIGHTS ON THE BANGOR AND PISCATAQUIS RAILROAD.*

LOCALITIES.	Feet.	LOCALITIES.	Feet.
Grade E. & N. A. depot in Oldtown, about, ...	105	Piscataquis river (low water) opposite Randall Hall's place in Sebec, ...	280
Average low water at Black Island (Pea Cove) Penobscot,	105	Depot grade, Foxcroft, ...	374
Freshet height, Penobscot, ...	114	Head of Foxcroft dam (estimated,)	370
Lake Boyd, Orneville, ...	303		
Orneville summit grade, ...	335		
Low water at Piscataquis crossing, about 40 rods above the mouth of Sebec stream, ...	271		

* Reported by L. H. Eaton, Res. Eng., from a survey by Col. A. W. Wildes, C. E.

HEIGHTS ON A CANAL ROUTE.*

LOCALITIES.	Feet.	LOCALITIES.	Feet.
Guilford Village, 70 feet above Sebasticook main stream between Cambridge and Ripley, about, ...	385	14 miles above Guilford, (13 feet to the mile,) .... Shirley mills, about.........	567 942

HEIGHTS ON THE BELFAST AND MOOSEHEAD RAILROAD.†

High tide at Belfast, ...	0	Dixmont Notch, ...	580
Webb's ledge, Brooks, ...	350	Dixmont Centre, ...	448

ELEVATIONS ON AND NEAR THE DIVIDE OF THE PENOBSCOT AND ST. JOHN WATERS.‡

Lewis's on Fish River road, No. 7, R. 5, ...	1,084	Thence south-southwest to the south line of No. 4, R. 17, ...	2,130 1,780 1,972 1,701 2,200 1,879 1,699 1,591 1,870
Between Milnokett and Seboois lakes,..............	778 1,119		
Divide between lake Pomgocquamoc and the Aroostook waters, No. 7, R. 11,......	1,049		
Water shed ridge east of Chamberlain lake, on line of Nos. 6 and 7, R. 11,.............	1,134	Height of ridge, Nos. 5 and 6, R. 17,...............	1,989 1,732 1,694 1,517
Telos canal, ...	914		
Two miles south of Telos canal,	1,125		
Between Telos and Cusabexis lakes, ...	1,029	Portage, No. 6, R. 17,......	1,492
Heights between Mud pond and Umbazooksus lake, ...	1,034 1,006 988		
Cauquomgomoc lake, about, ...	930		
Heights between Allaguash and the Couquomgomosis lakes, ...	1,860 1,710 1,223 1,075	Heights along the northwest head waters of the Penobscot,.............	1,742 1,644 1,707 1,558 1,808 1,888 2,012 1,995 1,857 1,600 1,800
Heights about Horn pond, No. 8, R. 15, at the head of Wadleigh brook,.........	1,734 1,835 1,509 1,735 1,633	Portage lake, west of Penobscot lake and west of boundary, ...	1,546
Divide, Nos. 6, and 7, R. 16,	1,612 1,750		

Geological relations.

Gneiss predominates as far north as Frankfort and Bucksport, with schists, granite and limestone intermingled. Thence northward to the Piscataquis, mica schist prevails, with granite about the Passadumkeag. North of the Piscataquis, clay slate; but on the left bank of the Penobscot, schist obtains to some distance north of the Mattawamkeag, where clay slate is struck. This last mentioned form of rock occupies much the larger proportion of the northern part of the basin, with granite abundant about Katahdin, with sandstone northeast of

* Documents, 1837. James Hall, C. E.
† Reported by A. L. Mortimer, Res. Eng., from a survey by Col. A. W. Wildes, C. E.
‡ From Col. Graham's map of N. E. Boundary.

Moosehead lake, and mica schist at the head of the main river, west branch. Slaty rocks are largely in excess of all other forms, and by far the most important, as locally of unsurpassed quality for roofing purposes.

Surface conditions.

The basin of the Penobscot is mountainous from the sea to above the head of tide; thence northward, gently undulating, to, into, and throughout the region of the east and Mattawamkeag branches, until it is insensibly blended with the valley of the Aroostook. On the main river, above Nicatou, it is more broken, and is singularly diversified with lakes, ponds, swamps, streams, hills, valleys and detached peaks. The Katahdin mountains, the highest in Maine, affording a prospect characteristic and sublime from the vast breadth of level country overlooked, lie upon the left bank. Further west the valley becomes merged with that of the Kennebec on the south and the Allaguash on the north, and terminates on the northwest at the highland boundaries of the State and in the swamps and lagoons which form the common reservoir of the St. John and Penobscot. As a whole the valley is uniform in its topographical features.

The surface materials prevailing in this district, or rather in the small part of it occupied, and from which returns have been received, are as follows, as indicated by responses to inquiries:

Gravel.	Sand.	Sandy Loam.	Loam.	Clay Loam.	Clay.
16	7	3	15	5	16

Showing that soils retentive of water are considerably in excess in the portions reported.

Including the unbroken wilderness about the head waters, and the wooded tracts of the nominally cleared districts, probably about two-thirds of the basin are still forest-covered.

Rainfall.

The sum of annual deposition upon the Penobscot basin, is estimated at 799,500,000,000. cubic feet

Section 2.—The Penobscot River.

Course.

As a whole, east of south; so, at least, all the branches of the river and the movement of the combined waters being taken into account.

Affluents.

The so-called *west branch* is properly only the continuation of the main river; it is the *upper Penobscot;* a name applicable to the stream from the Mattawamkeag to the

"Forks" in Pittston township, where the Penobscot takes origin. The *lower Penobscot* extends from the Mattawamkeag to Penobscot bay.

The *east branch*, so called, should be known as the *Mattagamon*,* after and in common with the lake from which it issues and the mountain in its vicinity. The various terms, west branch, east branch, northwest branch, etc., should be reserved for use about the head waters of the river, where indeed they are already applied. When used in both the mid and upper section they involve its nomenclature in confusion.

The principal tributaries of the Penobscot are subjoined:

	Name.	Where received.
From the right bank,	Kenduskeag,	Bangor.
	Pushaw,	Oldtown.
	Piscataquis,	Howland.
From the left bank,	Passadumkeag,	Passadumkeag.
	Mattawamkeag,	Mattawamkeag.
	Mattagamon,	Nicatou.

Name.	BASIN.			STREAM.	
	Length, miles.	Breadth, miles.	Area, sq. miles.	Length, miles.	Estimated discharge, cubic feet.
Kenduskeag,	27	13	190	34	7,410,000,000
Pushaw,	23	12	200	26	7,800,000,000
Piscataquis,	55	34	1,276	71	50,960,000,000
Passadumkeag,	27	20	320	35	12,480,000,000
Mattawamkeag,	64	30	1,375	85	53,625,000,000
Mattagamon,	50	33	841	63	32,799,000,000

Several of the tributaries of these rivers are so large as to require independent notice.

Name.	Branch of	BASIN.			STREAM.	
		Length, miles.	Breadth, miles.	Area, sq. miles.	Length, miles.	Estimated discharge, cubic ft.
Pleasant,	Piscataquis,	34	14	235	40	9,165,000,000
Sebec,	"	33	13	250	42	9,750,000,000
Molunkus,	Mattawamkeag	31	11	180	34	7,020,000,000
Baskahegan,	"	22	12	198	33	7,722,000,000
East Branch,	"	30	8	185	32	7,215,000,000

The west branch of the Mattawamkeag, so called, is simply and properly the upper Mattawamkeag,—is the upper section of the main river. It drains a considerabiy larger area of country than

* As suggested by Prof. C. H. Hitchcock.

the east branch. There are 1,604 streams represented on the State map in the Penobscot system. The word Piscataquis means "Branch," in Indian, and Nicatou signifies "Crotch." The Mattawamkeag is 300 feet wide at its mouth, and the Penobscot 500 feet wide at the same point. The Piscataquis is about 250 feet wide for 25 miles above its mouth. The mean width of the Penobscot for some miles above Bangor is about 800 feet.

Length.

The Penobscot from the confluence of the Mattawamkeag to the open sea is about 120 miles long; from the junction of the Mattagamon to the sea about 132 miles; from its extreme head waters about 260 miles, or including the local windings, 300 miles. The main water-power section extends from lake Chesuncook to Bangor, 120 miles, the fall being 900 feet; or, via the Mattagamon, from lake Mattagamon to Bangor, 115 miles, and a fall of about 850 feet.

Volume.

The annual discharge of the Penobscot is estimated as 319,800,000,000 cubic feet. Of this about 31,000,000,000 are received below the lowest mill privilege, yielding on its passage to the river important power.

Variations of volume.

The Penobscot naturally, and without the assistance of man, holds a position amongst the most highly favored rivers of the State in respect to uniformity of volume at different seasons of the year. This is due in part to the extent of its tributary area, in virtue of which the contributions of the various branches do not reach its chief manufacturing sites at the same time. It is due also to the more uniform surface aspect of the basin, in respect to which it has the decided advantage over the Saco, Androscoggin and Kennebec; it is due also, in common with the other large rivers of the State, to its extensive system of lakes and the vast breadth of forests upon its drainage surfaces.

H. F. Mills, C. E., estimating for the very dry seasons of '64 and '65, reports 117 thousand cubic feet per minute *in use* at Bangor for manufacturing, in addition to what was employed in passing rafts at the sluice, the amount of which he could not arrive at, and expresses the judgment that the total amount was at least 25 per cent. in excess of the above figures, or 146,250 cubic feet.

Assuming the minumum run at Bangor at 146,250 cubic feet per minute, the total low-run delivery of the river at its mouth is not far from 160,000 cubic feet per minute for the 24 hours. This continued day and night throughout the year, would convey off about 82.5 billion cubic feet, or somewhat over one-fourth of the estimated total annual delivery.

The mean run for the summer at Bangor, estimated from the lowest run with such ratio of excess thereover as has been found to obtain on the Kennebec at Augusta, is about 194,000 cubic feet per minute for the 24 hours.

Mr. Mills also reports 5,760,000 cubic feet per minute passing Treat's falls at Bangor in a "heavy freshet." [The discharge of the Connecticut at Turner's falls in the winter of 1866, varied, as Mr. Francis states, from 300,000 to 600,000 cubic feet per minute.] The figures indicate relatively less variation than occurs on the Kennebec; there undoubtedly is considerably less than upon the Saco and Androscoggin, relatively to the areas drained.

The range from lowest to highest water appears in the following table. The absolute range is of course greater than upon the smaller rivers, but a proportionally greater range is not to be inferred from this fact. The absolute range is, however, the incident that bears upon the manufacturing character of the stream, since the location of mills is in a measure determined by it:

Locality.	Feet.	Locality.	Feet.
Bangor,	12	Oldtown falls,	11
Black Island, Pea Cove,	9	Island rapids.,	11

Slope.

The descent of the river from the Mattawamkeag, where its elevation above tide is about 190 feet, to Bangor, a distance of 57 miles, is at the rate of 3.3 feet to the mile, or 2′.1 mile in angular measurement. Of this fall 92 feet are found in the first twelve miles above Bangor, and accordingly above this point—Milford—the river is mainly navigable, the chief interruption being the Piscataquis rips at Howland. From lake Chesuncook the depression of the surface to the tide is about 7.5 feet to the mile, or 4′.8; from lake Mattagamon, about 7.3 feet to the mile. The slope of the whole river from its remotest sources to its mouth is a little below six feet to the mile on the average.

Lakes.

The number of lakes and ponds in the basin of the Penobscot, represented upon the State map, is 467. The number due to its comparative extent is 385; so the per cent. of numerical excess is about twenty-one.

PRINCIPAL RESERVOIRS OF THE PENOBSCOT AND ITS TRIBUTARIES.

Name.	Connected with		Approximate area in square miles.	Present storage in feet.*	Additional storage feasible in feet.*
Little Seboosis lake,......	Piscataquis riv.		1.40	†	†
Endless "	do	do	4.25	-	-
Pond north of Endless,...	do	do	1.10	-	-
Pond northeast of " ...	do	do	1.20	-	-
Schoodic lake,...........	do	do	16.00	-	8
Seboeis "	do	do	12.00	-	-
Dover pond,.............	do	do	0.70	6	More feasible.
Harlow, 2 ponds,.........	do	do	0.50	6	Can cut down outlet.
Kingsbury pond,.........	do	do	3.00	10	More feasible.
Sangerville ponds,........	do	do	0.90	Dams.	-
Piper pond,..............	do	do	1.25	-	Dam feasible.
Upper Piper pond,........	do	do	0.35	-	Can have dam.
Spectacle "	do	do	1.10	Dam.	10
Lower Ebeeme "	do	do	2.25	-	-
Upper " "	do	do	1.25	-	-
Sebec lake,..............	do	do	14.00	6	4
Long pond,‡.............	do	do	1.00	-	4
Ship " ‡.............	do	do	3.00	Poor dam.	10
Hebron pond,............	do	do	2 00	Dam.	-
Monson pond,............	do	do	0.40	0	Several feet.
Bowdoin College, 3 ponds,.	do	do	2.00	-	-
Wilson pond, ...	do	do	2.25	7	Several feet.
Houston "	do	do	3.00	-	-
Pond in B, R. 11,........	do	do	1.00	-	-
Bald Mountain pond,.....	do	do	2.00	4	4
Shirley bogs, ...	do	do	8.00	7, upon 2 sq miles.	Can be made immense reser'rs.
Thirty ponds or more,	-		85.90	-	-

Name.	Connected with		Approximate area in square miles.	Present storage in feet.§	Additional storage feasible in feet.§
Cold Stream pond,........	Passadumkeag		6.00	A poor dam.	10 feet could be [held.
Second Cold Stream pond,.	do	river.,	0.95	8	
Clear Water pond,........	do	do	0.80	8	-
Escutassis, 2 ponds, ...	do	do	1.40	8, both.	-
Saponac pond,...........	do	do	1.30	-	-
Madagascal pond,........	do	do	1.70	7, good dam.	-
2 ponds above Madagascal,	do	do	0.25	6, the larger.	-
Spring pond,.............	do	do	0.20	-	-
No. 3 "	do	do	1.00	-	-
First Pistol lake,.........	do	do	1.00	6, good dam. [flows all.	-
Second, Third and Fourth Pistol lakes,...........	do	do	0.50	8, one dam	-
Porter pond,.............	do	do	0.20	-	-
Nicatous lake,...........	do	do	10.00	10, good dam.	-
Abamgamook or West lake,	do	do	2.00	7, mod. good dam.] 9	-
Duck lake,..............	do	do	2.00		-
Garbeus lake,............	do	do	1.00	6, mod. good dam.] 5	-
Coombs "	do	do	0.15		-
Ware pond,..............	do	do	0.80	-	-
Twenty-two ponds, ...	-		31.25	-	-

* Storage of the Piscataquis reported in part by Messrs. Calvin and Luther Chamberlain.
† Blanks, as above, indicate that the storage has not been reported.
‡ Ship pond and Long pond when flowed will cover several hundred acres of swamp land.
§ Storage of the Passadumkeag reported by Joseph W. Porter, Esq., of Burlington, with a map of the ponds and streams.

PRINCIPAL RESERVOIRS OF THE PENOBSCOT AND ITS TRIBUTARIES.

Name.	Connected with	Approximate area in square miles.	Present storage in feet.	Additional storage feasible in feet.
Mattakeunk pond,........	Mattawamkeag	1.50	Dam.	Can be made a
Mud "	do [river,	0.60	- *	great reservoir.
Molunkus "	do do	3.00	-	- *
Benedicta "	do do	0.75	-	-
Mackwacook "	do do	1.00	-	-
Wytopitlock "	do do	3.25	-	Can be made a
South pond, No. 3, R. 4,..	do do	0.75	-	great reservoir.
Hot brook, " "	do do	3.50	-	-
Baskahegan lake,........	do do	18.00	-	-
Pond in No. 3, R. 3,......	do do	1.00	-	-
Mattawamkeag lake,.....	do do	5.50	12	-
Caribou pond, Isl. Fls. pl.,	do do	1.50	-	-
Pond in centre Isl. Fls. pl.,	do do	1.00	-	-
Pleasant lake,...........	do do	3.50	-	Can have many
Sketicook "	do do	1.25	-	- [feet.
Spaulding's lake,.........	do do	2.50	-	-
Rockabema "	do do	2.25	5	Several feet at
Mud lake, above Rockabema lake,............	do do	1.25	8	little expense. -
Small ponds in Rockabema plantation,...........	do do	2.50	-	-
Twenty-one ponds,....	-	53.35	-	-

Name.	Connected with.	Approximate area in square miles.	Present storage in feet.†	Additional storage feasible in feet.†
Salmon-stream pond,.....	Mattagamon	2.00	-	-
Katahdin "	do [river,	0.65	-	-
Pond in No. 4, R. 7,......	do do	1.50	0	-
Bowlin pond,............	do do	1.10	-	Several feet.
Upper Bowlin, 2 ponds,...	do do	0.85	-	Several feet.
Mattagamon lake,........	do do	5.00	10	-
Mattagamonsis lake,......	do do	2.25	10	-
Third lake,..............	do do	1.75	6	-
Fourth lake,.............	do do	0.90	Dam 12 ft.	-
Flowage above Fourth lake,	do do	1.00	Several feet.	-
Snake pond, in No. 7, R. 11,	do do	1.00	Dam 7 feet.	-
Big Leadbetter pond, "	do do	0.80	Dam 10 ft.	-
Lower Shin pond,........	do do	2.25	-	-
Upper Shin "	do do	1.30	-	12 to 20
Pond in No. 5, R. 7,......	do do	1.00	-	-
First lake,..............	do do	1.10	5 to 6	-
Second lake,............	do do	1.10	5 to 6	-
Seboois "	do do	4.75	5 to 6	-
5 ponds in No. 6, R. 8,....	do do	3.00	-	-
Scraggly lake,...........	do do	3.00	0	-
Wassattiquoick pond,....	do do	1.50	-	-
Webster lake,...........	do do	3.00	10	-
Hudson and Wadleigh brook reservoirs,............	do do	1.50	Several feet.	-
Twenty-eight ponds,..	-	42.30	-	-

* Storage reported mainly by Messrs. E. S. Coe and Daniel Barker, of Bangor.
† Blanks, not reported.

PRINCIPAL RESERVOIRS OF THE PENOBSCOT AND ITS TRIBUTARIES.

Name.	Connected with.		Approximate area in square miles.	Present storage in feet.*	Additional storage feasible in feet.*
Pushaw lake, ...	Penobscot	river,	8.00	– †	6
Boyd "	do	do	1.75	–	– †
Little Pushaw pond, ...	do	do	0.90	–	–
Mud pond, ...	do	do	0.75	–	–
Pickerel pond, in Alton, ..	do	do	0.50	Dam.	Can be flowed 3 [ft. over 1.75 [square miles.
Nichols pond, ...	do	do	3.00	–	
Davis "	do	do	0.90	–	
Holbrook's pond, ...	do	do	0.90	–	–
Mattanawcook pond, ...	do	do	1.30	Dam.	–
Crooked pond, ...	do	do	0.70	Dam.	–
Folsom "	do	do	0.40	Dam.	–
Upper "	do	do	1.20	Dam.	–
Pond in Nos. 2 and 3, east of Chester, ...	do	do	4.50	–	–
Mattamiscontis pond, ...	do	do	2.00	–	–
Lower Mattamiscontis, ...	do	do	0.90	–	–
Cambolasse pond, ...	do	do	0.65	Dam.	–
Long "	do	do	1.00	Dam.	–
Caribou "	do	do	0.85	Dam.	–
Centre "	do	do	0.30	Dam.	–
Madunkeunk pond, ...	do	do	1.00	–	–
Nollesemic "	do	do	2.50	–	–
Quakish lake, ...	do	do	1.75	–	A 12-foot dam [feasible.
Shad "	do	do	0.75	–	
South Twin lake, ...	do	do	3.00	Several feet ‡	3
North Twin "	do	do	3.25	Dam of 16 ft.	3
Mattaceunk lake, in Molunkus, ...	do	do	2.50	–	–
Jo-Mary upper lake, ...	do	do	3.00	–	–
Jo-Mary middle "	do	do	2.50	–	–
Jo-Mary lower "	do	do	3.00	–	–
Pemedumcook "	do	do	16.00	Several feet ‡	3
Milinokett "	do	do	18.00	–	10 to 12
Katahdin pond, in No. 2, R. 9	do	do	2.00	–	–
First pond in No. 2, R. 10,	do	do	0.75	–	–
Second pond, "	do	do	1.00	–	–
Third " "	do	do	2.50	–	–
Nahmakanta lake, ...	do	do	3.00	8	–
Uusuntabunt "	do	do	3.75	4 to 6	–
Sourdnahunk "	do	do	3.75	0	4
Five ponds in A, R. 11, ...	do	do	4.75	Dammed in part.	–
Penobscot pond, in No. 1, R. 11, ...	do	do	1.00	–	–
Three ponds west of Namakanta lake, ...	do	do	2.50	2 flowed 4 to 6	–
Ripogenus lake, ...	do	do	2.00	–	–
Ripogenus pond, ...	do	do	4.00	–	–
Caribou lake, ...	do	do	6.50	–	–
Upper Caribou lake, ...	do	do	1.00	–	–
Ragged "	do	do	4.00		–
Chesuncook "	do	do	22.00	Dam, 12 to 13	2
Duck pond, ...	do	do	2 00	Several feet.	–
Cusabexis lake, ...	do	do	2.00	5 to 6	–
Umbazooksus lake, ...	do	do	2.25	0	Low banks abt. [the outlet.
Longley, in No. 6, R. 13, .	do	do	1.50	Dam, 7 feet.	
Black pond, ...	do	do	1.00	–	–
Shallow lake, ...	do	do	2.50	6	–
Poland "	do	do	0.75	–	–

* Storage reported mainly by E. S. Coe, Esq, of Bangor
† Blanks, not reported.
‡ By the North Twin dam.

PRINCIPAL RESERVOIRS OF THE PENOBSCOT AND ITS TRIBUTARIES.

Name.	Connected with	Approximate area in square miles.	Present storage in feet.*	Additional storage feasible in feet.*
Cauquomgomoc pond,.....	Penobscot river,	10.00	0	Outlet can be
Portage pond,...........	do do	1.25	-	[lowered sev-
Daggett "	do do	1.00	-	[eral feet.
Pond above Daggett,......	do do	0.75	-	-
Loon "	do do	3.00	0	Dam feasible.
Two ponds above Loon, ...	do do	1.25	-	-
Hurd, 2 ponds,..........	do do	1.50	0	-
Wadleigh pond,..........	do do	0.75	0	-
Pine Stream, 2 ponds, ...	do do	1.00	-	-
Lobster pond,...........	do do	6.00	0	0
Russell "	do do	1.00	5 to 6	-
Luther "	do do	0.90	-	-
Nulhedus pond,..........	do do	1.00	-	-
2 ponds, No. 3, R. 3, north of Thorndike township,.	do do	1.25	0	-
2 ponds in Bald Mountain township,.............	do do	1.50	-	-
Penobscot lake, in Hammond township,........	do do	1.50	-	-
2 ponds in No. 3, north of Hammond township,....	do do	1 50	-	-
Eighty-four ponds,...	-	182.40	-	-

The foregoing 185 lakes and ponds have a combined surface of 395.20 square miles, substantially the whole of which is susceptible of use for storage purposes, and is tributary to the water-power of the lower main Penobscot.

In addition to the above, the following lakes, which naturally belong to the Allaguash System, have, for practical purposes, in lumbering and of water supply, been added to the Penobscot series by means of dams, canals, etc.

PRINCIPAL RESERVOIRS ARTIFICIALLY TRIBUTARY TO THE WATER-POWER OF THE PENOBSCOT.

Name.	Connected. with	Approximate area in square miles.	Present storage in feet.†	Additional storage feasible in feet.†
Telos lake,..............	Mattagamon	2.75	10	-
Telosinis lake,..........	do river,	1.00	10	-
Chamberlain lake,........	do do	20 00	10	-
Leadbetter "	do do	0 60	8	-
Big Leadbetter bog,......	do do	0.75	Flowed.	-
Mud pond, with flowage, in No. 6,...............	do do	2.10	6-foot dam.	-
Doddle Brook flowage,....	do do	0.90	8-foot dam.	-
Allaguash lake,..........	do do	9.00	4	Seve'l ft. by dam
Mud pond, in No. 9, R. 15,	do do	2.00	-	[below outlet.
Nine ponds,.........	-	39.00	-	-

* Storage reported mainly by E. S. Coe, Esq., of Bangor.
† Storage reported by Messrs. E. S. Coe and Daniel Barker.

The following lakes and ponds are tributary to the main river below the lowest fall thereon, namely, at Bangor, and support very valuable water-powers on their outlet streams:

PRINCIPAL RESERVOIRS TRIBUTARY TO THE PENOBSCOT TIDE WATERS.

Name.	Connected with		Approximate area in square miles.	Present storage in feet.	Additional storage feasible in feet.
Alamoosuc pond, ...	Penobscot river,		1.90	Dam.	-
Craig's "	do	do	0.40	-	-
Toddy "	do	do	5.35	9	-
Fitz "	do	do	3 00	-	-
Bucksport, 6 ponds, ...	do	do	2.00	1 dam.	-
Brewer pond, ...	do	do	2.90	10	4
Field's "	do	do	0.60	-	-
Hermon pond,*	do	do	1.15	-	-
Etna "	do	do	1.00	Dam.	Can have higher
Pitcher, Andrews, etc., ...	do	do	4.00	-	Can be made ca-
Camden ponds, nine, ...	do	do	2.10	Stored in part	[pacious reser-
Goose pond, ...	do	do	3.00	Dam.	[voirs.
White's "	do	do	1.00	9	4
Pierce's "	do	do		9	Many feet.
Walker's pond, ...	do	do	3.00	4	2
Thirty ponds, or more,	-		31.40	-	-

This gives a grand total of 462.10 square miles of reservoir surface tributary to the water-power of the Penobscot and its affluents, 224 of the principal lakes and ponds out of the whole 467 alone being taken into the account.

The following lakes and ponds naturally connected with the Allaguash series, are by means of locks and canals made available in the *lumbering* operations of the Penobscot, though not tributary to its volume of water to any extent:

LAKES ARTIFICIALLY TRIBUTARY TO THE LUMBERING OPERATIONS OF THE PENOBSCOT.

Indian pond,	Spider lake,
Pomgoewahem lake,	Pleasant lake,
Heron lake, in No. 10,	Soper pond,
Heron lake, in No. 8,	Pomgocquamoc, 2 ponds,
Churchill lake,	Mud pond, in No. 9, R. 12.

These ponds have a combined surface of 42.75 square miles. The extent of the several ponds and the flowage thereon are given in the table of reservoirs connected with the Allaguash

The aggregate area of the lakes belonging to the Penobscot river.

* "Hermon pond, with the four others connected, cover at least 2.75 square miles, and can be flowed 3 1-2 feet. There are 1,500 acres of swamp land bordering the ponds that can be converted into reservoir at trifling expense."

system, estimated from the maps, is 585 square miles, or 1 square mile to each 14.0 square miles of basin. The lakes average 1.18 square miles each in area.

Telos canal. The artificial connection of the Allaguash and Penobscot waters, above mentioned, is on this wise :—Webster lake is the last *naturally* belonging to the Penobscot on the Mattagamon branch. A canal has however been constructed between Webster and Telos, and by means of a dam at the northern end of Chamberlain lake,—its natural outlet, the water is turned through Telosinis and Telos, these being on the same level with Chamberlain, into the Penobscot. Thus the surplus waters of 39 square miles of reservoir surface, are, as shown by the table before given, made tributary to the reserve supplies of the Penobscot. The Telos canal also has a dam 12 feet in height, which controls the flow of waters from the lakes above. The flow from Chamberlain lake, when logs are not being driven, is about equal at each outlet.

Still further: a dam of 20 feet head at the natural outlet, the northern end, of Churchill lake, flows that lake, and Pomgocquahem and Heron lakes, but not to the level of Chamberlain lake. Accordingly these lakes with those connected, as shown in the table before given, do not contribute their waters to the Penobscot. By means of a *lock*, however, logs are driven up into Chamberlain and thence down the Penobscot. The lock is temporarily out of repair and is not used.

Summary view of the Penobscot reservoirs. It will be seen that no single lake or compact and closely connected series of lakes in the Penobscot system, can compare on terms of equality with the Umbagog series on the Androscoggin or Moosehead on the Kennebec; much less, relatively to the size of the rivers, with the Schoodic series on the St. Croix, the Eagle lakes on the Fish river, or Sebago on the Presumpscot—as a reservoir of water-power material. Relatively to the size of the basin and of the the main drainage stream, the leading lakes are smaller; they are scattered one from another and cannot be commanded by so few artificial constructions.

It is therefore in a peculiar sense and emphatically true of the Penobscot, that its full capacity as a water-power river will be realized only, as the actual occupation of the interior districts of the State shall render possible the improvement for local purposes of the power of the very numerous streams and small lakes situated around and constituting its head waters. It will be only when this has been effected that the powers upon the main stream and its chief affluents will reach their highest efficiency.

Feasibility of artificial reservoirs.

The country about many of the Penobscot lakes, as in the district from Nicatou to Chesuncook lake, and on the Mattagamon, is low and flat, so that upon moderate elevations of their surface very large tracts are overflowed. Thousands of acres are even by the present use of the lakes for storage submerged the greater part of the year, as for example between lakes Mattagamon and Mattagamonsis. This indicates very unusual facilities for *artificial reservoirs*. The cost of flowage will continue to be for an indefinite period merely nominal. There are also quite extensive low and swampy tracts upon the upper sections of the river that can readily be converted into artificial reserve basins at low cost, whenever manufacturing necessities shall require it. So that the low run of the river can be indefinitely increased and its manufacturing capacities in proportion, whenever the expense shall be justified.

The passage of water to Bangor from the great lakes on the upper Penobscot, Pamedumcook, Milinokett and Chesuncook, is accomplished in forty to fifty hours; from Mattagamon lake on the Mattagamon in forty-five to fifty-five hours.

Power on the Penobscot.

On the upper Penobscot.

The section of the upper Penobscot between Chesuncook lake and the mouth of the Mattawamkeag combines in unusual degree the grand requisites of water-power—namely, great reservoirs close at hand and a large amount of fall, and will in time become the site of very great manufacturing industry. The total descent is not far from seven hundred feet, and is broken by numerous falls and steep rapids that can be improved at small expense. The lakes lying upon the river in the region are of large size and can be used to any amount for reservoirs. The area tributary to the lakes is so great that any required head of storage can be secured upon them, and the river thus be made constant to the demands of enormous manufacturing.

The Mattagamon, likewise, has a great amount of fall below the lake of the same name, and will draw from this lake and its feeders, including the reservoirs artificially connected with it, vast supplies of water.

On the lower section of the Penobscot. The volume of the river in the vicinity of Bangor, being assumed at 146,250 cubic feet per minute for the twenty-four hours, at the period of extreme low run, the power in the ninety-two feet fall from Milford to Bangor, would be 55,600 horse-power gross, or 2,224,000 spindles, for eleven hours per diem. But a small portion of this power is employed, the dams not being of sufficient height to hold the water back in the hours of non-use. The long tract of dead water above Milford will furnish the power with an immense reservoir close at hand.

Means of access. A railroad runs by the side of the power in question, and is constructing to Winn, thus opening up the entire lower section of the river.

A record covering the period from 1816 to 1866, shows that the earliest opening to navigation of the Penobscot at Bangor, for the period, was on March 21, and that during the whole time registered it opened in January and February but once—namely, in 1831, on January 9. The river remains frozen over for one hundred and twenty-five days yearly on the average.

CHAPTER XIX.

THE SYSTEM OF THE ST. CROIX.

Section 1.—The St. Croix Basin.

Location. In the southeast corner of the State in part, and in part in the southwest portion of the British province of New Brunswick.

Form. [See Map.]

Dimensions. Length, 70 miles; breadth, 50 miles; area, 800 square miles in Maine, 375 square miles in the adjacent province; total, 1,175 square miles. Of this all but about 20 square miles contributes to the main river above the lowest mill privilege.

Elevation. This is the least elevated of all the drainage districts on the Southern Slope of the State which extend so far into the interior. The following table from which a complete profile of the river might be constructed, indicates in its two right-hand columns of figures the elevations of the river at different points. The country about is of course higher than the stream, but how much, there are no data at hand for determining.

Table of the distance and elevation of various sections of the St. Croix river, commencing from Calais bridge and the levels from nearly low water: *

NORTHERN BRANCH.

LOCALITIES.	From station to station.		Whole distance from Calais.		From station to station.		Whole elevation from Calais.		Remarks.
	Miles.	Rods.	Miles.	Rods.	Feet.	Inches	Feet.	Inches	
Upper bridge, Milltown,............	1¾	8	–	–	72	7	–	–	–
Baring bridge,......................	3½	32	5¼	40	13	11	86	6	Land good. Banks uniform.
Foot of Sprague's falls, ...	5	20	10¼	60	6	8¼	93	2¼	" "
Head of " "	¼	34	10¾	14	25	5¼	118	7½	Land good. An excellent water-power.
Head of Enoch's rips,...	½	61	11¼	75	9	6¾	128	2¼	Another good mill privilege.
Pitch of Lower Grand falls, ...	7¾	58	19¼	53	17	9¼	145	11½	Land variable. Banks low.
Head of Upper Grand falls, ...	½	20	19¾	73	20	–	165	11½	Western branch enters St. Croix few rods above.
Foot Grand Chiputneticook falls,.....	2¼	–	22	73	3	11½	169	11	Low land, and mostly light.
Head of " " "	½	10	22¾	3	20	1	190	–	An excellent water-power.
Foot of Canoose rips, ...	7¼	16	30	19	10	8¼	200	8¼	Land good.
Head of " "	½	20	30½	39	11	3	211	11¼	Rocky channel; water shoal.
Foot of Haycock rips,...............	2¾	40	33¼	79	–	6½	212	5¾	– –
Head of " "	¼	45	33¾	44	6	–	218	5¾	Channel very rocky. Land light and gravelly.
Foot of Meeting-house rips, ...	1	–	34¾	44	–	2½	218	8¼	Good land, with small exceptions.
Head of " "	1	20	35¾	69	7	9	226	5¼	Channel very rocky. Banks rough.
Foot of Rocky rips, ...	½	40	36½	24	1	–	227	5¼	Land low.
Head of " "	3¼	40	39¾	64	24	8¾	252	2	Extremely rocky channel. Shores rough.
Foot of Mile rips,..................	10	24	50	8	83	3¼	335	5¼	Much good land. Banks regular.
Head of " "	1	–	51	8	22	10½	358	3¾	Water shoal. Channel rocky.
Foot of Kill-me-quick rips,..........	3	12	54	20	14	7	372	10¾	Low meadow land.
Head of " "	½	20	54½	40	9	8¾	382	7½	Entrance of Chiputneticook lake.
Head of Chiputneticook lake,........	20	–	74½	40	–	–	382	7½	Shores of this lake mostly rocky.
Stream into Mud lake,..	1½	72	76¼	32	44	3	426	10½	Meadow land at the entrance, then rocky.
Head of Mud lake,..................	4	64	80½	16	–	–	426	–	Water from 2½ to 10 feet.

* Anson's Survey, Documents, 1839.

NORTHERN BRANCH, (CONTINUED.)

LOCALITIES.	From station to station.		Whole distance from Calais.		From station to station.		Whole elevation from Calais.		Remarks.
	Miles.	Rods.	Miles.	Rods.	Feet.	Inches	Feet.	Inches	
Stream into Grand lake, ...	1¼	16	81¾	32	17	5¼	444	3¾	– –
Length of " "	12¾	–	94½	32	–	–	444	3¾	– –
Length of Thoroughfare, ...	1	56	95¾	8	–	–	444	3¾	– –
Up North lake to Monument brook,..	½	40	96¼	48	–	–	444	3¾	Land excellent on the American side.

Table of the distance and elevation of various sections to the head of Grand lake, commencing at St. Croix river:

WESTERN BRANCH.

LOCALITIES.	From station to station.		Whole distance.		From station to station.		Whole elevation.		Remarks.
	Miles.	Rods.	Miles.	Rods.	Feet.	Inches	Feet.	Inches	
Foot of Lewey's rips,...............	8½	24	–	–	12½	4½	–	–	Land low.
Head of rips or bridge on Houlton road,	½	16	9	40	7	3	19	7¼	Good mill privilege.
Foot of Grand Lake stream,.........	10	76	20	36	3	5¾	23	1	Channel 3½ to 30 feet.
Head of " "	2¾	37	22¾	73	82	5	105	6	Very rough channel. Good mill privilege.
Head of Grand lake,...............	11¾	–	34½	73	82	5	105	6	– –

The elevation of the following lakes on the west branch, is *estimated* from the *known* elevation of the lakes in the above table :*

Pocumpus lake,	105 feet.	Scraggly lake,	115 feet.
Sysledobsis "	120 "	Pleasant "	155 "
Upper Chain "	150 "	Clifford "	63 "
Sysledobsissis lake,	140 "	Tomah "	162 "
Junior lake,	115 "	West Musquash lake,	72 "
Bottle "	113 "	Musquash "	112 "
Cag "	110 "	Oxboook "	160 "
Horseshoe	120 "		

The St. Croix at the junction of the west branch is elevated 165 feet 11 inches above tide at Calais. The tide at Calais flows eight feet. The monument at the extreme head waters is elevated 538 feet.

Geological relations.

Granite prevails as far north as Baileyville, succeeded by mica schist, which obtains, with a narrow belt of clay slate interjected, to the Chiputneticook lakes. These lie in a region of granite touching mica schist in the northwest.

Surface conditions.

Surface forms, undulating to hilly, with mountains of moderate height about the head waters of the lake chains. "Four fifths of the basin are covered with forests, which consist largely of heavy valuable timber."†

Rainfall.

Upon the Maine portion of the basin, 77,000,000,000 cubic feet; upon the provincial portion, 35,000,000,000 cubic feet; total, 112,000,000,000 cubic feet.

Section 2.—The St. Croix River.

Course.

Southeast.

Affluents.

The river is formed by two branches, the northern or eastern, called the Upper St. Croix or Chiputneticook river, the outlet of the Chiputneticook lakes; and the western, called the Kennebasis river, which discharges the Kennebasis lakes. Both streams are in proportion to their length wide and voluminous, being in fact in a manner simply attenuated extensions of the lakes. There are 183 streams in the system, represented upon the State map.

Length.

From the head of North lake, at the mouth of Monument brook, to Passamaquoddy bay is about 97 miles by the course of the river. The Kennebasis river is 42 miles long from its extreme head waters to the Chiputneticook river, to the

* Oscar Pike, Esq., of Princeton, authority.
† L. L. Lowell, Esq., Calais.

bay 75 miles. The main water-power section is 42 miles long on the north branch, and 22 on the west branch.

Volume. Annual discharge estimated at 44,800,000,000 cubic feet. Nearly all is tributary to the power of the main river. The stream is five hundred feet wide for ten miles above tide.

Variations of volume. Naturally small, and capable of becoming less than upon any other of the large rivers of the State. Indeed only two rivers, the Presumpscot and the Fish, can challenge comparison with the St. Croix in this regard. Almost its entire flow is derived from lakes, and lakes readily improved as reservoirs. The land bordering the river and its tributaries is to a large extent low, and forms temporary receptacles for the volume of freshets, preventing excessive rises upon the river itself.

As regards the range from lowest to highest water, Anson in his survey, which took place in an extraordinary drouth in 1838, noted the summer level at numerous points 7 feet 9 inches below the very highest freshet marks. This is probably the greatest range ever occurring, and is comparatively small.

Slope. The fall from the lower Chiputneticook lake to the tide, a distance of 54 miles, is 382 feet, 7 feet to the mile, or 4′.5 by circular measurement. The fall from Kennebasis Grand lake on the west branch, to the tide, is 271 feet, or 6.3 feet to the mile, or 4′.1. Big lake of the Kennebasis series is 189 feet above tide, or 82 feet below Grand lake of the same series.

Lakes. The lacustrine system of the St. Croix is of really remarkable development even for this State, and as contrasted with average lake districts of equal extent elsewhere in the country, or in other countries, may justly be regarded as quite extraordinary. The north branch of the river for a half of its length is a continuous lake, highly elongated, and with its irregularities of form simulating the windings of a river. The west branch through five-sixths of its length is likewise lake, broken somewhat into separate members, and branching out into many connected ponds. So that the river might almost justly be described as a lake in motion.

The total number of lakes in the system is sixty-one, or three above the proportion due to the size of the basin.

PRINCIPAL RESERVOIRS OF THE ST. CROIX.

Name.	Connected with		Approximate area in square miles.	Present storage in feet.*	Additional storage feasible in feet.*
Lewey's lake, ...	Kennebasis		0.85	Slight.†	8
Long "	do	branch,	1.25	"	6
Big "	do	do	14.00	"	10
Grand "	do	do	17.00	lk. dm.] 8	Several feet.
Pocumpus lake, ...	do	do	2 50	6 ft. byG'nd	–
Machias "	do	do	2.00	3	–
Sysledobsis "	do	do	7.00	8	–
Sysledobsissis lake, ...	do	do	4.00	3	–
Horseshoe "	do	do	0.75	5	–
Oxbrook, "	do	do	1.00	3	–
Shaw "	do	do	1.75	–	–
Junior "	do	do	6.00	–	–
Mill-privilege "	do	do	0.75	6	–
Scraggly "	do	do	3.00	–	–
Pleasant "	do	do	2.00	4	6, with flowage.
Duck "	do	do	0.75	4	4
Chain, 2 lakes, ...	do	do	1.50	4	–
Little River lake, ...	do	do	0.80	3	–
West Musquash lake, ...	do	do	3.00	4	–
Musquash "	do	do	1.25	7	–
Farrer's "	do	do	0.75	4	–
Tomah, 3 lakes, ...	do	do	2.00	Dam.	–
Clifford 4 "	do	do	2.00	5	–
Twenty-two lakes, ...	–		75.90	–	–

Name.	Connected with		Approximate area in square miles.	Present storage in feet.	Additional storage feasible in feet.
Chiputneticook lower lake,	Chiputneticook		27.00	Dam 15 ft.	–
Chiputneticook Grand "	do	branch,	25.00	head.] 6	–
North lake, ...	do	do	3.50	3	–
Lambert's lake, ...	do	do	2.00	4	–
Enoch "	do	do	0.75	Slight.	–
Five lakes, ...	–		58.25	–	–

Eleven lakes and ponds belonging to the latter series are located wholly in New Brunswick, and the largest two of the same series constitute in their whole length a part of the eastern State boundary.

The name *Schoodic* which in the Indian tongue denotes low swampy ground, is applied to the St. Croix region in general, including its chains of lakes and its streams.

The sum total of lacustrine surfaces in the system is estimated not less than 150 square miles, or one square mile to each 6.5

* Storage reported by William H. Boardman, Oscar Pike, and others.
† Dam flows Lewey's, Long and Big lakes.

square miles of basin. A proportion so remarkable places the St. Croix at once and without controversy in the foremost position amongst the large rivers of the State as a manufacturing stream, so far as respects natural reservoirs, and in proportion to its magnitude and its area of basin. The lakes average 2.95 square miles each in surface, or more than twice the mean for any of the other *large* systems on the Southern Slope.

The power on the main river from below the junction of the West and North branches is already for the greater part well accommodated with railroad communication. The navigable portion of the river, below Calais, is closed by ice two months and twenty-five days.

CHAPTER XX.

THE SYSTEM OF THE ST. JOHN IN MAINE.

Section 1.—THE ST. JOHN BASIN IN MAINE.

Location. In the extreme northern part of the State, occupying all our domain north of the Penobscot district, and constituting the upper portion of the right bank of the river St. John, with a small strip of the upper left bank.

Form. Consolidated, and least broken in contour of all the great river districts in the State.

Dimensions. Greatest length—across its southern border—117 miles; greatest breadth, 90 miles; square dimensions, 7,400 miles; the area of the *whole* St. John basin is 26,000 square miles.

Elevation. Next to the Androscoggin this is the most elevated drainage area in Maine. But its height is due to a considerable altitude over its whole extent, rather than to an extreme elevation in any part. It is, therefore, indicative and productive of less fall and power on the streams, than are found upon equal areas of the Southern Slope.

The following details of elevation are appended :*

Localities.	Feet.
Monument at source of St. Croix,	538
Alder brook, at eastern boundary,	453
Mud " " "	487
Wirley " " "	531
Parks Hill, ...	814
South branch Meduxnakeag, at eastern boundary, ...	265
North branch Meduxnakeag, at eastern boundary, ...	326
Dead stream, at eastern boundary,	337
Presque Isle river, " "	322
Region of Mars Hill, ...	527
Gizarquit river, at eastern boundary, ...	460
River Des Chutes, at eastern boundary, ...	412
Camp brook, at eastern boundary,	694
Tobique road " "	775
Aroostook river " "	345
Limestone river, at eastern boundary, ...	399
Rapide de Femme, at eastern boundary, ...	597
River St. John, at eastern boundary, ...	419
Cleaveland lake of Eagle series, .	603
Sedgwick " " " .	587
Winthrop " " " .	578
About the mouth of Fish river, ..	556
River St. John northwest of north end of Cleaveland lake, ...	474
Divide between Portage lake and Little Machias pond, ...	998
Heights on the east of Eagle lakes from Cleaveland lake southward to foot of Sedgwick lake, ...	917 949 935 389 1,015 936 1,032 1,020 977 925 923 1,015 1,060 1,006 1,041 1,044
About the east end of Winthrop lake, ...	942 839 889
Fort Kent, ...	556
Mouth of the St. Francis, ...	606
Mouth of the Allaguash, ...	606
Glazier lake, ...	664
Beau lake, ...	713
Pohenagamook lake, ...	748
Little Millnoket lake, No. 7, R. 9, about, ...	700
Divide between Allaguash and Aroostook rivers at lake Pomgocquamoc, No 7, ...	1,049
Francis lake, No. 8, R. 16, ...	1,632
Upper St. John ponds, No. 4, R. 17, ...	1,989

Heights on the military road from the divide of the Penobscot and St. John basins to the St. John river.*

Localities.	Feet.
Crossing of road and the divide, ..	1,084
Near the first crossing of Masardis waters, ...	945
Near the second crossing of Masardis waters, ...	918
Near the third crossing of Masardis waters, ...	950
Two miles above crossing of road and the main Masardis, ...	701
Two miles below crossing of road and the main Masardis, ...	558
Squawpan lake, about	600
Near the crossing of Squawpan Lake stream, ...	540
Head waters Masardis stream, abt.	900
Heights near the Aroostook river, ...	884 727 518
Two miles north of crossing of road and Aroostook river, ...	807
Near southeast end of Portage lake, ...	879
Off northeast end of Portage lake, ...	658
Two miles north, ...	690
Near crossing of a branch of Fish river, ...	658
East of the south end of Long lake, ...	931
East of the north end of Long lake, ...	672 706 1,186
Near elbow of Winthrop lake, .	634
West of the outlet of Winthrop lake, ...	778
Near outlet of Wallagrass river, ...	563 911
Two miles above Fort Kent and west of the road to Fort Kent.	877 556

* Col. Graham's map of the N. E. Boundary.

Geological relations. The rocks prevailing in the St. John basin in Maine are in the eastern part lime slates; next in order, and covering with some patches of sandstone, quartz rock and granite, three-fourths of its whole area, clay slate; and lastly on the west, and bordering the river on both sides through the upper two thirds of its length, a tract of mica schist. The rock is less exposed than upon the Southern Slope, and building stone less readily procurable.

Surface conditions. The surface conformation of this basin is, as before noticed, of striking uniformity. In the eastern or lower portion bordering the river, the face of the country is very nearly level, and at a distance from it gradually becomes undulating and moderately hilly, until it subsides into and is merged in the flat country bordering the Aroostook river. Highlands of low elevation diversify its aspect in the mid district about the mouth of the St. Francis and Allaguash rivers. Beyond the confluence of these streams, the valley of the upper St. John is quite level nearly to the boundary highlands on the west and southwest. Accordingly large portions of it are swampy, the pitch of the water sheds not being sufficient to throw off the surplus water into the drainage channels.

The far greater proportion of the whole territory is covered with unbroken forests.

Rainfall. Estimated at the mean rate for the whole State, 710,500,000,000 cubic feet. This is doubtless considerably in excess of the actual fall, the yearly receipt of moisture being several inches less than upon the Southern Slope.

Section 2.—The St. John River in Maine.

Course. The mean direction of the streams of the St. John system in Maine, is east-northeast.

Affluents. The chief tributaries, specifying only those received in Maine, or the chief part of whose course is in Maine, are as follows:

	Name.	Where received.
From the right bank,	Aroostook,	New Brunswick.
	Fish,	Fort Kent pl.
	Allaguash,	No. 16, R. 10.

Name.	Basin.			Stream.	
	Length, miles.	Breadth, miles.	Area, sq. miles.	Length, miles.	Estimated discharge, cubic feet.
Aroostook, ...	75	38	2,100	117	81,900,000,000
Fish, ...	50	25	890	72	34,710,000,000
Allaguash, ...	55	35	1,484	100	57,720,000,000

The tributaries on the left bank in Maine are comparatively small. The number of streams in the system, represented on the State map is 1,524.

Length.

The total length of the St. John in Maine, is estimated as not far from 211 miles, including the more important meanderings. Its total length from its remotest sources to the sea is about 450 miles.

Volume.

The annual discharge from the basin of the St. John in Maine, estimated at the average rate for the State, is 284,000,000,000 cubic feet. The depth of water received is less than upon the Southern Slope, but evaporation is less also, and the discharge of the river probably equal to that of any other in the State, in proportion to its drainage territory.

Variations of volume.

Upon this point no explicit testimony has come to hand. As regards freshets, the general uniformity of the tributary surfaces favors only moderate rises on the central stream. But the moderate slope of the main stream, on the other hand, tends to large accumulations of water, the surplus not being passed off rapidly. The indications are that as regards dearth or exhaustion of water, the river and its tributaries must be unusually favored. The levelness of the drainage surfaces, which secure the retention of the water of precipitation and its copious absorption into the soil, the dense shade of the forests, protracted throughout the year, for the woods are mainly evergreen; the obstruction of atmospheric currents by the same agency, and the low annual temperature—must, it would seem, reserve an unusual share of water against the exhaustion of summer.

Slope.

The elevation, above tide, of the St. John, at the State boundary, is 419 feet; at the mouth of the St. Francis, 606 feet. The distance being 70 miles, the mean slope is at the rate of 2.6 feet per mile. The elevation of the stream at its point of formation, the junction of the northwest, southwest and Woolastaquaguam, is probably about 750 feet. The distance thence to the State boundary is 158 miles, and its mean slope in that distance, therefore, 1.8 feet per mile. Accordingly, the river is navigable in its whole length in Maine, and is of comparatively inferior value for the purposes of power.

The Allaguash falls from Chamberlain lake to the St. John about 308 feet, a very little over three feet to the mile.

Lakes. The total number of lakes in the St. John basin in Maine, appearing upon the State map, is 206. The number due to its size is 370, accordingly the per cent. of numerical deficiency is forty-five.

PRINCIPAL RESERVOIRS OF THE ST. JOHN IN MAINE, AND ITS TRIBUTARIES.

Name.	Connected with	Approximate area in square miles.	Present storage in feet.*	Additional storage feasible in feet.*
Chapman-plantation lake, .	Aroostook	1.00	– †	– †
Squawpan lake, ...	[river.	10.00	–	5
St. Croix lake, No. 8, R. 4,	do do	2.50	4	–
2 ponds in No. 8, R. 3, (Howe and Main inlet,).	do do	1.50	–	Dams feasible.
Pond in No. 7, R. 4, Tracy pond, ...	do do	1.30	–	Can have dam.
Umcolcus lake, ...	do do	3 00	–	–
Pond in No. 7, R. 6, ...	do do	1.25	–	[outlet of lower.
Sapompeag ponds, 2, ...	do do	2.50	–	Can have dam at
Millnokett lake, ...	do do	5.00	–	12
Little Millnokett lake, ...	do do	3.50	–	Can have dam at
No. 7 pond, above Millnokett, ...	do do	1.00	–	[outlet. –
Pond in No. 7, R. 10, near Winter road, ...	do do	1.10	–	–
Pond in Nos. 7 and 8, R, 10,	do do	1.20		
Mansungun lake, ...	do do	5 00	–	Can have dam.
Pond below Mansungun lake, ...	do do	1.00	–	–
3 ponds above Mansungun lake, ...	do do	1 50	–	Can have dams.
Pond north of Mansungun lake, ...	do do	1.10	–	–
Goddard's pond, ...	do do	0.90	–	Dam feasible.
Mooseleuk lake, No. 9, R. 8,	do do	3.00	–	Can have dam.
Big Machias lake, ...	do do	2.00	Dam 12 feet.	–
Pond south of Big Machias lake, ...	do do	1.00	–	–
Lake in No. 11, R. 8, ...	do do	3.00	–	–
Pond in No. 11, R. 9, ...	do do	1.10	–	–
Nashville plantation pond,	do do	1.00	–	–
Salmon-brook lake, ...	do do	1.00	–	Can have high dm.
Madawska "	do do	4.00	–	8
Thirty ponds, ...	–	59.95	–	–

* Storage reported by W. H. Rowe, Esq., of Masardis, and others.
† Blanks, not reported.

PRINCIPAL RESERVOIRS OF THE ST. JOHN IN MAINE, AND ITS TRIBUTARIES.

Name.	Connected with	Approximate area in square miles.	Present storage in feet.	Additional storage feasible in feet.
Keeobscus upper pond,....	Allaguash	1.00	–	–
Keeobscus lower "	do [river,	1.15	–	–
Pataquongomis lake,......	do do	2.75	–	–
The Five lakes,..........	do do	11.00	–	–
The Long lakes,..........	do do	10.00	–	– [feet.
Lake in 10, R. 13, ...	do do	3.00	–	Can be raised many
Chemquasabamtic lake, ...	do do	8.00	–	–
Heron, or Harrow lake, in No. 10,..............	do do	2.75	–	– [dam.
Churchill lake, ...	do do	8.00	–	Formerly a 21-foot
Heron lake, in No. 8,.....	do do	4.00	–	Formerly several ft.*
Pomgocwahem lake,......	do do	11.00	–	Formerly several ft.*
Indian lake,.............	do do	3.00	Dam 6 feet.	–
Spider "	do do	4 00	5 foot dam.	–
Pleasant lake, ...	do do	4.00	–	–
Soper flowage and pond,...	do do	2.00	10 ft. dam.	–
Smith brook flowage, ...	do do	3.00	12 ft. dam.	– [eral ft.
Pomgocquamoc lake, ...	do do	3.00	Dam.	Can be flowed sev-
Pillsbury pond, ...	do do	1.50	8 foot dam.	Several feet.
Mud pond, in No. 9, R. 12,	do do	1.50	8 foot dam.	–
Russell stream, 3 ponds, ..	do do	2 25	–	–
4 ponds above Spider lake,	do do	3.00	–	–
Twenty-eight, ...	–	84.90	–	–

Name.	Connected with	Approximate area in square miles.	Present storage in feet.	Additional storage feasible in feet.
Meduxnakeag lake, ...	Meduxnak'ag	3.75	Dam.	Can be raised 4 feet.
New Limerick, 3 ponds,...	do [stream,	1.50	Dams.	–
Caldwell lake, ...	do do	1.00	–	–
Spaulding's lake,.........	do do	2.25	–	–
No. 9, "	do do	1.00	–	–
B, "	do do	1 00	–	–
Eight lakes,.........	–	10.50	–	–

Name.	Connected with.	Approximate area in square miles.	Present storage in feet.†	Additional storage feasible in feet.†
Cleaveland, or Long lake,.	Fish river,	19.00	No dam.	Can have dam.
Second, or Bear "	do do	2.00	No dam.	Dam feasible.
Cross, or Preble "	do do	6 00	No dam.	Would be flowed by Square lake dam.
Square, or Sedgwick "	do do	15.00	No dam.	Can have dam, or be flowed by Eagle lake dam.
Eagle, or Winthrop "	do do	22.00	No dam.	Dam 20 ft. could be built for $20,000.
St. Froid, or Long "	do do	5.50	No dam.	Can have dam, or would be flowed by a high dam on Eagle lake.

* Formerly flowed by the Churchill dam.
† William Dickey, Esq.

PRINCIPAL RESERVOIRS OF THE ST. JOHN IN MAINE, AND ITS TRIBUTARIES.

Name.	Connected with		Approximate area in square miles.	Present storage in feet.	Additional storage feasible in feet.
Portage lake, ...	do	do	8.50	No dam.	Dam feasible.
Fish River lake,.........	do	do	7 00	-	-
Pond northwest of Spruce lake, ...	do	do	1.00	-	-
The long pond in 17, R. 6,	do	do	1.25	-	-
Ponds (5) above Fish River lake, ...	do	do	2,75	-	-
Fifteen lakes,.......	-		89.00	-	-

Name.	Connected with.		Approximate area in square miles.	Present storage in feet.	Additional storage feasible in feet.
3 ponds in 15, R. 7, ...	St. John riv.		1.50	-	-
Glazier's lake, ...	do	do	3.00	6	Several feet.
Beau "	do	do	5.00	4	Several feet.
Pohenagamook lake,......	do	do	4.50	-	Several feet.
Cascade brook, "	do	do	2.75	-	-
Cascade brook, upper lake,	do	do	1.00	-	-
Chimenticook lake, ...	do	do	4 50	-	-
Depot lake,...............	do	do	3.50	-	-
Ishaeganalshegeck,.......	do	do	1.75	-	-
Baker lake, ...	do	do	4.00	Dam.	-
Francis lake, ...	do	do	0.90	-	-
Lake north of Francis lake,	do	do	1.00	-	-
Turner brook lake,.......	do	do	1.10	-	-
Woboostook lake,........	do	do	2.50	-	-
Upper Woboostook lake, ..	do	do	1.00	-	-
2 lakes, No. 4, R. 17, ...	do	do	2 25	-	-
Nineteen lakes,......	-		36.65	-	-

The foregoing 100 principal lakes and ponds have a surface of 278.00 square miles. As before shown, some 36 square miles of lake surface naturally belonging to this district, have by artificial means been made tributary to the Penobscot.

The area of all the lakes in the St. John system, is 350 square miles, or one square mile to each 21.1 square miles of basin. The lakes average 1.75 square miles each in surface.

It is probable that a large number of small lakes and ponds in the wilderness districts of this basin are not represented upon the maps, and the numerical and surface proportion of its lacustrine waters is not represented at its true value. There is reason, however, for believing that owing to the disintegrable character of the rocks prevalent in this part of the State it has become more thoroughly channeled with water-courses than the Southern Slope, and that by consequence many lakes anciently existing upon it have become obliterated. There is hardly any question that the valley of the Walloostook (upper St. John) was once a continued lake, as also the valley of the St. John above the Grand falls for a long distance. In the whole kingdom of France, 200,000 square miles in area, whose rock formations are largely soft limestones, chalk, etc., there are but two lakes larger than mere pools, one being 29 square miles and the other three square miles in surface.

DIVISION II.

The Secondary or Seaboard Systems.

The river systems to be noticed in Division II. of Part II., are called *Secondary* as being smaller in size than the Primary systems hitherto noticed; and *Seaboard*, because lying as they do betwixt the outfalls of the Primaries, they rest upon the coast. Their accessibility by sea and their occupation by comparatively dense populations, give them a present relatively large importance.

As treated on the pages following, several of the systems are *composite*, consisting of a number of drainage tracts grouped together for convenience of representation, and to avoid too great a multiplication of divisions.

The seaboard systems will be noticed in the order of their location, beginning at the east.

CHAPTER XXI.

THE DENNYS, PEMAQUAN, ETC.

Section 1.—Basin.

Location and dimensions.

The drainage district of the Dennys, Pemaquan, and associated streams, is located in the southeast corner of the State. It is 33 miles long, 15 broad, and its area is 375 square miles. Of this, 150 square miles belong to the Dennys, about 40 to the Pemaquan, and the rest to various small streams.

Geological and surface conditions.

Quartz rock, trap and upper silurian predominate. Surface moderately undulating to level, with scattered low hills. Surface materials, clay loam subsoil, gravelly loam at the surface, with bog in localities. One half of the whole district forest-covered. Vast amount of lumber still remaining.

Rainfall.

Estimated, in cubic feet, 36,540,000,000.

Section 2.—Rivers.

The total number of streams in the district, represented on the State map, is 79; and their estimated annual discharge is 14,616,000,000 cubic feet.

Dennys river.

The principal river is the Dennys,* 25 miles long, with a fall of 250 feet from Meddybemps lake to the tide, the mean slope being, therefore, 10 feet to the mile, or 6′.5 in angular measurement. Volume uniform at different seasons, owing to the influence of the great lake at the head. Total range from low to high water, on Lincoln's dam at Dennysville, 5 feet. Water reaches the tide from the lake in 24 hours at a high stage of the river. The river is closed by ice about four months yearly, from December 1st to April 1st. Vessels get in earlier by assisting the ice to escape. Freight-laden vessels come within eight miles of Dennysville in mid winter, the lower portion of the bay not freezing over.

Lakes.

Whole number, 22; number due to the size of the basin, 18; combined area of the lakes 38 miles, or one square mile to each 9.6 square miles of basin.

PRINCIPAL RESERVOIRS OF THE DENNYS, PEMAQUAN, ETC.

Name.	Connected with	Approximate area in square miles.	Present storage in feet.	Additional storage feasible in feet.
Boyden's lake,	Little river,	3.25	4	4
Pemaquan "	Pemaquan riv.,	2 25	4	-
Round "	do do	0.50	3	By Pemaquan dam
Meddybemps lake,	Dennys river,	15.00	7	-
Little "	do do	0.75	Dam.	-
Harward "	do do	0.50	-	-
Cathance "	Cathance river,	7.00	6.5	-
Little Cathance lake,	do do	0.50	-	-
Rocky "	Holmes river,	2.50	-	-
Little Rocky "	do do	1.00	-	-
Orange, "	do do	.50	-	-
Indian "	do do	.35	-	-
Twelve lakes,	-	29.45	-	-

Meddybemps and Cathance lakes.

A storage of 7 feet upon Meddybemps lake, would yield in its descent through 250 feet to the tide, a gross power of 7,500 horse, or 300,000 spindles, for 10 hours a day,

* Facts furnished chiefly by Peter E. Vose, Esq., of Dennysville.

9

312 days per annum. It would operate upon the five powers (56 feet) on the line of Dennysville and Edmunds, about 77,200 spindles. To this is to be added the *natural* low-run of the river. It is estimated that for $600 or $800, the channel at the outlet could be lowered two feet, giving a storage of nine feet with the present height of dams. The tributary country will yield considerably more drainage than is now reserved upon the lake.

Cathance lake is "at least 200 feet above tide, doubtless more." It is fed by Cooper stream, an inlet of considerable magnitude, and by Munson's stream, which once carried a mill, so that it is in large annual receipt of water. The storage head now commanded upon it is 6.5 feet. The dams might be raised one or two feet higher at little expense, but channeling the outlet would involve considerable outlay owing to the ledgy character of the bottom. The tributary country furnishes considerably more water than the dams will now hold.

The storage upon this lake, in its fall to the tide, would yield about 2,600 horse power, gross, or 104,000 spindles for the working hours of the year.

CHAPTER XXII.

THE EAST AND WEST MACHIAS

The East and West Machias rivers are independent, having no more intimate connection than a common debouchure into an estuary which makes inland from the head of Machias bay, but are here treated together for convenience.

Section 1.—East and West Machias Basin.

Location, form and dimensions. The Machias basin is located in the southeast part of the State, at the head of the great bay bearing the same name. In form it expands symmetrically with removals from the sea, and projects northeast and northwest in two extensive ovals. It is 48 miles long, 28 miles broad, with an area of 800 square miles, of which all but 30 square miles is tributary to the power of the main rivers. The basin of the West Machias contains about 500 square miles, of the East Machias about 300 square miles.

The highest part of the district is in the northwest, where the mean height for a considerable extent is about 400 feet. The lower portion of the basin is occupied with quartz rock; granite succeeds, and to this mica schist about the head waters. The surface is moderately broken. Out of fifteen towns and townships watered by the West Machias eight are still forest-covered, and a very large amount of woods still remains in the residue. Including the East Machias district, probably nearly two-thirds of the whole territory is still wooded.

Elevation, geological, and surface conditions.

Annual deposition, estimated as about 78,000,000,000 cubic feet.

Rainfall.

Section 2.—East and West Machias Rivers.

Both rivers flow about southeast. The number of streams in the district, represented on the State map, is 93. The annual discharge is estimated at 31,200,000,000 cubic feet, of which 19,500,000,000 belong to the West Machias, and 11,700,000,000 to the East. Nearly all the delivery passes to the sea by the two main rivers.

Course, affluents, and volume.

Naturally rather inexcessive, as the surface conformation of the country is favorable to a gradual removal of surplus water, and the lakes and ponds equilibrate the flow. The extensive wooded surfaces, moreover, prevent the extreme exhaustion of water by summer heat. The delivery of the East Machias in particular is remarkably uniform. Its waters are drawn largely from lakes, and on their passage to the sea circulate through lakes, and lakes of great size relatively to the magnitude of the stream and the area of the basin. In an ordinary season, 15,000 cubic feet per minute, for the working hours of the day, are estimated to be commanded at Machias, for the summer months. The delivery of the East Machias, at East Machias, in a *dry* season, is considerably larger than of the West Machias at Machias. The West Machias ranges from low to high water, on the dam at Whitneyville, ten feet; at Centerville, seven feet.

Variations of volume.

Fifth lake on the West Machias is elevated 380 feet above tide. Thence the stream falls away to 275 feet at First lake. A fall of 380 feet in 75 miles, gives a mean slope of 5.8 feet to the mile, or 3′.7 circular measurement.

Slope.

The lacustrine system of the East and West Machias is of unusual extent. Total number of lakes and ponds, 56, nine above the proportion due to the size of the basin. The lakes are, some of them, quite large.

Lakes.

PRINCIPAL RESERVOIRS OF THE EAST AND WEST MACHIAS.

Name.	Connected with.	Approximate area in square miles.	Present storage in feet.*	Additional storage feasible in feet.*
Gardiner's lake, ...	East Machias [river.	8.50	Dam.	Storage might be greatly increased.
Hadley "	do do	3.50	Dam.	Storage might be greatly increased.
Second "	do do	0 60	Flowed.	†
Rocky "	do do	2.75	Dam.	–
Round "	do do	0.70	Dam.	–
Long "	do do	1.25	6	–
Spectacle, 3 lakes, ...	do do	.85	†	–
Love lake, ...	do do	1.75	5 to 6	–
Barrows lake, ...	do do	1.50	3	–
Crawford "	do do	2 75	9	–
Mud "	do do	0 50	–	–
Shining "	do do	5.00	–	Several feet.
Seavey, 2 "	do do	0.60	7	–
Patrick lake, ...	do do	.30	–	–
Seventeen lakes, ...	–	30.55	–	–

Name.	Connected with.	Approximate area in square miles.	Present storage in feet.‡	Additional storage feasible in feet.‡
Mopang, 2 lakes, ...	West Machias [river,	4.50	7	–
Lilly, 2 "	do	1.00	–	–
Chain stream, 6 ponds, ...	do do	5.00	Dam.	8
First and Second lakes, ...	do do	1.25	–	9
Third lake, ...	do do	3.00	10	–
Fourth "	do do	1.50	7	–
Fifth "	do do	2.50	7	–
Cranberry lake, ... } Lake in S. W. of No. 36, }	do do	1.30	–	–
Lake in centre of No. 36, ..	do do	0.50	5	–
Sabao lake, ...	do do	2.00	7	–
Green and Stiles lakes, ...	do do	1 50	–	–
Horseshoe lake, ...	do do	0.90	3	–
Machias lake, in 41, ...	do do	1 25	–	7
Bog "	do do	1.50	6	–
Marshfield lakes, ...	do do	2.00	Dam.	Several feet.
Twenty-six, ...	–	29.50	–	–

There are in the East Machias basin about 38 square miles of lake and pond surface, and in the West Machias about 32 square miles; total, 70 square miles, or one square mile of lake to each 11.4 square miles of basin. The lakes average 1.2 square miles in surface.

The lakes of this system, in particular of the West Machias, are to a noticeable extent situated at the remotest sources of the streams. They accordingly exert their equalizing effect upon the

* Storage reported by Messrs. P. S. J. and F. L. Talbot and N. W. Foster.
† Blanks, not reported.
‡ Storage reported by J. K Ames, Esq.

streams in their whole length, and upon improvement as reservoirs will add to their manufacturing capacities in their whole length. As thus situated they are of course not so valuable as *local* reservoirs to the powers on the lower sections of the rivers, but are of more value to the rivers as a whole, or will be when put to use for storage basins for manufacturing purposes. The lakes are now mostly dammed, but the water is used for only log-driving purposes. The lakes at the source of the West Machias have but short tributaries and therefore fill up slowly and cannot be counted upon for especially large amounts of reserve water.

The West Machias is closed to navigation by ice for four and a half months, yearly, from December 1st to April 15th on the average.

CHAPTER XXIII.

THE NARRAGUAGUS, PLEASANT, TUNK, ETC.

Section 1.—Basin.

Location and dimensions.

The drainage district of the Narraguagus, Pleasant, etc., is located next west of the Machias system, and at the head of several great bays, Mason's, Pleasant, Dyer's, Gouldsboro', etc. It is 40 miles long, 27 broad, and its area is 550 square miles. The Narraguagus drains about 215 square miles, the Pleasant about 110 square miles, the Tunk about 60, and the Chandler's about 50 square miles.

Geological and surface conditions.

Granite prevails along the coast and throughout the western portion of the district, with mica schist in the valley of the Pleasant river. Surface, level to undulating, with scattered low mountains. Surface materials, clay loam very abundant, except on the "plains," which are gravelly at the surface, though underlaid with clay. "One-half of the territory is covered with heavy timber forests; large areas are occupied with 'plains' or 'barrens;' considerable portions are burnt lands bearing now a growth of small birches. The proportion of cultivated land is very small."*

Rainfall.

In cubic feet, about 53,000,000,000.

* J. A. Milliken, Esq., Cherryfield.

Section 2.—RIVERS.

The number of streams in the district, represented on the State map, is 131. The annual discharge from the basin is estimated at 21,200,000,000 cubic feet. A considerable portion passes to the sea by various small streams which empty directly into the tide, and with their tributary country expand the district widely on the coast, as represented on the map.

The Narraguagus, etc. The largest river is the Narraguagus, which is fifty miles long. This river ranges from low to high water, six feet at Cherryfield, four feet at Deblois. It is 220 feet wide at and below Cherryfield. It is closed to navigation from about December 15 to March 25; above the falls, from three to five weeks longer. The Pleasant is 38 miles long, the Tunk 17, not including local windings.

Lakes. Whole number, 38; combined area, estimated from the map, 25 square miles. This gives one square mile of lake to each 22 square miles of basin.

PRINCIPAL RESERVOIRS OF THE NARRAGUAGUS, PLEASANT, TUNK, ETC.

Name.	Connected with	Approximate area in square miles.	Present storage in feet.	Additional storage feasible in feet.
Schoodiac pond, ...	Narraguagus [river.	0.65	*	*
Narraguagus pond, ...	do	1.00	–	–
Spruce Mountain pond, ...	do do	1.35	–	–
Chalk pond, ...	do do	0.35	–	–
Baker brook flowage, ...	do do	1.00	–	–
Third pond, ...	do do	0.50	–	–
Eagle "	do do	1.50	–	–
Deer "	do do	0.50	–	–
Spring run pond, ...	do do	1.00	–	–
Nine ponds, ...	–	7.85	–	–

Name.	Connected with	Approximate area in square miles.	Present storage in feet.	Additional storage feasible in feet.
Round pond, ...	Tunk river,	0.30	*	*
Great Tunk pond, ...	do do	2.00	11	–
Little Tunk "	do do	0.25	–	Several feet.
Long "	do do	1.50	12	–
Rocky "	do do	0.35	–	Several feet.
Downing "	do do	0.30	9	–
Six ponds, ...	–	4.70	–	–

* Blanks, not reported.

PRINCIPAL RESERVOIRS OF THE NARRAGUAGUS, PLEASANT, TUNK, ETC.

Name.	Connected with	Approximate area in square miles.	Present storage in feet.	Additional storage feasible in feet.
Donnell's pond, ...	Donnell's stre'm	1.50	11	*
Fox "	do do	0.25	4	3
Otter Bog pond, with flowage, ...	do do	0.25	0	6
Alder Brook pond, with flowage, ...	do do	0.44	10	-
Upper Shillalah pond, with flowage, ...	do do	0.35	6	4
Lower Shillalah pond, with flowage, ...	do do	0.20	10	5
Sullivan, 2 ponds, ...	do do	0.45	-	-
Eight ponds, ...	-	3.45	-	-

Name.	Connected with	Approximate area in square miles.	Present storage in feet.	Additional storage feasible in feet.
Chandler's pond, ...	Chandler's river	0.75	Dam.	*
Pleasant "	Pleasant river,	2.00	Dam.	-
Southwest "	do do	0.50	*	-
Jones "	Jones stream,	1 00	-	-
Flanders "	Flanders river,	1.00	-	-
Forbes "	Prospect river,	0.35	-	-
Six ponds, ...	-	5.60	-	-

The above 29 ponds have a combined surface of 21.60 square miles, as estimated from the map. The areas, as reported, are considerably larger.

CHAPTER XXIV.

THE UNION.

Section 1.—Basin.

Almost entirely within the limits of Hancock county, and at the head of Bluehill, Frenchman's, and other bays. Location.

Long and narrow, and contrary to the general law, diminishing in breadth at its head. It is to the last degree diversified on its ocean border with peninsular outreaches, bays and islands; so that the territory actually tributary to the Form.

* Blanks, not reported.

river above its embouchure into Bluehill bay, is not much over two-thirds of the whole drainage country betwixt the head of the basin and its outside limit on the open main.

Dimensions. Greatest length, from the head to the outfall of the river, 43 miles; to the open sea, 70 miles; breadth about 20 miles; square dimensions, of the area tributary to the main river above the Ellsworth falls, about 500 square miles; of the area below the falls and including the outlying islands, as represented on the maps, 250 square miles; total, 750 square miles.

Elevation. The country in the north part of the basin is elevated from 225 to 250 feet. The lowest part of the watershed ridge east of that point toward the Penobscot, is 257 feet, as determined by the surveys for the European and North American Railway.

Surface conditions. The district is bounded by a chain of bald granite mountains, which extends in the form of a horseshoe from Bluehill to Gouldsboro', Mt. Desert occupying the position of the *frog*, and in like manner towering in lofty granitic elevations. Accordingly, the interior of the basin is a strongly defined valley, of a rolling surface, encompassed on nearly all sides by rugged highlands. The scenery of the region, in particular of the coast, is unusually varied and grand.

Geological and surface conditions. The valley above mentioned is underlaid with mica schist; exterior to this upon all sides, as above stated, granite is found, occupying four-fifths of the whole area. The larger proportion of the lakes lie in the granite district. The surface forms have already been remarked. "Out of the 500 square miles lying above the lowest falls, at Ellsworth, probably four-fifths are forest-covered."

Rainfall. Estimated at 72,450,000,000 cubic feet.

Section 2.—River.

Course and affluents. The direction of the river is slightly west of south. Its tributaries are short. With the exception of the Presumpscot, it exhibits less of divarication and embranchment than any other stream in the State of equal size and importance, it being laterally restricted by the highland ranges above referred to. Total number of streams represented on the State map, on both the basin proper and the islands, 137, most of them quite small.

Length and volume. The river is fifty-two miles long to the bay or estuary into which its waters are discharged. Its annual delivery is estimated at 19,500,000,000 cubic feet, that for the entire district being 28,980,000,000 cubic feet.

Variations of volume.

Not excessive even in the state of nature, owing to the influence of the lakes, and capable upon reservoir improvement of being made comparatively small. In an ordinary summer season — cubic feet per minute, for the ordinary working hours of the day, are estimated to be passed over the dams at Ellsworth. The total range of water on the same dams is seven feet.

Slope.

The height of the lake in the north part of this basin is about 205 feet above sea level, the descent from which to the mouth of the river would be at the mean rate of four feet to the mile, or 2′.6 circular measurement.

Lakes.

The Union river is furnished with natural reservoirs of remarkable extent and number, the total count of which upon the proper basin of the river and upon the outlying islands, is 61, on the basin proper, 43, or 11 above the proportion due to its size. The combined area of the lakes and ponds, small and great, in the basin proper, as inferred from the map, is sixty square miles, or one square mile to each eight square miles of tributary country.

PRINCIPAL RESERVOIRS OF THE UNION.

Name.	Approximate area in square miles.	Present storage in feet.*	Additional storage feasible in feet.*
Branch pond,	3.75	10	10
Rocky pond, in Orland,	0.35	10	10
Reed's "	4.25	6	14
Beech Hill pond,	1.85	6	14
Mountain "	1.25	6	14
Hat Case "	0.50	-	-
Molasses "	2.25	10	2
Scammon, "	1.00	-	-
Abram's "	0.80	10	-
Webb's "	1.75	10	-
Spectacle "	2.10	8	3
Rocky "	0.40	10	5
Rocky " in No. 22,	1.15	-	-
2 Lead Mountain ponds, upper and lower,	2.00	6 and 8	3 and 4
Brandy pond	1.60	6	-
Great "	1.50	13	10
Long "	1.00	8	5
Alligator "	1.80	6	5
Morrison's pond,	0.35	8	-
Middle Branch pond, upper,	1.25	6	5
" " " lower,		5	5
Flood's pond,	1.00	9	5
Springy "	.60	9	5
Hopkins' pond,	1.75	No dam.	5
George's "	0 90	-	-
Twenty-six ponds,	34 85	-	-

* Storage reported by Eugene Hale and Seth Tisdale, Esqs.

The mean head now commanded upon the 22 of the above reservoirs whose storage is reported, is 7.7 feet. An additional head of 7.6 feet can be raised, as is estimated, upon 19 of the number, including nearly all the larger.

If we assume an average depth of only six feet upon 33 square miles—a head of over 15 feet being capable of reserve upon over 30 square miles, so far as regards the holding capacity of the lakes, the storage, amounting to 5,520,000,000 cubic feet, would yield for the working hours of the year, upon the Ellsworth falls alone, their height being assumed at 100 feet, a gross power of 5,600 horse, or 224,000 spindles. The amount of storage specified (six feet) it is judged can be secured from the surplus of the snow-meltings and fall rains, without impairing the working power of the stream during the process of accumulation. To the above would require to be added the *natural* low-run of the river to arrive at the aggregate of its constant manufacturing power at the point specified.

The following ponds are located in the district, below the outfall of the Union river, and are, or may become, sources of valuable local power:

RESERVOIRS TRIBUTARY TO THE TIDE WATERS OF UNION RIVER.

Name.	Connected with	Approximate area in square miles.	Present storage in feet.	Additional storage feasible in feet.
Patten's pond, ...	Patten's brook,	4.00	-	-
Patten's upper pond,......	do do	1.10	-	-
Flood's pond, ...	Flood's stream,	0.25	-	-
The "Four Ponds,"	Four Ponds [stream,	1.00	-	Several feet.
"Salt Pond,"............		1.50	-	-
Eagle "	-	0.75	-	-
Dening's pond, ...	Dening's "	0.75	Dam.	-
Great pond, and the two connected, ...	Gt. pond "	3.50	Dams.	-
Seal Cove pond,..........	Seal Cove "	0.75	Dam.	-
Twelve ponds,........	-	13.55	-	-

The river, below the falls at Ellsworth, is closed to navigation four months yearly.

CHAPTER XXV.

THE ST. GEORGE, SHEEPSCOT, MEDOMAC, ETC.

Section 1.—Basin.

Under the above title is massed together the entire district lying between and separating the southern points of the Kennebec and Penobscot basins. Location.

From its interior limit to the ocean, a length of 50 miles; breadth, 30 miles; area, including the various peninsulas and outreaching headlands, about 800 square miles. Dimensions.

Estimated at 78,000,000,000 cubic feet. Rainfall.

Section 2.—Rivers.

First, the St. George, which is 35 miles long from source to mouth, or 50 miles to the open main, and drains about 210 square miles above the lowest falls. Secondly, the Sheepscot, which is 37 miles from source to mouth, or 58 miles to the sea, and drains about 190 square miles above the lowest falls. Thirdly, the Medomac, 21 miles long, or 37 to the sea, draining about 62 square miles above the lowest falls. The Damariscotta river drains about 43 square miles above the lowest falls, and is of unusual importance as a manufacturing stream on account of the size of its natural reservoir, the pond of the same name. Dyer's river drains about 38 square miles above its outfall. Total number of streams represented upon the State map, 173. The St. George, etc.

The estimated yearly discharge of all the streams is 31,200,000,000 cubic feet. A less than usual proportion of this is available for power, so much of it passing directly from peninsulas and islands into the tide, without being massed in streams of economical size. The Sheepscot discharges about 7,410,000,000 cubic feet from the portion of its basin above the lowest falls; the St. George about 8,190,000,000 cubic feet; the Medomac 2,418,000,000, and the Damariscotta about 1,677,000,000 cubic feet. Volume.

The whole number of lakes in the district, represented on the State map, is 72, 38 being the number due to its size. The greater number are small. Nearly all are Lakes.

sources of valuable local power, and in the aggregate will hold in reserve a vast amount of water. The combined area of all the lakes and ponds is 50 square miles, one mile to each 16 square miles of basin. The lakes average 0.7 of a mile in area.

Damariscotta pond, assumed from the maps at 10 square miles, if covered with storage to the depth of four feet would yield for 312 days per annum, 10 hours per day, a gross power of 572 horse, 22,880 spindles, at "Damariscotta falls." This would of course be increased by the amount of the *natural* low-run of the stream. The actual rise upon the pond in the spring and fall is from four to six feet, which might be reserved for power purposes. The mill owners let the water off to avoid paying damages, the present use of the power not justifying the expense of flowage.

PRINCIPAL RESERVOIRS OF THE ST. GEORGE, SHEEPSCOT, MEDOMAC, ETC.

Name.	Connected with.	Approximate area in square miles.	Present storage in feet.	Additional storage feasible in feet.
South pond,	St. George riv.,	1.15	–	–
North "	do do	0.50	–	–
Seven Tree pond,	do do	1.10	–	Several feet.
Crawford's "	do do	1.05	Dam.	Several feet.
Round "	do do	0.35	–	Several feet.
Western "	do do	0.30	–	–
Senebec "	do do	1.15	–	Several feet.
Quantabacook pond,	do do	2.00	–	Can have high
True's pond,	do do	0.30	6	– [dam.
St. Georges pond,	do do	2.00	Dam.	–
Stevens' "	do do	0.75	Dam.	–
The "Lake,"*	do do	2.00	4	2
Lermond pond,	do do	0.50	8	0
Hobbs "	do do	0.25	4	2
Southern Hobbs pond,	do do	0.75	0	2
Fish pond,	do do	0.40	6	1
Sixteen ponds,	–	14.35	–	–

Name.	Connected with	Approximate area in square miles.	Present storage in feet.†	Additional storage feasible in feet.†
Medomac pond,	Medomac river,	0.75	‡	‡
Little Medomac pond,	do do	0.25	–	–
Washington pond,	do do	1.25	–	–
Clark's "	do [river,	0.50	–	10
Damariscotta "	Damariscotta	10.00	6	–
Muscongus "	Muscongus st'm	0.50	Dam.	Several feet.
Biscay "	Pemaquid river,	1.00	–	Can be raised 3
Pemaquid "	do do	2.00	–	feet, and outlet
Duck "	do do	0.30	–	lowered 3 feet.

* Storage and areas of ponds in Hope reported by Isaac Hobbs of Hope.
† Storage reported by H. P. Carleton, John Bodge, Dr. O'Brien, and others.
‡ Blanks, not reported.

PRINCIPAL RESERVOIRS OF THE ST. GEORGE, SHEEPSCOT, MEDOMAC, ETC,

Name.	Connected with	Approximate area in square miles.	Present storage in feet.*	Additional storage feasible in feet.*
Dyer's Long "	Dyer's river,	1.20	6	4, with flowage,
Dyer's "	do do	0.20	†	†
Pleasant "	Sheepscot river,	1.10	-	4 to 6
Travel "	do do	0.60	-	6
Patricktown "	do do	1.00	-	Outlet can be lowered 10 ft.
James' "	do do	0.30	Several feet.	Outlet lowered several feet.
Sheepscot Great pond, ...	do do	1.50	Dam.	6, by higher dams and lowering outlet.
Sixteen ponds,.......	-	22.45	-	-

The above 32 principal lakes and ponds have a surface of 36.80 square miles.

CHAPTER XXVI.

THE PRESUMPSCOT.‡

Section 1.—BASIN.

Betwixt the Saco and the southern part of the Androscoggin basin. Location.

Highly elongated, and like the Union district, diminishing in breadth at the head. Form.

Greatest length, 52 miles; greatest breadth, 18 miles; area about 520 square miles. Dimensions.

The streams setting from the immediate vicinity of the northern part of this basin, north toward the Androscoggin at Bethel, and east into Greenwood, have at their points of discharge, a height of about 600 and 700 feet, respectively, above tide. Accordingly the upper portion of the basin must be inferred to have a mean elevation at least from 800 to 900 feet above sea level. Songo pond, occupying of course one of the lowest points, is two feet higher than the Androscoggin river near the mouth of Pleasant river (as shown by surveys for a canal) or about 630 feet. Sebago lake, midway the basin, has usually been Elevation.

* Storage reported by H. P. Carleton, John Bodge, Dr. O'Brien, and others.
† Blanks, not reported.
‡ The Royal and Nonesuch districts are noticed at the end of this chapter, they being massed with the Presumpscot on the map.

estimated 280 feet above tide, but has been found by J. F. Anderson, C. E., to be but 247 feet above high water at Portland. So that as a whole the district is considerably elevated, and the fall of its surplus waters correspondently large.

The table annexed gives all the specific facts that have come to hand:

LOCALITIES.	Feet.	LOCALITIES.	Feet.
Cumberland station,	64	Gorham and Buxton boundary,	192
Falmouth "	32	Buxton Centre,	175
Gorham "	220		

Heights on a railroad route to Lake Champlain. [State Docs.]	Feet.	Heights on a Trial Section of the same railroad.	Feet.
Near northwest end Canada hill, Windham,	192	Pond north of the village of Saccarappa,	70
Crossing of Pleasant river,	175	Mouth of Ink-Horn brook,	73
Turtle pond, Windham,	300	Coleright's brook,	74
Parker pond,	426	Horsebeef falls,	101
Saturday pond, Otisfield,	522	Opposite Great falls, Pleasant river,	221
Pierce's mill pond,	435	Boody's tavern, Windham,	297
Divide of Presumpscot and Androscoggin,	668		
Songo pond, about,	630		

Geological and surface conditions.

From the sea to Sebago lake the basin is underlaid chiefly with mica schist, the river itself however for nearly half the distance flowing in a narrow belt of gneiss. Around and above Sebago lake granite prevails exclusively. Excellent building stone abundant in nearly all parts. The southern portion of the basin is undulating and moderately hilly, the northern rugged and mountainous. Surface materials predominating, as shown by returns, sandy and gravelly. The southern part is pretty thoroughly cleared of forests; the northern is still quite heavily wooded.

Rainfall.

The annual receipt of moisture is estimated in cubic feet 51,000,000,000.

Section 2.—RIVER.

Course.

Very nearly southeast, and, regarded as continued in Crooked river, remarkably direct, or free from extensive windings, from its source to its mouth, so that its drainage area is, as before noticed, very long in proportion to its breadth. But the main stream above Sebago lake is to a most extraordinary degree diversified with local and minute sinuosities, which parallel fully the eccentricities of course of the celebrated river of the east, Meander.

Affluents. Important only as connecting the river and several of its reservoirs, and as furnishing the sites of many small water-powers.

Length. The Presumpscot proper, from Sebago lake to the tide, by the course of the river, is about 22 miles long. Crooked river is estimated to be 42 miles long.

Volume. Estimated discharge of the river for the year, 20,400,-000,000 cubic feet.

Variations of volume. These are, and even in the state of nature would be, comparatively small upon the Presumpscot proper, owing to the great extent and compensating influence of the grand reservoir at its head. The natural uniformity of the stream is assisted by the artificial control of the delivery of the lake, so that for the practical purposes of extensive manufacturing it is constant throughout the year. The volume employed at Cumberland Mills, estimated from the statement of the Superintendent, George W. Hammond, Esq., is about 50,000 cubic feet per minute. This run continued throughout the working days of the year, for ten hours a day, would carry off about 9.5 billion cubic feet. The range from lowest to highest water is found to be, on the several dams in Westbrook, from four to five feet; at the Outlet dam, four to five feet.

Slope. The descent of the river from the lake to the tide, 247 feet in 22 miles, is at the mean rate of 11.2 feet per mile, or 7′.3 circular measurement.

Lakes. Total number in the system, 45, or 17 above the proportion due to the size of the basin. Combined area, 97 square miles. There is one square mile of lake surface to each 5.3 square mile of basin. The lakes average 2.1 square miles in surface.

PRINCIPAL RESERVOIRS OF THE PRESUMPSCOT.

Name.	Approximate area in square miles.	Present storage in feet.	Additional storage feasible in feet.
Sebago lake,	50.00	4	4
Trickey pond,	0.75	*	*
Peabody "	1.50	–	–
Brandy "	1.25	–	–
Long "	12.00	Dam.	Several feet.
Pleasant "	2.25	–	– [ble,
Panther's "	2.75	–	High dam feasi-
Rattlesnake, 2 ponds,	2.75	–	–
Little Sebago pond,	5.00	7	5

* Blanks, not reported.

PRINCIPAL RESERVOIRS OF THE PRESUMPSCOT.

Name.	Approximate area in square miles.	Present storage in feet.	Additional storage feasible in feet.
Crotched pond,	2.75	5	2
Adams' "	0.30	4	2
Holt's "	0.30	Dam.	*
Stearns "	1.00	*	4
Anonymous "	0.75	Dam.	–
Woods "	1.50	6	Outlet can be
Thomas "	1.15	Dam.	[lowered 3 ft.
Long pond, Waterford,	1.00	–	–
Bear "	0.75	1	4
Moose "	0.75	–	–
Songo "	0.85	–	–
Stone, 2 ponds,	1.10	–	–
Twenty-three ponds,	90.45	–	–

Sebago lake. There is a dam eight feet high at the outlet of Sebago lake, by which a head of four feet is now commanded over the whole surface. It can be raised four feet more, as I am informed by Mr. Hammond, without incurring more than very trifling damage for flowage. A head of six feet, giving a volume of 8,363,520,000 cubic feet, would supply 44,600 cubic feet per minute for the ordinary working hours of the year. This (the storage alone be it observed) would yield on a fall of 20 feet, as at Cumberland mills, a gross power of 1,688 horse, for the time specified. It would yield in its fall of 247 feet to the tide, a gross power of 20,846 horse, 833,840 spindles, throughout the year. To this requires to be added the power due to the *natural* low-run volume of the river, to arrive at the constant aggregate of its manufacturing power from Sebago lake to the sea.

W. H. Jackson, Esq., President of the Oriental Powder Company, writes as follows in regard to the volume of water that can be had from the tributary country: "I have run water at Wescott's falls, where the lake waters enter the river, for 32 days, through four gates four feet square each, and one six feet square, under a ten-foot head, with a flow four feet deep over the dam eighty feet long, and even then have not succeeded in preventing the water from rising six to nine inches above the four feet head on the dam, which is all the dam will now safely carry." These figures indicate an enormous waste of water, much the greater part of which, with a suitable dam, can be reserved for manufacturing use.

* Blanks, not reported.

The water of Sebago lake is shown by analysis to approach as near to absolute purity as any mass of water of large volume in the world, so far as known. It is therefore particularly adapted to use in chemical and bleaching works.

Of the 20 to 30 thousand horse-powers available upon this river, unsurpassed in all respects, but a small proportion is yet in use. The absolute immunity of the power from dearth or freshet, the superiority of the natural sites for improvement, the proximity to market, conspire to give this river unusual attractions to the manufacturer.

The Royal and Nonesuch.

This is situated between the southern points of the Presumpscot and Androscoggin basins, and is named for its chief river. It is about 21 miles long, 12 broad, and 170 square miles in area. Its elevation is small.

Drainage district of the Royal.

Localities.	Feet.	Localities.	Feet.
New Gloucester station,.........	100	Yarmouth Junction,..........	75
Pownal "	120	Summit Yarmouth and Cumberland, on Grand Trunk R. R..	113
North Yarmouth "	95		

Its surface is moderately undulating to hilly. Surface materials chiefly loam and clay. Somewhat over one-fourth of the surface wooded. Gneiss occupies the southern part of the basin, mica schist the northern three-fourths. Royal, the principal stream, length 28 miles, including the chief windings. Total number of streams represented on the map, 38. Six small ponds. Range from lowest to highest water, six feet at Yarmouth. Annual rainfall, about 16,500,000,000 cubic feet, of which about 6,600,000,000 are discharged by the rivers. Large artificial reservoirs about the head of the main river, are about to be constructed.

Situated south of the Presumpscot basin, covering the tract between the southern point of the Saco basin and Casco bay. Area, about 125 square miles. Two small ponds represented on the State map. Principal streams, Nonesuch and Stroudwater. Estimated discharge, 4,800,000,000 cubic feet. Portland lies in this district.

Drainage district of the Nonesuch.

CHAPTER XXVII.

THE MOUSAM, ETC.

Section 1.—BASIN.

Location and dimensions. The drainage district of the Mousam and its associated streams, is located in the southwest part of the State, between the lower sections of the Saco and Piscataqua basins. Its greatest length is 32 miles; breath, 27 miles; area, 260 square miles; the Mousam drains about 120 square miles, and the Kennebunk about 50 square miles.

Elevation. Moderate, as shown by the following figures; these are, however, below the mean for the surrounding districts, as they express the heights of water surfaces and points upon railroads:

LOCALITIES.	Feet.	LOCALITIES.	Feet.
Kennebunk station,.............	122	Alfred station,...............	264
Wells "	200	Mousam river at railroad crossing in Sanford,............	214
South Waterboro' station,.......	264	About the level of Springvale,.	262
Shaker pond,..................	223		

Geological and surface conditions. Granite is almost the exclusive rock. It is quarried at Kennebunk extensively and of most superior quality. The general surface of the basin is level and moderately undulating. Surface materials are gravel, sand and sandy loam, with clay locally. Forests have been removed from over two-thirds of the whole area.

Rainfall. In cubic feet, for the whole district, about 25,000,-000,000.

Section 2.—RIVERS.

Total number of streams in the district, represented on the State map, 28; the estimated yearly discharge of which is 10,000,000,000 cubic feet.

The Mousam. The longest river is the Mousam, which is about 25 miles long, and has an estimated yearly discharge of 4,680,000,000 cubic feet. The statement for Kennebunk, in Part III. of the Report, indicates a volume of over 13,000 cubic feet per minute, at low run. This continued 11 hours per day, 312 days per year, would carry off 2,800,000,000 cubic feet.

Lakes.

Whole number, 14; combined area, estimated from the county map, about 10 square miles; one square mile to each 26 square miles of basin. The lakes average 0.71 of a square mile each in surface.

In consequence of the comparatively level character of the basin and the general improvement of the lakes and ponds for reservoirs the streams are very constant.

PRINCIPAL RESERVOIRS OF THE MOUSAM AND KENNEBUNK.

Name.	Connected with	Approximate area in square miles.	Present storage in feet.	Additional storage feasible in feet.
Kennebunk pond,........	Kennebunk riv.	0.85	4	*
Swan "	do do	0.75	*	-
Shaker's "	Mousam river,	0.40	2	-
Bunganut "	do do	0.50	Several feet.	-
Mousam "	do do	2.75	Several feet.	-
Square "	do do	1.00	-	-
Loon "	do do	0.20	-	-
Seven ponds,..........	-	6.45	-	-

Power on the Lower Section of the Mousam.

If a mean volume of 10,000 cubic feet per minute for the ordinary working hours, can be counted upon, on the Mousam river, from about Springvale to the tide, the power due to the descent of 262 feet is 4,978 horse-power, gross, or 199,120 spindles. In the report for Sanford, Part III., it is estimated 10,000 spindles can be operated on a 14-foot fall, throughout the year. A small part of the power is in use.

* Blanks, not reported.

CHAPTER XXVIII.

THE PISCATAQUA.

Section 1.—BASIN.

Location. The drainage district of the Piscataqua is located in part in the extreme southwest part of the State, and in part in the southeast corner of New Hampshire.

Dimensions. Greatest length, 43 miles; greatest breadth, 23 miles; area, 550 square miles, 240 in Maine, 310 in New Hampshire. About 230 square miles only are drained into the river, from both Maine and New Hampshire, above the lowest falls on the Salmon Falls branch.

Elevation. The following points are upon railroads or water surfaces, and are therefore below the mean:

LOCALITIES.	Feet.	LOCALITIES.	Feet.
Kittery station,	17	Great Falls Co.'s mill-pond Berwick,	107
Elliot "	21	Mast Point reservoir, Berwick,	180
Great Falls Junction,	90	Deering's pond, Lebanon,	350
South Berwick station,	93	Foot of Three ponds, Lebanon,	353
North " "	135	Level of " " "	367
Portsmouth Co.'s mill-pond, South Berwick,	32	Horn pond, Acton,	479
Salmon Falls Co.'s mill-pond, So. Berwick,	73	Northeast pond, Acton,	499

Geological and surface conditions. Granite greatly in excess of all other rock, with mica schist and quartz rock in localities. Surface aspect, undulating to hilly. Surface materials, gravel and sand, with some clay. Forests more than two-thirds cut off.

Rainfall. Estimated, in Maine, 23,000,000,000 cubic feet; in New Hampshire, 31,000,000,000 cubic feet; total, 54,-000,000,000 cubic feet.

Section 2.—RIVERS.

Course, affluents and length. Course, south-southeast. The river is formed of three main tributaries, the Cocheco, Salmon Falls, and Great Works rivers. The first is in New Hampshire; the second constitutes in its whole length, with the main Piscataqua, a part of the western State boundary; and the third is situated in Maine.

One-half only of the water-power of the Salmon Falls river, accordingly, is in Maine. The tributaries in Maine, represented on the map, number 19; in New Hampshire, 54; total, 73. The length of the river from the sources of the Salmon Falls branch to Piscataqua bay is about 40 miles. The Salmon Falls river is properly the upper Piscataqua.

Volume, and variations of volume.

Estimated yearly discharge of all the streams, 21,600,000,000 cubic feet. The amount employed at Great Falls, for manufacturing purposes, at the rate of 409 cubic feet per second, 11 hours a day, 312 days a year, is 5,053,000,000 cubic feet. This constitutes a very large proportion of the total estimated discharge of the basin tributary to the stream at and above that point, which is 8,970,000,000 cubic feet. Accordingly it is evident that the water is carefully and successfully husbanded against waste, and that its volume is remarkably uniform at all seasons. "A variation of three feet on the dams is very unusual."

Slope.

The fall from Northeast pond to the tide is 499 feet, which gives a mean descent of 16.6 feet to the mile, or 10′.8.

Lakes.

The larger lakes in the Maine portion of the basin number 9, in the New Hampshire portion 13, total 22, or five below the proportion due to the size of the district. With the exception of Northeast pond, the reservoirs are all small. Their combined surface is about 16 square miles, 1 square mile to each 34 square miles of basin; they average 0.72 of a square mile in extent.

The area of the several ponds used as reservoirs to the Salmon Falls branch is 3,759 acres, or a little less than six square miles. The following are the most important:

PRINCIPAL RESERVOIRS OF THE SALMON FALLS BRANCH OF THE PISCATAQUA.

Name.	Connected with	Approximate area in square miles.	Present storage in feet.	Additional storage feasible in feet.
Northeast pond,.........	Salmon Falls [river,	3.00	24	None.
Garvin's "	do	0.65	These ponds can on the average be stored to the depth of 10 ft.	"
Horn "	do do	0.35		"
Wentworth "	do do	0.55		"
Northwest "	do do	0.20		"
Five ponds,.........	–	4.75	–	–

Bonny Big pond, connected with Negutaquis river, has 2.50 square miles of surface, and is dammed.

Power of the Salmon Falls river.

From the statement for Berwick in Part III., it appears that at Great Falls a volume of 24,540 cubic feet per minute is commanded at low run, being supplied by the reservoirs chiefly, and by the natural flow of the river in part. If 16,000 cubic feet of this, on the average, be assumed to be available from the foot of the reservoirs to the tide, the total power due to the descent through [about] 480 feet is 14,500 horse-power, or 580,000 spindles, for the working hours of the year. A large proportion remains unused.

SUMMARY.

The combined areas of the various river basins before noticed is 32,575 square miles. Of this, 1,825 square miles are beyond State. The remainder, 30,750 square miles, being subtracted from 31,500 square miles, the nominal area of the State, leaves 750 square miles to be absorbed in island surfaces, small peninsulas, etc., not reckoned in the estimates for the river districts.

PART III.

The Water Powers of Maine.

DIVISION I.

Miscellaneous and General Views of the Water Powers.

CHAPTER XXIX.

EXPLANATORY AND INTRODUCTORY OBSERVATIONS.

Section 1.—Water Powers and their Measurement.

The water-powers treated by themselves.

The water-powers of the State are treated in a distinct division of the general subject and apart from the rivers, because they require to be exhibited with comparative fulness, and because powers of no inconsiderable consequence are found upon streams too small for particular notice in this Report.

In what points considered.

The features of each water-power proper to be set forth, as affecting its economical value, are the following:—Its location, as regards settlements, villages, or established industries in the town, and also as regards other powers with attendant facilities for associated manufactories; the formation of the fall, whether of abrupt or gradual descent, and the number of feet of both vertical pitch and horizontal run; its formation also with respect to bottom and banks, whether rock, pan, clay, gravel, sand, or otherwise, as affording suitable substratum for dams and mills, and affecting the construction of canals, raceways, etc.; the width of the stream, as determining the required length of dams and influencing the rise of water in freshets; lay of the land about the falls, with reference to the convenient location of mills and workshops and the laying-out of a town; security of the various constructions against ice and freshets; the volume of water, the maximum of freshets, the mean flow for the year, and most important of all, the volume at lowest run; the volume now used, if any;

total range of water, in feet, at the fall or on the dam, from lowest to highest pitch during the year; reservoirs, both natural and artificial, lakes, ponds, swamps, etc., both those already in use and those that can be brought into use, the expense of improvement, and the results realized or anticipated; the amount of power available in mill-powers, horse-powers, or where such definiteness is not attainable in the estimated capacity of accomplishment in sawing lumber, grinding grain, or other forms of labor; accessibility of the power with respect to markets of supply and demand, including proximity to roads, railroads, canals, navigable rivers, or the sea; improvements already made; annual production; ownership; building materials, including brick clay, stone, lime and lumber; fuel; productiveness of the surrounding district; whether its population would furnish operatives in considerable part; adaptedness of the power to any particular manufacture.

It was of course to be expected that this outline could be filled out for but few of the water-powers of the State, so large a proportion of which, even of the greatest, remain in a condition of total unimprovement, and so very few of which have ever been subjected to such thorough examination as to be properly regarded *surveyed.* The statistics hereinafter given will be found, however, in the majority of cases, it is believed, sufficiently full to give a tolerably clear idea of the condition and capabilities of the powers.

The measurement of water-power. The mechanical horse-power.

The dynamical unit employed in the measurement of water-powers,—the *horse-power,* is the power developed by the fall of 8.8 cubic feet of water one foot in one second. This standard applied *at the dam,* gives the gross or theoretical power. The proportion of the gross power that can be netted, i. e., brought to bear effectively *in the mill,* varies with the conditions of application and the perfection of machinery.* With first-class machinery two-thirds of the power can in general be utilized. Stated otherwise, for each 12 cubic feet of water at

* Mr. Francis, of Lowell, gives the following figures indicating, first, the cubic feet of water required to develop a net horse-power in connection with the specified classes of wheels; and, secondly, indicating what proportion of the gross power applied to the wheels can be utilized.

STYLE OF WHEEL.	Cubic feet of water.	Per centage utilized.
First-class turbines,	11.76	75
Good ordinary wheel,	14.70	60
Ordinary to inferior wheel,	22.05	20 to 40
Old-fashioned tub wheel.	88.20	10

the dam, falling one foot in one second, a horse-power of force can be commanded in the mill. Unless specified to the contrary, water-powers in this report are rated in gross horse-powers.

In cotton and woollen mills.

The power employed in cotton mills is usually estimated by the number of spindles, the number varying from 30 to 100 per horse-power, the average being 60 to each net horse-power, or 40 to each gross horse-power. The power of woollen mills is commonly reckoned by the number of sets of cards, at the average rate of one set to each eight net horse-powers.

In grist mills and saw mills.

It requires about one and one-third horse-powers to grind a bushel of corn of ordinary hardness to an average fineness. A horse-power will cut, as is estimated in our saw-mills, at the rate of one and one-tenth square feet per minute of ordinary pine lumber.

The horse-power compared with the strength of man and the horse.

A man of ordinary strength will produce a useful effect in eight hours' time of 1,157,740 foot pounds. A horse of average strength will produce an effect in the same time of 8,400,000 foot pounds. The mechanical horse-power will produce in the time specified an effect of 15,840,000 foot pounds. Accordingly the mechanical horse-power is equal to about thirteen man-powers and to the force of nearly two ordinary horses.

The mill-power.

The *mill-power* is frequently employed, as a larger and more convenient unit than the horse-power, for the rating of large water-powers. The standard employed in this country—the Lowell standard—is the power generated by the fall of 750 cubic feet of water one foot in one second—equal to 62.5 net or 85.2 gross horse-power.

Section 2.—Summary View of the Water Powers of Maine.

Number of the powers.

There are 878 municipal districts in the State, including cities, towns, plantations and townships. Of these, 595 are represented, partially or wholly, in the syllabus following, 471 being cities, towns and plantations, and 124 townships. The number of powers cannot be given in a precise figure, some of the towns reporting their privileges indefinitely as "several" or "numerous;" there are certainly 3,100.

Condition as to improvement.

Of the above, probably half are entirely unused. Amongst these is the greater proportion of the largest powers in the State. Thus of the great powers on the Penobscot above Oldtown, on the lower main river, on the Mattawamkeag, Mattagamon, and the upper main river, they being numbered by the score and being first-class as to magnitude, not one, with insignificant exceptions, is in use. The great powers on the Kennebec, also, above Skowhegan, unsurpassed in all regards, are substantially unused. The same is true of much the larger proportion of the privileges on the Androscoggin, the Saco, St. Croix, and Machias rivers, the Union, St. George, Presumpscot and Salmon Falls rivers, and of all on the Aroostook, Allaguash, St. John, and Fish rivers (with one exception for the last.) Many of these privileges are fully equal to that at Lowell in improvability, and several exceed it in natural power. Very many of them are sufficient to sustain thrifty manufacturing villages of fifteen or twenty thousand inhabitants each—all of them, the great and the small alike, in a state of total unimprovement.

Of the powers nominally improved there are next to none whose capacities are fully developed, and of very few are they even approximately developed. Their tributary lakes and ponds remain unused, at least for other than log-driving uses, the natural flow of the streams exceeding the present demands upon it for manufacturing purposes. The dams are leaky, the water-wheels of primitive patterns and to the last degree wasteful of power, and the working equipment in nearly all particulars of the cheapest and simplest sort. A carding-machine, shingle-mill, or grist-mill will be found in exclusive occupancy of privileges upon which a series of first-class cotton factories or woollen mills could be operated the year through, and so in multitudes of instances.

It is not necessary to say in respect to the use of our water-force and the equipment with which that use is conducted, that *some* of our powers are furnished with accessories in all particulars, dams, canals, machinery, buildings, fully on a par with the very best constructions in the country or the world; as examples of which it is necessary only to refer to Lewiston, Saco and Biddeford. The saw mills of the Penobscot have no superiors on the globe in all the appurtenances necessary to the more elementary manufacture of lumber.

Accessibility of the powers.

Upon this topic nothing will be said in this connection. The statements in Part I., Chapter XII., touch the essential points.

The powers can be had at low cost.

For many years the proprietors of water-power, sharing in the preposterous and ignorant hostility to manufacturing corporations, begotten and sustained by the policy of the State, either refused to sell their property for improvement at any rate, or held it at such figures as virtually excluded it from market. All this is now changed. Really responsible parties having in view the actual improvement of powers, can get possession of them at rates merely nominal as compared with prices beyond State, and in many cases can secure them *free of cost.*

The returns from the several towns, embodied in the last Division of this Report, contain, at length, statements to the following effect:—"The proprietors will sell upon very favorable terms to any parties who will improve the power." "Any parties who come amongst us with a view to improvement of our power will meet a hearty reception and substantial coöperation." "The proprietor will *give* the power outright to any responsible person of sufficient means to improve it and who will improve it," etc., etc. Unquestionably privileges that in the older States would be held at thousands of dollars can be purchased for scores in this State; privileges of great capacity, well situated, improvable at small outlay, and which are thus in the market at a merely nominal rate simply because their *owners have not the means for their development.*

Exemption from taxation.

The law of the State allows any town to exempt from taxation for a period of ten years manufacturing establishments of whatever character, located therein, together with all the machinery and capital employed in operating the same. This policy of the State has in many cases already been ratified, and in all cases may be regarded as certain of ratification whenever occasion shall call for it.

Towns invest in manufactories.

Towns are adopting the practice of coöperating with parties improving their water-power, by subscribing in their corporate capacity, under suitable conditions, to the capital stock employed in the manufactures. The Legislature grants permits to this effect without reluctance in the majority of cases.

Liberal flowage statutes.

The law of the State allows land to be taken for flowage purposes upon payment of damages, the amount of which in case of dispute is to be determined by a commission. So that it is not possible in this State, as it is in some others, for an obstinate and selfish land-holder to prevent the improvement of large and valuable water-powers by the obstruction of antiquated and unfriendly flowage statutes.

Reservoirs.

The extraordinary resources of our water-power as regards storage basins, have already been set forth in detail in Part II. and need not be be dwelt upon in this connection. The returns from the various towns given upon the following pages, testify explicitly to the advantages accruing.

In point of *supply of water* the testimony is to the following purport:—"Abundant water at all seasons owing to the ponds;" "never any lack of water when the dams on the ponds are kept in order;" "the lakes and ponds yield an unlimited supply of water;" etc., etc.

As regards *freshets,* the testimony is full to the following intent:—"Total range of water insignificant;" "freshets harmless, the water being kept back in the ponds;" "no damage from freshets, the water being under perfect control;" "loss from freshets unknown, all considerable rise being prevented by the reservoirs;" etc., etc.

As regards *ice,* "no trouble from ice, the water being warm from the pond;" "the stream never freezes at the outlet, and but very little for miles below, the water being fresh-drawn and warm from the pond;" "the water from the lake is so warm that the wheels need no protection from the cold;" "the formation of ice is prevented by the water being let on warm from the pond;" etc., etc.

As regards the *cost of developing the reservoirs,* the testimony is explicit in proof of its comparative insignificance:—The sums specified are $200, 300, 600, 1,000, etc.; or in general terms, "cost trifling;" "expense insignificant;" "can be made a great reservoir at moderate cost;" "cost of flowage nothing;" etc.

Artificial reservoirs.

Artificial reservoirs are demonstrated by the testimony of the returns to be feasible in remarkable degree. The cost of flowage is comparatively trifling, rainfall is everywhere in excess of evaporation, the brokenness of the State surface affords innumerable receptacles for storage, and the impermeability to water of our rocks prevents its dispersion and loss by underground percolation; lastly, as just noticed, the laws interpose no obstacles.

The practicability of artificial reserve basins should be taken into particular account in connection with the *small* powers and the powers which are represented in the Returns as *intermittent* for a part of the year. There can be no question that nine-tenths of these are susceptible of being respectively very greatly augmented and of being made efficient throughout the year by reservoirs. As is well known, there are numerous privileges in Massachusetts,

Connecticut, etc., upon which cotton mills and woollen mills now operate for the whole year, the motor material of which in the summer, consists almost entirely of water impounded in artificial receptacles. The proportion of reservoir water is in many cases eighty or ninety per cent. of the entire low run of the streams; in other words, the volume of the streams in the summer is artificially augmented variously from four hundred to nine hundred per cent. over and above what it would be in the state of nature. Indeed, considerable mills are now run all the year in the districts referred to, upon streams which before the construction of reservoirs went almost literally dry in summer. It is in view of such facts that the small powers and intermittent powers are exhibited so fully in the Digest of Returns, these being nearly all susceptible of conversion into constant sources of mechanical force, and of being increased, many of them, by hundreds per cent.

It is obvious that the improvement of the small powers by the means in reference will react upon the large and vastly increase their capacity at low run, and this without any additional expense to the proprietors of the large powers.

Natural water supply.

The bulk of annual rain in Maine, has been shown to be unusually large, its fall to be uniform at different parts of the year, and the residuum of evaporation to be great. So that, aside from the reservoirs, the natural flow of the rivers of the State is comparatively copious and constant.

Building material.

In much the larger proportion of the towns granite is specified as attainable close at hand, either as the prevalent rock or occurring in isolated patches or sporadic in boulders and detached masses. In next to none is there a dearth of stone suitable for ordinary construction purposes. Lime of the best quality is a characteristic product of the State, also slate for roofing purposes, and brick clay.

Lumber is of course abundant and cheap. The returns testify to the fact that great breadths of forest still remain in the close vicinity of large numbers of our water-powers. These forests contain every variety of soft and hard lumber appropriate to the region, procurable at small expense, and susceptible, by the fortunate proximity of the water-powers, of being worked up inexpensively into any forms which such woods are made to assume for any of the purposes of civilization. The forests in many cases stand close upon railroads or on the seaboard, and the articles manufactured from them are thus easily transportable to the markets of the world.

Operatives.

Operatives of the best character and in any required number, can be procured from amongst the sons and daughters of our farming population; accustomed to labor, robust, trustworthy, and intelligent, and glad for employment within their native State at moderate compensation.

DIVISION II.

Statistical and Descriptive View of the Water Powers.

"A" TOWNSHIP, R. 7—PENOBSCOT COUNTY.

Statement of Daniel Barker, Esq., of Bangor.

Numerous Powers.

First, on the Penobscot river (west branch), "Rocky Rips," above Rockabema rips, no perpendicular fall, but very swift water for 100 rods.

Second, "Dolby Rips," above, fall eight feet in ten rods, a first-class site.

Third, "Ledge Falls," above, and half a mile above mouth of Schoodic stream, about 100 rods long, fall 12 or 15 feet, one pitch six feet; river wide, but banks high.

Fourth, Fifth, Sixth, etc.; from the head of Ledge falls to the outlet of "Shad pond"—an expansion of the Penobscot river—there are three miles of swift water, at the head of which and at the outlet of Shad pond is a pitch of five feet descent in four rods. A storage head of eight feet can be held on Shad pond at this point; river quite wide. The whole series of privileges are called the "Pond Falls."

Hundreds of square miles of lakes and ponds situated further up the river can be and already are improved for storage, the water being used for log-driving, so that a constant power of many thousand horse can be had in this town.

All the privileges unimproved.

"A" TOWNSHIP, R. 13—PISCATAQUIS COUNTY.

Statement of Hon. Abner Coburn, of Skowhegan.

One Power.

At the foot of Lower Roach pond, a dam giving ten feet head.

The pond covers about five square miles, is flowed eight feet, and can be raised four feet more, securing an enormous volume of water. Five square miles of ponds above are tributary to the lower pond.

ABBOT—PISCATAQUIS COUNTY.

From Selectmen's Returns, and a Plan of the Streams.

Six Powers.

First, on Piscataquis river near the centre of the town, and near the bridge. Saw, shingle, and shovel-handle mills. A very superior power. Side canals can be constructed upon this privilege, and mills located thereon for twenty rods down the river.

Second, on the south branch of the Piscataquis, not far from its mouth and near the bridge. Grist, carding and clothing mill, and blacksmith shop. A very good and safe power.

Third, on the outlet stream of Piper pond, near its junction with the south branch of the Piscataquis; saw, clapboard, and shingle mills. Piper pond covers about one and a fourth square miles, and can be dammed at trifling expense so as to furnish abundant water to Nos. Three and Four throughout the year. Six or more ponds, above, in Kingsbury and Blanchard, can have dams.

Each of the powers above specified will cut 2,000,000 feet of lumber yearly.

No specifications respecting the other powers, except that one is near the main road, and the other near a cross road.

The height of the various falls is respectively about fourteen feet in a distance of three to five rods.

Range from low to high water, four feet. In a very dry season the mills are obliged to hold up for a short time, owing to the non-use of the reservoirs.

Annual products, $10,000. Less use made of the powers than formerly.

Market, Bangor. The main road from Bangor to Moosehead lake passes directly by two of the above privileges, and the best two.

ACTON—YORK COUNTY.

From Selectmen's Returns.

[See also "Acton and Newfield."]

Eight Powers.

Five on the Salmon Falls river, which forms the western boundary of the town. Water sufficient at each of the privileges to run a large cotton mill all the year. Privileges all owned by the Great Falls Manufacturing Company. The company have constructed works at the cost of $40,000 by which they draw down the Great Acton pond to the depth of 24 feet, using the water in time of dearth at their factories at Great Falls.

Sixth, Seventh, and Eighth, sufficient to saw lumber or grind grain a third of the year.

Market, Saco, Great Falls, and Boston, by rail.

Acton and Newfield—York County.

From the Returns of Acton and Newfield.

[See also "Acton," and "Newfield."]

One Power.

On the Little Ossipee river, "Balch's Mills," on the Acton side. Power sufficient to run a cotton mill of medium size the year round. Saw and grist mill now upon it. Balch's pond, with its flowage covers 2.50 square miles; a dam at the outlet gives a head of eight feet over its whole surface, giving great steadiness of flow to the river below.

Addison—Washington County.

From the Returns of D. M. Wass, Esq.

Two Powers.

First, on the "Basin Stream," formerly two saw mills, now rotted down, one succeeding the other. Unused for several years. A saw mill can run about one-fourth of the year. Good site for dam at little expense; ledge bottom. Twelve feet head and fall. No ponds.

Second, "Half Tide Falls" on Indian river, a very good power for a small one; no lakes or ponds, except the mill pond, about 1,000 acres. Fourteen feet head and fall. Saw, grist, lath, and shingle machinery. Site for dam very good; ledge bottom all the way, and short distance to build, good stone very handy. Water sufficient for the mills about half the time, and sufficient with a tight dam for one mill through a drouth. One or two dams could be built to hold back a large amount of water. Vessels of 300 tons burden can load within twenty rods of the mills.

ALBANY—OXFORD COUNTY.

From Selectmen's Returns.

Six Powers.

First, on Crooked river, fall twelve feet; saw, shingle, and lath machinery; 300 square inches of water; 300,000 feet of boards and 300,000 shingles and laths in an ordinary season.

Second, a mile below, fall twenty feet, 300 square inches of water, 300,000 feet of lumber yearly, saw mill.

Third, four miles below, fall eight feet. Saw mill when in repair will saw 900,000 feet of lumber; an addition of water supplied by Songo pond.

Fourth, two miles below, fall nine feet, unimproved.

Fifth, in the south part of the town, on Stone-pond river, twelve feet fall, 300 square inches of water; saw, shingle, stave and lath machinery; can saw 500,000 feet of lumber yearly.

Sixth, stave and shingle mill, on the outlet of Kneeland's pond; fall eight feet.

ALBION—KENNEBEC COUNTY.

From Selectmen's Returns.

Six Powers.

First, at the village, on Fifteen-mile river, tannery.

Second, on the same river, at "Puddle Dock," grist and saw mill.

Third, a mile above, saw mill.

Fourth, one and a fourth miles above, saw mill.

Fifth, on a branch of Fifteen-mile river, saw mill.

Sixth, on a tributary to Lovejoy's pond, saw mill.

ALEXANDER—WASHINGTON COUNTY.

From Selectmen's Returns.

One Power.

At the outlet of Lake Beautiful, saw and shingle mills; operate about half of the year. Old-style wheel. The lake contains 400 to 500 acres. One-fourth of the basin covered with woods.

Market, Calais, turnpike.

ALFRED—YORK COUNTY.

Statement of E. H. Tripp, Esq., of Lyman.

Five Powers.

First, the "Shaker Mills," on the outlet stream of Bunganut pond, saw and grist mill; pond covers half a square mile, and is flowed several feet.

Second, three miles below, on the outlet stream of Bunganut and Shaker ponds, saw, grist, and woollen mills; blankets, three sets cards, about 36 horse powers, operates all the year.

Third, Fourth and Fifth, on the outlet stream of Middle-branch pond; three saw mills.

ALNA—LINCOLN COUNTY.

From Returns of Hiram P. Carleton, Esq.

Three Powers.

First, "Sheepscot Falls," saw and grist mill, operate on the ebb tide.

Second, "Head-of-Tide Falls," five miles above Sheepscot falls, wooden dam, head and fall about 10 feet; can be increased to 13 feet readily by clearing channel below the dam. Grist, stave and shingle mills. Large building adjoining, would make an excellent carriage shop or factory in connection with still another building attached, formerly used as fulling and cloth-dressing mill.

Excellent chance for a stone dam, the bottom and sides being rock, with a high ledge on one side, from which stone for the dam can be taken. By improving the numerous lakes and ponds above, the power can be made sufficient for large manufacturing.

The site is an admirable one for a cotton or woollen factory. Proprietors not anxious to sell, but will sell on very liberal terms to induce parties to improve the power.

Third, the "Rapids," the head of which is two miles above the "Head-of-Tide Falls," and which have a fall of twenty-five feet in one mile, with steep banks on both sides. Formerly a saw mill upon this privilege, now decayed. A dam might be built at the lower end of the Rapids, so as to flow them out, and give a head and fall of nearly thirty feet, and a pond, above, two miles long.

See page 141, Part II., for reservoirs tributary to the Sheepscot river.

"Two and a half million feet of logs were run through this town in 1866, besides what were sawed in the mills on the stream."

ALTON—PENOBSCOT COUNTY.

From Selectmen's Returns.

[See also "Alton and Argyle."]

Two Powers.

First, "Alton Village Mills," on Dead stream, two up-and-down saws, grist and shingle mill. Height of falls not ascertained; but "the privilege is a good one."

Second, "Lewis' Mills," on Pushaw stream, single saw and shingle mill. Six up-and-down saws have run on this privilege, but the mills were burned down. Stream fed by the Pushaw lake, which contains ten or twelve square miles.

Market, Bangor.

ALTON AND ARGYLE—PENOBSCOT COUNTY.

Statement of Isaac Foster, Esq.

[See also "Alton," and "Argyle."]

Two Powers.

"Long Rips," on Birch stream, good power, long tract of dead water above.

"Short Rips," two and a half miles below; dead water above; excellent privilege.

ALVA PLANTATION—AROOSTOOK COUNTY.

Statement of H. O. Perry, Esq., of Mars Hill.

Several Powers.

The Presque Isle river of the St. John runs three or four miles in the town; it is rapid in its whole course, and affords several good mill sites. Rocky bottom in nearly its whole length, so that dams can be located at almost any desired point. Good banks in all parts.

There is no improvement at present. It has been proposed to improve an excellent site near the north line of the town. Various mills on the stream just across the Province line. A good grist mill is very much needed. Any responsible party who will build and carry on a really good mill, will be welcomed and substantially aided. A woollen mill also is very much needed.

AMHERST—HANCOCK COUNTY.

From the Selectmen's Statement, and a Plan of the Streams.

Six Powers.

First, "Buzzell's Tannery," which operates all the year and uses 1,500 cords bark. Saw mill which operates six months. Situated on the west branch of the Union river. Abundant water except in a severe drouth.

Second, above on the same stream, about midway its course in the town, "Silsby Falls," not now used. Mills burned down.

The west branch of the Union river is fed, at and above this point, by eight or more considerable lakes and ponds, the area of which is not less than eight square miles, all of which are improved for reservoirs, the mean head of storage thereon being not far from seven feet, and all being susceptible of much more reserve than is now held. Storage now used for log driving purposes. See page 137, Part II.

Third, upon Spring brook, a site for four shingle mills, power six months of the year; not used.

Fourth, upon Half-mile brook, power for a shingle mill four months; not used.

Fifth, on Warm brook, power for a shingle mill four months; not used.

Sixth, on Chick's brook, grist and shingle mill; water six months.

Amity—Aroostook County.

Statement of J. O. Smith, Esq., of Hodgdon.

One Power.

Good but not large, of capacity to carry a saw mill and one run of stones the year through; situated on a branch of the Meduxnakeag stream, which drains quite a large territory.

The fall is about 10 feet.

Andover—Oxford County.

From Selectmen's Returns.

Eleven Powers, and More.

First, the "Corner Mills," on the West branch of Ellis river; fall 15 feet in 10 rods; grist, saw and shingle mills and starch factory. Power all used, with such machinery as is now employed.

Second, two miles above, unemployed, and of equal capacity with the Corner power.

Third, the "Ellis Falls," on the East branch of Ellis river; fall 25 feet in four rods. Not improved. Title in dispute.

Fourth, the "Brickett Falls," below, 20 feet fall in 10 rods, granite ledge foundation. Unimproved.

Fifth, a good granite dam at the "Goddard Site;" saw, shingle, lath, and other machinery. Fall 10 feet.

The East branch is fed by Ellis pond, three by one and a half miles, and by Garland pond, one by one miles, both of which are dammed. It is constant, owing to the ponds and swamp land connected. The West branch is more variable, being fed by springs and mountain streams. Both branches are so rapid in descent that the water can be used over many more times than are specified.

Also several powers on tributaries to Ellis river, as follows:

Sixth, on Black brook, in the northeast part of the town.

Seventh, on Sawyer's brook, in the north part of the town.

Eighth, on Frye's brook.

Ninth, on Stony brook.

Tenth, on Lone brook, formerly used.

Eleventh, on Gardner brook, starch factory, with capacity to manufacture 100 tons in three months.

These "tributary" powers have from 15 to 30 feet fall each, and are estimated each equal to operating a grist mill with two runs of stones in any drouth, and much more in any ordinary season. Granite abundant and good. Lay of the land favorable, chief part of the basin of the streams wooded.

Eighty-six tons of starch were made and 200,000 feet of lumber sawed last year. Small part of the available power used.

Market, Portland, by road to Bryant's pond station, and thence by rail.

ANDOVER NORTH SURPLUS—OXFORD COUNTY.

Two Powers.

First, on a tributary of Ellis river, "Falls," below "Dunn's Notch," not occupied.

Second, on Black brook, saw mill.

ANDOVER WEST SURPLUS—OXFORD COUNTY.

One Power.

The "Cataracts" on the West branch of Ellis river. Not occupied.

ANSON—SOMERSET COUNTY.

From the Statements of D. D. Mann, M. D., the Selectmen, and others.

[See also "Anson and Madison."]

Nine Powers.

First, on the Fahi brook, the outlet of Fahi, Sandy, Mud and Lily ponds, and of a large tract of swamp land; grist mill and saw mill.

Second, on Mill stream, at the village, saw and carding mill; the stream is fed by the great Embden pond, 2.50 square miles, Hancock pond, and the Fahi-stream ponds. A dam at the outlet of the Embden pond could be of sufficient height without any considerable damage from flowage, or outlay, to maintain a good flow of water all the year. The pond is fed by a large extent of drainage territory, and naturally has a large supply of water. The outlet stream is unaffected by freshets or drouths.

Third, on a tributary to the Carrabasset, in the northeast part of the town, a saw mill.

Fifth, on the Lemon stream, in the southwest part of the town, a saw mill.

Sixth, below, a grist mill.

Several large and valuable powers are situated on the Carrabasset at the village. The river falls 50 feet in a third of a mile above the "basin;" the bridge is near the foot of the fall. The bottom and banks are solid ledge; the opportunities for canalling are first-class. The river at this point is fed by 290 square miles of drainage territory, and by ten or twenty square miles of reservoirs, including large and small. The Embden-pond stream empties into the Carrabasset about two-thirds of the way up the fall.

A very small part of the power is now used. The following privileges are more or less improved:

Seventh, at the head of the Carrabasset fall, a dam, seven feet head.

Eighth, below, head not reported.

Ninth, "Albee's privilege," below, eight feet head, saw mill. A canal can be cut from this privilege to the "basin" below, 25 rods, and a fall of 30 feet secured. On the side opposite the mill a canal 14 rods long in ledge will give a fall of 12 feet.

The "Upper Carrabasset Falls," four and a half miles above the lower falls, "a splendid water-power," with only a saw mill and grist mill upon it.

The best of granite, and excellent slate quarries close at hand on all the falls.

Railroad from West Waterville now in process of construction.

ANSON AND MADISON—SOMERSET COUNTY.

From the Returns of Madison.

[See also "Anson," and "Madison."]

One Power.

"Madison Bridge Falls," on the Kennebec river.

There is a fall of 87 feet from the head of Madison Bridge falls, two and a half miles to the south town line. The fall consists of two principal and several subordinate pitches, with swift water between. The illustration accompanying this statement represents simply the upper pitch, the only part of the fall improved at all, and shows scarcely one-fourth of the whole descent. Dams can be located at any point as may be required, the bottom being ledgy.

At the upper pitch an inferior dam has been maintained for years. Here a dam could easily be constructed that would control the entire river, and at the same time be perfectly safe, having a ledge for its foundation across the channel, and being buttressed at both ends by the solid rock rising several feet above the surface of the water. Upon the eastern bank, a canal could be opened and carried nearly one hundred rods down the river, the further end of which could have an elevation of thirty feet or more above the bed of the river adjacent to it, and the land traversed would furnish the stone for the purposes of construction.

The lower pitch is also favorable to the construction of a permanent dam and for canalling to any extent desired.

The extreme drouth run at this point, assumed to be thirty-nine per cent. less than at Augusta, or 103,700 cubic feet for 11 hours a day, that at Augusta being estimated at 170,000 cubic feet for the same time, would yield, if only 60 feet of the whole fall were improved, a gross power of 11,650 horse, for the hours specified, or 465,600 spindles. The realization of this power would require, of course, works on a sufficient scale to control the whole volume of the river.

The amount of increase of which the natural low-run power at this point is susceptible, may be inferred from inspection of the tributary reservoirs on the Carrabasset, Dead and Moose rivers, pages 94 and 95, and on the upper Kennebec, page 96; in particular, Moosehead lake, page 98.

The power is pretty well guarded naturally against danger from freshets, the land upon the falls being high and ledgy, and it can be made at small expense entirely safe.

Madison-Bridge Falls, Anson and Madison.

The only use made of the power at present is to drive the machinery of a few mills,—a grist mill, a saw mill, sash and blind factory and a starch factory; all of which draw but slightly upon its resources.

The railroad now constructing to this point, soon to be in running order, passes by the side of the power. There could be no finer site for any form of manufacturing, in particular for the extensive manufacture of lumber.

Among the islands a little above, logs can be held back or safely stored to any amount, and floated down with ease when wanted. This place is also the centre of a wool-growing district, where more wool of the finer grades is raised, it is supposed, than in any other equal portion of the State. It is also the centre of a large agricultural district of unsurpassed productiveness.

Appleton—Knox County.

From Selectmen's Returns.

Twelve Powers.

Three on the St. George river, one on Pettengill river, two on the Medomac, three on Medomac branch, and three on St. George branch.

These are, Smith's mills, 15 feet fall in one mile; McLain's mills, (upper), fall 15 feet in 1.5 miles; (lower), fall 12 feet in 50 rods; Cutler, Burkett's, Lermond's, Stubbs', Hills', Burkett's, Conant's, Gushee's, and Simmons', mills.

Only part of the power is used. With good dams the powers of St. George river can operate all the year. Machinery by no means of good construction.

The streams are connected with lakes and ponds, which are susceptible of cheap improvement as reservoirs. Artificial reservoirs possible. Abundant and good stone for building. But little forest on the basin of the streams.

Market, Belfast, Rockland, by road.

Argyle—Penobscot County.

Statement of Isaac Foster, Esq., and the Selectmen.

[See also "Alton and Argyle."]

Three Powers.

First, "Comstock Rips," near the mouth of Hemlock brook; 20 feet fall can be had; shingle mill.

Second, "Lunt Rips," three miles above, 15 feet fall; no improvement. Artificial reservoirs of 100 acres connected with the stream.

Third, on Hoyt brook, saw and shingle machine; 500 acres of reservoir; drawn down in summer.

Powers operate from six to eight months. Good stone for building. Basin mostly heavily wooded.

Market, Bangor, by road, railroad and boat.

ARROWSIC—SAGADAHOC COUNTY.

From Selectmen's Returns.

Three Powers.

All are tide powers, one being situated on the Kennebec river, and two on Back river, so called.

Mills will cut about 200,000 of lumber per month. Operate about ten months in the year. Best machinery for the sort of power.

ATHENS—SOMERSET COUNTY.

From the Statement of William McLaughlin, Esq., with Plan of the Water-Powers.

Five Powers.

First, on the outlet of Wentworth pond, a tributary of the Wesserunsett river, about a mile and a quarter below the pond, 12 feet fall; a dam and saw mill.

Second, just below, nine feet fall; grist and shingle mill.

Third, below, 11 feet fall; shingle mill.

The above mills, known as "Fellows' Mills," are all within a distance of 30 rods. The pond covers 325 acres, and by small outlay might be converted into a reservoir ample for the supply of the mill at all seasons of the year.

Fourth, at the village, on the Wesserunsett river, 10 feet fall, part natural, with machinery for manufacturing lumber; carding and fulling mill.

Fifth, 20 rods below, 14 feet fall; flour mill, large lumber mill, planing machine, etc. Only part of the power used. This is regarded an excellent site for a cotton or woollen mill.

ATKINSON—PISCATAQUIS COUNTY.

From Selectmen's Returns.

Four Powers.

First, on Alder stream, in the centre of the town, saw, grist, and shingle mills; operate six months.

Second, on Dead stream, in the southeast corner of the town, saw and shingle mills; five months.

Third, on Dead stream, near the centre of the south line of the town, saw and shingle mills; operate five months in the year.

Fourth, in the northeast part of the town. Not occupied.

The fall on each of the above powers is about 10 feet in 25 rods. The power at each is sufficient to cut 100,000 long lumber, and 200,000 short; at the centre to do all the local grinding of grain. All poorly improved, with leaky dams, and inferior equipment. Freshets harmless.

Market, Bangor, by road; distance, 27 to 30 miles. The Piscataquis Railroad is building within three to five miles of all of said mills.

Attean Township—Somerset County.

Statement of Heman Whipple, Esq., of Solon.

One Power.

A fall of 10 feet between Little Wood and Wood ponds. Can be made a good power. Large and small ponds above for reservoirs.

Auburn—Androscoggin County.

From the Statements of Edward A. Little, Esq., President Agawam Manufacturing Company, and of C. B. Stetson, Esq.

Seven Powers.

First, Second and Third, the "Auburn Falls," on the Little Androscoggin river, east of the railroad and parallel to it in their entire length. The foot of the falls is about one-fourth of a mile from the Androscoggin river.

Total height of the fall, 70 feet, obtained in a running distance of 150 rods. It is proposed to divide the descent into three parts by dams. The dams will be each about 125 feet in length.

The bottom of the stream is a solid ledge, and affords unsurpassed sites for the firm establishment of dams. The banks are steep and ledgy; and at the first and second dams offer good sites for mills on the west side, and at the third dam on both sides.

The volume of water employed at Mechanic Falls, a few miles above, is, as reported, nearly 20,000 cubic feet per minute for the ordinary manufacturing hours, at the low stage of water. It is probably reasonable to infer the low run at Auburn to be 22,000 cubic feet per minute for the same hours, as the contributions of several ponds improved for reservoirs, as well as of various streams, are received below Mechanic Falls. This would give a gross power of 2,870 horse on the whole fall, or 114,800 spindles. This result, so remarkable for a stream which drains only 280 square miles, is obtained by the improvement of its numerous and capacious reservoirs. The capacity of these storage receptacles is by no means fully developed. See page 83, Part II.

There are 175 acres of land connected with these privileges, which is all for sale or any part of it. All of the property is situated directly opposite the city of Lewiston, and is owned by Edward A. Little, Esq. It is intended this season to erect a dam upon the middle site, and to lease a part of the power for a flour mill. There are at present only a saw mill, box mill, and batting mill on the privileges: these operate all the year.

Fourth, on Taylor brook, the outlet of Taylor pond, which covers about two square miles, has four feet of storage; about 50 rods from the Maine Central Railroad track, 12 feet fall; is capable of carrying three runs of flour stones under a nine-foot head in the summer months: owned by Edward A. Little.

Fourth, "Ryerson's Privilege," on the Little Androscoggin river, eight miles below Mechanic Falls, and three miles from Lewiston. Twenty feet head can be had. There is no improvement. There were formerly a saw mill, grist mill, shingle machine and clapboard machine. Owned by Nicholas Ryerson. This privilege is in receipt of all the water commanded at Mechanic Falls, and the available power is inferred to be about 840 horse power, or 33,600 spindles.

Fifth, near the outlet of Little Wilson pond, a saw mill. The pond is used for a reservoir.

Sixth, below, near Wilson pond, a saw mill.

Seventh, at the outlet of Wilson pond or Lake Auburn, seven feet fall, can be increased to 12 feet; peg, saw, grist and box mills, and furniture factory. The pond covers 1,968 acres, upon which a head of eight feet is commanded.

AUGUSTA—KENNEBEC COUNTY.

From the Statements of Col. H. A. DeWitt and Judge Samuel Titcomb, and from Articles in the Kennebec Journal.

Five Powers.

First, the "Kennebec Dam," on the Kennebec river at the head of tide, and within the limits of the city proper.

Kennebec Dam, Augusta.

Height of fall.—The present fall is 15 feet, part vertical, and part on a sloping apron 40 feet wide. So far as regards flowage or interference with privileges above, the dam can be raised six feet or more. It is now contemplated to raise it three feet for the present.

Volume of water.—The volume of water recorded by measurement during the summer of 1866 was 130,000 cubic feet per minute for the 24 hours, in the extreme low run, and 175,500 cubic feet for the mean run throughout the summer season. By reference to Part II of this Report, pages 91 and 92, it will be seen that the minimum volume of the river for that summer must have been considerably in excess of the minimum summer volume in the average of years. Upon supposition that the excess was, for the three months of ordinary lowest run, 40 per cent., the *minimum drouth* volume of the river at this point, ever observed, may be estimated as 170,000 cubic feet per minute for 11 hours a day. This would yield, on a fall of 15 feet, for the hours specified, a gross power of 4,830 horse-power, or 193,200 spindles, or about 300,000 spindles with preparation on print cloths.

The power can be increased by raising the dam, as above noticed. This would not only give a higher head, but would put the whole volume of the river under control for a distance of 17 miles, to the foot of Ticonic falls in Waterville.

It can be increased enormously, also, by the use of the 300 square miles, more of less, of lakes and ponds tributary to the Kennebec above this point. See Part II, pages 94—98. It can be further increased by the construction of artificial reservoirs of large size, at low cost, so that the present minimum power is very greatly in defect of what can be readily commanded.

Lay of the land.—By no means favorable for the erection of mills with the appurtenant boarding houses, yards. etc.; but understood to be susceptible of improvement adequate to all practical necessities.

Construction material.—The best of granite close at hand; also unlimited quantities of clay for bricks; the country above furnishes lumber in all required amounts.

Proprietorship.—Owned by the A. & W. Sprague Manufacturing Company; Agent and Engineer, Col. H. A. DeWitt.

Improvements.—Improvements on this power on a vast scale are now in prospect and in the early stage of execution. Six hundred acres of land have been purchased, extending a mile and a half on the east side of the river and a mile and a quarter on the west side. A brick yard is in operation capable of producing 100,000 bricks per week. Townships of timber land have been purchased, saw mills bought and built, etc., so that a great manufacturing city may reasonably be looked for as certain speedily to arise upon this privilege.

The power of the Kennebec dam is already employed as follows:

At the east end an extensive saw mill, Lancy & Smith, proprietors; about fifty hands employed; annual product, $40,000.

At the west end of the dam, an excelsior mill, J. W. Longfellow & Co.; annual product about $3,000. Also a clapboard planer, capable of planing 5,000 clapboards a day.

A saw mill, Charles Milliken, proprietor; twenty-five hands; product, $75,000 to $100,000.

A saw mill, D. G. Baker & Co.; fifteen hands; product, $25,000.

Sash, door, and blind factory, Banks & Mosher; thirty-five hands; $60,000 per annum.

Barrel-head factory, Freeman Barker, $7,000 per annum.

Scoles' grist mill, 25,000 bushels per annum.

O. W. & W. G. Emery, planing and job mill.

E. Atkins & Co., boxes and shooks, $12,000 a year.

Furniture factory, A. Cowee & Son, $25,000.

Furniture factory, David Knowlton, $2,000.

Broom and brush handle factory, Smiley & Church, $5,000.

Kennebec mill, A. & W. Sprague Manufacturing Company, 10,000 spindles, 300 looms; 2,400,000 yards light sheeting; hands, 175, of whom 125 are females; value of product, $275,000 in 1866.

The present season, 1869, the Sprague Manufacturing Company are building a new cotton mill of 30,000 spindles.

Second, Third, Fourth and Fifth, upon the Bond brook, four dams in two miles, mills upon each, room for others. Stream rather variable in volume, but capable of very great improvement by artificial connection with large ponds in the vicinity.

Upper dam occupied by Abner Coombs, grist mill and saw mill; former operates all the year; the latter fall and spring.

Second dam, excelsior factory, E. C. Coombs, proprietor; annual product, $5,000.

Third dam, grist mill, Russell Eaton, proprietor; 11,000 bushels per annum.

Lower dam, factory of doors, sash and blinds, J. P. Wyman & Son, proprietors; 13 feet fall; 60 hands; annual product, $100,000.

Accessibility.—Augusta is connected with the seaboard by a line of railway, is about three hours distant from Portland, and eight from Boston. For about eight months of the year the river is open to the city, admitting the approach of vessels drawing 10 feet.

Population of Augusta, 1867, 8,000; valuation, $5,500,000.

AVON—FRANKLIN COUNTY.

From Selectmen's Returns.

Three Powers.

First, "Russell's Mills," on the outlet stream of Mount Blue pond, manufacture lumber. Operate four months in the year.

Second, one mile below, "Haines' Mill," manufactures lumber. These powers might be materially improved by a dam at the outlet of the pond, and raising the water some three or four feet, which the proprietors of the first power are authorized to do, there being a surface of more than three hundred acres. Rocks mostly granite, suitable for building purposes. The falls are each about fifteen feet.

Third, on a stream in the westerly part of the town, one and a half miles from Phillips village; lumber mills. Mills operate about three months. Fall less than fifteen feet.

The "Mount Blue Pond" drains an area of about fifteen hundred acres, two-thirds being forest; a large amount of spruce, hemlock, bass, maple, birch, suitable for manufacture and easy of access. Aggregate production, $4,000. Market, Farmington and Lewiston.

BAILEYVILLE—WASHINGTON COUNTY.

From the Statement of the Selectmen, the Returns of Calais, and Anson's Report of Survey.

Three Powers.

First, "Sprague's Falls," on the St. Croix, five miles above the Baring mills. Fall about twenty-five feet. "A magnificent water-power." At the head of the falls an island divides the river, and the St. Croix Log Driving Company have built a dam across the western channel. The power is unimproved. The Lewey's Island Railroad passes close by this privilege.

Second, "Enoch's Rips," one-half mile above Sprague's falls. Height of fall, nine feet. It is unimproved.

Third, the "Grand Falls," six miles above, just below the junction of the West and North branches. The falls consist of two pitches about half a mile apart, each pitch having a descent of about eighteen feet, and in combination constituting a power of the first magnitude. At the head of each fall is an island, with a dam from the island to the English side. It is unimproved.

A storage of four feet upon the two great Chiputneticook lakes would yield on the above falls, for ten hours a day, 312 days a year, a gross power of nearly 4,000 horse, or 160,000 spindles.

The extraordinary constancy of the volume of the St. Croix, its susceptibility of improvement in natural and artificial reservoirs of great size, the convenient lay of the land adjacent to the above falls, the abundance of building material in their vicinity, and their position not remote from navigable waters, with a railway in their neighborhood,—render the above mentioned privileges of the first value and of the highest capacity with reference to economical improvement. See reservoirs, page 119.

BALDWIN—CUMBERLAND COUNTY.

From Selectmen's Returns.

[See also "Baldwin and Hiram" and "Baldwin and Limington."]

Ten Powers

On Break-Neck brook, a stream in the west part of the town.

First, the "Burnell Privilege," on town road. Fall, in 100 feet, 20 feet, and a head of seven feet additional. Various saws. Stream falls rapidly from the mill. Water from bottom of dam runs a twenty-foot overshot wheel. If the mill were further down stream, there might be a larger wheel. Dam could be made higher. The water used to the best advantage would run the machinery now on the premises night and day the year round, or nearly so. The pond, as now flowed, about three acres. Mill very safe. Considerable lumber in vicinity.

Second, below, "Richardson's Privilege." Grist, shingle, and saw mills. Now run about half the year. Might be made to run the whole year by day. Head seven and a half feet, pond two acres. Dam could be raised two feet, and pond would flow three acres.

Third, below, "Little Falls." Not improved. Six feet fall, good chance to flow, a fine little privilege.

Fourth, below, "Bowers' Privilege," on town road; formerly a saw mill and grist mill; privilege not now occupied. Fall eight

Great Falls, Baldwin and Hiram.

feet; chance for a small pond with several feet head, and for another pond, above, of fifteen to twenty acres. Well situated, a good water-power.

Fifth, below, "Wetfoot Privilege." Not improved. Few feet fall; but high dam and large flowage feasible. A grist mill, or other light machinery, could be run the year round.

Sixth, on Dug-hill brook, "Clark's Mills," nine feet head, pond small, rake factory, saws, &c.; would run light machinery nearly or quite the year round.

Seventh, just above, "Harding's Privilege;" rake factory. Head nine feet, and water sufficient for the business.

Eighth, above, "Harding's Privilege." Dam eight feet, five feet water in the flume. Saw mill and rake factory; operate two or three months in the year. With help of upper pond, 22 acres, can run light machinery nearly the year round.

Ninth, above, "Flint's Privilege." Twenty-four-foot overshot wheel; shingle and spoke machine, saws, &c. Runs nearly the year round.

Tenth, on Quaker brook, "Dyer's Water-power." Fall and head ten feet. Saw mills. With tight dam and good machinery, might run an up-and-down saw nine months. Good privilege and very well situated.

BALDWIN—CUMBERLAND COUNTY, AND HIRAM—OXFORD COUNTY.

From the Surveys of Cyrus Ingalls and George Wadsworth, Civil Engineers.

[See also "Baldwin," and "Hiram."]

Two Powers.

First, "Great Falls," on Saco river, two and a half miles below Hiram bridge. Total fall 72 feet three and one-half inches in 55 rods. The distance and fall are divided as follows: The first 30 rods have a fall of 28 feet five and one-half inches; the next 15 rods, a fall of 23 feet; and the last 10 rods, a fall of 20 feet 10 inches.

The river for some distance above and below the falls is the boundary line between Hiram and Baldwin. Its bed and shores are mostly solid ledge the whole extent. The banks are high and bold; the land upon the east side rises to considerable height, but upon the west side is nearly level with high water mark. The river seldom overflows its banks.

The volume of water in a drouth is, in the present condition of the reservoirs of the river, comparatively small, probably not over 12,000 cubic feet per minute, that at Saco being 18,000 cubic feet. A dam of six feet at the falls would send the water back for nearly fifteen miles, and form a pond of at least a thousand acres, and greatly increase the available power, though at some expense for flowage. There are, as shown in Part II., page 77, fifteen or twenty square miles of lakes, ponds and swamps, in Hiram, Brownfield, Denmark, and other towns above, which could be at small expense turned into reservoirs, and the river made equal to the demands of very extensive manufacturing at the Great Falls.

If 12,000 cubic feet of water per minute can be realized in a drouth, the power of the whole fall is 1,614 horse, or 64,560 spindles; or 3,520 horse, or 140,800 spindles for 11 hours a day.

The average range from lowest to highest water at the Great Falls is about 12 feet.

Some years ago, the Water-Power Company of Saco cut a channel through the head of these falls, on the west side, and put in locks for the purpose of letting down water through the dry season of the year. There is no dam or other improvement.

The land upon the west bank is favorable for setting mills and factories a distance from the shore or bank, and taking water from the river. It is also quite favorable on the east side.

Second, half a mile below the foot of the "Great Falls," and extending nearly half a mile. The river is only six rods wide at the head of this fall and is rock bound. It widens to eight or ten rods lower down and has good banks on both sides. A fall of eight to ten feet. The Baldwin side is owned by the Saco Water Power Company and the Hiram side by Benjamin Goodwin. This fall has long been known as the "Great Falls' Wife," and offers a capital privilege for heavy operations. No improvement.

Building material of all sorts abundant.

Market, Portland, with which railroad connection will undoubtedly very speedily be effected. Stages now pass directly by the powers.

BALDWIN—CUMBERLAND COUNTY, AND LIMINGTON—YORK COUNTY.

From the Returns of Baldwin and Limington.

[See also "Baldwin," and "Limington."]

One Power.

"Highland Rips," on the Saco river, about midway the north line of Limington; height 15 feet in a horizontal distance of 40 rods. Width of river, 200 feet.

If the volume of the river at this point be assumed to be, in a drouth, 5,000 cubic feet per minute less than at Saco, or 13,000 cubic feet per minute for the 24 hours, the power of the fall is about 375 horse-power gross, day and night, or about 800 horse-power, 32,000 spindles, for 11 hours a day. It can be greatly increased by the use of reservoirs. See page 77, Part II.

It is unimproved.

Granite abundant and suitable for building close at hand.

Market, Portland.

BANCROFT PLANTATION—AROOSTOOK COUNTY.

From Assessors' Returns.

Three Powers.

First, "Bancroft Mills," on Baskahegan stream, half a mile above its junction with the Mattawamkeag river. Fall 26 feet in 75 rods. Grist and various saw mills. Small part of the available power used. A storage of four feet upon Baskahegan lake, tributary to the stream, would yield upon these falls, for the ordinary working hours of the year, a gross power of 1,250 horse or 49,000 spindles. To this should be added the *natural* low run of the stream. The storage could be used in four months, if desired, the natural flow sufficing for the rest of the year.

Second, "Holbrook Falls," on the outlet stream of Holbrook pond, which covers 3.50 square miles. Unimproved.

Third, "Ledge Falls," on Mattawamkeag river, about seven miles above the mouth of the Baskahegan stream, height fifteen feet in fifty rods. There are a great number of lakes and ponds above, that might be or already are used for reservoirs. See page 108, Part II. The river drains several hundred square miles of territory, so that the volume of water is large, and may be made comparatively constant at all seasons. Unimproved.

Underlying rock, limestone. The lay of the land about the falls favorable for the location of mills.

Market, Bangor, by military road, steamboat and railroad.

BANGOR—PENOBSCOT COUNTY.

From the Mayor's Returns.

[See also "Bangor and Brewer."]

Six Powers

On the Kenduskeag stream, viz., "Drummond's Mills," "McQuestion's Mills," "Bruce's Mills," "Hatch's Mills," "The

Four Mile Falls," and "Six Mile Falls." These are mentioned in their order, going up the stream.

Fall from ten to fifteen feet for each power. The first four flow back the Kenduskeag about one mile each; the Six Mile fall flows back over two miles.

The power of the series is indicated in the fact that Bruce's mills could saw from 2,500,000 to 3,000,000 feet of lumber annually.

There is a dam at each of the six powers except at Four Mile falls. Four of the powers are improved with mills, to wit: Drummond's, McQuestion's, Bruce's and Hatch's mills. One of said mills manufactures lumber and plaster, grinds grain, and has a trip hammer and wool carding machinery; one manufactures lumber and salt; the others, lumber only.

The mills run about seven months annually with full power; and for some time longer with less than full power.

Some of the machinery is of the best construction for economizing power. The Robbins wheel is used; also the old Stearns wheel, and several others. The centre-vent turbine wheels are generally used; some reacting.

The powers are owned by Messrs. Morse & Co., (two powers,) Stetson & Co., (one power,) Merrill and Sons, (one power,) and J. R. Lumbert, (two powers.)

The Kenduskeag stream is naturally connected with a few small ponds; and, artificially, could be readily connected, by an inexpensive two-mile canal, with the Pushaw pond, distant about three and a half miles from the stream. The Pushaw pond now covers an area of about twelve square miles; and, at little expense in the erection of dams, etc., could be converted into a reservoir of much greater area, wherein the water could be raised and held, five to seven feet above its natural level, to supply the Kenduskeag stream during drouth, or low water towards the end of summer. The stream is rapid, rises from eight to twelve feet during freshets, but is considered comparatively safe. The supply of water is not large during part of the summer.

The out-cropping and underlying rocks are slate, easily quarried, and much used as rough building material.

The lay of the land at *all* the various falls is *suitable,* and at most of the falls extremely favorable, for convenient location of mills and workshops. A small part of the basin of the stream is wooded.

Market. Lumber is shipped from Bangor direct, to almost every port where there is a sale for it; but the principal markets are Boston, New York and the West Indies. The Penobscot river (when not closed by ice) is the usual, as well as best and cheapest, channel of transportation.

The soil is mostly clayey loam, with some small areas of gravel, and has generally a hard pan of clay. In most localities the soil is very retentive of water, and is relieved only by thorough drainage.

Bangor and Brewer—Penobscot County.

From the Returns of Mayor Wakefield of Bangor, and from the Survey of Hiram F. Mills, Engineer of the Hydrographic Survey for the Eastern Division.

[See also "Bangor," and "Brewer."]

One Power.

"Treat's Falls," on the Penobscot river, one mile above the harbor proper of Bangor, and within one mile of the city Post Office. The falls are now flowed by high tide, but to what depth is not stated. The total range of the ebb and flow in the harbor one mile below, is from twelve to eighteen feet; range from lowest to highest water on the river proper (above tide) about twelve feet. A dam fifteen feet above mean high tide will pond the water back about four miles. The privilege is owned by Messrs. Leavitt, Weston, and others. For further information respecting the privilege, I subjoin the statement (or the essential portions of it) of Hiram F. Mills, C. E.

"The circumstances under which my determination of the volume of the river was made were these: In the spring of 1866 I examined the river and made inquiries of the men connected with the mills from Milford to Bangor, for the purpose of determining the least quantity that flowed in the river in the extremely dry seasons of 1864 and 1865, and the greatest quantity in time of freshet. The latter I succeeded in getting quite to my satisfaction, as one of the greatest freshets known occurred during my observations, when there was flowing 96,000 cubic feet per second.

The actual quantity flowing in the greatest drouth could not at that time be determined; but I was fortunate in obtaining data by which I could, by measurements made at this time, determine the quantity actually *used* in that dryest time, and thus know a quantity which could, with certainty, be relied upon in an extreme drought, and one upon which estimates could be based with safety. This quantity I found to have been 1,950 cubic feet per second, exclusive of that used at the sluice for passing rafts.

The quantity here excluded I could not at the time form a judgment upon, as the quantity required was not only that for passing the rafts through the sluice but over the rapids between the sluice and the race from the mills. This was evidently in excess of the quantity that would be required at a well constructed sluice at Treat's falls for the passage of rafts; hence I could report that at Treat's falls there would be supplied constantly through the twenty-four hours, in the greatest drought, the quantity necessary for the passage of rafts, together with 1,950 cubic feet per second, that could be applied to manufacturing purposes; and having to report without seeing the river in its lowest stage, I could only, from the data gathered and my measurements, express my confidence that the quantity that can be relied upon is in excess of this, probably twenty-five per cent., possibly fifty per cent.

This quantity was, however, the base of my computation of results, providing, of course, room for the use of any further quantity that could be realized.

With a constant fall of fifteen feet and no pond, the amount of power that could be derived from this water would be, in gross, 3,315 horse-powers.

With the proposed dam at Treat's falls to a height of fifteen feet above mean high tide, with flash boards two feet high in time of drought, the above amount used in connection with the pond and so much of the tide as can be used to advantage, will furnish during the working hours of the dryest day a power in gross of 9,000 horse-powers, leaving the surface of the water at evening level with the top of solid dam.

During the night the pond will fill to top of flash boards, besides allowing the constant use of 1,473 horse-powers.

The advantage that can be taken of the tide in connection with the large pond above the dam, with the use of turbine wheels, is shown in this increase of power from 3,315 horse-powers to 9,000 horse-powers. This result is derived from calculating the experience of the worst day of a dry season in which the circumstances would be, 1,950 cubic feet of water per second being supplied by the river, and high tide a half hour after starting the factories in the morning, the pond being full to top of flash boards.

This is one of the many cases in which in an unimproved river the quantity of water flowing and the fall are items by themselves quite inadequate to present the capabilities of the river for the development of power.

The 9,000 horse-powers that can be derived from the Penobscot by the construction of a dam at Treat's falls, can be increased to 13,500 horse-powers at this point by constructions up the river, similar to those upon the Merrimac.

The site selected for the dam at Treat's falls is underlaid by a continuous ledge of good quality throughout, and there is no question of the practicability of constructing a dam there which shall be permanent, and never require repairs that will interfere with the daily use of the water of the river.

The length of the overfall designed is 828 feet. The total length of canals will be a little less than half that in Lowell to supply the same power to the same area, and the expense of constructing them here will be very light. The wheels will deliver their water directly into the river, thus obviating the expense of constructing long races at a low level.

The area for factory sites directly below the dam is ample for the use of the power when fully developed, and remarkably well adapted for this use. Entire safety in time of freshets will be secured.

The material for foundations is very good, being over the greater part of the area ledge, at a convenient depth, and where not of ledge of hard gravel and clay.

Building stone of superior quality for foundations is found in available positions in the immediate vicinity, and the excellent Brewer bricks are manufactured close at hand.

The expense of constructing factories on these sites will be unusually small, and there will be the great and unusual advantage of both railroad communication and of free navigation in deep tide water to and from the factory yards."

Baring—Washington County.

From the Returns of C. F. Todd, Esq., of Calais.

One Power.

"Baring Mills," on the St. Croix, three miles above the mills at Milltown, (Calais.) A dam extends across the river at this point, and gives about 10 feet head at a high stage of the river. Improvements are as follows:

English side.	*American side.*
Six gangs; three single saws, six lath machines, three shingle machines.	One gang; one lath machine, one shingle machine, one carding machine (not in operation.)
Will cut 15,000,000 of long lumber, 15,000,000 laths, 2,500,000 shingles.	Will cut 2,000,000 feet lumber, 2,000,000 laths, 1,000,000 shingles.

A building has recently been erected, 40 by 60 feet, three stories high, for a woollen mill.

BARNARD—PISCATAQUIS COUNTY.

From Selectmen's Returns.

Several Powers.

"Bear Brook" has fall sufficient at several points to run a considerable amount of machinery the entire year, except in an extremely dry season.

Saw and grist mill in operation at one point. Saw and shingle machine on the east or main branch of the stream. Also a saw mill at Egery & Williams' slate quarry on the West branch of the stream. This stream is not half so large as Bear brook proper, or East branch; yet they expect to saw heavy lumber and run machinery for quarrying purposes.

Valuable power for quarrying purposes on the Green brook, as there are several slate ledges and veins along its banks. Also on Front and Wells brooks.

The best of slate in this town. The Egery and Williams' quarry has been in operation one year, and so successfully, that it could not be purchased for ten times its cost one year ago. The product is fully equal if not superior to any slate in this country. There are specimens of slate about five feet square, and about one-fourth of an inch thick, as it came from the ledge.

An immense amount of lumber of all kinds, especially spruce, hemlock and cedar. Hemlock is almost inexhaustible. We do not think there is another place in the State where the *Extract of Hemlock* could be manufactured with a greater certainty of success. Land is now very cheap in this town.

BATH—SAGADAHOC COUNTY.

From the Returns of James Wakefield, Esq.

Three Powers.

"Sewall's Mill," a tide power, fall 13 feet, twenty horse-powers, will grind 10,000 bushels of grain, and saw 200,000 of lumber. One saw operates eight months. Two wheels, H. Blake's patent, thirty and thirty-six inches in diameter each.

"Rogers' Mill," a tide mill on Whiskeag stream, sixteen horse-powers, will saw 300,000 of lumber. One saw, operates nine months yearly. Kendall wheel.

"Winnegance Mill Dam Company's privilege," a tide power, three hundred and thirty-three horse-powers, will saw 16,000,000 of lumber, operates nine months. Kendall wheel.

Market, Bath, Portland and Boston, by rail and sea.

Two-thirds of the above power (Winnegance) is in Phipsburg; one-third in Bath.

Belfast—Waldo County.

Returns of John H. Quimby, Esq.

Ten Powers, and More.

On "Goose river," which empties into Belfast bay, directly opposite the wharves of the city, on the eastern side of the harbor. Fall 185 feet in three-fourths of a mile, the river running that distance over a ledge. It flows from Goose pond, in Swanville, six miles from Belfast, which pond contains thirteen hundred acres, with a great depth, and a large water shed draining into it. It is also fed by springs from its bottom which makes a steady supply of water during the entire year.

At the outlet of this pond, there is a solid stone dam, so that there never has been or can be any freshet upon the river to do damage to buildings or dams, that are or may be erected thereon. About one-half of the powers upon said river are now occupied.

First. At the mouth of the river near the bay, there is now in process of construction a stone dam, which, when completed, will be, on top, 300 feet long and 20 feet wide; and 26 feet wide at the bottom, 30 feet in height, built upon a ledge. The salt water flows at full tide at the face of this dam, 10 feet, leaving a head of water in the pond at full tide of 20 feet, and at or near low tide of 30 feet.

There are also wharves being built upon each side of said stream, extending from the dam 325 feet to the bay, one of which will be 140 feet wide; they will be of solid rock and gravel, and vessels drawing from 12 to 14 feet of water can load or discharge at the wharves at the foot of this dam.

The pond at this dam will contain 15 or 20 acres, and the main travelled road from Belfast to Searsport crosses the pond about 50 rods above the dam. The volume of water at this dam will be equal to 185 horse-power, (this power being calculated upon a turbine wheel about five feet in diameter.) This privilege is not occupied.

Second. The next fall above on said river has 48 feet head, equal to 850 horse-powers, and is not occupied.

Third. The next above this has 15 feet head, equal to 114 horse-powers, with a stone dam, and is occupied for a grist mill.

Fourth. The next fall above has 14 feet head, equal to 100 horse-powers, has a stone dam, occupied for manufacture of paper.

Fifth. The next fall has 10 feet head, equal to 62 horse-powers, has a stone dam, is occupied for the manufacture of paper.

Sixth. The next has 18 feet head, equal to 150 horse-powers, has a nice stone dam, is occupied for the manufacture of paper.

Seventh. The next has 10 feet head, equal to 62 horse-powers, has a stone dam, is occupied for axe factory.

Eighth. The next has 10 feet head, equal to 62 horse-powers, has a stone dam, is occupied for an axe factory, ("Whiting's axe factory.")

Ninth. The next has 13 feet head, equal to 92 horse-powers, has stone dam, and is occupied for the manufacture of paper.

Tenth. The next and last, the "Mason dam," has a fall of 25 feet head, equal to 240 horse-powers, has a stone dam, and is unoccupied.

The powers on the stream used for the manufacture of paper, are occupied by the Messrs. Russell, from the firm of William Russell & Sons, Lawrence. The axe factories by Messrs. B. Kelley & Son, and Isaac L. Dunton.

The power used for a grist mill with those below, including the dam at the outlet, are the property of Hiram E. Pierce, Esq.

There are also several other small water-powers within the limits of the city, but none that in size or volume can compare with this, and they are mostly located at such points, that no heavy manufactory could be established upon them; they are mostly occupied for saw, stave, shingle, grist and plaster mills.

BELGRADE—KENNEBEC COUNTY.

From Selectmen's Statement.

Three Powers.

First, "Belgrade Mills;" fall ten feet; saw, shingle and grist mills, which have constant employment; also a factory for the manufacture of thread-spools and excelsior, which does a large amount of business, using annually 5,000 cords of birch and poplar wood.

The power is very inadequately employed, considering the great supply of water and excellence of the location, it being situated at the outlet of Great pond, which is about eight miles in length, and has an average width of two and a half miles, and is supplied by North, McGraw, and other ponds, besides numerous large and small streams. This power is situated six miles from the Maine Central Railroad station at Belgrade.

Second, at the outlet of McGrath pond, at the present time undergoing improvement, there having been erected the present season, 1867, a building forty by fifty feet, three stories high, intended for machinery of various descriptions; already in operation, various saw mills, and grist mill, with room and power for more mills during a portion of the season. Height of fall, ten feet.

Third, below the above powers, on the outlet of McGrath pond, formerly saw, and shingle machine; at present not used. A valuable power.

BELMONT—WALDO COUNTY.

From Selectmen's Returns.

Three Powers.

First, on "Tilden Stream," the outlet of Tilden pond; fall twenty-four feet in half a mile.

Second, on "Green Stream;" fall twenty feet in a half mile.

Third, on "Cross Stream;" fall fifteen feet in one-fourth mile.

The above streams are connected each with a pond two miles in circumference. Two mills upon them, which operate about six months. Capacity of the lakes can be increased by dams. One-fourth of the basin wooded.

Market, Belfast, by road.

BENEDICTA PLANTATION—AROOSTOOK COUNTY.

Statement of the Assessors.

There is no water power in this plantation.

BENTON—KENNEBEC COUNTY.

From Selectmen's Returns.

Five Powers.

The "Lower Falls," on the Sebasticook river, about half a mile from the south line of the town. Height twelve feet in half a mile. Works all the year. Grist and various saw mills, and brush-handle factory.

The "Upper Falls," half a mile above the Lower falls. Height ten feet in one mile. Works all the year. Saw mill and match factory.

The "Nine Mile Rips," about one mile above the Upper falls. Height from eight to twelve feet in one mile. No improvements. Could work all the year if improved.

"Hunt's Mill," on the Fifteen-Mile stream. Fall nine feet, horizontal run one mile. No improvements.

"Hanscom's Mills," on Fifteen-Mile stream. Height fifteen feet in two miles. Improvements, various saws, planing, last, and shingle machines, and tannery.

The mills on the Fifteen-Mile stream operate about three-fourths of the year; the tannery all the year.

Machinery not of the best sort for economizing power. Kimball, Tuttle, and Atkins wheels; the last regarded the best.

The power on the Sebasticook could be greatly increased by the improvement of the ponds for reservoirs. An artificial reservoir of 1,000 acres could be readily constructed on Fifteen-Mile stream, above Hanscom's Mills. This stream also connects with Albion pond. See reservoirs, Part II, pages 95–96.

No danger from freshets; range of water on the Sebasticook a little over six feet; on the Fifteen-Mile stream about six feet.

Rocks, granite and slate; excellent for building purposes. Lay of the land about the falls convenient for the erection of mills.

Value of Aggregate Products. At Hanscom's mills, $27,000; Sebasticook lower falls, $10,000; Sebasticook upper falls, $6,000.

Accessibility.—The Sebasticook upper and lower falls are about two miles distant from the depot of the Maine Central Railroad at Kendall Mills. Hunt's and Hanscom's are about four miles from the depot of the same railroad at Clinton. Lumber goes to Augusta and other points by water.

BERWICK—YORK COUNTY.

From the Returns of the Selectmen.

Six Powers.

All on Salmon Falls river, the first four constituting the "Great Falls," and the last two the "Salmon Falls." More definitely—

No 1, the Mast Point Privilege,		8 feet fall.
No. 2, Great Falls Manufacturing Co.'s	upper level,	33 "
No. 3, " " " "	2d "	33 "
No. 4, " " " "	3d "	33 "
No. 5, Salmon Falls, " "	upper "	19 "
No. 6, " " " "	lower "	22 "

Total, 148 feet, of which 107 are obtained in two miles, and 41 in about 50 rods.

No. 1 is simply a feeder for the next three. It is filled by night and drawn down by day, and thus no water runs to waste by night. It is supplied by the reservoir ponds above, from which is drawn in twenty-four hours what the mills of the Great Falls Manufacturing Company use in eleven. This quantity is 409 cubic feet of water per second, which if used on a fall of eight feet would give an absolute power of 371 horse-power, but the great variation in the head renders it of little value for operations at dam No. 1.

The above quantity flows to Nos. 2, 3 and 4, successively, and would give 1,530 horse-powers to each, or 4,590 horse-powers to the three. It then flows to Nos. 5 and 6, and would give respectively 880 and 973 horse-powers. As the thread of the Salmon Falls river is the boundary line between this State and New Hampshire, only one-half this power, or 3,221 horse-powers, is in this State.

The power on Nos. 2, 3, 5 and 6, or 5,913 horse-powers, is all taken up by cotton mills, and about a quarter of No. 4 by a small woollen mill. Three-quarters of this, or 1,148 horse-powers, are as available in this State as in New Hampshire.

The mills run all the year. The wheels are turbines and breast, and the useful effect is two-thirds of the power expended, i. e., the power above given.

The first three privileges, and the ponds mentioned below, are owned by the Great Falls Manufacturing Company, and the last two by the Salmon Falls Manufacturing Company.

The stream is fed by eight ponds, all used as reservoirs, and containing 3,759 acres, mostly in this State. The above are all the ponds connected with the stream. Dams are already erected as high as possible without serious damage to rail and highways.

Destructive freshets are unknown. By the exercise of its right of controlling the reservoirs, the Great Falls Manufacturing Company maintains a uniform stream the year round. In the spring freshets a rise of three feet is an unusual occurrence.

Underlying rocks, granite and trap. Brick clay is also abundant. No difficulty in locating mills, &c. One-eighth of the basin covered with woods.

As regards the effect of the improvement of the power, there was little more than a bare settlement before the building of the mills. Estimates from the census of 1860 show that in Berwick, Somersworth and Rollinsford, a population of about 9,000 has been brought together by the erection of mills on the falls above described.

Annual production in 1856, for example, 27,534,255 yards cloth, valued at the mills at $910,571.49.

Market, Boston, by rail or water, after four miles of teaming.

Several small powers in town, as Horn's saw mill, Goodrich's saw mill, Spencer's shingle mill, all on Little river; Guptill's saw mill and shingle mill on Beaver Dam brook; McIntire's sash, door and blind factory on Salmon Falls brook, etc.

BETHEL—OXFORD COUNTY.

From the Statement of C. F. Walker, Esq., and of the Selectmen.

Seven Powers.

Five on "Alder Stream," which is the outlet of ponds covering 1,000 acres, and has a descent of 70 feet in one-fourth of a mile.

First, the upper, Hodsdon & Brown's saw and shingle mill; fall 12 feet; works about five months in the year. With improved machinery could operate all the year.

Second, Russell's Bedstead and Furniture Mill; fall 11 feet; works all the year. Machinery not economical of power. Capable of turning out with best machinery 10,000 bedsteads per annum. L. & L. W. Russell.

Third, Walker's grist and flour mill; fall 15 feet; three runs of stones; works all the year. Very superior building. Machinery good, but not the best for economizing power. Would grind 100,000 bushels per annum with best wheel. Owned by C. F. Walker.

Fourth, Ripley's shingle and threshing mill, fall six feet. Machinery of poor construction. Would saw 2,400,000 shingles with suitable wheel.

Fifth, unimproved; fall about six feet.

All the above powers are situated within three or four rods of the Grand Trunk Railway, which runs beside the stream for some distance. They are all perfectly safe against freshets or ice, the stream being fed almost wholly by ponds. The largest pond could be raised four feet or more for a reservoir, at little expense.

Sixth, Chapman Brook power; fall 20 feet.

Seventh, on "Mill brook," in Bethel village.

Granite abundant.

Market, Portland, by Grand Trunk Railway.

BIDDEFORD—YORK COUNTY.

Statement of J. G. Garland, Esq.

[See also "Biddeford and Saco."]

Two Powers.

First, "Swan-Pond Falls," on the outlet stream of Swan pond, a short distance from Saco river; eight feet head and fall, 20 horse-power for eight months of the year. Saw mill.

Second, "Curtis Falls," on Little river, not far from its mouth; eight feet head and fall, 15 horse-power for eight months of the year. Saw mill.

BIDDEFORD AND SACO—YORK COUNTY.

From the Returns of the Mayor of Saco, and from the Statement and Plan furnished by J. G. Garland, Esq., of Biddeford.

[See also "Biddeford," and "Saco."]

Two Powers.

First "Saco Falls," on the Saco river, four miles from its mouth and at the head of tide. There are two pitches; the upper eight feet; the lower 32 feet; about an eighth of a mile apart. The river is divided at the lower falls into two channels; the "main river" and the "east branch."

Volume of water.—In the time of extreme low water, in a drouth, 18,000 cubic feet per minute for the 24 hours are commanded, or about 40,000 cubic feet for 11 hours a day. The water is so carefully husbanded and the machinery is so excellent, that the power realized is 150,000 spindles for the class of goods now manufactured.

13

Upon reference to Part II, page 77, it will be seen that the development of the reservoirs of the river would increase the power at this point very greatly. The more important improvements however, as the storage of Gt. Ossipee pond to a larger depth, and the conversion into reservoirs of the low lands above Great Falls, would be attended with considerable expense for flowage.

In ordinary seasons there is much more power at lowest run than the above specified; and in all seasons a far greater amount for nine or ten months of the year.

Lay of the land.—Naturally only moderately favorable, the banks being rough, high, and composed of tough ledge. The best of granite within a mile.

Accessibility.—The falls are a short distance only from railroad to Portland and Boston; and as stated above, are at the head of tide, vessels drawing 10 feet coming to the foot of the lower fall. River open to navigation eight or nine months of the year.

Improvements.—On the Saco side:—On the upper fall a gang saw mill turning out 30,000 feet lumber per 24 hours; single saw 7,000 feet; box machines making 300 sugar-box shooks per day; heading machines capable of turning out 500 pairs hogshead heads daily.

On the lower fall and main river the York Corporation, 454 horse-powers. H. Temple, agent, five mills, 25,000 spindles, capital stock, $1,200,000; employing 300 males at an average of $1.50 per day; 600 females at $1.00 per day. Goods furnished, tickings, denims, pantaloon stuff, etc. Also on the lower fall, east branch of the river, a grist mill with three runs of stones; a plaster mill; a manufactory of carriage wheels; planing, turning; also unemployed water-power, 50,000 spindles thereof, available nine months of the year.

Annual production of all the powers in Saco: of the cotton manufactures, $1,000,000; of the lumber manufactures, $250,000. Power on the Saco side, owned by the Saco Water-Power Company; agent, Thomas Quimby, Biddeford. About 40 horse-powers of steam-power are employed in Saco in tanneries and brick yard. Population of Saco, 6,000; six churches; 13 school-houses; 20 school-rooms; expenses for schools, 1866, $7,456.02. Valuation, 1866, $3,358,460.

Power on the Biddeford side, owned by the Laconia Company, Pepperell Company, and Saco Water-Power Machine Shop Company. Products for 1867 about $7,000,000.

Second, "Little Falls," on Saco river, five feet four inches fall in 80 rods. The channel is straight and smooth and about five feet deep. Not improved.

Bingham—Somerset County.

From Selectmen's Returns.

[See also "Bingham and Moscow."]

One Power.

"Holway's Shingle Machine," on Fall brook. Works about three months.

Market, Skowhegan, and other points on the Kennebec.

Bingham and Moscow—Somerset County.

From the Returns of Bingham and Moscow.

[See also "Bingham," and "Moscow."]

One Power.

"Goodrich's Mills," on the Austin stream. Three-fourths of the dam is in Moscow; saw, grist, shingle, clapboard and lath mills, in Bingham. Operates the whole year; but owing to a leaky dam has to stop in a severe drouth.

Numerous and large ponds above on the stream. See page 96, Austin ponds. Freshets heavy. Slate rock abundant about the fall. Basin of the stream nearly all covered with forests.

Market, Skowhegan, twenty-five miles distant.

Blanchard—Piscataquis County.

From Selectmen's Returns, and a Plan of the Streams.

Several Powers.

The Piscataquis West branch for the distance of a mile has a fall of 200 or 300 feet, and is a violent torrent. The banks are very rough and ledgy, so that only a part of the power could be put to use except at considerable expense. These are the so-called "Grand Falls." They are situated below the forks of the west branch.

"Blanchard Village Power," eight feet fall; water for saw, shingle, and grist mills, nine months of the year.

In the southwest corner of the town, on Thorn brook, the outlet of ponds; formerly used for saw and shingle mills, not in use at present; large reservoirs feasible.

Numerous lakes in connection with the streams, all susceptible of improvement at little cost. See last part of the first Table, Part II, page 107. Freshets harmless. Building stone abundant and good.

Market, Dexter, twenty miles distant.

BLUEHILL—HANCOCK COUNTY.

From Selectmen's Statement.

Numerous Powers.

Several on the outlet stream of the "Four Ponds;" ponds, 300 acres, can be flowed sufficiently to run two saws the entire year. The extreme length of stream and ponds three and one-half miles. Upper pond elevated about 200 feet above the mouth of the stream. Two falls *occupied* on the stream.

"Allen's Mill," at its mouth, about three and one-half miles from Bluehill village. An old-fashioned fly wheel. Can be run about four months in the year, and will cut about 300,000 feet of lumber.

About two miles from Allen's mill, and about one and three-fourths miles from the village, "Grindle & Stover's Mills," saw and shingle. Stave mill has a horizontal paddle wheel, saws about 200,000 staves per year.

Several upon the "Head of the Bay Stream." Stream is about six miles in length. The "upper dam," about one and one-fourth miles from the mouth of the stream, flows 100 acres as a reservoir. 100 or 125 feet fall from dam to mouth of stream.

Four mills on this stream, on as many different dams, all within 100 rods of its mouth, viz: saw, grist, shingle, and stave mills; each having a head and fall of about 12 feet. Mills operate four months yearly.

One or more on Noyes' pond stream, with a pond of about 50 acres. A saw mill at its mouth, old-fashion fly wheel. Abundance of water for one saw in the wet season of the year, but fails soon.

Some are located upon McHeard's stream, three and a half miles in length, and connected with a pond of about 30 acres, which holds out most of the year. Saw, shingle, and stave mills. Old-fashion fly and tub wheels run about half the time.

As many more and quite as eligible falls unoccupied on the above named streams.

"Tide Mill," 10 acres of pond, grist mill, horizontal paddle wheel, with ordinary tides, has sufficient water to drive all its machinery.

About 200 rods south of the tide mill, are situated "Bluehill Falls." This, as a tide-water power, is probably unsurpassed in the State. The full flow of the tide rushes through a passage about 175 feet in width at high water mark, into a basin or pond, about two miles in length and half a mile in breadth. Tributary to the pond are the Four Ponds stream, above named, and one other stream nearly as large, besides several smaller ones. This fall can be easily dammed, there being abundance of good granite within one-fourth of a mile.

BOOTHBAY—LINCOLN COUNTY.

From Selectmen's Returns.

Three Powers.

First, at the outlet of Adams' pond, a saw and carding machine. Former operates four months.

Second, at the outlet of Reed's pond.

Third, on Mill-Cove stream.

Artificial reservoirs of medium capacity are feasible. Suitable rocks for building.

BOWDOIN—SAGADAHOC COUNTY.

From Selectmen's Returns.

Nine Powers.

First, on Eaton stream in the east part of the town, carding, fulling and threshing machines. Fall about 15 feet.

Second, below, a very good privilege, old grist mill not used, fall of 12 feet. The above would run half of the time throughout the year.

Third, in the northeast part of the town, saw and shingle mill on Dead river. Fall about eight feet. If the dam were good, would saw three-fourths of the year. Large quantities of hemlock, spruce and all kinds of hard wood near this mill.

Fourth, two miles below, on the Cathance stream, the "Huff Mill." Head of 10 feet, and the best mill privilege in town.

Fifth, Sixth, etc. Two or three good privileges for mills of any kind on this river, with enough water to carry a saw mill three-fourths of the year.

Eighth, a grist mill at the outlet of Cæsar's pond; fall 10 feet. Mill operates about half of the time.

Ninth, saw, grist, shingle, picket and threshing machines on Purington stream; fall eight feet; water enough to carry most of the machinery about one-half of the time.

BOWDOINHAM—SAGADAHOC COUNTY.

Selectmen's Statement.

The water-power in this town is unimportant.

BOWERBANK—PISCATAQUIS COUNTY.

From Selectmen's Returns.

Several Powers.

On Mill brook, Long-pond and Buttermilk streams. None are employed.

Long pond covers 1.50 square miles. A 20-foot fall, in Howard, on its outlet.

The Buttermilk stream is tributary to Long pond. There are three ponds upon said stream.

At the foot of the lower is a privilege upon which by fluming a fall of twenty feet can be had.

A good site above, at the foot of one of the ponds.

Ponds can be flowed, also swamp land. Abundant stone for building; basin of streams nearly all forest-covered.

"We are in great need of mills, as the nearest are six miles off."

Market, Dover, by road.

BOWTOWN TOWNSHIP—SOMERSET COUNTY.

Statement of Joseph Clark, Esq., of Carratunk.

[See also "Bowtown Township and Forks Plantation," also "Bowtown Township and Township No. 1."]

Several Powers.

Situated on the outlet stream of Pierce pond. Stream is very rapid throughout, and at several points can be used advantageously for power. The pond covers 3.50 square miles, and is raised 10 feet, forming a large reservoir. Storage now used for log-driving.

Powers all unimproved.

BOWTOWN TOWNSHIP AND FORKS PLANTATION—SOMERSET COUNTY.

Statement of J. M. Haynes, Esq., of Augusta.

[See also "Bowtown Township," and "Forks Plantation."

One Power.

"Stand-Up Rips," on the Kennebec river, one mile above the Forks, 20 feet fall in 100 feet, ledge bottom, good site for dam, ready of access, would operate heavy machinery the year through.

No improvement.

BOWTOWN TOWNSHIP AND TOWNSHIP NO. 1—SOMERSET COUNTY.

Statement of J. M. Haynes, Esq., of Augusta.

[See also "Bowtown Township," and "Township No. 1."]

Several Powers.

The "Dead River Rapids," on the Dead river, between the Forks and Grand falls, a distance of twelve miles. The descent is gradual, the current swift, with good sites for dams; the volume of water, by the use of the numerous ponds above, can be made constant and large at all seasons; the ponds are already to a considerable extent improved for storage for log-driving. See page 95.

None of the privileges improved.

BRADFORD—PENOBSCOT COUNTY.

From the Selectmen's Returns, and a Plan of the Streams.

Ten Powers, Small.

Four on the west branch of Dead stream, each of which will run a saw for half the year. One in the north part of the town. Three in the east part of the town. Two on Farber brook in the west part of the town, which will operate about four months.

No lakes or ponds in the vicinity. Total products, in value, about $8,000.

Market, Bangor.

BRADLEY—PENOBSCOT COUNTY.

[See Appendix.]

BRASSUA TOWNSHIP—SOMERSET COUNTY.

Statement of Heman Whipple, Esq., of Solon.

One Power, or More.

About two miles above the lake, fall ten feet; more may be had. Good site for dam. Several small falls above.

Quite a number of small ponds on various streams for reservoirs.

BREMEN—LINCOLN COUNTY.

From Selectmen's Returns.

Four Powers.

First and Second, on the outlet of Muscongus pond. Upper power is about a mile above the lower, and the lower is at the head of tide. Fall of forty feet in a mile. The upper power is improved in a saw and grist mill. The lower power is not used. About 1,500,000 of lumber are cut annually. Mills operate about seven months.

Third, a tide power, "Keen's Mill Pond," near the centre of the town. Not improved.

Fourth, a tide power, "Broadcove Mill Stream," in the northern part of the town. Not improved.

The tide flows and ebbs about ten feet. Muscongus pond is a mile long and half a mile wide; can be made a good reservoir. Artificial reservoirs feasible at small expense. Rock, mostly granite. Basin one-half wooded.

Market, all points by water.

BREWER—PENOBSCOT COUNTY.

From Selectmen's Returns.

Seven Powers.

All situated on Segeunkedunk stream, within a running distance of two and a half miles. The height of the falls, beginning at the lower, is twenty, fourteen, four, twelve, ten, fourteen and twelve feet respectively.

One gang of saws, two single saws, and a shingle mill, all upon tide water at Brewer village. This power is estimated at 150 horse; an excellent site for cotton or woollen factory.

The shingle and grist mills operate all the year; the saw mills about eight months. Breast wheel.

Stream connected with two ponds, one three and five-tenths by one mile, the other one by one mile; it has also the flowage of 2,200 acres of meadow. The large pond has a dam ten feet high; could have four feet more head.

Freshets harmless; stream very constant; in full working condition even when the mills on the Penobscot are stopped for want of water.

The saw mills cut about 4,000,000 feet of lumber annually. Small part of the power used.

Market, all points by sea; vessels load at wharves close by the mills.

BRIDGTON—CUMBERLAND COUNTY.

Selectmen's Statement.

Twenty-Two Powers.

First to Twelfth, inclusive. On Stevens' brook, the outlet of Crotched pond; capable of working machinery from that of a saw and grist mill to a large woollen factory. Dam at outlet of pond will reserve five feet of water. First, "Cumberland Mills," 12 feet fall. Second, four feet fall; sash and blind factory, both owned by R. Gibbs. Third, saw mill, carriage factory, and foundry; B. Walker. Fourth, 12 feet fall, "Pondicherry Mills," machine shop, and grist mill; Storer Bros., Davis & Littlefield. Fifth, "Johnson's Falls," 12 feet; saw mill. Sixth and Seventh, sites for two dams, fall 28 feet; unimproved. Eighth, 12 feet fall, "Forest Mill, No. 1." Ninth, 12 feet fall, "Forest Mill, No. 2," all owned by Taylor & Perry. Tenth and Eleventh, sites, fall 25 feet; unimproved; owned by S. F. Perley, Esq. Twelfth; site, 20 feet fall; owned by H. Little; unimproved. Total fall about 150 feet in one and one-half miles.

Thirteenth and Fourteenth. On Wood's pond outlet. First, 10 feet fall; saw and grist mill, Berry Bros. Second, 10 feet fall; grist mill.

Fifteenth and Sixteenth. At North Bridgton. First, 20 feet, bedstead and furniture factory, saw and grist mill; Hon. L. Brown. Second, 16 feet fall; tannery and shingle mill, F. W. Tarr.

Seventeenth and Eighteenth. On Bear brook. First, 12 feet fall; saw and grist mill, A. Sampson. Second, site, fall not reported; unimproved; E. Adams.

Nineteenth. On Adams' pond outlet, South Bridgton; 12 feet; carriage factory, O. J. Libby.

Twentieth, Twenty-First and Twenty-Second. On Ingalls pond outlet, three dams. First, 20 feet fall; saw mill. Second, eight feet fall; grist mill, by Fosters. Third, 10 feet; machine shop, by Knapps.

The dams on Stevens' brook are chiefly of granite laid in cement; those on the other streams with very few exceptions are permanently made of stone and gravel. Generally the best of machinery is employed.

Annual production of the various mills, $600,000.

Amount of water in Stevens' brook, from Crotched pond to Pondicherry mills, 300 square inches, under 12 feet fall; including said mills to Long pond, 450 square inches, under 12 feet fall. The Woods pond outlet falls into Stevens' brook above Pondicherry mills. Power of the other streams is sufficient to drive all the machinery that is employed, during ordinary seasons.

Stevens' brook is supplied by Crotched pond, area of about three square miles, and that by Stevens' pond, of one square mile. Also by Woods pond, of one and a half square miles, and that by another of 50 acres. Brown's is supplied by Moose pond, area one and a half square miles. Sampson's by Bear pond, of one square mile. Libby's by Adams' pond, three fourths square mile. Reservoirs of 100 to 500 acres could be made, and at trifling cost. Several of said ponds could be raised. Perhaps 50 per cent. of the above power is in use. There is a constant supply of water, with one or two exceptions, for all the powers named in the foregoing list.

Granite in ledge and boulders sufficient for all building purposes. Buildings principally of wood above the basement. Clay in abundance for making the best of brick.

Fifty per cent. of the basin of the streams covered with forest. Lay of land for building, above the average.

Market, Bridgton and adjoining towns; Portland and Boston; conveyance, canal in summer, team and railroad in winter.

BRIDGEWATER—AROOSTOOK COUNTY.

From Selectmen's Returns.

Five Powers.

First, the "Bond Power," on the Presque Isle stream of the St. John, forty rods from Maine State line. The dam is chiefly natural, and the artificial part rests on solid rock. Grist, saw and two shingle mills. Properly managed, this power would run twelve months in the year a grist mill, a gang saw mill, two shingle machines, a machine shop, and a large woollen and cotton factory. Immediately above the mill the Whitney brook connects with the stream forming a part of the mill pond. There are no lakes of any account on the Presque Isle stream. Small proportion of this power used.

Second, "Whitney Brook Power," a natural privilege just across the point made by the Presque Isle stream and Whitney brook. A good site for dam (which would be very short) on a rock. Large flowage and plenty of reservoirs at the head of the brook. This would drive the machinery of a large woollen factory, machine shop, &c., all the year.

Third, Fourth, and Fifth, good privileges on the Presque Isle stream, from one to four miles above. All are capable of supplying water for a small amount of machinery nearly all the year, if properly managed. Lumber of the best quality on the streams, which would furnish work for two saw mills twenty years.

BRIGHTON—SOMERSET COUNTY.

From Selectmen's Returns.

Four Powers.

First and Second, upper and lower "Weeks' Falls," on the Wesserunsett river. The lower fall has thirty feet descent in four rods, with a stone dam at the head; no mills. Upper fall has saw, grist and shingle mills.

Power sufficient to carry all the machinery the year round. On the lower fall a breast wheel, 34 feet, may be used.

Third, the Cooly falls, on the same stream.

Fourth, on the Wyman brook. Unimproved.

The Wesserunsett is fed by Weeks' pond, which has a dam six feet high at its outlet, and has an area of over a square mile; range of the stream, from lowest to highest, four feet. Sites for mills most excellent. Basin thickly covered with woods.

Not ten per cent. of the power used.

Market, Skowhegan, by road.

BRISTOL—LINCOLN COUNTY.

From the Returns of O. St. C. O'Brien, M. D.

Seven Powers.

The Pemaquid river falls 50 feet in the first 500 of distance from tide water, and 100 feet in the first two miles, or from "Bristol Mills" to the salt water.

First, the 50 feet constitute the "Pemaquid Falls." The privilege can be advantageously divided into four or more sites. The only improvement at present is a grist mill and carding machine, using an insignificant portion of the power. The remnants of two ancient dams are found here, of the history of which no one in the vicinity has knowledge. Privilege is regarded an excellent site for a manufacturing enterprise of considerable magnitude. The lower privilege discharges its waters directly into tide. Vessels load and unload within 50 rods of the present mill. Excellent opportunities for locating mills and dams, on a coarse granite which underlies the stream and banks for two miles back.

Second, a mile and a half above, "Hatch's Saw Mill."

Third, "Bristol Mills," half a mile above, grist and two saw mills; dam and grist mill are stone; considerable expenditure making by the proprietors, in various improvements, and the power is quite fully used.

Fourth, "Upper Saw Mill," near the outlet of Biscay pond.

Forty years ago a dam at the outlet of Pemaquid pond secured abundant water at Bristol mills for two saw mills, a grist mill and woollen factory, all summer, with old-fashioned wheels. For reservoirs, see page 140, Part II.

Artificial reservoirs feasible, but would be expensive on account of flowage. The stream is naturally constant, the moderately undulating character of the country, and the capacity of the surface soil for water, favoring the retention of water.

Sixth, "Call's Tide Power."

Seventh, "Paul's Tide Power."

Considerable oak and Norway pine in the vicinity of the powers. Abundant granite in boulders, and excellent quarries within five miles.

Pemaquid stream strongly resembles in volume, location, etc., Pemaquan stream, on which the Pembroke Iron Works are located, and the Pemaquid falls are judged well adapted to a similar use, on account of remarkably easy access.

BROOKLIN—HANCOCK COUNTY.

Selectmen's Statement.

No water-power in this town. Fisheries and porgy oil manufacture, the leading industries.

BROOKS—WALDO COUNTY.

From Selectmen's Returns.

Eight Powers.

Four on Marsh stream, two on Sawyer stream, and two on Ellis stream.

Average height of the falls 15 feet. Power not all improved. Rose wheel. Mills operate about seven months. Six or more saw, one grist, with several shingle mills, etc.

Ellis stream is connected with a pond and affords water most of the year. The pond might be raised considerably more by a dam. An artificial reservoir of large extent might be constructed on the

"Sawyer Stream," which would also benefit all the powers, but one, on the Marsh stream.

Streams rise and fall suddenly except the Ellis. Not much forest.

Market, Belfast, seven miles, by road.

Brooksville—Hancock County.

From Returns of Selectmen and of J. B. Goodwin, Esq.

[See also "Brooksville and Penobscot."]

Seven Powers.

First, at the outlet of Walker's pond, which covers 2,000 acres; a woollen factory with six looms. A grist and shingle mill operated there several years until they were burned. Now carding, shingle and stave machines. Two dams; at the upper, a head of four feet, which can be increased to six feet. Head and fall at the lower dam 18 feet, which can be increased to 20 feet. Power only partially used.

Second, "Parker's Privilege," at the outlet of a pond, operates saw, grist and shingle mills. Operates only half the year when the water is drawn off the surrounding meadows.

Third, Fourth and Fifth, "Blodgett's Privileges," at the outlet of two ponds. Ponds so much elevated above tide that the water can be used three times. Now entirely idle, dams all gone.

Sixth, "Smith's Cove," a tide mill. Formerly a saw mill and a grist mill that could grind 100 bushels a day. Mill now idle. Can operate 16 hours out of the 24.

Seventh, "Bakeman's Privilege," a tide mill, capable of doing a large amount, but now idle. Nature almost completed the dam. Good building and machinery upon it. Can operate 16 hours out of the 24.

The capacity of the ponds can readily be increased by the use of suitable dams, except Walker's which would not rise much. Machinery all very inferior. Freshets harmless. Lay of the land favorable.

Market, any point accessible by sea.

Brooksville and Penobscot—Hancock County.

From the Statement of the Boards of Selectmen.

[See also "Brooksville," and "Penobscot."]

One Power.

"Davis's Narrows" or "South Bay Meadow Dam," on the Bagaduce river, an inlet of Penobscot bay, five miles above Castine, and four miles below Walker's mills in Brooksville. A company was some years ago incorporated under the name of the South Bay Meadow Dam Company, with power to build a dam across the river for the purpose of draining the channel above the dam to make meadow for the cultivation of hay. The river extends five miles above the dam with an average width of 80 rods. The company built a stone dam across the river on the head of a fall where the river is about 15 rods wide with a fall of 10 feet in five rods horizontal distance. The dam has a passage through it 26 feet long, closed by gates that open on the ebb tide and shut on the flood. The company succeeded in draining the river of the tide water, but the numerous streams flowing into it prevented further operation in that direction. They then obtained a charter for a toll bridge on said dam, and at present it is used only for the bridge. It is said by skilful millwrights that if another dam were erected on a similar fall one mile below on said river, with gates as before described, so as to drain the river between the dams for a reservoir to receive the water received by the mills on the upper dam, so that what accumulated on the flood would run out on the ebb tide, there would be a never failing supply of water. If the fresh water streams should fail at any time, the flood gates could be set open and the river above filled in 24 hours. It has been estimated that the river when full above would last one week without the help of any of the streams. The river above could be filled while the mills are shut down on the Sabbath. The Meadow dam is now the head of navigation on the river; vessels drawing 12 feet of water can come up to the dam.

BROWNFIELD—OXFORD COUNTY.

From Selectmen's Returns.

Ten Powers.

First, "Tyler's Mill," in the village on Shepard's river. Can grind 75 bushels of grain daily, and for four months of the year saws 2,000 feet of boards, and cards into "rolls" about 7,000 pounds of wool.

Second, the "Tannery Mill," 40 rods below. Three tons of leather per week.

Third, "Thorn & Seavey Mills," half a mile from No. 1, on same stream, 8,000 shingles per day for six months, 3,000 feet boards daily for four months, and 50 bushels grain ground daily through the year.

Fourth, at outlet of Ten-Mile pond, 100,000 boards and staves yearly, valuable power, only partially improved.

Fifth, "Marston Mills," on the Little Saco river; same amount of business as No. 4, though a much smaller power.

Sixth, "Linscott's Mill," on south branch of Shepard's river; does about the same as No. 4.

Seventh, "Cram & Whitney Mill," on Shepard's river; grinds 2,000 bushels, saws 200,000 shingles.

Eighth, "Hurd & Blake's Mill," on south branch Shepard's river; not employed, formerly sawed 50,000 feet yearly.

Ninth, "Bradeen's Mill," southeast branch Shepard's river; cabinet and furniture manufactory.

Tenth, "Brown's Mill," tub and kit factory.

The Ten-Mile pond is one mile long and half a mile wide; the storage can be increased greatly. Artificial reservoirs feasible. Shepard's river is variable, but no damage need occur. The powers can be doubled by employment of the best machinery and proper use of the water. There are no considerable *falls*, only rapids; the dams vary from six to fifteen feet. Rock granite, good for rough work. Lay of the land excellent for all purposes. Basin one-eighth wooded.

Market, Portland, 40 miles, by road; railroad looked for.

Brownville—Piscataquis County.

From Selectmen's Returns.

Three Powers.

First, at the village on Pleasant river. Head and fall 12 feet. Saw, shingle, clapboard and grist mills. Work all the year.

Second, below, and near the south line of the town. Not improved.

Third, on Pleasant river, about four miles above the village.

The river connects with a number of large ponds, Lower and Upper Ebeeme, Houston, Furnace, and others, and its manufacturing capacity can be very greatly increased and at little expense by the use of these for reservoirs. "There is water enough to carry a great many wheels."

The well-known slate quarries are about half a mile distant from the village, and building stone of all dimensions can be procured thereat in any quantity.

Market, Bangor.

BRUNSWICK—CUMBERLAND COUNTY.

From Selectmen's Returns.

[See also "Brunswick and Topsham."]

One Power.

"Gatchell's Mills," a small carding mill.

BRUNSWICK—CUMBERLAND COUNTY; TOPSHAM—SAGADAHOC COUNTY.

From the Returns of the Selectmen of the Towns, from Col. Loammi Baldwin's Report of Survey, and from various other sources.

[See also "Brunswick," and "Topsham."]

Two Powers.

First, the "Pejepscot Falls," on the Androscoggin river, at the head of tide; total height of fall about 41 (40.83) feet above common high tide; whole horizontal distance, 1,980 feet. The fall can be increased to 55 feet by raising the upper dam, and the damage from flowage would be comparatively inconsiderable, the land on both sides of the river for eight miles to Little River village being mostly high.

Formation of the Falls.—The natural falls consist of coarse graphic granite and gneiss. The rock upon the middle fall projects above the water at several points, serving as natural abutments to the several sections of the dam. Shad Island, the former site of mills, divides the lower fall about midway. There are three pitches. The lowest has a vertical descent of about 15.49 feet, the middle of 14.04, the upper 11.30.

The view accompanying this statement is of the middle pitch alone.

Volume of Water.—The amount of water commanded at Lewiston at low run is 94,000 cubic feet per minute for 11 hours a day. The Little Androscoggin is estimated on the basis of returns from Mechanic falls, to yield at its low stage the truly remarkable volume of 22,000 cubic feet per minute to the Androscoggin, so at least for the average per-diem working hours. If the estimate for the powers on the Sabattus river, in the report for Lisbon, is to be relied upon, that stream yields 6,000 to 8,000 cubic feet per minute for the ordinary working hours. So that with the additional contributions of the Little river and other smaller streams, the volume of water available for manufacturing at Brunswick must be estimated at 125,000 cubic feet per minute for 11 hours a day, at extreme low summer run, in a dry season.

Pejepscot Falls, Middle Pitch, Brunswick and Topsham.

Amount of power.—The amount of power due to 125,000 cubic feet per minute on 41 feet of fall is in gross 9,676 horse power, or 397,000 spindles. A dam securing 55 feet head would give a gross power of 12,980 horse, or 519,200 spindles.

The above estimate is based upon the present volume of the river, the great lakes remaining unimproved for summer storage. The enormous increase of the power attainable, may be seen upon reference to pages 83–86, Part II. It will be borne in mind that the storage of the lakes is, with a few unimportant exceptions, now used for only log-driving purposes.

Lay of the land.—Unsurpassed upon both sides of the river. Ample accommodations for a great manufacturing city, with all of the appurtenant mills, workshops, boarding-houses, yards and dwellings are found upon either bank. On the Brunswick side, below the village, the ground lies in three extensive levels of such height and form as to admit of improvement without grading. A natural "run" leads from the required site of the upper dam to these levels, and could be converted into a grand canal at very small expense, it already serving for a water course for considerable part of the distance. There would be little or no rock excavation.

The stone in the immediate vicinity of the falls is suitable for foundations, and other coarse work. Building granite of excellent quality within two miles, and excellent clay for bricks close at hand. Lime burned in town.

The privilege is owned by about fifteen different proprietors, resident in the vicinity.

Improvements.—Two dams constructed of wood, leaky at present, as indeed they always have been. The power has been so much in surplus that the leakage has been of no importance. The upper or third dam rotted down and was carried away a few years ago. The machinery employed is by no means of the best construction for economizing power or in other respects. This statement does not apply, however, to the cotton mill. This is located on the middle dam on the Brunswick side, a natural site for a mill of 50,000 spindles being close by it on the same dam, and is the property of the Cabot Manufacturing Company, organized 1857, capital $400,000 ; mill recently enlarged, best of machinery put in, 25,000 spindles, employs about 500 hands, manufactures fine and coarse sheetings and drills. The company own 30 acres of land on the two sides of the river, and 75 tenements. Agent, Benjamin

Greene, Brunswick. There are also on the Brunswick side two flour mills and two saw mills. Upon the Topsham side the Topsham Paper Company are just completing a first-class paper mill, of brick with slated roof, 232 × 68 feet, three stories; heated with steam, equipment for which is already in; $68,000 has already been spent; just getting into operation; estimated capacity six tons of paper per day. There are also two saw mills, a flour mill, and other small machinery.

The proportion of the power now used is insignificant. Thirty saws formerly were run, now only four single saws and a gang.

Second power, "Quaker Mill pond," on the Androscoggin, three miles above the Pejepscot falls, will furnish power for a number of saws. It may in time serve a purpose of great importance as a reservoir against the *day drouths* at Brunswick, caused by the stoppage of the run at Lewiston by night in the low-water season.

Accessibility.—Brunswick and Topsham are connected by railroads with Portland, Bath and the interior. Vessels of 1,000 tons can come within five miles of the falls, but from that point would be obliged to "lighter up," the channel being obstructed with shifting sands. The river is "frozen for four and a half to five months yearly." From the falls to Casco bay is three miles, the country a dead level; a railroad could be built at small expense, opening upon excellent harborage.

"Any parties who come amongst us with a view to the improvement of our water-power, will meet a cordial reception and substantial coöperation on both sides of the river."

BUCKFIELD—OXFORD COUNTY.

From the Statement of Virgil D. Parris, Esq.

Ten Powers.

Four on the Nerinscot or Twenty-mile river, at Buckfield village. Fall 64 feet in 100 rods. Three dams, on which are "Harlow's Flour Mill," 75 barrels capacity per day besides custom grinding; also plaster, carding, saw, and two shingle mills, tannery, shovel-handle factory, carriage factory, etc.

The power is wastefully employed; the dams are old and leaky; the machinery not economical of power.

The stream is fed by Abbot, Washburn, Half-Moon, Shag, Pleasant, Tautrabagus, North and South ponds. Three only improved for reservoirs, and they but partially. A thousand dollars outlay in dams on the ponds would quadruple the power at Buckfield in a drouth, and make it unfailing and ample for the demands of a large manufacturing business.

Fifth and Sixth, at North Buckfield, on the same river, 25 feet fall in 40 rods horizontal. On the upper, Col. W. Heald, flour, saw, and shingle mills, powder-keg machinery, etc., etc. On the lower, Messrs. Keen, large carriage and sled factory, not yet in full operation.

Seventh, half a mile above, "Marble's Powder Mill," 90 tons, or 6,000 kegs powder per annum; capacity for double the amount.

The above powers are all within two and a half miles of Buckfield depot, and have therefore facilities of access to market for products. They are alike and equally with the village powers susceptible of increase by the use of the ponds above referred to.

Eighth and Ninth, on the east branch of Nerinscot river, half a mile from Buckfield village, fed by the outlet streams of Bungamuck, Northeast, Swan, Great and Little Labrador ponds; power not heavy, but can be made constant by the use of the reservoirs, and indeed is already comparatively free from variation.

Tenth, half a mile below Buckfield village, at the junction of the East and West branches of the Twenty-mile river, four feet perpendicular fall, ledge bottom and banks, river not over 65 feet wide, banks bold and high; inexhaustible quarry of the best of granite within 150 rods of the site, with descending grade. No better possible location could be found for a large factory, as power, building material, accessibility to market, and unusual facilities for economical improvement are combined.

Market, all points, by rail.

Bucksport—Hancock County.

From the Statement, and from a Plan of the Water-Power, Presented by W. H. Pilsbury, Esq., at the Request and with the Endorsement of the Selectmen.

Nine Powers.

A valuable stream of water runs through the eastern part of Bucksport village to tide water, (see plan accompanying this paper.) It is valuable because, first, of the number of times the water can be used over—the banks being high and formed of rocks; because, secondly, of its immediate contiguity to navigable tide water; because, thirdly, of the supply of water; because, fourthly, of the readiness and ease with which all the requisite building material may be obtained—the wood being at hand, the brick within a few miles, and plenty of granite by water about five miles distant, from quarries which supply the material for Fort Knox and for other government works both in and out of the State; and because, fifthly, of the opportunity for building, especially on the eastern side of the stream, from dam No. 8 to tide water in the harbor.

First, No 1 dams the pond making the head water. The dam may be raised three feet with but very little expense, and with little damage; then the head will be ten feet, and the pond will cover, at low water, about 150 acres, and at high water at least 350 acres, with a very short dam.

The accompanying plan will show the number of dams that *may be* erected, with the *distance* and *fall* from dam to dam and to tide water. The dams, less one, have all been erected, though two are now in a state of decay and have been abandoned.

From the plan referred to I digest as follows:

Second, 230 rods below the first, and just below Centre street in the village, fall 19 feet.

Third, 18 rods below the second, 11 feet fall. A small building upon it, which has been used as an edge tool factory.

Fourth, 82 rods below the third, fall eight feet. Used for a tannery.

Fifth, 15 and three-fourths rods below, fall 15 feet. Dam in contemplation.

Sixth, eight rods below, fall 12 feet. Dam in contemplation.

Seventh, four and one-third rods below, fall 13 feet. Grist mill, with a 16-foot overshot wheel.

Eighth, eight rods below, eight feet fall. Clothing mill and carding machine, ten-foot breast wheel taking the water on the top.

Ninth, eight rods below, nine feet fall. A saw mill that takes up logs from tide water. From the Ninth to the tide, ten rods and sixteen feet fall.

With very small expense the water of another pond in Bucksport can be turned into pond made by dam No. 1, and by damming the pond referred to (a very short dam) this water can be held in reserve. This addition will make the stream a source of constant and valuable manufacturing power.

BURLINGTON—PENOBSCOT COUNTY.

Selectmen's Returns.

In the town of Burlington there is but very little water-power, and no mills of any description. The Madagascal lake, which covers 1,000 acres, has a head of seven feet raised upon it by a dam, the storage being used for log-driving purposes.

BURNHAM—WALDO COUNTY.

From Selectmen's Returns.

[See also "Burnham and Clinton Gore," also "Burnham and Pittsfield."]

Three Powers.

First, on the Twenty-Five-Mile stream, one-fourth of a mile from the Sebasticook river, in the northwesterly part of the town. The falls were formerly known as the Ferguson falls, (not to be confounded with the Ferguson rips on the Sebasticook between Burnham and Clinton Gore,) and have a twelve-foot head and fall in ten rods at a medium stage of water. Tannery, grinding from 3,000 to 4,000 cords of bark, and tanning about 35,000 sides of leather per year; two shingle machines, sawing from 400,000 to 500,000 shingles, running from eight to ten months; also a saw mill, sawing from 800,000 to 1,000,000 feet of lumber, running from four to six months.

The machinery is of good construction. Stearns and Rose wheels. The stream is fed by the Twenty-Five-Mile pond, which is four by two miles in extent. There are now two feet head of storage on the pond; two feet more might be had by channeling the outlet, which could be done at small expense. No destruction by freshet. Total range from low to high water, twelve feet. The rock about the falls is granite, suitable for building purposes. The land very convenient for shops and more mills. About half the basin of the stream covered with forest.

Second, in southeasterly part of the town, on Bog brook, three feet fall in four rods; 200,000 to 400,000 feet of lumber, and from 200,000 to 300,000 shingles; Rose wheel. Works four months in the year. Power could be greatly improved by buying flowage, so as to hold the water in the summer.

Third, in the northerly part of the town, on the Meadow brook; three feet fall in six rods; from 400,000 to 600,000 shingles; operates three to four months in the year.

Market, all points, by rail.

BURNHAM—WALDO COUNTY; CLINTON GORE—KENNEBEC COUNTY.

From the Returns of Clinton Gore.

[See also "Burnham," and "Clinton Gore."]

One Power.

The "Ferguson Rips," on Sebasticook river; ten feet fall in fifteen rods distance; half a mile from the Maine Central Railroad, one and one-half miles from the village of Burnham.

The banks are favorable for the location of mills. The bottom and sides of the stream are excellent for dams.

For reservoirs tributary to this power, see Part II, pages 95–96.

No part of this privilege is employed.

BURNHAM—WALDO COUNTY; PITTSFIELD—SOMERSET COUNTY.

From the Returns of Burnham and Pittsfield.

[See also "Burnham," and "Pittsfield."]

Two Powers.

First "Eel Weir Rips," on the Sebasticook river; fall eight feet in eighty rods; unimproved.

Second, "Thirty Mile Rips," on the same river; fall 35 feet in 480 rods. This is a most valuable power. The banks are in all respects favorable for the location of manufacturing establishments; the bottom and sides of the river will admit of the building of dams first-class in all particulars at small expense. No part of it is improved.

For reservoirs, see last table, page 95, Part II.

Market, all points, by rail.

BUXTON—YORK COUNTY.

Statement of the Selectmen, based upon the Survey of Daniel Dennett, Esq.

[See also "Buxton and Dayton," "Buxton and Hollis," also "Buxton, Hollis and Standish."]

Four Powers.

Two on the outlet of Bonny Eagle pond. Volume of water at ordinary low stage, nearly two square feet. The quantity for use might be considerably increased by a dam three or four feet in height at the outlet of the pond, which could be constructed at inconsiderable cost, and with little or no expense for additional flowage. The pond contains about one hundred and ninety acres.

First, "Bog Mills," about half a mile from the pond. Fall about 15 feet in six rods. At the head a dam of stone about 11 feet high. Grist, shingle, lath, and heading mills. Situated one mile from West Buxton village and Bonny Eagle village.

Second, half a mile below. Fall 15 feet in three rods. Formerly occupied for a chair and furniture factory, now unoccupied. Situated on the road about half a mile below Bonny Eagle village and one mile above West Buxton village.

Small powers on Little river, as follows:

Third, near Buxton Centre, "Leavitt's Mills," grist, stave and shingle. Stone dam 10 feet high; head and fall 11 feet. Water-wheel, Howd patent. At lowest run not sufficient power to operate.

Fourth, about 50 rods below, "Ward's Carriage Shop;" fall 14 feet. "Tuttle centre vent wheel." Not sufficient water to carry the machinery at lowest water.

BUXTON AND DAYTON—YORK COUNTY.

From the Joint Statement of the Selectmen of Buxton and Hollis, based upon the Survey of Daniel Dennett, Esq.

[See also "Buxton," and "Dayton."]

Two Powers.

First "Union Falls," on Saco river, 12 miles, following the course of the river, and eight miles by the most direct road, above Saco falls, in Saco. A good stone dam here was built by the Saco Water-Power Company in 1856, with 15 feet fall in low water. A good bridge 200 feet below the dam. This power is entirely unoccupied, with the exception of a small grist and shingle mill.

If the volume of water at this point in a severe drouth, be assumed to be 1,500 cubic feet per minute less than at Saco, or 16,500 cubic feet per minute, the gross power of the fall is 465 horse-powers for 24 hours, or over 1,000 horse-powers for 11 hours a day, or over 40,000 spindles.

Granite, in convenient localities for use, abounds within a mile or two of the falls.

On the west side there is below the dam an intervale of sixty acres, convenient for building mills; the back lands are high, of granite soil, and are productive. On the east side the soil is more clayey, but not less productive than that on the west. Abundance of good clay for bricks in the immediate vicinity.

The land in the vicinity is to a great extent under cultivation, though there is an abundance of wood, and of pine and oak timber. There are also in the neighborhood large peat beds of good quality.

This power is now held by the Biddeford and Saco Water-Power Company.

Second, "Union Rapids," extending half a mile below Union falls, the descent in that distance being eight or nine feet. Power in proportion as above.

The capacity of these powers can be immensely increased by the use of reservoirs on the river. See page 77, Part II.

BUXTON AND HOLLIS—YORK COUNTY.

Joint Statement of the Boards of Selectmen, Based upon the Survey of Daniel Dennett, Esq.

[See also "Buxton," and "Hollis."]

Three Powers.

"Salmon Falls," on Saco river. The head of these falls is two miles, by the course of the river, above Union falls. A log dam has been erected here about 20 feet high. From this dam the water dashes through a narrow rock-bound channel for a distance of something above 200 rods to the foot of the falls. The whole fall is 62 feet.

If the extreme low-run volume of water at this point be assumed to be 2,000 cubic feet per minute less than at Saco for the 24 hours, the gross power of the fall, day and night, is 1,860 horse-power, 74,400 spindles; or 4,050 horse-power for 11 hours a day, 162,000 spindles.

The east bank is high and precipitous, except near the dam, where is a favorable mill site which is now partially occupied by saw mills, containing in all four saws, capable of cutting 4,000,000 feet of lumber per annum. On the west side of the river in Hollis, the bank of primitive rock is not so high or precipitous, and has convenient sites for mills and manufactories, now only occupied for a grist mill and one shingle and heading machine. At the foot of the falls, both in Buxton and Hollis, are good sites for mills, and in the immediate vicinity an abundance of good clay for bricks. About two miles west of these falls there is a large supply of granite, easily accessible, suitable for building purposes. Salmon Falls village, situated at the head of these falls, is upon a direct road from Alfred to Portland. The surrounding country furnishes a large supply of agricultural productions. The soil, like other localities by the river in these towns, is of various qualities, principally, however, a clay or sand loam, and quite productive. The head of these falls is situated fifteen miles, road distance, from Portland, and nine miles from Saco and Biddeford. The Portland and Rochester Railroad passes within one and one-fourth miles. Power is owned by the Biddeford and Saco Water-Power Company.

Second, "Bar Mills Falls," situated at the village of Bar Mills, 420 rods, by the river, above Salmon falls. The fall here is 18 feet in a running distance of 60 rods.

The total power of the fall in a drouth, with water as above, is 540 horse-power, gross, or 1,178 horse-power, gross, for 11 hours a day, or 47,120 spindles.

The banks are low on either side, furnishing excellent sites for the erection of manufactories and mills. There is an old wooden dam at the head of the falls, which allows a great waste of water, while the power now available is only partially used. There are here 11 saws, capable of sawing at least 11,000,000 feet of lumber. In connection with the saw mills, there are several heading machines, and machines for manufacturing sugar-box shooks. In addition to the foregoing there are a grist mill and plaster mill. The water-wheels are the spiral vent, excepting four of the old style under-shot wheel. A county road crosses the river here over a bridge 250 feet long, and the Portland and Rochester Railroad crosses the river near the falls. Good granite quarries are open within two miles of these falls, with an abundant supply. The falls are 15 miles from Portland, and 10 from Saco.

Third "Moderation Falls," at West Buxton village, five miles by the course of the river above Bar Mills falls. Fall 14 feet in 36 rods running distance.

If the lowest volume of water at this point be assumed to be 2,300 cubic feet less per minute for the 24 hours than at Saco, the constant gross power at minimum run is about 420 horse-power, or 16,800 spindles. This is but a small part of the power that can be realized upon use of the reservoirs above for storage. See page 77, Part II. The storage is equally available upon the other powers.

At the head is an old log dam, through which at lowest water more than one-half of the water of the river escapes. The river here has a rock bed, and the banks on either side furnish excellent sites for building mills for a considerable distance below the falls, to which the water might be carried with slight expense and labor, by means of canals, penstocks, or flumes. Within two miles are now two brick-yards, where a large number of bricks of superior quality are annually manufactured. Good granite for building purposes may be obtained on the banks of the river about one mile above. The soil in the immediate vicinity of the falls is a clay loam, while further from the river a sandy loam prevails. The out-cropping rocks on the west or Hollis side of the river are granite; on the east or Buxton side the rocks are chiefly mica schist. No granite except detached rocks or boulders. Wood and timber are abundant for fire and for building purposes.

This power is now partly improved by two woollen manufactories; two double saw mills, containing three single saws and one gang, capable together of sawing annually 11,000,000 feet of lumber. There are besides, four machines for manufacturing sugar-box shooks, two shingle mills, several heading machines, one grist mill and one plaster mill. Water-wheels, spiral vent and turbine. A county road here crosses the river over a good bridge 240 feet in length.

The market of this place, as well as the principal market of those doing business at either of the falls in these towns, is Portland, and is reached by way of the Portland & Rochester Railroad.

These falls are situated 18 miles from Portland, 14 miles from Saco, and five miles from the nearest station on the Portland & Rochester Railroad.

BUXTON AND HOLLIS—YORK COUNTY; STANDISH—CUMBERLAND COUNTY.

Statements of the Boards of Selectmen, based for Buxton and Hollis upon the Survey of Daniel Dennett, Esq.

[See also "Buxton," "Hollis," and "Standish."]

One Power.

"Bonny Eagle Falls," in Hollis on the west and Standish and Buxton on the east side, situated at Bonny Eagle village, one and one-fourth miles by the river above "Moderation Falls." Their total height is forty-eight and one-half feet. That descent is attained within a running distance of 160 rods. Twenty-five feet of fall are obtained in 50 rods. The water of the river divides at the head of the falls and runs in two channels to the foot of the falls, forming an island containing about 60 acres. By the main or western channel, the water descends through a narrow passage bounded by rocks, in a succession of falls and rapids, while by the other or eastern channel, the descent, though rapid, is continuous. The banks of the western channel, though not rising to a great

Bonny-Eagle Falls, Buxton, Hollis and Standish.

height, are precipitous through a part of the distance, though furnishing in some places eligible sites for mills and reservoirs. The bed of the eastern channel or "New River," so called, is of rock, with low banks, sufficiently high however to serve as a protection from freshets. The banks and the lands extending back from them, furnish excellent sites for building mills, and seem to be especially fitted for the easy and cheap construction of aqueducts and reservoirs, particularly upon the island above named.

At the head of the main channel the power is partially improved. On the Standish side there is one double saw mill, containing two single saws, with other machines sufficient to manufacture into headings and sugar-box shooks the boards sawed at the mills. This machinery is capable of manufacturing 2,000,000 of lumber annually. On the Hollis side of the falls are two saw mills, owned by Messrs. Abijah Usher and M. M. Came, with other machinery capable of manufacturing into headings and box shooks 2,000,000 feet of lumber. Standish report says, "Three million feet of lumber manufactured annually." Total range of water from lowest to highest on the dam, six feet.

If the volume of water at this point, in extreme summer drouth, be assumed to be 2,500 cubic feet per minute less than at Saco, or 16,500 cubic feet per minute for the 24 hours, the gross power of the fall is 1,504 horse-power, 60,160 spindles; or 3,263 horse-power, 130,520 spindles, for 11 hours a day. See page 77, Part II, for a list of the reservoirs that may be improved for the further development of this power.

The out-cropping rocks at the falls and in their neighborhood, are chiefly granite of good quality for building purposes, and easily accessible. The soil in the vicinity is of various qualities and generally of good quality for agricultural purposes. Wood and timber are abundant. There is also good clay for bricks in the vicinity, and a brick-yard now being worked within a half mile of the falls.

Bonny Eagle village, at the head of the falls, is upon the county road which formerly was the great thoroughfare from Dover, N. H., and Alfred, Me., to Augusta and the east. Bonny Eagle is distant from Portland 18 miles; from Saco by road 16 miles; from the nearest station on the Portland & Rochester Railroad, six miles.

BYRON—OXFORD COUNTY.

From a Statement, and Plan of the Streams, furnished by Stephen Taylor, Esq.

Twelve Powers, and More.

It is hardly practicable to enumerate all the powers in this town as Swift river, the most important stream, is so steep in its descent, that a mill could be run upon every ten rods of its length in this town. The twelve enumerated are the most important.

First and Second, on Mill brook, formerly grist and saw mills, now out of use; quite a large pond can be had at No. 1. At No. 2 10 feet fall, rocky bottom, and four square feet of water at average run, and one and one-half to two square feet at low-water.

Third, on Mott branch, saw mill, more machinery going in.

Fourth, on Swift river below the west branch; cuts out over 3,000 clapboards in 24 hours at a good pitch of water; about four square feet water at low run, and at high water, the river full, which is from 40 to 60 feet wide.

Fifth, on the same, a saw mill forty years ago; not now used.

Sixth, below, one-third of a mile above the bridge, formerly a saw and grist mill; now unimproved.

Seventh, a few rods below, grist and saw mill in construction. River is about 60 or 75 feet wide, ledgy bottom, with a natural canal on the left bank; 12 to 14 feet fall; about six square feet water at low run.

Eighth, below, at the bridge, natural ledge fall 10 to 14 feet high; a deep cut in the ledge just below the fall, with a bridge resting upon it at either end, perhaps 100 feet from the water.

Tenth, below, saw mill 30 or 40 years ago. Not now used.

Eleventh, below, a very good power, ledge on one side, rocky bottom.

Twelfth, on East branch, a good power, ledge falls, a dam would give 10 or 12 feet head; about two and a half feet water at low pitch.

C TOWNSHIP—AROOSTOOK COUNTY.

Statement of H. O. Hussey, Esq., of Monticello.

There are water powers in this township on the Meduxnakeag river. Enormous amounts of lumber close about them.

C TOWNSHIP—OXFORD COUNTY.

One Power.

A dam on the outlet of Richardson lake gives a head of 12 feet over the entire surface of about 20 square miles. Storage now used for only log-driving purposes. Lake fed by 35 or more square miles of lakes above, which are dammed.

CALAIS—WASHINGTON COUNTY.

From the Statement of Levi L. Lowell, and William H. Boardman, Esqs.; and of C. F. Todd, Esq., of Milltown.

Eight Powers.

First, the "Salt Water Falls," on the St. Croix river just above the bridge; fall ten feet; the power is now used to propel only a grist mill; formerly a saw mill was situated on the dam, but this is discontinued, owing to the rise of tide which suspends operations about half the time.

Second, about a half mile above, the "Union Falls;" seldom obliged to stop on account of rise of tide. At this point a dam extends across the river, on which dam are situated improvements as follows:

English side.	*American side.*
Five gangs; five lath machines. Will cut twelve million feet of long lumber and twelve million laths.	Two gangs; one shingle machine; two lath machines. Will cut five million long lumber; five million laths; five hundred thousand shingles.

Third, "Salmon Falls," about one mile further up, on which are improvements as follows:

Very fine power unimproved.	A machine shop and grist mill.

Fourth, "Lower Dam at Milltown," one-fourth mile above Salmon falls, with improvements as follows:

Three gangs; two single saws, three lath machines, one sash and blind factory, one shingle machine, a planing machine, one saw factory, two axe factories, two grist mills. Will cut eight million long lumber, two million laths, and manufacture 600 dozen axes.	Two gangs; one single saw. Will cut six million feet lumber and six million laths.

Fifth, "Upper Dam at Milltown," forty rods above Lower dam, with improvements as follows:

Six gangs; six lath machines.

Will cut fifteen million long lumber and fifteen million laths.

Three gangs, three single saws, three lath machines, two shingle machines, one planing factory, one grist mill.

Will cut nine million long lumber, nine million laths, one million five hundred thousand shingles.

Aggregate annual production, about 100,000,000 of lumber sawed, and 70,000 bushels of grain ground. The power is ample to double or treble the amount. Not more than half of the power is improved, if so much. Value of annual products about $2,000,000. The saw mills operate from April 1st to November 25th, they however do partial work for a larger proportion of the year. The grist mills operate all the year. Various forms of wheels used; centre vent reputed the best. Machinery in general excellent. The power is owned chiefly by manufacturers of lumber resident in the vicinity.

The great lakes at the source of the river on both its branches can be flowed to almost any extent, securing an indefinite increase of power. Artificial reservoirs also are peculiarly feasible, there being a large amount of low land upon the river susceptible of ready conversion into storage basins at moderate expense. The delivery of water can be made practically constant. For table of reservoirs, with the storage thereon, see page 119, Part II. The storage is now used for driving lumber. A storage of only four feet upon 100 square miles of lakes connected with this river, would yield for 10 hours a day, 312 days per year, on the Calais falls alone, 72 feet, a gross power of over 8,000 horse, or 320,000 spindles.

Freshets can be controlled readily, the low banks further up the stream overflowing after a certain rise is attained, and relieving the pressure. No logs have ever been lost on the St. Croix. The extreme total range from lowest to highest water is about nine feet.

Underlying and surrounding rock, granite and slate, adapted to building uses. The lay of the land upon the privileges is most excellent for the accommodations of mills and workshops, the natural surface being about on a level with the highest run of water in freshets. Probably five-sixths of the basin of the stream is forest-covered, much of it being timber land.

Inadequately as the power has been improved, it has been sufficient to draw about it and settle a population of 20,000 souls within a radius of five miles.

Being situated at the head of tide upon navigable waters, markets are at all points accessible by sea where lumber is wanted; in particular the ports of the United States, the West Indies and Europe. Records from 1831 to 1867 in possession of L. L. Lowell, Esq., show that the river closes with ice on the average the 25th of December, and opens the 20th of March.

Sixth, on Beaver lake stream. No specifications. The lake covers about a square mile according to the State map.

Seventh and Eighth, on Magurrewock stream, the outlet of the Magurrewock lakes. No details. The lakes cover an aggregate of three or four square miles according to the State map.

CAMBRIDGE—SOMERSET COUNTY.

From Selectmen's Returns.

Several Powers.

First, at the village, on Ferguson stream, which rises in large bogs; head and fall thirteen feet; saw and flour mill; former operates about half of the time, the latter all the year.

Other small powers not occupied.

CAMDEN—KNOX COUNTY.

From the Statement of T. R. Simonton, Esq., and from a Plan of the Water-Power, both based upon a Survey by Nathaniel Crooker, Esq.

Twenty-One Powers.

The most important are on the Megunticook stream, which flows from Canaan or Megunticook pond into Penobscot bay. The length of the stream, following its course, is about three miles and a half; but the distance on a straight line from the pond to tide waters at Camden harbor is about two and one-half miles. By means of the dams at the source of the stream a full and abundant supply of water is reserved for the dry months of summer.

The number of falls available for manufacturing purposes on the stream is 14, and the amount of head of all the falls is about 150 feet.

First, three rods from tide waters at Camden village is located the large anchor factory owned and operated by H. E. & W. G.

Alden. Nine feet head at high tide and 15 feet at low tide. Two buildings, 50 by 90 feet, and 35 by 60 feet. Wheel, Reynolds' turbine. Three thousand pounds of anchors per day, or 350 tons per year, can be made by the machinery now used.

Second, six rods from tide waters, grist mill, Messrs. Carleton and others. Twelve feet head and 50 horse-power. Twenty thousand bushels ground per annum.

Third, 41 rods from tide waters, Moody's cracker bakery; four feet head, $12,000 annual manufacture. Kneading, etc., done by water-power. The surplus water is conducted by a flume to the carriage factory of William J. Farrar, and there used in driving machinery for sawing and turning materials employed in repairing and manufacturing carriages.

Fourth, 59 rods from tide waters, "Bryant's Marble Works;" four feet head. Nearly all the gravestones sold in Belfast, Camden and Rockland, are polished at this establishment. Shafting is connecting with an adjoining building, where the manufacture of Collins' glass cylinder pumps is carried on.

Fifth, 66 rods from tide waters is the large factory for manufacture of felting used in the manufacture of paper, carried on by Johnson, Fuller & Company, being the only establishment of the kind in the United States. Factory building 40 by 100 feet, has two stories and two basements; operatives employed, 35; sales, $60,000; head, 13 feet and 55 horse-power; two sets of machinery with 800 spindles; Reynolds' turbine. The surplus water is conducted by a canal to the tannery some 40 rods below, owned and carried on by Thorndike & Scott. This power has eight feet head. Three large buildings; 34 tan vats. Sales yearly, $25,000.

Sixth, 86 rods from tide waters, "Alden's Oakum Factory." Eight feet head and 34 horse-power. Reynolds' turbine. Two large buildings. Sales $25,000 per year. A carding machine.

Seventh, 98 rods from tide waters, "Knowlton & Co.'s Machine Shop;" 12 feet head and 50 horse-power in drouth. Reynolds' turbine. Five buildings averaging 40 by 60 feet. Manufactures are ships' iron pumps, capstans, steering wheels with iron rims and locust spokes, force pumps, windlass purchases, geared and gipsy winches, composition work, iron spikes, galvanized spikes, vessels' blocks; also Reynolds' turbine water wheels with gearing, shaftings, iron pullies, &c. One of these power capstans, the vessel pumps and a windlass purchase, were invented by David

Knowlton, one of the firm. Sales, $75,000 to $100,000 per year. Operatives, 35 to 45.

Eighth, 239 rods from tide waters, "Hemingway Falls," head about 10 feet. Have never been used, but are available for manufacturing purposes.

Ninth, 340 rods from tide waters is "Gould's Plug and Wedge Factory," head 13 feet. Two buildings, 25 by 30 feet, and 31 by 50. Sales, $5,000 per year.

Tenth and Eleventh, at the distance of 412 and 432 rods from tide waters, occupied by D. H. Bisbee & Co., in the manufacture of powder. Two dams, head 20 feet; at the lower dam eight, at the upper dam 12 feet. The buildings, eleven in number, one story, vary in size from 28 by 38 to 12 by 12. Powder manufactured yearly, 8,000 kegs, $30,000 to $40,000.

Twelfth, 544 rods from tide waters are the falls on the Conant farm, having a head of 10 feet. Unoccupied.

Thirteenth, 797 rods from tide waters, with 11 feet head, also unoccupied.

Fourteenth and Fifteenth, at the source of the stream, 1,107 rods from tide waters, the "Molineaux Mills." Two privileges as now occupied, one for a grist and one for a saw mill. Head of 12 feet. Should a dam be built, say 12 rods below these privileges, and they united, a head of water could be obtained of 20 feet or 85 horse-power. This privilege would be an excellent one for a paper factory, the water being pure and well adapted for the manufacture of a superior quality of paper. A number of enterprising gentlemen have been talking of building such a factory for a year or two past.

In addition to the water-powers on the Megunticook stream already named, there are others of minor importance in different parts of the town, which have been or are now occupied for various branches of manufacture.

Sixteenth, on Spring brook stream, two and a half miles from Camden village, on the road to Belfast; head 50 feet, available during a part of the year. Formerly a stave and shingle mill. Now unoccupied.

Seventeenth, on the brook running from Harrington's meadow into Canaan pond; head 16 feet. Operates a stave and shingle mill during the fall and spring months.

Eighteenth, on Goose river stream, which runs from Hosmer's pond to Rockport village; power available during a large part of the year. Formerly a grist, saw, and two stave and shingle mills. Now in operation a stave and shingle mill.

On the outlet of Oyster river pond, several powers available in wet seasons during all the year, and in dry seasons during the largest part of the year.

Nineteenth, near Oyster river pond, nine feet head; used eight or nine months of the year for a stave and shingle mill.

Twentieth, a little over a mile below, twenty-three feet head, available during most of the year, some years all the year; stave, shingle and grist machinery. Three-fourths of a mile below, saw mill and grist mill; head ten feet. Operates nearly all the year.

Twenty-First, at Rockville village, formerly a tannery, stave and shingle mill, and a sash and blind factory; not in operation at the present time.

The scenery of Camden is to a remarkable degree varied and beautiful, combining the charms of inland, ocean and mountain prospect. There are extensive beds of limestone in the town, and large quantities are quarried at various points. There are nine ponds, with an area of 1,335 acres.

The population of Camden by the census of 1860 was 4,588, and its valuation $1,062,228. It is considered a moderate estimate that the next census will give a population of 5,500, and an increase of valuation from 50 to 75 per cent. There are two good harbors, one at Camden and the other at Rockport, both clear of ice except during a few of the coldest days of winter.

Camden has devised liberal things for those willing to assist in developing her manufacturing resources, by exempting from taxation the property invested, for a period of five or ten years.

CANAAN—SOMERSET COUNTY.

From Selectmen's Returns.

Six Powers, and More.

First, "Barnes' Mill," on the outlet stream of Morrill pond, which has high banks and can be converted into a reservoir with 10 feet head; it is one and a half by three-quarter miles. A dam, small saw mill, with 14 feet head, are the only improvements.

Second, in Canaan village, on Sebattas stream, the outlet of Sibley's pond. The pond is one by two miles, receives contributions from Morrill pond, also from Black stream and Bog stream. Head seven feet, shingle and planing mill; operates about three-fourths of the year.

Third, in Canaan village, on the Sebattas stream, 18 feet head, grist, carding, bark and fulling mills; operate the year round.

Fourth, in Canaan village, on the same stream, head eight feet; saw and shingle mill which operates nearly all the year.

Fifth and Sixth, "Moore's Mills," one mile below Canaan village; the upper, a head of six feet; a saw mill which operates about six months of the year. Lower dam 10 feet head; saw, shingle and grist mills; operate nearly all the year.

The power on Sebattas stream is only part improved. It will furnish 100 horse-powers the year round. Black stream and Bog stream are both very constant in their flow. The dams can all be raised several feet so as to furnish more head.

Other dams, also, at other points, might be built, so as to afford safe and valuable power. Wheels, Tuttle's centre-vent with patent regulator. The soil of the town is very productive as appears by census statistics.

CANTON—OXFORD COUNTY.

From the Statement of the Selectmen.

Six Powers.

First, Capen's Rips," on the Androscoggin river. Fall six to ten feet in ten rods. A saw mill was formerly operated at this point. A substantial dam can be erected here, and an excellent water-power established.

Second, "Canton Mills," upon the outlet of Whitney pond. Fall eight feet in three rods. Various saws operate from three to six months. Also tannery, and a grist mill which operates the whole year.

Whitney pond is nearly two and a half by three-quarter miles. By means of dams the power can be increased, with damage by flowage. No loss by freshets when the dam is in good order.

Third, 15 rods below the saw and grist mill, a fall of three feet vertical, with a dam to add seven feet head. A foundry, with the first right to draw the water, two large planers, one small do., one iron lathe, one wood do., and various saws, all of which may be propelled at the same time. Across the stream is a carriage manufactory with necessary saws and lathes.

Fourth, "Stubbs' Mill," upon the outlet of Dix pond; fall 20 feet; overshot wheel, on which 29 cubic inches of water carry the board saw. Various saws.

Fifth, between this and the pond, has the same altitude and is not used. A dam controls the water in the pond without damage to any land owner and might be made to hold it still higher. Pond is fed by springs and is about half a mile in length.

Sixth, "Howe's Mill," on Howe's stream; fall 15 to 20 feet; stream small, and a dam would cause the flowage of a large tract of valuable meadow; saw and grist mill which operate part of the year.

Market, Portland, by the Portland & Oxford Central and the Grand Trunk Railroads, also by the Androscoggin Railroad and its connections.

CAPE ELIZABETH—CUMBERLAND COUNTY.

From Selectmen's Returns.

Four Powers.

First, "Clark's Mills," on Long creek. Fall 18 feet in half a mile, operates 10 months, breast wheel 18 feet in diameter.

Second, on Mill creek, a tide power. Stone dam; grist mill, nine-foot tub wheel. Tide rises and falls from five to eight feet; mill operates from 10 to 12 hours a day, and can grind 150 bushels in the time.

Third, a tide power at Spurwink. Unimproved.

Fourth, a tide power of large capacity can be secured by a dam at the mouth of the estuary into which Long creek empties.

Two artificial reservoirs of large capacity can be constructed in connection with the powers.

Market, Portland, close at hand.

CARMEL—PENOBSCOT COUNTY.

From Selectmen's Returns.

Seventeen Powers.

Upon the Ruggles stream, three; Kingsley do., four; Sowadabscook do., four; Harvey do., four; Kenduskeag do., two.

There are no falls of any note; the power is produced chiefly by dams; is judged sufficient to cut yearly 5,000,000 feet of boards and 4,000,000 shingles. It is not all improved; in part, in mills, as follows: Ten board, eight shingle, one lemon-box, one cloth-dressing and carding, and a grist mill. The mills do not work all the year; about one-half work six months, and the other half one-third of the year.

The Sowadabscook stream is connected with a pond two by one miles, the Kenduskeag with a pond somewhat smaller. The capacity of the ponds could be very much increased at small expense by the erection of dams. Freshets moderately heavy. In ordinary seasons there is sufficient in the Sowadabscook throughout the year to operate nearly all the mills upon it. Three-fourths of the town are covered with forests.

Yearly product, $25,000. Market, Bangor.

CARRATUNK TOWNSHIP—SOMERSET COUNTY.

Statement of Joseph Clark, Esq.

[See also "Carratunk Township and Township No. 1."]

Numerous Powers.

Several of the above are on the outlet stream of Pleasant pond. Stream is three miles long and falls 100 feet in that distance.

First, at the outlet, "Clark's Saw Mill," head and fall 12 feet, abundant water all the year may be had; pond covers over three square miles. Most excellent site for mills. Small part of the power used.

Second, half a mile below, fall 12 feet; unimproved.

Third, Fourth, Fifth, below, good privileges, unimproved.

Sixth, below, near the road, "Brown's Mills," saw, grist, axe, and other machinery; 12 feet head and fall; more may be had.

Seventh, below the road, near the Kennebec river, head and fall 12 feet, unimproved.

Five of the above are below the inlet of the Moore's Bog stream, which is very constant and has three or four ponds, all of which can be flowed for reservoirs.

Pine, cedar, spruce and hardwood lumber in vast quantities.

A flat-bottomed steamer could be run on Kennebec river from Carratunk falls in Solon, to the Forks, passing in the close vicinity of the powers.

Eighth, Ninth and Tenth, or the outlet stream of the Baker ponds, two privileges below the second pond, and one below the lowest pond. Thirty feet fall on the last, large amount of fall at the upper two. Unimproved, except a dam at the outlet of the lower pond, which flows it eight feet.

CARRATUNK TOWNSHIP AND TOWNSHIP NO. 1—SOMERSET COUNTY.

Statement of E. W. Parlin, Esq., of Pleasant Ridge.

[See also "Carratunk Township," and "Township No. 1."]

One Power.

"Carrying-Place Rips," on the Kennebec river, at the mouth of the Carrying-Place stream. The natural fall is moderate, but canals could be constructed on either shore, which would give a large amount of power. Banks high, but not so crowded upon the river as to forbid the location of mills. Rock bottom and banks. Fully developed this would make a valuable power.

CARROLL—PENOBSCOT COUNTY.

Statement of J. A. Larrabee, Esq.

Two Powers, or More.

First, "Lowell's Mill," near the outlet of Buck's pond; operates four months.

Second, saw mill on the west branch of the Baskahegan inlet, operates four months.

No other powers now used in the town of Carroll.

CARTHAGE—FRANKLIN COUNTY.

From Selectmen's Returns, and the Statement of Robert Potter, Esq.

Ten to Twenty Powers.

The whole volume of Webb's river can be used from 10 to 20 times. The river is a constant succession of rips for several miles. The amount of power is indicated by the fact that there are upon *one* of the dams a saw mill, grist mill with two runs of stones, two shingle mills, and other machinery; and that there is abundant water for them all, when any sort of precautions are taken to use it economically.

Webb's pond, the source of the stream, covers three square miles; its outlet can be lowered six feet, and its surface raised three feet, thus securing nine feet head over the whole surface. The pond is fed by seven different streams and many small brooks, and thus drains a large tract of country.

The privilege at the foot of the pond, owned by Robert Potter of Portland, offers first-rate facilities for improvement. There are near the outlet 1,000 acres or more of very thrifty second-growth pine.

One-third of a mile below the outlet, owned by Robert Potter, formerly used for various mills, all of which are now burned down. Dam gone. Ten or twelve feet fall.

One-fourth mile below, as good as the above, no improvement.

One-half mile below, saw mill and threshing machine.

Various privileges below not used.

About one mile below the saw mills, and at the village, grist and saw mill, and other machinery.

Various privileges below, not improved.

Flutter and centre-vent wheels.

Granite abundant, also clay for bricks, and vast quantities of excellent limestone. Sites for mills excellent, the land mainly level.

Three-fourths of the basin covered with woods.

Market, Portland, by Androscoggin railroad, from North Jay depot, 10 miles distant from water-power.

CASCO—CUMBERLAND COUNTY.

Statement of Albion Cobb, Esq.

[See also "Casco and Naples," and "Casco and Raymond."]

Twenty-One Powers.

First, at the foot of Pleasant pond, which serves as a mill pond, various saws, and grist mill.

Second, below, a dam, tannery and starch factory, with other mills now idle.

Third and Fourth, below, two equally good powers; unimproved.

Fifth, below, various saws.

Sixth and Seventh, below, and within two miles, good powers; unimproved.

Eighth, below, grist and plaster mill, and various saws.

Ninth, just below, various saws.

Any one of the foregoing powers is sufficient to drive a large amount of machinery the year round. The stream is very little affected by either drouth or freshets. The pond has an area of 2.25 square miles and has a storage of —— feet. It is fed by Parker's pond.

Tenth, "Decker's Mill," on the outlet of swamps; saw mill, water enough for six months; poor wheel.

Eleventh, at the outlet of Dumpling pond, formerly a saw mill, power now idle, the dam is used for storage.

Twelfth, just below, grist mill, and various saws. Part of the machinery runs the year round.

Thirteenth, thirty rods below, lumber-working machinery.

Fourteenth, immediately below, carriage manufacturing, small pond, good privilege.

Fifteenth, just below, good privilege, with an excellent place for a mill pond; unimproved.

Sixteenth and Seventeenth, below, the water might be used with breast or overshot wheels, but the mill ponds would be small.

Eighteenth, below, unimproved, with an excellent chance for a mill pond.

The stream on which the last eight powers are situated, is little more than a mile in length, but in that distance descends about 200 feet. The stream is little affected with freshets, and since the water of the ponds, Dumpling and Coffee, is controlled by tight dams, not greatly affected by drouth.

Nineteenth, on the outlet stream of "Hog Meadow Pond," a power of extraordinary excellence. An overshot wheel of twenty-two feet diameter is used; a stave mill.

Twentieth, said to be a good one, on a small stream emptying into the northeast corner of Rattlesnake pond. Unimproved.

Twenty-First, "Pinkham's Mill," on a small tributary of Pleasant pond; fails in summer.

Market, principally Portland, distance 25 miles by road.

Casco and Naples—Cumberland County

Statement of Washington Bray, Esq., of Naples.

[See also "Casco," and "Naples."]

Two Powers.

Both situated on Crooked river below Edes' falls. Each has a fall of about eight feet.

The volume of the river at mean run is about 1,593 inches under a head of 9.5 feet, giving on an eight-foot fall about 100 horse-powers. River very constant, fed by ponds.

Casco and Raymond—Cumberland County.

Statement of Albion Cobb, Esq., of Casco.

[See also "Casco," and "Raymond."]

One Power.

On the outlet stream of Thomas pond, a very excellent power, unimproved. The pond covers 1.15 square miles, and is flowed by a dam.

Castine—Hancock County.

Selectmen's Statement.

One Power.

A tide power; a grist mill and shingle mill upon it in working order. Work all the year. Machinery of the best construction for a tide mill. Height of tide at this point about 12 feet.

Centerville—Washington County.

From the Statement of James Pope, Esq., and the Selectmen.

Two Powers.

First, the "Great Falls," on Machias river, about five miles above Whitneyville Dam, and nine miles from Machias tide water. There is railroad connection between Whitneyville and Machiasport.

The fall is 20 feet in 60 rods. A dam 12 feet high near the head of the fall, would pond back the water two or three miles, and could be built with small outlay. An island in the middle of the river would serve as an abutment to the sections of the dam. No granite nearer than two miles, but abundance of trap suitable for foundations and other rough work. Good brick clay close at hand.

The left bank at the falls is a hard wood ridge somewhat broken in surface, but affording an excellent and ample site for a manufacturing town. The shore is rocky and about ten feet above the stream in a freshet. The right bank is flat but not boggy. It is underlaid with rock.

The bed of the river at the falls is rocky, and at one point a continuous ledge extends from bank to bank, affording an unsurpassed natural foundation for a dam.

On the right bank the facilities for canalling are most excellent, cannot in fact be excelled. The growth on this bank is spruce, pine and hemlock.

There is no settlement within three miles, and the privilege has no improvement whatever upon it. The country above is unbroken wilderness.

The power and the township are owned by the Whitneyville Agency; Agent, James Pope, Esq.

If the volume of water at mean summer run in an ordinary season, be assumed to be 14,000 cubic feet per minute, that at Machias being 15,000, the gross power of the Great Falls, with a dam as above, is 832 horse, or 33,280 spindles. It can be increased several fold by use of the reservoirs upon the river. See page 132, Part II.

Second, on the west branch of Chandler's river, eight feet fall, saw mill operates six months.

CHARLESTON—PENOBSCOT COUNTY.

Four Powers.

First, on a branch of Kenduskeag river, in the west part of the town, a saw mill.

Second, on the west branch of the Pushaw river, a saw mill.

Third, below, on the same stream, a shingle mill.

Fourth, on the east branch of the Pushaw river, near the south-east corner of the town, a saw mill.

CHARLOTTE—WASHINGTON COUNTY.

From the Selectmen's Returns, and a Plan of the Streams.

[See also "Charlotte and Township No. 14."]

Eight Powers.

First, "McGlaughlin's Mills," on Damon mill brook; fall ten feet; shingle mill, operates five months.

Second, "Granger's Mills," on Moosehorn stream, twelve feet fall; shingle and clapboard mills, operate six months.

Third, above, two miles from the county road, 18 feet fall.

Fourth, on Fisher's mill brook, a short distance above Round pond, fall 12 feet.

Fifth, above; by means of a canal conducting the water across the county road, a fall of 40 feet can be secured.

Sixth, above, and very near the county road, by means of the same canal a fall of 30 feet can be secured.

Seventh, above the county road, a fall of 12 feet.

Eighth, short distance above, fall 12 feet.

A large bog above might be converted into a reservoir, though with some damage by flowage. Powers operate five to six months. A 15-foot back-shot wheel. The Moosehorn is derived from bogs and low lands, and is constant. One-third of the basin covered with woods.

Market, Pembroke and Calais, by road.

CHARLOTTE AND TOWNSHIP NO. 14—WASHINGTON COUNTY.

From the Statement of T. W. Allan, Esq., of Dennysville, and a Plan of the Streams furnished by the Selectmen.

Three Powers, or more.

First, a dam at the head of Gilman's rips, on Dennys river, eight feet fall; flows the river to the lake. No other improvement.

Second, "Gilman's Rips," on Dennys river, four and a half miles below Meddybemps lake, 12 feet fall.

Third, below, and nearly continuous, "Gardner's Rips."

The above are a series of rips and ponds, which with Brights-Island rips between Dennysville and No. 14, have an estimated fall of 30 feet.

The lake above, 15 square miles in area, with seven feet of storage, constitutes a great reservoir. The powers can be made constant throughout the year.

Chelsea—Kennebec County.

From Selectmen's Returns.

Nine Powers.

Seven on the outlet of Worromontogus pond in Augusta.

First, about ten rods below the south line of Augusta, a dam seven feet high, and five rods long, which flows several square miles, with banks which admit of raising the dam to any desired height. This dam is for a reservoir.

Second, 20 rods below, dam and falls, fifteen feet, saw and shingle mills, which cut all the available lumber, although the dams are old and leaky, and the wheels are the old-fashioned ladle pattern.

Third, half a mile below, a good stone dam 12 feet high, with shingle and grist mill nearly new, operates all the year.

Fourth, half a mile below, formerly a saw mill, destroyed by fire many years ago. Fall from the third mill to this privilege, about 18 feet. Unoccupied.

At this point is received an additional stream called "Chase Meadow Brook," which takes its rise from "Greely Pond" in Augusta.

Fifth, three-fourths of a mile below the 4th, fall 14 feet, has been occupied by two sets of saw mills.

Sixth, 80 rods below, fall 16 feet, formerly "Searle's Mills." Privilege now unoccupied, flows about five acres, has a ledge foundation, which runs far into the banks, for dam and mills. The stone wings of the old dam are now standing. Here an additional stream comes in, known as "Long Meadow Brook," with large space for flowage.

Seventh, one mile below, fall 15 feet, formerly "Jewett's Saw Mill;" burned many years ago; privilege not occupied.

The total fall of the "Togus" stream in Chelsea is about 98 feet in three miles. No damage from freshets to dams for the last 35 years. Properly improved the stream would carry a large amount of machinery.

Granite suitable for walls and underpinning. The surface around the falls is generally very convenient for the location of mills, and other necessary buildings, with good roads passing Searle's, Dorr's, Baker's and Lewis' falls. Clay and sand are quite abundant near the river, with good privileges for making brick, and a large amount are manufactured annually.

Eighth, on Gardiner Meadow brook; formerly a saw mill, operated two months. Unimproved for the last 12 years.

Ninth, on a small stream, fall 30 feet, close by the Kennebec river. An overshot saw and shingle mill, did business for a few years. Now unimproved.

Market, Pittston, Gardiner, Hallowell, and Augusta, from one-half to seven miles distant.

CHERRYFIELD—WASHINGTON COUNTY.

From Selectmen's Returns.

Six Powers.

The above taken together constitute the "Cherryfield Falls," on the Narraguagus river.

First, at the head of tide, in the village, a privilege of six feet fall, owned by A. Campbell & Co., who contemplate building a dam. An excellent power for machine shops, etc., for village use. Excellent sites for building on the east bank.

Second, the "Lower Dam," so called. Nine feet head, 80 rods horizontal run. Occupied, east side, grist mill, planing mill, sash, door and blind factory, a machine shop and foundry. West side, gang, edge and lath mill. Gang cuts on the average 25,000 lumber per day, lath mill about 25,000 per day. Owned, east side, by A. Campbell & Co.; west side, one-half by the same, one-quarter by J, O. Nichols & Son, and one-quarter by S. Campbell, agent.

Third, "New York Dam," so called, at the upper bridge; 11 feet head; horizontal run 60 rods to the next dam above. Owned by John W. Coffin & Co. Occupied, east side, gang and single saw, edge and lath mill; west side, grist mill. A very fine power.

Fourth, "Wakefield Dam," head seven feet, horizontal flow 50 rods to the dam above. Occupied by two shingle mills, two machines each, with cut-off saws, etc. Owned, east side, by T. P. Wiley; west side, by Lewis & Godfrey.

Fifth, "Hall Dam," 10 to 11 feet head, 90 rods horizontal flow to dam above. Occupied, west side, gang, single saw, edge and lath mill; east side, shingle mill with two machines and cut-off saw, carding mill.

Sixth, "Stillwater Dam," nine feet head, horizontal flow three miles. The east and west branches of the Narraguagus river form junction half a mile above this power. The land in the vicinity being low and flat, has been flowed by the dam, forming a very large reservoir. All the mills upon this power were burned in July, 1866. The dam has since been thoroughly repaired, and a gang and single saw, edge and lath mill, erected on the west bank. These mills are very superior and of large capacity. The gang has cut in twelve hours 52,000 of two-inch plank, would average 30,000 daily. The reservoir formed by this dam is so large as to sustain the stream, and by consequence all powers upon it in the severest drouths, the accumulations of the night meeting the drain of the day.

The mills work all the year save the winter and early spring, at which time the ponds freeze so that the logs cannot be floated to the slip. Very extraordinary summer drouths sometimes suspend the mills for a short time. The power of the river is capable of great increase by the improvement of the lakes connected with it for reservoir purposes. An extensive heath in Beddington could at little expense be converted into an immense reservoir.

Freshets, less severe than formerly, since the lakes were dammed. Range from lowest to highest water about six feet.

Special pains have been taken to construct the best mills and secure the best machinery. The centre-vent wheels are much preferred.

Production.—Each dam occupied by a gang and single and lath mill is capable of sawing 5,000,000 of long lumber and 5,000,000 of laths each season. For the last three years the annual product in long lumber has been worth at the wharf here $400,000; shingles, $30,000; total, $430,000. When our power shall come to be improved for regular manufacturing purposes to the extent of its capacity, we have the assurance of great increase in wealth and population.

The lumber is marketed in New York and Boston mainly, though pine boards are shipped of late directly to the West Indies.

Accessibility.—Vessels approach within five and a half miles of the falls, at Millbridge, to which point lumber is floated in scows and rafts. The river is open to navigation eight and a half months of the year.

CHESTER—PENOBSCOT COUNTY.

Statement of Daniel Barker, Esq., of Bangor.

[See also "Chester and Winn."]

Five Powers.

All on Medunkeunk stream.

First, half a mile from mouth, 20 feet perpendicular fall, width of stream 150 feet, ledge bottom; once occupied by saw, grist, clapboard and shingle mills. Mills now decayed.

Second, two miles above, eight feet head, flows five miles, dam 125 feet long, ledge bottom; power good for the whole season; formerly occupied.

Third, on Eber-horse branch, 10 feet head, dam 25 feet long, stone wing 100 feet, built for grist and shingle mill; grist mill not complete.

Fourth, half a mile above, 10 feet head, dam 125 feet, flows four miles. Saw and shingle mills burnt two years ago.

Fifth, above, at the north line of the township, old dam 50 feet long, 10 feet head, flows two square miles.

CHESTER AND WINN—PENOBSCOT COUNTY.

Statement of Joseph S. Bowler, Esq..

[See also "Chester," and "Winn."]

One Power.

The "Island Rapids," on the Penobscot river, all within one mile of the village. The total fall is judged not less than 15 feet in 100 rods, and may be increased to any required amount by a dam, the banks above being of ample height to prevent flowage. The fall is broken into two pitches, the "Babcock Rips," amongst the islands, and the "Five Island Falls" at the foot of the islands. There are five small islands in the river, which are above water at all seasons, and would constitute natural abutments to the dam and sites for mills. The river is about 900 feet wide, and the bottom on the crest of the pitches is nearly on a level all the way across the river. The banks below are high, 20 feet or more, above the river. Range of water 10 to 12 feet. The power of this privilege suitably developed would doubtless net six or eight thousand horse-power, or 400,000 spindles.

Unimproved.

CHESTERVILLE—FRANKLIN COUNTY.

From Selectmen's Returns.

[See also "Chesterville and Farmington."]

Four Powers.

First, at North Chesterville, on Wilson's stream. Fall 12 feet in 30 rods. Grist and carding mill. Water sufficient for all the machinery six months, and for the grist mill with two runs of stones the whole year. Centre-vent wheel. High banks, level back from the stream.

Second, at Chesterville Centre, on Little Norridgewock stream. Twelve feet fall; saw mill, salt-box factory. Flutter, Tuttle and Blake wheels.

Third, below, at Chesterville Center; fall eight feet. The power on the two falls is judged equal to 100 horse-powers. The mills run nine months. Four ponds, averaging one mile by one half mile. Artificial reservoirs of large capacity can be constructed. Ponds, also, can be improved for reservoirs by dams. Perfectly safe in freshets. Range of water on the upper dam, six feet; on the lower, three feet.

Fourth, fall 35 feet; saw and grist mill, etc. Large reservoirs could be constructed. Power is not all used.

The lay of the land good; excellent granite. "Millions of pine lumber still remaining in the town. Fine grazing town."

CHESTERVILLE AND FARMINGTON—FRANKLIN COUNTY.

From the Statement of the Boards of Selectmen.

[See also "Chesterville," and "Farmington."]

One Power.

"Farmington Falls," on the Sandy river; head and fall 16 feet. Power not now and at no former time half put to use, except perhaps in extreme drouth.

The outlet stream of two large ponds situated in Wilton, joins the river above the dam; each pond contains about 300 acres.

On the Farmington side of the river, "Davis' Saw Mill;" formerly a grist mill, which was burned three or four years ago. The mills being situated upon a canal may be regarded as safe from freshets.

On the Chesterville side there are two saw mills, a spool factory, a factory for the manufacture of drums and horse-rakes.

CHINA—KENNEBEC COUNTY.

From Selectmen's Returns.

Several Powers.

These are nearly all upon the west branch of the Sheepscot river, once occupied by grist and saw mills. None can operate all the year. Very large ponds in town, which serve as reservoirs to powers in adjacent towns.

"The water-powers are of local value and use, but not such as would influence capitalists to invest upon them with a view to permanent profitable business."

CLIFTON—PENOBSCOT COUNTY.

Statement of Benjamin Penney, Jr., Esq.

Four Powers, or more.

First, on Great Works stream, fall 12 feet, not occupied.

Second, on the Park's pond stream, saw and shingle mill; 2 to 300,000 feet of lumber, and 5 to 1,200,000 shingles; water six months.

Third, below, "Penny's Mill;" 50,000 clapboards, and 1,500, 000 shingles.

Fourth, below, not occupied; head nine feet.

CLINTON—KENNEBEC COUNTY.

From Selectmen's Returns.

Three Powers.

First, "Hunter's Mills," in the southeast part of the town on the Sebasticook river, dam seven feet; can be raised several feet more by paying small damages. Double, single, and shingle saws, also grist, sash, door and blind, carding and cloth-dressing, and brush-block machinery. About 3,800 inches of water are used. With a good dam there would be plenty of water for all the mills the year round. In great freshets the water rises only about three and a half feet in the mill pond. Underlying rock slate; the dam and mills both rest upon solid ledge; granite boulders that may be split for building purposes abundant within a half mile or mile. The land bordering the stream is but a few feet above the level of the water in time of freshet, is level and very convenient for building.

The figures given above indicate a volume of water approximating 20,000 cubic feet per minute, which if ten feet head can be obtained would give about 370 horse-power gross, or 19,800 spindles. For reservoirs, see pages 95–96.

Second, on Black stream in the northeast part of the town; grist and saw mill. Saw mill operates six months. Dam ten feet high.

Third, on the Twelve-Mile stream; stone dam, about ten feet high; slate-ledge foundation; water about four months of the year.

Market, Portland, by Maine Central railroad; depot one-half mile from the principal mills.

CLINTON GORE PLANTATION—KENNEBEC COUNTY.

From Assessors' Returns.

[See also "Burnham and Clinton Gore."]

One Power.

On the Powers brook, ten rods from the railroad, and half mile from Burnham depot. Shingle mill, runs four months, cuts 500,000 shingles.

CODYVILLE TOWNSHIP—WASHINGTON COUNTY.

Statement of Peol Tomah.

Several privileges on the Tomah streams, the outlets of ponds covering two square miles, and admitting of dams. One is now dammed. None are improved.

COLUMBIA—WASHINGTON COUNTY.

From Selectmen's Statement.

Two Powers.

First, "Saco Falls," on Pleasant river. Height fifty feet in two hundred yards. Power not all improved. A dam; shingle, lath, saw, and grist mills upon it. Mills can work all the year, but do not; or rather the grist mills operate all the year, the saw mills but part.

Second power, "Little-River falls" on Little river. Height, presumed from the statement given to be the same as of the above Saco falls.

Land about the falls well adapted to improvement. Streams connected with lakes; one, 3' by 1 miles.

Market, Boston and New York, by coasters.

COLUMBIA FALLS—WASHINGTON COUNTY.

From the Selectmen's Returns and a Plan of the Streams.

Seven Powers.

First and Second, "Columbia Falls," at Columbia village on Pleasant river, at the head of tide, which here rises and falls from 12 to 15 feet. Total descent about 16 feet in 300 yards, divided into two pitches. On the upper pitch there are a gang and single saw and lath machine, cutting about 3,500,000 of long lumber and about 5,000,000 laths. Owned by George Harris & Co. On the lower pitch are a single saw mill, lath mill, grist mill, carding mill and fulling mill. The power here is equal to the first. Owned by Samuel Bucknam and others. The grist mill operates all the year, the saw mills are idle in winter, and usually for a short time in the lowest stage of water in summer are shut down, there not being water sufficient for a full business.

Third, two and a half miles up the river is the "Burnt Mill Rips," fall eight feet in 150 yards. The power is equal to either of the above. No improvement.

Volume of water.—Pleasant river is bridged between the pitches at the village, the abutments being about 45 feet apart. At the lowest water the stream pours through this space eight inches deep and six miles an hour. At highest water the space is filled about ten feet deep. The rise of the river is slight, owing to the large extent of heath and low intervale bordering the stream, which overflows in freshets and holds back the water. The land adjacent to the stream and its bordering intervale is to a considerable extent sandy plain, somewhat elevated, at the base of which are countless never-failing springs of water, which contribute to sustain the river.

If the mean velocity of *four* miles an hour should actually be realized, betwixt the abutments, as above, 10,560 cubic feet per minute must pass the point, which would give a gross power of 320 horse on the 16 feet of fall, or 12,800 spindles.

Fourth and Fifth, on Lower Little river, a tributary to the Pleasant, about two miles above the village. Lower fall about ten feet in 40 feet, the upper a gradual descent but an excellent power. No improvement upon either of the powers.

Sixth and Seventh, small powers on Peckey branch, a tributary of Chandler's river.

At the head of Pleasant river is a lake 3 by 1.5 miles; several small ponds also contribute to it. There is a dam at the outlet of the lake. Capacity of the lake could not be increased; but very large artificial reservoirs can be had at small cost. Rock about the falls "shelly" and not suitable for building. Land lies well for the erection of mills and shops.

Value of annual products about $80,000. The improvement of the power has increased the population somewhat, and has added considerably to the wealth of the town.

Market, all points by water. The village powers are at the head of sloop navigation; vessels of 150 tons load at wharves.

Concord—Somerset County.

From Selectmen's Returns.

Two Powers.

First, on Chase's stream, an excellent power; saw, shingle, lath and clapboard mills; it will run all the saws five months in the year, and either one alone all the rest of the time; five feet fall; poor machinery; the power used would do much more with good equipment.

Second, saw and grist mill; machinery poor. Twenty feet fall and water enough to run all the year. Four mills could be built on the stream, and seven small ponds with a large amount of bog land about them, can be converted into reservoirs.

Two-thirds of the land covered with timber; hilly with plenty of rocks for building dams and buildings. Lumber manufactured yearly, 200,000 feet, which might be increased to five times the amount. Five miles from Somerset railroad.

Cooper—Washington County.

From Selectmen's Returns.

Two Powers.

First, "Cooper's Mills," in the west part of the town; a saw mill, which does but little in comparison with what it might; old-fashioned wheel. Streams connected with ponds which might be greatly improved for reservoirs by dams.

Second, on Dead stream, in the east part of the town. No improvement whatever. Streams connected with ponds that might be converted into reservoirs.

Both streams rise and fall quickly, owing to the non-use of the ponds for storage basins. Basin of Cooper stream nearly covered with woods. Capital and enterprise could find good investment on these privileges.

Market, Calais, Machias, etc.

CORINNA—PENOBSCOT COUNTY.

From Selectmen's Returns, and a Plan of the Streams.

Eleven Powers.

First, on the Dexter stream, "Moody's Mills," eight feet head, various saws.

Second and Third, below, unoccupied; ten feet head each.

Fourth, "Lincoln's Mill," ten feet head, two shingle mills, privilege capable of doing much larger business.

Fifth, "Village Mills," 12 feet head, grist, shingle, cloth-dressing and carding mills; an old saw mill not running needs to be rebuilt.

Sixth, unoccupied, about eight feet head.

The above privileges have all the water received from Dexter, and in addition the contributions of numerous brooks tributary to the stream on its course through the town.

Seventh, on Alder stream, "Shepherd Mill," has carried a saw and shingle machine spring and fall; now unoccupied.

Eighth, "Welch Mill," below, nine feet head, a good saw mill operates spring and fall; in the summer the water is drawn off on account of flowage.

Ninth, "Burrill Mill," below, a shingle machine, seven feet head; can be used only when the Welch mill is in operation.

Tenth, "Nickerson Mill," in the south-west corner of the town, on a brook, shingle mill, operates spring and fall.

Eleventh, "Stubb's Mill," on a brook in the east part of the town, saw mill, operates in the spring, now out of repair.

Town will exempt manufacturing capital from taxation. Railroad runs by the side of the powers, the whole length of the town. The streams are both connected with ponds which are improved or susceptible of improvement as reservoirs.

Market, for produce, Newport; for lumber, Bangor.

CORINTH—PENOBSCOT COUNTY.

From Selectmen's Returns.

Four Powers, or More.

First, on Kenduskeag stream; two saw and shingle mills.

Second, on Kenduskeag stream; a grist mill.

Third, on Crooked brook; saw and shingle mill.

Fourth, on Bear brook; saw and shingle mills.

The saw mills cut about 300,000 each, but might do more. The McGregory mill saws nearly twice that. A new and good grist mill about to go up in place of an old one. The mills operate three-fourths of the year, grist mill all the year. Slate rock, with granite in spots. Little forest.

Market, Bangor, by road.

CORNISH—YORK COUNTY.

From the Selectmen's Returns, and a Plan of the Town.

[See also "Cornish and Hiram."]

Three Powers.

First and Second, "Thompson's Falls," on Little river; first, 33 feet descent in 361 feet run; second, 12 feet perpendicular. Stream 18 feet wide, one and one-half feet deep; velocity of current 60 feet per minute. The upper not improved. The lower improved in a grist mill.

Third, "Brown's Falls," on Brown's brook; 11 feet fall in 118 feet run. Stream 18 feet wide, one and one-half feet deep; current 60 feet per minute; saw mill and shingle machine.

Powers operate all the year except in severe drouths. Wheels, overshot and breast.

Brown's brook is fed by Long pond. Spruce brook can be turned into Little river, doubling its power. Long pond can be flowed. Freshets not destructive. Rock, gneiss and mica schist. Land convenient for building. Basin one-fourth wooded.

Improvement of powers here would benefit the town greatly.

Market, Portland, thirty miles by road, soon by P. & O. R. R.

CORNISH—YORK COUNTY, AND HIRAM—OXFORD COUNTY.

From the Returns of Cornish and Hiram.

[See also "Cornish," and "Hiram."]

Two Powers.

First, "Allen's Falls," on Great Ossipee river, half a mile above the Saco, fall three and a half feet in 12 rods. River 155 feet wide, six feet deep, velocity of current 60 feet per minute. The privilege is not now used. There was formerly a grist mill upon it, with dam 10 feet high.

Second, "Warren's Mill," about one mile and a fourth from Cornishville. It was burned in 1849, and has not been rebuilt. There were both saw and grist mills. The river is from six to eight rods wide and has a fall of eight to ten feet in half a mile.

CORNVILLE—SOMERSET COUNTY.

From Selectmen's Returns.

Four Powers.

All situated on the east branch of the Wesserunsett river.

First, two miles south of the north town line; saw mill and shingle machine.

Second, two miles below; saw and shingle mills.

Third, one mile south of the above; a grist mill.

Fourth, sixty rods below; shingle machine.

There are no considerable falls; a succession of rapids. The mills operate nearly all the year; all can work ten months. The power is only partially improved. The stream is the outlet of Wentworth pond, in Athens, two by three miles. Granite abundant and of good quality. Basin one-fourth covered with woods.

Market, Skowhegan, nine miles from the upper mill by road.

CRANBERRY ISLES—HANCOCK COUNTY.

From Selectmen's Statement.

One Power.

A tide power on Great Cranberry island, at the mouth of a creek or inlet, where a dam might be built so as to enclose a vast body of water with which to operate at low tide. Not improved. Situated near Great Cranberry harbor, which is open at all seasons. Would operate a large amount of machinery.

CRAWFORD—WASHINGTON COUNTY.

Statement of F. Loring Talbot, Esq., of East Machias.

Five Powers.

First, on the East Machias river, "Ripplings at Bridge," 10 feet fall.

Second, "Pokey Dam," nine feet fall, on the East Machias river, at the outlet of "Pokey" or Crawford lake.

Third, the "Barstow Dam," one mile below, 12 feet fall.

The above powers are fed by Crawford lake, which has nine feet head of flowage over its surface of 2.75 square miles, and also by Shining lake, which has a surface of six square miles.

Fourth, on "Barrows'-Lake Stream," 12 feet fall; the lake has a surface of 1.50 square miles.

Fifth, on "Seavey's Mill Brook," eight feet fall.

The water-power and township are owned by M. J. Talbot, Esq., of East Machias.

Crystal Township—Aroostook County.

Statement of E. F. Dinsmore, Esq., of Island Falls Plantation.

One Power.

On the outlet stream of Crystal lake, which is three miles above, a fall of fifteen feet. An abundant supply of water can be had by flowing the lake.

Cumberland—Cumberland County.

Statement of the Selectmen.

Three Powers.

Two up-and-down saws driven by water, will operate part of the year, and one carding machine.

Cushing—Knox County.

Selectmen's Returns.

One Power.

A stave mill upon it, running about half the year.

D Township—Aroostook County.

Statement of Harrison O. Hussey, Esq., of Monticello.

Water-power in this township on the tributaries of the Meduxnakeag. The main stream is fed by a pond of considerable size.

Dallas Plantation—Franklin County.

Statement of Abner Toothaker, Esq., of Phillips.

One Power.

At the outlet of Gull pond, a good privilege; pond covers 0.65 square miles, and can be flowed several feet. Unimproved.

Dalton—Aroostook County.

From Selectmen's Statement.

Two Powers.

First, on Big Machias stream, saw mill and grist mill; power sufficient to drive an up-and-down saw, and clapboard and shingle machine, and two runs of stones the year through.

Second, on Little Machias stream, will drive machinery, as above, eight months of the year. Saw mill and grist mill now upon it. The Big Machias is connected with several lakes of considerable size, and drains a large extent of territory.

DAMARISCOTTA—LINCOLN COUNTY.

Selectmen's Returns.

One Power.

A tide power; 10 feet fall at low tide; not improved. Proprietorship unknown.

DANFORTH—WASHINGTON COUNTY.

One Power.

"Butterfield Privilege," on the Baskahegan stream, 10 miles above its junction with the Mattawamkeag river.

The dam is about seven feet high and may be made two feet higher if needed. On the dam a single saw and a shingle machine. Sufficient power to drive one single saw, a shingle and clapboard machine, four runs of stones for grinding grain, a carding and clothing mill, and probably more. The dam flows a pond some eight miles in length and one-third of a mile in width. The privilege may also have all of Baskahegan lake, containing about eighteen square miles, for a reservoir, by maintaining a dam at the outlet, which would treble the power for the whole year.

Good markets for products.

DAYTON—YORK COUNTY.

Statement of Z. G. Staples and J. R. Haley, Esqs.

[See also "Buxton and Dayton," and "Dayton and Hollis."]

Seven Powers.

First, Second, Third, Fourth, etc., on Hill's brook, which flows from a remarkable natural fountain or spring, and abounds in falls sufficient to turn a grist or shingle mill.

Fifth, "Goodwin's Mills," on Goodwin's or Swan-pond stream, fall about 33 feet. Various mills.

Sixth, "Wadlin Privilege," a few rods below, large fall; unimproved.

Seventh, ten rods below, "Hanson & Pierce Mill," 16 feet fall, grist and saw mills.

DAYTON AND HOLLIS—YORK COUNTY.

Statement of Z. G. Staples and J. R. Haley, Esqs., of Dayton.

[See also "Dayton," and "Hollis."]

Several Powers.

On Cook's brook, which flows mostly from Bartlett's pond in

Waterborough. Excellent privileges, especially those situated near the Saco river.

Two are improved, "Clark's Mills," grist, stave, and shingle.

One mile below, "Kimball's Mills," 40 feet fall, saw mill; power not all used.

Water sufficient to operate mills nearly all the year.

Dayton Plantation—Aroostook County.

Statement of John Gardiner, Esq., of Patten.

One Power.

On Crystal stream, a saw mill. No others known to the reporter.

Dead River Plantation—Somerset County.

Statement of Hon. Abner Coburn.

One Power.

"Hurricane Falls," near the northwest corner of the township, a descent of eight or ten feet, banks high, dead water above for five miles.

Deblois—Washington County.

From Selectmen's Statement.

Numerous Powers.

First, the "Great Falls," on the Narraguagus river, and on the county road leading to Beddington on the north and Cherryfield on the south, about eleven miles from tide water, and where the village, comprising about 120 inhabitants, is located. The falls extend about half a mile, with an aggregate descent, it is estimated, of nearly 50 feet, embracing a succession of mill privileges equal, if not superior, to any to be found at the same distance from navigable waters within the county. They are so situated as to afford superior facilities for erecting factories of almost any description. The banks on either side are high, the channel of the river narrow and its bed ledgy, so that the expense of dams would be comparatively trifling.

Within a short distance of Great Falls there are over 3,000 acres of forest, one-half of "black growth," pine, spruce, hacmatac and cedar timber; the other half of old-growth hardwood, beech, yellow, white and grey birch, oak, rock and white maple, ash, &c. Vast quantities additional suitable for cord wood, and millions of feet of hardwood large enough for plank stock and ship timber. The timber adjacent is sufficient to run saw mills of various kinds for many years, and to justify the investment of tens of thousands of dollars with prospect of a generous return.

The soil is excellent, is free from rocks; roads are constructed with the utmost ease; large natural meadows abound; great numbers of cattle, from all the region about are pastured within the town; muck of the best quality is abundant. "We are anxious to have capitalists come in and improve our water-power, and industrious workingmen to cultivate our excellent soil. The proprietor of these lands, Wm. Freeman, Jr., of Cherryfield, offers the highest inducements as to terms, to farmers, millmen, or manufacturers."

There are other valuable privileges on the Narraguagus river in this town, none of which are employed. Also smaller powers on other streams which might be turned to useful and profitable account. The only improvement on the Great Falls is a shingle mill, which operates without the aid of a dam, by the natural force of the current.

DEDHAM—HANCOCK COUNTY.

From Selectmen's Returns.

Five Powers.

Five already in use, with several employed, and therefore not reported, all situated upon Fitts pond stream.

First and Second, the "Fitts Mills"; two dams, each with head and fall of 15 feet, giving a total fall of 30 feet in less than one-fourth of a mile. Saw, shingle and lath mills.

Third, Fourth and Fifth, "Dedham Tannery"; three dams, 12, 15 and 12 feet high, respectively, and total fall of 39 feet in about 40 rods distance. Saw, shingle, lath, stave, and flour mills, and tannery.

The mills operate all the year, and the power can be greatly increased at little expense, the stream being fed by four ponds, one large and three small. The tannery privileges have two additional ponds, and all can be converted into reservoirs of great capacity. Freshets are not serious. The largest pond is on the dividing ridge betwixt the Penobscot and Union basins, and when greatly swollen pours off its surplus into the Union river, the natural and usual outlet being into the Penobscot.

Rocks, coarse granite, suitable for rough constructions. Lay of the land, suitable for mills, etc.

Two-thirds of the basin covered with forests. Improvement of the power has more than doubled the valuation of the town.

Market, Bangor, by road.

Deer Isle—Hancock County.

From Selectmen's Returns.

Several Powers.

All but one are tide powers; one, with dam already built, can carry a large amount of machinery. A carding mill on a brook. Two tide grist mills. The tide privileges are mainly unemployed. Various ponds of an aggregate surface of 400 acres might be turned to account for reservoir purposes. Wheels, two overshot and one spiral.

Denmark—Oxford County.

From the Report of Survey of Cyrus Ingalls and Joseph Bennett, Esqs.; Procured and Endorsed by the Selectmen.

Fifteen Powers, or More.

The most important are on the outlet stream of Moose pond, which covers about 1,700 acres, is about seven miles long and from 40 to 275 rods wide.

First, at the outlet, at "Denmark Corner," the "Outlet Dam." Thirteen feet head and fall. A good stone dam 70 feet long extends from the west bank, the remainder of the dam being of wood for log slips and flumes for the use of the mills. Saw, grist, stave, and shingle mills.

Second, 26 rods below, head and fall nine feet. Good stone dam 80 feet long, and a mill 26 by 56, three stories high, in which are various saws, etc.

Third, 37 rods below, a new stone dam nearly completed, intended for a starch factory. Head eight feet.

Fourth, 30 rods below; head and fall 15 feet, good split-stone dam, 90 feet in length laid in cement upon solid ledge. Dam flows about 700 square rods. Stave, shingle, clapboard, planing and kit machines, and various saws. Also a large cooperage.

Fifth, 55 rods below, "Long Falls," 20 rods long; head and fall 10 feet. Bed of the stream and the shores are smooth, solid ledge. A dam at the head of the falls, 75 feet long, would reach from bank to bank, and pond back a large body of water; the land above the head of the falls lies nearly level with the surface of the stream at high water in the spring.

Sixth, 66 rods below, "Symonds' Dam," head and fall of 10 feet; banks high, a dam 60 feet in length, would flow an area of 400 square rods.

Seventh, at the foot or outlet of Little Moose, "Webster's Falls," which are 40 rods long. In 1807 a dam was built at the foot of this pond, making a head of ten feet, for the purpose of driving logs down the Moose Brook canal into Saco river; dam now nearly rotted away. This is the most valuable privilege on the whole stream, for head and fall, and amount of water. There are many small streams emptying into Moose brook, between here and the upper mills. The tract of land upon the west side is covered with a heavy growth of pine and white oak timber, the best in the county.

Eighth, "Lower Falls," three miles below; head and fall 15 feet.

Ninth, Tenth, etc., several good mill privileges between Webster's falls and the Lower falls.

Moose brook, from the upper mills at the foot of Moose pond, to Saco river, runs parallel with, and distant about 200 rods from the county road leading from Denmark corner to Hiram bridge. No estimate of the volume or power of the stream furnished, other than which is involved in the statement of the capacity of the reservoir. A large area of country and several streams are tributary to the pond.

Twelfth, "Holt's Privilege" at West Denmark village, on a pond of six acres which is fed by a pond of 120 acres. Fall 12 feet; abundant water nearly all the year for saw and grist mill.

Thirteenth, at the foot of Granger pond; 64 feet fall in 264 rods; a good privilege for light machinery or a grist mill. Pond can be raised six feet by a dam without damage. Good site for a flour mill, which is greatly needed, as all the wheat now goes out of town several miles to be ground.

Fourteenth, on the outlet of Fish pond, 25 acres and fed by a pond of eight acres; fall 10 feet; a shingle mill.

Fifteenth, a mile below, a dam flowing a large tract of land; 12 feet head and fall may be had. Two ponds empty into the stream a short distance above the dam, making an excellent privilege.

Granite abundant in all the town, some of it excellent. Sufficient clay for bricks in various localities. Inexhaustible peat bogs of the best quality. Soil excellent for fruit and corn. Two-thirds covered with forests, pine, hemlock, spruce, white and red oak, bass, etc. The Portland & Ogdensburgh railroad will pass in our close vicinity. Transportation now by Cumberland & Oxford canal and by road. Market, Portland, 35 miles distant. Wood, $1.25 to $3.00 per cord. Labor, $1.00 to $2.00 per day, exclusive of board.

"We offer the highest inducements to capitalists; and any parties coming in to improve our water-power will be received with the utmost favor, and will meet the most liberal advances."

Dennes Township—Somerset County.

Statement of Heman Whipple, Esq., of Solon.

Five Powers.

First, at the outlet of "Little-Big" Wood pond, a fall of 35 feet in half a mile. Good chance for dams. Pond covers 1.35 square miles, and is dammed seven feet.

Second, half a mile below the east line, fall 10 feet. Small ponds above for reservoirs.

Third, "Dennes Falls," on Sandy stream, in the east part of the town, 10 feet fall, formerly a grist mill. Good site. Small pond above, can be flowed.

Falls above on the branches, 10 and 12 feet.

Dennysville—Washington County.

From the Returns of Peter E. Vose, Esq.

[See also "Dennysville and Edmunds."]

Two Powers.

First, on "Wilson's Stream," a shingle mill. The stream is not constant, having no reservoir; a shingle mill might run four to five months in the year.

Second, the stream empties into tide waters close by the county road leading to Pembroke, where machinery might be conveniently located, to be propelled by say an overshot wheel of 16 feet diameter. The tide flows to the mills on Dennys river in this village.

Dennysville and Edmunds—Washington County.

From the Returns and from a Plan of the Water-Power, Furnished by the Selectmen of Dennysville.

[See also "Dennysville," and "Edmunds."]

Five Powers.

All on Dennys river, the outlet of the great Meddybemps lake.

First, "Dennysville Falls," at the village of Dennysville, near

Cobscook bay. On the dam at the village, which has a head of ten feet and a good pond, there are a single saw mill, one gang saw mill, and a lath machine attached to each; also shingle machines for winter sawing, one grist mill, one bone mill, two pail and churn manufactories. These last are carried on by Lincolns & Eastman, while the mills are the property of Edmund, Thomas and Elizabeth Lincoln. There is water sufficient to operate these mills, &c., three-fourths to seven-eigths of the time from the first of April to the first of December, day sawing. They will cut from 2,500,000 to 3,000,000 feet of long lumber per sawing year, and 1,000,000 to 2,000,000 of laths and shingles. The pail factories are capable of turning out 100 dozen pails or 50 dozen churns per week, and the grist mill can grind 150 to 200 bushels corn per day.

Second, one mile above; a total fall of twenty feet in —— rods. Unimproved.

Third, one-half a mile above; a fall of eight feet in ————. Unimproved.

Fourth, one mile above; a fall of eight feet. No improvement.

Fifth, about one mile above; ten feet fall. Not improved.

The foregoing powers are owned by the Lincolns aforesaid, as also nearly all the banks of the river on both sides for several miles. Good roads most of the way to two of them. A gang saw mill once started on one of the privileges, which was destroyed by fire. The total fall of the river from the lake to its mouth, about twenty miles, must be 250 feet. Several small streams empty into the river in its course, upon some of which logs can be driven.

The volume of water in time of freshets is judged to be from two to three times the ordinary volume. No serious damage has ever been caused by them. The river, with the water held in the lakes by the dams, can be depended on, excepting in an unusually dry time. The lay of the land is such in connection with the powers, that mills and workshops can be conveniently located. More than half of the basin must be covered with forests, though it has been mostly cut over. But timber enough is left, if fires do not destroy it, to supply the mills for many years. The rocks in the vicinity are suitable for building purposes, and the soil is generally a clayey loam. If our water-power could be brought into use, our population and wealth would rapidly increase.

Lumber-laden vessels of 200 tons come within half a mile of the mills.

DENNYSVILLE AND TOWNSHIP NO 14—WASHINGTON COUNTY.

Statement of T. W. Allan, Esq., of Dennysville.

Three Powers.

First, half a mile from the north line of Edmunds, "Stodder Rips," on Dennys river. Three-fourths of a mile long; total fall 25 feet. Good chance for dam at the head. Owned by T.W. Allan and the Lincolns. No improvements.

Second, three-fourths of a mile above, "Clark's Rips," 40 rods long; fall six feet. No improvement. Pond in the river two miles long; a dam would make the pond half a mile wide; green timber land, old growth. Owned by T. W. Allan and the Lincolns.

Third, two and a half miles above Clark's rips, "Bright's Island Rips"; fall estimated ten feet. No improvement.

DETROIT—SOMERSET COUNTY.

From Selectmen's Returns.

One Power.

The "Rips," on the Sebasticook river; fall 30 to 40 feet in one-fourth of a mile. Power estimated equal to sawing 8,000,000 or 10,000,000 lumber. Power only partially improved; a tannery, two saw mills and a shingle mill upon it. Mills work or may work all the year. See reservoirs tributary to this power in last Table page 95, Part II. The power can be greatly increased by the use of these. Machinery of ordinary construction. Rocks, granite and limestone, suitable for building. Total products, $100,000 or $150,000 per annum. The improvement of the power has resulted in a large increase of the wealth of the town.

Market, Bangor and Portland, by Maine Central Railroad.

DEXTER—PENOBSCOT COUNTY.

From the Statement, and from Elaborate Plans of the Water-Power, Furnished by Josiah Crosby, Esq.

Twenty-eight Powers.

Sixteen of the above are situated upon the outlet stream of Dexter pond. Height of the falls 142 feet in three-fourths of a mile, or 160·5 feet in two miles. These are classed together as "Dexter Falls."

First, next below the outlet, J. & G. Abbott's woollen factory; head and fall 18 feet.

Second, J. & G. Abbott's saw mill; head and fall 18 feet.

Third, H. C. Parson's carriage shop, occupied by J. C. Grant; head and fall nine feet.

Fourth, C. W. Curtis & Co., carpenters' and sash and blind shop; head and fall nine feet.

Fifth, Geo. Bailey's carriage shop; head and fall nine feet.

Sixth, N. Dusten & Co.'s machine shop and foundry; head and fall 12 feet.

Seventh, Pennington & Tibbetts' furniture factory; head and fall 10 feet.

Eighth, J. & G. Abbott's grist mill; head and fall 22 feet.

Ninth, Dexter mills machine shop; head and fall 16 feet.

Tenth, Dexter mills woollen factory; head and fall 20 feet.

Eleventh, Charles Shaw's tannery; head and fall nine feet.

Twelfth, Dexter mills picker house; head and fall 11 feet.

Thirteenth, Dexter mills woollen factory; head and fall 16 feet.

Fourteenth, Dexter mills woollen factory; head and fall 17 feet.

Fifteenth, lemon-box factory, occupied by Reuben Flanders.

Sixteenth, Francis Hill's woollen factory, occupied by ——— Campbell.

As appears in the above statement, all the falls have some machinery upon them, but very much might be added. The amount of manufactures might be nearly doubled. An excellent site for a cotton or woollen mill in place of the saw mill; also of the grist mill. The stream, or rather the pond, will furnish forty horse-powers under an 18-foot head all the year. The dam at the foot of the pond usually flows it about eight feet in the spring. Area of the pond not far from three and a half square miles. No freshets, water all kept back. Machinery mostly excellent. The best wheels are an overshot, John Tyler, and Reynolds' turbine.

Seventeenth, on the same stream, just below its junction with Spooner's pond stream, unoccupied; head and fall six feet.

Eighteenth, on the same stream, near the south line of the town, Libbey's saw and shingle mill; head and fall 10 feet.

There are a number of privileges upon the Sebasticook main stream in the north part of the town. The stream is rapid and rather inconstant. Will give 20 horse-powers five months of the year. Never has been a tight dam or good machinery upon it. Large quantities of hemlock, hardwood, and cedar on its bordering territory. On this stream are five privileges, as follows:

Nineteenth, Silver's saw mill; fall 10 feet.

Twentieth, below, unoccupied; fall eight feet.

Twenty-First, about a mile below; 10 feet fall.

Twenty-Second, somewhat south of the west line of the town, unoccupied; fall 12 feet.

Twenty-Third, Charles Jumper's saw and shingle mill; fall 10 feet.

Twenty-Fourth, on a branch of the main stream, Silver's shingle mill; fall 20 feet.

Twenty-Fifth, at the outlet of Spooner's pond, saw mill and shingle mill; fall 13 feet.

Twenty-Sixth, a short distance below on the same stream, unoccupied; six feet fall.

Spooner's stream will furnish 15 horse-powers from five to seven months of the year. A good dam at the outlet of the pond. The Kenduskeag stream will furnish 10 horse-powers four months in the year. Two privileges on said stream noticed as follows:

Twenty-Seventh, unoccupied; 10 feet fall.

Twenty-Eighth, on a branch; 20 feet fall; formerly a saw mill upon it.

Abundant slatestone on all the privileges, which is sometimes used for building; two stories of the largest factory are built of it. The improvement of the power has doubled the population and trebled the wealth of the town.

Market, Portland and Boston, by Dexter & Newport Railroad, and connections.

Dickeyville—Aroostook County.

From the Assessors' Returns.

Nine Powers.

First, on the Dufour brook, not employed; at low water about two feet square in bulk. Good site for grist and saw mill. The fall averages about one in nine. Rocky.

Second and Third, on Gagnon brook, about three feet square in bulk, and if the upper part were cleared would be considerably more. One saw mill three miles back, and two other mills near St. John river, grist and saw, small branch coming from the northwest joining at lower mill. Sandy soil; much buckwheat raised.

Fourth, on Rosignol brook, size as No. 1, stream takes its rise from a small lake six miles in the interior. Privilege is not employed, but is an admirable one.

Fifth, on Bourgoin brook, size as No. 1; not employed; good facilities for building; one mile from last mentioned.

Sixth, on Cyr brook, small saw mill near river St. John. Runs only in high water.

Seventh, on Gagnon brook, a grist mill; power not quite as strong as first named.

Eighth, takes its source from the two small Bourgignon lakes. About a foot square at low water.

Ninth, runs a small saw mill, and is about same force as last named at low water.

The above brooks are capable in high water of running considerable machiney; but the parties owning the privileges are poor, and have means to erect buildings and machinery, merely to supply their own wants. The powers work only in summer time, spring and fall. On some of these, reservoirs could be built cheaply, to supply the mills all winter. No. 6 ground 12,000 bushels grain last year with one set "burrs." No export; all for home consumption.

DIXFIELD—OXFORD COUNTY.

Statement of the Selectmen.

Seven Powers.

First, on Webb's river, at its junction with the Androscoggin, not of the largest class, but not excelled as to quality, in the State. It will operate throughout the year a saw, grist, shingle, carding and threshing mill, a carriage factory and tannery, all of which are in active operation. A woolen factory, in operation here thirty years, was burned down in spring of 1868.

Fall from the dam to the Androscoggin river, 29 feet in 200 of run. The bottom, sides, and bank of the stream are solid granite, and are favorable for the location of structures. The dam can be raised several feet higher, if so desired. The mill pond connected above is five miles long, four rods wide, and 12 feet deep on the average.

The power and the beautiful village connected are 18 miles from Bryant's-Pond Railroad Station, and 13 miles from North-Jay Railroad Station.

Second, five miles above, unoccupied. Volume of water three-fourths of No. 1; fall six feet in 100 of run. Easy of access, by land or water.

The outlay of a few hundred dollars in building a dam at the outlet of Webb's pond, would render both the above powers constant even in the most extreme drought, and very greatly increase their efficiency. The pond is six miles long and one and a half miles wide. A head of nine feet could be raised upon it.

Third, on Newton brook, "Wells' Mills," saw, shingle, and threshing; 200,000 feet boards, and as many shingles; with good dam and wheels, double might be done; head and fall 11 feet; six to eight months.

Fourth, above, fall nine feet; volume nearly equal to No. 1; a saw mill in former years.

Fifth, above, saw mill and thresher; few months. 250,000 feet boards; head and fall 15 feet. This stream overflows in freshets, producing much grass.

Sixth, on "Seven Mile brook," at East Dixfield; saw and grist mill; operate respectively four and 12 months; 150,000 feet of lumber; stream subject to heavy freshets from mountains. Three miles to North-Jay Station.

Seventh, an overshot power on "Siberia Brook;" saw and shingle mill; fall 20 feet.

Several more small powers in town unoccupied.

Market, Lewiston and Portland, chiefly by rail.

DIXMONT—PENOBSCOT COUNTY.

Statement of W. B. Ferguson, Esq., and the Selectmen.

Four Powers.

First and Second, Dixmont Centre Falls. One is fed by a pond covering 200 acres which is raised eight feet; the other by the same and by another pond of 100 acres which is flowed 10 feet.

Third, a power at North Dixmont; fed by a pond of 75 acres, which is flowed 10 feet.

Fourth, at the outlet of Skinner pond, fall of 20 feet may be had; formerly a dam and mill; pond covers 300 acres, and can be flowed 10 feet, together with a large tract of swamp. Unimproved.

Improvements: three saw mills, one axe factory, two shingle and one grist mill. The saw mills run about four months, grist mill nine months.

Market, Bangor, by road.

DOVER—PISCATAQUIS COUNTY.

Statement of the Selectmen.

Ten Powers.

First, "Dover Great Falls," at Dover village, on Piscataquis river; falls 23·5 feet in 325 feet.

Improvements: one woolen mill of 100 horse-power, one grist mill, four runs of stones of 80 horse-power. This is not more than half of the power of the falls in a common season. There can be dams upon the head waters of said river so as to raise the power at these falls to 600 horse.

Second, on Piscataquis river, 100 rods below the bridge at Dover village; height of fall, six feet. Unoccupied.

Third "Dover Lower Village Falls," on Piscataquis river, at East Dover; height of dam nine feet.

Improvements: saw, grist, shingle and clapboard mills. This commands all the water that passes the "Great Falls" at Dover village. The dam at East Dover flows the river two miles.

Fourth, "Dover South Mills," on Black stream, dam 12 feet high.

Improvements: saw and shingle mills, operate all the year.

Fifth, "Sias-Brook Power," suitable for a shingle mill. Not occupied.

Sixth, "Ayer's Falls," on Black stream, not occupied.

Seventh, on Alder stream, a shingle mill.

Eighth, Ninth, Tenth, etc., on Black stream and Alder brook, suitable for shingle mills. Not used.

Union, Stearns, and scroll wheels. Rock, granite, lime and slate; land level about the river and of a superior quality for farming.

Market, Bangor, 35 miles; railroad building, open in fall of 1869.

DRESDEN—LINCOLN COUNTY.

From Selectmen's Returns.

Six Powers.

First and Second, on Goud stream; former 30 feet fall in 100 of distance; latter 10 feet in 40 feet. Grist and saw mill; operate six months; percussion wheel, formerly an overshot, which gave much more power. A large bog, 175 acres, could be flowed eight feet at little expense. Range of water about six feet. Would cut 100,000 of lumber, and grind 9,000 bushels of grain.

Third, Fourth, Fifth and Sixth, on Gardiner stream, averaging each about 25 feet in a total distance of two miles; small part of the power used. Formerly a good grist mill and saw mill; both now greatly dilapidated; would saw 300,000 to 400,000 of lumber. Stream could work six months with the present volume of water. Poorest sort of wheels.

Stream connected with two ponds; Gardiner pond 150 acres in extent and 20 feet deep; also a large bog between the lake and mill, 500 acres, which might be flowed four or five feet with ease. Second pond about 70 acres. The stream might be made to carry two or three saw mills.

Stone not good for building. No forest on basin; stream low in summer.

Market, at home.

Drew Plantation—Penobscot County.

Statement of D. Butters, Esq., of Prentiss.

Three Powers.

First, "The Falls," on Meadow brook, one overshot wheel of large diameter could be operated.

Second and Third, further up; a dam eight or ten feet would flow at each point a very large tract of low flat land, perhaps 500 acres. There is no improvement at any of the privileges. Stone suitable for building close at hand.

Duck-Trap-Grant Plantation—Penobscot County.

Statement of the Assessors of Independence Plantation.

Several Powers.

The "Jimsketticook Rapids," on the Mattawamkeag river, just below the mouth of the Crossuntic stream. The fall, which is judged to be from 30 to 40 feet in a mile, affords several points at which dams could be located; the banks are high on each side, dead water above for 12 miles. In the drouth of summer the water at the fall is 15 rods wide, and from two to five feet deep.

The Mattawamkeag at this point drains 1,100 square miles, and is fed by numerous large lakes and ponds. In addition, by building a dam at the falls, a breadth of land 30 to 40 rods wide on the sides of the river can be converted into reservoir, and a bog three or four thousand acres in extent, which now are flowed from four to twelve feet in freshets. There is unquestionably power enough here, readily commanded, to build up a great manufacturing city.

The European & North American Railway will pass directly by the powers.

Enormous amounts of lumber in the region, hemlock bark for tanning, etc.

None of the power is used.

DURHAM—ANDROSCOGGIN COUNTY.

From Selectmen's Returns.

Three Powers.

First, on the outlet of a small pond in the western part of the town; grist mill, and saw mill which cuts 40,000 feet yearly.

Second, in the northeast part of the town; grist and shingle mill; small stream.

Third, near Southwest Bend; grist, saw, shingle, and clapboard mills, cut 40,000 feet boards annually.

Mills work about eight months in the year. Large peat bogs in the westerly part of the town.

Market, Lewiston, ten miles, by road.

DYER-BROOK PLANTATION—AROOSTOOK COUNTY.

Statement of S. D. Philpot, Esq.

Two Powers.

First, on Dyer brook.

Second, on a brook not yet named.

E PLANTATION—FRANKLIN COUNTY.

From the Assessors' Returns.

Numerous Powers.

There are two sets of falls on the Sandy river. The upper have a descent of about 30 feet; the lower consist of four successive pitches, which average about 20 feet each. They are capable of carrying a large number of mills, and have an abundant supply of water the greater part of the season. They are located on the road leading from Phillips to Rangely lake. There is any amount of timber in their vicinity, which can be got to the privileges on a down-hill grade; there is also a good market for manufactured lumber.

Other falls are situated on the north branch of the Sandy river, the descent of which is ninety feet.

EASTBROOK—HANCOCK COUNTY.

Two Powers, or More.

First, on the outlet stream of Molasses pond, "Macomber's Saw Mill;" the pond covers 2.25 square miles and 10 feet depth of storage are already commanded upon it; two feet more are feasible.

Livermore Falls.

Second, at the outlet of Scammon pond, a saw mill. Scammon pond covers one square mile, storage not reported. It is fed by Abram's pond, 0.80 square mile, 10 feet storage, and by Molasses, area and storage as above.

No others in use.

EAST LIVERMORE—ANDROSCOGGIN COUNTY.

From Selectmen's Returns.

[See also "East Livermore and Livermore."]

Two Powers.

First, a privilege on the Johnny brook; a small power; works about half the time.

Second, a privilege on the Norris brook; a small power; works about half the time.

EAST LIVERMORE AND LIVERMORE—ANDROSCOGGIN COUNTY.

From Returns of the Selectmen, and the Statements of H. W. Hutchins and Hollis Turner, Esqs., and of James Bridge, Esq., of Augusta.

[See also "East Livermore," and "Livermore."]

One Power.

"Livermore Falls," on the Androscoggin river; height of the natural fall 22 feet in 30 rods, upper fall 14 feet, then eight feet fall in 30 rods. The dam located on the crest of the upper fall is seven feet high, making the total head and fall 29 feet. It can be raised seven feet more.

The power due to the total available fall, 36 feet, the volume of water being assumed 15 per cent. less than at Lewiston, or 79,900 cubic feet per minute at lowest run, is 5,436 horse-powers gross, or 217,440 spindles. The increase to be derived upon use of the reservoirs tributary to the river, above, may be inferred from inspection of pages 84–86, Part II.

During the summer of 1867, the proprietors built a very excellent dam, of crib work, filled in with stone in its whole extent, as strong a construction as can be made except of split granite. It was built with a view to future enlargement, and can be raised seven feet without damage from flowing.

The land on both sides of the river is peculiarly well adapted to the location of manufacturing establishments. A company from Massachusetts, years ago, negotiated for the privilege, with a view to canalling and improvements on the Livermore side, but failed to make any arrangement on account of disagreement as to price.

The rock in the immediate vicinity of the falls is fit for foundations and other rough work. Very excellent granite is abundant within two miles. Bricks of excellent quality for building were delivered at the falls, 1868, for $6 per thousand.

Of the 5,436 horse-powers, probably not over one hundred are in use, operating a saw mill, grist mill, and some other small establishments.

The Rocomeka Company are the chief proprietors of the power. They own, in addition to the saw mill, a building, nearly new, 80 by 30 feet, three stories high, and a fifty horse steam boiler attached for heating purposes. Building has been used for the condensation of milk; but sufficient quantities not being procurable in the vicinity, the manufacture will probably be abandoned, and the whole property put into the market.

The privilege is regarded by experts as second to none on the river except that at Lewiston, and to that only in sum of power, not in availability and facilities for improvement.

Market, all points, by railroad, which passes close beside the power.

The view accompanying this statement represents but little more than the fall produced by the dam.

East Machias—Washington County.

From Selectmen's Returns.

Six Powers.

All of the above are within two miles of tide water, four of them on the main (East Machias) river, and two on Chace's stream.

The four privileges on the main river are situated between the head of tide and Hadley's lake, a distance of three miles; total descent in that distance, 47 feet.

First, "Lower Mills," at the head of tide; height of mill pond, 9.8 feet above mean high water; three saw mills with lath mills, not much used at present, two grist mills and one planing mill.

Second, "Upper Mills," 2,000 feet by the course of the river above the lower; height 15.8 feet, or 25.6 feet above tide; two double saw mills or four single saws, and two lath mills. Three saws are about constantly employed.

Third, between these two dams, the water is rapid; a dam might be thrown across at any point. At present the privilege is occu-

Lower Falls, East Machias.

pied only by a gang and a single saw mill, with grist mill and lath mill.

Fourth, "Jacksonville Mills," one and three-fourths miles by the river above the upper mills, with a further elevation of about 12 feet; thence to Hadley's lake, about one mile, and a further elevation of about 10 feet.

The above privileges are of very unusual excellence. The form of the land and the condition of the bottom and banks are such as to admit of the economical development of the power. The grand reservoirs situated just above furnish a great supply of water close at hand. The powers are near tide water and have ready access to the sea. Freshets are unknown, the great lakes equalizing the flow of water; no damage of any sort has been caused by flood for 60 years.

Upon reference to page 132, Part II, it will be seen that 22 square miles of lakes and ponds, not including the smaller, are tributary to this power, nearly all of which are already flowed for log-driving purposes. A storage of six feet upon 20 square miles would yield, for 10 hours per day, 312 days a year, upon the fall from Hadley lake to the tide, a gross power of 1,600 horse, or 64,000 spindles. To this should be added the *natural* flow of the river to arrive at its constant manufacturing power. But in fact the storage could be used in six months or less, the natural flow of the river sufficing all demands for the rest of the year.

Fifth and Sixth, at the outlet of Gardiner's lake on Chace's stream, which enters the main river above the Upper falls. Stream is three-fourths of a mile long, and its descent in that distance to the main river is 30 feet; two single saws, two lath mills, one shingle mill. At the point of confluence the main river is 30 feet above tide; Gardiner's lake, therefore, is 60 feet above sea level. Upon this stream are two single saws, two lath mills, and one shingle mill.

Gardiner's lake covers 8.50 square miles. If stored to the depth of six feet, it would yield for the working hours of the year upon the whole fall to the tide, a gross power of 840 horse or 33,600 spindles. This is the storage alone. Remarks as to availability of the privileges upon the main river apply here also.

Not over one-fourth of the whole power upon these various privileges is now employed in saw and grist mills. The dams are not tight; there is no economy in the use of water; the machinery though good, is not the best for economizing power.

Mills operate from the 15th of March to the 15th of December; might work all the year but for the difficulty of getting stock to the mills after the ponds are frozen.

The water of both the main river and Chace's stream being purified by subsidence in the lakes above, is admirably adapted for paper-making and for chemical and bleaching purposes.

Granite is abundant on Hadley lake. Lumber and other building material are of course abundant and cheap.

Parties proposing the development of this power will meet with substantial aid and coöperation. The privileges are all owned in the vicinity.

Market, all points reached by sea where lumber is wanted.

The view given in connection with this statement is that of the "Lower Falls," with a mere glimpse of the "Upper Falls" under the bridge.

EASTON—AROOSTOOK COUNTY.

From a Statement, and a Plan of the Streams, Furnished by Albert Whitcomb and David R. Marston, Esqs.

Four Powers.

First, "Wartman's Saw and Shingle Mills."

Second, "Marston's Mills," on the Presque Isle river of the St. John, dam 10 feet, could be 25; saw, shingle and lath mill, located on a good road, or at the crossing of two roads. Saw mill and shingle mill can operate all the year.

Third, half a mile above, on a good road; dam could be 14 feet high.

All the machinery is of inferior quality; small ponds; basin is heavily wooded.

Fourth, below Marston's mill; not occupied.

EASTPORT—WASHINGTON COUNTY.

From the Selectmen's Returns, and a Plan of the Town.

Three Powers.

First, "Big Cove," contains 100 acres, bare at low tide, depth at mouth 20 feet, would require a long dam.

"Price's Cove," would require dam 250 feet long, would be buttressed by rock at each end. Dam could be built easily.

"Shackford's Cove," would require dam 200 feet long, rock at both ends. Dam could be built easily. Mean rise and fall of the tide 18 feet; powers could operate 16 hours out of the 24. None of the privileges are in use.

EATON-GRANT PLANTATION—AROOSTOOK COUNTY.

From the Assessors' Statement.

Four Powers.

First, "one of the best unoccupied water-powers in the county," on the Little Madawaska stream, which is 200 feet in width and 40 miles in length. Its last two miles of length are in this plantation, and in each mile it falls 40 feet.

The power is of unusual excellence. The stream is comparatively constant in its supply, and the facilities for improvement are first-rate. Mills are needed in this region. Good soil, vast amount of lumber.

Second, Third and Fourth, smaller powers.

EDDINGTON—PENOBSCOT COUNTY.

From Selectmen's Returns.

Four Powers.

On the Davis stream, total fall 45 feet in three-fourths of a mile.

The power is sufficient to saw 2,500,000 long lumber and 5,000,000 shingles. On the first dam, saw, shingle and clapboard mills. On the second dam, shingle, three grist, and carding machines. Mills operate all the year except in severe drouths. Stream connected with two ponds of about 1000 acres. Rock abundant. Basin one-fourth covered with woods.

Market, Bangor, six miles, by road; and by water for long lumber.

EDEN—HANCOCK COUNTY.

Four Powers.

First, "Hadley's Mills," in the west part of the town; stream fed by a pond.

Second, above, "Higgin's Saw Mill."

Third and Fourth, on Eagle-pond stream, two saw mills; stream fed by three or four small ponds.

EDGECOMB—LINCOLN COUNTY.

From Selectmen's Returns.

Four Powers.

First, on branch of Sheepscot river, a mile from Wiscasset village; tide grist mill, 80 bushels per day; pond of five acres; fall eight feet. Kendall wheel.

Second, on a pond in centre of the town; grist and shingle mill, fall 18 feet, 300 bushels of grain per day; will work without cessation; pond about 200 acres. Blake wheel. Power only part used.

Third, below, a grist mill; fall 15 feet, 60 bushels per day. Works about six months; pond about 20 acres. Tub wheel.

Fourth, on branch of Sheepscot river, four miles from Wiscasset, formerly saw, grist, clothing and carding mills, now in ruins; fall 15 feet. A reservoir might be formed, of 500 acres, and receive all the water from Second and Third mills. If said water-power were improved, it would be one of the most valuable in Lincoln county.

EDINBURG—PENOBSCOT COUNTY.

Statement of S. E. Batchelor and Isaac Foster, Esqs.

[See also "Edinburg and Passadumkeag."]

Six Powers.

"Labalister Rips," near the south line of the town on Hemlock stream, 10 feet fall; not improved.

"Little Falls," above, 15 feet, no improvement.

"Long Rips," above, 12 feet, no improvement.

"Slate Falls," above, 11 feet, no improvement, dead water above, which may be made a large reservoir.

Also two powers on Pollard brook. Not used.

EDINBURG AND PASSADUMKEAG—PENOBSCOT COUNTY.

From the Statement of S. E. Batchelor, Esq.

One Power.

"Passadumkeag Rapids," on Penobscot river. The fall is seven feet in —— rods.

The bottom of the river is solid ledge, well adapted to the location of a dam. Length of dam required, about 200 feet.

The west bank in Edinburgh is about 15 feet, and the east bank about four feet above the river at a high stage; the east bank is ledge. The land lies level. Canals can be constructed with ease.

The privilege is owned by Isaac Foster of Argyle. It is regarded an excellent location for mills of any description; especially for a tannery, as vast quantities for tanning material are readily procurable in the vicinity.

Edmunds—Washington County.

From the Returns of Peter E. Vose and T. W. Allan, Esqs., of Dennysville, and of the Selectmen of Edmunds.

[See also "Dennysville and Edmunds."]

Nine Powers.

First, on Cathance stream, the "Mill Seat," one mile from the mills at Dennysville; ten feet head; not improved. Rock bottom and sides to the stream; good chance to locate mills.

Second, Third, Fourth and Fifth, "The Flume," within three miles of the Mill Seat, fall averaging from six to 15 feet each. No improvements; good chance to improve.

Sixth, "Great Works," four miles from Dennysville by the river; a gang saw mill, recently erected, owned by Hobart, Vose and others. The head and fall here are about 11 feet, and the pond has an area of at least 1000 acres. This mill, taking into consideration the amount of water, head and speed, ought to cut 2,500,000 to 3,000,000 feet of long lumber per sawing year. There is also a lath and shingle machine connected with the same. This is a good power,—is owned in Dennysville. The lumber is hauled to and shipped from Dennysville, vessels of 100 tons taking it at the wharves.

The Cathance lake is the reservoir, six or seven square miles in extent, the outlet dam having six feet head.

Fourth, a saw mill and a lath machine, in the same building, on Bell's Meadow brook.

Fifth, on Burnt Cove stream, unimproved; a privilege of some capacity for a part of the year.

Sixth and Seventh, on Little-Falls stream; both good privileges. One, the "Rock," one mile from tide water at Cobscook bay, with a dam of about 40 feet in length and eight feet in height, would carry a number of machines for manufacturing purposes. The other privilege, the "Falls," is of about the same capacity as the "Rock."

Eighth, at the mouth of Little-Falls stream, an excellent tide privilege, pond covers 30 acres, can saw 14 hours per day; will cut 500,000 of lumber yearly with single saw.

Ninth and Tenth, of somewhat less capacity, but if located in some parts would be improved to profit.

ELLIOT—YORK COUNTY.

Statement of the Selectmen.

There is no water-power in the town of Elliot, large or small.

ELLIOTSVILLE—PISCATAQUIS COUNTY.

Several Powers.

One only improved, on Wilson stream, a saw mill.

Stream fed by Wilson pond, covering three square miles, and by four or five smaller ponds, which sum two or three square miles.

ELLSWORTH—HANCOCK COUNTY.

From the Statement of Hon. Eugene Hale, and from the Returns of the Board of Selectmen.

Thirty-Nine Powers.

First to Fifth, inclusive, on Card's stream, upon which there have been two saw, one shingle, one grist, and a carding mill. Not in operation for several years.

Sixth to Tenth, inclusive, on Beach-Hill-pond stream; one only improved; a dam and shingle mill.

Eleventh to Sixteenth, inclusive, on Reed's-pond stream; two dams and mills; the others unoccupied. Height of the fall, sixty feet in half a mile.

Seventeenth to Twenty-Eighth, inclusive, on Branch-pond stream; fall 90 feet in three miles.

Twenty-Ninth to Thirty-Ninth, inclusive, "Ellsworth Falls," the principal power in town, situated on the Union river, at Ellsworth village and above, the total fall being 85 feet in about two miles, or "one hundred feet in two and a quarter miles." Above this point the river is level for a long distance, the upper dam flowing the current back about ten miles and slackening it 12 or 15 miles.

For a statement of the reservoirs tributary to this series of powers, see pages 137–138, Part II, of this Report. The enormous storage now held upon the ponds is used almost exclusively for log-driving purposes.

Freshets have caused but trifling damage upon this river, and none for the past 25 years worth mentioning. The range from low to high water may be perhaps six feet, where the river is narrow. The water now being employed wastefully sometimes runs low in severe drouths.

Upper Dam, Ellsworth.

The mills work about seven months in the year; lie still in the winter and early spring. They might be worked all the year, so far as regards supply of water.

The machinery has not been applied with any view to economizing power; the wheels, etc., are quite ordinary.

Rocks in the vicinity, talcose slate, suitable for building. Lay of the land about the falls for almost the entire two and a quarter miles on the main river is favorable for the location of mills, workshops, boarding-houses, etc. Excellent opportunities offer for canalling and dividing the waters of the river. At one point, rather more than a mile from tide waters, a canal can be run for over half a mile, with a fall of 32 feet, and in no way interfering with the privileges above.

The power is employed almost exclusively in the manufacture of lumber. The mills have been running 50 years; have largely increased in numbers in the last 20 years, during which time the population of the town has increased from 2,000 to 5,000, and its valuation in corresponding ratio.

Average annual production, 35,000,000 feet of long lumber, 200,000 sugar-box shooks, 2,000,000 laths, 5,000,000 shingles, 200,000 clapboards, and a large quantity of smaller stuff. Value of annual production estimated from $700,000 to $950,000.

Accessibility—The falls are situated upon tide waters and can be approached by vessels drawing —— feet of water. The river below the fall is frozen about four months of the year.

Market, New York, Boston, Portland, and Cuba; all reached by sea.

Embden—Somerset County.

[See also "Embden and Solon."]

From Returns of Selectmen, and of William Atkinson, Esq.

Five Powers, or More.

First, 12 rods below the outlet of Embden pond, two saws, shingle and treshing machine, and turning lathe. The fall from the outlet to the mill is 13 feet. The dam at the mills raises no head on the pond.

Second, 80 rods below, saw and grist mill and other machinery. Lay of the land excellent upon both privileges. Freshets have no effect. Very small part of the power used.

The Embden pond covers 2.50 square miles, is fed by a large extent of tributary country, and by several ponds. It can be made a reservoir of very great capacity when needed. The water from it is warm in winter, so that there is no trouble from ice; it never freezes at the outlet nor in fact for miles below it.

Third, abundant and quite valuable power, upon the Seven-Mile brook.

Fourth, Fifth, etc.; sufficient to drive a considerable amount of small machinery nearly all the year.

"We have all the natural advantages here for a great manufacturing community, climate, soil, labor, agricultural productions, and water-power."

The Somerset Railroad is now building to this point.

EMBDEN AND SOLON—SOMERSET COUNTY.

From the Returns of Joseph P. Buswell, millwright, of Solon, Endorsed by the Selectmen.

[See also "Embden," and "Solon."]

One Power.

The "Carratunk Falls," on the Kennebec river, one mile distant from the bridge across Fall brook in Solon village. Fall 20 feet perpendicular, at the head of which a dam ten feet high can be made, giving about 30 feet head and fall, or equal to the head and fall at Lowell.

The volume of water at this point, estimated as 43 per cent. less than at Augusta, would yield for the extreme low summer run in a very dry season, 96,900 cubic feet per minute for 11 hours a day, giving on a 30-foot fall a gross power of about 5,500 horse, or 220,000 spindles.

The volume of water can be more than trebled by the use of the reservoirs above for storage. See reservoirs of the Dead, Moose, and upper Kennebec rivers, pages 95–97; also page 98, Part II.

The facilities for canalling by the falls and along the river bank a distance of three-quarters of a mile, are very good. Nature apparently has done the grading completely; no engineer could form the ground better. The panel of land, 160 acres or more, within the bounds of the county road on the east, the Falls road on the north, the river on the west, and Fall brook on the south, about one mile north and south by one-fourth mile in breadth, is equally well graded for the erection of buildings sufficient to accommodate the population necessary to work all the mills that the whole power of the Kennebec may drive. If more room is wanted, a level plain extends about two miles north and south by half a mile wide, east of the county road, affording ample space for a good-sized city.

Carratunk Falls, Embden and Solon.

The northerly two-thirds of the 160 acres, lying between the county road and the river, is owned by three or four individuals, who reside on the road and whose lots extend west to the river. The westerly half of this plain along the river's bank is covered with young wood and no doubt may be purchased at a fair value.

Coolidge and Bodwell own some half a dozen acres abreast of the falls, including the water-power. B. F. Rowell of South Solon, owns the power on the west side of the river, in the town of Embden.

There is plenty of stone suitable for mortar walls, and an excellent granite quarry on the river bank fifteen miles above, with good facilities for boating down the river. Brick clay and sand are abundant in almost every direction within a mile or a mile and a half of the falls.

The terminus of the Somerset railroad, now constructing, will be in the immediate vicinity of the falls.

Enfield—Penobscot County.

From Selectmen's Statement.

[See also "Enfield and Howland."]

Four Powers.

On the outlet of Cold-Stream pond; which has an area of about six square miles. The entire series of privileges is called "Treat's Mills." The height of the falls is about 50 feet in 80 rods. There have been four dams upon the falls within the distance above named. There are now, saw mills, shingle and grist mill upon the privilege. Machinery inferior; old style "ladle-board" wheel. Capacity of the pond can be increased by the erection of dams. Freshets have no effect.

Rocks, granite in part, good for building. Lay of the land excellent. One-half the basin of the stream covered with forests; lumber was formerly manufactured here; less now.

Market, Bangor, by railroad and river.

Enfield and Howland—Penobscot County.

From the Statement of the Boards of Selectmen.

[See also "Enfield," and "Howland"

One Power.

"Piscataquis Falls," on Penobscot river. Height of fall, 21 feet eight inches. The river is about 900 feet wide. Dams can be firmly established. Banks are about 25 feet above the river, so that its surface can be raised as required. A lock is built upon one end of the fall, to pass steamboats and river craft. A long tract of dead water, above, would serve for a feeder. The power is that due to the entire volume of the Penobscot river at this point, which on a fall of 20 feet, is some thousands of horse-powers.

The European & North American Railway is now constructing by the side of this privilege.

No part of the power is improved.

Etna—Penobscot County.

Two Powers.

First, a shingle mill on Kinsley stream,

Second, a saw mill on Kinsley stream, in the east part of the town.

Both intermittent, operating only at time of high water.

Eustis Plantation—Franklin County.

Statement of J. M. Haynes, Esq., of Augusta.

Six Powers.

First, on Dead river, "Eustis Falls," six miles above Flagstaff, one-half mile below the confluence of the North and South branches, fall 12 to 20 feet.

Second, on South branch or Saddleback river, "Buttermilk Falls," 10 feet, good site; large flowage.

Third, "Bloomfield Rapids," above, 50 feet in 100 rods, good site.

Fourth, "Sawyer Falls," above, 25 feet in 20 rods; good site, large flowage.

Fifth, on the North branch, "Eustis-River Falls," 12 feet, excellent site; dam, saw and grist mill.

Sixth, on Stratton brook, "Stevens' Mill," saw and shingle.

Exeter—Penobscot County.

From Selectmen's Returns.

Ten Powers.

First, on Kenduskeag stream, shingle and grist mill, fall 10 feet, capacity, 500,000 shingles per year; grist mill runs eight months.

Second, on the same, saw mill, fall 12 feet, capacity 500,000 of lumber a year, could do more.

Third, on the same, saw and shingle mill. Saw mill capacity, 600,000 per year; shingle machine, 300,000; fall 11 feet, could do more.

Fourth, a shingle mill on the same, fall 10 feet; capacity 300,000 per year.

Fifth, on the same, saw and shingle machine, and two runs of stones; fall, 12 feet; saw mill capacity, 300,000; shingle mill about 300,000.

Sixth, on the same, shingle mill, a nine-foot fall.

Seventh, on the same, grist mill, machine shop, carriage shop and tan yard; fall 11 feet.

Eighth, on the same, not now in use, formerly a shingle mill; fall 12 feet; of one-fourth greater capacity than either the other privileges.

Ninth, shingle and grist mill upon the "Andrew's Brook;" fall nine feet; can cut 200,000 shingles, can grind about four months.

Tenth, on the "Atkins' Brook," capacity as No. 9.

FAIRFIELD—SOMERSET COUNTY.

From Selectmen's Returns.

Five Powers.

First, at "Kendall's Mills," a dam across the Kennebec river gives a fall of 22 feet in three-fourths of a mile; works all the year; is owned by the Kendall's Mills Water-Power Company, C. H. Foss, Secretary. The value of yearly products is estimated at $250,000. The principal market is Portland, Boston and New York.

Second, at "Somerset Mills," a dam across the Kennebec river produces a fall of 12 feet; on this dam are located seven saw mills and other machinery; works all the year; is owned by Silas Bates and E. & E. J. & G. W. Lawrence. Estimated value of yearly products is $75,000.

The extreme low run in a drouth, assumed as 31 per cent. less than at Augusta, or 117,300 cubic feet per minute for 11 hours a day, would yield, for the hours specified, on the total fall of 34 feet, a gross power of 7,540 horse, or 301,000 spindles.

Not over half of the power at Kendall's Mills, and not over one-fourth at Somerset Mills, is now used. The power is susceptible of very great increase by the use of reservoirs above. See storage basins of the Sandy, Carrabasset, Dead, Moose, and upper Kennebec rivers, pages 94–97; also page 98.

Third, on Martin stream, about 100 rods from the Kennebec river and Somerset Railroad; fall 15 feet in about 10 rods; sufficient power to carry four saw mills the most of the year; unimproved.

Fourth, on the same stream at Blacknell's Mills, so called, North Fairfield, a saw mill, grist mill, and other machinery; works nearly all the year; located on the centre road leading to Skowhegan.

Fifth, about four miles up the stream from this point, located on the road leading to Norridgewock; fall about 12 feet in ten rods; of sufficient power to carry four saw mills the greater part of the year; saw mill, a tannery and other machinery. The power might be very much increased by removing obstructions at the head of the stream. The principal timber in the vicinity is hardwood, hemlock and cedar. A very good granite quarry within a mile of the stream. The water powers are located in the best farming section of the town, the soil being a clay loam.

FALMOUTH—CUMBERLAND COUNTY.

From Materials Furnished by Hon. F. O. J. Smith, and by the Selectmen.

[See also "Falmouth and Westbrook."]

Four Powers.

First, "Presumpscot Falls," on the Presumpscot river, two and a quarter miles by the course of the river from Casco bay, being the lowest water-power upon the river. This privilege is owned by a corporation known as the Presumpscot Land and Water-Power Company. The corporation propose erecting a dam at the falls, 900 feet in length and 22 feet above mean low tide, and conducting the water from the pond thus formed, by canal, to a point in the "lower harbor" of Portland, where eleven feet of water are found at mean low tide. The flats from the adjacent shore out to this point will be filled in, and extensive accommodations for mills and factories be thus formed, where ships can discharge into and receive cargo directly from the buildings.

The power at Cumberland mills a few miles above, is 2,013 horse power gross on 20 feet of fall. The power of "Falmouth Falls" will not probably be found to exceed 2,400 horse-power at a low stage of river and at low tide. This at least in the present condition of the reservoirs.

The increase of power that can be commanded at this point by the use of the storage basins, may be seen upon reference to pages 143–44, Part II, of this Report.

The canal is already considerably advanced toward completion, being 100 feet wide at its base and narrowest points, and 130 broad at its surface, and ten feet deep in the shallowest parts.

A hydraulic dock is contemplated, into which vessels with or without cargoes can be lifted by means of a lock 350 by 60 feet, and the dock being discharged at low tide, if so required, the vessels be left high and dry upon a cradle or outspread bed timbers. The dock will contain 25 acres. Other basins and reservoirs above this will be formed by the canal embankment, with an aggregate area of 50 acres

The Grand Trunk railway runs by the side of this property. The main improvements will be within about a mile of the Victoria wharves in Portland harbor.

The water-power being that resulting from the volume of the whole Presumpscot river, will be to a remarkable extent characterized by equability, by exemption from both freshets and low water.

Material for the best of bricks is afforded by the entire body of soil in the vicinity; granite (gneiss) is abundant and accessible, and building materials of all sorts can be dropped from the railway upon the premises of the corporation.

The corporation intend to build only a saw mill and several ice-houses, and for the present to supply privileges by sale or rent, and to leave to individual capitalists and corporations the work of erecting the required superstructures.

The above statement is condensed from the printed report of the company, which may be had upon application to the Hon. Francis O. J. Smith of Portland, a member of the corporation. The report sets forth the singular advantages of the privilege with great perspicuity and force.

This corporation, or rather the member referred to, holds a charter, granted March 15, 1836, by the Legislature of Maine, authorizing the construction of a canal from the Androscoggin river at Bethel to Songo pond, the head waters of the Presumpscot river, which canal should command the delivery of the Pleasant river, a branch of the Androscoggin, for its feeding. The charter further authorizes the building of a dam across the Androscoggin at any point in Bethel, which shall not raise the surface thereof at any point over four feet, and which shall not direct the water of the river (Androscoggin) into the canal aforesaid. The construction of the canal would therefore not affect the manufacturing capacity of either the Androscoggin or the Presumpscot, except to the amount of substracting the delivery of the Pleasant river from the one and adding it to the other. This would be the case at least except perhaps in times of great freshets upon the Androscoggin. The canal would be from four to five miles long, and could be "constructed with insignificant cost."

Second, the "Lower Falls." on the Piscataqua river; a good dam, a grist mill, and spoke-and-hub manufactory; fall 15 feet in 60. Machinery operates all the year. Centre-vent wheel. The stream is connected with Goose pond. Freshets quite heavy, no damage to the mills. The lay of the land for mills, &c., is good. Yearly products of the spoke-and-hub manufactory, about $4,000.

Third, "Piscataqua Upper Falls," one-fourth of a mile above, fall 14 feet; saw mill cuts 250,000 lumber per year, with water enough to saw double the amount, and half the year water enough to run double the present machinery. Wheel, spiral-vent.

Fourth, an excellent tide power, dam 280 feet, about seven feet head, a first-class grist mill, can run 15 hours in 24, grind 400 bushels in the time with one run of stones. The mill has made 60 bushels of meal in an hour. Pond about six acres terminating in a creek into which the tide flows about one and a half miles, and which receives the drainage of more than 1,000 acres by numerous brooks. Vessels drawing eight and one-half feet can go to the mill.

FALMOUTH AND WESTBROOK—CUMBERLAND COUNTY.

[See also "Falmouth," and "Westbrook."]

One Power.

It has been contemplated to build the Martin's-point bridge solid, and by the means to convert the pond above into a reservoir for a tide power. The area of the cove above the bridge is about 768 acres, estimated from the county map. The mean rise and fall of the tide is about nine feet. An important part of the construction material required is on the spot in the abutments of the bridge. The lay of the land is such on the left bank as will admit of the location of any number of mills under the most favorable conditions. The parties interested propose to build the dam, the county furnishing toward it only the cost of a common pile bridge, and to keep it in good repair for a roadway (constructed on the dam) free of all expense to the county for a period of 99 years.

Objections to the plan, based upon the presumed injury to Portland harbor, are believed to be of no considerable weight. The Presumpscot being derived from a lake, whose waters are purified by subsidence, yields but very little silt at the utmost, and the great part of this would settle in the reservoir above the dam. A dredging machine would remove in a few days all such accumulations as would make below the dam in a long period of years.

The power being close upon the Grand Trunk Railway, and upon navigable water, would be, it is believed, of unusual value for milling purposes, and other adapted uses.

FARMINGDALE—KENNEBEC COUNTY.

Statement of Selectmen.

There is no water-power in this town.

FARMINGTON—FRANKLIN COUNTY.

From Selectmen's Returns.

[See also "Chesterville and Farmington."]

Three Powers, etc.

First, on the Temple stream, saw and grist mill; the former runs fall and spring, and the latter all the year.

Second, three miles above, saw mill.

Third, on the Fairbanks mill stream, grist and saw mills. Operate part of the year.

Abundant and excellent rock, for building purposes, and an immense quarry of granite in the immediate vicinity of Farmington Falls.

Other small powers of no present importance.

FAYETTE—KENNEBEC COUNTY.

From Selectmen's Returns.

Five Powers.

First, "Fayette Mills," owned by R. B. Dunn, 14 feet fall in a run of 12 feet; is about half improved by scythe-shops, running ten trip hammers, with required machinery to finish scythes. Mills work all the year; the machinery is not of the best construction for economizing power. The stream is connected with and fed by nine large ponds. See second Table, page 84. The rocks about the fall are of a slaty character and are good for building purposes. The lay of the land is good for the location of mills and workshops.

Second, in the west part of the town, 14 feet fall; power to drive three saws, two turning lathes, planer and moulding machine. Mills operate all the year. Stream connected with three ponds of considerable size; the land around the falls is adapted to improvement.

Third, in the northerly part of the town, 11 feet fall; spare power, improved in four saws; works nine months; one pond.

Fourth, in the southerly part of the town, 20 feet fall, would carry three saws and a shingle saw; works six months; fed by the Berry pond, which might be cheaply dammed so as to carry the mills the year round.

Fifth, fifty rods below, 15 feet fall; not improved.

Flagstaff Plantation—Somerset County.

Statement of J. M. Haynes, Esq., of Augusta.

One Power.

On the outlet stream of Flagstaff pond, grist mill and saw mill; pond covers 2.75 square miles.

Forestville Plantation—Aroostook County.

From the Statement of Dominicus Harmon, millwright.

Seven Powers.

First, on Otter brook near the Aroostook river, fall ten feet; shingle mill.

Second, a short distance above, a fall of ten feet can be had. No improvement.

Third, on Cane brook, a good site for a grist mill on the bank of the Madawaska. Unimproved.

Fourth, on Greenlow brook, a good mill-site near the Madawaska. Not used.

Fifth, Sixth, and Seventh, mill sites of unsurpassed excellence on the Little Madawaska river, adapted to any sort of manufacturing, lay of the land favorable, foundation for dams good. Ten feet fall at each of these privileges. None employed.

The Madawaska river drains a large extent of country, at least 250 square miles, and holds out well in dry seasons; nearly all the basin is covered with heavy forests.

A dam at its outlet will flow the Madawaska lake eight feet; it would cost not over $2,000. Lake would thus make a good reservoir, as it covers four square miles.

FORT FAIRFIELD—AROOSTOOK COUNTY.

From Selectmen's Returns.

Two Powers.

First, "Randall's Mills," on Fitzherbert stream; grist mill, 15,000 bushels of grain annually; saw, clapboard and shingle machinery; in operation about half the year, intermitting in the drouth of summer and the dead of winter.

Second, "Barnes' Mills," on Lovely brook; grist, carding and clothing mills. There being no woollen factories in the county, wool from a large circuit is carded and the cloth dressed at these mills, the machinery being in operation night and day from early spring to late autumn. All the mills driven with work.

Lake connections upon Fitzherbert stream. Freshets, at least ten times the ordinary volume of water; never have caused any serious damage.

Market, "Boston, Mass., or St. John, N. B., for the practical reason that the province of N. B. affords us an outlet to the 'outer world' by both rail and water, both of which are denied us in our own State."

FORT KENT PLANTATION—AROOSTOOK COUNTY.

From the Statement of William Dickey, Esq.

Four Powers.

First, "Fish River Mills," on the Fish river, one mile above its junction with the St. John; 18 feet fall. At extreme low run there are 20 feet of water—i. e., a penstock five by four feet full. The low-run volume of water, by the improvement of 82 square miles, more or less, of lake surface above, might be increased several hundred per cent. A dam at the outlet of the lower lake alone, Eagle lake, which covers not less than 22 square miles, would give a vast amount of water at all seasons.

All of the lakes can be converted into reservoirs and almost any amount of head raised upon them, the cost of flowage being very small. See page 125, last Table.

This power is now improved in several single saws and a gang, also a fine grist mill with four runs of stones.

The water in winter is warm, being fresh from the lake; ice never gives much trouble. The power is never injuriously affected by freshets.

With suitable improvements on the lake above, this would make a power admirable in all respects and adequate for the uses of a large manufacturing corporation.

Second, "Fish River Rapids," on the St. John river, about a mile below the confluence of Fish river. This upon improvement would make a very fine power.

The bottom of the river is ledgy and affords an admirable foundation for a permanent dam. A fall of 16 feet could be secured. The lay of the land on either side of the river is not surpassed for the convenient and safe location of factories. A lock would be required for the passage of lumber rafts and tow-boats.

This privilege is supplied by the contributions of the Fish river, with its immense reservoirs, as above specified; also of the Allaguash and upper St. John. See reservoirs of, pages 125 and 126. It can easily be converted into one of the safest, most convenient and constant of water-powers and equal to the heaviest operations.

This power taken together with the Three great privileges on Fish river, one in Fort Kent, and two in Wallagrass Plantation, affords abundant power for the establishment of a series of large manufacturing towns. The power, land, reservoirs, and all sorts of building material can be had at comparatively insignificant cost.

Third, on D'Aigle brook, saw mill, a grist mill going up, abundant water for both mills for eight months; 144 square inches at lowest run, sufficient for grist mill; breast wheel.

Fourth, on "Perley Brook," of about the same size; not far from Fish River Mills. This and the foregoing were in D'Aigle Plantation before its incorporation with and conversion into Fort Kent.

FOXCROFT—PISCATAQUIS COUNTY.

From Selectmen's Returns.

Several Powers.

First, "Foxcroft Dam," on Piscataquis river, at the village. Upon this are located mills as follows:

	Sq. in.	Head.
Carding mill, ...	100	12 feet.
Saw, shingle and clapboard mill, .	500	12
Tannery, ...	.	9
Woollen factory, . . .	156	12

The above are never obliged to shut down for lack of water except in severe drouth.

The following three mills use the surplus water from the same dam; are generally obliged to shut down five weeks in the year from scarcity of water:

	Sq. in.	Head.
Sash and blind factory, . .	144	10 feet.
Iron foundry, . . .	144	10
Machine shop, . . .	144	14
"Blethen's Mills," as follows:		
"Blethen's saw and shingle mills," . .		9
Operate four months annually.		
"Jordan's grist mill," . .	36	14

Operates all the year. Could have 100 inches nine months of the year.

Second, "Pratt's Rips," on Piscataquis river, a mile above the Foxcroft dam. It is well nigh as valuable as the latter, is well situated and adapted for improvement. The land lies favorable for the location of mills. No part of the power is used.

Quite a large number of small ponds tributary to the river above this point, are or might be, employed for storage. See Table page 107. Also immense bogs in Shirley as shown in the Table; also a large artificial reservoir in Abbot, 12 miles above. Much of the present storage is used for log-driving.

Third, Fourth, Fifth, etc., upon Weston and Chase brooks. Former drains Weston pond, one by three-fourths miles, which could be raised six feet without flowing more than two acres. The latter drains Snow's pond, one-half by one-fourth miles; pond might be raised indefinitely. The mills upon these brooks could operate nearly all the year, if the water were suitably used and economized. Stream runs dry in summer, when the reservoir dams are not kept in order on the ponds.

There are several privileges upon the Hammond brook.

Abundant granite for building purposes, accessible conveniently.

Market, chiefly in the county. The products of the woollen factory go in part to Boston and New York. A railroad from this town (the terminus) to Bangor, in running order autumn 1869.

FRANKFORT—WALDO COUNTY.

Statement of J. N. Atwood, Esq.

Two Powers.

First, on Marsh river, at Marsh village, 16 miles from both Bangor and Belfast. Head and fall 15 feet; dam of wood on ledge foundation. Power only part improved now, in various saw, and a grist mill; is capable of running a large amount of machinery. Mills can operate all the year except in severe drouth.

The stream is connected with lakes and ponds, two of which are of considerable magnitude, and by the aid of artificial reservoirs, which could be cheaply constructed, the capacity of the power could be very largely increased.

The land is convenient for location of mills and workshops, and stone and wood building materials can be easily procured, there being two extensive granite quarries within a mile and a half of the location, and wharves within one-half mile of the mill, on Marsh river, where large vessels come, and flat-boats to the mills.

Second, "Flat-Rock Falls," about one and a half miles above, now unoccupied; a very excellent locality for factories.

FRANKLIN—HANCOCK COUNTY.

From the Statement of R. F. Gerrish, Esq., Agent of the F. L. M. & W. Co., and a Plan of the Lands, Streams, and Ponds.

Six Powers, and More.

First, "Donnel Pond Privilege," 12 feet head, and more can be had; privilege fed by Donnel and several small ponds, all of which are used as reservoirs.

Second, "Alderbrook Privilege,"' 14 feet head, supplied from the above ponds.

Third, "Hog-Bay Privilege," below, and fed by the same ponds; 10 feet head, 10 more can be had.

Tributary to the above powers are reservoirs as follows:

"Fox Pond," 150 acres, is flowed four feet, and can be raised three feet more.

"Otter-Bog Pond," can be raised so as to flow 150 acres six feet deep.

"Upper Shillalah," now flowed six feet, can be raised four feet more, and would then cover 200 acres.

"Lower Shillalah" is now raised 10 feet, and might be flowed five feet more, covering 100 acres.

"Donnell" or "Great Pond," flowed 11 feet; several hundred acres.

"Alderbrook Pond," flowed 10 feet; area, when flowed, 300 acres.

"Duck Pond," 80 acres; six to ten feet storage can be had.

These ponds, taken in connection with the natural run of the streams, yield a large and constant supply of water. Freshets are kept under perfect control.

Fourth, on the outlet stream of Little or "Breeches" pond in Township 9; 15 to 20 feet head can be had near Hog-Bay and near the mouth of the stream. Pond covers 100 acres and can be flowed several feet.

Fifth, Sixth, etc., "Taunton," "Egypt," "Scammon," and several minor powers in this vicinity.

The first three powers operate all the year, or the first two all, and Hog-Bay nearly all. The others operate from one-half to two-thirds of the year.

The larger powers are capable of manufacturing many millions of lumber yearly. There are dams, mills, etc., on each of the first three where long lumber, etc., is manufactured extensively annually. The others manufacture laths, shingles, clapboards, staves, headings, pickets, etc.

Wheels mostly in use are an old style of iron wheel, that uses water without stint. At Hog-Bay some more modern machinery has recently been put in.

Donnel pond and Alderbrook privileges, land and mills, are owned by the "Franklin Land, Mills and Water Company;" the Hog-Bay mills, by Messrs. West & Macomber; "Egypt," by William Salisbury; Taunton, by various parties; Scammon, by Gladding, Hoyt & Co.; others variously.

Rock, hard blue slate, boulders, and a large amount of superior granite, close at hand.

Lay of the land good, almost without exception; at "Donnel" and "Alderbrook" ample and eminently convenient.

Vast quantities of hardwood, spruce, pine and hemlock, sufficient to stock the mills for many years; ship timber abundant; the growth is more than eqivalent to present demand.

The improvement of the power has gradually and permanently increased population, and has added to the wealth of the place. Sixteen new dwellings erected, 1867.

Annual production for the past four years, about ten millions of lumber yearly; double could be done annually. Market, mainly Boston and New York; occasionally Philadelphia, and the coast, by sea.

The Franklin Land, Mills and Water Company, have one of the most liberal charters from the Legislature of our State; a present capital of $32,000, with the right to extend it to $50,000. Its lakes, streams and water-powers, are so completely within its own territory, that any flowage now required, or that would be, is entirely within its own control; tribute for water privileges being paid only to the company. The powers are near the head of tide-water on "Frenchman's Bay," and are approached by vessels of 500 tons and upwards. A ship of 1,200 tons has been built and launched here; vessels are built here annually. In fine, but few places, comparatively, offer superior inducements to capitalists who wish to invest in these interests, to Franklin, and especially the lands, some twelve thousand acres of which belong to said company.

FRANKLIN PLANTATION—OXFORD COUNTY.

Statement of the Assessors.

Five Powers.

Situated upon Spear's stream, a tributary to the Androscoggin river. Said stream furnishes sufficient water for sawing about half of the year.

First, fall 11 feet, shingle machine.

Second, fall 16 feet, saw mill.

Third, fall 20 feet, unoccupied.

Fourth, fall 14 feet, unoccupied.

Fifth, fall 20 feet, unoccupied.

FREEDOM—WALDO COUNTY.

From the Report of A. J. Billings, Esq.

Five Powers.

Situated upon a stream issuing from a pond that at high water covers about a square mile, and at low about one-third of that area. Total fall, 70 feet. Sufficient water to use 100 square inches under 10 feet head, during 10 hours in each day, through the dry season.

First, 22 feet head; a flour mill.

Second, 14 feet head; a corn mill. About 14,000 bushels of grain manufactured in the two grist mills jointly, yearly.

Third, 12 feet head; saw mill, shingle mill, etc. Production, $700.

Fourth, 13 feet head; carding machine, machinery for manufacturing cloth. Production, $1,100.

Fifth, nine feet head; tannery. Production, $1,000.

Freshets harmless. Stream very constant. Area of the pond could not be increased. Machinery excellent; the Boston wheel and close wheel.

Freeman—Franklin County.

From Selectmen's Returns.

Three Powers.

First "Oliver Falls," in the north part of the town, on a branch of Seven-Mile brook.

Second, "Starbird Falls," on a branch of Sandy river.

Third, "Crosby Falls," in the centre of the town, on a branch of Sandy river.

Improved in saw, threshing, and clover mills. Turbine wheels. No lakes or ponds.

Market, Farmington, by road.

Freeport—Cumberland County.

From Selectmen's Returns.

Two Powers.

First, at the head of tide waters on Harrasekett river; fall, 40 feet; stone dam. Power has been sufficient to run a grist mill with three runs of stones, and a saw mill with other machinery attached. Mills have been destroyed by fire; privilege for sale.

Second, on the east branch of Royal river; grist mill and saw mill; run a part of the year.

Friendship—Knox County.

From Selectmen's Returns.

Six Powers.

First and Second, on Goose river and Goose pond; fall 20 feet.

Third, on Beckett's brook; fall, 20 feet in 30 rods.

Fourth, Fifth and Sixth, tide privileges; one with a good stone dam.

One privilege only is improved, in saw and stave mill. The fresh-water powers operate 10 months; salt water, 12 hours per day the year through. The streams are connected with two small ponds; artificial reservoirs feasible; good stone for building.

Market, Thomaston, by road.

Fryeburg—Oxford County.

Statement of E. C. Farrington, Esq.

Six Powers.

First, "Merrill's Mills," on Kezar river, saw, grist and shingle; run only 6 months, proprietor not having the right to flow meadow lands above the mills.

Second, on "Ballard's brook," "Locke's Mills," saw and grist.

Third and Fourth, on Evans' brook, near Fryeburg village, on one a carriage shop; on the other a grist mill.

Fifth, on Elkin's brook, grist and saw mill.

Sixth, by far the largest, unoccupied, "Swan's Falls," situated upon the Saco river, within a mile of Fryeburg village, and one and a half miles of the contemplated P. & O. R. R. Direct fall of eight feet, with rapids extending several rods. River 200 feet wide. The privilege is judged equal to heavy operations. The river is variable in its volume in this section.

Fryeburg is a town of very unusual agricultural excellence, the intervales upon the Saco being productive of immense quantities of hay. There is a large amount of lumber in the region.

GARDINER—KENNEBEC COUNTY.

From the Returns of R. H. Gardiner, Esq., and from Articles in the Kennebec Journal.

Eight Powers.

All of these are situated in the city of Gardiner on the Cobbossee Contee river, within one mile of the mouth thereof, and taken together are called the Cobbossee Contee Falls. The total height of the falls is 127 feet above high tide; and 133 feet above low tide in the Kennebec river.

The power of the whole fall, estimated by a skillful hydraulic engineer, during the year ending July, 1866, being the year of the greatest drouth ever known in New England, and during October, the driest month of that year, is 1,200 horse. This power is realized, the reservoirs of the river being comparatively unimproved.

All of the mills work throughout the greater portion of the year by day and by night. Upon the dams where all the power is used, a portion of the machinery is sometimes obliged to lie idle for two or three months. In ordinary seasons everything is running.

About half of the power is employed.

The machinery is not of the best construction for economizing power. The Blake wheels are mostly used.

Six of the eight privileges, upon all of which are strong well-built stone dams, are owned by the heirs of the late Hon. R. H. Gardiner; one is owned by F. G. Richards, and one by S. D. Warren, of Boston, Mass.

For reservoirs tributary to this power, and the storage now held or judged feasible thereon at moderate cost, see Part II, page 97,

Dam No. 5, Gardiner.

second Table. Artificial reservoirs are entirely feasible at moderate cost, and would vastly increase the power.

Owing to the extent of its reservoirs the stream is very safe from freshets; the total range of water on the crest of unoccupied dams seldom exceeds two feet.

Stone and other building material abundant. Lay of the land about the falls excellent for the location of buildings. Sufficiency of land connected with each dam for all required building purposes.

Six of the eight dams, including land and privileges, are for sale; or a large amount of power to rent. Proprietors would assist in surveys required for the development of the power.

First power, reckoning from the foot of the falls; dam one foot, head 18.28 feet. Eleven establishments, engaged chiefly in the manufacture of lumber as follows:

Saw mill, N. O. Mitchell, 40 hands; annual product four to five million feet of lumber, $175,000.

Saw mill, Arthur Berry, 40 men; annual product $150,000; in long lumber, shingles and clapboards.

Sash, blind and door factory, Joseph L. Mitchell & Co., six hands.

Saw mill, Daniel Grey, 16 hands; product 2,000,000 lumber long and short, $80,000.

Sash and blind factory, P. S. Robinson, six hands; 1,000,000 clapboards and $2,000 of sash and blinds.

Cabinet shop, James Nash, $8,000; also Cabinet shop, Morgan and Wadsworth, $10,000.

Gardiner Plaster Mill, $7,000.

Lumber manufacture, H. W. Jewett, 35 hands, $70,000; also in same business, Hooker, Libby & Co., $60,000.

Gardiner Flour Mill, manufacturing 40,000 bushels of wheat yearly. In the same building, Bartlett, Dennis & Co., a grist mill, 60,000 bushels a year. Power all occupied.

Second power, dam two feet, head 11.01 feet. Power about half employed, as follows:

Machine shop, foundry, etc., P. C. Holmes & Co., 28 hands, annual product $45,000.

"Blake" water-wheel manufactory, Atwood & Howland, $8,000.

Third power, dam three feet, head 19.01 feet. About half occupied, as follows:

J. E. Ladd & Co., millwrights; fancy goods manufactory, Chas. Swift, $10,000; mill work, H. Scriber, Jr., $8,000 iron work; E. Drake, $10,000 wood work.

Woollen factory, I. N. Tucker, six sets of cards, 40 hands; 450 yards per day; $120,000 yearly product.

Washing machine factory, R. W. George, $5,000,

Broom factory, Moore & McCausland; broom handles, Augustus Lord; mill work, Joseph Perry, eight hands, $24,000.

Saw mill, Joshua Gray, 25 hands, total product, $60,000, long lumber and short.

"People's Grist Mill," 7,000 barrels flour, $100,000.

Fourth power, dam four feet, head 16.18 feet, half occupied, as follows:

Two small saw mills, Lincoln Perry and R. T. Hayes & Co.

Carriage spring factory, Wentworth & Butler, six hands, $15,000.

Axe factory, Elbridge Berry, $7,500.

Forge, owned by P. C. Holmes & Co.

Fifth power, dam five feet, head 16.30 feet; wholly unoccupied. See view of.

Sixth power, dam six feet, head 16.69 feet: Copsecook paper mill, owned by S. D. Warren of Boston; paper for books and newspapers. Annual product 550 tons, $175,000. Thirty-eight hands; power about half employed.

Seventh power, dam seven feet, head 15.51 feet; fully occupied. Paper mills, Messrs. Richards & Co., yearly product 900 tons, $400,000. Seventy-five hands.

Eighth power, dam eight feet, head 13.38 feet; wholly unoccupied.

Total number of hands employed 410. Total annual product, $2,000,000.

GARLAND—PENOBSCOT COUNTY.

From Selectmen's Returns.

Ten Powers.

All, with one exception, situated on the head waters of the Kenduskeag stream. No precipitous falls, but a gradual descent from the west line of the town to the southeast corner.

First, at the west side of the town; fifteen and one-half feet head; saw mill, Hopkins' wheel, operates four months; will cut 600,000 of lumber; shingle mill, Tub wheel, six months cutting about 500,000; grist mill, Carleton wheel. The dam flows about a mile.

Second, 40 rods below; saw mill, turbine wheel, 10 feet head; 200,000 feet.

Third, 15 rods below; planing mill and rake factory; six feet head, Tub wheel, earning $1,200. On the same, a machine shop, carding mill, cloth dressing and weaving; turbine wheel.

Fourth, shingle mill, below; 10 feet head; Stearn's wheel; 500,000 feet; runs six months.

Fifth, below; saw, Tub wheel; 13 feet head; cuts 500,000; runs four months. Planing mill, with saw, and other machinery; earns about $1,000; full time. Also grist mill, Carleton wheels; pond flows one and a half miles; full time.

Sixth, below; tannery; six and one-half feet head; Stearn's wheel; $5,000.

Seventh, below; saw; Stearn's wheel, six months; cuts 500,000; nine and one-half feet head; flows three-fourths of a mile. Also shingle mill; Stearn's wheel; one-half time; cuts about 500,000.

Eighth, unoccupied; seven feet head; below.

Ninth, 50 rods below; saw, scroll wheel; 12 feet head; earns $1,000. Shingle mill; scroll wheel; $800.

Tenth, on Black stream, seven feet head; a shingle mill; Tub wheel.

Rocks, argillaceous slate.

Market, at home, and Bangor, by teams.

Georgetown—Sagadahoc County.

From the Returns of B. F. Hinkley, Esq.

Five Powers.

First, a tide power on Robin Hood's cove; saw and shingle mill; also shingle and grist mill; large amount of business.

Second, a tide power on Eastern branch of same cove, will carry three or four saws. Unimproved.

Third, "Wyman's Privilege," a tide power, unimproved.

Fourth, on the outlet of Nichols' pond; carding and shingle mill; room for an overshot wheel 15 feet feet in diameter.

Fifth, in connection with a great meadow, whose outlet has a long and steep descent; can be greatly improved by a dam.

Machinery very good. Turbines.

Market, Boston, by water.

GILEAD—OXFORD COUNTY.

From Selectmen's Returns.

Three Powers.

First, a grist mill on Pleasant brook; can operate two runs of stones a few months yearly. Not now in operation.

Second, a saw mill on Chapman's brook; can operate but a short time yearly. Not now in operation.

Third, a stream with abundant water but uncontrollable, called Wild river; dam after dam has been swept away by freshets, and a mill formerly upon it was carried off; it is now not used at all for power.

GLENBURN—PENOBSCOT COUNTY.

Statement of the Postmaster, Selectmen, and others.

Two Powers, More feasible.

First, on Kenduskeag stream, two miles above Bangor line; formerly improved, dam carried away on account of bad construction; not rebuilt, as until recently, no ready access to the privilege was possible, and the lumber had to be rafted down river. Roads now built near the site. More water than at Kenduskeag village, Black branch coming in below the village.

Second, a shingle mill, on Lancaster brook.

A canal from Pushaw lake to the Kenduskeag river has been proposed, the lake to be dammed at its natural outlet in Oldtown, and also at a low point in Orono where water escapes in freshets. It is alleged that 12 square miles of reservoir on the lake and surrounding low land can be had with six feet of storage thereon. This would yield on total fall of 100 feet to the tide a gross power of 1,900 horse for the working hours of the year, or 76,000 spindles. Length of canal three and half miles; cost, 4 by 12 feet, including dams, about $9,000.

A statement from the Messrs. Coombs, Civil Engineers, of Bangor, communicates the following facts: 1st, that the lake is *not* now used for the storage of waters; the dam on the natural outlet stream, below the Rips, "exercises scarcely any appreciable effect upon the body of water in the lake." 2nd, "by a few comparatively inexpensive dams, etc., the water could be raised several feet on the pond; no surveys have yet been made to ascertain the resultant flowage." 3rd, "the channel of the outlet is ledge and can be lowered without heavy expense; this at least is our judgement and recollection without actual survey."

Glenwood—Aroostook County.

One Power.

"Wytopitlock Falls," 100 rods below the Wytopitlock lake; fall ten feet in ten rods.

Good circular board saw, clapboard and shingle machine; a grist mill is needed very much.

The power being fed by a lake, four by two miles, is constant throughout the year. It can be made to saw 3,000,000 feet annually with ease. Only a part of the power is used; freshets entirely harmless.

Good rock for building. The whole country above the mill is an unbroken forest of the best of lumber. It has built up an incorporated town out of the wilderness in five years.

Market, Bangor, for short lumber; the country above for long.

Gorham—Cumberland County.

From Selectmen's Returns.

[See also "Gorham and Windham."]

Six Powers, Small.

First, near centre of town, on Little river, "Davis Mill," 12 feet head, and 20 horse-power. Saw, grist, and stave mills; centre-vent wheel; mills work half the year; falls formed by cut through solid ledge. No ponds.

Second, two miles below, "Cloudman's Mill"; eight feet head and 20 horse; saw and threshing mill. Centre-vent and spiral wheels; saw mill used all the year.

Third, "Curtis's Mill," south part of town, on Stroudwater river; ten feet head and 25 horse; stone dam; saw, grist, carding and shingle mills. Tuttle wheel, highly esteemed. Will run one mill all the year. Fall formed by cut through solid ledge; a small pond.

Fourth, "Shaw's Mill," on north branch of Little river; ten feet head, and 20 horse; saw mill, shingle mill, &c. Mills run four months.

Fifth, one and a half miles below, "Libby's Mill," 14 feet head, twenty horse; unimproved; formerly a saw mill. Fall 22 feet, would run a saw mill the greater part of the year.

Sixth, on Little river, formerly a mill, now unimproved. Several other falls upon which formerly were mills of various kinds, have long been unimproved.

Streams are very variable in their volume; generally unconnected with ponds, and flow through cleared land. Artificial reservoirs would be expensive.

GORHAM AND WINDHAM—CUMBERLAND COUNTY.

From the Reports of the Boards of Selectmen,

[See also "Gorham," and "Windham."]

Nine Powers.

All of the above are situated on the Presumpscot river, which forms the common boundary of Gorham and Windham.

First, "Harden's Falls," one mile from the outlet of Sebago lake; 11 feet head. The power on the Gorham side is owned by Goff & Plummer, and is improved in part, the improvements consisting of one double saw mill, a keg mill, and other machinery that is used in connection with saw mills. Windham side, owned by the Anderson heirs; unimproved.

Second, one mile below Harden's falls, "Great Falls," with 16 feet head. The power is owned on the Gorham side by John Lindsey, and improved in part with grist mill, plaster mill, saw mill, &c. Windham side is owned by William H. White and Walter Corey; improved by Mr. White with two saw mills, one gang of saws, grist mill, box mill, &c.; by Mr. Corey with a chair factory.

Third, half a mile below Great falls are "Whitney's Falls," with 14 feet head. The falls are unimproved, and owned on Gorham side by Jefferson Mayberry and others, and on Windham side by Joseph W. Parker and J. Walker.

Fourth, half a mile below Whitney's falls, "Island Falls," with ten feet head. This power is unimproved, and owned on Gorham side by Solomon Libby, and on Windham side by O. Haskell.

Fifth, nearly a mile below Island falls, "Dundee Falls," with 18 feet head. The power in unimproved, and is owned on Gorham side by Solomon Libby, and on Windham side by Frank Mayberry.

Sixth, nearly a mile below Dundee falls, "Leavitt's Falls," with 12 feet head. This power is unimproved and is owned entirely by the Oriental Powder Company.

Seventh, a mile below Leavitt's falls, are "Gambo Falls," with 16 feet head. This power is improved, in part, and owned entirely by the Oriental Powder Company. The improvements consist of the extensive powder works of this company.

Eighth, a mile below Gambo falls, "Little Falls," with 17 feet head. This power is unimproved and is owned by Watson Newhall.

Ninth, half a mile below Little falls are "Mallison Falls," with 18 feet head. This power is owned on Gorham side by Stevens and Ray, and improved in part with a grist and saw mill. On Windham side the improvements consist of a woollen mill, and are owned by the Mallison Falls Manufacturing Company.

The head on the above falls is susceptible, in several cases, of being nearly or quite doubled. The horizontal, or running distance in which the descents above specified are attained, varies in the different cases, from one-fourth to one mile.

No estimate, by measurement, has ever been made of any of these powers, other than a survey of the head at each fall, which was made several years ago. But a small part of the power at either falls is used. With scarcely an exception the mills work all the year. The machinery is not of the best construction for economizing power. At Harden's falls, the Centre-vent and Spiral wheels are used; at Great falls, the Centre-vent and Kendall wheel; and at Gambo, 13 water wheels are run, from tubs to turbines.

For reservoirs tributary to these powers, see Part II, pages 143–44.

The head waters being so entirely under control, there are no freshets. The stream is almost entirely uniform throughout the year, varying from low to high water not over two feet. The out-cropping and underlying rocks, about the falls, consist of granite, mica schist, &c., and are regarded as very suitable for building purposes. The lay of the land, about the falls, is excellent for the location of mills, workshops, &c.

About one-third of the basin of the stream forest-covered.

At Little falls, formerly there were a cotton factory and saw mill. The former was burned down several years ago and has never been rebuilt.

Market, Portland, distant from the different falls from 10 to 15 miles; by road, or the Cumberland and Oxford canal, which, on the Gorham side, passes in close proximity to the falls. The P. & O. R. R. is constructing to the last four powers.

Gouldsborough—Hancock County.

From Selectmen's Returns.

Four Powers.

First, at Prospect harbor, on Prospect Harbor stream, the outlet of Forbes' pond. The pond is about a mile square, and is about a mile above the privilege. Fall 20 feet in 600. Unimproved.

Second, at Winter harbor, on Winter Harbor stream. Fall 20 feet in 600; unimproved. Privileges close upon tide.

Third, at West bay, on West Bay stream, which runs from low land; no pond. Saw, two shingle, and grist mills; operates half of the year.

Fourth, at West Gouldsborough, on Jones' stream, the outlet of Jones' pond; pond is two by one miles. Fall 40 feet in 40 rods; saw, grist, and shingle mill, and cabinet shop. Power partially improved; mills operate all the year.

None of the machinery, on the above powers, is economical of power; privileges are owned by various parties in the vicinity; the ponds are susceptible of large improvement for reservoir purposes; artificial reservoirs are feasible; freshets not destructive; lay of the land good, in all cases, for building. The improvement of the power has been of considerable benefit to the town; might be of much greater.

Market, chiefly Boston, by water; this applies to all the points specified. Aggregate annual products, $10,000.

GRAFTON—OXFORD COUNTY.

From Selectmen's Returns.

Two Powers.

First, "Screw-Augur Falls," on Bear river, in southeast part of town; fall 50 feet in 100; saw mills.

Second, "Brown's Falls," on Cambridge river, in west part of town; fall 50 feet in 195; saw mills.

Both powers operate nine months. With better machinery and improvement of the reservoirs, which can be very cheaply effected, they can work all the year. Miller, Tuttle & Co., N. Y.

First quality of granite; land about the falls convenient for building; enormous quantities of lumber in the region; improvement of the power, though only partial, has added much to the prosperity of the town.

Market, Bethel, and thence to Portland.

GRANT ISLE PLANTATION—AROOSTOOK COUNTY.

Two Powers.

First, in the north part of the township, a grist mill. Stream is fed by a pond nearly a mile square.

Second, a grist mill at Grant Isle in the St. John.

GRAY—CUMBERLAND COUNTY.

From Selectmen's Statement.

Eight Powers.

Four on Collyer stream, the outlet of Dry pond.

First, "Dry Mills," saw, grist, shingle and stave mills; run two-thirds of the year; fall eight feet.

Second, "Webster's Mills," at North Gray, saw, grist, shingle, and sash and door mills; run all the year.

Third, "Mayall's Mills," of brick, Olfene & Thurlow, ladies' cloths; one building at present unoccupied. Water the year round; fall 11 feet. Estimate of power 40 years ago, 40 horse. Centre-vent wheel.

Fourth, "Weymouth's Falls," the best power in town, a fall of 30 feet can easily be made.

Fifth, still further down, "Morse's Mills," long since gone to decay. The capacity of Collyer's branch can be largely increased at a small expense, by artificial means.

Sixth, on the great Sucker brook, stave mill; runs most of the year.

Seventh, a mill at West Gray, recently built, various saws, &c., runs most of the year, and derives its power from artificial means, back flowage, &c.

Eighth, formerly saw and grist mill, the "Ramsdell Mill," on Meadow brook. Privilege now unoccupied, mills gone.

Plenty of building material, some timber, &c.

Market, Portland, by road. Railroad at Pownal, five miles.

GREENBUSH—PENOBSCOT COUNTY.

From Selectmen's Returns.

One Power.

"Oleman Mills," on Olemon stream, near its mouth, fall 12 feet; made by a dam which ponds the water back about five miles.

Power operates two saws, a grist, shingle, clapboard and lath machine, all the summer, and with an additional foot to the dam will drive them all the year. Large improvements just made.

No lakes near. No injury from freshets; granite good for building; lay of the land good.

Market, Bangor, by Penobscot river; E. & N. A. R. R. passes within 40 rods of the mill.

GREENE—ANDROSCOGGIN COUNTY.

From Selectmen's Returns.

[See also "Greene and Turner."]

Four Powers.

First, on Sabbatus stream, 15 feet fall from top of dam to vent of wheels; two-thirds of the fall is secured by the dam.

Second, on Meadow brook, saw and shingle mill; operate fall and spring.

Third and Fourth, on the outlet stream of Allen's pond. Neither is employed now, but they are more valuable than either of the others. Formerly grist, shingle, and carding mill upon them. Water holds out the year round; fall 20 and 25 feet; excellent chance for dams. Saw mills and a grist mill; former operate four months, latter all the year. No damage from freshets; annual production $7,000.

Market, Lewiston and Portland, by rail.

GREENE AND TURNER—ANDROSCOGGIN COUNTY.

Statement of M. T. Ludden, Esq., of Turner.

[See also "Greene," and "Turner."]

One Power.

"Turner Centre Falls," at Turner Centre bridge, on the Androscoggin, ten miles above Lewiston; 12 feet fall; excellent opportunity for canals and dam; hard bottom and banks; abundant stone.

If the volume of water at low run be assumed to be five per cent. less than at Lewiston, or 89,300 cubic feet per minute, 11 hours per day, the gross power of the fall is about 2,030 horse, or 81,200 spindles.

The power can be vastly increased by use of reservoirs; see pages 85 – 86, Part II, of Report. No improvement.

GREENFIELD—PENOBSCOT COUNTY.

Statement of Jeremiah Towle, Esq.

Five Powers.

First, on Olemon stream, shingle and clapboard mill.

Second, 25 rods above, unimproved; formerly saw and grist mills.

Third, on Sunkhaze stream, saw and shingle mill, called the "LeBallister Mill."

Fourth, one mile above, the "Crocker Falls," unimproved; formerly clapboard and shingle mill.

Fifth, one and one-half miles above, "Big-Dam Falls," a dam for log-driving; no other improvement.

Greenville—Piscataquis County.

From Selectmen's Statement.

Four Powers.

First, on Wilson's stream; fall 100 feet in 1.5 miles; will saw 1,000,000 feet of boards; saw mill formerly,—carried away by freshets in 1846; owned by the town.

Second, on Eagle stream; six feet fall in 25; will saw 75,000 feet boards; saw mill; two months.

Third, on West Bay stream; fall 10 feet in 10 rods; saw, shingle, clapboard, and grist mill; will saw 250,000 of boards; eight months. Fed by a brook.

Fourth, on Whitcomb brook; fall 10 feet in 20; saw mill; will saw 50,000 boards.

Wilson's stream is fed by several ponds, a constant and large supply of water may be had. An immense quantity of excellent slate for roofing purposes.

Old-fashioned Flutter wheels. Power only partially improved. Slate rocks for building.

Market, Bangor, by road.

Geeenwood—Oxford County.

From Selectmen's Statement.

Eight Powers.

First, at the outlet of Hick's pond.

Second, "Richardson's Mill," on Sanborn river.

Third, "Hick's Mills," saw and shingle, at the outlet of Twitchell's pond.

Fourth, at the "McKenney Falls," on the Morgan stream, height 100 feet.

Fifth, "Bacon Falls," on a branch of the Little Androscoggin river, height 50 feet; unimproved.

Sixth, on the Little Androscoggin; unimproved, a large and constant supply of water from various ponds above.

Seventh, "Lock's Mills," grist, saw and carding mill, excelsior factory, etc. This is upon Alder river, which issues from ponds covering 1,000 or more acres, and is a valuable and steady power, perfectly safe and constant at all seasons. The larger pond can be raised four feet by a dam for a reservoir. Grand Trunk Railway track close by.

Eighth, a saw mill, in northwest part of town.

GREENWOOD PLANTATION—AROOSTOOK COUNTY.

Statement of W. H. Bryson, Esq., of Haynesville.

One Power.

On "Scaggrook" stream; fall 20 feet in a mile. No improvement. Stream drains quite a large extent of country.

GUILFORD—PISCATAQUIS COUNTY.

From Selectmen's Returns.

Four Powers.

First, "Guilford Village Falls," on the Piscataquis river; fall 14 feet; mills run all the year, except in an extremely dry season. A saw, two shingle, two clapboard, one lath, one grist mill, two carriage shops, a blacksmith's shop, and one woollen factory with two sets of machinery, all in full operation. 600,000 of lumber per year, 4,000,000 shingles, 1,500,000 clapboards, 1,000,000 laths, 30,000 bushels of grain, with carriage, planing, and smith work done by water. Power owned by the Guilford Manufacturing Company; woollen factory by Hobart & Young.

Second, at the outlet of Davis pond, fall 11 feet; saw, shingle, and clapboard machinery; 500,000 feet of lumber, 3,000,000 shingles, 400,000 clapboards. Stream fed by three ponds; power good 10 months, and by a higher dam at the outlet of pond could be made available all the year, at a trifling expense.

Third, on the outlet stream of Salmon pond, two shingle mills, 200,000 shingles yearly; works about eight months.

Fourth, on the Piscataquis river, two miles west of Dover village, a fall of 20 feet in 30 rods, an admirable site for a cotton or woollen factory. This power is wholly unimproved.

Various ponds and sites for reservoirs above, which if duly improved would give a large supply of water.

Freshets on the Piscataquis, quite heavy; range of water, 10 feet. The banks of the stream are high so that little or no damage is done.

Rock, limestone and slate; lay of the land excellent at Guilford village. The improvement of the power has greatly increased the wealth of the town; the village contains one-third of the whole taxable property of the town, and it is nearly all the result of the utilization of the power.

Value of annual products of the water-power alone, $300,000.

Market, Bangor, via Dexter & Newport Railroad, station 12 miles distant. Bangor & Piscataquis Railroad, now building to Dover and Foxcroft, station six miles distant.

HALLOWELL—KENNEBEC COUNTY.

Nine Powers.

The "Vaughan Stream Falls." The total descent is 188 feet in about a third of a mile. No estimate of the power has ever been made with any degree of accuracy. On one of the falls, upon which there is an overshot wheel 20 feet in diameter, and a grist mill with three runs of stones, grinding can be done 11 months of the year. Three only of the privileges are improved, using 55 of the 188 feet. Overshot and breast wheels employed, and no others. The power is owned by William Stickney and Simon Page. The stream is naturally variable. Artificial reservoirs of almost any desired magnitude could be constructed, and a vast amount of water kept in reserve.

Rock, granite, suitable for building purposes, in some respects the best variety quarried in this country if not the world.

Some 25 hands are employed in the mills the year through.

Market, Portland by rail, Boston by steamboats, four times a week; vessels drawing 12 feet can come within 100 rods of the stream.

HAMLIN PLANTATION—AROOSTOOK COUNTY.

From Assessors' Returns.

Four Powers.

First, "Hammond Privilege," on Hammond brook; large quantities of spruce lumber in the basin of the stream. Unimproved.

Second, on Duboy brook, about 40 feet perpendicular descent. A large amount of machinery might be kept in motion throughout the year by means of an overshot wheel 28 feet in diameter.

The stream is fed by a small pond. Another small lake in the vicinity which now discharges its waters into Black brook, and thence into the Aroostook river, might at a small expense be connected with the Duboy brook. The privilege probably belongs to the State.

Third, a small power below the above, near the river St. John.

Fourth, a power on Stony brook, an active stream, which would keep considerable machinery in motion by means of an overshot wheel.

HAMLIN'S-GRANT PLANTATION—OXFORD COUNTY.

Statement of the Assessors.

There are no streams of any considerable size in Hamlin's-Grant Plantation, and none whatever suitable for milling purposes.

HAMPDEN—PENOBSCOT COUNTY.

From a Statement and Plan of the Streams furnished by Daniel Crosby, Esq.

Six Powers, or More.

First, on Sowadabscook river, near its junction with the Penobscot. Fall at low water nine feet; various lumber, shingle and lath saws; four American turbines, 150 inches water each, or 35 horse-power in all; a fulling mill, six horse-power.

Second, above, a paper mill of four 30-inch engines, three turbines, 400 inches water, 50 horse-power. Head and fall 13 feet.

Third, above, paper mill of six 30-inch engines, three turbines, 400 inches water, 65 horse-power. Head and fall 17 feet.

Fourth, Fifth and Sixth, between this mill and Stetson's pond, two and one-half miles, one occupied by saw, lath and shingle machines; head 10 feet; head at the other two privileges eight feet; not occupied.

The Sowadabscook is the outlet of various ponds, area 1,000 acres; not improved for storage on account of flowage. At the foot of Stetson's, the lowest pond, a ledge in the channel prevents the *drawing-down* of the pond. The attempt to construct a cut or channel at this point resulted in a law suit on part of mill owners on the *Kenduskeag* stream, between which and the Sowadabscook there is a natural thoroughfare with the water flowing forth and back at different seasons—and ultimately in an abandonment of the scheme. The use of these ponds with the flowage feasible would add greatly to the value of the powers. As now used the ponds serve neither river for reserve purposes. The river is naturally constant. Scanty water only for two months.

HANCOCK—HANCOCK COUNTY.

From Selectmen's Returns.

Three Powers.

First, "Graves' Privilege," on Skilling's river, at tide water. Unimproved.

Second, "Joy's Privilege," above, one-third mile from tide water. Unimproved.

Third, "McFarland's Privilege," above, one-half mile from tide. From McFarland's privilege to salt water is a continuous fall of 10 feet in 100. Unimproved.

Power of 20 horse the year round. Formerly grist, saw, and shingle mills; went to decay, dams finally swept away by freshets.

One small pond. An artificial reservoir three miles by one could be constructed. Stream comparatively constant at all seasons.

The power being located upon tide, is favorably situated as regards accessibility.

Rock, suitable for rough work.

HANOVER—OXFORD COUNTY.

From Selectmen's Returns.

Numerous Powers.

On the outlet stream of Howard's pond, which falls *three hundred and sixty-five feet* in its course of one and a half miles to the Androscoggin.

One-fourth of the power is improved. There is but one dam, at the outlet of the pond. Wheels, overshot. The mills work all the year: annual product, $5,400.

The pond is three-fourths by half a mile; its capacity could be doubled at an expense of $500. The mills on the stream now constitute about one-fourth of the valuation of the town. Freshets harmless.

Mills are within seven and a half miles of the Grand Trunk Railway. Market, for the products of the mills is now at the mills.

HARMONY—SOMERSET COUNTY.

From Selectmen's Returns.

Four Powers.

First, "Harmony Village," on Higgins' stream; 500,000 of boards, 150,000 shingles, and a machine shop. Part of the mills operate all the year. Power only partially used.

Second, below, carding and cloth-dressing machine.

Third, at Main Stream village, on Sebasticook main stream; 500,000 feet of boards, 1,000,000 shingles, and a good grist mill. Operates all the year.

Fourth, on "Main Stream Falls," below; unimproved.

A bog six miles by three-fourths mile, is flowed by a dam, in connection with Higgins' stream. Stream can be made to yield abundant water all the year; Main stream also, by proper dams.

Good building stone. Market, Skowhegan, Newport, by road.

HARPSWELL—CUMBERLAND COUNTY.

From Statement of the Selectmen, and of Messrs. True & Co., of Portland.

Several Powers.

All are tide powers, several very excellent ones being unimproved.

First, "Casco Bay Mills," at the lower Narrows of the "Basin," in the southwest part of the town. Length of dam 275 feet; height above low water, 12 feet; mean rise of tide, nine feet. Area of pond, 200 acres; about one-fourth filled at low water to about 15 feet depth. Mill, 45 by 50 feet, three storied; Ryder turbine, 50 horse-power. Building will accommodate three wheels and six runs of stones. Capacity of privilege fully developed, estimated at 600 horse-power. Privilege situated on an excellent harbor; vessels of 8,000 bushels grain capacity discharge directly into the mill. Fourteen miles from Portland. Owned by George W. True & Co., Portland.

Second, at "Mill Cove," grist mill and saw mill.

No information respecting the other privileges.

HARRINGTON—WASHINGTON COUNTY.

Selectmen's Returns.

Two Powers.

First, on Mill river, fall ten feet, stream very rapid; water spring and fall.

Second, on Great Marsh stream; fall about ——— to the mile; will carry one saw the year round.

Saw, lath, and shingle mills. Rock, limestone, "which should be tested."

Harrison—Cumberland County.

From Selectmen's Returns.

Four Powers.

First, at the outlet of Anonymous pond, at Harrison village, fall twelve feet; "Tolman & Co.'s wire-factory"; product $50,000 per annum.

Second, on Bear river, at the village, fall 21 feet. The Harrison Water Power Company have just commenced building a dam for a factory.

Third, on the same river, just below, fall ten feet; unoccupied.

Fourth, at Bolster's mills, on Crooked river, fall eight feet, dam ponds the water back 60 rods; saw, grist and shingle machine; wheels overshot, centre-vent, and Leffel's American double turbine.

Bear river is the outlet of Bear pond; Crooked river is connected with numerous ponds above; no damage by freshets; abundant supply of water except in severe drouths. Rock; granite, abundant and of good quality; lay of the land very good.

Market, Portland, by canal, and road.

Hartford—Oxford County.

From Selectmen's Returns.

Three Powers.

On Bungermuck stream; fall respectively 9, 15, and 20 feet. They are not improved.

Hartland—Somerset County.

From Selectmen's Returns.

Three Powers.

First, "Upper Sebasticook Falls," in the village of Hartland, on the west branch of the Sebasticook river, about one mile from the outlet of Moose pond; fall 30 feet in 75 rods.

Second and Third, smaller powers about three miles from the village.

Improvements upon the above powers, three dams, saw, shingle and grist mill, carding machine, woollen factory, carriage and blacksmith shop; powers operate all the year; Tuttle wheel used.

A storage of six feet on Moose pond, assumed at 10 square miles, will yield for 10 hours a day, 312 days per year, 480 horse-power, gross, on the Upper Sebasticook falls, or 19,200 spindles. The storage could, however, be used in six months or less, and the power increased in proportion, the natural run sufficing all demands the residue of the year.

Artificial reservoirs of very great extent can be constructed; freshets perfectly harmless; range of water about five feet; water abundant at all seasons.

Rocks, granite; one-half basin forests; lay of the land good.

Market, Bangor, by road to Pittsfield, seven miles, and thence by railroad.

HAYNESVILLE AND LEAVITT PLANTATIONS—AROOSTOOK COUNTY.

From the Statement of W. H. Bryson, Esq., of Haynesville.

One Power.

At "The Forks" of the East and West branches of the Mattawamkeag river, within a half mile of the road from Bangor to Houlton. A dam 400 feet long would give a head of eight feet. The bed of the river is ledge. The great Mattawamkeag lake, 5.50 square miles, 12 miles above, on the West branch, is an immense reservoir, having a dam at its outlet which raises a 12-foot head. Unimproved.

HEBRON—OXFORD COUNTY.

From Selectmen's Return.

Several Powers.

"Matthews Pond Falls," height 140 to 180 feet in 100 rods. Only one mill upon it. The power fully employed would saw 800-000 of lumber. Could be worked all the year with a suitable dam.

Machinery now used of the poorest construction; old-fashioned wooden wheel. Area of the two connected ponds, 470 acres. Their capacity could be doubled by a dam, and at a trifling expense. Rocks, coarse granite, suitable for building dams. Lay of the land convenient.

Market, West Minot and Mechanic Falls.

HERMON—PENOBSCOT COUNTY.

Selectmen's Returns.

Two Powers.

First, "Shaw & Harding Mill," on Cold brook. Fall eight feet. Dam and mill upon it; mill out of repair; operates four months. Situated close by the Maine Central Railroad, and three miles from the business part of Bangor.

Second, on the Wheeler stream, "King's Mill-Dam"; five and a half miles from Bangor. About equal to the first-mentioned in capacity. No other improvement than the dam.

Hinkley Township—Washington County.

Statement of Peol Tomah.

[See also "Hinkley Township and Township No. XXVII."]

Several Powers.

On the East and West Musquash streams, the outlets of the lakes of the same name. There is a fall of 60 feet from West Musquash, and 100 feet from East Musquash lake to Big lake. The lakes are dammed four and seven feet respectively, and yield a large volume of water.

Hinkley Township and Township No. XXVII—Washington County.

Statement of Oscar Pike, Esq., of Princeton, and Anson's Survey.

Several Powers.

The outlet stream of Grand lake, on the west branch of the St. Croix, or the "Grand Lake Stream," has a fall of about 80 feet in its descent to Big lake. At its head the St. Croix Log Driving Company built in 1867, a dam to hold about eight feet head.

A storage of only four feet on the lake, will yield on the whole fall 1,480 horse-power, for ten hours a day, 312 days per annum, or 59,200 spindles. In addition, the various lakes above are dammed, and the supply of water can be much increased thereby. The storage could be used in six months or less, the natural flow sufficing the rest of the year.

The lower privilege at the head of steamboat navigation on the Big, Long, and Lewey's lakes, is furnished with an almost complete dam by nature; a ridge of rock running across the river leaves only about 25 feet to be constructed. A head of 15 or more feet can be had readily. Solid rock bottom and sides. Most excellent chance for mills. Quite a large eddy above serves as a natural pond.

The sites above are likewise very superior. All unimproved.

HIRAM—OXFORD COUNTY.

From the Report of Surveys of Cyrus Ingalls and George Wadsworth, Esqs.

[See also "Baldwin and Hiram," "Cornish and Hiram," and "Hiram and Parsonsfield."]

Twenty-Five Powers.

Nine of the above are situated upon Hancock brook, which is a chain of eight or more considerable lakes and ponds.

First, 100 rods from Hiram bridge, Allen's mill and privilege; various saws; head and fall eight feet.

Second, 25 rods above, Clark & Co.; various saws and a grist mill; head and fall 16 feet.

Third, 20 rods above, a dam seven feet, can be made ten feet; pond of five acres. Formerly a shingle machine. It is held as a reserve for the mills below.

Fourth, three-quarters mile above, Rankin's saw mill and privilege; head and fall 10 feet.

Fifth, Sixth, and Seventh, above the Rankin's mill, excellent sites for mills of large capacity. Dams twelve feet high can be made at small expense, as the banks are closely adjacent and the foundation rock. Two wooden dams are used for log-driving.

Eighth, two miles above, the "Barker Dam," at the outlet of Barker pond, head and fall eight feet, and at an altitude of 275 feet above the Saco river at Hiram bridge. Pond contains over 500 acres. From this pond, northeasterly, one mile, is the Pickerel pond, 25 acres.

Ninth, from this pond up, three-fourths of a mile, at the foot of the "Great Hancock Pond," stone dam 50 feet long, eight feet high; pond contains 500 acres. From the upper end of this pond, four rods further, the foot of the "Upper Hancock Pond" is reached, which contains about 100 acres. Three-fourths of a mile east of this pond, are four other ponds, some of which are of considerable size, and flow into the Great Hancock pond.

The ponds connected with this stream taken together have an area of not less than 2,500 acres, and at small expense could be made reservoirs to the Saco for extensive operations.

Tenth, on Wadsworth Canal brook, various saws; 13 feet head and fall, pond four acres. Water six months.

Eleventh, two miles above, "Hatch and Warren's Mill," ten feet head and fall, pond four acres, various saws.

Twelfth and Thirteenth, on Hunter's brook, fall for overshot wheels 25 feet diameter, could operate about all the year. Good sites for light machinery, and accessible.

Fourteenth and Fifteenth, on Barnes' brook, 30 to 40 feet fall can be had at each. Great amount of hemlock and hard wood.

Sixteenth, above, at the "Barnes place," formerly a saw mill. Not used.

Seventeenth, a mile above, "Wadsworth's Mill," stave and shingle. Operates part time nearly all the year.

Eighteenth and Nineteenth, on Meadow brook, formerly grist mills; dam 12 feet high, feasible; water for small machinery, nearly all the year.

Twentieth, half a mile above, "Pierce's privilege," suitable for an overshot wheel, and light work.

Twenty-First and Twenty-Second, on Mill brook; one near the Fryeburg stage road, has an overshot wheel 22 feet in diameter, and eight feet fall from the dam above. Formerly operated a grist mill, now various lumber saws.

Twenty-Third and Twenty-Fourth, etc., good privileges, above.

Twenty-Fifth, on "Spring-Schoolhouse brook," at crossing of road, might operate nearly all the year by use of reservoirs.

Hiram—Oxford County, and Parsonsfield—York County.

Statement of George Wadsworth, Civil Engineer, of Hiram.

[See also "Hiram," and "Parsonsfield."]

Two Powers.

On the Great Ossipee river, between the site of "Warren's Mill," and Kezar Falls. Head of 12 feet can be had at each. These sites are regarded as valuable in their degree as Kezar Falls.

The river is very permanent, being fed by large ponds which are already improved for storage, and are susceptible of greater improvement. See page 77, second Table.

Hiram and Porter—Oxford County.

Statement of George Wadsworth, Civil Engineer.

[See also "Hiram," and "Porter."]

Four Powers.

On the outlet stream of Spectacle and other ponds.

First, the lowest near Ossipee river, "Stanley's Mill," various saws and planer. Nine feet head and fall. Can operate all the year.

Second, "Milliken's Mill," above, grist mill, and various saws, operating all the year.

Third, above, at outlet of Spectacle and Trafton ponds; formerly saw and grist mills. Now unoccupied; except dam for reservoirs. Ten feet head and fall can be had, the best privilege on the stream.

Fourth, "Merrifield's Mill," at outlet of Jay-Bird pond, stave and shingle machinery. Head and fall, now five feet, can be doubled.

HODGDON—AROOSTOOK COUNTY.

From Selectmen's Returns.

Three Powers.

Good privileges, on the Meduxnakeag river, and all in a running distance of one mile; the upper two 50 rods apart.

The upper two, "Jewett & Dunell's Mills"; the lower, "Hutchinson's Mills."

Upper fall 11 feet; second, six feet; lower, nine feet. No natural ponds in the vicinity. The upper dam ponds back the water three miles; the lower about a mile.

Economically applied, the power would carry a considerable amount of machinery nearly all the year. Poorly applied at present.

On the upper dam, various saws, a carding and fulling and grist mill.

On the second dam, a shingle mill.

On the lower dam, various saws, and planing machine.

The grist mill works all the year; the saw mill two-thirds of the year; the lower mill nearly all the year; the shingle machine was erected recently.

The machinery is not economical of power; centre-vent and reacting wheels.

An artificial reservoir, five miles by four, could be constructed at small expense above the upper dam, and the land it would flow is nearly useless; freshets harmless; total range from lowest to highest water, about eight feet.

HOLDEN—PENOBSCOT COUNTY.

From a Statement of the Selectmen, and a Plan of the Streams.

Six Powers.

Four situated on Dead river the outlet of Fitz pond, which is four miles by half a mile. All good privileges, and sufficient to run an up-and-down saw throughout the year except in a severe drouth.

First, a shingle mill.

Second, a saw mill and tannery.

Third, saw mill and shingle mill.

Fourth, a shingle mill.

Fifth, on Budge's stream, a saw mill.

Sixth, on the same, a saw mill.

The powers on Budge's stream run about four months in the year.

Annual product, about $10,000. Market, Bangor, seven miles distant.

Holden Township—Somerset County.

Statement of Heman Whipple, Esq., of Solon.

Six Powers.

First, on Heald stream, three-fourths mile above south line, 16 feet fall can be had; grist mill to be built.

Second, a mile above, 15 feet fall, saw mill.

Third, three-fourths mile above, 10 feet fall, dam.

Fourth, "Dog-Hole Falls," above, 12 feet. No improvement.

Pond above, one-half square mile, flowed eight feet.

Fifth, one-half mile from south line, fall 10 feet, dam.

Sixth, one mile above, 10 feet fall, dam.

Pond above for reservoir, one-half square mile.

Holeb Township—Somerset County.

Statement of Ex-Governor Coburn.

Two Powers.

First, on Moose river in the extreme southeast corner of the township, "Holeb Falls," 48 feet fall in 80 rods. Very fair chance for dams and mills, granite bottom and banks. No improvement.

Second, on Barrett brook, 15 feet in 30 rods. Good site for dam and mills. Small pond, which can be dammed.

Hollis—York County.

[See also "Buxton and Hollis," "Buxton, Hollis and Standish," and "Dayton and Hollis."

Three Powers.

First, a saw mill on a brook running from Hollis Centre to Barker's-Pond stream.

Second, a saw mill on a tributary to Kelliok pond, about three-fourths of a mile above the pond.

Third, on the same stream, about a mile above, a saw mill.

HOPE—KNOX COUNTY.

From the Selectmen's Returns and a Plan of the Streams.

Ten Powers, and More.

Four at the foot of the Hobbs and Fish ponds, all within three-fourths of a mile; average head upon each privilege 10 feet.

First, on the dam at the foot of the ponds, various saws and a grist mill.

Second, below, saw mill, water for a large business 10 months.

Third, on the next dam, saw, threshing, grist, and machine shop equipment; water the year round.

Fourth, on the next dam, various saws.

Fifth and Sixth, below, unoccupied.

Lay of the land good for building; abundance of rocks, and quite heavily wooded. Mills located at the foot of the above named ponds; see page 140, second table.

Seventh, at the foot of the Mansfield pond; saw for staves and heading; eight months in the year; head 14 feet; a great amount of lumber.

Eighth and Ninth, below, unoccupied.

Tenth, mill for staves and heading; three months. Other privileges below, superior to this, unoccupied. These privileges are at the upper end of the Hobbs and Fish ponds. Mills located from 10 to 12 miles of Rockland, and seven to nine miles of Camden; both good markets.

HOULTON—AROOSTOOK COUNTY.

From Selectmen's Returns.

Seven Powers.

Upon the south branch of the Meduxnakeag river and its tributaries, known as the "Cary," the "Page and Madigan," the "Ham," "Logan," "Mansur," "Cressey" and "Houlton" water-powers. The Cary privilege has a fall of about 30 feet; the others of about 12 feet.

"Power is sufficient for the largest manufactories; water abundant all the year." Improved in two grist, four saw, and two carding mills; two cabinet shops, one tannery and a machine shop and foundry. Numerous lakes and large streams; the lakes can be converted into large reservoirs at small expense.

Freshets never destructive; sites for building very excellent; rock suitable for building close at hand.

"There is a most excellent opportunity for factories, especially woollen factories. We raise the best of wool, in great quantities, which now goes to Boston and then comes back to us in cloth. Other manufactories are greatly needed, and we can offer the highest inducements." The soil in this region is a deep rich loam, underlaid by clay.

Market, Boston and Bangor; the former by the St. Andrews Railroad and steamboat. "Our great trouble, in years past, has been means of access to the rest of the world. The railroad above mentioned has begun to give us relief. The opportunities and necessities for manufacturing here are very unusual."

HOWARD TOWNSHIP—PISCATAQUIS COUNTY.

Statement of Luther Chamberlain, Esq., of Atkinson.

Eight Powers.

First, on the Ship pond stream, about 30 rods above Sebec lake; a head of 10 feet can be had perpendicular, and by flumes a fall of 20 feet in 200 of run.

Second, Third, Fourth, above, rapids; from 8 to 12 feet on each can be had.

Fifth, on the outlet stream of Long pond, a fall of 18 feet can be had.

Sixth, on Wilson stream, about a mile above Sebec lake; a fall of 15 feet can be had perpendicular; rock bottom and banks. Good site for mills. Formerly a mill.

Seventh, a short distance above, a perpendicular fall of 15 feet can be had; solid ledge, good chance for mills.

Eighth, a saw mill on the outlet of Beaver pond.

Ship pond covers three square miles, is fed by other ponds, and is a grand reservoir. Long pond covers a square mile.

HOWLAND—PENOBSCOT COUNTY.

From Selectmen's Returns.

[See also "Enfield and Howland."]

Two Powers.

First, the "Howland Falls," at the mouth of Piscataquis river.

Height 20 feet, produced by a dam, which ponds the water back six miles or more to the privileges in Maxfield. The dam is 300 feet long, is built of logs, and is of great strength, with a sluice for ice at the east end, 40 feet long and two feet deep. Five saw mills are already built upon the privilege; there is room with abundant power for five more.

Upon the south side of the river there is a *natural canal* through which the river could be turned with insignificant cost. The land upon the canal is level, and but little elevated above high water. It affords sites for any number of mills, of unsurpassed excellence and easily and cheaply improved.

Enormous quantities of lumber remain upon the river above, especially of hemlock. No more favorable opportunity could possibly be afforded for tanning on an extensive scale. The "extract of bark" for tanning purposes could also be made here under the most favorable conditions. The privilege is owned by Messrs. N. J. Miller of Portland, and Albert Emerson of Bangor.

The Piscataquis at this point drains 1,276 square miles, or only about 100 square miles less than the Saco at Saco; it is fed by over 74 square miles of lakes and ponds, including only 29 of the larger. The surface of the basin is generally moderately uneven and undulating, so that the surplus drainage is not thrown off with rapidity, and a comparatively large volume is reserved for use in the summer season. A storage of six feet upon the Schoodic, Sebec, Seboois and Endless lakes alone, 47 square miles, would furnish 1,580 horse-powers, 63,200 spindles, for 10 hours a day, 312 days per year, on this fall. But the storage could all be used in three to six months furnishing a two to three fold greater power, to sustain which, for the rest of the year, the *natural* run of the river would be more than sufficient. The lakes specified are comparatively near at hand. To the above figure for the power attainable in a drouth by storage, should be added the *natural* low run of the river, which at this point would probably be 400 to 500 horse-powers, on a 20-foot fall.

Second, a power on the Seboois river; unimproved.

These, taken in connection with the enormous power on the Penobscot river, carry up the manufacturing resources and capabilities of this town to a figure not surpassed.

Hudson—Penobscot County.

Statement of Joel Mann, Esq.

One Power.

At Hudson village, in the centre of the town, on the outlet stream of Little Pushaw lake, two saw, a shingle and grist mill, and other machinery, and power sufficient to carry as much more.

Lumber is manufactured the year round.

The Little Pushaw lake covers nearly a square mile, and is fed by numerous and considerable streams.

Independence Plantation—Penobscot County.

Statement of the Assessors.

Several Powers.

On the Crossuntic stream, large enough to operate saw mills and shingle and clapboard machines. There are swamps and ponds that might be converted into reservoirs of considerable capacity.

None improved.

Indian Township—Washington County.

Statement of Oscar Pike, Esq.

Two Powers.

First on the Tomar stream, three miles from the river, fall 10 feet; dam and shingle machine.

Second, one and a half miles above, 10 feet fall; excellent chance for dam. Not used.

Stream fed by the Tomah ponds which cover two square miles, and can be flowed.

Indian-Pond Township—Somerset County.

Statement of Messrs. J. M. Haynes of Augusta, and Heman Whipple, of Solon.

Several Powers.

From the dam at the foot of Indian pond to the mouth of Chace's stream, the Kennebec river is a violent torrent, constituting the well-known "Rapids," the upper half of which is in this township. The fall is not less than 150 to 200 feet in a run of four and a half miles. The banks are very high and steep, and together with the bottom and sides of the river are solid ledge. There are points, however, where dams could be constructed and facilities for access secured.

At the head of the rapids, "Indian-Pond Dam," flows five miles, large reservoir, dam 200 feet long, 24 gates; good site for development in all respects.

Between the two ponds, which are classed together as Indian pond, is quick water for one-half mile, with a good site for improvement. Upper pond two miles long.

There are several privileges upon other streams, as follows:

First, at the foot of the lower pond on Chace's stream, a most excellent site, where 20 feet fall can be had; a dam already built. Below this the stream is very swift, but the height and steepness of the banks render it almost unimprovable.

Second, Third, etc., above, good sites, with large and numerous reservoir ponds. Not used.

Fifth, Sixth, etc., on Indian stream; reservoirs above. Not used.

INDIAN PURCHASE TOWNSHIP (EAST)—PENOBSCOT COUNTY.

Statement of Daniel Barker, Esq., of Bangor.

Eleven Powers, or More.

First, Second, etc., "Grand Falls," on the Penobscot river, one mile of swift water; lower pitch 15 or 20 feet.

Fourth, Fifth, Sixth, etc., above Grand Falls, "Island Falls," two miles long. One pitch 20 feet in 20 rods.

Seventh, "Rhine's Pitch," ten feet fall.

Eighth, at outlet of Quakish lake, a dam can be built 12 feet high; lake about a square mile and a half.

Ninth and Tenth, from Quakish lake to North-Twin Dam about one mile of rough water; fall about 25 feet.

Eleventh, "North Twin Dam." The dam is about 400 feet long, 16 feet high, and has 22 gates. It flows North Twin lake, five square miles, South Twin, four square miles, Pamedumcook six square miles, and Amjejus four miles, holding an enormous store of water.

INDUSTRY—FRANKLIN COUNTY.

From Selectmen's Statement.

Two Powers.

First, at the outlet of Clear-Water pond, "Allen's Mills"; 33 feet fall in 55 rods. Eight hundred inches of water, under a 12-foot head, operates 12 hours per day through the year; machinery not of the best construction; grist, saw, shingle, clapboard and lath, and shovel-handle machinery; also a tannery, with water privilege sufficient to use 100 cords of bark per year; the dam, at the foot of pond, may be raised three feet; abundant stone for building purposes; the pond contains from 1,500 to 2,000 acres; water deep and clear; absolute immunity from danger by freshets.

Six miles from Farmington depot, good roads; 15,000 dozen shovel handles manufactured last year, and hauled to depot for two cents per dozen.

Second, "West's Mills," 30 feet fall in 50 feet distance; saw and shingle machine, two months per year; grist mill, ten months per year. Ten miles from Farmington depot.

Island Falls Plantation—Aroostook County.

Statement of E. F. Dinsmore, Esq.

Three Powers.

First, on the Mattawamkeag, west branch, fall 20 feet, with a chance for flowage of some hundreds of acres, by a higher dam. Water enough at all seasons to carry a large amount of machinery.

There are at present on this privilege a saw, shingle, and grist mill. The stream drains a large extent of rolling country, is fed by numerous ponds, and is therefore comparatively constant.

Second, on "Cold Brook," saw and grist mill.

Third, on Dyer brook, water sufficient for saw and grist mill. Unimproved. This and the foregoing power are situated near the stage road.

Islesborough—Waldo County.

From Statement of the Selectmen.

Six Powers, or More.

First, at the outlet of a pond of 12 acres, which may be increased to twice that size by means of a cheap dam; an eight-foot greater head than the present may be had and water sufficient to carry a grist mill two-thirds of the year. Pond lies one-third mile from sea shore.

Second, on the same stream, just at its mouth; with another dam, the water may be used again to as good advantage as at the pond. Unimproved.

Third, Fourth, etc., from the pond to the sea line there is a total fall of 60 feet, which might be improved in two or three privileges. Unimproved.

Fifth, a tide power at the head of Sabbath-day harbor, quite a reservoir, with a very narrow entrance, which could be dammed at trifling expense. Unimproved.

Sixth, a tide power at the head of Gilkey's harbor, with a large reservoir which could be dammed at not unreasonable expense, and a large amount of work done. Unimproved.

Rocks, shale.

JACKMAN TOWNSHIP—SOMERSET COUNTY.

Statement of Heman Whipple, Esq.

One Power.

About half a mile from lake, "Churchill Falls," fall 10 feet, excellent chance for improvement; good land all about. Not used.

JACKSON—WALDO COUNTY.

From Selectmen's Returns.

Six Powers.

First, on Hadly brook, saw mill; fall fourteen feet.

Second, on Hadly brook, fall 20 feet.

Third, Fourth, Fifth and Sixth, on Marsh stream; total fall of the four combined, 60 to 70 feet in three-fourths mile; two saw, one grist, and a shingle mill; operate from one-third to one-half of the year. Power only partially improved.

Rose wheel. Two ponds at the head of Hadly brook; each will cover twenty-five acres. Artificial reservoirs feasible to some extent. Basin one-third wooded. Mills cut in 1867, 600,000 feet hemlock boards, 1,000,000 shingles, 25,000 feet vessel plank. Total value, $7,800.

Market, Belfast, by road; "hope soon to have a railroad."

JAY—FRANKLIN COUNTY.

From Selectmen's Returns.

Five Powers.

First, "Jay Bridge Falls," on the Androscoggin river, three miles above Livermore Falls, and several miles below Capens' Rips in Canton on the same river.

Formation.—The bottom and banks of the river at this point consist of solid ledge, extended both above and below the falls. An island, fifteen acres in extent, divides the fall into two parts and serves for abutments to the sections of the dam. A first-class dam was erected in 1867, and commands a head of 12 feet. Its

Jay Bridge Falls.

sections are respectively 150 and 200 feet long. The river is rapid both above and below, and exhibits a well defined pitch a short distance above the dam where another island divides the river into two channels. There is also a pitch a short distance below.

Volume of Water and Power.—If the extreme drouth run at this point be assumed to be 20 per cent. less than at Lewiston, or 75,200 cubic feet per minute, the gross power of the falls, if so much as 30 feet be available, is 4,260 horse-power gross, or 170,-400 spindles; that developed by the present dam is about 69,000 spindles. The power can be increased by raising the dam, 10 feet or more, as may be desired, no loss from flowage being entailed thereby. It can also be enormously increased, in common with the other great powers upon the river, by the use of the reservoirs above. See pages 84–87, Part II.

Lay of the land.—Unsurpassed upon the east bank, there being an extensive slope of evenly graded surface and of suitable height for improvement, upon the margin of which a canal could be constructed down river to any distance required, and mills advantageeously located thereon. The island also is of such height that factories can be placed upon it favorably, a natural run extending through it, which could be inexpensively converted into a canal, and mills located in connection. The substratum of both the island and banks being mainly ledge, affords the best possible basis for the firm establishment of dams, mills, and all required structures. The territory bordering the privilege also lies well for the accommodation of boarding houses, and other appurtenances of a manufacturing town.

Building materials.—The island is a body of granite of first-rate building quality. A quarry of excellent granite is also adjacent on the bank of the river. Good brick clay is close at hand. Lumber can of course be procured in unlimited quantities from up river.

Proprietorship, etc.—The privilege is owned by Hon. John Lynch of Portland. The only improvement upon it at present is the dam and a saw mill. The line of the Androscoggin Railroad is within one and a half miles. The privilege is declared by experts to be unsurpassed upon the river as respects feasibility of development and as a site for heavy operations.

Second, about one mile below Jay bridge, "French's Falls," on the Androscoggin. Total height 10 feet; no part of the power is improved.

Third, below the above named falls, the "Otis Falls," on the Androscoggin, situated about one-half mile above Livermore falls. The total height of said falls is fourteen feet, within a running distance of six rods; no part of this power is improved, either by mills or dam. It is owned by Capt. Ezekiel Treat of Livermore falls, and Dr. Kilburn of Lewiston.

The power of these two privileges is, in proportion, as above.

Fourth, "Stubb's Mill," in the east part of town; stream small.

Fifth, "Look's Saw Mill," in north part of town; small stream; operates several months.

JEFFERSON—LINCOLN COUNTY.

From the Statement of the Selectmen, and a Plan of the Streams.

Ten Powers.

First, on Dyer's river, saw and shingle machinery; fall 11 feet eight inches. Cuts equal to 300,000 of lumber. With a good dam (easy to construct) mill could be run eight months. Good chance on one side for a grist mill, or other machinery. The forest adjacent consists of pine, about 3,000,000 or 4,000,000, white and red oak, maple, birch, &c.

Second, two miles above; grist, carding and fulling, stave and shingle mills; fall ten feet; water to grind most of the time.

Third, above, an old saw mill about rotted down; a good privilege; fall nine feet. It is the outlet of Dyer's pond. The pond is three by one-half miles, with another pond tributary to it, one by one-half miles.

Fourth and Fifth, on the brook connecting the ponds, one seven feet, the other ten feet.

Sixth and Seventh, on the Weeks stream; two saw mills; fall eight feet. The two could saw about 500,000 a year.

Eighth, "Jackson's Mills," on Jackson's stream, head and fall 12 feet, dam flows pond one-half mile long; saw, and stave machine; 400 square inches water; five months.

Ninth, below, "Bond & Jackson's Grist Mill," eight feet head and fall, 144 square inches of water.

Tenth, below, "Deshon's Mills," eight feet head and fall, stave and threshing machines, operating eight months and three months, respectively.

Eleventh, below, grist mill, eight feet head and fall, operates nearly all the year.

The foregoing mills on Jackson's stream have stone dams on ledge foundation.

Twelfth and Thirteenth, etc., good sites below.

Fourteenth, "B. Weeks' Saw Mill," above Dyer's Long pond; small mill pond.

Fifteenth, "Caldwell & Brown's Mill," stave, on a branch of this stream.

Sixteenth and Seventeenth, stave and shingle mills, small capacity.

JERUSALEM TOWNSHIP—FRANKLIN COUNTY.

Statement of Abner Toothaker, Esq., of Phillips.

One Power.

Dam at the forks, flows river back one and one-half miles; also Reddington pond is raised several feet for a reservoir.

JONESBOROUGH—WASHINGTON COUNTY.

From a Plan of the Streams furnished by J. D. Parker, Esq., of Steuben.

Three Powers.

First, the "Great Falls," on Chandler's river, a dam, no other improvements.

Second, "The Mills," at the village, and at the head of tide.

Third, on a creek tributary to the estuary of Chandler's river, near the village, a mill.

JONESPORT—WASHINGTON COUNTY.

From Selectmen's Returns.

One Power.

On Indian river; fall 10 feet; only partially improved, in dams and mills; mills operate half the time. Turbine wheel. No ponds. No artificial reservoirs feasible.

Underlying rock, syenite. Little forest. Market, all points, by sea.

K TOWNSHIP—AROOSTOOK COUNTY.

From the Statement of Dominicus Harmon, Esq., of Forestville Plantation.

Two Powers.

First, on the Little Madawaska river, a good mill site; fall ten feet. Unimproved.

Second, on the same river, a good mill site. Unimproved.

The river has a large and comparatively steady volume of water, as it drains 250 square miles of territory. The Madawaska lake, four square miles, can be dammed eight feet, making the powers constant throughout the year. Vast amount of lumber.

KENDUSKEAG—PENOBSCOT COUNTY.

From the Selectmen's Returns, and a Plan of the Streams.

Four Powers.

First, "Kenduskeag Village Power;" "Garland's Mills" on the east side, "Hodsdon's Mills" on the west side of the stream, fall 11 feet; water at medium stage of the river, 600 square inches; width at dam, 200 feet.

"Garland's Mills;" production, 1,500,000 feet board measure, 4,000,000 shingles, 40,000 bushels grain. "Hodsdon's Mills;" production, 1,000,000 shingles, 300,000 staves, 100,000 heading boards, 12,000 pounds wool, carded.

Second, "Higgins' Mill," one and a quarter miles above the foregoing power; production, 700,000 board measure, 1,500,000 shingles; fall nine feet; 600 square inches of water at medium stage; width at dam, 200 feet.

Third, "Young's Mills," on Bog brook; production, 800,000 shingles.

Fourth, "Piper's Mills," on Bog brook; production, 200,000 board measure.

Grist mills work all the year; the others might, but do not probably more than half the year. Machinery of the best construction. Tuttle's centre-vent wheel.

"For the last five years all the mills on Kenduskeag river could have run all the year round. The volume of the stream seems to have increased."

Market, Bangor, by turnpike, ten miles distant.

KENNEBUNK—YORK COUNTY.

From Selectmen's Returns.

Seven Powers.

First, Second and Third, "Mousam Village Falls," at the head of tide on Mousam river, two and a half miles from the sea. Divided into three pitches; total height of fall 40 feet. The lower, to the foot of which the tide flows, has no dam. The second has a sash and blind factory, machine shop, saw mill, shingle machine, with circular saws. The upper has 17 feet fall; two cotton mills and a grist mill.

Fourth, two miles above, on the same stream, "Lord's Cotton Mills," eight feet fall.

Fifth, one-half mile above, "Davis' Lumber Mill," nine to ten feet fall.

Sixth, one mile up, "Varney's Falls;" 12 feet fall.

Seventh, one mile further up, "Great Falls," fall 45 feet, with a natural stone dam and some "twelve hundred horse-powers; one of the best powers in the State;" entirely idle; owned by Dana, Fitch & Thompson.

From Great falls to Mousam Village falls, is 150 feet descent, the distance five miles. In this distance the gross power is estimated, including Great Falls, to be about 3,600 horse power, or 144,000 spindles, for 11 hours a day, 312 days per annum.

The stream is very constant. See page 147, Part II. The power could be increased one-fourth by the improvement of the ponds for reservoirs; total range of water from low to high, 3.5 feet. The falls are bounded all about with ledge; one-fourth of the basin covered with woods.

Market, Boston and Portland, by rail, also all parts by sea.

Kennebunkport—York County.

From Selectmen's Returns.

Eight Powers.

First, John Smith's saw mill; fall 10 feet; saws quite an amount of lumber.

Second, Jacob Curtis' saw and shingle mill; fall 10 feet; both in middle part of town, on small streams.

Third, Moses Nason's saw and carding mill, on Kennebunk river.

Fourth, Edwin Hutchins' shingle and clapboard mill; saws 50,000 per year; on a small stream.

Fifth, Goff's mills, Andrew Merrill's shingle, saw and grist mill.

Sixth, Perkins' mill; fall 12 feet; near the sea.

Seventh, Goodwin's mill; saw mill; small stream; does but little.

Eighth, tide mill, James D. Perkins, in village; grist mill, valuable.

Some of the above operate only at high water.

KINGFIELD—FRANKLIN COUNTY.

Statement of William Dolbier, Esq.

Thirty Powers, or More.

The Carrabasset river from the north line of the town to below the village, a distance of five miles, is exceedingly rapid, and good sites for mills are found at nearly every point, the whole number available is not less than 20, of 10 feet fall each.

On the lower privilege at the village, a fall of 12 feet in 50 rods, four saws can be driven the year through. Only a part of the power has ever been used. The mills, burned last year, are now rebuilding.

The river is connected with several lakes and ponds, which are already in part, and can be in a higher degree improved for reservoirs. The sum of available power is great, as the fall is very large, and the bottom and banks of the stream admit of cheap improvement.

Several located on the outlet stream of Tuft's pond, 300 acres, and can be flowed several feet.

Several on the outlet stream of Dutton pond; on one a saw mill; pond is flowed several feet; one of the falls is 50 feet perpendicular.

This pond and stream are tributary to the powers on the Carrabasset.

Several on Rapid stream, and one or more on Indian stream. As a whole, the water-power of this town is of quite unusual dimensions, considering the size of the streams. The streams are subject to considerable rise, but hold out well, being fed by springs about the bases of the mountains and by ponds.

A large proportion of the basin of the stream still wooded. Total yearly products, $8,000.

Market, Farmington, by road.

KINGSBURY—PISCATAQUIS COUNTY.

Statement of Leonard Hilton, Esq.

Six Powers, and More.

Three situated on the outlet stream of the Kingsbury pond, or ponds, three square miles, fed by a large extent of tributary country, and an excellent and copious reservoir.

First, at the foot of the pond, fall 14 feet; saw, clapboard, grist, shingle and lath mills. Power is sufficient to drive double the machinery the year through.

Second and Third, on the same stream, not improved ; stone and lumber close at hand for building, fall 16 feet each.

Fourth, Fifth and Sixth, on Thorn stream, fall 14 feet each.

Vast quantities of spruce and cedar in the vicinity of the above powers.

Market, now Skowhegan, 28 miles ; will be at Solon as soon as railroad is built, 12 miles by road.

KITTERY—YORK COUNTY.

Statement of J. H. Sanborn, Esq.

Two Powers.

First, a tide power on Spruce creek, sufficient for a saw and grist mill.

Second, a tide power, at Cate's island, sufficient for a grist mill. Operate the whole year.

LAGRANGE—PENOBSCOT COUNTY.

Digested from Selectmen's Returns.

Four Powers.

First and Second, on Dead stream ; Third, on Birch stream ; Fourth, "Slate Falls," upon Hemlock stream. Fall at each averages eight feet in three rods.

Two mills on Dead stream, valuable powers ; operate three fourths of the year ; capacity not known to the reporter. No mill on Hemlock stream. Formerly a mill on Birch stream, not now in use.

Two small ponds connected with Birch stream. They can be improved for reservoirs. Dead stream connected with lake Boyd which covers two or three square miles and is a capacious reservoir. The basin of Hemlock stream heavily wooded.

Market, Bangor, by road. Railroad is building into the region.

LEBANON—YORK COUNTY.

From Selectmen's Returns.

Three Powers.

Situated on the Salmon Falls river. The upper is opposite the Three Ponds village in Milton, and is known as the "Three Ponds Privilege." Two miles below, is the "Skates & Lyman Privilege." Below this, directly opposite East Rochester, is the "East Rochester Privilege."

Upon the lower fall, on the Rochester side, are two woollen mills, one of brick, the other wooden; each four stories high, 150 feet in length, and 54 feet wide, in which are 11 sets of woollen machinery. These mills run the whole year and have a full supply of water. The capital is $100,000, and $500,000 worth of goods are manufactured per year. The Cocheco Manufacturing Company own these mills.

The total height of the falls, on each of these powers, is 20 feet to about 900 feet in running distance. The power is not all improved. There are a saw mill, grist mill, &c., on the upper, and nothing on the two lower, on the Lebanon side. Each of the powers is capable of carrying as much machinery as is now used at East Rochester; there are two dams now constructed. The mills work all the year. The machinery is of the best construction. The upper dam is owned by the Great Falls Manufacturing Company; the middle by Skates & Lyman, and the lower by the Cocheco Manufacturing Company. For reservoirs see page 149.

The rocks about the falls are not suitable for building purposes; the land would be convenient to locate mills upon. The forests about the stream have been considerably cut off. The building of mills on the New Hampshire side, has increased the population in our town and made the real estate more valuable. The land and farms in the vicinity of the power, have already increased one-half in value. Market, Great Falls and East Rochester.

LEE—PENOBSCOT COUNTY.

From Selectmen's Returns.

Four Powers.

On the west branch of the Mattakeunk river, the "Mattakeunk Falls." Total descent 100 feet in two and a half miles.

Only a small part of the power is improved, in dams and mills; part of the mills operate all the year, part one-half, part one-fourth. Stream fed by Mattakeunk lake, which covers 1,000 acres. Its capacity can be readily increased. No rocks. One-half of the basin of the stream covered with woods.

Market, Bangor, by road.

Leeds—Androscoggin County.

From Selectmen's Returns.

[See also "Leeds and Turner."]

Eight Powers.

First, on Cushman's Mill stream; grist mills; in former years used also for saw mills.

Second, fifty rods below; shingle machine, etc.

Third, on Coffin's Mill stream; saw and shingle mills.

Fourth, on Bridgham stream, unimproved; formerly grist mill and carding mill. A considerable pond connected.

Fifth, on Mason brook, not used, formerly a grist mill.

Sixth, on a small stream in the north part of the town; a shingle mill.

Seventh, not used, in northwest part of the town; operates a shingle mill.

Eighth, a small but good power in southwest part of the town; formerly a saw mill. Not used.

The Androscoggin pond, on the confines of Leeds, is connected with the Androscoggin river by Dead stream, and the pond lying upon the same level as the river, the waters flow in and out according to the stage of the river. Could be stored at high water, and held for reserve.

The water-powers, though not large, are susceptible of much more use than is now made of them.

Market, Lewiston, by road or rail.

Leeds and Turner—Androscoggin County.

From the Returns of Leeds and Turner, and of M. T. Ludden, Esq.

[See also "Leeds," and "Turner."]

One Power.

The "North Turner Falls," at North Turner bridge, 16 miles above Lewiston, fall 13 feet. The natural force of the water is so great that a saw mill has been run here by its means.

Sites for mills excellent. Facilities for canals first-class. Building materials abundant. An island in the river diminishes the required length of dam. Firm bottom and banks for dams, and other structures. Railroad station within four miles.

If the volume of water at low run be assumed 10 per cent. less than at Lewiston, or 84,600 cubic feet per minute for 11 hours a day, the gross power of the fall, at 13 feet, is 2,080 horse-power, or 83,200 spindles.

For reservoirs tributary to this power, see pages 84–86, Part II. Unimproved.

LEVANT—PENOBSCOT COUNTY.

From Selectmen's Returns.

Five Powers.

On Black stream, and its tributaries.

First, "Wiggin's Mills," at Levant village, fall ten feet in 125 rods. Saw, shingle, and lath machines, run six months, and some of the machinery the whole year, manufacturing long and short lumber of an aggregate value of $7,000.

No natural lakes or ponds, but by constructing a dam half a mile above the mills, thereby forming an artificial pond several miles in length, the power would be available throughout the year, and one of the best in the State. The stone about the falls is a coarse slate, easily rifted, used in the vicinity in the construction of dams, cellar walls, &c. The land slopes gently for ten rods to the brink of the stream, and is quite favorable to the erection of mills, work-shops, &c.; about one-half the basin of Black stream is covered with forest.

Second, at South Levant, "Weston's Mills," fall 15 feet in 200 rods. Saw, shingle, grist, and clapboard mills, which run about half the year, employing nearly all the power, excepting at times of high water, and manufacture about $7,500. Ponds and lay of land as at Wiggin's.

Third, shingle mill, on "Horseback Road"; fall eight feet in 100 rods, can cut yearly about 500,000 shingles, but at present is not employed to any extent.

Fourth, at West Levant, "White's Mill," fall 20 feet in half a mile; saw and shingle mill, 300,000 long lumber and 300,000 shingles, capable of doing much more. Operates five months.

Fifth, in the west part of Levant, "Emerson's Mills," fall 22 feet in 20 rods, saw mill, formerly two saw mills; will operate one mill four months per year. Manufactures 200,000 to 300,000 feet of long lumber.

Market for lumber, Bangor, by road.

LEWISTON—ANDROSCOGGIN COUNTY.

Digested from Memoranda furnished by A. D. Lockwood, Esq.

Five Powers.

First, "Lewiston Falls," on the Androscoggin river, 20 miles

Lewiston Falls.

above its junction with the Kennebec, and 40 miles by the river from the ocean.

How Formed.—By a ledge of gneiss and mica schist, crossing the river diagonally, which is so extended as to form the bottom and sides of the stream both above and below the falls, and which projects above the level of the water in several small rocky islets, that serve as abutments to the dams.

Height.—Of the *natural* fall, 38 feet, which with dams of an average height of about 12 feet, produces an available power of fully 50 feet head. This descent is attained in a horizontal distance of 600 feet.

Volume of Water.—Volume at lowest stage, 94,000 cubic feet per minute, 11 hours a day. The water is under such perfect control that the total run of the river in drouth is economized, none going to waste by night or Sundays. The enormous increase in the volume of water that can be realised at this point may be seen upon reference to Part II, pages 84–87. The volume of water now used is 58,000 cubic feet per minute.

Power.—At lowest run, 8,900 horse, gross measurement, or 356,000 spindles. Of this 5,450 horse are now in use. The available power can be, as shown in Part II, doubled or trebled, as required. It is perfectly secure against all possible contingencies of ice or flood. Total range from lowest to highest water on the dams, about eight feet.

Lay of the Land.—Exceedingly favorable for the location of manufacturing establishments, there being two natural levels on the margin of the river, the lower allowing 22 feet fall, the upper 28 feet; and there being also abundant room for factories employing the whole power. The levels are sufficiently distant from the river and from each other to afford ample space for the largest establishments, with their yard room, boarding-houses, etc.

The territory removed from the river is favorably disposed for the location of streets and building lots, and for the growth of a large city. Seven acres have been elegantly laid out as a public square.

Incidentals.—Firm foundations for the large mills are easily obtained at trifling cost. Bricks of the best quality are made close at hand. Stone is procurable in unlimited quantities. Lumber is supplied by the country above and adjacent. The surrounding native population of farmers furnishes the operatives for the greater part.

Accessibility.—Lewiston is connected with the seaboard by two lines of railway, and is within six and a half hours of Boston, one and a half of Portland, and one hour and a quarter of Bath. Cotton can be brought to its warehouses, from Mobile or New Orleans, as cheaply as to Lowell or Lawrence; and transportation of either raw material or manufactured goods can be effected at as little cost, as to or from any other of the large interior manufacturing towns of the country.

Improvements.—Four dams, 850 feet in aggregate length. Guard locks, with seven sluiceways, 9 by 12 feet; main canal 64 feet in average breadth in the clear, and designed for 12 feet depth of water. Cross canal 40 feet broad in the clear, 10 feet of water. The dams and guard locks are constructed of split granite, in the most solid and substantial manner.

Proprietorship.—The power is owned by the Franklin Company. Office at Lewiston; agent, A. D. Lockwood.

Corporations.—The various manufacturing companies now in occupation of the power, are as follows, viz:

Bates Manufacturing Company, David M. Ayer, Agent. Incorporated 1850. Commenced operations 1852.

Capital stock,	$1,000,000
Mills, Cotton, 2,	40,000 spindles.
Mills, Woollen, 1,	8 sets machinery.
Females employed,	850
Males, "	350
Horse-power,	800
Water-wheels,	6 turbines.
Buildings,	Brick.
Goods manufactured,	Cotton and woollen.
Production—Cotton,	5,707,372 yards cloth per year.
	1,417,949 pounds " " "
Woollen,	226,155 yards cloth per year.
	146,912 pounds " " "

Hill Manufacturing Company, Josiah G. Coburn, Agent. Incorporated 1850. Commenced operations 1854.

Capital stock,	$700,000
Mills,	2
Spindles,	51,200
Females employed,	800
Males, "	200
Horse-power,	800
Water-wheels,	4 turbines.

Buildings, ... Brick.
Goods manufactured, ... Cotton.

Production, { 7,037,353 yards cloth per year.
1,753,770 pounds " " "

Androscoggin Mills, Amos D. Lockwood, Agent. Incorporated 1860. Commenced operations 1860.

Capital stock, ... $1,000,000
Mills, ... 2
Spindles, ... 50,000
Females employed, ... 788
Males, " 312
Horse-power, ... 800
Water-wheels, ... 5 turbines.
Buildings, ... Brick.
Goods manufactured, ... Cotton.

Production, { 6,500,000 yards cloth per year.
1,750,000 pounds " " "
1,800,000 grain bags " "
1,800,000 pounds " " "

Continental Mills, Stephen I. Abbot, Agent. Incorporated 1865. Commenced operations 1866.

Capital stock, ... $900,000
Mills, ... 1
Spindles, ... 27,360
Females employed, ... 395
Males, " 175
Horse-power, ... 440
Water-wheels, ... 3 turbines.
Buildings, ... Brick.
Goods manufactured, ... Cotton.

Production, { 5,600,000 yards cloth per year.
1,400,000 pounds " " "

Franklin Company, A. D. Lockwood, Agent. Incorporated 1854. Commenced operations 1857.

This company owns the water power, canals and the adjoining land around the falls on both sides of the river, also several hundred acres of land in and around the more thickly settled portion of the city. They also own the following property, viz:

Lincoln Mill, J. K. Piper, Agent.

Mills, ... 1

Spindles, ... 20,000
Females employed, ... 285
Males, " 143
Wheels, ... 2 turbines.
Buildings, ... Brick.
Goods manufactured, ... Cotton.
Production, { 2,800,000 yards cloth per year. 750,000 pounds " " "

Grist Mill building, occupied by Bradley & Co., manufacturers of flour and meal.

D. Cowan & Co., manufacturers of woollen goods, also dyeing and bleaching woollen and cotton yarns, employing 27 females, 25 males.

H. H. Dickey, manufacturer of belting and covering rollers, employing 10 men.

Wheels, ... 3 turbines.
Saw mill, occupied by S. R. Bearce & Co., manufacturers of lumber.
Water wheels, ... 5
Lewiston Bleachery and Dye Works, occupied by H. W. Farrell.
Capacity for bleaching and dyeing, ... 8 tons per day.
Females employed, ... 14
Males, ... 204
Water-wheels, ... 1 turbine.

Mechanic shops, occupied by O. B. Morse, stair builder; David Scott, manufacturer of weaver's reeds; O. H. Littlefield, doors, sash and blinds; L. W. Gilman, bobbins and spools; Rufus Stevens, machinist.

Water wheels, ... 2 turbines.

Lewiston Mills, Marshall French, Agent. Incorporated 1853. Commenced operations 1853.

Capital stock, ... $500,000
Mills, ... 2
Spindles, ... 17,880
Females employed, ... 460
Males, ... 211
Horse powers, ... 450
Water-wheels, ... 3 turbines.
Buildings, ... Brick.
Goods manufactured, ... Cotton and Jute.
Production—Cotton, { 764,619 yards cloth per year. 1,241,776 pounds " " "

Jute used,..........................1,679,281 pounds per year.
Cotton and jute bags.........................1,233,423 per year.

Lewiston Falls Manufacturing Co., John M. Frye, Agent. Incorporated 1834. Commenced operations 1834.

Capital stock,......................................$60,000
Mills, ...2
Sets machinery, ...6
Females employed,...45
Males, " 40
Horse-power, ...100
Water-wheels,..2
Buildings,..................................Brick and Wood.
Goods manufactured,................................Woollen.

Production,	225,000 yards cloth per year. 200,000 pounds " " "

General Statistics and Summary.

Number of manufacturing companies, ...15
Capital invested $5,000,000
Number of cotton mills,.......................................9
Spindles,..220,000
Water-wheels,...33

Power used for cotton mills,	3,666,	6,666 horse.
" " " other purposes,	500,	
Power not used,	2,500	

Females employed, ...3,664
Males; 1,660

Annual production—28,409,344 yards cotton cloth; 8,313,495 pounds cotton cloth; 451,155 yards woollen cloth; 346,912 pounds woollen cloth; 3,033,423 grain bags; 1,679,281 pounds jute used.

Population of Lewiston,...............................13,000
" " Auburn,...............................8,000
Valuation of Lewiston, ...$5,500,000
" " Auburn,.............................$1,680,000
Number of churches in Lewiston, ...7
" " school-houses,...............................27
" " schools, ...38
Expenditures for school purposes, 1866–7,............$53,278.58

In 1850, when operations commenced for the improvement of the power, the population was only about 4,000, and the total valuation $625,596. It is not presumed that the growth of the city has, by any means, reached the limit due to even the present improvement of the power; but even at its present stage it strikingly illustrates the rapidity with which water-power, when adequately improved, under favorable conditions, accumulates wealth and augments population. If all the available lake surfaces of the Androscoggin were as thoroughly improved as those of the Merrimac now are, the population of the city would probably go up to over 40,000, and with Auburn, which is divided from Lewiston only by the Androscoggin, would probably reach at least 50,000.

It will be seen that the population of Lewiston and Auburn is 21,000, and a part of the growth of Auburn is the result of the improvement of the water-power here, for though there are no factories there, many live on that side of the river who do business in Lewiston.

Second, "Lewiston Lower Power," two miles below Lewiston Falls, on the Androscoggin river, of 1500 horse, which has not yet been improved.

Third, two miles up the river, at "Deer Rips," there is unimproved power of at least 2,500 horse; the two together being sufficient to drive cotton mills containing about 250,000 spindles.

Fourth, "Barker's Mills," on Barker's Mill stream; fall 20 feet in 20 rods, saw and grist mill; both operate three months, and the grist mill nearly the whole year. Stream fed by Berry pond. J. B. Ham & Co.

Fifth, at the outlet of Noname pond, fall 12 feet in 12 rods, power sufficient to drive one run of stones the whole year. Pond is flowed a little, can be flowed so as to cover 300 acres, with considerable damage.

LEXINGTON—SOMERSET COUNTY.

Several Powers.

First, a saw mill on Sandy stream in the north part of the town.

Second, on Alder brook, the outlet of Butler and other ponds, a saw mill.

Other powers not improved. A large extent of pond surface available for reservoirs to any desired extent.

LIBERTY—WALDO COUNTY.

From Selectmen's Returns.

Twenty-Five Powers.

On the St. George and Sheepscot rivers. First to the Fifteenth (inclusive) in the first mile below the outlet of St. George's pond. The fall in that mile is 150 feet. Improvements, tanneries, saw mills, grist mills, stave and shingle mills, shovel handle factory, and many others. Part of the mills operate all the year; a part stop two or three months for want of water.

Streams connected with many lakes and ponds; artificial reservoirs feasible; freshets not very destructive; few rocks. The use of the power has greatly benefited the town.

Market, Belfast, by road.

Limerick—York County.

From a Statement, and a Plan of the Streams furnished by H. H. Burbank, Esq.

[See also "Limerick and Waterborough."]

Eight Powers, or More.

First, "Holland's Factory," on Brown's brook; woollen goods; fall of 12 feet in five rods, with a dam of 12 feet head besides. About half of the power is improved; works the year round; runs 1,144 spindles, could carry 2,300 spindles; iron machinery; breast wheel, 20 feet. Stream is connected with three ponds, two of which are one and one-half by one and one-half miles; and one is one by one-half miles. At the outlet of two of these, dams could be easily constructed; the other has a dam; granite around the falls; good location for shops and houses near the mill; basin of stream nearly all cleared. Twelve years ago the owner bought the power, then not in use for some years; he now pays heaviest tax in town. Annual value of his manufactures, $150,000; made for Boston and New York markets; situated ten miles from line of Portland and Rochester Railroad; and 30 miles from Portland.

Saw mill on the same fall, and shingle machine, both working the year round; each having one saw.

Second, "Bradbury's Mill," one-fourth mile below, grist mill and shingle machine; two feet fall, (natural,) in eight rods; small dam of three feet head; mainly worked with waste water of Holland's; could be much improved; good banks; worked the year round.

Third, "The Enterprise," formerly "Old Foster Mill Privilege," about one mile below; unimproved; fall five feet in 20 rods; once used; had dam with ten feet head in fair condition; stream about two rods wide, steep banks, rocks enough for building purposes.

Fourth, "Folsom's Mill," grist mill, runs about three-fourths of the year; proprietor intends to improve the power and build saw mills.

Fifth, "The old Jackson Mill Privilege," on Staples' brook; formerly, but not now, improved. Fall 11 feet in 12 rods; steep banks; excellent opportunity for building dams; plenty of rocks; small stream; not connected with lakes or ponds; good location for shops.

Sixth, "Durgin's Mill," on Staples' brook; small power, for sawing lumber.

Seventh, on Fogg's brook, "The Fogg Mill Privilege," not now improved; fall 16 feet in 80 rods, with quick water above and below; narrow current; steep banks for 80 rods or more; any quantity of rocks on and in the banks; the old dam had head of 11 feet.

Eighth, a mile below, "Dole & Gilpatrick's Saw Mill," cutting lumber nearly the year round; three feet fall in ten rods.

There are, besides the estimated powers, some privileges for sawing lumber and grinding grain sufficient for the adjacent neighborhood, but not worthy of note in this communication.

LIMERICK AND WATERBOROUGH—YORK COUNTY.

From the Returns of H. H. Burbank, Esq., of Limerick.

[See also "Limerick," and "Waterborough."]

Two Powers.

First, on Little Ossipee river; privilege occupied by the Waterborough Manufacturing Company on the south side, and by Stimson's grist mill on the north or Limerick side; grist mill has three runs of stones; operates the year through. Two feet fall in 20 rods; dam, seven feet head; gradual rapids for some distance below points measured, (in the survey made by Mr. Burbank.)

Second, the "Scratch" privilege, on the same river; unimproved; formerly used. Natural fall, four feet in 20 rods, with rapids above and below. For a mile above the termini of the 20 rods, the river rises six feet, and for a mile below falls 10 feet; all quick water; steep banks; no damage will be done by flowage; narrow current.

LIMESTONE PLANTATION—AROOSTOOK COUNTY.

Statement of E. J. Pattee, Esq.

Two Powers.

First, "Getchell's Mill," on Limestone stream, saw and clapboard mill.

Second, "Pattee & Jones' Mill," saw and clapboard mill. The latter is new; the power has been sufficient to drive the clapboard mill all summer, and saw mill part of the time.

LIMINGTON—YORK COUNTY.

From Selectmen's Returns.

[See also "Baldwin and Limington," and "Limington and Standish."]

Five Powers.

First, on Little Ossipee river, in the southeast part of the town, "Nason Falls"; height, 60 feet; length, one-fourth of a mile; width of the river, 175 feet. Improvements, grist, shingle and saw mills on each.

Second, three miles further down and near Limington falls, "Chase's Falls"; height 35 feet; length 40 rods; width of the river, 175 feet. Improvements, saw, box and shingle mills on each.

Third, on "Small's Mill Pond," at the outlet of Horn pond; length, 350 feet; width 30 feet; height 20 feet; saw mill and grist mill.

Fourth, a power on Salmon brook; grist mill and tannery.

Fifth, a power on Kellick pond; saw mill, clapboard and shingle machine.

The power is not all improved. The mills on the river work all the year; on the ponds, nearly all the year.

Large ponds connected with the stream, which can be converted into reservoirs at little expense. See page 77. Rocks, granite, suitable and close at hand for building, on the rivers.

Market, Portland.

LIMINGTON—YORK COUNTY; AND STANDISH—CUMBERLAND COUNTY.

From Returns of the Boards of Selectmen.

[See also "Limington," and "Standish."]

Three Powers.

First, "Steep Falls," at the northeast corner of Limington, four miles below the rips between Baldwin and Limington, on the Saco river; height, 40 feet in three-fourths of a mile. River at this point 150 feet wide and 10 feet deep. Improvement, a box machine, formerly a double saw. Two million feet lumber sawed annually.

If the volume of water at this point be assumed to be 5,000 cubic feet per minute less than at Saco, or 13,000 per minute for the 24 hours, the gross power day and night due to 40 feet fall, is about 1,000 horse power, 40,000 spindles; or about 2,180 horse power, 87,200 spindles, for 11 hours a day.

Second, "Union Falls," on the Saco river, in the close vicinity of Steep falls; height, 26 feet in 80 rods; width of the river, 200 feet.

The power at this point, with water as above, is 650 horse power gross, day and night, or over 1,400 for 11 hours a day.

Third, "Limington Falls," one mile further down; height, 65 feet in one-third of a mile; width of the river 250 feet. Improvements, a saw mill, a box machine and shingle machine.

The estimated power on this fall is 1,625 horse power gross for 24 hours, or 3,540 horse power for 11 hours a day, or 141,600 spindles.

Total power of the several falls, 7,120 horse power, gross, for 11 hours a day, or 284,000 spindles. An insignificant portion of the power is now used. The greater part of it can be put to use with ease, the lay of the land, the state of bottom and banks all favoring development.

Railroad communication with Portland is confidently looked for.

LINCOLN—PENOBSCOT COUNTY.

From Selectmen's Returns.

Seven Powers.

First, Second and Third, on the Mattanawcook stream at and near Lincoln village, and all within one mile of the Penobscot river. Dams are erected on two of these, each with 15 feet head and fall; and the same head and fall might be secured upon the third by a dam.

The power is used only in part; grist mill and cabinet maker's shop on one dam; on the other, saw, clapboard, shingle, and carding mills.

There are four lakes upon this stream, one flowed by the grist mill dam, and covering 600 acres; the others flowed by reservoir dams of about the same extent of flowage. The stream is exceedingly constant; freshets harmless.

Fourth, a fall of 60 feet in the first 60 rods below the upper and longest lake on the Mattanawcook stream; not improved at all.

Fifth and Sixth, on the Cambolasse stream, which has about half the capacity of the former stream; saw, clapboard and shingle mill, upon one dam; grist mill upon the other dam, with a reservoir dam above. This stream is connected with several large ponds, and is very constant.

Seventh, at the outlet of Second Cold-Stream pond, dam flows both lakes, above, eight feet; saw mill; lakes have an area of 1.75 square miles.

All the lakes and ponds are capable of great improvement as reservoirs. Granite abundant in the form of boulders; ledges of slaty rock suitable for building. Basin of streams nearly all covered with woods.

Market, Bangor; the European & North American Railway crosses the Mattanawcook between the mills. Also via Penobscot river.

Lincolnville—Waldo County.

From Selectmen's Returns.

Six Powers.

First, "Ducktrap Falls," on Ducktrap stream, the outlet of several large ponds. Descent of the stream nearly 300 feet in three miles. The power in question is situated about 20 rods above Ducktrap bridge, and 40 rods from high water mark. There is now a wooden dam upon it, built in 1852, about 13 feet high; the banks of the stream are high, and the dam can be raised to any required height, "short of 100 feet," at comparatively small expense.

A canal could be made, at little outlay, to conduct the water below the bridge, where factories could be built close upon tide water, so that vessels could load and unload by their immediate side. The harbor receives vessels drawing 12 feet.

Power upon this river within two miles of its mouth, with feasible improvement, estimated equal to 75,000 spindles.

Twenty-eight hundred acres of pond surface, all within a few miles, are available for reservoir purposes. The capacity of the ponds could be greatly increased by dams.

One grist mill on this power; no other improvements; the proprietor will *give* the privilege outright to any responsible party who will improve it. Proprietor, D. Howe.

Second, a power on the McCobb stream.

Third, a power at the outlet of Kendal pond; stave mill.

Fourth, a power at Gould pond; saw mill.

Fifth, a power at Andrews' point, owned by David P. Andrews; a saw mill.

Sixth, a power at Stetson's pond; a stave, shingle and saw mill.

The mills, on the greater part of the before mentioned powers, work only a portion of the year, the water being drawn down on account of flowage, there not being work enough for the mills, at present, to pay damage for flowing. No damage ever occurs on the stream from freshets; no power in the State can be superior in this respect.

Abundance of excellent granite; and the best lime, the Coleman white lime, in the market; also abundant clay of the best quality for brick at tide water; convenient locations for mills.

LINNEUS—AROOSTOOK COUNTY.

Statement of P. P. Burleigh, Esq.

Four Powers.

First, on Bither brook; not improved.

Second, on Mill brook; not improved; will operate 3 months.

Third, on Beaver brook, in the southwest part of the town, small pond above, flowed by a dam; a large tract of bog also can be flowed. Unoccupied.

Fourth, on Meduxnakeag stream, in the northwest part of the town; quite a large stream; will saw six months. Unoccupied.

LISBON—ANDROSCOGGIN COUNTY.

From the Statement of G. C. Moses, Esq., of Bath, and the Returns of the Selectmen of Lisbon.

Eight Powers.

First, "Lisbon Falls," on the Androscoggin river, in the southeast corner of the town of Lisbon; 11 miles from Lewiston, 17 from Bath, and 30 from Portland.

Height and Formation.—There were, originally, two falls about 900 feet apart, giving together a natural fall of 31 feet in the distance of 1,800 feet, which fall is increased by the elevation of the dam to 33 feet.

The upper fall, just below which the dam was located, is formed by a ledge of granite making directly across to an island about 300 feet distant, thence to the opposite shore, 650 feet farther. This ledge extends for more than half a mile down the river, on both sides, giving the best possible foundation for manufacturing establishments.

The dam is in two sections, each resting on the island. It is built on the ledge about eight feet lower than the brow of the natural fall, and being an average height of ten feet, raises the water but two feet above its natural level. It is constructed of hewn timber,

Lisbon Falls.

in the form of crib-work, the lower tier of which is fitted to all the irregularities in the surface of the ledge, and firmly secured with bolts. The cribs are filled with rock ballast and covered with hard wood plank. The whole work and materials were designed to make it equal or superior to any dam in the country not built of stone. It is believed to be strong enough to withstand any force to which it may be subjected.

Volume of Water.—Volume in the dry season of the year, estimated from the volume at Lewiston, with allowance for the additions of the Little Androscoggin and Sabattus rivers, 122,000 cubic feet of water per minute, during working time of 11 hours per day, six days in the week. The improvement of the lakes, by which the run of water at Lewiston would be increased, would operate to the same extent in favor of the power at this point. See pages 83–86.

Power.—Without any increase as above named, in the dry season, equal to 7,623 horse power, gross, or 305,000 spindles. But a trifling amount of this large power is yet in use. The expense of making the balance available has been pronounced, by competent engineers, very small, compared with the expenditure at other points of corresponding importance as to extent of power.

Lay of the Land.—Favorable for manufacturing establishments, with sufficient room for using the whole power. The surrounding territory is inhabited by farmers who furnish abundance of produce for the support of a large population.

Accessibility.—The Androscoggin Railroad runs through the land of the company, giving ample conveniences in the way of side tracks, to warehouses for storage of raw materials, fuel, &c., and for shipment of manufactured goods without drayage. By railroad Lisbon Falls is 30 minutes from Lewiston, one hour from Bath, one and a half hours from Portland, and six hours from Boston. Raw materials and manufactured goods can be transported to and from the mills as cheaply as from other interior manufacturing towns.

Proprietorship.—The power is owned by the Androscoggin Water Power Company, Oliver Moses, President; G. C. Moses, Treasurer. This company also own the real estate along the river, the toll bridge, saw and grist mill on the lower fall, and other property in the vicinity.

Improvements.—The only company now in occupation of the power is the *Worumbo Manufacturing Company*, F. Gutmann, Agent. Incorporated 1864.

Capital stock,	$250,000
Number of mills,	2,—10 sets of cards.
Goods manufactured,	All-wool beavers.
Females employed,	70
Males "	100
Power used,	150 horse.
Wheels,	2 turbines.
Buildings,	Brick.
Production per annum,	120,000 yards 6-4. 225,000 pounds of finished cloth.

Incidentals.—Building materials of all kinds are to be obtained in the immediate vicinity at reasonable cost. The Water-Power Company own two saw mills, supplied with abundance of pine and hemlock from the surrounding country. Brick of excellent quality are made upon the land of the company. Abundance of stone suitable for foundations and canal walls can be had on the spot where it is wanted. The village is yet small, but growing, and a commendable improvement in schools and churches is already manifest. To make an increased supply of water at Lewiston available at this point, it would only be necessary to provide means to hold back the water, left in the river between the two places after close of work at Lewiston, for use the next day, as the arrangements there would of course be complete for holding all the water coming down to that point in the night. The reservoir above the dam at Lisbon falls being very large, but slight elevation would be requisite. With this increase the power would be nearly double that now used at Lewiston, and would support a population of 40,000 persons.

Second and Third, at Factory village, on Sabattus river, owned by N. W. Farwell of Lewiston. The upper one has a fall of 10 feet; is under improvement; double turbine wheel; power 175 horse. Lower fall not improved, save in an old grist and saw mill. Fall, 20 feet; power, 325 horse. Stream connected with the Great Sabattus pond; water constant; freshets not destructive.

Fourth, at Lisbon plains, on the same river, about one-third of a mile from the Androscoggin river; 20 feet fall; unimproved; owned by B. Farnsworth and others.

Fifth, about one-fourth mile above; fall 12 feet; the property of the Paper Company; mill built 1866; manufactures one and a half tons newspaper per day; machinery best quality.

Sixth, next above, the property of the Farnsworth Manufacturing Company; fall, 13 feet; woollen mill, built 1865; first-class machinery; manufactures 30,000 yards per month of "three-fourths" goods; spare power except in drouth.

Seventh and Eighth, on Little River stream, near its junction with the Androscoggin. No details.

LITCHFIELD—KENNEBEC COUNTY.

From Selectmen's Returns.

Eight Powers, or More.

First, on Patten Mill stream, which rises in swamps; a saw mill; operates six months.

Second, Third, Fourth and Fifth, on Potter Mill stream, the outlet of Loon pond; not improved by reservoir dams, but holds out well in dry seasons. On the lower dam a grist mill; above on the other dams, are carding, shingle, saw, and grist mills. The lower privilege is a good one; 12 feet head and six feet fall.

Sixth, Seventh, and Eighth, on the outlet of Purgatory ponds, four in number, which cover over a thousand acres and drain three thousand acres. A dam at the outlet of the lower pond, holds back a part of the surplus water. The outlet channel might be deepened and a higher dam built at no great cost, and the power rendered available all the year.

The upper power has 12 feet head and six feet fall; saw mill, 200,000 feet of long lumber, and a shingle machine about 200,000 shingles; grist mill, large custom.

The lower power is operated by E. Plimpton & Sons, in the manufacture of forks and hoes; 12 feet head and four feet fall. The machinery is run from October to July.

Several smaller powers in town, capable of operating small machinery a portion of the year.

LITTLETON—AROOSTOOK COUNTY.

From Selectmen's Returns.

Several Powers.

Three on the Big brook, "several" on the South branch of the Meduxnakeag river, and one on a branch thereof.

The powers on Big brook are each sufficient to drive a saw mill or grist mill the year round. Those on the Meduxnakeag "can propel any amount and size of machinery."

Only one of the powers is improved; a saw mill operates part of the year, for local and settlers' uses.

The Meduxnakeag drains a large area of country and is connected with several large ponds; artificial reservoirs of very large capacity can be cheaply constructed on Big brook, and doubtless on the river also. Freshets are not very heavy; lay of the land about the powers most excellent for mills and workshops; basin mostly wooded.

Market, Houlton, and Richmond station.

LIVERMORE—ANDROSCOGGIN COUNTY.

From the Statement of Hollis Turner, Esq.

[See also "East Livermore and Livermore."]

Twelve Powers.

Five on a stream from Long pond.

First, a saw mill, near the outlet; fall nine feet; square inches of water in use, 600.

Second, a grist mill, below; fall 12 feet; 300 square inches of water.

Third, pill-box factory; fall 10 feet.

Fourth, rake-factory; fall 12 feet.

Fifth, saw mill; 15 feet fall.

On a stream, from Turner pond, are two powers, improved; also, three unimproved, as follows:

Sixth, at the outlet, unimproved; fall eight feet; capacity 1,200 square inches; ownership, Hollis Turner.

Seventh, a short distance below, a grist mill; fall 15 feet; capacity 1,200 square inches of water; Hollis Turner; centre-vent wheels.

Eighth, just below, various saws in one building; fall nine feet; capacity, 2,500 square inches; ownership, Lewiston Company. This mill does a good business at flood of water, spring and fall.

Ninth, about a half a mile below, on the same stream, the same company own another water-power, not improved, equal to, or better, in many respects, than that before described.

Tenth and Eleventh, smaller powers, on separate streams; a shingle mill on each.

Twelfth, on the same stream, upon which is the last mentioned grist mill; opposite the mill is another privilege not improved, with a capacity equal to that of the grist mill. Ownership, Hollis Turner.

LONG-POND TOWNSHIP—SOMERSET COUNTY.

Statement of J. M. Haynes, Esq., of Augusta, and Heman Whipple, Esq., of Solon.

Four Powers.

First, on the Lower Churchill, "Lower Churchill Falls," 40 rods from lake, 10 feet fall; dam; good site.

Second, above, good site. Ponds above, flowed for reservoirs.

Third, "Parlin Stream Falls," on Parlin pond outlet, near the line of the town, 15 feet fall. Solid ledge; land favorable. An excellent privilege. Parlin pond, above, covers 2.75 square miles, and has been flowed five feet and can be flowed three feet more.

Fourth, at the outlet of Long pond, which covers eight square miles, a dam giving eight feet head. Twenty square miles of ponds above this point that can be flowed for reservoirs. See reservoirs, middle table, page 95.

LOVELL—OXFORD COUNTY.

From the Statement of the Selectmen.

Six Powers.

First, "Lovell Village," on Kezar river; an excellent privilege; numerous saws and a grist mill with four sets of stones. Water more than abundant through the year. Fall 15 feet; width of stream at dam, 100. Power not all improved.

Second, Alder-brook privilege at "Number Four;" 10-acre pond; a superior power for one of its capacity, can furnish an ordinary power all the year. Fall eight feet; carriage, gun, planing and turning machines. Power not wholly improved.

Third, "Kezar Falls," on Kezar river; fall 20 feet, nearly perpendicular; entirely unoccupied.

Fourth, at "Slab City;" Heald's pond the reservoir, 30 acres; grist, saw, and stave mills, run all the year.

Fifth, "Succor Brook;" small pond; can run in spring and fall; saw mill.

Sixth, at outlet of Andrew's pond, "Cushman's Mills"; stave and shingle.

"Lovell Village" is fed by the ponds called Five Kezars. See Part II, page 77.

Rock abundant for building purposes. Lay of the land convenient. The power is as a whole comparatively undeveloped.

Market, at home. Nothing is carried beyond a circuit of 15 miles.

LOWELL—PENOBSCOT COUNTY.

From Selectmen's Returns.

Ten Powers.

First, on Passadumkeag river, "Passadumkeag Rips," 16 feet fall; not improved.

Second, on Passadumkeag river, "Little Falls," 16 feet fall. Improvements, "Lord's Mill" and "Webb & Co.'s tannery." Fall extends one mile; dam has 12 feet head.

Third, on Passadumkeag river, "High Ledge," 9 feet fall; not improved.

Fourth, on Passadumkeag river, "Lightning Rips," 7 feet fall; not improved.

Fifth, on Eskutassis stream, "Varney's Mills," fall 14 feet; mill not now in use.

Sixth, "Porter's Grist Mill," fall 10 feet; grist mill and shingle machine.

Seventh, "Porter's Saw Mill," fall 10 feet.

Eighth, "Woodman's Mill," 10 feet fall; mill not now in use; "mill and dam both run down."

Ninth and Tenth, sites, unoccupied.

The total fall on Eskutassis stream is 70 to 80 feet in four and a half miles; total fall on the Passadumkeag not known.

No estimate of the power has ever been made by accurate measurement.

Each power on the Passadumkeag will run four saws through the whole sawing season. Those on the Eskutassis will run one saw four months of the year. The grist mill and tannery work all the year; machinery not of the best construction.

The capacity of both streams can be greatly increased by the use of the connected lakes for reservoirs. See Part II, page 107.

Granite abundant for all building purposes; the leading rock, slate. Lay of the land about the sites, level and good; 99 hundredths of the basin of the Passadumkeag covered with forests; annual product about $100,000.

Market, Bangor, by county road to Passadumkeag, thence by boat to Oldtown, and by railroad to Bangor; or by rafts direct from Lord's mill to Bangor, by the river.

Lowell Township—Somerset County.

Statement of Heman Whipple, Esq., of Solon.

Several Powers.

First, "Lowell Falls," on Moose river, a mile from the town line, 30 feet fall in 60 rods. Most excellent site for dam and mills; ledge bottom and banks; dam would make considerable dead water above.

Second, above, about midway the town, 50 feet fall in about a mile. Hard bottom, good banks.

Ponds in the Gore above which can be made reservoirs; also in the township.

Good sites on the "Upper Gulf Stream." Little ponds above, which can be dammed.

Lubec—Washington County.

Statement of E. A. Davis, Esq.

Eight Powers.

First, at West Lubec, a tide saw mill.

Second, on the tributary to the pond of the above, formerly lath and box mills; now unoccupied; will run eight months in the year.

Third and Fourth, on McDaniel's stream; unoccupied; formerly operated saw mills.

Fifth, at the mouth of the same stream, a dam, not now used.

Sixth and Seventh, near West Quoddy head, sufficient to carry a saw mill each.

Eighth, at "Lubec Mills," a tide power, formerly plaster mills; the largest power in town; pond over 100 acres; head about 15 feet. "Power here, 100 horse, and the others combined as much more."

Ludlow—Aroostook County.

Selectmen's Statement.

One Power.

One small power on Small's mill brook; a saw mill that works fall and spring and during occasional seasons of high water.

LYMAN—YORK COUNTY.

Statement of E. H. Tripp, Esq.

Eight Powers.

First, "Goodwin's Mills," on Wadlin-pond stream, saw and two grist mills, shingle machine, etc. Operate all the year, in part. Pond covers 0.35 square miles, flowed 10 feet, can be raised more at some expense, covering a large tract of land.

Second, two miles above, a shingle machine.

Third, at the outlet of the pond, saw mill.

Fourth and Fifth, on the southern outlet of Kennebunk pond; one formerly used; mill burned; both good privileges; five feet fall each.

Sixth, on the northern outlet of the pond, various mills; operate two-thirds of the year on both outlets. Kennebunk pond covers 0.50 square miles, and is flowed four feet.

Seventh, one and one-half mile below the point of junction of the outlets, five feet fall; saw mill.

Eighth, a mile below; fall six feet; mills going up.

LYNDON—AROOSTOOK COUNTY.

From the Statement of J. B. Hayes, Esq.

Seven Powers.

Four, upon Caribou stream, at Caribou village, and within half a mile of its mouth. Height of the series, 50 feet.

First, (upper) saw, clapboard and lath machine.

Second, grist mill, three runs of stones, operates all the year; planing mill.

Third, unoccupied at present; privilege sold and a woollen factory to be erected next season.

Fourth, very good; dilapidated grist mill, unused; shingle machine in operation part of the year.

Very small proportion of the power now used; the grist mill alone now operates all the year; the others might so far as regards supply of water. The stream is connected with only one pond 1.5 by 0.5 miles in extent. On one branch a small artificial reservoir might be constructed; on the other a very large one. The basin of the river is large and lies in easy swells, consequently freshets are neither high nor sudden; no damage from high water for twenty years. By means of artificial reservoirs a great amount of machinery might be run all the year.

Underlying rocks, a mixture of slate and lime, not suitable for building purposes, yet the bed of the stream and the banks, (which are all solid ledge,) endure aqueous and atmospheric action persistently. The slate stands fire well also. The lay of the land about the falls, the very best possible for the location of mills, shops, etc.

Seven-eighths of the basin of the stream are covered with woods. "Climate rendered singularly humid by the lakes and surrounding rivers and adjacent high ridges of land."

Influence of the improvement of the power upon the town very great. A thriving and beautiful village has sprung up within the last four years; several buildings now going up; a church erecting to cost $2,500, "all paid for in advance by ourselves." An Academy in contemplation.

Market, Tobique, on the St. John river, 15 miles, thence by river to the seaboard, or by State road to Houlton; thence to Bangor by said road; or by St. Andrews Railroad, to the ocean. Trade mostly by the latter.

Fifth, Sixth and Seventh, upon brooks, operating a saw mill each, about half the year.

Machias—Washington County.

From the Statement of H. L. Hill, Esq.—Endorsed by the Selectmen.

Four Powers.

The water-power in this town consists of a series of falls on the Machias river, naturally divided into four general privileges, each containing from one to three special privileges, or ownerships; and a dam thrown entirely across the river a distance of 130 rods up from the lower falls, making a second fall, 12 feet 6 inches, from the surface of the lower pond.

These privileges are located at the head of navigation, six miles from the river's mouth and three miles above its junction with the East Machias river. The difference of level from high water at average tides, to surface of lower pond, is 20 feet 6 inches. The fall is distributed as follows: the fall at upper dam, 12 feet 6 inches; fall at extreme lower falls, where about one-half the lower machinery is located, 20 feet 6 inches; the remaining one-half a fall of 15 feet. There is a canal from the upper dam, running parallel to the river bank, a distance of 60 rods, upon which are a planing mill, and sash, door and blind factory. The embankment of this canal is lower than the dam, but the conformation of the river bank is such that two-thirds its length may be raised to the same level as the dam, thereby making the fall from the canal equal to that from the upper pond.

The volume of the river at lowest run, is 15,000 cubic feet per minute, which, with the use of wheels that will give 70 per cent. of the theoretic power of water, yield 630 horse-power; the gross power is about 937 horse. The whole amount of long lumber and laths sawed in 1866 by water-power, (allowing 500 feet cut surface per 1000 laths,) was 38,266,000 feet, allowing that amount of work to be done in 182 days of 10 hours each, (which is maximum length of sawing season,) requires 350 horse-power. Allow for driving grist, carding, and planing mills, and sash, door and blind factory, 50 horse-power, makes an aggregate of 400 horse-power, leaving a balance of 230 horse-power for the 182 days, and the whole power the balance of the year surplus.

It is not to be understood that there is a surplus of power during all the working season, as the wheels in use are not generally of the best construction for economizing power, nor has full advantage been taken of the fall in their location. The wheels in use are all of the turbine class, representing (comparatively) a large variety of style, amongst which are the Perry, Stearns, Union, Close & Rider wheels; the last two being considered best.

The power is owned in town.

For reservoirs tributary to this power, see Part II, page 132, second table.

No material damage of property caused by freshets; total range from high to low water, eight feet.

Extreme low water prevails one-sixth of the year; extreme high water, one-twelfth; the balance of the year the volume is from two to three times the before given estimate. The outcropping and underlying rocks are trap, but there is an extensive granite quarry within three miles of the falls. The lay of the land in reference to the erection of mills and workshops, is favorable.

Total length of the river is 70 miles, draining 15 towns and townships, eight of which, except locally, are still entirely covered by forest, from which an average of 40,000,000 feet of lumber are taken per annum; a bountiful supply still remains. The residue of towns and townships also retain npon their surface a large portion of forest.

Annual export, by sea, to Boston, New York, the West Indies and South America, $650,000 worth of lumber. This amount shows no falling off from former years, either in total annual product or value, but rather an increase. Vessels of 600 tons burthen lie at the lower falls with full cargo.

Within the last 17 years the capacity of the town to accommodate its growing population has been increased three-fifths, yet the demand for tenements is greater than ever before; our mechanics and laborers are constantly employed, and our business men invite capitalists to unite with them in opening new avenues of industry.

MACHIASPORT—WASHINGTON COUNTY.

Selectmen's Statement.

There is no water-power in this town.

MADAWASKA—AROOSTOOK COUNTY.

One Power.

A grist mill and saw mill on a stream tributary to the St. John river.

MADISON—SOMERSET COUNTY.

From Selectmen's Returns.

[See also "Anson and Madison."]

Five Powers.

Five dams upon the outlet of Madison pond, furnishing a fall of 50 feet within a running distance of one mile from the outlet.

For half the year the pond would supply 1,000 inches of water; the remaining part of the year it would average 300 inches for 10 hours per day.

One fall of 10 feet is not improved. Two saw, four shingle, and two grist mills, one sash and blind factory, several lath machines, and a tannery in operation.

The grist mill and sash and blind factory operate nearly all the year; the shingle mills run over three-fourths of the time; saw mills run about three-fourths of the time. Machinery good; Gould wheels.

Madison pond contains 2,000 acres, flowed six feet by a dam at the outlet. Freshets are controlled, stream is perfectly safe and very constant. Rocks about the falls, hard slate. Market, for the products of the mills, Skowhegan depot, six miles distant, by road.

MADRID—FRANKLIN COUNTY.

From Selectmen's Returns.

Five Powers.

First, on the west branch of Sandy river; grist, and various mills; fall seven feet. Power in the drouth of summer or in the dead of winter, is now scarcely sufficient to carry more than one run of burr stones. Stream rises in several ponds, 500 acres, near Saddleback mountain, whose storage capacity might be doubled by dams. Seven-eighths of the basin of the stream covered with forest.

Second, on the Perham stream; various saws; the head is produced solely by the dam. No chance for artificial reservoirs. Mills run three months, and cut 300,000 of lumber. Nineteen-twentieths of the basin of the stream covered with forest, a large part of which is spruce.

Third, on the Oberton stream, "Great Falls"; unoccupied; fall 100 feet in 10 rods. Volume of water small,—would in a drouth all run through a spout less than 10 inches square, without head. The entire basin of the stream is an unbroken wilderness. A good location for a lumber mill, and about 11 miles from Phillips village. An artificial reservoir, 50 acres, might be constructed on this stream at small cost.

Fourth, on the Sargent stream; unoccupied; volume of water smaller than the last mentioned; fall about eight feet. No chance for artificial reservoirs.

Fifth, various saws, above; seven-eighths of the basin of the stream wooded.

So steep are the water declivities in this town, that a head of water might easily be raised almost anywhere on the streams, sufficient to carry a saw mill or other machinery. The volume of water in all the streams varies greatly from lowest to highest water.

Old-fashioned flutter wheels. Each of the three saw mills cuts 200,000 feet of boards per year. With improved machinery, they might do double the amount. Rock, the coarsest granite.

MANCHESTER—KENNEBEC COUNTY.

From Selectmen's Returns.

Three Powers, or More.

First, in the north part of the town, saw mill, two months; 30,000 feet.

Second, near centre of town; carriage factory; overshot wheel, circular saw and other machinery.

Third, on the Cobbosseecontee river. An excellent dam across the stream, a few rods below the outlet. This would, undoubtedly be a valuable power, holding as it does such large reservoirs of water. See page 97, second Table.

"Several small streams could be made useful in driving machinery for a portion of the time, by forming ponds and reservoirs; they are all of very gradual descent, without any very considerable falls or rapids."

MAPLETON PLANTATION—AROOSTOOK COUNTY.

From Assessors' Returns and a Plan of the Streams.

Three Powers.

First, on the Presque Isle stream, about midway its course in the township, a rapid, ten feet fall might be had, a valuable privilege; unoccupied.

Second, two miles above, "Ball's Mills," 10 feet fall, saw mill; 3,000 feet of boards, 10,000 shingles, and 1,500 clapboards per day; operates nine months per year; abundant lumber in the vicinity.

Third, on a brook tributary to the Presque-Isle stream, would operate part of the year.

Market, Presque Isle, by road.

MARIAVILLE—HANCOCK COUNTY.

From Selectmen's Returns.

Five Powers.

First and Second, on West brook, one improved in tannery and saw mill; the other, in saw mill and shingle mill.

Third, on East brook, saw mill.

Fourth, on Hopkins' brook, saw mill and shingle mill.

Fifth, on the west branch of Union river; unimproved.

West brook is connected with two quite large ponds; their capacity can be much increased.

Market, Bangor, 20 miles; Ellsworth, 13 miles, by road.

MARION—WASHINGTON COUNTY.

From Selectmen's Returns.

Nine Powers.

First, on the Cathance river; 10 feet head; saw and lath mill, old wooden machinery; 600,000 long lumber per year. With improved machinery, would yield four-fold. Owned by T. W. Allan & Son of Dennysville.

Second, three-quarters of a mile above; rips of 10 feet fall; unimproved. Owned by John Smith of Dennysville.

Third, "Lath Mill Dam," one-quarter of a mile above; head 13 feet; natural privilege—scarce any dam needed; shingle mills and lath mills. Owned by Allan & Smith.

Fourth, "Saw Mill Dam," 10 rods above; nine feet head; saw mill; owned by T. W. Allan of Dennysville.

Fifth, Sixth, etc., on Clifford's stream, on which are five falls or pitches, with no lakes or ponds above. A chance to flow a small pond at each fall. Stream exceedingly variable.

The falls on Clifford's stream with improvements and modern machinery, would run mills two-thirds of the time.

The Cathance stream is the outlet of Cathance lake, which covers seven square miles. There is a dam at the outlet which holds in check six feet depth of water, so that the powers are comparatively constant, and may be rendered still more so.

MARSHFIELD—WASHINGTON COUNTY.

From Selectmen's Returns.

Eight Powers.

On Marshfield stream; from the tide two miles by the county road to Mark Longfellow's lake.

At the different mills the head and fall are from seven to ten feet. The power is only partially improved, in saw lath and grist mills, flour mill and carding machine; the grist mill alone operates all the year; wheels mostly old style; some, Stearns' cistern wheel.

The stream is connected with four ponds; one a mile long, which flows a large body of water. The power, if improved properly, would furnish abundant water all the year; slight damage from freshets. The best of granite; lay of the land convenient.

Market, Machias, by land or sea.

The privilege at T. B. Getchell's mill, at the outlet of the lake, is a good site for a woollen factory or other machinery.

Mars Hill—Aroostook County.

Statement of H. O. Perry, Esq.

Several Powers.

The Presque Isle of the St. John runs three miles in this town and is a rapid stream in the whole distance. Abundant water the year round to run a large factory. Artificial reservoirs are feasible, but there are no lakes or ponds.

The privilege that could be at present most advantageously improved is near the stage road. At least 12 feet fall. Rocky bottom and good banks; a privilege that can be readily and cheaply improved.

There are several other sites that can be developed without difficulty.

Two sites on the Rocky brook, both improved, saw mills, lath mill, planing machine, etc.

A grist mill is very much needed; the proprietors of the privilege near the road will give the site and land adjacent to any party who will build and carry on a really good mill of this sort. Citizens also will coöperate substantially. A woollen mill also will do well; vast quantities of wool, and good market for the manufactured goods.

Masardis—Aroostook County.

From Selectmen's Returns.

Three Powers.

First, "Reed & Clayton's Privilege," on the Masardis stream, a branch of the Aroostook river, ten feet head above low water mark.

Second, "Trafton's Privilege," on Squawpan stream; Squawpan lake is ten miles long, and can be flowed three feet by a dam, forming a great reservoir.

Third, "Clayton's Privilege," on the Aroostook river. "Fall sufficient for any machinery."

No improvement of any kind. No mills of any sort in the town, except a circular saw on a little brook for sawing sash and other small stuff. "Sum of power unknown, but it is very great." Water abundant and constant.

Nearly all the lakes and ponds on the Aroostook and tributaries above this point, can be dammed and a vast body of water held in reserve, including the Millinokett, Little Millinokett, Mooseleuk, Sapompeag and other considerable lakes. See Part II, page 124.

MASON—OXFORD COUNTY.

From Selectmen's Statement.

Four Powers.

All upon Pleasant river; chief fall, 35 feet in 20 rods. Grist, saw, and two shingle mills; operate all the year on the largest fall; on the others, six months; centre-vent and Rose wheels.

No lakes or ponds. No artificial reservoirs feasible. Basin seven-eighths covered with woods.

Market, Portland, by Grand Trunk Railroad.

MATINICUS PLANTATION—KNOX COUNTY.

Statement of the Assessors.

This is an island at the mouth of Penobscot bay, 800 acres in extent; has no water-power, but fish innumerable in the surrounding sea; natural cranberry meadows, and a glorious prospect. There could be no finer summer resort.

MATTAWAMKEAG—PENOBSCOT COUNTY.

From the Statement of George W. Smith, Esq.

[See also "Mattawamkeag and Winn."]

Seven Powers.

First, "Slugunda Falls," on the Mattawamkeag river, above the mouth of the Gordon brook. A dam is built to facilitate the driving of logs.

Second, "Scataract Falls," about a mile above. A dam is built part way across the river for log-driving purposes.

Third, a short distance above, a mill privilege, no improvement.

Fourth, above, a short distance below the mouth of Whitten brook, "Ledge Falls," no improvement.

Fifth, above, and a short distance above the mouth of said brook, a mill privilege No improvement. Ledge bottom.

The rise from Gordon brook to Mattagordus stream on the line of the European & North American Railway is 70 feet, and this amount of fall is to be distributed, as is presumed, amongst the powers above noted, and the "Jimsketticook Falls" in Independence Plantation.

The Mattawamkeag here drains about 1,200 square miles, is a comparatively constant stream, and can be made by the use of reservoirs to furnish a vast amount of power at low run.

The several falls are nearly all underlaid with ledge, so that stone dams could be built for indefinite duration. The lay of the land about the several falls is excellent for the location of mills and work shops.

Sixth, on Mattaceunk stream, just below the military road, saw mill, which operates half of the year.

Seventh, on Mattaceunk stream, just above the military road. No improvement.

Tenth, two miles above, no improvement.

Mattaceunk pond covers 2.50 to 3 square miles, is fed by a large tributary country, is dammed 10 feet, "could be 14 or 16 feet," and thus forms a capacious and valuable reservoir. See Part II, page 108, for reservoirs of the Mattawamkeag.

The country all about is nearly covered with woods, and vast amounts of lumber remain to be worked up.

Market, Oldtown and Bangor, by road; and by the river, "running lumber in rafts, or singly by the log."

Mattawamkeag and Winn—Penobscot County.

From the Statement of the Selectmen of Winn, and of George W. Smith, Esq., of Mattawamkeag.

[See also "Mattawamkeag," and "Winn."]

Two Powers.

The "Gordon Falls" extend for a considerable distance along the Mattawamkeag river, which at this point crosses the town lines four different times. The total rise between Mattakeunk stream and Gordon brook on the line of the European & North American Railway is 32 feet, and this fall, it is presumed, is available on the river also and constitutes the Gordon falls.

First, "Lower Pitch," where the river for the second time passes into Winn from Mattawamkeag; a dam has been constructed at this point to facilitate the driving of logs.

Second, "Upper Pitch," at the point where the river first passes from Winn into Mattawamkeag. No improvement.

For reservoirs, see Part II, page 108.

River underlaid with ledge, lay of the land favorable for the establishment of mills and workshops.

MAXFIELD—PENOBSCOT COUNTY.

From Selectmen's Returns.

Three Powers.

First, "McIntosh's Falls," on the Piscataquis river; height, eight feet in 20 rods. No improvement.

Second, "Whitney's Falls," on the Piscataquis river; height, eight feet in 20 rods. No improvement.

The enormous development of which these powers are capable by the use of reservoirs, may be seen upon reference to Part II, page 107.

Third, a power on Hardy brook, fed by a lake. No improvement.

Market, Oldtown and Bangor, by road and river.

MAYFIELD—SOMERSET COUNTY.

Selectmen's Statement.

Five Powers.

First, operating a saw and shingle mill four months yearly, in the southeast part of the town.

Second, shingle and lath mill in the southwest part of the town, operates four months.

Third, Fourth and Fifth, good mill-sites on the Austin stream, in the northwest part of the town. Unoccupied. Stream fed by four ponds, whose area is, all together, three square miles, all of which can be flowed for reservoirs.

MAYSVILLE—AROOSTOOK COUNTY.

From the Statement of Solomon Parsons, Esq., of Bangor.

Two Powers.

First, on the Presque Isle river, three-quarters mile below the mills at Presque Isle, ledge on one side, gravel bank on the other, power sufficient for a factory, saw mill or grist mill. In freshet flows back to the Presque Isle mills. Some back water from the Aroostook for a few days in high freshets. Privilege formerly improved, not now in use. It is an excellent location for a woollen factory, also for shingle machines for sawing cedar, which may easily be run down the Aroostook, and taken in rafts to the machines.

Second, on a brook, fails in drouths, and is stopped by back water in moderate rises of the Aroostook, "Kennedy's Mill," for sawing small lumber.

Meddybemps—Washington County.

From Selectmen's Returns.

Two Powers.

First, at the outlet of Meddybemps lake; fall 20 feet in one-eighth of a mile. Power will carry three gangs of 12 saws each; operates all the year; owned by Benjamin Lincoln & Co., of Dennysville. The lake which feeds this power has 15 square miles of surface, upon which seven feet of storage are raised. See also pages 129–130, Part II.

Second, "Bearce's Privilege," at the outlet of Bearce's lake; fall about 20 feet in one-eighth of a mile; will carry a gang of 12 saws for the whole year. Lake is raised by dam — feet.

Overshot and vent wheels. No damage from freshets. Range of water six feet from highest to lowest. Granite abundant and good; lay of the land good; basin mostly cleared.

Medford—Piscataquis County.

From Selectmen's Returns and a Plan of the Streams.

Four Powers.

First, "Schoodic Falls," on Piscataquis river, just below the mouth of the Schoodic stream, fall 15 feet in 100 rods. Stream 15 rods wide, 18 inches deep at low water; ledge bottom, projecting above the surface, at points, at high water. "One of the best privileges in the State, safe and convenient for manufacturing." It is unimproved.

Second, "Little Falls," on Piscataquis river, below Meadow brook, fall 10 feet in 30 rods; 13 rods wide, 14 inches deep at low water. It is unimproved.

Third, "Schoodic Stream Falls," on the outlet of the Great Schoodic lake; fall 22 feet in 35 rods. It is unimproved.

Fourth, on Cold brook, about a mile above its junction with Piscataquis river, fall 10 feet in 30 rods; saw mill and shingle machine; operate about half the year. Stearns' wheel used.

The power on the Piscataquis is sustained by the whole volume of the river which is, in this town, not far from its mouth, draining a very large area of country, and is fed by numerous large lakes and ponds. See page 107, Part II.

The Schoodic lake alone stored to the depth of six feet, would yield on the "Schoodic Stream Falls" and the "Schoodic Falls" combined, a gross power of about 1,000 horse, for the working hours of the year. But the storage could be used in six months if needed, the natural run of the streams sufficing all demands for the other six, thus doubling the power.

Artificial reservoirs, also, are feasible at small expense. Slate rock; lay of the land level and favorable.

Market, Bangor, by road.

MERCER—SOMERSET COUNTY.

From Selectmen's Returns.

[See also "Mercer and Starks."]

Two Powers.

On Bog stream; first fall 15 feet in 10 rods; the other not so great. Improvements, mills, tannery, and starch factory. Machinery will operate about eight months. Rocks, "flint;" lay of the land good.

Market, Skowhegan, by road.

MERCER AND STARKS—SOMERSET COUNTY.

From Returns of the Boards of Selectmen.

[See also "Mercer," and "Starks."]

One Power.

"Dickerson's Rips," on Sandy river; in two pitches; first, 3.5 feet in 20 rods; second, 4.5 feet in 30 rods, and fall continued a long distance below. Owned by James Davis. Formerly mills upon the privilege; dam fallen to decay. Range of water six feet.

Upon comparison with the power estimated and realized upon the same river at New Sharon, it may be inferred that the power at this point, if fully developed, and if 10 feet of fall be available, would be not less than 500 horse-powers gross, or 20,000 spindles.

Privileges are but a few miles from the Somerset Railroad now constructing.

MEXICO—OXFORD COUNTY.

Statement of Selectmen.

One Power.

"Kimball's Mills," on Swift river; fall 50 feet in half a mile. Only improvement, a saw mill, which works all the year. A large amount of power unused.

MILFORD—PENOBSCOT COUNTY.

[See Appendix.]

Millbridge—Washington County.

Selectmen's Statement.

No water-power in town, except upon small brooks, and none sufficient to drive a mill for grinding grain.

Milo—Piscataquis County.

From the Statement of Phineas Tolman, Esq.

Two Powers.

First, the "Sebec Falls," at Milo village; nine feet head and a fall of 14 feet in the distance of about 20 rods below the dam. Grist, saw, and shingle mills, and small woollen factory, occupied by James & William Gifford, all in operation.

The power is fed by Sebec lake, 14 square miles, Ship pond, three square miles, and many square miles of smaller ponds, 18 or more in number. A storage of six feet on Sebec lake alone would furnish, 10 hours per day for the year, 552 gross horse powers, 22,000 spindles on a total fall of 23 feet. Not one-tenth of the power is now improved.

The stream is always warm, the water being derived from the lakes. There is no trouble from ice.

The land about the stream is very convenient for building. Slate rock. No machinery has ever been injured or carried away by freshets.

Second, on the Pleasant river, on the road from Milo to Brownville, about two miles from Brownville village; not occupied; judged to be a very good one. It was reserved by Mr. J. Lake for power purposes, when he sold the land near it.

Pleasant river at this point drains 235 square miles, and has ten or more square miles of lakes and ponds tributary to it, so that a large supply of water can be had at low run.

An immense amount of lumber about the Sebec lake and its tributaries.

Milton Plantation—Oxford County.

From the Statement of the Assessors.

Four Powers.

On Concord river, the outlet of Great and Little Concord ponds; water enough to drive a saw mill most of the year; by damming the pond, capacity might be much increased. In the driest time known, stream carries water enough to grind 40 bushels per day.

First, on the Great Concord river, in the northerly part of the plantation, "Swett's Saw Mill and Shingle Machine;" a carriage shop now building.

Second, about half a mile above, is "The Falls;" descent 30 to 40 feet in about 20 rods; is called, by mill-men, a grand water-power. Unimproved.

Third, about a mile above, a fall of some 20 feet; is called a good water privilege. Unimproved.

There is, in the vicinity of the powers, timber enough to wear out quite a number of mills; mainly spruce, hemlock, and hard wood. The mills are situated about eight miles from Bryant's Pond station, on the Atlantic & St. Lawrence Railroad, by a level road. The country around is well adapted to farming purposes.

MINOT—ANDROSCOGGIN COUNTY.

From Selectmen's Returns.

[See also "Minot and Poland."]

Three Powers.

First, on Bog brook, "Faunce's Mill;" fall 12.5 feet in 50 feet; operates part of the year.

Second, "West Minot Falls," on Bog stream; fall 22.5 feet in 500 feet.

Third, "Hillburn Falls," on Bog stream; power not used.

First and Second partially improved in saw mills and a planing mill. Stream will run the planing mill all the year. One-third of the basin covered with woods.

Market, Portland and Lewiston, by rail and road.

MINOT AND POLAND—ANDROSCOGGIN COUNTY.

From Joint Statement of the Boards of Selectmen, based upon the Survey of S. F. Waterman, Civil Engineer.

[See also "Minot," and "Poland."]

Four Powers.

Situated on the Little Androscoggin river.

First, "Mechanic Falls," fall 37 feet in 950 feet distance; velocity of current 96 feet per minute. Area of cross section 270 square feet. Power not half improved; partially improved in paper making. A first-class stone dam at the head of the fall; a wooden dam midway and space for another dam below. Turbine wheels. Power owned by A. C. Denison & Co.; mills operate all the year.

On the upper dam, 14 feet head, 11 turbine wheels now operate, of 405 horse-powers; hence the volume of water, for the working hours of the day, must be equal to 20,000 cubic feet per minute, and the power of the whole fall, for the same hours, 1,053 horse.

Second, "Page's Mills," fall 14 feet in 1,500 feet distance. Volume of water same as at Mechanic Falls, less Waterhouse brook, which is 3,000 cubic feet per minute. Power partially improved in sawing lumber, in the manufacture of sash and doors, and grist mill; mills operate all the year; power owned by Moses Page and A. A. Buckman.

Third, "Hackett's Mills," fall 13 feet in 250. Volume of water same as at Mechanic Falls, plus Bog brook, 1,500 cubic feet per minute. Improved in part in saw mills; power owned by J. T. Waterman and Willard Buck; mills operate all the year.

Fourth, "Minot Corner," fall 11.5 feet in 500 feet run. Volume of water same as at Hackett's mills, with the addition of a small tributary. Improved in part in saw and grist mills; mills operate all the year. Owned by A. S. Freeman, Willard Buck, et. al.

For reservoirs tributary to these powers, see Part II, page 83.

Sites for building upon the privileges excellent. Freshets harmless, the reservoirs holding back the great body of the water.

Market, all points, by rail.

MONMOUTH—KENNEBEC COUNTY.

From Selectmen's Returns.

Nine Powers.

Four on Wilson stream, at North Monmouth; total descent, 50 feet in one-third mile.

First, on the upper dam, webbing factory, $25,000 per annum; also, a shovel-handle factory, 40 dozen shovel handles per day; shoe-peg factory, 3,000 bushels pegs annually; saw mill, 300,000 of lumber annually.

Second, on the second dam, webbing factory, heel-iron works, and spinning-frames for spinning woollen yarn, the latter two doing $25,000 per annum.

Third, 1,200 to 1,500 dozen of shovels, and some 800 dozen hoes, annually.

Fourth, grist mill, custom business.

Wilson stream is very safe; no damage has occurred by freshets for 50 years; double the business could be done that is now, if the water were properly husbanded. Some 150 men and women are engaged in the several shops and mills. Stream is fed by three ponds, area three or more square miles. Mills operate the whole year.

Fifth, Sixth, Seventh and Eighth, on the Cochnewagan stream at Monmouth Center, four dams, fall 60 feet in one-fourth mile. On the first, a grist mill; on the second, 20 rods below, a shingle and jobbing mill, which runs two-thirds of the time; on the third, a sash, door and blind factory; on the fourth and last, a saw mill, which cuts from 300,000 to 500,000 feet of boards, &c., during the year. Double the business might be done on this stream that there now is. In moderately favorable seasons there is water enough to run the mills the entire year. Pond one and one-half by three-fourths miles. The several mills are worth about $9,000; operate about three-fourths of the year.

The Juggernaut stream, at East Monmouth, has one dam, saw and shingle mill upon it. Most ample supply of water furnished by some eight or more ponds of the Cobbosseecontee series. The dam might be raised so as to give 10 feet head and fall, with some damage for flowage, and then a large factory might be run the entire year.

The Blake wheel is chiefly used; a small amount of stone suitable for building; lay of the land for building quite good; no forests of importance. Annual production, $125,000.

Market, all points, by rail.

MONROE—WALDO COUNTY.

From Selectmen's Returns.

Fifteen Powers.

First, "Willis' Mills," on Marsh river, head and fall 15 feet; wood and stone dam on ledge foundation; saw mill, 400,000 lumber, 800,000 shingles; grist mill, four runs of stones, etc. A good privilege for a small factory.

Second, half a mile above, head and fall 10 feet, saw, fulling and carding mills.

Third, half a mile above, saw and stave mill, 10 feet head and fall. Dam of wood, on ledge foundation; excellent and safe water-power.

Fourth, two miles above, saw and shingle mills; 15 feet head and fall; plenty of lumber at hand. Several good reservoirs, two to three miles up the stream. Mill runs a large portion of the year.

Fifth, a little below, fall 15 feet in 10 rods; unimproved. The above powers are all very safe, as respects freshets.

Sixth, "Thurlough Mill," on the outlet of Northern pond; good stone dam, eight feet high, at the head of the fall; water is taken from the pond to a point 120 feet below, where is a fall of 18 feet. The water ponds back one and a half miles. Pond contains 70 acres, and could be flowed to cover 100 acres, by a dam eight feet high; also, another pond and bog might be flowed to cover 25 acres or more; the dams would not be expensive. Capacity of this power, 200,000 of lumber.

Seventh, 10 rods below, chance for a dam 12 feet high; unimproved; also, other powers below, on the same stream.

Eighth, at the outlet of the Thomas-Chase bog; stone dam eight feet high, which ponds the water over several hundred acres, two hundred of which are flowage, constituting a valuable reservoir. The bog has the drainage of the Dixmont hills. Unimproved.

Ninth, one mile below, formerly a saw mill. Unimproved.

Tenth, half a mile farther down, formerly saw, lath, shingle and stave mills. Unimproved.

Eleventh, "Mayo Mills," a first-class grist mill, 12 feet head and fall. Pond and reservoir in the town of Swanville.

Twelfth, "Emery Mills Privilege," on the Emery Mills stream, near the centre of the town. A dam could be built between two ledges with but little expense, to raise a head of 15 feet at head of falls, and flow some 30 acres. Saw and stave mill.

Thirteenth, 20 rods below, a dam could be raised to give a head of 10 feet.

Fourteenth, in the next 20 rods below, a head and fall of 40 feet, or more, could be secured. This is one of the best chances for a factory that can be found in the State; and flowing a bog a half mile above the falls, would be very much such a water-power as that in the town of Dexter, where they have so many factories. It will be seen that in a distance of some 40 rods there are from 55 to 60 feet head and fall. Years past, there was a grist mill here that operated the year round, and a few years since a pail factory.

Fifteenth, half a mile above, and at the outlet of Jones' bog; formerly a saw mill. A suitable dam at the outlet would raise a head of ten feet, and flow some 700 acres.

With this reservoir in connection with several others in the town of Brooks, which are now used, machinery on the falls, twelfth to fifteenth inclusive, could be driven the year round, and would be one of the safest series of water-powers that could be found.

"The town will remit taxes upon capital invested in the improvement of the water-power. The people, also, would be disposed to render direct aid. The town has paid all its debts and is above-board in all financial respects ; this, in connection with our large water-power and opportunities for reservoirs, make our facilities worthy the attention of manufacturers."

Market, Bangor, Winterport, Bucksport, Searsport. Railroad soon to Belfast.

MONSON—PISCATAQUIS COUNTY.

From Selectmen's Returns.

Ten Powers, or More.

First, Second, Third, Fourth, and Fifth, on the outlet stream of Hebron pond, pond is three by one miles. All good privileges. Other sites on the same stream, below. Grist mill, two saw mills and two shingle machines, the only improvements.

Sixth, Seventh, Eighth, etc., on the "Rapids" at the mouth of Spectacle pond, total fall 70 feet in 70 rods.

Ninth, on the same stream, a short distance above Monson pond, a good power.

Tenth, "Barrow's Falls," on Piscataquis river, good banks of solid ledge, and a large volume of water. This is regarded a valuable privilege, and capable of a large amount of manufacturing.

No damage from freshets except upon the Piscataquis river. Rocks, slate. The country mainly covered with forests.

Market, Bangor, by road, and rail from Dexter, and soon from Foxcroft.

MONTICELLO—AROOSTOOK COUNTY.

Statement of H. O. Hussey, Esq.

Three Powers.

First, the "Wellington Mills," at Monticello village, on the Meduxnakeag; saw, grist, clapboard and shingle mills. Sufficient water to carry this machinery the whole year, by keeping the dam in good condition. Mill and dam now badly out of repair.

Second, on Dead stream, an old saw mill; but little is done or has been for several years.

Third, on Dead stream, two miles above; new building for saw, clapboard and shingle machines.

The mills on Dead stream are close by the line of New Brunswick.

Lumber in great abundance on these streams but few miles above the mills.

Montville—Waldo County.

From Returns of Hon. Ebenezer Knowlton.

Two Powers.

First and Second, "True's Mills," in the south part of the town; upper fall, ten feet; lower, seven feet; grist mill that will grind 15,000 bushels per annum; carding machine that will card 15,000 pounds wool; saw, stave and shingle mills that will cut 600,000 of lumber. Grist mill operates all the year; carding machine, five months; lower saw mill and stave machine, all the year.

Stream connected with three ponds, four square miles, and therefore quite uniform.

Granite abundant and good for building; lay of the land convenient; basin one-fourth covered with woods. The power has made seven-eighths of the business of the place. Annual product of the power, $150,000 to $200,000.

Market, Belfast, Camden and Rockland, by road.

Morrill—Waldo County.

From Selectmen's Returns, and a Plan of the Streams.

Four Powers.

Three on the Sacasawakie stream. The fall upon two of the privileges is ten feet each, upon the other two about nine feet each. Improved in part by saw, shingle and stave mills; about 500,000 shingles and 200,000 boards are or can be cut at each mill yearly; mills operate six months in the year.

About half of the power is used. Atkins, Breast, and Tuttle wheels; Atkins considered best. One small pond; range from lowest to highest water on the stream, six to ten feet. One-half of the basin of the stream covered with woods.

Market, Belfast, by road.

Moscow—Somerset County.

Statement of the Selectmen.

[See also "Bingham and Moscow," and "Moscow and Pleasant Ridge Plantation."]

Nineteen Powers.

First, "Austin Falls," near the eastern line of the town, fall 100 feet in half a mile. Powers sufficient to saw many millions of lumber in a year. A dam has been constructed near the head of the falls, which flows the stream back more than two miles, creating a pond of a thousand or more acres. Saw, shingle, clapboard and planing mills were in operation here for a number of years, but a short time ago they were destroyed by fire, and have not since been rebuilt. Water enough all the year.

For reservoirs tributary to this power, see Part II, page 96. An inexhaustible supply of water can be had, and the fall being so great, a vast amount of power realized.

Rocks about the falls, hard slate. The lay of the land about the head of falls is favorable for the erection of mills and dwellings; but at the foot, is rough and less favorable.

Second to Thirteenth, inclusive, below the "Falls," good and economical powers.

Fourteenth, "Temple's Mills" and "Temple's Wagon Works," on a brook emptying into the Kennebec river. Mills run spring and fall; fall 50 feet; pond contains some 25 acres, with opportunities for creating other reservoirs.

Fifteenth, "Basset's Shingle Mill," on the east branch of Chase stream.

Sixteenth, a few rods below, fall 30 feet in 200 rods. Artificial reservoirs could be created above, covering 100 acres, with slight expense; country densely wooded.

Seventeenth, "Chase Mill," on Chase stream, near the centre of the town, old saw mill with a 12-foot fall. Chase pond, half a mile above, 200 acres, a short dam at the foot of the pond would raise the water eight or ten feet. Another reservoir might be had by damming the little Baker pond, situated a mile above—and a mile in length.

Eighteenth, "Great Falls," below, fall 40 feet; never has been improved.

Nineteenth, "Carney's Saw Mill," on Carney's brook, not far from the Kennebec river; fall 12 feet in 10 rods. Several large ponds, above, for reservoirs.

Nineteen-twentieths of the whole region covered with heavy forests. The rocks are a hard slate, with veins of quartz, which yield small quantities of gold. Rose water-wheel.

MOSCOW AND PLEASANT RIDGE—SOMERSET COUNTY.

Statement of the Selectmen of Moscow.

[See also "Moscow," and "Pleasant Ridge."]

Several Powers.

"The Kennebec river flows some eight miles between Moscow and Pleasant Ridge, and in the distance there are several points where the river could be tapped by canals, and the *whole volume of the river* used for power purposes.

MOUNT CHASE TOWNSHIP—PENOBSCOT COUNTY.

[Monterey Plantation on the Map.]

Statement of John Gardner, Esq., of Patten.

One Power, or More.

On the outlet stream of the Upper Shin pond, a fall of 12 to 20 feet in 60 rods; banks rather low; bottom rocky. The pond above covers 1.30 square miles, and can be flowed 12 to 20 feet. A large extent of territory tributary to the pond.

MOUNT DESERT—HANCOCK COUNTY.

From Selectmen's Returns.

Four Powers.

On the Somes stream; fall 30 feet in 50 rods.

Power improved by mills; mills work about 10 months of the year. Old-style flutter, tub, and Stearns' centre-vent wheels.

The stream is connected with three ponds; the largest, five by one and one-half miles; the others each three and one-fourth by one-half miles. The power could be increased very considerably, and is in fact sufficient for mills of any description, by using the best styles of wheel and machinery. Freshets harmless, the water being kept back by dams.

An excellent harbor at the place, vessels can load and unload within 10 rods of the outlet of the stream, nine or ten months of the year; for the other two or three months there is some obstruction by ice, but the place can at all seasons be approached by sea within five miles. Packets are plying continually between this point and Boston, Portland, etc., for nearly the whole year.

MT. VERNON—KENNEBEC COUNTY.

From Selectmen's Returns.

Eight Powers.

First, the "Village Mills," on the Whitten stream, at the outlet of Flying pond; grist mill; saw mill, with five saws; carriage and repair shop, a spade-handle factory, tannery, and various saws. An excellent privilege, in the midst of a wealthy agricultural community.

Second, a mile below, buildings suitable for a tannery. Unused water-power, with good facilities for building.

Third, two miles below, the "Walton Privilege," at the outlet of Parker's pond. A very superior privilege, with 15 feet head, an abundance of water in the driest time, building material and firewood plenty and cheap, with an excellent site for a cotton or woollen mill, or other machinery, which can be bought for a fair price. On this privilege is a lumber mill with various saws.

Fourth, 60 rods below, is a large building, in which are a grist mill, a planing mill and a boot and shoe box factory, operating three circular saws. The dam and buildings here are all nearly new.

Fifth, about half a mile below the junction of the Walton and Whitten streams, saw mill, eight saws, and handle factory, repair shop and pump factory, carding and clothing mill. Abundance of water at all seasons; some trouble by back water.

Sixth, on the Quimby stream, grist mill; water for about two-thirds of the year.

Seventh, one mile below, lumber mill, five saws. The water here is all economized and the mill does a large business.

Eighth, below the outlet of Long pond, new first-class lumber mill, does a large business; chiefly timber for railroad cars. Unlimited amount of water for all purposes, a very beautiful site for building a first-rate, permanent dam, and a plenty of available land, adjoining, for all purposes. This is one of the most desirable openings for capital that can be found in this part of the State. It is situate on the McGaffey road, 10 miles from Augusta.

See Part II, page 84, for reservoirs tributary to these powers,—Parker's Long, and other ponds.

NAPLES—CUMBERLAND COUNTY.

From Selectmen's Returns.

[See also "Casco and Naples."]

Six Powers.

First, "Edes Falls," upon Crooked river, in the easterly part of the town, power all taken up, works all the year.

Whole fall in Crooked river, from top of dam at Edes falls to low water mark in Songo lock, 36.19 feet. Perpendicular height from top of dam to the mudsills of the old George Pierce dam, 19.22 feet.

The volume of water equals 1,593 inches, or 11.625 feet, flowing under a head of 9.5 feet; being equal, rejecting fractional estimate, to 110 horse-powers. This is at the mean flow of the river.

Second, "Chaplin's Mills," upon Muddy river. Power all taken up.

Third, "Symm's Mills," upon Muddy river; a dam; no other improvements.

Fourth, "Berry's Falls," upon Muddy river; a dam; no other improvements.

Fifth, "Songo Rips," upon Songo river; a dam; no other improvements.

Sixth, "Mitchel's Mills," at the outlet of Trickey pond. Power all improved. Works part of the year.

All the streams fed by ponds; Crooked river is very constant.

Rock, granite wholly, abundant and good.

Market, Portland, by road and Cumberland & Oxford Canal.

Newburgh—Penobscot County.

From Selectmen's Returns.

Four Powers.

"Gillmore's," "Bickford's," "Adams'," and "Rogers'."

Improvements, saw, shingle, fulling and cloth-dressing, two saw, and two shingle mills.

Fall, of Adams', 50 feet in 12 rods; of the others, 8 to 16 feet in about the same distance. 300,000 feet lumber, 600,000 shingles, 8,000 pounds wool, carded. Net earnings, including labor, about $1,500.

Power nearly all improved; works from four to six months.

Market, Bangor, Hampden, etc.

Newcastle—Lincoln County.

From Selectmen's Returns.

[See also "Newcastle and Nobleborough."]

Six Powers.

Two on Mill brook, formerly two saw mills and one grist mill; not employed at all now. The mills operated the greater part of the year.

Two upon Dyer's river; saw and shingle mill, and match factory; mills operate most of the year.

Fifth, a tide-power at Sheepscot.

Sixth, grist and bark mills, upon Meadow brook, that operate about eight months of the year.

Market, Boston and Portland, by water. Abundant and good granite.

NEWCASTLE AND NOBLEBOROUGH—LINCOLN COUNTY.

From the Statement of the Boards of the Selectmen.

[See also "Newcastle," and "Nobleborough."]

One Power.

"Damariscotta Fresh-water Falls," at the outlet of Damariscotta pond; height 52 feet in 20 rods. The stream is 22 feet wide and 2.5 feet deep.

The power now operates two saw mills, two grist mills, and a match-splint factory, the year through. The machinery is all old-fashioned.

As shown on page 140, the storage alone of the pond, would operate 22,880 spindles for the working hours of the year. The storage could however be used in six months or less, the natural run sufficing for the rest of the year. Undoubtedly 50,000 spindles could be operated on the privilege in the driest time.

The power is unaffected by freshets. Granite, in the vicinity, suitable for building. This is a most admirable site for a cotton factory.

NEWFIELD—YORK COUNTY.

From Selectmen's Returns.

[See also "Acton and Newfield," and "Newfield and Shapleigh."]

Five Powers.

First, "Dam's Mills," on the Little Ossipee river; six mills and two carriage shops; ten feet head and fall, and if the dam were suitably located there would be 12 feet.

Second, 70 rods above, the best privilege on the river; formerly a saw mill; not now improved.

Third, about 30 rods below Dam's, "Ham Mills;" grist and carding mill; nine feet head and fall.

Fourth, saw and grist mill, in the western part of the town, on a small stream; water spring and fall. Ten feet head and fall.

Fifth, shingle and clapboard mill, on a small stream in the south-east part of the town; 11 feet head and fall. Water spring and fall.

NEWFIELD AND SHAPLEIGH—YORK COUNTY.

From the Returns of Newfield and Shapleigh.

[See also "Newfield," and "Shapleigh."]

Three Powers.

First, on the Little Ossipee river, head and fall eleven feet. "Hargrave's Woollen Mills," on the Shapleigh side; four sets machinery; cassimeres and flannels; annual production, $125,000. On the Newfield side, a good building, 30 by 80 feet, formerly used for iron work; not now used. About 80 horse-power.

Second, 80 rods below, "Twombly's Privilege," 14 feet fall. Formerly a grist mill and saw mill on the Newfield side; not occupied, except by a shingle mill. Owned by the Paper Mill Company.

Third, Newfield Paper Company's privilege, 50 rods below, 18 feet head and fall; stone dam 12 feet; mill 30 by 80 feet, with wings 30 by 50 feet; manufacture leather board for inside soles, ton a day; $45,000 per annum.

Stream very constant; Balch pond at the source, with ten feet head, commanded by a dam.

New Gloucester—Cumberland County.

From Selectmen's Returns.

Nine Powers, or More.

Eight, on Royal river, and all within a running distance of one-fourth of a mile; total descent, 50 feet.

The power is only partially improved, in mills; centre-vent wheels employed.

Some small ponds are connected with the stream which can be used for reservoirs. The improvement of the power has operated favorably for the wealth of the town.

Market, Portland and Lewiston, by rail.

One power on Lovewell's brook.

New Limerick—Aroostook County.

From Selectmen's Returns.

Nine Powers.

Six, on the north fork of the south branch of the Meduxnakeag river.

First, 12 feet head and fall; saw mill.

Second, at the foot of Berry's lake, 10 feet head and fall; shingle machine, with power to drive a great amount of machinery.

Third, Fourth, Fifth and Sixth, below, all of them capable of doing good service with any kind of machinery.

Seventh, Eighth and Ninth, on the south fork of the Meduxnakeag stream, supported by Drew's lake, 2,000 acres; dam at the outlet can be raised four feet without damage. On the Seventh are saw, shingle, and lath saws; an excellent privilege; lime quarry close at hand. The Eighth is not occupied. The Ninth is a good privilege for small machinery. Not occupied.

Enormous quantities of timber in all the region. Granite sufficient for building. Excellent limestone. Overshot wheels used on all the privileges.

NEWPORT—PENOBSCOT COUNTY.

From Selectmen's Returns.

Three Powers.

First, on the Stetson stream; saw mill and shingle mill.

Second, on the Milliken stream; saw mill and shingle mill.

Third, by far the most important, the "Newport Village Power," at the outlet of Newport pond; fall 14 feet in 78 rods. It is improved in part, in flour, saw, and shingle mills. The power was formerly wholly used by a tannery and foundry. The power can operate all the year, though it is not now generally used throughout the year.

Wheels, turbine, tub and Gould. The power is sustained by the Newport pond, which covers eight square miles. Dam now raises a head of four feet on the pond; can be raised still higher; entire safety from freshets; no damage has ever been done; granite abundant and good; lay of the land convenient for improvement; basin one-fourth wooded. The power, though inadequately improved, has built up a flourishing village; annual production, $75,000.

Eight feet of storage on the pond would give 252 horse-power, gross, on the whole fall for 10 hours a day, 312 days in the year, or about 10,000 spindles. The storage could however be used in six months or less, the natural run sufficing the rest of the year; thus giving power for perhaps 30,000 spindles.

Market, Portland, Lewiston, etc., by Maine Central Railroad; junction of said road with the Dexter & Newport Railroad, is at this point.

NEW PORTLAND—SOMERSET COUNTY.

From Selectmen's Returns.

Five Powers.

First, "Gilman Stream Falls," would carry a saw, shingle, and grist mill, with three runs of stones, all the year; saw and shingle mill, carding and fulling mill, planing machine, circular saws, etc., now upon it.

Second, "New Portland Falls," on Carrabasset stream, would do as much as the above; saw and shingle mill, threshing machine.

Third, Fourth and Fifth, on Lemon stream, would each do about half as much as either of the above; saw, shovel handle, and shingle machinery upon one; grist and carding and clothing mill, upon another; saw, shingle, clover-seed, and threshing machinery, upon the third.

Gilman-stream privilege operates all the year; the others about half; undershot and centre-vent wheels; Gilman and Lemon streams connected with ponds; as Gilman pond, four by one-fourth miles; Porter pond, two by one miles; Lilly pond, one by one-half miles. The latter could be made a reservoir at little expense.

Freshets, on the Carrabasset 10 to 15 feet—have been destructive; the Gilman stream is quite constant. Rock, granite and slate; two-thirds to three-fourths of the basin of the streams covered with woods. The powers have increased the wealth of the town one-third or one-half.

Market, Skowhegan and Farmington.

NEWRY—OXFORD COUNTY.

From Selectmen's Returns.

Three Powers.

First, on Bear river; fall sufficient for a large overshot wheel; grist mill.

Second, on the east branch of Bear river; a saw mill.

Third, on Sunday river; mill, dam.

Streams variable. Several millions of spruce lumber near the water-powers on both streams.

Rocks, granite, and the town ledgy for a considerable part. Amount of business, far less than might be with the power.

Market, Bethel Hill, 10 miles; a good road.

NEW SHARON—FRANKLIN COUNTY.

From Selectmen's Returns, and a Plan of the Stream.

Several Powers.

First, "New Sharon Falls," on Sandy river, at New Sharon village; head and fall, ten feet. Volume of water stated to be 2,722 inches under the head and fall, giving a gross power of 320 horse, 12,800 spindles. The mills now in use are estimated to require 150 horse power. With a tight dam the available power would probably be nearly or quite twice greater. On the south side of the river there is an intervale, which would be an excellent site for mills, much better than the north side, on which they now stand.

Improvements.—A dam in poor order, saw, grist, shingle, chair, and machine-shop equipment. Wheels, Kendall and Tuttle.

Second, "Lower Falls," below; vastly superior in every respect.

The lay of the land hereabout most excellent for the location of bridge, mills, dwellings, etc., far better than at the upper site. This power is totally unimproved.

Third, Fourth, etc., below, of considerable height, with convenient locations for building; none of them improved.

For the lakes and ponds connected with the Sandy river, see Part II, page 94. Artificial reservoirs, if required, could be constructed without large expense. No damage from freshets when the dam is in proper order.

Sixth, "Weeks' Mill," on Muddy brook, a considerable stream, issuing from Clear-Water pond in Industry, 1.75 square miles, and raised eight feet by a dam. Saw mill.

Seventh, Eighth, etc., on Muddy brook; none of them employed.

Rock, gneiss, slate, and an inferior limestone.

Market,—"We are about five miles from the railroad station at Farmington."

NEW VINEYARD—FRANKLIN COUNTY.

From Selectmen's Returns, and a Partial Survey under their Direction.

Twenty Powers, and More.

Six, of the principal, situated on the outlet stream of Porter's pond, near the centre of the town; saws in successful operation.

First, at the outlet, head and fall, ten feet.

Second, 20 rods below; head and fall, eight feet.

Third, one mile below, at the village; head and fall, nine feet.

Fourth, one hundreds rods below; head and fall, nine feet.

Fifth, half a mile below the third; head and fall, 12 feet.

Sixth, one and a quarter miles below the village; head and fall, 12 feet. The back water of each power, except No. 5, at high water, extends to the power above; (No. 5 may be easily raised to No. 4); so that the whole stream is converted into a series of falls and reservoirs.

Seventh and Eighth, "at the village, coming down from the mountain," No. 7, tannery, fall 25 feet in six rods. Head and fall on the Eighth, 40 feet in seven rods; volume of water four inches square to 12 inches square, common height.

Ninth and Tenth, not now in successful operation, and not surveyed.

Eleventh, on the Barker brook; 12 feet head and fall.

Twelfth, on the Hillman Mill stream; both in the southwestern part of the town, and both streams tributary to the Fairbanks mill stream. Head on the Twelfth, 17 feet; fall 19 feet in two rods.

Thirteenth, on the Fairbanks mill stream, on the county road.

Fourteenth, on the outlet of a meadow of considerable extent.

Fifteenth, Sixteenth, Seventeenth and Eighteenth, below No. 14, and within three-fourths of a mile of it.

Nineteenth, on the McLerny mill stream.

Power No. 1, at the outlet of the pond, will run the saw mill upon it three-fourths of the year. Power No. 3, at the village, runs saw mill two months in the year, and the grist mill during the year. Nos. 2, 4, 5 and 6, though having more water, run only as the business requires. None of the powers in operation are fully improved; much water runs to waste.

The Bow wheel used at power No. 1, and does one-fourth more work than the old paddle wheel formerly used; the other powers use the centre-vent wheel chiefly.

Porter's pond is 640 acres in extent, and the flowage around is secured to the original proprietor; no additional reservoirs, of much extent, could be constructed. The capacity of the pond could be increased by raising the dam at the upper mill, so as to elevate the whole surface four feet higher than it now is, at an expense of $600.

At No. 14, a meadow could be flowed 200 acres in extent, for $200; and Nos. 15, 16, 17 and 18, are on the same stream, and within three-fourths of a mile. All the other powers on this stream would have small reservoirs.

All the powers are safe as to freshets, except No. 13; all except 1, 2, 3, 4, 5, 6 and 13, would be inconstant, and would run machinery only three to nine months in the year.

Outcropping and underlying rocks, granite boulders and limestone. Nos. 14, 15, 16, 17 and 18, have good facilities for building stone dams. Considerable forest and timber.

Market, Farmington, 4 to 11 miles distant from the powers.

NICATOU TOWNSHIP—PENOBSCOT COUNTY.

Statement of Daniel Barker, Esq., of Bangor.

Four Powers.

First, "Salmon Stream Falls," on the Penobscot river near the mouth of the Salmon stream, 12 feet fall in 75 rods. Unimproved.

Second, above, "Jo-Mary Rips," fall 8 to 10 feet. Unimproved.

Third, on the Upper Penobscot or West branch, a short distance above the confluence with the Mattagamon or East branch, "Rips," 100 rods long, formerly a dam 12 feet high; rocky bottom. Unimproved.

Fourth, above, "Rockabema Rips," 8 feet fall in 15 rods. Unimproved.

Each of the foregoing is a power of the first magnitude. The lakes and ponds above, which can be used for reservoirs, cover many scores of square miles, and would furnish a vast supply of water at all seasons. The two powers on the main river would be rather expensive to improve; but at and upon all the sites, dams can be placed upon rock bottom and mills upon ledge foundations.

The principal reservoirs tributary to these powers, either wholly or in part, may be seen upon reference to Part II, pages 108–9–10.

NOBLEBOROUGH—LINCOLN COUNTY.

From Selectmen's Returns.

[See also "Newcastle and Nobleborough."]

Three Powers.

First, on Oyster creek.

Second, on Winslow's stream.

Third, on Jones' stream.

NORRIDGEWOCK—SOMERSET COUNTY.

From Selectmen's Returns, and the Statement of E. S. Waters, Civil Engineer.

Two Powers.

First, "Bombazee Rips," on the Kennebec river, three miles above Norridgewock bridge; total height from the foot of the rapids to the head of the upper pitch, precisely 8 feet. There is an excellent location for a dam, by means of which a head and fall of 12 feet can be secured.

On the west bank the land lies favorable to the reception of mills. Range of water at this point, 15 to 20 feet.

If the extreme minimum volume of water for the summer in a dry season be assumed to be 36 per cent. less than at Augusta, or 108,800 cubic feet per minute, for 11 hours a day, the power with a head and fall of 12 feet would be 2,472 horse, or 98,880 spindles.

Second, "Sawtelle's Mills," at the mouth of Sawtelle's mill stream, in South Norridgewock; fall ten feet in 20 rods; power estimated sufficient to grind 16,000 bushels of grain, and saw some 200,000 feet of lumber; saw and grist mill upon it. The grist mill operates all the year; the saw mill all but winters. Occasional suspensions of both in very severe drouths.

The improvement of the power has had a marked influence, though variously estimated; as having built up a village of 300 inhabitants; as having increased the value of real estate in the vicinity 25 per cent.; as having resulted in a gross increase of property of $75,000.

The Somerset Railroad is now constructing on the bank of the river.

North Berwick—York County.

From Selectmen's Returns.

Ten Powers.

Eight situated upon the Great Works river, and two upon the Negutaquis river. They vary in height from ten to 35 feet, in a distance of 10 to 25 rods.

The power is not all improved. Partially improved in saw mills, grist mills, etc., and one cotton factory. The mills operate nearly all the year; the machinery employed is, in part, very good; turbines.

Power is owned by the North Berwick Company and others.

The main stream is connected with one pond which contains from two to three square miles. Artificial reservoirs not feasible. Rocks excessively hard; lay of the land, about the falls, good. One-third of the basin of the stream covered with forests. The improvement of the power has been of decided advantage to the town.

Market, Portland, Boston, by railroad.

Northfield—Washington County.

From Selectmen's Returns.

Four Powers.

First and Second, "Holmes' Falls," on the Machias river, which consist of two rapids about half a mile from each other, the upper having a fall of 15 feet, the lower of 13 feet; each capable of propelling machinery equivalent to eight saws for manufacturing lumber.

If the volume of water be assumed to be 10,000 cubic feet per minute at low run, that at Machias being 15,000 cubic feet, the gross power of the whole fall is about 550 horse, or 22,000 spindles. For reservoirs, see page 132, Part II.

Third, "Black Cow Meadow Rips," on Bog stream, fall 13 feet. The source is Bog lake, 1,000 acres, and affording power for two saws the year round.

Fourth, on Bog stream, near its exit from the lake, saw, lath and shingle mills. With a suitable wheel this power will operate the season through.

None of the privileges above mentioned are put to use except the Third.

Other points are noted as having power, "Dick's Falls," "College Rips," and "Brown's Rips."

NORTH HAVEN—KNOX COUNTY.

From Selectmen's Returns.

Two Powers.

First, saw and grist mill on Luce's tide stream.

Second, at the outlet of Beaver pond; by the construction of a dam, a fall of 10 feet could be secured, without serious flowage of the surrounding farming land, and a power of local value produced.

Market, Rockland, 12 miles, by sea.

NORTHPORT—WALDO COUNTY.

From the Selectmen's Statement.

Four Powers.

First, on Little river, at the head of tide; average volume of water six square feet, bottom of stream solid ledge, banks almost perpendicular and also ledge, head and fall of 15 feet feasible, excellent chance for reservoirs; privilege accessible by tide water; formerly used, not now improved.

Second, Third and Fourth, on Sucker brook, in the northwest part of the town; saw and shingle mills; average volume of water three square feet, bottom ledge, fall eight to 12 feet.

North Yarmouth—Cumberland County.

From Selectmen's Returns.

Two Powers.

First, "Porter's Mills," on Royal river.

Second, "Masters' Mills," on the east branch of Royal river.

The power is sufficient to drive a saw and two runs of stones the year round.

Market, Portland.

Norway—Oxford County.

From Selectmen's Returns.

Eleven Powers.

The "Pennassawassa Falls," on the outlet stream of Pennassawassa pond, in Norway village, constitute six of the above. Total fall 76 feet in one mile.

First, below the outlet, "Bennett's Mills," fall 13 feet; saw, shingle, and flouring mills.

Second, "Pennassawassa Mills," fall 11 feet; a two-set woollen mill, carding and cloth-dressing mill, (independent of the others, for custom work,) and machine shop.

Third, no improvement except dam; 15 feet fall.

Fourth, fall 15 feet; grist, plaster, shingle, carding, and job mills.

Fifth, seven feet fall; no improvement except a dam.

Sixth, fall 15 feet; saw and planing mill, kit, shingle, and clapboard machinery.

Seventh, between the second and third dams, fall four feet; can be made available only by flowing the meadows west of and contiguous to the village. The last-named five powers are called "Steep Falls," and are all within a horizontal distance of 15 rods.

Volume of water, with 11 feet head on the second dam, four feet square, (16 square feet) for 13 hours per day, throughout the year.

The foregoing powers work all the year; the ponds, three in number, connected with the stream, have an aggregate surface of 2,500 acres, upon which 10 to 15 feet depth of water can be commanded. The power and mills are owned by a large number of different owners. Machinery generally good; wheels, centre vent; one overshot on the fourth dam.

Freshets entirely indestructive when the dams are kept in order; total range of water, four feet, or thereabout; supply constant, even when all other powers in a radius of 16 miles have failed.

Eighth, at the outlet of North pond, in the northeast corner of the town, with constant supply of water and a fall of 12 feet.

Ninth, Tenth and Eleventh, upon small streams in different parts of the town, with saw mills upon them, and sufficient water for use during three or four months of the year.

Market, Portland and Boston; station of the Grand Trunk Railway distant one mile at South Paris.

OLDTOWN—PENOBSCOT COUNTY.

[See Appendix]

ORLAND—HANCOCK COUNTY.

From the Selectmen's Returns, and an elaborate Plan of the Streams, prepared by R. T. Osgood, Esq.

Sixteen Powers, or More.

Several of these are situated upon the outlet stream of Toddy pond. Said pond covers an area of 5.33 square miles of deep water, nine feet of the depth being commanded by a dam, by which the powers below are rendered perfectly constant and secure at all seasons of the year, as well as furnished with a great supply of water.

First, 16 rods below the outlet dam, mill, 12 feet three inches fall.

Second, 22 rods below, mill, 14 feet fall.

Third, 22 rods below, mill, 12 feet three inches.

To this point there is a total head and fall of 48 feet, the distance being 60 rods. From this point to the Great pond below is a distance of 146 rods, and a fall of 99 feet nine inches, making the grand total from the surface of Toddy pond reservoir to the surface of Great pond, 147 feet nine inches, and the distance 206 rods. The 40 rods of the distance next above Great pond is too flat for dams.

In this whole distance the opportunities for dams are unsurpassed, their required length is about 150 feet each, the banks being on each side about 25 feet high. The land on the west side of the stream, from Toddy to Great pond, slopes gradually and uniformly, and furnishes an unrivalled field for building operations. It will be seen that there is sufficient fall for eight privileges, over 12 feet each in height.

Thirteenth, at the foot of the Great pond, where the Lock and Sluice Co.'s mills are located, head and fall 15 feet eight inches to

Oldtown Falls.

the stone dam at tide water. The pond covers 1.90 square miles and receives the contributions of Toddy pond, of two streams, one large one, and of various small ponds.

Fourteenth, the dam at the head of tide is substantially built of granite, head and fall 10 feet, ponding the water back two miles to the Great pond dam; saw, grist, and stave mills.

The total fall from Toddy pond to the tide flats is 174 feet.

Fifteenth, on the outlet stream of Craig's pond, a shingle mill, head and fall 22 feet.

Sixteenth, "Swazey & Co.'s Mills," on Dead river, the outlet stream of Long, Fitz, Hothole, and other ponds; head and fall 12 feet.

The ponds can all be cheaply improved for reservoirs, their mouths being narrow. Artificial reservoirs of large capacity can be formed, if needed. Freshets entirely harmless, owing to the lakes and ponds. A very insignificant portion of the power now used. Annual product about $50,000. Rocks suitable for building purposes.

The power is eminently accessible, the first dam being, as before stated, at the head of tide. Proprietors will coöperate substantially for the improvement of the power.

ORNEVILLE—PISCATAQUIS COUNTY.

Three Powers.

First on Dead stream, the outlet of lake Boyd, which covers two or three square miles, and is a capacious reservoir, "Cushman's Grist Mill." Considerable power unappropriated.

Second, on the Middle branch of Dead stream, "Hall's Shingle Mill;" stream fed by Pleasant pond, which covers half a square mile.

Third, on the West branch of Dead stream, saw and grist mill.

Ponds can be used for storage, and the available power greatly increased.

ORONO—PENOBSCOT COUNTY.

From the Returns of N. Wilson, Esq.

Five Powers.

First, the "Upper Stillwater Dam," on the western *chute,* or channel, of the Penobscot river, which here is divided and broken by large islands; said channel is called the Stillwater river, and is fed by Pushaw river, the outlet of the great Pushaw lake.

Second, the "Lower Stillwater Dam," upon the same river. Total head upon these two dams, 16 to 22 feet.

Improvements; upon these two dams are now 22 single saws, 10 gangs, five rotary saws; 12 lath, three shingle, and four clapboard mills; also two planing machines, one machine shop and one grist mill, and ample space and power for more.

Third, "Ayer's Falls," on the chute, or channel, of the Penobscot, lying betwixt Ayer's island and the right bank of the river. The mills upon this privilege are called the "Basin Mills." Head, nine to 14 feet. The total *fall* from Hammett's mill, (so-called,) to the foot of Ayer's island, is 31.53 feet.

This power commands the entire volume of the Penobscot, by means of a low dam extending from the head of Ayer's island to the left bank of the main river, which, at low water directs the whole current down the channel aforesaid.

Improvements; eight single saws, four gangs, two lath, two clapboard, one shingle, two rotary saws and a machine-shop.

This privilege is unsurpassed in respect to its combined advantages for mills, cheapness of dams, security from freshets, and amount of power. Chief owner, heirs of Gen. Samuel Veazie.

Fourth, "The Stillwater Canal Power;" by means of a canal leading from the Stillwater channel above the upper dam, to the "Basin," a vast amount of power would be made available, as the water could be used several times over.

Fifth, "The Basin Canal Power;" a canal extending from the Basin down the right bank of the river two miles, and conveying, as it might, the total volume of the Penobscot, would afford privileges for mills and factories its whole length, totally secure from ice or freshets. The improvements upon the three privileges, as above set forth, consume but a small part of the available power.

The mills operate, for the most part, only from April to December. Total annual production, 65,000,000 feet of lumber, besides laths, clapboards and shingles.

Market, Bangor, seven miles distant, by canal, by the river, and by the European & North American Railway.

Population of Orono, 3,300; three churches; the best of public schools, and excellent society. The State College of Agriculture and Mechanic Arts is located here, about one mile from the village, on the east bank of the Stillwater river, in a beautiful and commanding situation.

ORRINGTON—PENOBSCOT COUNTY.

From Selectmen's Returns.

Six Powers.

On Segeunkedunk stream, the outlet of Orrington Great pond.

The "Fall at East Orrington," is the most important, being about 16 feet; upon the other privileges is from eight to 12 feet. The upper fall is backed by about two miles of dead water; the other powers by from one-fourth to three-fourths of a mile.

The best privilege runs two saws through the year; No. 2, a tannery; Nos. 3 and 4, grist mills, and will grind an indefinite amount. Four only of the privileges are improved; smallest are unimproved. The mills operate all the year, except in very dry seasons, when a month is sometimes lost. The powers are all owned in Brewer and Orrington.

The stream is connected with two ponds; combined area according to the county map 3.50 square miles, by the State map six square miles; 12 square miles according to the Selectmen. There is a dam at the outlet of Great pond, and if this were in good repair, the water would be ample to run all the year, however severe the drouth. Stream steady; freshets in spring about five times ordinary volume; no damage, to any amount, has ever occurred.

If six feet head can be commanded upon five square miles of the pond surface, the storage amounting to 836,000,000 cubic feet, would furnish on the series of falls, their combined height being assumed at 46 feet, for ten hours a day, 312 days a year, 393 horse-power gross, or 15,720 spindles; to this should be added the *natural* low run of the stream to arrive at the low-run power available. The storage could however be used in three or four months, at least doubling or trebling the power, the natural flow of the stream sustaining the power at this figure for the rest of the year.

The falls are protected with ledge, but rock is not sufficient in the immediate neighborhood for extensive building. The lay of the land is excellent in every locality.

The improvement of No. 1, was the up-building of the eastern portion of the town; No. 2, has had a similar effect; and both together have increased population and wealth ten per cent.

Market, great local market, lumber shipped at Brewer village and Orrington, by hauling one and a half miles; produce, at Bangor, by road, two miles.

Power No. 1, at East Orrington, is well situated in the centre of

25

the village, and within three rods of the road, which is easy of access from the mill at all times. It is a *natural* site for a mill, and the power is sufficient to run a first-class factory. It is considered one of the best locations for the investment of capital, with profit, that there is in the State.

The other powers, between East Orrington and Brewer village, are excellent; grinding 40 bushels of corn per hour, at a single run of stones.

OTIS—HANCOCK COUNTY.

From Selectmen's Returns.

Six Powers.

First "Remick's Falls," at the foot of Flood's pond; fall 75 feet in 20 rods. Clapboard and shingle mill, 2,000,000 shingles, 100,000 clapboards, works all the year, machinery not of the best construction. Not one-fourth part of the power employed. Flood's pond covers one square mile according to the county map; over two square miles according to the State map. It has nine feet head of storage raised by a dam, and can have five feet more.

Second, half a mile below, saw mill, can run all the year, not now in use.

Third, one mile below, shingle and clapboard machine; cuts about the same as the first mentioned. Power all improved.

Fourth, at the outlet of Springy pond, formed by dams which raise the surface of the pond. A shingle machine, can run half the year, dam now out of repair, power not in use. The pond covers 0.60 square miles according to the county map; has nine feet head of storage, and can have five feet additional.

Fifth, at the foot of Beach-Hill pond, saw mill, 500,000 long lumber, board measure, per annum. Fall 20 feet in 30 rods; power about half improved. The pond covers 1.85 square miles according to county map; 3.00 square miles according to State map. It has six feet storage, and can have 14 feet additional.

Sixth, at the foot of Mountain pond, fall same as the above. Shingle and clapboard mill, can run all the year, and cut 1,500,000 shingles and 100,000 clapboards. The pond covers 1.25 square miles according to county map; has six feet storage, and can have 14 feet additional.

Market, Ellsworth and Bangor. Ample room and power for other mills and factories, on the above privileges. Centre-vent wheel employed.

OTISFIELD—CUMBERLAND COUNTY.

Four Powers.

First and Second, on the outlet stream of Saturday pond, saw mills.

Third, saw mill in the southwest part of the town.

Fourth, one-half of Bolster's mills power, on the Crooked river, is in this town.

OXBOW PLANTATION—PENOBSCOT COUNTY.

Statement of W. H. Rowe, Esq, of Masardis.

One Power.

On the Umcolcus stream, the outlet of Umcolcus lake and several ponds. A saw mill. Large supply of water, as the Umcolcus covers three square miles, and the other ponds about two square miles.

OXFORD—OXFORD COUNTY.

From the Statements of Wm. S. Dodge, Esq., and of the Municipal Officers.

Three Powers.

First, at Oxford village, at the outlet of "Thompson Pond," owned and improved by the "Robinson Manufacturing Co.;" three woollen mills, 12 sets machinery, manufacturing 2,200 yards three-quarter cloth per week; one saw mill, fall 13 feet; pond 10 miles long, average width one and one-fourth miles; annual product of woollen mills $250,000. Distance from mill to railway (Grand Trunk) one and one-half miles; 800 square inches of water used, more might be had by clearing the outlet channel.

Second, below, at Oxford village, 100 rods easterly from the Robinson Manufacturing Co.'s privilege; fall 10 feet; owned by Hon. J. J. Perry, and improved by Messrs. S. Rawson & Co. in the manufacture of hoe, shovel and fork handles, shingles, staves, &c. Annual product,$50,000. Also, sash and blind factory, grist mill, stave machine, &c. Value of annual productions, $25,000. Uses 700 square inches of water when in full operation.

Third, at Welchville, on the Little Androscoggin river, 10 feet fall, never failing supply of water; owned and improved in part on the north side by John Harper, Esq., proprietor of "Monitor Woollen Mills," four sets machinery; cassimeres, tweeds and repellants; annual value, $100,000. On the south side, owned by

Messrs. A. C. Denison & Co., and Emery Andrews, Esq., who are now preparing to set up a paper mill, grist mill, &c.; distance from railroad (Grand Trunk) one and two-thirds mile; 1,200 square inches of water.

This is probably the most valuable privilege on the river, as the supply of water is inexhaustible, with power enough to operate six or eight woollen mills of four or six sets capacity.

By vote of the town, capital invested in manufacturing, to the amount of $5,000 and upwards, is exempted for 10 years from taxation.

Market, Portland, Boston and New York.

PALERMO—WALDO COUNTY.

From Selectmen's Returns.

Ten Powers, or More.

First, "Marden's Stave and Shingle Mill;" power to drive two runs of stones eight months of the year.

Second and Third, on Little river.

Fourth, on the main Sheepscot river; fall about 13 inches to the rod for 15 rods; dam broken, mills in decay. Power sufficient to drive four runs of stones nearly, or quite, all the year; stream fed by ten or more ponds. The privilege is about a quarter of a mile below Sheepscot Great pond; three by one miles; stream ranges from six to eight feet, from lowest to highest water. The lakes can be improved readily for reservoirs.

Fifth and Sixth, on a tributary of the West Branch of the Sheepscot; saw and shingle mill.

The other powers are not specified.

One-half of the basin of the stream covered with woods; granite in the form of boulders; flint rock, and a sort of sandstone.

Market, Belfast, Rockland and Augusta, by road.

PALMYRA—SOMERSET COUNTY.

From Selectmen's Returns.

Three Powers.

First, at the outlet of White's pond, on Village Mill stream; "Shaw's Shingle Machine;" four to six months.

Second, on Madawaska stream, Nay & Runnels; saw and shingle machine; four to six months.

Third, on Indian stream; a building once used for a peg factory, now unoccupied; circular saw on the other side of the stream; eight or ten months.

Paris—Oxford County.

Returns of S. P. Maxim, Esq., Selectman.

Twelve Powers.

First, "South Paris Privilege," on Little Androscoggin river; flouring, saw, shingle, planing, and barrel machinery; Charles Bailey & Co.; annual production, estimated, 15,000 barrels flour; capacity, 20,000 barrels; now grinding 700 bushels of wheat every 24 hours. Saw mill, 100,000 feet boards, 100,000 shingles, and materials for 15,000 barrels. Power all used, except in periods of high water. A deficiency, usually, in mid-summer.

Second, "West Paris," on Little Androscoggin river; flouring-mill, Andrews & Dean; annual production, 3,000 barrels flour.

Third, "Willis' Privilege," on Little Androscoggin river; saw and shingle mill, Willis Brothers; annual production, 75,000 feet of boards, and 75,000 shingles.

Fourth, "Barnes' Privilege," on Little Androscoggin river; three-fourths mile south of West Paris station; saw mill, P. C. Fickett; capacity, estimated, 100,000 feet of boards.

Fifth, "Snow's Falls," on Little Androscoggin river; furniture factory, S. L. Howard; capacity, estimated, 3,000 barrels flour.

Sixth, "Jackson's Privilege," on Little Androscoggin river; saw and grist, shingle and stave mills; I. H. Jackson. Capacity, estimated, 3,000 barrels of flour.

Seventh, "North Paris Privilege," on Moose pond stream; grist mill, E. W. Murdock; 1,000 barrels flour.

Eighth, one-fourth mile below, saw and shingle mill, Ira Bartlett; 50,000 feet of boards, and 50,000 shingles.

Ninth, "Iron Foundry Privilege," on Stony brook, near South Paris. Foundry and machine shop, F. C. Merrill & Co. Capacity estimated, 500 barrels flour.

Tenth, "Royal's Privilege," on Stony brook; grist mill, carriage shop, William Royal; production, estimated, 500 barrels flour.

Eleventh, "King's Privilege," on Stony brook; saw, shingle, and "Dead-Eye" machinery; S. M. King; production, estimated, 50,000 feet of boards, and 100,000 shingles.

Twelfth, "Hammond's Privilege," on Smith brook; saw mill, M. Hammond; 50,000 feet of boards.

The aggregate annual production of all the powers enumerated above, is 26,000 barrels flour; 400,000 feet of boards, 200,000 shingles.

The proportion of forest is estimated at one-sixth; but little old-growth forest left. The market connections are at Paris Hill, South Paris, West Paris, North Paris and Snow's falls; principally at Grand Trunk stations at South Paris and West Paris.

PARKMAN—PISCATAQUIS COUNTY.

From Selectmen's Returns.

Four Powers.

First, "Cumming's Brook," head and fall (with a dam eight feet high) 24 feet, water for four months. Its capacity could be doubled by the construction of two dams above.

Second, "Pingree's Mills," on Mill stream, shingle mill; formerly grist and saw mill, also; works four months in the year; situated near the centre of the town.

Third, "Holbrook's Mills;" four saws; grist mill, six months. Capacity of the above two powers might be doubled by a cheap dam, which would flow a very large bog. Situated near the centre of the town.

Fourth, "Pease Mills," on the south branch of the Piscataquis river; a good power with a good dam; saw and shingle mill recently burned. Sometimes a lack of water, but at a trifling outlay a lake two miles above might be converted into a reservoir and ample water secured all the year. Situated in the northwest corner of the town.

"Good roads to all the powers, and a good farming town."

PARLIN-POND TOWNSHIP—SOMERSET COUNTY.

Statement of Heman Whipple, Esq., of Solon.

Two Powers.

On the Parlin-pond stream; fall 10 feet each; one dam; good sites. Pond covers 2.75 square miles, and can be flowed eight feet.

PARSONSFIELD—YORK COUNTY.

From the Returns of the Selectmen.

[See also "Hiram and Parsonsfield," and "Parsonsfield and Porter."]

Four Powers.

Situated upon brooks which are supplied by Long, Spruce, and Mudgett ponds. Three of the powers are occupied by mills.

PARSONSFIELD—YORK COUNTY, AND PORTER—OXFORD COUNTY.

From the Returns of Parsonsfield and Porter.

[See also "Parsonsfield," and "Porter."]

Three Powers.

On Great Ossipee river, First, "Kezar Falls;" fall 50 feet in one mile. One perpendicular saw will cut 1,000,000 feet lumber annually; a part of the power is improved as follows: planing, stave, and shingle machines; bobbin factory; grist mill; saw mill; two dams.

All the mills and machines work the whole year. Dry times do not interfere with the working of the machiney, as there is always an abundance of water. The volume of water might be somewhat increased by further improvement of the reservoirs. Centre-vent and spiral-vent wheels. Power owned by Moses Sweat, A. P. Benton, and others.

The bed of the stream, at the falls, is very stony and many large rocks are found; but of a quality not suitable for building purposes. In the vicinity of the falls, however, granite is found in quantity sufficient for all buildings which may be erected. The river flows in an easterly direction; the southern shore is a gradual slope to the river the entire length of the falls, which gives an excellent location for mills or shops. The northern shore descends to the river by a steep bank, the greater part of the length of the falls, and would be a good location for mills. The river is very constant. In dry seasons all other mills in this section are obliged to suspend operation, while the machinery on this stream runs with the same regularity and power as at any other time; and during such periods receives the patronage of people at a great distance; not improved on the Porter side.

Second, "French's Falls," above; fall nine feet; not improved.

Third' "South River Falls," above; descent eight feet; not improved.

The river, at the above sites, about 200 feet wide.

No mills have ever been damaged by freshets; ordinary rains have but little or no effect upon the stream. The country not being mountainous, the stream rises and falls slowly. Total range from low to high water three to five feet.

The Portland & Rutland Railroad will run on the bank of the river for ten miles by the side of the water-powers.

PASSADUMKEAG—PENOBSCOT COUNTY.

Statement of Selectmen.

[See also "Edinburg and Passadumkeag."]

There is no water-power within the limits of this town.

PATTEN—PENOBSCOT COUNTY.

From Selectmen's Returns.

Four Powers.

First, the "Upper Dam," on Fish stream; 12 feet head, saw mill, planing mill, &c.; water for the saw mill four months; 200,000 of boards annually, and 30,000 clapboards.

Second, the "Lower Dam," a grist mill; head 12 feet; sufficient water to carry the mill eight months, on an average.

Third, on the "Hersey Brook," a grist mill; fall 22 feet; over-shot wheel 18 feet in diameter. Two runs of stones, one flour bolt. Sufficient water about four months.

PEMBROKE—WASHINGTON COUNTY.

From the Statement of C. B. Blanchard, Esq.

Five Powers.

First, on Pemaquan river, three and a half miles from tide water, "Little Falls," saw, shingle, lath, and clapboard machines; run the entire year, excepting a few weeks in extreme drouth; fall 18 feet.

Second, two and a half miles below; Pembroke Iron Company, rolling mills, furnaces, &c. Operates throughout the year, assisted during seasons of drouth by steam. Annual manufacture, 9,000 tons iron, 3,600 casks of nails; fall 30 feet.

Third, one-fourth mile below, gang saw mill, shingle, lath, and stave machines connected; runs throughout the year; fall seven feet. A good privilege.

Fourth, one-quarter mile below; "Leavitt's Grist Mill;" power not all used; fall six feet.

Fifth, one-half mile below, and on tide water; grist and planing mill, sash and blind factory; obliged to shut down five hours per day on account of tide. Convenient location, as vessels discharge directly into the mill.

The entire stream, with the exception of the first grist mill site named, owned by Pembroke Iron Company.

Penobscot—Hancock County.

From Selectmen's Statement.

[See also "Brooksville and Penobscot."]

Seven Powers, and More.

Upon Wardwell's stream and Winslow's stream. Wardwell's stream is fed by Pierce's pond, which is half a mile in diameter and half a mile from tide water. Three falls on said stream, which have been improved, all but one have been abandoned for want of lumber.

First, nearest the pond, used to drive a single saw and a grist mill with two runs of stones, stave, lath, and shingle machines. Old-fashioned paddle wheel and breast wheel; 10 feet head. Can be worked six months. The saw mill does but little business for want of logs; the stave machine has cut 600,000 staves the present year.

Second, below, has been used for a carding and clothing mill, driven by an overshot wheel 15 feet in diameter. The fall is obtained by carrying the water eight rods horizontally; does no business at present.

No information given respecting the third power on Wardwell's stream.

Granite in abundance on the premises; bricks manufactured within 50 rods of either power. Vessels of 200 tons burthen come within one mile; small vessels and scows come to the brick yard, within 50 rods. The dam at Pierce's pond is 90 feet long. The pond might be raised to any height by building the dam higher.

Fourth, Winslow's stream, six miles long from tide water to the head of Wight's pond, 75 acres. At its foot, single saw and grist mill; 10 feet fall, dam 60 feet long and six feet high in the middle. More fall might be easily obtained if needed.

Fifth, below, within 50 rods of tide water, formerly a shingle machine. Fifteen feet fall feasible. The location is convenient for mills; 10 rods to the stage road; vessels of 200 tons burthen have been built within 50 rods. Plenty of granite suitable for building within 100 rods. The quarry has been worked.

Sixth, etc., other powers on said stream have been improved in years gone by, but the lumber has been cut off, and for the want of capital and experience in other manufacture than lumber, they are and remain unimproved. The last three powers by the flowing of a meadow would do a large amount of business all the year.

PERKINS—SAGADAHOC COUNTY.

Statement of the Selectmen.

One Power.

The "Little Narrows," between two islands, about 75 feet wide, through which the tide runs with rapidity. Fifty years ago a wheel was set which worked well, but from want of means or some other cause not now known, mills were never erected. The privilege is now unimproved.

PERRY—WASHINGTON COUNTY.

From Selectmen's Returns.

Five Powers.

On Little river, the outlet stream of Boyden pond, and all within horizontal distance of two miles. Pond is five by two miles, and has a dam at its outlet.

First, "Gibson's Privilege," 12 feet fall; grist mill and carding machine.

Second, "Gates, Duren & Co.'s Privilege;" fall 25 feet; gang saw mill.

Third, "Chadbourne's Privilege;" lath machine; fall 22 feet.

Fourth "—— Mill," lath machine; fall 10 feet.

Fifth, "Rapid;" six feet fall.

The powers work about eight months of the year; artificial reservoirs might be constructed of size to supply water all the year; wheels, high breast.

Gates, Duren & Co., upon one power, saw 3,500,000 of lumber yearly. Their mill is within three-fourths of a mile of the landing place of vessels of 200 tons.

Rock; sandstone. Land on each side of the stream cleared, level, good for building, and productive of hay; the town is generally fertile. The lots remaining after the removal of the timber, 200 acres each, will make each two good farms.

The power is not all employed. The amount of it may be judged from the working capacity of Gates, Duren & Co.'s work upon one power.

Market, New York, Boston, and all points by sea.

PERU—OXFORD COUNTY.

Statement of Jonas Greene, Esq.

Nine Powers.

First, on the outlet of Worthley pond; fall 25 feet in 25 rods;

"Ripley's Saw and Shingle Mill;" with small outlay in improvements could run through the year, as it is fed from this large pond.

Second, one mile below; fall eight feet; "Howard's Shingle and Lath Mill;" runs a few months; can be greatly improved.

Third, below, fall 10 feet in a few rods; "Bemis' Grist Mill," and other small machinery; short of water a portion of the year.

Fourth, at the centre of the town on a large brook, near its outlet into the Androscoggin river; Hayford & Son; fall 20 feet in four rods; grist mill, threshing machine, with various lumber machinery. Saw mill going up with the contemplated improvements can be operated a large portion of the year.

Fifth, 20 rods below, unoccupied, six feet fall.

Sixth, on Spear's stream, at West Peru; fall in 80 rods 35 feet; grist, saw and shingle mills, and machine shop. Grist mill runs most of the year; saw mill spring and fall.

Seventh, above, "Jennie Falls;" unoccupied; fall, six or eight feet.

Eighth, on said Spear stream in west part of the town or Brookline, so called; John C. Wyman, Jr.; fall 12 feet in three rods; saw, shingle and lath mill, also threshing machine. Runs about four months; with improvements could do much more.

Ninth, on Winthington brook, in the north part of the town, Elbridge Austin, saw mill, shingle and threshing machine. Overshot wheel; two-thirds the year.

Stone abundant and near all the privileges. Considerable timber in the vicinity of all, and large amount of hard timber in town.

Market, Lewiston and Portland.

Phillips—Franklin County.

Statement of Abner Toothaker, Esq., and the Selectmen.

Numerous Powers.

On the Sandy river in a running distance of three and one-half miles. The river in the whole descent is a *torrent,* and the total fall is judged not less than 300 feet. Mills could be operated its entire length. Three privileges are improved.

First, "Wing's Mills," the upper of the series, head and fall 12 feet, saw and clover mill, shingle machine; old leaky wooden dam that wastes two-thirds of the water at low run.

Second, two miles and a half below, "Whitney's Saw Mills" use 144 inches of water; estimated power, 30 horse at lowest run, which is about one-fourth of the quantity running. Operate part of the year. Improvements, planing, shovel-handle, and small lumber machinery.

Third, one mile below, as the stream runs, and 60 feet lower, vertically, "Beedy's Grist Mill," operates all the year. Improvements, grist and carding mill.

Flutter, Blake's, and Tub wheels. More dams could be cheaply constructed, a vast amount of unused power; freshets cannot affect the present mills. Rock, granite; lay of the land good; three-fourths of the basin covered with forest.

Market, Farmington, 18 miles by road, and at home.

PHIPSBURG—SAGADAHOC COUNTY.

Statement of Samuel D. Reed, Esq.

Ten Powers.

First, a good tide privilege at the "Basin," on New Meadow river; has carried saw, corn, carding and fulling mills; not in use for a great number of years; stone dam remains good; vessels can load at the mills. Situated 25 miles from Portland, by inside navigation among the islands of Casco Bay, and ten miles from Bath. Good second growth in the vicinity. Good granite near, and a good lime quarry within a mile on the same basin of water, and plenty of wood in the vicinity. Lime burning could be made very profitable, as the limestone is situated near the shore. A superior emery found here. All owned by Samuel D. Reed and others of Phipsburg.

Second, a small tide power at Small Point; saw and shingle mill; also a quarry of good mica slate, which can be got out in large sheets. Third, a small tide power on a branch of Morse's river; has been a saw mill.

Fourth, at "Parker's Head," on the Kennebec river, a very great tide power, has carried ten up-and-down saws with the usual complement of small machinery. With the best wheels, the power would carry double the amount. It "is considered the best privilege on Kennebec river," being open all winter to navigation; is three miles from the mouth of the river and Fort Popham, and ten miles from Bath. Logs come down river to supply the mills. Eight of the mills were burned down in September, 1866, leaving the dam in good condition. The privilege is for sale. Good quarry of granite and flagging stone about one mile to the west of Parker's Head village, the stone splits well, and works up to a fine edge.

Fifth, a tide power at the centre village, on Kennebec river, now occupied by two up-and-down saws, some small machinery, and a grist mill; power sufficient to carry more mills. Used in part for sawing ship timber for vessels built near the mills. The mills are seven miles from Bath and six miles from the mouth of Kennebec river.

Sixth, double saw mill at Drummore, vessels load at the mills.

Seventh, "Drummore Bay" might be dammed so as to make a very large tide power.

Eighth, on a fresh-water stream which enters Parker's Head mill pond, has been a saw mill; afterwards a shingle mill, worked by an over-shot wheel.

Ninth, a fresh-water power, at the basin, 60 feet feet from the pond to high water mark; not perpendicular fall. The stream enters the basin, then passes into New Meadow river.

Tenth, "Winnegance Tide Mills," three miles from Bath and four miles from Phipsburg-centre village, a large reservoir, 16 saws, and some machinery for small lumber. Nine mills are on the Phipsburg side of the pond, and seven on the Bath side. Supplied with logs from up Kennebec river, mostly. It is controlled by a corporation. Winslow Morse, President.

Pittsfield—Somerset County.

From Selectmen's Returns.

[See also "Burnham and Pittsfield"]

Three Powers.

First, "Douglass Ledge," on the west branch of the Sebasticook river; fall 14 feet in 150 rods. Unimproved.

Second, on the same stream, "Hathorn's Mill;" fall 14 feet in 40 rods; capacity 4,000,000 shingles, 2,000,000 long lumber, 10,000 bedsteads, grind 100,000 bushels of grain. This is about one-fifth of what all would do if improved. Centre-vent wheels.

Third, "Call Rips," on the same stream, 17 feet in 200 rods. Unimproved.

Several lakes and ponds, amongst them Moose pond, eight by one miles. All can be converted into reservoirs. A storage of six feet depth on Moose pond, will yield for 312 days per annum 10 hours a day, a gross power of 675 horse, on the above series of falls, or 26,800 spindles. This is the storage alone, it will be observed, to which the *natural* low run of the stream requires to be added, increasing the present available power two or three fold.

Granite boulders, suitable for building. One-half basin of stream covered with woods.

Market, Bangor, Lewiston, Portland, by Maine Central Railroad.

PITTSTON—KENNEBEC COUNTY.

From Selectmen's Returns.

Two Powers.

First, on Worromontogus stream, a very substantial stone dam 15 feet high; various saws, 500,000 long lumber, 1,000,000 shingles, clapboards and laths in the same proportion.

Second, on a branch of Eastern river; saw mill, grist mill; former operates five months, latter about all the year.

PITTSTON TOWNSHIP—SOMERSET COUNTY.

From the Statement of Hon. Abner Coburn.

One Power.

"Canada Falls," on the Penobscot river below the forks, over 20 feet descent. Unimproved.

PLEASANT RIDGE TOWNSHIP—SOMERSET COUNTY.

Statement of E. W. Parlin, Esq.

[See also "Moscow and Pleasant Ridge."]

Numerous Powers.

On Houston stream. The stream is a torrent for nearly two miles. The lower three-fourths of a mile is a continuous rapid, with a pitch of eight feet at the foot. At the head of the three-fourths mile, the "Grand Falls," 50 feet perpendicular; a most beautiful cascade. For half a mile above the Grand Falls there are rapids all the way. Good sites for dams at any point. Chance to flow 300 acres of intervale at the head of the upper rapids; also a considerable pond on the south branch of the Houston stream. Total fall judged to be 300 feet.

Mill site at outlet of Rowe pond, 0.70 square miles.

Also at the foot of Jewett pond, 25 feet fall can be had. Very large supply of water by dams on the ponds.

PLYMOUTH—PENOBSCOT COUNTY.

Statement of the Selectmen.

Five Powers.

On Martin stream, all improved save one.

First, "Martin Stream Falls," at Plymouth village; saw, shingle and grist mill; 500,000 of lumber. Grist mill usually full of business, especially in dry seasons.

Second, 60 rods below; a large tannery, 8,000 cords of bark and 5,400 cords of wood.

Third, 120 rods below; carding and clothing mill which is never idle in the season of business. Recent improvements added.

Fourth, unimproved, two miles below.

Fifth, two and a half miles below; saw and shingle mill.

The fall is sufficient for a 15-foot head on either of the powers named. A judgment of the capacity of the stream for manufacturing may be formed from the fact that it is sufficient to run the saw mills, shingle mills and grist mill a greater portion of the year in the driest seasons

Machinery modern; "Rose," or "Thurlow," and "Scroll" wheels; cannot be recommended for economising power.

Martin stream is connected with two ponds within two miles of the falls, Plymouth and Little ponds; ponds are flowed by the dam at falls together with a large extent of land comprising with pond some 1,800 acres. The large volume of water held in reserve is used as needed and renders this power among the best in the State.

Formerly a dam in Dixmont, four miles southeast of this village, upon which were mills; mills burned and dam gone to ruin; dam flowed a large area of land and added much to the capacity of the power at Plymouth. This might again be built if deemed necessary.

If six feet head can be commanded upon four square miles of reservoir, the gross power of the series of falls, at 15 feet each, arising from the storage alone, is 486 horse-powers, or 19,440 spindles, for 10 hours a day, 312 days per year. The storage can all be used in six months or less, the natural run sufficing the rest of the year, doubling or trebling the power.

The stream is very uniform on account of reservoirs. The stream at falls runs on a compact ledge. The land above falls lies but little elevated above high water mark on dam for quite a distance, and the site for factories, worshops, &c., is convenient and easy of access. The proportion of basin of stream covered by forests about one-half.

Market, all points by Maine Central Railroad, station three and a half miles north of village.

POLAND—ANDROSCOGGIN COUNTY.

From Selectmen's Returns, based upon the Survey of S. F. Waterman, Esq.

[See also "Minot and Poland."]

Three Powers.

First, "Poland Corner Privilege," on Waterhouse brook; fall 18 feet in 350 feet; velocity of current, 100 feet per minute; area of cross section, 30 square feet. Improved in part, by a grist mill and saw mill; a good stone dam across the head of the falls; mills operate all the year; about 75 horse-power, gross.

Second, "Shaker Mill;" fall 42 feet in 250 feet distance. A 30-foot overshot wheel runs a large amount of machinery all the year; for grinding, sawing, planing, machine shops, carding, &c.

Third, "West Poland Mill Company," on Saunder's brook, an 18-foot overshot wheel, saw mill, operating half the year. Power could be increased, to some extent, by flowing meadows.

PORTER—OXFORD COUNTY.

From Selectmen's Returns, and the Statement of G. G. Stacy, Esq.

[See also "Hiram and Porter," and "Parsonsfield and Porter."]

Seven Powers.

First "Stanly's Mills," at the foot of Robert's pond; head and fall eight feet.

Second, "Colcord's Mill," at the foot of Colcord's pond; eight feet fall.

Third, "Gentleman Mill," on the Mill brook which runs by Porter village; fall seven feet.

Fourth, "Robbins' Mill," on West Branch brook; fall five feet.

Fifth, "Weeks' Mill," on the outlet of Spectacle pond, stave and shingle mill; formerly a large saw mill.

Sixth, "Davis' Privilege."

Seventh, "Norton & Davis Privilege."

Abundant and good granite. Two-thirds of the basin wooded. Market, Portland, by rail and road.

PORTLAND—CUMBERLAND COUNTY.

Statement of the Proprietors.

One Power.

The "City Mills," a tidal grist and salt mill; three runs of stones; works 12 hours a day; can grind 150 bushels per day; 30 acres of pond.

The above privilege is situated near the head of Back Cove, an arm of the sea, nearly 800 acres in extent, with a narrow entrance which might be dammed at no great expense, and a tide power of great capacity and of great value for flour mills and other adapted purposes be established.

Pownal—Cumberland County.

From Selectmen's Returns.

Two Powers.

First, "Haskell's Mills," on the southeast branch of Royal river, near Poland Centre; fall, with a dam 10 feet high, 12 feet. Saw and grist mill; dam out of repair; machinery old-fashioned and poor; power sufficient to run both mills all the year, with improved machinery and good dam. Rocks, coarse granite.

Second, "Merritt's Mills," on the northeast branch of Royal river, near north Pownal village; a saw mill might run the year round with good dam and modern machinery; fall, with a dam 12 feet high, 14 feet; ponds the water back about two miles; formerly a grist mill upon it.

Prentiss—Penobscot County.

From Selectmen's Returns.

Two Powers.

First, "Mattagordus Falls," on Mattagordus stream; fall 40 feet in one-fourth mile, the main road crossing where the dam should be placed. Power not improved; very large tract of low land upon the stream could be converted into reservoir at little expense: ne suitable for foundations and dams close at hand.

Second, on Mud brook, saw mill; basin of stream seven-eighths forest. Annual production $500. "Before the mill was built a board could not be got within ten miles." Soil stony and productive.

"Large and valuable water powers in the unincorporated places surrounding us. They will be of great value in time. The whole region needs survey; it will stand the test."

Presque Isle—Aroostook County.

From Selectmen's Returns.

Two Powers.

First, at "Presque Isle Village," on Presque Isle river of the

Aroostook. Fall ten feet in one-fourth mile; dam, saw and grist mill. Reynolds' turbine wheels, highly esteemed.

Second, on Alder brook, a dam and saw mill; Tuttle's wheel, also esteemed.

The above, chiefly the river, will saw 3,000,000 feet, and grind 100,000 bushels, yearly.

No lakes or ponds in the neighborhood; the dam on the river ponds the water back five miles. Land about the falls very convenient for building; basin, one-half wooded. Wealth and population of the place have been doubled by the improvement of the power.

Market, St. John, N. B., and Boston, by St. John river and St. Andrews Railroad.

PRINCETON—WASHINGTON COUNTY.

From Selectmen's Returns.

Four Powers.

First, "Foot of the Lakes Privilege," on the West branch of the St. Croix river; fall eight feet; large tannery, woollen factory, two gang saw mills, six shingle mills, grist mill and other machinery.

Second, three miles below, unoccupied; fall about six feet.

For reservoirs tributary to these powers, and the storage held thereon, see Part II, page 119. The storage is now used for log-driving purposes. The supply of water can be made inexhaustible to the demands of extensive manufacturing.

Third, on Dry brook; power to carry a saw mill, with the machinery usually attached. Unoccupied.

Fourth, on Lewey's brook; of equal capacity with the foregoing. Unoccupied.

PROSPECT—WALDO COUNTY.

From Selectmen's Returns.

Three Powers.

On Grant's river; head and fall about eight feet to each; saw mills on each; only one saw mill now in use; a grist mill, also, on one dam.

Mills operate about three-fourths time; would saw 300,000 of lumber and do all the grinding of grain for the county; stream variable.

Porphyritic granite; no old-growth forest.

Rangely—Franklin County.

Statement of Abner Toothaker, Esq., of Phillips.

Numerous Powers.

First, at the outlet of Rangely lake, a dam 13 feet high, can be increased to 17 feet; short dam required, solid ledge bottom and banks; the lake covers about 14 square miles, and is flowed four feet; excellent land all about it; hard-wood growth; site favorable to the location of mills. The privilege is unsurpassed. Owned by E. S. Coe, Esq., of Bangor. Unimproved.

Second, on the outlet stream of Quimby pond, 35 feet fall in 10 rods, clapboard and shingle machine. Pond covers 0.30 square mile, can be flowed four feet.

Third, on the outlet stream of Dodge pond, 10 feet head can be had, pond covers 0.75 square miles, and can be raised 10 feet. Good privilege. Unimproved.

Fourth, at the outlet of Round pond; a dam flows the pond six feet, eight feet fall; pond covers 100 acres and is fed by five or more small ponds; all these small ponds can be made reservoirs.

Fifth, on Kennebago river, half a mile from its mouth, ten feet fall can be had; good chance for dam; dam will flow the stream back four miles. Unimproved.

Numerous mill sites on small streams.

"Vast forests. Good soil. Heavy rains, and no drouth at any time."

Raymond—Cumberland County.

From Selectmen's Returns.

[See also "Casco and Raymond."]

Six Powers.

First, "Plummer's Mills," on Panther river, fall 16 feet, operate nearly all the year; numerous saws, a planer, grist and plaster mill. About half of the power used.

Second, "Fulton's Mill," on Radoux river; fall 15 feet.

Third, "Jordan & Adams' Mills," on Nubble brook; fall sufficient for overshot wheel; several circular saws; operate part of the year.

Fourth, "Nason's Mill," on Nason's brook; overshot wheel, several circular saws; operates part of the year.

Fifth, "Spiller's Mill," on Little Rattlesnake river; overshot wheel, several circular saws; operates part of the year.

Sixth, "Getchell's Mill," on Little Rattlesnake river; overshot wheel, circular and up-and-down saws; operates part of the year.

Streams connected with ponds, three of which have an area of nearly six miles, all of which can be improved for reservoirs. See page 143. A dam, at the outlet of Panther pond, would make the privilege a most excellent one; there is now abundant water at this privilege all the year with great waste; streams very constant; freshets entirely harmless. The water-power, if suitably improved, would benefit the town largely. One-third to one-half of the basin of the streams covered with forests.

Market, Portland, by road and canal.

READFIELD—KENNEBEC COUNTY.

From Selectmen's Returns.

Three Powers.

Upon Factory stream, height of the series 40 feet in 160 rods; mills operate in general all the year.

Stream connected with a pond covering one and a quarter square miles; its capacity can be increased.

REED PLANTATION—AROOSTOOK COUNTY.

Statement of W. H. Bryson, Esq., of Haynesville.

One Power.

On Wytopitlock stream; fall 15 feet, a dam upon it; no other improvement.

The Wytopitlock stream draws its contributions from a large extent of country, and is fed by a lake of the same name, and by various ponds. The lake covers 3.25 square miles; it can be raised several feet by a dam and thus made an unfailing reservoir.

RICHMOND—SAGADAHOC COUNTY.

From Selectmen's Returns.

Two Powers.

First, on Abagadassett river, fall 14 feet; no part of the power improved; would carry two runs of stones nine months of the year.

Second, on Mill brook; fall 10 feet in half a mile; no part of the power used. Streams regular; good stone for building; lay of the land good. One-half of the Abagadassett basin covered with forest; one-fifth of the Mill brook, do.

RILEY PLANTATION—OXFORD COUNTY.

Statement of the Assessors.

Three Powers.

First, "Lock's Falls," on Bull branch, fall 25 feet. Unimproved.

Second, on Bull branch, fall 25 feet. Unimproved.

Third, on west branch of Sunday river, fall 20 feet in 50 rods. Unimproved.

Nine-tenths of the basin of the streams covered with a fine forest of pine, spruce, hemlock and hardwood.

Market, Bethel, 10 miles, good road, and thence to Portland by rail.

RIPLEY—SOMERSET COUNTY.

From Selectmen's Returns.

Four Powers.

On the outlet of Roger's pond, in the south part of the town; fall 50 feet in 160 rods. If suitably improved would saw 1,000,000 feet of boards per annum; three fourths of the power improved in saw and shingle mills; mills operate about one-third time; machinery of poor construction for economizing power; centre-vent, Stearns, and flutter wheels.

Pond two by five-eighths miles; its capacity cannot be increased by dams. No out-cropping rock about the falls; one-third of the basin of the stream is covered with forests; annual product of the power about $1,400.

Market, Newport and Bangor by road, and by railroad from Newport.

ROBBINS PLANTATION—WASHINGTON COUNTY.

Statement of Peol Tomah.

Several small powers on the Tomah streams, the outlets of the Tomah ponds. Ponds cover two square miles, and can be dammed.

ROBBINSTON—WASHINGTON COUNTY.

From Selectmen's Returns.

Nine Powers, or More.

First, on Low's brook; formerly a saw mill, now out of use; fall 10 feet; 864 square inches; stream supplied by Shattuck's lake, 60 acres, and Cranberry lake, 30 acres.

Second, a short distance above the flow of the tide at Mill cove, in South Robbinston, below the junction of the Western and Eastern Lake streams, (the lakes have an area of 80 acres), "Vose's Saw Mill;" at present operations suspended; capable of cutting at least 10,000,000 feet boards in the usual sawing season, besides laths, pickets, &c. Overshot wheel, 24 feet diameter; water about 1,628 square inches; head and fall, 30 feet. The tide flows to the foot of the mill, which is about 40 rods from the county road.

Third, at Mill cove, formerly a tide-mill; an eligible site for one.

Fourth, 50 rods above Vose's mill, on the Western Lake stream; shingle, plug and wedge, tannery, lath and carding machines; overshot wheel nine and one-half feet diameter; head and fall 12 feet; dam founded on a ledge and about five rods long; 1,152 square inches.

Fifth, Sixth, etc., on the Western Lake stream, equally eligible with those described above.

Seventh, Eighth, etc., "several good privileges" on the outlets of Rand Lake and Money-makers' lake, 30 and 35 acres, respectively.

Ninth, a good site, on the outlet of Eastern lake, 35 acres.

ROCKABEMA PLANTATION—AROOSTOOK COUNTY.

Statement of John Gardner, Esq., of Patten.

Nine Powers.

First, on Darling brook, a saw mill, 20 feet fall, overshot wheel; pond above.

Second, Third, Fourth, on the outlet stream of Mud pond, two and a half miles to Rockabema lake, and very rapid current all the way; good bottom and banks; pond covers 1.25 square miles, and is flowed eight feet. It is fed by other ponds above, the largest of which, 1.35 square miles, is flowed six feet by the Mud pond dam.

Fifth, Sixth, Seventh, etc., on the outlet stream of Rockabema lake, situated between the outlet and the Aroostook road.

Eighth, "Jackson's Sluice," about two miles below the road, a large fall and readily susceptible of improvement, excellent banks and hard bottom.

Ninth, near the south of the town, "Warren's Falls," a good power.

Rockabema lake covers 2.25 square miles, and is flowed five feet, and can be raised considerably more with some expense.

Rockland—Knox County.

From the Mayor's Returns.

Two Powers.

First, at the outlet of Chickawakie pond. This pond supplies the city with water, and the power is used only when there is a surplus. A grist mill located upon it. Mill and privilege both owned by the water company. Volume of water could not probably be increased.

Second, a power on Boggy brook; two mills, a single saw and stave; runs about four months of the year.

"Manufactures of this place, lime and vessels;" over 1,000,000 casks of the former annually.

Rome—Kennebec County.

From the Statement of the Selectmen.

One Power.

Situated upon a small stream that leads from one pond to another; saw and grist mill on the same, which run about three months out of twelve.

Roxbury—Oxford County.

From Selectmen's Returns.

Numerous Powers.

The principal two on Swift river, "Walker's Narrows," and "Weeks' Falls;" fall 16 and 18 feet respectively, attained in 15 rods in each case; average velocity of current one rod per seven seconds; area of cross section taken in same locality as the velocity, 45 feet; so it will be perceived that the stream is narrow and shallow, but very rapid.

"Weeks' Falls," have never been improved, but Walker's Narrows have been improved to a considerable extent. Mills destroyed by fire in 1860. They were saw, grist, clapboard, shingle mills and thresher.

Water always sufficient for running a saw mill at each, throughout the year.

Few ponds. "On account of the variableness of the stream it would be difficult to construct artificial reservoirs of any considerable capacity. Freshets swell the stream to perhaps a greater extent than any other stream in the State;" they are not destructive as the banks are very high. Plenty of granite.

RUMFORD—OXFORD COUNTY.

From Selectmen's Returns.

Five Powers.

"Rumford Falls," on the Androscoggin river, the largest water-power in New England.

Height of the falls 162 feet eight inches, in a running distance of one mile.

Power, that of the whole Androscoggin river at that point. The river is but 90 feet wide and could be dammed at comparatively small expense. The bottom and sides of the stream are granite ledge; the rocks are suitable for building purposes.

The power is owned by Chaplin Virgin and others. Proprietors are disposed to sell.

Improvements, saw and grist mill, and some other small works. An insignificant fraction of the power is employed.

If the volume of water be assumed to be 25 per cent. less than at Lewiston, or 70,500 cubic feet per minute at low run, the power of the whole fall in a drouth is not less than 21,546 gross horse power, or 870,000 spindles. For reservoirs see pages 85–6.

Four small powers, concerning which no information is given.

ST. ALBANS—SOMERSET COUNTY.

From Selectmen's Returns, and a Plan of the Streams.

Eight Powers.

First, at the outlet of Indian pond, a stone dam ten feet high, flowing the pond with its flats, 1,500 acres in all; no machinery upon it.

Second, below, a stone dam, seven feet high; shovel-handle, carriage shop, sash and door, and shingle machinery.

Third, 50 rods below the upper dam, grist and saw mills.

Machinery on the middle dam runs nearly all the year; the saw mill on the lower dam runs about nine months.

Fourth, a mile below, "Lothrop's Mills;" fall 15 feet; saw and grist mill, and tannery; eight months.

Fifth, on the main branch of Indian pond stream, in the north part of the town; fall 60 feet in half a mile; only a shingle mill upon it; fed by Rogers' pond in Ripley.

Sixth, fall 20 feet in 30 rods, on the east branch of the stream; shingle mill, fed by a pond.

Seventh, on a branch of Footman brook, fall 25 feet in 50 rods; formerly occupied but not now.

Lower Falls, Rumford.

Eighth, on another branch of Footman brook, fall 25 feet in 50 rods; formerly occupied but not now.

Each of the foregoing two powers is capable of running a saw mill half the year. One has a good dam and a building for a shingle mill upon it. Expense of dams at either of the powers would be small, and there is no liability to damage from freshets. Rogers' pond, before mentioned, might be made a valuable reservoir. A head of six feet upon Indian pond and flowage ground, would give upon 40 feet of fall on the stream below, 160 horse-power gross for the working hours of the year, or 480 horse-power for four months, or 19,200 spindles. The ordinary natural run of the stream would yield as much, or more, during the residue of the year.

Manufactures, 200,000 shingles, 400,000 feet boards and timber, 8,000 dozen shovel handles, and 75 to 100 tons of leather.

Market, all points by rail from Newport.

Saco—York County.

From the Mayor's Returns.

[See also "Biddeford and Saco."]

Two Powers.

First, on Little river, fall six feet; single and circular saws operate three months in the year; cut 60,000 lumber and 50,000 fish-barrel staves.

Second, on Nonesuch river; fall 20 feet in one-tenth of a mile, single saw and circular saw; run nine months in the year; cut from 300,000 to 400,000 lumber, and 150,000 shingles annually.

St. George—Knox County.

Selectmen's Statement.

There is no water power in this town.

Salem—Franklin County.

From Selectmen's Returns.

One Power.

On Curvo stream; height of dam 14 feet; ponding the water back half a mile. Will run an up-and-down saw and grist mill all the time. Howard, Centre-vent, and Rose wheels. Does all the sawing and grinding for the region seven miles about.

Market, Farmington, by road.

SANDWICH-ACADEMY GRANT—SOMERSET COUNTY.

Statement of Governor Coburn.

Six Powers, or More.

First, three-fourths mile below the west line of the town, on Moose river; fall 10 feet, much more can be had.

Second, Third, Fourth, etc., "Moose River Rapids," extending two miles below the above falls; total fall of perhaps 40 feet. Several good sites. A dam formerly on the fall, eight feet high, commanded four feet on Long pond, two feet on Wood & Attean ponds, thus forming a reservoir of immense capacity.

Also a good privilege on Stony brook, half a mile from Moose river, 12 feet or more fall, small ponds above for reservoirs; large amount of flat land above the fall that can be flowed for storage.

Also, on Misery stream, in the southeast corner, a fall of six feet, dam, can be raised to any desired height.

SANDY-RIVER PLANTATION—FRANKLIN COUNTY.

Statement of Abner Toothaker, Esq., of Phillips.

Several Powers.

The outlet stream of Long pond falls 200 feet in its total length of one and a half miles. The pond covers about a square mile; three feet head of storage are raised upon it, and five feet more can be.

There are upon the stream quite a number of excellent privileges, good chance for dams, and mills. All unimproved except one upon which are saw, grist, clapboard, and shingle mills.

Several good but small privileges on the outlet of the Sandy-river ponds; bottom and banks ledge. Unimproved.

SANFORD—YORK COUNTY.

From the Returns of M. W. Emery and James O. Clark, Esqs.

Sixteen Powers.

Located upon the Mousam river.

First, the upper, "Merrifield Fall," near Jillison's bridge, fall 30 feet; entirely unimproved.

Second, "Hemmingway & Lord's Fall," 10 feet; a wooden dam; saw, grist and threshing machinery.

Third, "Kimball's Privilege," below, and a mile above Springvale; fall 10 feet; was used for a grist mill; now out of use.

Fourth, "Factory Privilege," fall 15 feet; located at Springvale; stone dam; cotton mill about 100 feet long, three and one-half stories high; manufactures print cloth.

Fifth, a saw mill privilege, just below, fall 10 feet; wooden dam.

Sixth, "Print Works Fall," fall 12 feet; stone dam; grist mill and cabinet manufactory in operation.

Seventh, "Low's Privilege," fall 10 feet; entirely unimproved; half a mile below Springvale.

Eighth, "Gowen Privilege," three-fourths mile above Sanford corner; was used for a saw and grist mill; now run out; fall nine feet.

Ninth, "Goodall's Privilege," stone dam; fall 15 feet; saw mill on one side, on the other side, a mill three stories high, 100 feet long, with a large L, and will be used to manufacture carriage lap-robes.

Tenth, just below, same proprietor, stone dam; fall 14 feet; grist and flour mill; these falls taken together would give a fall of about 36 feet; located at Sanford corner.

Eleventh, "Chadbourn Privilege," one-fourth of a mile below, formerly a saw mill; now run down; fall nine feet.

Twelfth, "Willard Privilege," at South Sanford; fall eight feet, stone dam, saw mill and box mill.

Thirteenth, "Linscott's Privilege," two miles below, fall 10 feet, wooden dam, saw mill.

Fourteenth, "Estes Privilege," one mile below, fall nine feet, wooden dam, grist mill.

Fifteenth, "Whitches Privilege," one mile below, fall 14 feet, stone dam, saw mill.

Sixteenth, "Hills' Mill," immediately below, fall 12 feet, grist mill, wooden dam.

The aggregate fall, within the limits of the town, is about 200 feet. With 14 feet fall, the river would drive 10,000 spindles, of woollen machinery, all the year. All the mills on the river work the whole year, if they have work to do; the water has never failed when the dams have been in good condition. See page 147, Part II.

The lay of the land about nearly all the falls, is well adapted to the erection of mills. Above half of the basin is forest.

The water-power "has been the making of Springvale, and is now building up Sanford Corner."

Principal market, Boston; the railroad now runs within eight miles of the centre of the town; Portland and Rochester railroad now constructing through the town.

SANGERVILLE—PISCATAQUIS COUNTY.

From Selectmen's Returns.

Nine Powers.

Five on the Northwest-pond stream, and in close proximity to Sangerville village, as follows: "Weymouth Dam," six feet, flows back one-fourth of a mile; "Factory," 14 feet, flows one-eighth of a mile; "Carleton," 17 feet, flows 20 rods; "Fulling Mill," 12 feet, flows 20 rods; "Thissell," 12 feet, flows 15 rods. All the above have been improved, and each dam flows as near as practicable to the next above.

On the Carleton dam, grist and saw mill and tannery; grind ten bushels per hour at lowest water, and for the most part 30 bushels per hour, and leave sufficient water to run saw mill and tannery.

No. 2 a woollen factory, and No. 3 a saw and grist mill and tannery, 12 and eight months respectively.

Ponds about 500 acres in extent, which could be doubled, and new reservoirs made on the stream that supplies the pond in Parkman, helping the privileges in that town equally with those in Sangerville.

If eight feet head can be commanded upon three square miles of reservoirs, the storage would yield on the total fall of 61 feet, a gross power of about 360 horse for 10 hours a day, 312 days a year, 14,400 spindles. To this should be added the *natural* low run of the stream. The storage can all be used in four months, vastly increasing the power, the natural flow sustaining the power without assistance for the rest of the year.

Freshets never destructive, the ponds and swamps taking up the water and passing it off gradually.

Rock, lime slate. Mills may at the same time connect with the dam as a part of their foundation, and be adjacent to a good road running parallel to the stream. Nearly one-half of the basin of stream is covered with forest and timber.

Sixth and Seventh, on Black stream, total fall 30 feet, mills on each, operate all the year; stream fed by Dover pond.

Eighth, on Centre-pond stream; fall 14 feet; saw and shingle mill.

Ninth, on the same stream; fall 12 feet; saw and shingle mill, all the year.

Market, Bangor by road, 33 miles, soon by rail from Foxcroft.

SCARBOROUGH—CUMBERLAND COUNTY.

From the Statement of the Selectmen, and of W. S. Milliken, Esq.

Three Powers.

First, a saw mill privilege with a small volume of water. Will operate only in wet times. Situated near the post road.

Second, on Alger's brook, "Alger's Falls," on the Dr. Milliken farm; fall 15 feet; ledge bottom, good site for dam; not occupied, formerly a saw mill; chance for artificial reservoir above. Good opportunity for a butter or cheese factory.

Third, "Carter's Falls," one-fourth mile above, no improvement; formerly grist mill.

SEARSMONT—WALDO COUNTY.

From Selectmen's Returns.

Fifteen Powers.

Eight on the west branch of the St. George river and seven on the east branch and tributaries.

First, "Woodman's Mills," on the west branch, saw and stave mill; operates only a part of the year on account of the flowage of meadow land.

Second and Third, two miles below, the two "Boynton Privileges," both unoccupied. A head of 16 feet can be raised at these points and flow a large pond.

Fourth, one mile below, the "Muzzy Mills;" saw and stave mill and tannery.

Fifth, below, the "Muzzy Privilege," unoccupied.

Sixth, eight rods below, "Hezeltine Mills," at Searsmont village, saw, grist, carding and clothing, stave and shingle mills; operate all the time except in drouths; a head of 18 feet can be had.

Seventh, two miles below, and below the junction of the east branch, "Dyer Mills; saw and stave, operate part of the year at present.

Eighth, half a mile below, "Canal Dam," unoccupied; head of 25 feet can be raised. This power and the one above can be made capable of large use throughout the year, by means of a dam at the outlet of Quantabacook pond, situated on the east branch. Pond covers 1.25 square miles.

Ninth, north part of town on the east branch, "Thompson's Saw Mill."

Tenth, one mile below, "Wallace Dam," unoccupied; flows a large meadow.

Eleventh, 100 rods below, "Jewett Mill;" saw and stave.

Twelfth, in the west part of the town, "Arnold's Privilege."

Thirteenth, 100 rods below, the "Morse Stave Mill."

Fourteenth, half mile below, "Woodcock Mill;" saw and stave, cabinet shop.

The Fifteenth not specified.

The lay of the land on the main river very convenient for the location of mills. Abundant rocks suitable for dams and other constructions.

Market, Belfast, ten miles.

SEARSPORT—WALDO COUNTY.

From Selectmen's Returns.

Eight Powers.

On Big Meadow stream and Half Way stream, all small.

Power nearly all improved; one grist, two flouring, two stave, three shingle, and various saw mills.

Privileges owned by the "Mill Company," and private parties in town. Underlying rock, granite, and good for building purposes. Market, at home.

SEBAGO—CUMBERLAND COUNTY.

Statement of S. R. Porter, Esq.

Six Powers.

First, at the outlet of Peabody pond, formerly saw mills. Not used now.

Second, one and a half miles below, "Folly Privilege," mills formerly. Not in use now.

Third, two and half miles below, the site of the "Liberty Mills."

Fourth, one mile below, the site of the old "White Mill."

Fifth, half a mile below, "Fitch's Mills," saw and flour.

Either of these five falls has power enough to run a saw mill eight months in the year; six months in the year there is power enough to run eight saw mills.

Peabody pond, the reservoir of the foregoing powers, has an area of 1.50 square miles.

Sixth, a small power on the outlet of Brown's pond, grist and shingle mill. Power enough more than half the year to run a good grist mill.

SEBEC—PISCATAQUIS COUNTY.

From the Returns of Augustus Williams, Esq., and others.

Two Powers.

First, at the foot of the lake, "Sebec Village Power," 18 feet fall in 25 rods; woollen mill, 4 sets machinery, saw, clapboard, shingle and lath mills, carriage shop, etc. Mills operate all the year. Not half of the power used.

Second, two miles below, "Half Mile Rips," fall 25 feet in half a mile. Unimproved.

The above powers are fed by Sebec lake, the area of which according to the maps is not less than 14 square miles, but which is judged fully 18 square miles, and by 20 or more ponds, the combined area of which is certainly equal to that of the lake.

A head of six feet on the lake, at 14 square miles area, would furnish, ten hours per day for the year, 432 horse-power gross on the upper fall, and 600 on the lower, or 41,280 spindles on both. The storage could however be used in six months or less, the natural run sufficing for the rest of the year, thus doubling or trebling the power. The power can be still further augmented by the use of the other lakes and ponds for reservoirs. The capacity of these lakes and ponds can be increased greatly.

The water of the lake is so warm that the wheels need no protection from the cold; the water in the pond, for a half mile above the dam, seldom freezes over, and never remains frozen but a few days at a time. No damage from freshets.

Underlying rock, a hard "blue rock," suitable for rough constructions; the lay of the land, at both privileges, is as good as could be desired; nearly all the basin of the stream is covered with woods. "Where our village stands, a forest would probably have stood, but for our water-power."

Market, Bangor, by road, and in fall 1869, by rail from Dover.

SEDGWICK—HANCOCK COUNTY.

From Selectmen's Returns.

Five Powers.

First, at the outlet of Frost pond; saw, stave and shingle mills.

Second, on Thurston's brook; a saw mill.

Third, on Black brook, the outlet of Black pond; a saw mill.

Fourth, on Camp stream, a saw, shingle and stave mill.

Fifth, grist mill on Sargent's stream.

Sixth, a saw and stave mill, also a grist mill, driven by tide power, on Benjamin's river, a valuable power.

Only the tide mills operate all the year, water being too low a part of the year at the others. Some of the powers could be much improved by raising the dams at the outlets of the ponds.

SHAPLEIGH—YORK COUNTY.

From Selectmen's Returns.

[See also "Newfield and Shapleigh."]

Four Powers.

First, "Emery's Mills," on Mousam river; fall 14 feet; saw, shingle and planing mills; mills operate or can operate all the year. A good site for a factory as there is abundant water, constant at all seasons, perfectly manageable and safe from freshets.

Fourth, near Emery's mills, not occupied; abundance of good stone; lumber sufficient for building purposes.

Market, Wells, the nearest railroad station now, distance 16 miles. The Portland & Rochester Railroad now building within three miles.

SHERMAN—AROOSTOOK COUNTY.

[Golden-Ridge Plantation on the State Map.]

From Selectmen's Returns.

Three Powers.

First, "Upper Falls," Molunkus stream, fall 10 to 14 feet; unimproved.

Second, "Centre Falls," Molunkus stream, 10 to 14 feet fall; single saw and grist mill.

Third, "Lower Falls," "improved," but not stated how; fall 10 to 14 feet.

These powers work about eight months in the year. A dam at the Upper falls might flow a large bog eight feet, and secure water enough for the whole year. Range from lowest to highest water, four feet. Rock, slate; nine-tenths of the basin of the stream covered with forests. The improvement of the power has added 75 per cent. to wealth and population of the place.

Market, Bangor, by boat and road.

SHIRLEY—PISCATAQUIS COUNTY.

From Selectmen's Returns and a Plan of the Streams.

Six Powers.

First, "Hulling-Machine Falls," on the west branch of the Piscataquis, a mile and a half above the south line of the town; fall 28 feet in 20 rods. Unimproved.

Second, "Hale Falls," above, about midway the town, fall 25 feet in four rods. Unimproved.

Third, above, one and a half miles, "Bog Falls." Unimproved.

Fourth, "Buck-Basin Falls," on the east or north branch of the Piscataquis, about a mile above the south line of the town; fall 25 feet in one rod. Unimproved.

Fifth, "—— Falls," above, about midway the town. Unimproved.

Sixth, "Shirley Mills Falls," above, at the village; fall 40 feet in 30 rods.

Thousands of acres of bog can be flowed by means of dams, securing a vast supply of water. The fall being so great an immense amount of power can be realized. Considerable ponds also, above, that can be used for storage.

Rocks, slate, and good for building. Land level about all the falls and convenient for location of mills.

Market, Bangor, 60 miles by road. Town free from debt; school fund of $3,000.

SIDNEY—KENNEBEC COUNTY.

From Selectmen's Returns.

Thirteen Powers, and More.

First and Second, on Dyer brook; good mill sites; one ten feet fall, the other 17; saw and shingle mill on the latter; 300,000 shingles and 100,000 of boards; Blake wheel, 24 horse-power. The other site has never been occupied. Brook fed by Ward's pond, three-fourths by three-eighths miles; at the outlet a dam that commands all the water to the depth of 11 feet.

Third and Fourth, on branches of Lovejoy stream; saw mill sites, fall 10 or 12 feet; unoccupied.

Fifth to Tenth, inclusive, on Lovejoy stream, fall 10 to 20 feet each; only one or two have been occupied. One within 75 rods of the Kennebec river, has a fall of 20 feet or more, and would cut from 200,000 to 500,000 boards annually.

27

Eleventh, on the Thayer brook; formerly saw mill; has any amount of fall desirable, could cut from 150,000 to 200,000 feet of lumber annually.

Twelfth, Thirteenth, etc., on the Delano brook; mill site with falls sufficient for any purpose, formerly a saw mill on one.

Streams are affected by drouths in summer, except the Dyer.

SKOWHEGAN—SOMERSET COUNTY.

The Statement of William Philbrick, Esq.

Four Powers.

First, "Skowhegan Falls," on the Kennebec river.

Height and Formation.—The total fall is 28 feet in half a mile, a considerable proportion of which is perpendicular, with swift water below. The fall can be increased by dams as may be required.

An island, the head of which is at the crest of the fall, divides the river into two channels, and serves at once as a natural pier to the sections of the dam and as sites for mills. The bottom of the river is solid ledge, as are also the banks, both of the island and the bordering main land. Various masses of rock upon the brink of the fall project in such a manner as to support the dam and make it of impregnable strength.

Lay of the Land.—The general disposition of the land about the falls is only moderately favorable for the location of mills; some of the sites, however, are in their natural state, good; and room for all structures that may be needed for the use of all the power, can be secured by canals or by shafting. The rock is suitable for dams, foundations and other coarse work.

Volume of Water, and Power.—If the minimum volume of water available at this point in a drouth, be assumed to be 35 per cent. less than at Augusta, or 110,500 cubic feet per minute for 11 hours a day, the gross power of the fall for the hours specified, in a severe drouth, is 5,852 horse-powers, or 234,000 spindles.

The enormous increase of power that can be had upon use of available reservoirs may be seen upon reference to Part II, pages 94–9. The storage of the reservoirs is now used almost exclusively for log-driving purposes. Not over half of the power at present available is employed.

Incidentals.—Bricks of the best quality are made close at hand. Lumber is furnished by the river in unlimited quantities. The population is almost exclusively agricultural, and would furnish

North-Channel Dam, Skowhegan.

operatives of the best class in any desired number. The town is the natural centre of trade for all upper Somerset, and for a part of Franklin and Piscataquis counties, and now commands a large and rapidly increasing wholesale and retail trade. It is the terminus of the Portland & Kennebec Railroad, extensions of which into the interior will further increase the business of the place.

Improvements.—The "North Channel Dam" runs from the upper end of the island to the north bank, (the river at this point runs east and west) being planted on the solid ledge crest of a natural fall. Its cost is quite insignificant, the fall being nearly all natural. At its north end is a large brick flour mill; $82,000; Messrs. Tuttle, Kidder & Co., with power and sites for a large amount of machinery, both by locating mills and shops over the power, and by shafting taken to lots adjoining, high and dry from any risks from freshets.

At the south end of the dam, on the island, which is also in the centre of the village, there are now, circular, clapboard, shingle and lath machines; Weston and Baker; run all the year on hemlock, and all kinds of hardwood, which is hauled in from the surrounding country, and pine timber from the lake (Moosehead) and streams above; $35,000. A carding and cloth-dressing mill; Messrs. Stinchfield; who design manufacturing cloths, in addition to their other business. An old flour mill, owning a large amount of power, now partly used for a bedstead factory; Weston and Varney; $5,000.

The mills on the island are all on a *natural canal,* extending through the upper end of the island, walled in by native rock, and emptying below the falls. These privileges are very desirable in every particular, are safe from freshets, and contain a large amount of unemployed power, which can be used, like that on the north side, by shafting running inland.

The north channel dam turns the water down the south side of the island, at the foot of which the "South Channel Dam" crosses on solid ledge to the south shore, with a gateway conveying the water down the south shore by a side dam and wall.

On the north end of the dam, on the island, a bedstead factory; $7,000; F. Turner. On the south end and on the wing dam and wall are the following mills and shops: First, building 100 by 40 feet, three stories high, Abba Abbot, planing mill; $4,000; and for grinding slate rock for paint for oil cloth manufacture. This property is now in the market for sale. Also another planing mill, door, sash and blind factory; H. K White; $20,000; a custom flour mill; a paper mill; R. E. Lyon & Co.; $100,000; a skate and chisel factory, running ten trip hammers, lathes, drilling machines, grindstones, &c.; C. A. Williams & Co.; $50,000; an axe factory, running eight trip hammers, grindstones, &c.; Steward Williams & Co.; $75,000; also another axe factory, Barnet Wharff, running two trip hammers, grindstones, &c.; $15,000; large foundry, (building of stone) and a first-class machine-shop owned by S. L. Gould & Co., fitted up with lathes, planers, drills, &c., for the manufacture and repair of all kinds of machinery, and the manufacture of the Gould water-wheel, which is used in most all the mills and shops in the town.

At the "Basin," a short distance below the mills, an unsurpassed site for improvement now lies vacant. At this point canals can be constructed with ease, and mills located advantageously, the banks of the river being in all respects well formed for improvement.

Second, Third and Fourth, on the Wesserunsett stream; occupied, one by a tannery, and one by two saw mills, which operate fall and spring; these will run small machinery all the year.

SMITHFIELD—SOMERSET COUNTY.

From Selectmen's Returns.

One Power.

On "Greeley's Mill Stream;" eight feet head; dam flows East pond, which covers 2.50 square miles.

Saw, lath, shingle, and carding machinery; mills operate, or can operate, three-fourths of the year. The mills are thought capable of sawing 150,000 short lumber and 500,000 long per annum. Two Gould wheels used, excellent, the others worthless.

Range of water about five feet. Power has recently passed into new hands, "and it is hoped will now be of some benefit to the town."

Market, at home and adjoining towns.

SMYRNA—AROOSTOOK COUNTY.

Statement of T. B. Stewart, Esq.

One Power.

On the east branch of the Mattawamkeag river, a good privilege, formerly a mill; the dam made about nine feet head; dam now gone, mill out of repair. It is the only privilege in town, and is regarded as a very valuable one.

SOLON—SOMERSET COUNTY.

From a Statement, and a Plan of the Streams furnished by Joseph P. Buswell, Millwright, Endorsed by the Selectmen.

[See also "Embden and Solon."]

Nine Powers.

Five on Fall brook, a rapid stream with steep banks, four rods in width when full, with solid ledge bottom and banks, which empties into the Kennebec river at Solon village, falling 100 feet in one-fourth of a mile. At the head of the falls a reservoir dam about eight feet high flows the stream back about a mile through the plain which borders the Kennebec river, upon which Solon village is located.

The falls average about 20 feet each and are nearly equi-distant from one another. Each will give a power of 20 horses for 10 hours a day in the time of drouth, with very few exceptions, by the use of a high-breast pitch-back wheel, provided the dams are kept tight and the water is used with discretion.

In proof of the power and durability of the stream the results of actual trial in a single case are given: A grist mill, with four runs of stones and all the apparatus for flouring, was driven by a high-breast wheel eighteen feet in diameter, with four feet and two inch elbow buckets, measured inside the rims, and a twelve-inch shroud, and ground for each of seven successive years 20,000 bushels per year. "We never lacked for water during the whole period of seven years, and in our opinion the same may be done again if the dams are kept tight and the same care and attention are again given."

There are several other privileges in the town of Solon, on small streams where sufficient power to drive an up-and-down saw some three or four months in a year may be had at small expense, as follows:

Sixth, on Baker pond brook, in the northeast corner of the town.

Seventh, at the southeast corner.

Eighth, now occupied, on Michael stream, three miles or more east from the village, where a saw mill and lath machine are now run at good advantage.

Ninth, a mile below this, in a dense forest, a beautiful waterfall, where at a very small expense some 25 feet perpendicular fall may be obtained, and a few rods above some 40 or 50 acres of meadow land may be flowed, forming a reservoir sufficient to sustain a mill of eight or ten horse-powers some six months or more per year, and some seasons giving a constant supply the year round. It is about three miles distant from Solon village, in a southeast direction, near the centre of the town, on Michael stream, and is surrounded with lumber sufficient to wear out one mill or more.

The power on Fall brook is, as a whole, only partially occupied; if suitably improved it would do a great amount of business and give employment to a large number of hands.

Solon, with 400 inhabitants, two meeting-houses, schools, 15 stores, etc., is a centre of trade for several towns; has a first-class grist mill, various saw mills, a cloth-dressing mill, tannery, etc., and is one of the most beautiful villages in the Kennebec valley.

It is the terminus of the Somerset railroad now constructing.

SOMERVILLE—LINCOLN COUNTY.

From Selectmen's Returns.

Nine Powers.

Two on Travel stream, stave and shingle mills.

Three on Lovejoy stream, upon each of which there have been saw mills; only one of these is now in operation, there not being sufficient lumber to employ all three. Would saw 100,000 of lumber yearly.

Three on small streams, shingle machines.

One on Sheepscot river, fall 12 feet in 50 rods; properly managed with a tight dam it would saw 200,000 of boards per annum and keep the grist mill upon it in operation throughout the year. Grist mill has three runs of stones.

The stream is connected with the Patricktown pond a mile long and half a mile wide, in the town, and with the various ponds above in other towns. The outlet of Patricktown pond can be lowered eight or ten feet by blasting, and for $1,000. This would injure no mill privilege. The pond cannot be raised more than 2 feet above its present height without considerable damage. The mill pond is two miles long and half a mile wide. Freshets harmless by reason of the size of the pond.

Rocks suitable for mill purposes close at hand.

Market, the Kennebec towns and Portland, by road and rail.

SOUTH BERWICK—YORK COUNTY.

From the Returns of Edward S. Goodwin, Esq.

Three Powers.

First, "Quamphegan Falls," on the Salmon Falls river, which here meets the tide-waters of the Piscataqua.

The falls are owned and occupied by the Portsmouth Company, whose works, besides other necessary buildings, consist of a four-story brick cotton mill of about 7,000 spindles, using about 1,300 bales of cotton, and turning out annually about 2,000,000 yards of cotton sheetings.

This company was incorporated in 1831, and the factory erected and put in operation in 1832, since which time the hydraulic power of the company has been greatly enlarged by the erection of a substantial dam, raised 11 feet higher than the old dam, and 275 feet in length, giving a head and fall of 19 feet above high water mark in the Piscataqua river at ordinary high tides, and affording a surplus power sufficient to drive 20,000 additional cotton spindles.

This, the main branch of the Piscataqua river, naturally afforded a copious supply of water; but its hydraulic power has been immensely augmented by the operations of the Great Falls Manufacturing Company on the river and its branches, thus insuring an ample supply of water at all seasons of the year. See pages 149–150. The power is used only in part.

Second, "Newichawanick Falls," on Great Works river, about a mile above its conflux with the Salmon Falls river. The total height of the fall is 60 feet; the descent is divided into three pitches by as many dams; upon these dams are two woollen mills with 10 sets of machinery, and one saw mill.

The power is reckoned equal to 600 horse. The supply of water is ordinarily good. The river is connected with several small ponds. Privilege and improvements owned by the Newichawanick Company. The power is not all used.

Third, at the junction of the Great Works and Salmon Falls rivers, "Yeaton's Mills;" dam 17 feet high; saw mill, grist mill, plaster mill; power estimated at 250 horse. Power used only in part and superior facilities for further improvements.

The above privileges are situated in close proximity to the Boston and Maine, Portland, Saco and Portsmouth, and the Great Falls and Conway Railroads, and have accordingly superior facilities for transportation.

SOUTHPORT—LINCOLN COUNTY.

Statement of Selectmen.

Two Powers.

Both are tide powers. One is capable with improved machinery of running two saws and a grist mill, the other with the best machinery will operate a saw mill and grist mill. Neither is improved.

SOUTH THOMASTON—KNOX COUNTY.

From Selectmen's Returns.

One Power.

The "Weskeag River Tide Power;" width of stream at the mill is 320 feet; power estimated at about 400 horse.

A good stone dam; grist, stave and heading mill in operation; grist mill could grind 50,000 bushels per annum. The stave mill and heading machine employ eight men and saw four to five cords wood per 24 hours; 1,200 cords wood about one year's stock.

Mills run the year round, and less than half the power is improved. Machinery is of good construction; the wheels are iron, of the Union patent.

Power owned by the Weskeag Mill Company, and all or a part for sale, or the balance of the power not occupied. The dam ponds the water back two miles, pond covers about 200 acres.

Quarry of granite easy of access by land or water, good for building purposes; very convenient location for mills and shops. Vessels can come alongside the mill and discharge cargo. A good chance to put in a flour mill and good market to sell in. The product of the stave and heading machine for the past year is about $22,000. The stave mill and heading machinery are new, and have furnished a large amount of business to residents.

Market, Rockland, by water or land.

SPRINGFIELD—PENOBSCOT COUNTY.

Four Powers.

First, "Blanchard's Mill," on west branch of Mattakeunk stream, fed by two ponds.

Second, on Mattagordus stream, "Trask's Mill," two small ponds.

Third, saw mill, on a branch of Mattakeunk stream, small pond at the village.

Fourth, below, grist mill.

STANDISH—CUMBERLAND COUNTY.

From Selectmen's Returns.

[See also "Limington and Standish," and "Standish and Windham."]

Seven Powers.

First, "Paine's Mill," on the outlet stream of Great Watchic pond; fall 12 feet.

Second, "Rich's Mill," on a brook tributary to the Sebago pond; fall 14 feet.

Third, "Dow's Mill," on Josey's brook; fall 12 feet.

Fourth, "Dresser's Mill," on Josey's brook; fall 10 feet.

Fifth, "Shaw's Mill," on Shaw's brook.

Sixth, "Moody's Mill," on Stickey river; fall 8 feet.

Seventh, "Blake's Mill," on Josey's brook; fall 10 feet.

The above powers are all small, the chief powers being upon the boundary rivers of the town.

The total production of all the mills in Standish, including those upon the Saco and Presumpscot, is in value not far from $300,000.

Rock, granite; lay of the land, about the chief falls, excellent; three-fourths of the basin of the streams covered with woods.

STANDISH AND WINDHAM—CUMBERLAND COUNTY.

From the Statement of W. H. White, Esq., of Windham.

[See also "Standish," and "Windham."]

Four Powers.

These are all valuable, being situated on Presumpscot river, the outlet of Sebago lake.

First, "Wescott's Falls," at the outlet of the lake, fall 14 feet; an excellent power. Controls the delivery of the lake. Unimproved on the Windham side, improved on the Standish side by double saw mill, and powder-keg factory. Owned by William H. Jackson, Salem, Mass.

Second, "Eelweir Falls," below, 12 feet fall. Unimproved. Owned on the Standish side by Levi Wescott, and on the Windham side by H. Proctor.

Third, "Hubble Falls," eight feet fall, owned on the Windham side by S. D. Page, on the Standish side by Levi Wescott. Unimproved.

Fourth, "Steep Falls," 12 feet fall, owned on the Windham side by J. Mabry, on the Standish side by John Lindsey. Unimproved; has been occupied by saw mill; dam on the same.

For an account of the reserve capacity of the lake tributary to the above powers, see pages 143–44, Part II, of this Report.

STARKS—SOMERSET COUNTY.

From Selectmen's Returns, and a Plan of the Streams.

[See also "Mercer and Starks."]

Five Powers, and More.

First, on Lemon stream, at the village, "Sawyer's Mills;"

200,000 boards, 200,000 shingles, besides laths and pickets; grind 5,000 bushels grain; could grind 25,000 bushels. Operate 11 months of the year for grinding; for sawing, spring and fall; fall five feet in five rods.

Second, "Lemon's Mills," on Lemon stream; four feet fall in four rods.

Third, on the same stream.

Fourth and Fifth, on Chase's brook.

Several others on the above streams, not occupied. The fall is rapid, for a considerable distance, at each of the privileges. The streams are much swollen by freshets.

Suitable stone for building; "blue ledge." Land on the falls, level and dry. Small part of basin covered with woods. Mills have been profitable to the owners, and extremely convenient for the public; villages have sprung up around them.

Market, Skowhegan, by road, and home.

STETSON—PENOBSCOT COUNTY.

From the Statement of J. D. Maxfield, Esq.

Seven Powers.

Three on the outlet stream of Stetson pond, which covers about 2.50 square miles, and supplies abundant water to the several privileges the year through. The power is perfectly exempt from damage by freshets or inconvenience from rise of water.

First, (below the bulkhead) shingle mill, 25,000 per day, 1,500,000 manufactured this year; head eight feet.

Second, 40 rods below, saw and grist mill; 2,000,000 feet, board measure. Four runs of stones; 50,000 bushels of grain ground yearly; head and fall 14 feet.

Third, unimproved, about 60 rods below the Second, fall 14 feet.

Fourth, saw and shingle mill, water four or five months; 13 feet head.

Fifth, half mile below, 12 feet head; unoccupied.

Sixth, shingle mill, seven or eight months; 10 feet head.

Seventh, good power for eight months on Buzzell stream; unoccupied; 10 or 12 feet head.

STEUBEN—WASHINGTON COUNTY.

From the Returns of J. D. Parker, Esq., and a Plan of the Streams.

Eighteen Powers.

Fourteen on Tunk river, which is fed by ponds, the aggregate surface of five of which is not less than six square miles, and which are all susceptible of improvement as reservoirs. The river empties into one of the most magnificent harbors in the world; has sufficient water at low tide to float the largest vessel ever constructed, and excellent and ample holding ground.

First, "Head of Tide Power," a few rods from the wharves; eight feet head; gang saw mill, 30,000 of lumber per day.

Second, a short distance above, not now occupied; formerly by saw and grist mill.

Third, a short distance further up; shingle and grist mill on a wing dam.

Fourth, 150 yards above tide; not improved. A dam, if constructed here, will flow about 200 acres. The whole fall to the tide is about 25 feet; may be made 30 by a dam. By means of a canal the whole series could be converted into one large and valuable power. A bridge here.

Fifth and Sixth, one and a half miles above, the "Rips;" not now improved; formerly a saw mill.

Seventh, one and one-fourth miles above, a dam; shingle mill, etc.

Eighth, 20 rods further up, a dam; shingle, stave and spool mills, etc. A bridge here.

Ninth, a mile and a half above; not a very good power, as a great length of dam would be required.

Tenth, outlet of Round pond; formerly a mill; high banks on the pond.

Eleventh, 80 rods up the river; formerly a mill, now burned down.

Twelfth and Thirteenth, just above, eight feet head each; no improvements.

Fourteenth, a short distance above, the "Lath Mill."

Fifteenth, Sixteenth and Seventeenth, on Whitten stream, west part of town; various saws on each. Sixteenth now out of repair.

Eighteenth, on Pinkham's stream, a mill formerly at its mouth, now gone; the dyke now protects a marsh. Power could be used for a last or shovel-handle factory. A meadow above can be dammed for reservoir.

Abundant stone near each of the privileges for rough construction, and a quarry of beautiful granite near the mouth of Tunk river. A bed of clay, for bricks, at the water's edge; can be put directly from kilns into vessels. With one exception the required dams can all be short. Privileges can all be bought very cheap.

The power is very constant on Tunk river, freshets of course harmless; total range of water not over four feet. There are about 2,500 inches under an 8-foot head; 780 horse-power, gross, on the whole fall of 30 feet, or 31,200 spindles; if the water were economized, there would be considerably more the year round. A small proportion of the power employed. Wheels, spiral-vent, Wakefield centre-vent, a powerful wheel; Atkins wheel.

Town will exempt from taxation for ten years $50,000 invested in manufactories.

Market, all points, by sea.

STOCKTON—WALDO COUNTY.

From Selectmen's Returns.

Three Powers.

First, the "Tide-Mill Power," at Stockton village; fall about eight feet. Just completed, a saw mill, shingle mill, block shop, grist mill, and sash, door and blind factory. Much addition to the property and business of the town is anticipated from these improvements.

Second power, "Perkins' Mill," at Sandy Point; stream small, but never-failing; a carding and cloth dressing establishment upon it; fall eight feet.

Third power, "Roberts' Mill," on Seavy stream; fall eight feet; saw mill and shingle machine; eight months.

STONEHAM—OXFORD COUNTY.

Statement of S. Evans, Esq.

Twelve Powers, or More.

First, on the outlet stream of lower Stone pond, saw, grist, shingle, stave, and clapboard mills; quite a large business done, particularly in manufacturing staves for flour barrels.

Second, half a mile west, on the same outlet, saw, stave, and shingle mill, can do a large amount of business.

Third, one-fourth of a mile west, at the outlet of the pond, a saw mill, an excellent power.

Fourth, about two miles west, on the outlet stream of upper Stone pond, shingle and stave mill.

Fifth, 40 rods west, on the same stream, a shingle, stave and bobbin mill.

Sixth, Seventh, Eighth, etc., in the immediate vicinity of the above-mentioned; unoccupied. Good privileges.

Ninth, at West Stoneham, on Beaver brook, a saw mill.

Tenth, Eleventh, Twelfth, etc., good privileges on the above-mentioned stream, unoccupied.

The two Stone ponds have a joint area of over a square mile, and are good reservoirs.

STOW—OXFORD COUNTY.

From Selectmen's Returns.

Two Powers.

On Little Cold river. One fall ten feet in ten rods; saw mill and grist mill. The other fall seven feet in 150 rods; shingle and clapboard mill; mills operate about three months.

STRONG—FRANKLIN COUNTY.

From Selectmen's Returns.

Five Powers.

First, "Pierpole Falls," on Sandy river; fall 12 feet in 18 rods; would run two up-and-down saws and a gang, eight months of the year; unimproved.

Second and Third, on northeast branch of Sandy river, "Porter Falls," "Morton Falls;" 12 feet fall in 20 rods.

Fourth, on McCleary stream; fall as above; two saw, grist, clover, planing, batting, starch, and shingle mills; operate generally part of the year, some of them all the year.

Small lakes and ponds; limestone; half of the basin wooded; improvement of the power has largely built up Strong village.

Market, Farmington depot.

SULLIVAN—HANCOCK COUNTY.

From Selectmen's Returns.

Nine Powers, or More.

First, etc., on Flander's stream; three stave, a shingle, and saw mill; two or three privileges not occupied; water year round supplied by a pond; head 10 to 20 feet; lower mill distant from salt water about 100 rods; lumber growing scarce; excellent power for manufacturing purposes.

Fourth, Fifth, etc., on Morancey stream; carding and fulling, stave and saw mills. A number of sites for mills not occupied; water low in drouth of summer.

Eighth, on Gordan's stream; carding and fulling mill; water most of the year; good privilege for light manufacturing purposes.

Ninth, on Simpson's stream; grist and lath mill combined; water low in dry weather.

SUMNER—OXFORD COUNTY.

From Selectmen's Returns.

Five Powers.

First, at Jackson village, West Sumner, on the outlet of Pleasant pond; grist, saw, and shingle mill, carriage factory, rake factory, and machinery for hand-sleds. Morton & Bates, who employ 30 or 40 men. Grist mill operates the whole year, the other machinery not the whole year.

Second, "Powder Mill," on the west branch of the Twenty-Mile river, near the south part of the town.

Third, on the east branch of Twenty-Mile river, at Sumner flat; grist, shingle, and saw mills.

Fourth, on the outlet of Labrador pond; saw and grist mill.

Fifth, on the outlet stream of Shag pond, in the northwest part of the town; saw, grist, shingle and clapboard mills; the pond is in Woodstock.

SURRY—HANCOCK COUNTY.

From Selectmen's Statement.

Nine Powers.

On the outlet stream of the Upper and Lower Patten's ponds, 3,800 acres; four miles from the lower pond to sea-shore, the descent in that distance being, as is estimated, 212 feet.

None of the nine sites have a "head and fall" of less than 11 feet, and one has a fall of 30 feet, 15 feet of which are perpendicular and at a point where the stream is but 22 feet wide. It is easy of access, and is one of the best unoccupied privileges in the State.

Three of the sites only are occupied, the proprietors not having been willing to sell; it is now in the market.

By constructing a dam some miles below the lower pond, at the foot of a great meadow, a reservoir at small cost could be made to hold an unfailing supply of water during the severest drouth.

The storage of six feet depth upon six square miles of reservoir, would give over 2,000 horse-power, gross, upon a fall 212 feet, for the working hours of the year, or 80,000 spindles.

Patten's bay, one of the best of harbors, is the outlet of said stream.

Hon. Charles J. Abbott, Castine, is the agent for the proprietors.

Swan's Island Plantation—Hancock County.

From Assessors' Returns.

Two Powers.

First, on the east side of the island, formerly a grist mill, during the rainy season.

Second, at "Cold Harbor;" a tide power; mean rise of the tide 12 feet; pond 40 acres; formerly grist and saw mill; now vessels pass through the dam, drawing 12 feet of water.

No part of the power is improved.

Swanville—Waldo County.

From Selectmen's Returns.

Three Powers.

First, "Swanville Mills," on the outlet stream of Swan lake (Goose pond on the State map); fall 10 feet; stone and cement dam; saw mill owned by the Belfast Paper Mill Company, and worked only when the paper mills need water, the lake serving as a reservoir to said mills. Power sufficient to drive an up-and-down saw all the year. The lake contains three square miles.

Second, "Nickerson's Saw Mill," on Dead brook; fall seven feet; operates six months.

Third "Mardin's Privilege," on the same stream; unimproved; fall nine feet.

No damage from freshets; Swan lake rises and falls about four feet. Two small ponds, also, connected with the streams.

There is no ledge near either dam; dams are built in "pin" gravel; basin one-fourth wooded.

Market, Belfast, by road.

Sweden—Oxford County.

From Selectmen's Statement.

Two Powers.

First, the "Stearns Pond Privilege;" fall 25 feet in 50 rods; the power is not improved. There is an old dam, formerly saw and grist mill; capable of running a grist mill all the year and a saw mill half the year.

Second, "Keyes Pond Privilege;" fall 150 feet in 75 rods; power not improved; an old dam; no buildings; estimated equal to the First.

Ponds could be raised three or four feet at trifling expense.

Rocks, coarse granite, suitable for building purposes; lay of the land excellent for the erection of mills.

Market, Portland, by Grand Trunk Railroad from South Paris.

TALMADGE TOWNSHIP—WASHINGTON COUNTY.

Statement of Peol Tomah of Indian Township.

Several Powers.

Located on Tomah stream, the outlet of Tomah ponds. The ponds cover one to two square miles, one is dammed and the other two can be readily.

Also on the east Musquash stream, the outlet of Musquash lake, which covers 1.25 square miles, and is dammed seven feet.

Also on the west Musquash stream, the outlet of west Musquash lake, which covers three square miles, and is dammed four feet.

Large tracts of low land on the streams above the falls, which can be made great mill-ponds. Abundant water can be had at all seasons, and good locations for dams and mills.

An excellent power on the Musquash stream about midway the township, formerly used, mill now burned; 12 feet fall.

TAUNTON AND RAYNHAM ACADEMY GRANT—SOMERSET COUNTY.

Statement of Heman Whipple, Esq., of Solon.

Three Powers.

First, on Moose river; fall 10 feet, half mile below the lake. Enormous reservoirs above, so that an unlimited supply of water can be had.

Second, on Misery stream, about five miles from the lake, a fall of eight feet; dam. Large lake above, dammed.

Third, on Western outlet, a fall of eight feet, more fall can be had by a dam. Two or three reservoir ponds. The outlet is dammed at its head.

TEMPLE—FRANKLIN COUNTY.

From Selectmen's Returns.

Five Powers.

First, on a branch of Temple stream, saw mill, 20,000 a year, might four times that amount; 12 feet fall.

Second, on the outlet of the Staples pond, which might be made to hold more water at small expense. Privilege not in use now; formerly threshing mill.

Third, on the main Temple stream, "Temple Mills;" grist and saw; fall 11 feet; grist mill runs the year round; saw mill cuts 250,000 per annum, operates six months.

Fourth, at Temple mills, a very good privilege; not now used; formerly a starch factory.

Fifth, one-fourth of a mile below, grist, threshing, rake, lath, shingle, and other machinery; fall 12 feet.

Thomaston—Knox County.

Statement of the Selectmen.

Three Powers.

First, the "Lower Dam," on Mill river, grist and stave mills.

Second, "Clark's Mill," two miles above, stave and grist mills; stream fed by the Chickawakie pond.

Third, on Oyster river, a tide power, with a flowage back of three miles, and an average tide rise of about nine feet; width of river from 100 to 150 feet. Mills could be run 16 hours out of 24. By building a dam 15 feet high, they could be run most of the year with fresh water. Privilege not occupied.

Thorndike—Waldo County.

Statement of Joseph Higgins, Esq.

Three Powers, or More.

Small, operate only three or four months in the year, up-and-down saws, and three shingle machines.

Thorndike Township—Somerset County.

From a Plan in possession of St. John Smith, Esq., of Portland.

Six Powers.

Four on the Lower Churchill stream, the outlet of the Churchill ponds, which cover about two square miles.

First, at the outlet of the largest pond a dam four feet high might be built to give a head of four feet over the largest two ponds, there being three closely connected.

Second, at the outlet of a small pond half a mile below the above, a dam might be built to raise a considerable head of water (the banks being high) and flow a swamp surrounding the pond; three-fourths of a mile square of reservoir might be secured at this place.

Third, about a mile below, a dam might be built giving a good head of water. There is no pond at this point or opportunity for artificial reservoir of much capacity.

Fourth, above the falls at the south line of the town, "Clark's Dam," used for log-driving purposes.

Fifth, on the "East Branch" of Lower Churchill stream (not represented on the State map) which enters the stream north of the centre of the town and which is fed by two ponds covering together about a square mile, at the outlet of the upper pond, a good site for a dam.

Sixth, below, and three-fourths of a mile above the mouth of the branch, and at the outlet of a second pond, a good site for a dam. This dam would flow a large swamp bordering the pond and give a large body of water.

None of the above dams would be difficult or expensive to construct.

The whole township covered with valuable timber.

TOMHEGAN TOWNSHIP—SOMERSET COUNTY.

Statement of Heman Whipple, Esq., of Solon.

Two Powers.

Two or more falls on Tomhegan stream. One dam. Stream fed by Tomhegan pond, which covers 0.50 square miles. Pond can be raised six or eight feet.

TOPSFIELD—WASHINGTON COUNTY.

From Selectmen's Returns.

Five Powers.

First, "Eaton's Privilege," on East Musquash stream; fall ten and a half feet in 30 rods; fed by Musquash lake, two and a half by one miles; not improved.

Second, "Farrer's Mill," on Farrer's stream, the outlet of Farrer's lake; fall 66 feet in 200 rods; a saw mill which supplies local demand; operates six months. Lake two by one-half miles.

A dam at the outlet of Musquash lake flows seven feet for log-driving purposes. Dams can be built cheaply on Farrer's stream. Total range of water never over three feet.

Three small powers; no details.

TOPSHAM—SAGADAHOC COUNTY.

Statement of Warren Johnson, Esq.

[See also "Brunswick and Topsham."]

Four Powers.

On Cathance river; the lower is of considerable size and volume, the others are small.

TOWNSHIP No. 4, R. 3—AROOSTOOK COUNTY.

Statement of E. F. Dinsmore, Esq., of Island Falls Plantation.

Several Powers.

First, at the outlet of Mattawamkeag lake, judged equal in every respect to "that at Hartland on the Sebasticook." The supply of water can be made practically unlimited for all the purposes of extensive manufacturing. Vast quantities of lumber in all the region remain to be worked up. The dam raises a head of 12 feet. The lake is fed by a large number of streams and ponds, and receives the surplus drainage of a large extent of country. It is a reservoir of first-class excellence. Its area is from 5.50 to six square miles.

Second, Third, Fourth, Fifth, etc., situated at the outlet and on the outlet stream of Pleasant lake, which covers 3.50 square miles. The fall is not less than 80 feet in as many rods, affording sites for the use of the water several times over. There is a dam at the outlet of the lake, raising a head of several feet. The lake can be flowed many feet. It is fed by large streams which are themselves fed by lakes and ponds, and can therefore be made a reservoir of the utmost value.

Vast quantities of lumber of hard and soft wood remain in the region.

All unimproved.

TOWNSHIP No. 8, R. 3—AROOSTOOK COUNTY.

Statement of H. O. Hussey, Esq., of Monticello.

Several Powers.

On the Meduxnakeag river. Small ponds for reservoirs; abundant lumber.

Unimproved.

TOWNSHIPS NOS. 7 AND 7, RANGES 3 AND 4—AROOSTOOK COUNTY.

Statement of W. H. Rowe, Esq., of Masardis.

Several Powers.

On the main inlet, tributary to the St. Croix lake at its south end. Stream fed by two or three ponds above.

Not improved.

TOWNSHIP NO. 3, R. 4—AROOSTOOK ,COUNTY.

Statement of E. F. Dinsmore, Esq., of Island Falls Plantation.

One Power.

On the outlet stream of Caribou lake, a very fine privilege, with, "as is reported," a fall of 20 feet. "Several square miles of flowage above" are to be had. The flowage of the *lake* alone, as represented upon the State map, would not exceed two square miles.

Not improved.

TOWNSHIP NO. 7, R. 4—AROOSTOOK COUNTY.

Statement of W. H. Rowe, Esq., of Masardis.

Several Powers.

On the Tracy brook, the outlet stream of Tracy lake. Said lake covers 1.30 square miles and can be made a good reservoir by a dam.

Unimproved.

TOWNSHIP NO. 8, R. 4—AROOSTOOK COUNTY.

Statement of W. H. Rowe, Esq., of Masardis.

Several Powers.

First, on the Masardis stream, or St. Croix river of the Aroostook, half a mile below the outlet of the St. Croix lake. The dam is at the head of the falls and flows the lake three or four feet. Stream fed by several square miles of lakes and ponds, all of which can be used for storage.

Not improved.

Second, Third, etc., on Howe brook, tributary to the St. Croix lake, on the east side, about one and a half miles above the outlet of the lake. Stream fed by Howe pond.

Not improved.

Township No. 9, R. 4—Aroostook County.

Statement of W. H. Rowe, Esq., of Masardis.

One Power.

On the Masardis stream, or St. Croix river of the Aroostook. Stream fed by the St. Croix, Tracy, and other ponds, all of which can be dammed for reservoirs. Great supply of water.

Not improved.

Township No. 10, R. 4—Aroostook County.

Statement of W. H. Rowe, Esq., of Masardis.

One Power.

On Black-Water brook; five miles of dead water can be flowed three or four feet.

Not improved.

Township No. 14, R. 6—Aroostook County.

Statement of Daniel Barker, Esq., of Bangor.

Several Powers.

The thoroughfare at upper and lower portions thereof between Portage and Eagle lakes is principally dead water, but midway is quick water over ledges of limestone and conglomerate four miles. River clay in sufficient quantity to make bricks. Unimproved.

Two branches of Beaver brook on east side of town, with fair water-power on each. Old driving dams, 75 feet length and five or six feet height, flow large tracts of low land. No other improvement.

Mosquito brook in southwest quarter of town, two rods wide, with high, steep banks. Power sufficient to drive mills most of the season. Unimproved.

At mouth of Portage lake, site for dam 200 feet long five feet high.

Large tract of bog land near the lake. Whole flowage thereupon two square miles. Large part of soil good farming. Spruce and cedar abundant.

Unimproved.

Township No. 12, R. 8—Aroostook County.

Statement of Daniel Barker, Esq., of Bangor.

Several Powers.

Dam at Machias lake 100 feet long and 12 feet high, would flow two square miles; now improved for driving; banks good.

Twenty-Mile brook empties into Machias lake just above dam on north side; is about four rods wide with high steep banks and rapid water. Two good sites within one mile of lake. One at crossing of Allaguash road. Unimproved.

Township well timbered, with much good farming land.

TOWNSHIP NO. 18, R. 10—AROOSTOOK COUNTY.

Statement of William Dickey, Esq., of Fort Kent.

One Power, or More.

The power at the mouth of the St. Francis river is very superior. Thirty feet head can be had by suitable improvement; and the lakes and ponds above, all of which are susceptible of use as reservoirs, will furnish a copious supply of water at all seasons.

No improvement.

TOWNSHIP NO. 13, R. 14—AROOSTOOK COUNTY.

Statement of Daniel Barker, Esq.

Three Powers.

Two good powers on the main St. John river; rapids quite strong; bank on east side of river very high and steep; west bank rises gradually. Would require dam 20 rods long; water could be used twice in a half mile. River large at this point and the powers first-class.

On Moose brook in southeast corner of town, a power sufficient for small machinery the larger part of the season.

All unimproved.

TOWNSHIP NO. 14, R. 14—AROOSTOOK COUNTY.

Statement of Daniel Barker, Esq.

Two Powers.

"Priestly Rapids," principal powers in this town; from one-half to three-fourths mile long, quick and rough; ledge bottom and banks, with channel of river from eight to ten rods wide. Water sufficient in all seasons. Fall sufficient for two dams in a hundred rods that would control the whole river.

This has been one of the greatest pine-timber towns in the county, and has now an almost inexhaustible quantity of coarse pine and other timber.

Unimproved.

Township No. 15, R. 14—Aroostook County.

Statement of Daniel Barker, Esq.

Numerous Powers.

On Big-Black river eight or ten strong rapids. The series of ledges which causes these rapids is no doubt the same as that in the main St. John river called "Big Black Rapids." Bottom and banks mostly ledge, and all excellent powers. River six rods wide. Large flow of water at all times.

Priestly brook, a stream three rods wide, has fall sufficient for five or six different sites. These are all small powers and would answer only in the season of high water.

All unimproved.

Township No. 12, R. 15—Aroostook County.

Statement of Daniel Barker, Esq.

Five Powers.

Near the centre of the town on the main St. John river is a very excellent power; river rather wide and rapids long, but an abundance of water. Fall sufficient for two sites.

Near the north line of the town is another power of about the same magnitude; river very rapid but smooth.

A brook with two small ponds comes in on the west side of the river near this point, which would afford two or more small powers; stream narrow and rapid but not large.

All unimproved.

Township No. 13, R. 15—Aroostook County.

Statement of Daniel Barker, Esq.

Five Powers, and More.

First, on the main St. John river below Seven Islands. Dam could be raised 10 or 12 feet, and flow slack water about Seven Islands and be made to control the whole river.

Second and Third, on Depot stream, in the northwest corner of the town; stream quite large and rapid, with slack places; two good sites might be improved; stream fed by a large pond. This stream is a branch of Big-Black river.

Fourth and Fifth, etc., on a small stream running through the middle of the town into the main river; stream small and rapid; could be improved in three or four different places, but would probably lack water in the dry season.

All unimproved.

TOWNSHIP No. 14, R. 15—AROOSTOOK COUNTY.

Statement of Daniel Barker, Esq.

Two Powers.

This town is mostly low and water sluggish. Two small rapids on Depot stream or south branch of Big Black, are all the falls of any account; situated in the southwest part of the town; are large enough for all purposes of saw-mill improvement.

Unimproved.

TOWNSHIP No. 15, R. 15—AROOSTOOK COUNTY.

Statement of Daniel Barker, Esq.

Several Powers.

On east branch of Big Black; it is all rapid water from the boundary three miles down the stream. Banks most of the distance quite high. Could be improved many times within the distance. Stream is not large, but sufficient for most of the season.

All unimproved.

TOWNSHIP No. 11, R. 16—AROOSTOOK COUNTY.

Statement of Daniel Barker, Esq.

Several Powers.

The main St. John river passes through this town from southwest to northeast, is very rapid, with good banks and rather narrow bed, and fall sufficient for six or eight good powers.

The river is quite uniform in its course, and the several sites nearly equal in power and cost of improvement. Should consider the town superior to any other in the vicinity, for extent of power.

Much sapling and other timber in the township.

Privileges all unimproved.

TOWNSHIP No. 12, R. 16—AROOSTOOK COUNTY.

Statement of Daniel Barker, Esq.

Several Powers.

Three good powers on the main St. John river, and one on Nine-mile brook. Those on the river are first-class powers; banks high and good, and water abundant.

That on Nine-mile brook is sufficient to drive a common saw mill; the descent is very rapid, and brook narrow; could be improved at moderate cost. The brook is formed from four or five branches each sufficiently large for small machinery.

Privileges all unimproved.

Township No. 13, R. 16—Aroostook County.

Statement of Daniel Barker, Esq.

Four Powers.

On Depot stream, a branch of Big Black river. At the head of the stream is a lake three miles long. An old dam about five feet high; rapid water below dam. Fall suitable for two powers.

Also in northeast corner of town on same stream, two rapids, each making a good power.

Stream is not large, but has slack places for reservoirs and would be considered a fair stream in any settled town.

Water might fail in the dry season.

All unimproved.

Township No. 14, R. 16—Aroostook County.

Statement of Daniel Barker, Esq.

Four Powers, or More.

Depot stream, very rapid; water can be used two or three times, though it runs but a short distance in the town.

On Middle branch are two rapids each constituting a very excellent power. A saw mill has been in operation many years on this stream, on the Canada side. The stream is narrow, with steep banks, and could be improved at little cost. Should consider the powers abundant for spring and fall.

Privileges unimproved, save one.

Township No. 7, R. 17—Aroostook County.

Statement of Daniel Barker, Esq.

Numerous Powers.

One good site on Carry branch in southwest quarter of town; fall ten feet.

Half a mile below the head of "Sline Rapids," three miles long; banks high, water could be used many times, with a good head at each site. A small lake above the head of the rapids.

Another good fall at outlet of Baker lake; dam 300 feet long and six feet high will flow lake; area of lake 4.5 square miles.

On same stream, below, near town line, two other falls with good banks. These last two sites are thought to be the best in the town. Also a long stretch of rapids.

Township well covered with timber of all kinds.

All unimproved.

TOWNSHIP No. 8, R. 17—AROOSTOOK COUNTY.

Statement of Daniel Barker, Esq.

Four Powers.

Three good sites near the south part of the town on the Woolastaquaguam river; four or five miles of dead water above the falls; a good head can be obtained at either site with a short dam.

On Turner brook, half mile above the mouth, is a fall, very steep, with excellent banks. This stream is quite large, and would afford water most of the season. Town well timbered.

Privileges unimproved.

TOWNSHIP No. 9, R. 17—AROOSTOOK COUNTY.

Statement of Daniel Barker, Esq.

Fifteen Powers, or More.

In this town the Boundary branch forms a junction with Baker-lake branch. On the Boundary branch, above the junction, are as many as seven good mill sites. There are also two or three falls on Baker branch, and three on main branch below the junction, in all as many as fourteen or fifteen good mill sites. The town seems covered with fine water-powers almost the whole length of the river.

All unimproved.

TOWNSHIP No. 10, R. 17—AROOSTOOK COUNTY.

Statement of Daniel Barker, Esq.

Several Powers.

Water in this town somewhat sluggish except near the north line. Here is a rapid fall and a very fine power; water could be used many times over; river not very wide; banks high.

The rapids extend along the line between the two towns for some miles. Water abundant at all seasons. Town well timbered.

All unimproved.

TOWNSHIP No. 11, R. 17—AROOSTOOK COUNTY.

Statement of Daniel Barker, Esq.

Numerous Powers.

The Northwest branch runs southeasterly through this town, and forms a series of rapids almost the entire distance from the lake at the boundary to its confluence with the main St. John river. This is a very fine stream with high banks and rapid current, about three rods wide.

Scarce a half mile can be found without sufficient fall for a good power.

The lake at the boundary would be sufficiently large for a reservoir through the dry season.

Privileges all unimproved.

Township No. 8, R. 18—Aroostook County.

Statement of Daniel Barker, Esq.

Several Powers.

On the Southeast branch, Rapids about two miles long, can be improved in many places with little cost, and for small machinery.

Unimproved.

Township No. 7, R. 19—Aroostook County.

Statement of Daniel Barker, Esq.

Several Powers.

Good rapid on Boundary branch, two miles from north line of town. Water could be used two or three times over in the distance of a mile. The stream is swift the whole length of the town.

The sites in this town are too many to enumerate, but they are all small powers, as they are so near the sources of the river.

Unimproved.

Township No. 8, R. 19—Aroostook County.

Statement of Daniel Barker, Esq.

Several Powers.

On the Southeast and Boundary branches; each has sufficient rapids for two or three powers. The streams are not large, but have a very steady flow of water; are generally boatable as long as the river below. Powers are capable of driving any common mill machinery.

An abundance of timber on the township.

Unimproved.

TOWNSHIP No. 3, R. 1—FRANKLIN COUNTY.

Statement of Abner Toothaker, Esq., of Phillips.

Several Powers.

First, on South Bog stream, two miles above Rangely lake, pond just above, which covers 200 acres, and can be flowed several feet.

Second, Third, etc.; the stream is swift for the whole distance to the lake, and can be used for power advantageously.

All unimproved.

TOWNSHIP No. 3, R. 4—FRANKLIN COUNTY.

Statement of Abner Toothaker, Esq., of Phillips.

One Power, or More.

First, on the Kennebago river, half mile below the Kennebago pond, a fall of 25 feet can be had, abrupt; ledgy bottom and banks, excellent site for mills. Pond covers four square miles and can be flowed several feet. It is a most admirable privilege.

Stream in the upper part of the township is rapid, with eight small ponds about the head waters above, which can be improved for reservoirs.

All unimproved.

TOWNSHIP No. 1, R. 5—FRANKLIN COUNTY.

Statement of Hon. Abner Coburn.

Two Powers.

On Dead river, not far from midway its course in the township, "Ledge Falls," 12 feet descent. A long stretch of quick water above to the Chain-pond dam.

Second, above, "Swampscot Falls," 10 feet, good site, large flowage.

Both unimproved.

TOWNSHIP No. 1, R. 6—FRANKLIN COUNTY.

Statement of Hon. Abner Coburn.

One Power.

On Dead river, "Chain-Pond Dam," at the outlet of the Chain ponds, eight feet high, ponds the water back over the whole series of ponds, covering five square miles, and thus reserves a large body of water.

Township No. 3—Hancock County.

Statement of J. W. Porter, Esq., of Burlington.

Nine Powers, or More.

The "Grand Falls" on the Passadumkeag river comprise and constitute four of the above, situated near the west line of the township, and extending about 200 rods, the total fall being about 100 feet. The lower pitch is nearly perpendicular, and has about 20 feet descent. From this point, inclusive, to the head of the series are a number of sites of unsurpassed excellence as respects either opportunity for dams, locations for mills, or for villages adjacent. They could have from 15 to 18 feet head each. There is a dam on the lower pitch, which gives a 20-foot head, and flows back not more than ten rods. No other improvement on the whole series of privileges. These powers are seven miles from Burlington Post Office, and 15 miles from the European & North American Railway.

There is an abundance of good building granite in the vicinity for construction purposes. The entire basin of the stream above, is covered with forests. Proprietors of the power, Thomas W. and R. R. Porter, of Burlington.

Settlement near the falls of about 100 inhabitants, mostly farmers. Soil in the region good. A county road is about completed from Burlington to the falls. Falls are within three miles of the proposed Milford & Burlington turnpike.

Fifth, Sixth, etc., "Nicatous Falls," on the outlet stream of Nicatous lake, and situated about a mile below the lake, extending about a half mile, and have a total fall of 40 feet.

Eighth, a dam at the outlet of Nicatous lake, gives a head of 10 feet storage over the whole lake. Used only for log-driving purposes.

Ninth, a dam at the outlet of the First Pistol lake, gives a head of six feet over the whole surface of 600 acres. Lake is fed by three lakes above which have a head of eight feet each, raised by one dam; used for log-driving only.

The extent of the reservoirs tributary to the "Grand Falls," as well as the others mentioned, may be seen upon reference to Part II, page 107.

TOWNSHIP NO. 4—HANCOCK COUNTY.

Statement of J. W. Porter, Esq., of Burlington.

Two Powers.

First, at the outlet of Duck lake, a dam which raises a head of nine feet over the whole surface of the lake. Lake covers 1,200 acres or more.

Second, a dam at the outlet of the Second Pistol lake, flows the three upper lakes eight feet. Lakes have an area of over 300 acres combined.

TOWNSHIP NO. 7—HANCOCK COUNTY.

[West of Steuben.]

Statement of J. D. Parker, Esq., of Steuben.

One Power.

On West-Bay stream, not at present improved.

TOWNSHIP NO 10—HANCOCK COUNTY.

[West of Cherryfield.]

From the Statement of J. D. Parker, Esq.

Five Powers.

First, at the outlet of Downing's pond, head 10 feet, two mills.

Second, on Bog brook, head eight feet or more.

Third, on Spring river, head eight feet, and three or four feet fall.

Fourth, at the outlet of Long pond, head 13 feet.

Fifth, at the outlet of Big Tunk pond, 11 feet 5 inches head, 13 feet can be had.

Mostly unimproved.

TOWNSHIP NO. 35—HANCOCK COUNTY.

Statement of J. W. Porter, Esq., of Burlington.

One Power.

At the outlet of Coombs' pond, a dam which flows the lake five feet, lake covers 100 acres.

TOWNSHIP NO. 40—HANCOCK COUNTY.

Statement of J. W. Porter, Esq.

One Power.

At the outlet of West or Abamgamook lake, a dam which raises a head of seven feet over the whole lake. Lake covers 500 acres.

TOWNSHIP NO. 41—HANCOCK COUNTY.

Statement of J. W. Porter, Esq.

One Power.

At the outlet of Garbeus lake, a dam which raises a six-foot head over the entire lake. Lake covers 600 acres or more.

TOWNSHIP NO. 5, R. 2—OXFORD COUNTY.

From the Statement of John H. Wilson, Esq., of South Columbia, N. H.

Several Powers.

"Ariscoos Falls," on the Magalloway river, are situated near the centre of the township, extending along the river nearly two miles. Mills have been built at the foot of the falls; but are now gone or dilapidated. The dam, at this point, can be raised to the height of 15 feet, if necessary.

About a mile above the dam is a sudden pitch of eight or ten feet with a ledge on the right bank and bottom, and a steep bank on the left, admitting a head and fall of about 18 feet, with an opportunity for a canal below on either side.

Near the head of the falls the river drops 80 or 90 feet in 60 or 70 rods, an island extending that distance, which leaves a broad deep gulch along the right bank. On this bank a canal can be made, on one level, for more than half a mile, and the dam at the head of the island can be built at small expense.

At the head of the falls, 60 or 70 rods above the island, a dam eight feet high would check the water of the river more than 20 miles above, and could be raised to any desired hight by winging a short distance on each side.

The great volume of head water secured by this dam, together with the storage of lake Parmachenee and various ponds, would raise the constant power on these falls to a very high figure.

The Magalloway drains about 400 square miles, or 44 per cent. more than the Little Androscoggin. A bridge crosses the river at the foot of the falls.

TOWNSHIP NO. 2—PENOBSCOT COUNTY.

[West of Mattawamkeag.]

One Power.

On Eber-horse stream, a shingle mill and clapboard mill.

TOWNSHIP No. 3, R. 1—PENOBSCOT COUNTY.

[Next east of Burlington.]

Statement of J. W. Porter, Esq., of Burlington.

One Power.

A dam at the outlet of the upper Madagascal lake, flows its surface of 100 acres, six feet.

TOWNSHIP No. 4, R. 1—PENOBSCOT COUNTY.

Statement of Peol Tomah of Indian Township.

Three Powers.

The Sysledobsissis outlet stream falls 30 feet, and affords three sites suitable for powers. The lake covers four square miles, is dammed three feet, and can be raised several feet more.

Unimproved.

TOWNSHIP No. 5, R. 1—PENOBSCOT COUNTY.

[Junior Lake Township.]

Statement of Peol Tomah.

Several Privileges.

The Junior-lake stream falls 10 feet from lake to lake.

There is a fall of 50 feet on the outlet stream of Mill-privilege lake. Good sites for dams, banks high. Lake covers three-fourths of a square mile, and is raised six feet.

There is a fall of 15 feet on the Shaw-lake outlet. Lake covers nearly two square miles and is raised three feet. A dam 60 rods below the lake.

Unimproved.

TOWNSHIP No. 3, R. 6—PENOBSCOT COUNTY.

Statement of John Gardner, Esq., of Patten.

Two Powers.

On Mud brook, a saw mill. "Probably other privileges above."

A power on Swift brook, two miles below the north line of the town. Small ponds above. Unimproved.

TOWNSHIP No. 2, R. 7—PENOBSCOT COUNTY.

Statement of Daniel Barker, Esq., of Bangor.

Two Powers.

Both situated on the Mattagamon or East branch of the Penobscot.

First, "Crowfoot Falls," two miles above Grindstone, five feet fall, river 15 or 20 rods wide.

Second, "Whetstone Falls," eight feet fall, river 15 rods wide, ledge bottom and banks.

These are both powers of the first magnitude. Water abundant at all seasons; easily controlled, and expense of improvement small for the amount of power obtained.

For reservoirs see Part II, page 108.

Unimproved.

Township No. 5, R. 7—Penobscot County.

From the Statement of G. H. Davis, Esq., of No. 6.

One Power.

"Outlet Falls," at the outlet of the lower Shin pond; a dam, seven rods long, would raise a head of 10 feet on the lake, and flow about 1,600 acres; pond is fed by the upper Shin pond in Monterey plantation. This is five miles from the Great falls below, on the Shin pond stream.

Unimproved.

Township No. 6, R. 7—Penobscot County.

From the Statement of G. H. Davis, Esq.

Three Powers.

The "Great Falls," on Shin Pond stream, the outlet of the Shin ponds, which cover nearly four square miles.

The falls are divided into three pitches, first two ten feet each, the third 35 feet in about 100 feet. A dam at the head of the first pitch would raise the head five feet more, giving 60 feet fall in a little over 100 feet run.

A storage of eight feet upon the two ponds would furnish 540 horse-power gross on the 60 feet fall, or 21,600 spindles, for the working hours of the year. This is the storage alone.

Unimproved.

Township No. 5, R. 8—Penobscot County.

Statement of Daniel Barker, Esq., of Bangor.

Three Powers.

All situated on the Mattagamon or east branch of the Penobscot.

First, "Bowlin Falls;" pitch eight feet, 15 rods wide, banks steep and ledgy.

Second, "Hulling Machine Falls," 12 feet descent, dam 50 feet long, channel cuts through deep ledges; can be easily improved and controlled.

Third, "Grand Falls;" 20 feet perpendicular pitch, width 30 feet, high ledgy banks.

These are the best privileges on the east branch of Penobscot, and are truly magnificent water-powers. The river is very narrow in the immediate pitches but widens into broad basins between, affording reservoirs for a steady flow of water at all seasons.

For reservoirs tributary to the river, see Part II, page 108.

All unimproved.

TOWNSHIP NO. 6, R. 8—PENOBSCOT COUNTY.

Statement of Daniel Barker, Esq.

Three Powers.

Situated on the Mattagamon river or east branch of the Penobscot.

First, "Pond Pitch;" nine feet fall, river 70 feet wide, ledgy.

Second, "Haskell Rock," 15 feet fall, eight rods wide.

Third, "Stair Falls;" 15 feet fall, six rods wide; fall composed of successive pitches, four or five feet each, over smooth ledges.

Five miles from this point is Grand lake; river very rapid the entire distance.

For reservoirs, see Part II, page 108.

The above powers are unsurpassed. All unimproved.

TOWNSHIPS NO. 2—PISCATAQUIS COUNTY; AND NO. 1, R. 7—SOMERSET COUNTY.

Statement of J. M. Haynes, Esq., of Augusta.

[See also "Township No. 1, R. 7, Somerset County."]

From the dam at the outlet of Moosehead lake to the head of Indian pond, a distance of five miles, the Kennebec river is extremely rapid. There is, at least, 125 feet fall. The bottom and sides of the river are mostly ledge and are rocky in all parts. The banks are high and abrupt, chiefly of ledge.

Three-fourths of a mile above the head of Indian pond is a site called "Ledge Falls," with excellent opportunity for dam and extensive development. At other points also, it is judged, mills could be located without extreme difficulty.

Privileges unimproved.

TOWNSHIP NO. 3—PISCATAQUIS COUNTY.

[Next west of Greenville.]

Statement of Caleb Holyoke, Esq., of Brewer.

A dam on the line of No. 3 flows the ponds above, four in number. Privileges on the stream below, that can be readily improved.

None are used.

TOWNSHIP NO. 2. R. 9—PISCATAQUIS COUNTY.

Statement of Daniel Barker, Esq., of Bangor.

Two Powers.

"Ambejejus Falls" and "Passamagamon (Passagamook) Falls," both upon the Penobscot river.

Ambejejus falls are about 160 rods long, very rough and broken.

Passamagamon falls 15 rods long, very rough and swift. A dam at the head of this fall can be made to flow Debskoneag lake.

Both of these are powers of the first magnitude. Unlimited supplies of water can be had at all seasons by the use of the scores of square miles of lakes and ponds above. See reservoirs of the Penobscot, page 109, from Ripogenus on.

Both unimproved.

TOWNSHIP NO. 6, R. 9—PISCATAQUIS COUNTY.

Statement of Daniel Barker, Esq.

Several Powers.

First and Second, on Webster stream, known as the "Main Falls," each from 10 to 15 feet perpendicular; the bed of the stream is very narrow with high perpendicular ledge banks. Few natural privileges surpass these in excellence. For reservoirs tributary to them, see last Table, page 110, Part II.

Third and Fourth, this reef of ledge extends across to the Mattagamon, or east branch of Penobscot river, where two other falls are formed.

None of these are used.

Fifth, Sixth, etc., two other streams (Boody brook and Trout brook) have each powers of considerable capacity. Dams for driving purposes have been built on each. "Trout Brook Farm" lies in this township.

TOWNSHIP NO. 2, R. 10—PISCATAQUIS COUNTY.

Statement of Daniel Barker, Esq.

Numerous Powers.

Several are situated on the Penobscot river.

First, Second, etc., "Debskoneag Falls," near the east line of the town, one mile long; all rough, swift water.

Third, "Pockwockamus Falls," above, three-fourths mile long; very rough.

Fourth, "Aboljackomegus Falls," 160 rods long; very rough; lower pitch exceedingly rugged and swift for 15 rods.

Fifth, "Sourdnahunk Falls," short, lower pitch eight feet perpendicular, upper pitch four feet; 40 rods of very rough water. Long reach of dead water above the falls for reservoir.

Sixth, Seventh, Eighth, etc., two streams; Aboljacknagesic and Aboljackarmeguscook flow down from Katahdin through this town, on beds of granite, and have as much fall and afford as much power as any streams in the State of corresponding size for the same distance.

The powers on the Penobscot are of the first magnitude, being furnished with reservoirs of vast capacity on the river above; scores of square miles of lakes and ponds can be flowed several feet at little or no expense. See page 109, from Ripogenus on, for reservoirs.

Privileges all unimproved.

TOWNSHIP NO. 3, R. 10—PISCATAQUIS COUNTY.

Statement of Daniel Barker, Esq.

Numerous Powers.

On the Sourdnahunk stream, a series of falls extending some four miles, with successive pitches from five to twenty feet high. Bottom and banks formed of abrupt ledges, and in many places the channel is narrowed up to a very few feet. Many wide basins between pitches suitable for reservoirs. One could hardly enumerate the number of powers in this distance. Sourdnahunk pond covers 3.75 square miles. In the easterly part of the town the two considerable streams (mentioned in No. 2, R. 10) flowing south from Katahdin mountain to the Penobscot river, have 10 or 12 powers to the mile. In many places the stream rushes through a channel of three or four feet width with a fall of 30 or 40 feet nearly perpendicular.

All unimproved.

Township No. 6, R. 10—Piscataquis County.

Statement of Daniel Barker, Esq.

Numerous Powers.

Several are situated on the outlet stream of Webster lake. Dam at the outlet is 400 feet long and 12 feet high, and controls all the water coming through Telos Cut. Surface of lake three square miles. Below the dam for the distance of three miles the stream is very rapid. Fall sufficient for a head every half mile. Near the east side of the town are two considerable falls over nearly perpendicular ledges. Bed of stream narrow, and easily controlled.

Wadleigh brook, Hudson brook, Braley brook and Thissell brook have each, one or more powers with sufficient water for common saw or grist mills. These streams have all been driven, and two of them (Hudson and Wadleigh brooks) have dams with large reservoirs.

For reservoirs tributary to the Webster stream, see last Table, page 110.

Privileges not used.

Township No. 7, R. 10—Piscataquis County.

Statement of Daniel Barker, Esq.

Several Powers.

On the Mattagamon or Penobscot east branch in this town, are four first-class powers.

First and Second, situated below Third lake, the river breaking over perpendicular ledges six or seven feet high; narrow channel; short dams only required.

At Third lake a dam 200 feet long and 12 feet high controls the lake and its tributaries; lake covers about two square miles.

Fourth, one mile above the lake, a ledge fall of five or six feet, with a dam flowing a large flat tract above.

Fifth, Sixth, etc., Braley brook, Snake brook, and Turner brook, tributaries of the East branch, and Aroostook brook, a branch of Aroostook river, are each sufficiently large for water powers, and have had dams constructed for driving purposes.

This town contains a large amount of timber and some good soil.

Privileges not used.

TOWNSHIP NO. 8, R. 10—PISCATAQUIS COUNTY.

Statement of Daniel Barker, Esq.

Fifty Powers, or More.

This town has three streams running through it sufficiently large to drive mill machinery, with ponds at the head of each. The streams are very rapid, rising on the high lands and falling so precipitously as to render them difficult driving. There are no doubt 50 small but excellent powers on the three streams ; in some places seven or eight may be found within the space of a mile.

The main lake in this town has no fall at the outlet.

Privileges all unimproved.

TOWNSHIP NO. 3, R. 11—PISCATAQUIS COUNTY.

Statement of Daniel Barker, Esq.

Twenty-Five Powers, or More.

All are situated on the Penobscot river.

First to Tenth, inclusive, the "Horse Race," no steep pitch, but a continuous and rapid descent for two miles, with sufficient fall for 8 or 10 powers in the distance. Hard bottom and high banks for the most part.

Eleventh, Twelfth, Thirteenth and Fourteenth, "Ambajemackomus Falls," next above, half mile long, and very rough. One mile of quick water above this to "Little Ambajemackomus Falls," which extend a hundred rods.

Fifteenth, Sixteenth, Seventeenth, etc., etc., the "Ripogenus Falls," three miles of Niagara ! This surpasses all description. Whole fall, 215 feet, over a rough bed of slate and quartz rock, with perpendicular banks rising in some places 50 or 75 feet above the water. Near the foot the river is divided into three channels, with banks 20 feet high, one channel making a perpendicular fall of 20 feet, and the others rushing on in a series of pitches to the junction below where all unite and make another perpendicular fall of many feet.

An almost unlimited supply of water can be held upon the lakes and ponds above ; these are already used for the storage of water for log-driving purposes. See page 109, from Ripogenus on.

Privileges unimproved.

Township No. 4, R. 11—Piscataquis County.

Statement of Daniel Barker, Esq.

Two Powers.

One on Wadleigh brook, stream two rods wide, banks high, and large flowage. The stream is formed from two considerable branches, each of which has been driven and had dams for that purpose. The principal power is on main brook just below the forks.

Another power on Soudnahunk stream near its exit from the town. Stream four rods wide, with granite bed and smooth falls, three or four feet to a rod. Water above, sluggish, and land low. A large lake at the head of the stream covering three square miles.

Both unimproved.

Township No. 5, R. 11—Piscataquis County.

Statement of Daniel Barker, Esq.

Six Powers, or More.

This town is situated on the height of land between Allaguash and east and west branches of Penobscot river. Water drains from the centre in all directions, crossing each of its exterior lines.

Thissell brook in the northeast corner, and a small stream flowing into Telos lake near the center of the town, are each sufficiently large for common mill privileges. The latter stream has high banks, is very rapid, and could be used four or five times within the distance of a mile from the mouth.

Telos brook in the northeast corner of the town has one good power; dam nearly new, 50 feet long and eight feet high. A small pond on one branch of the stream above. Water very rapid below the dam.

Privileges unimproved.

Township No. 6, R. 11—Piscataquis County.

Statement of Daniel Barker, Esq.

Six Powers.

First, Second and Third, the principal power in this town is at Telos cut. Dam 125 feet, head 12 feet. Length of cut from Telos to Webster lake, about 200 rods, with a fall of 50 feet. This water could be used three or four times over in the length of the cut with a head six or eight feet at each dam. For reservoirs see last Table, page 110.

Fourth, Fifth and Sixth, in the southeast corner of the town. Telos brook flows into Telos lake. Has a dam one mile from the lake 80 feet long and eight feet head; brook very swift below the dam. Has fall sufficient for two other sites below. These powers (on the brook) are small and would fail in mid summer.

Privileges not used.

TOWNSHIP No. 7, R. 11—PISCATAQUIS COUNTY.

Statement of Daniel Barker, Esq.

Numerous Powers.

First, at outlet of Fourth lake; dam 60 by 12 feet; flows 500 acres.

Second, on a small branch coming into north side of Fourth lake. Dam 75 feet by 10; flows a mile square of pond and bog; 100 rods of rapids from dam to Fourth lake.

Third, Fourth, Fifth, etc., three miles below Fourth lake, a chain of rapids and falls capable of driving a large amount of machinery.

Sixth, at outlet of Snake pond; dam 50 by 7 feet; pond about one mile square.

Seventh, at foot of Big Leadbetter pond; dam 125 by 10 feet; flows three-fourths of a square mile.

Privileges not used.

TOWNSHIP No. 8, R. 11—PISCATAQUIS COUNTY.

Statement of Daniel Barker, Esq.

Four Powers.

First, on Smith brook, at foot of Pockwockhamock lake; dam 50 feet at bed of stream, and can be carried to any height by extending length; can flow lake three miles long and one mile wide; lake fed by springs from mountains and never fails in summer.

Second, on north branch below Pillsbury pond, dam 125 feet, eight feet high; flows one and a half square miles of pond and low land; dam partially burnt.

Third, about one mile below the pond, a steep ledgy fall, channel narrow and banks high; low flat land above falls; a superior natural power.

Fourth, on Soper brook, old dam 40 feet, and 10 feet head; flows a large tract of flat land; may fail at low water.

One-third of town good soil. Timber abundant.

Privileges unused.

TOWNSHIP NO 4, R. 12—PISCATAQUIS COUNTY.

Statement of Daniel Barker, Esq.

Several Powers.

This township has two streams,—Red brook and Ripogenus stream, each large enough for common mill privileges. Red brook, four miles from the mouth, has a low flat space of dead water for reservoir, and another two miles higher where dams have been built for driving. At the lower place, bed of stream two rods wide and seven feet head.

Ripogenus stream is about three rods wide, is fed from numerous ponds, has many falls sufficient for good water-power. The principal site is at the foot of a long reach of dead water with rapids below, four or five miles from the mouth. Here a dam with 10 to 12 feet head has been built for driving purposes and affords a great supply of water.

A large amount of timber in this vicinity.

Privileges unused.

TOWNSHIP NO. 5, R. 12—PISCATAQUIS COUNTY.

Statement of Daniel Barker, Esq.

Four Powers.

Three are situated on Cussabexis stream.

First, in the southeast part of the town, improved for driving purposes; dam 100 feet long, 10 feet high; low flat land half mile above; banks gravelly.

Second, in north half of township, at foot of a long tract of dead water; dam 150 feet long, six feet high; flows the stream from two to three miles.

Third, at foot of lake; dam 75 feet long and six feet high; will flow one mile square.

Fourth, on Duck pond, in southwest quarter of township; dam built recently; 75 feet long, eight high; flows some two miles of pond; located in thick pine timber. Larger portion of soil poor.

Privileges used only for storage.

TONWSHIP No. 6, R. 12—PISCATAQUIS COUNTY.

Statement of Daniel Barker, Esq.

Three Powers.

First, old dam on Doddle brook, 50 feet long, eight feet high; flows 400 or 500 acres low land; stream not large.

Second, at outlet of Mud pond, dam 100 feet long, six feet high; flows pond and low land say two square miles; banks hard pan. Stream from Mud pond to Chamberlain lake (about half a mile) very rapid.

Third, 80 rods below the pond, dam 80 feet long, eight feet high; dam cut away. Water sufficient for the season. Township heavily timbered with pine, spruce and juniper. Soil poor.

Privileges used only for storage.

TOWNSHIP No. 7, R. 12—PISCATAQUIS COUNTY.

Statement of Daniel Barker, Esq.

Six Powers.

First, at outlet of Indian pond, dam 60 feet long, six feet high; nearly decayed; flowage, 2,000 acres, mostly pond. Pond lies on the back side of Chamberlain farm.

Second, on Little Leadbetter brook, pond half mile by a mile; old dam at outlet, 75 feet long, eight feet head; banks good. Half a mile of quick water between this pond and Chamberlain lake.

Third and Fourth, two other dams formerly built on this stream, 50 or 60 rods apart, about the same size as that at the pond; both now decayed. All three sites good except in drouth of summer.

Fifth and Sixth, on Big Leadbetter; one dam near the mouth, 100 feet long, 10 feet high; flows three-quarter square mile of bog land. Upper site near east line of town, nearly but not quite so large. Both dams partially decayed. Sapling pine near these streams, too much to estimate.

Unimproved.

TOWNSHIP No. 8, R. 12—PISCATAQUIS COUNTY.

Statement of Daniel Barker, Esq.

Three Powers.

First, on Smith brook, two miles above the mouth. Rapids 80 rods long with high banks and narrow channel at the head. Old dam 50 feet long, 12 feet high; can be carried much higher; flows some three square miles of low land. Water abundant.

Second, on Soper brook, half mile above mouth; fall six feet over ledge bottom; bed of stream 40 feet, banks rise to any height; low meadow land for two or three miles above the falls.

Third, at Soper pond, near east line of town; pond one mile square, and has as much more low land around it that could be flowed. Old dam 50 feet long, 10 feet high; banks very high.

Township mostly timber land.

Privileges used only for storage.

Township No. 9, R. 12—Piscataquis County.

Statement of Daniel Barker, Esq.

Two Powers.

First, on South Twin stream at outlet of lake, and two miles from Churchill lake. Old dam 75 feet long, eight feet head; flows one and one-half square miles of lake and low land; banks steep and good, and water rapid below.

Second, at outlet of Spider lake, which covers two square miles, and has two tributaries with small lakes at the head; dam 150 feet, five feet high; water rapid to Churchill lake.

Privileges used only for storage.

Township No. 10, R. 12—Piscataquis County.

Statement of Daniel Barker, Esq.

Numerous Powers.

The old dam at foot of Churchill lake, 700 feet long, 21 feet high, flows 20 miles across Churchill and Eagle lakes to Chamberlain Locks; dam mostly gone; bed of river and banks gravelly.

First, Second, Third, etc., "Rapids" below this dam for three-fourths of a mile, the fall 45 feet.

The waters of these lakes are inexhaustible. Ten large tributaries empty into them, each from 10 to 20 miles in length, and sufficient to drive any amount of machinery.

Fifth, Sixth, Seventh, etc., Harrow lake, in east part of the town, (some three miles long), flows into Allaguash river just below Churchill dam; has a good power at foot of lake, and four or five others along the stream below.

Privileges unused.

TOWNSHIP No. 5, R. 13—PISCATAQUIS COUNTY.

Statement of Daniel Barker, Esq.

Three Powers.

First, "Pine Stream Rapids," on the Penobscot river, three miles above Chesuncook lake, one of the best water-powers in the county; fall 12 or 15 feet in 100 rods; bed and banks of river solid ledge; channel 200 feet wide and a wide basin above the rips capable of holding a very great supply of water. The principal power is at the upper pitch, as the lower pitch is flowed out in the spring by the dam at foot of Chesuncook lake.

Second and Third, on the Cauquomgomoc stream, very superior powers; one a few rods above the mouth of the stream, or confluence with the Umbazooksus, and the other a mile or so further up.

These two falls are very much alike, each breaking over a perpendicular ledge 10 or 12 feet high, where, by a short dam, the whole volume of the stream could be controlled with ease. The stream is fed by a long chain of large lakes and has a great and constant supply of water.

There is a small settlement in this town at the head of Chesuncook lake.

Privileges all unused.

TOWNSHIP No. 6, R. 13—PISCATAQUIS COUNTY.

Statement of Daniel Barker, Esq.

Six Powers, or More.

Three are situated on the Umbazooksus stream. Longley pond, one mile by a mile and a half, at the head of the stream has an old dam at the outlet, 60 feet long, seven feet high. About a mile of quick water below this pond to Umbazooksus lake.

Umbazooksus lake is some three miles long; shores at outlet rather low; bed of stream 50 feet wide; height of banks five feet; bottom of lake sandy.

Two miles below the lake is a little portage 100 rods long; water in the stream very rapid; banks very steep and high, and the stream narrow.

A long space of dead water and low land above these rips. Should consider this much the best power in the town. Water might be used two or three times over in the 100 rods.

Chesuncook lake flows to the foot of these rapids.

Privileges unused.

TOWNSHIP NO. 7, R. 13—PISCATAQUIS COUNTY.

Statement of Daniel Barker, Esq.

Three Powers, or More.

The dams familiarly known as the "Chamberlain Lake Locks," are situated in the northeast quarter of this town, at the outlet of Chamberlain lake. Main dam 400 feet long, 12 feet high. Controls the waters of Chamberlain and Telos lakes (flowing back 20 miles to Telos cut) and all the head waters of Allaguash river. The lock dam is about 50 rods below this at the head of Eagle lake.

Ellis brook, taking rise in a chain of ponds on No. 7, R. 14, and running through this town into Chamberlain lake, has two very good powers. Two miles above the mouth a dam could be built at the foot of a long space of dead water that would flow two or three square miles of low bog land; width of stream about four rods; water very rapid below.

Half a mile from the mouth of the stream is a narrow channel with high banks where the water could be easily controlled, and a good power constructed at small cost, with abundant water for the season.

This town has a large amount of spruce, juniper and sapling pine.

Privileges used only for storage.

TOWNSHIP NO. 8, R. 13—PISCATAQUIS COUNTY.

Statement of Daniel Barker, Esq.

Twelve Powers, or More.

This town embraces a series of rapids on Allaguash river above Chamberlain lake.

First, "Main Fall," which breaks over a perpendicular ledge 15 feet high; small pond one-half mile square at head of falls. This is one of the finest natural powers on the river. All the dam necessary is across channel 25 feet wide through the solid ledge.

Second, just below the ledge, a large basin with an island in the channel at the foot, and a fall sufficient for another dam on either side the island. Width of either channel not over 75 feet.

Third, Fourth, and Fifth, still below this, three reefs of ledges with falls from three to seven feet, affording the whole power of the river by dams 75 or 100 feet each.

Sixth, Seventh, etc., main channel, below, very rapid to Chamberlain lake.

Eighth, Ninth, Tenth, etc., Russell brook, runs through the northwest quarter of the town into Eagle lake; is fed by a chain of ponds in adjoining towns; has a rapid current and narrow ledgy bed, and many nearly perpendicular falls of four or five feet. As many as five of these falls could be improved, and each command the whole power by a dam of 40 feet length.

Much of the soil in township is good for farming. One large farm on an island in Eagle lake, and two on main land, occupied for lumbering some years ago. Large amount of timber still on the town.

Privileges all unimproved.

TOWNSHIP No. 9, R. 13—PISCATAQUIS COUNTY.

Statement of Daniel Barker, Esq.

Numerous Powers.

Three large streams, Snare brook, Churchill brook and Thoroughfare brook, flow from west to east through this town into the lakes. Dams on each of these streams have been constructed for driving purposes. Scarce a half mile on either can be found without sufficient fall and banks for a good mill site. Water very rapid.

Soil fair for farming purposes. Timber abundant.

Privileges used only for storage.

TOWNSHIP No. 10, R. 13—PISCATAQUIS COUNTY.

Statement of Daniel Barker, Esq.

Five Powers, or More.

First, Second and Third, on the outlet stream of a large lake in the center of the town, said lake being three miles long and three-fourths mile wide. Stream at outlet very narrow and rapid with high steep banks. Dam 50 or 60 feet length would give any amount of flowage for manufacturing purposes. Fall sufficient to use the water two or three times over in the first half mile.

Fourth, Fifth, etc., small powers on Thoroughfare brook in southwest corner of the town. Stream two rods wide, good banks, and slack places for flowage, with rapids below.

Soil mostly poor. Large amount of spruce and pine.

Privileges unused.

Township No. 3, R. 14—Piscataquis County.

Statement of Daniel Barker, Esq.

Three Powers, or More.

On Moose-horn stream on the east side of Penobscot river; stream of small capacity, not over two rods wide, with no great fall. Some small sites sufficient to drive a common saw mill might be improved at no great cost.

Lobster stream and the west branch of Penobscot are both dead and sluggish through the entire town.

Unimproved.

Township No. 4, R. 14—Piscataquis County.

Statement of Daniel Barker, Esq.

Several Powers.

This town is traversed from south to north by the main west branch of Penobscot. The general width of the river is some 20 rods. Current quick but not much broken.

First, at Big island (an island dividing the channel into two nearly equal parts) the current is exceedingly rapid, and the banks, both upon the island and main land, are high and bold. Here either or both channels could be easily improved and any amount of power secured for driving the heaviest kinds of machinery.

Second, Third, Fourth, etc., many other sites might easily be improved within the length of the town and the whole river controlled.

Sixth, two miles above the island, the Ragmuff stream joins the the main river. Twenty rods from the mouth the stream breaks over a perpendicular ledge of six or seven feet through a channel of 20 feet width; banks exceedingly high. A long reach of slack water above the fall convenient for holding large reserve. This is a very extra power with abundance of water for common mill machinery.

Privileges unused.

Township No. 5, R. 14—Piscataquis County.

Statement of Daniel Barker, Esq.

The only streams on this town are Big Scott brook, emptying into Cauquomgomoc, and Ragmuff, emptying into the Penobscot. Neither is very large, or has reservoirs for holding surplus water to any great extent. Beds of streams about 40 feet wide. Dams of seven or eight feet height have been built on each with flowage sufficient for spring driving. Such streams fail early in a dry season.

TOWNSHIP No. 6, R. 14—PISCATAQUIS COUNTY.

Statement of Daniel Barker, Esq.

Numerous Powers.

A stretch of two miles or more of very rapid water on the stream of Cauquomgomoc lake, with fall sufficient for a head every 60 or 70 rods. Stream eight or ten rods wide with a large flow of water. The banks at the lake are too low to obtain a great head, but at slight expense the channel could be lowered and the lake be drained many feet below its natural level.

Loon stream and Little and Big Scott brooks afford powers to considerable extent. Dams have heretofore been erected on these for driving.

Privileges unused.

TOWNSHIP No. 7, R. 14—PISCATAQUIS COUNTY.

Statement of Daniel Barker, Esq.

Numerous Powers.

First, a small power in east part of the town, at outlet of lower pond on Ellis brook.

Second, at outlet of Shallow lake, two square miles, that can be controlled by a short dam at trifling cost.

Third, at outlet of Daggett pond, about the same as above.

Fourth, at foot of Lower pond; this pond is fed by both branches and affords a large supply of water.

The streams from these ponds are rough and rapid, and have a great number of good powers. In many places the water could be used over five or six times in half a mile distance. All kinds of timber abundant. Soil poor.

Privileges unused.

TOWNSHIP No. 8, R. 14—PISCATAQUIS COUNTY.

Statement of Daniel Barker, Esq.

Two Powers, or More.

This township contains the larger portion of Allaguash lake, covering nearly one-quarter of the town. At the outlet of this lake the bank on the south side is a high steep ledge, and on the north side a low sea wall, only six or seven feet above the lake, for a long distance. A dam was formerly built here, but the water broke through the wall at the end and carried away one wing, widening the channel to nearly twice its former breadth. A few rods below the lake the stream becomes narrow and the banks sufficiently high for a head to overflow the present dam. This would require a dam 75 feet long and 12 high.

Another good power is at the northeast corner of the town, on Russell brook; bed of stream 25 feet, through ledge; banks high and current rapid below; numerous ponds above to supply a head.

Privileges unused.

Township No. 9, R. 14—Piscataquis County.

Statement of Daniel Barker, Esq.

The only powers in this town are on Russell brook, a small stream taking its rise from various little ponds. Lumber has been driven from three of these ponds, and dams constructed at their outlets. These powers are each small but would afford sufficient water for driving common mill machinery through the spring and autumn.

No timber has ever been cut on the town except the large pine. The balance still remains in its natural state.

Township No. 10, R. 14—Piscataquis County.

Statement of Daniel Barker, Esq.

There is no stream sufficiently large for water-power, except Thoroughfare brook, and this would serve only during the wetter part of the season.

Township No. 2, R. 2—Somerset County.

Statement of E. W. Parlin, Esq.

Two Powers.

First, on the Sandy stream, below the inlet of the Rowe pond, a fall of 30 feet can be had; dam.

Second, a mile below, a fall of 50 feet can be had. Ledge bottom, good banks, good sites in all respects. Very large supply of water can be had by use of various ponds above, on the branches.

Unimproved.

TOWNSHIP No. 1, R. 3—SOMERSET COUNTY.

Statement of Joseph Clark, Esq., of Carratunk.

Several Powers.

On the outlet of Pierce pond. Stream violently rapid, capable of improvement at various points. Pond is a very large reservoir, 3.50 square miles, and can be raised 10 feet.

Several privileges on the outlet of the lower Carrying-place pond, stream is swift, good banks; pond can be made a good reservoir.

Unimproved.

TOWNSHIP No. 3, R. 4—SOMERSET COUNTY.

[North of Dead River plantation.]

Statement of J. M. Haynes, Esq., of Augusta.

Two Powers.

First, "Grand Falls," on the Dead river, in the northeast corner of the township, 40 feet fall, nearly perpendicular; an excellent power, capable of great development. The dam one-half mile above flows the river six miles to Long Falls.

Second, "Long Falls," one mile long, two pitches, 15 feet each, good bottom, banks, excellent site for mills, and a flowage of 10 miles above on the river. Great supply of water can be had at all seasons.

Both unimproved.

TOWNSHIP No. 4, R. 4—SOMERSET COUNTY.

[West of Hammond.]

Several Powers.

At the mouth and on the outlet stream of Penobscot lake, a series of rapids and pitches; total fall — feet. Stream narrow, excellent chance for dam at the outlet. Area of pond two and a half square miles. Abundant and excellent spruce forest.

All unimproved.

TOWNSHIP No. 1, R. 5—SOMERSET COUNTY.

Statement of Joseph Clark, Esq., of Carratunk.

Several Powers.

Several privileges on the Cold stream, the outlet of the pond of the same name. Pond covers 1.25 square miles and can be raised 12 feet.

Two or three privileges on Salmon stream. Formerly a mill on one; there is a dam giving 14 feet head, used for log-driving. No ponds, but large flowage.

Privileges not used.

TOWNSHIP NO. 1, R. 5—SOMERSET COUNTY.

Statement of Joseph Clark, Esq.

[See also "Townships Nos. 1 and 1, R. 5—Somerset County."]

Eight Powers, or More.

First, 10 rods below the outlet of dam of Moxie lake, 16 feet fall, ledge bottom and banks, lay of the land excellent. Unimproved.

Second, two miles below, a dam flowing the river back one and a half miles six feet, ledge bottom and banks, favorable location for mills. Ten feet head may be had.

Third, three-fourths of a mile below, "Rankin's Falls," 30 feet fall in six rods, and rapid slope for half a mile below. Good bottom and banks.

Fourth, a fall of 15 feet perpendicular; excellent privilege in all respects.

Fifth, 60 rods below, the "Moxie Falls," 95 feet fall perpendicular.

Moxie pond, the feeder of the above privileges, covers seven square miles, and is fed by other ponds and several important streams. A head of six feet is commanded on the pond, constituting a reservoir of very large capacity. Water under perfect control; freshets unknown; water abundant at all seasons.

Sixth, Seventh, etc., on Black stream, good privileges, easily improved, ponds above cover nearly two square miles, and are used for reservoirs. A bog above the upper pond, has had 12 feet of water held on it, covering half a square mile. A large amount of fall from the ponds to the Kennebec river. Timber in large quantities.

Privileges not used.

TOWNSHIPS NOS. 1 AND 1, R. 5—SOMERSET COUNTY.

Statement of J. M. Haynes, Esq., of Augusta.

Two Powers, and More.

First, "Moxie Rips," on the Kennebec river, three miles above the Forks, 15 feet fall in 20 rods; excellent site for dam and means of access; dam would be eight rods long.

Second, above, seven miles from the Forks, at the confluence of the Kennebec and the Black brook, the "Black Brook Rips," 20 feet fall in 30 rods; excellent situation for development.

Two miles above these rips commence the "Rapids," extending nine miles, and in the whole distance the river is a violent torrent, foaming and boiling; the fall is judged not less than 300 feet in the distance. About half the fall is between the two townships now under consideration. The shores are bold, in part precipitous and rising to the height of 100 feet on either side. Dams could be built at any point, and at several points roads can be constructed and mills located.

None improved.

TOWNSHIP No. 2, R. 5—SOMERSET COUNTY.

Statement of Heman Whipple, Esq., of Solon.

Numerous Powers.

First, on Enchanted stream, three-fourths mile from south line, an admirable site, 10 feet fall, flowage above.

Second, three-fourths mile above, fall at foot of pond 12 feet, large flowage on pond.

Third, one mile above, fall of eight feet; large tract of flowage above.

Fourth, above, near north line of town, fall of 15 feet, large pond above which can be flowed to any extent. The fall on the Enchanted stream is 100 feet or more.

Numerous privileges on the Stony brook; total fall 150 feet or more; six or more ponds all of which can be flowed; three or four already flowed.

All unimproved.

TOWNSHIP No. 4, R. 5—SOMERSET COUNTY.

Statement of Ex-Governor Coburn.

Dam flows the Spencer stream back three miles, head eight to ten feet. Quite large ponds above, which are or can be flowed.

TOWNSHIP No. 2, R. 6—SOMERSET COUNTY.

Statement of Heman Whipple, Esq.

Several Powers.

On the Cold stream; numerous reservoirs above; several already dammed; large supply of water; good sites.

Several privileges on Salmon stream; dam on one, formerly a mill on one; two or three ponds for resesvoirs.

Privileges not used.

Township No. 3, R. 6—Somerset County.

Statement of Heman Whipple, Esq.

Three Powers, or More.

One or two on Horse brook, fed by a pond covering three-fourths of a square mile; can be dammed.

One good site on the outlet of Bitter brook pond; pond covers three-fourths square mile, and can be flowed.

Not improved.

Township No. 4, R. 6—Somerset County.

Statement of Heman Whipple, Esq.

One Power.

At the foot of the Great Spencer pond, a fall of 20 feet can be had. Ledge bottom, admirable chance for a dam; banks favorable, level, and of just the right height for improvement. The dam would flow the pond 12 feet for several square miles. Pond is fed by other ponds and large tract of country.

Not used.

Township No. 1, R. 7—Somerset County.

Statement of Heman Whipple, Esq.

[See also "Townships No. 2, Piscataquis County, and No. 1, R. 7, Somerset County."]

One Power.

On Western outlet, at the foot of a pond, eight feet fall. Pond can be flowed.

Not used.

Township No. 2, R. 7—Somerset County.

Statement of Heman Whipple, Esq.

One Power.

On Misery stream, just below the outlet of the pond, eight feet fall; dam can be raised to any height.

Misery pond covers about two square miles, and is flowed two feet; can be raised more.

Not used.

TOWNSHIP NO. 4, R. 7—SOMERSET COUNTY.

From the Statement of Hon. Abner Coburn.

One Power.

"Attean Falls," at the head of Attean pond, 15 feet descent, and swift water below; a long range of sluggish water above, serving as a reservoir.

Not used.

TOWNSHIP NO. 1—WASHINGTON COUNTY.

[South of Vanceboro'.]

Statement of Peol Tomah, of Indian Township.

Two Powers.

On the outlet stream of Lambert's lake, which falls 20 feet from lake to river. Lake covers two square miles, and is dammed four feet.

Not used.

TOWNSHIP NO. 5—WASHINGTON COUNTY.

[Sysledobsis lake township.]

Statement of Peol Tomah, of Indian Township.

Several Powers.

Situated in part on the outlet stream of the Chain lakes. The total fall from the Upper Chain lake to Sysledobsis is 30 feet.

There is a fall of 15 feet from Sysledobsis to Pocumpus lake.

Unimproved.

TOWNSHIP NO. 6—WASHINGTON COUNTY.

[West of Talmadge.]

Statement of Peol Tomah.

Three Powers.

The Pleasant lake stream falls 40 feet to Scraggy lake, and has three dams upon it. Lake covers two square miles, and is dammed four feet; can be raised more with some flowage.

Used only for flowage.

TOWNSHIP NO. 6—WASHINGTON COUNTY.

[Grand lake township.]

Statement of Peol Tomah.

Several Powers.

The outlet stream of Ox brook pond falls from 50 to 100 feet to the lake, and affords several good sites for dams. The pond covers one to two square miles, and is dammed three feet.

The outlet stream of Wawbawsoos or Machias lake falls 40 feet from lake to lake. There is one dam at the outlet, which raises the lake three feet. A second dam about half a mile below. The lake covers about two square miles.

Used only for flowage.

Township No. 9—Washington County.

[East of Danforth.]

From the Returns of Calais.

Several Powers.

The Chiputneticook Grand Lake stream, connecting Chiputneticook Grand lake with Chiputneticook lake, is about three miles long. It has in that distance a fall of 60 feet. At the outlet of Grand lake there is a great dam, upon which a large tannery was built about three years ago, and about which quite a large settlement has clustered. There are undoubtedly several sites on this stream susceptible of improvement and use for power purposes.

A storage of four feet on the lakes above would yield on the whole fall of 60 feet, for 10 hours a day, 312 days a year, a gross power of 1,800 horse or 70,000 spindles.

Township No. 14—Washington County.

[West of Dennysville.]

Statement of T. W. Allan, Esq., of Dennysville.

Three Powers.

First, "Long Rips," on Cathance river, one-half mile above the south line of the township, one mile long; fall, estimated at 15 feet; chance for a dam, at the head 10 feet high; no improvements; dam would make large pond, two miles long.

Second, three and a half miles above, "Upper Rips," 100 rods long, eight feet fall, not including the dam at the outlet of the lake.

Third, "Outlet Dam," six and a half feet head on the lake, 4,000 or 5,000 acres.

The storage of Cathance lake will yield on these falls together, for the working hours of the year, a gross power of 300 horse, or 12,000 spindles. This is the storage alone.

TOWNSHIP No. 18—WASHINGTON COUNTY.

[North of East Machias.]

Statement of N. W. Foster, Esq., of East Machias.

Several Powers.

A number of good mill sites on the East Machias river, situated in a stretch of rips extending two and a half miles below Second lake. Formerly mills upon them.

"Munson Rips," on the East Machias river, a mile above Second lake, six feet fall, a dam at the head giving seven feet flowage over Round and Rocky lakes, total head and fall 13 feet. A most excellent power.

The water-power and the township are owned by S. W. Pope & Co., of East Machias.

Privileges used only for flowage.

TOWNSHIP No. 19—WASHINGTON COUNTY.

[South of Crawford.]

Statements of F. Loring Talbot and N. W. Foster, Esqs., of East Machias.

Seven Powers, or More.

First and Second, on the outlet stream of Spectacle lakes. Not used.

Third, at the outlet of Long lake, a dam six feet high. Lake covers 1.25 square miles. Fed by ponds above that are also dammed.

Fourth, the "Great Meadow Rips," on the East Machias river, fall 30 feet, very extensive artificial flowage over adjacent meadows. Not used.

Fifth, about a mile below the outlet of Love lake, six feet fall can be had. Unimproved.

Sixth, one mile below, a fall of six feet; formerly a shingle mill; unimproved.

Love lake covers 1.75 square miles and is flowed five or six feet; it is fed by Barrows' lake which can be flowed several feet. Large supply of water.

Power and township owned by C. Burrell, Esq., of East Machias.

Township No. 21—Washington County.

Statement of F. Loring Talbot, Esq., of East Machias.

Two Powers.

A dam on Allen's stream.

On Huntley brook a dam, five to seven feet, flows a large tract.

Used only for log-driving.

Township No. 24—Washington County.

Statement of J. K. Ames, Esq., of Machias.

One Power.

On the Mopang stream, near the line of No. 25, "Six Mile Dam," about six feet head, flows back two miles; stream narrow.

Used only for log-driving.

Township No. 27—Washington County.

Statement of Peol Tomah.

[See also "Hinkley Township and Township No. 27—Washington County."]

Several Powers.

The outlet stream of Clifford lakes falls 40 feet to Big lake, and has several good mill sites. The lakes cover two square miles and are dammed five feet.

Also on Little river a dam six feet high, used for log-driving. Stream fed by a pond covering three-fourths of a mile, and dammed three feet.

Privileges used only for log-driving.

Township No. 30—Washington County.

Statement of J. K. Ames, Esq., of Machias.

Six Powers.

First, "Robinson Dam," a mile and a half below the first, Mopang lake; flows the lake.

Second, "Gravel Dam," at outlet of second Mopang lake, seven feet head on the pond. High land all about; can raise the pond indefinitely.

Third, Fourth, Fifth and Sixth, on Crooked river, seven feet on the lower, the "Robinson Dam," six feet on "Fletcher Dam," above, six feet on "Pope Dam," above, and seven feet on "Elwell Dam."

TOWNSHIP NO. 36—WASHINGTON COUNTY.

Statement of J. K. Ames, Esq., of Machias.

Several Powers.

On the west branch of the West Machias river; stream is rapid, rocky, and narrow; several sites for dams. One dam already built.

TOWNSHIP NO. 41—WASHINGTON COUNTY.

Statement of J. H. Ames, Esq., of Machias.

Two Powers.

First, "Knight Dam," two and a half miles below Fifth lake. Six feet head.

Second, about half a mile below Fifth lake. "Fifth Lake Dam" flows the lake seven feet.

Used only for log-driving.

TOWNSHIP NO. 43—WASHINGTON COUNTY.

Statement of Peol Tomah.

One Power.

On Little river, north branch, half a mile below the lake, a dam four feet high. Pond covers nearly a mile square, and is dammed three feet.

TREMONT—HANCOCK COUNTY.

From Selectmen's Returns.

Ten Powers, and More.

First and Second, on "Heath's Stream," the outlet of Seal Cove pond, and emptying into Seal Cove, a convenient and safe harbor. Upon one a saw mill; upon the other a grist mill. The productions of these mills can be shipped without the expense and inconvenience of trucking. Annual lumber produced about 250,000; several hundred thousand staves; with proper machinery much more could be done. Total fall, 40 feet in one-fourth of a mile; two dams; mills work about three-fourths of the year, but with proper improvements could be run the whole season. Heath's stream connected with two ponds. Formerly a carding and fulling will on this stream, working successfully, but was worn out and suffered to go to ruin by the owner.

Third, Fourth, etc., on Heath's stream, never been improved. The water could be carried along the banks in flumes with but little expense; stream is narrow and runs over a rocky bed and between ledgy banks; the eastern bank is very high, while the western is not too high for the convenient erection of mills; it is but little affected by freshets, never enough to cause damage to dams or mills. All along the eastern shore of the ponds and on the slopes of the mountains near the ponds are forests of spruce, fir and pine.

Fifth, Sixth, etc., on Bass Harbor stream; shingle mill, six months. The stream five miles in length, and has a fall in the whole distance of about 60 feet. There are several points in its course at which improvements could be made so as to run successfully machinery for the manufacture of small lumber.

Seventh, Eighth, etc., on large brooks, with sufficient power to manufacture shingles, laths, clapboards, staves, &c.

Ninth, Tenth, etc., tide privileges, none of which are improved.

Trenton—Hancock County.

Selectmen's Statement.

One Power.

A tide-mill that does some business at sawing boards, staves, and herring boxes.

There is no fresh water-power in town of sufficient volume to warrant the construction of dams.

Trescott—Washington County.

Three Powers.

First, on Moose cove, a tide power, a saw mill.

Second, on Wiggin's stream, a saw mill.

Third, on a stream tributary to the south branch of Cobscook bay, a saw mill.

Troy—Waldo County.

From Selectmen's Statement.

Ten Powers.

First, at the foot of Carlton bog, which contains about 1,000 acres and has five important tributary streams, "Carlton Mills;" saw, shingle, clapboard, and grist mills; 300,000 of lumber, shingles 350,000, clapboards 30,000; grist mill 1,600 bushels; head and fall 13 feet. With a tight dam four times the present business might be done. With small expense there might be an upper dam built to raise the head four feet and flow from 2,000 to 3,000 acres, making power for any business.

Second, 40 rods below, site for another dam, nine feet head, with good location for mills, and easy of access; hard bottom and sides; rocks plenty.

Third, one mile below, falls 60 or 70 rods long.

Fourth, "Myrick Falls," in southwesterly part of the town; saw mill, 150,000 board measure; head and fall, 12 feet; water sufficient for nine months; good farming lands up to the edge of the pond; hard bottom.

Fifth, 20 rods below, shingle machine, 300,000 per year; could run three-fourths of the year; more machinery could be run.

Sixth, below. Not used.

Seventh, on Martin stream; saw mill, 150,000 board measure; shingle mill, 150,000 per year; might do a great deal more; could run nine months in the year.

Eighth, below, quite as good, hard bottom; land around good for farming.

Ninth, clover mill, on Shaw brook, 10 or 12 tons of seed per year; runs about six months; head and fall 11 feet; could do a great deal more by building dams; good farming land all about; banks of pond and stream hard; plenty of stone.

Tenth, half a mile below, shingle machine, 200,000 per year; could run eight months; bottom hard; good farming land. Considerable timber left.

TURNER—ANDROSCOGGIN COUNTY.

From Selectmen's Returns.

[See also "Greene and Turner," and "Leeds and Turner."]

Six Powers.

First, on the Martin stream, at the outlet of Bear pond, saw mill, can cut 600,000 feet annually; fall 10 feet.

Second, at North Turner village, three-fourths of a mile below, lumber, grist and carding mills; also carriage factory. Could cut 1,000,000 feet annually; fall 10 feet.

Third, "Chase's Mills," saw and shingle mill, and hub and bowl factory.

Fourth, at Turner village, on the Twenty-mile river, a woollen factory, grist mill, lumber mill and carriage factory. Fall about 12 feet; all the mills doing a large amount of business.

Fifth, at Bradford village, on the same river, unimproved; fall 12 feet; if properly improved would do a large amount of business.

Sixth, at the mouth of the Twenty-mile river; fall 11 feet; saw and grist mill; power enough to do a large business.

Plenty of good clay for brick.

Union—Knox County.

From the Statement, and a Plan of the Water-Power, furnished by William Gleason, Esq., Surveyor.

[See also "Union and Washington."]

Fifteen Powers.

Four on Crawford's river, the outlet of Crawford's pond and tributary to Seven Tree pond. The distance from pond to pond is 152 rods, and the declivity or fall 73 feet seven and one-half inches.

First, nearest the outlet; fall 12 feet; cabinet shop, $5,000 annual product.

Second, stave mill, eight feet fall.

Third, 18 feet fall, foundry, saw mill, shovel factory, axe factory; product, first, $3,000, second, $175.

Fourth, machine shop, 10 feet fall; 25 feet 11 inches not occupied.

The ponds which find their outlet at this place are judged to cover an area of more than 2,000 acres, none of which have any artificial works for reservoiring water except Fisk and Lermonds, and these are used as mill sites rather than reservoirs. The privileges on Crawford's river are not subject to sudden rise of water, and are among the best in this section to hold out in the dry season of the year. The outlet of Crawford's pond is only about 40 feet wide, and a dam could be easily constructed, costing but little, and the flowage of meadow would not exceed 75 acres. The privileges Three and Four have rock banks and bottom. A section of the stream was taken 19 feet nine inches long and 20 feet wide, depth in the middle, 20 inches, and sides 12¼ inches, and the velocity was found to be six seconds in the distance, (19 feet 9 inches.) The above described power is situated in South Union, and is known as the South Union water-power.

The next two powers are situated on the St. George river, below Senebec and above Round pond. The declivity from Senebec pond to the falls at Bachelder mills, measured to the bed of the river, near to, and on the west side of the flume at the grist mill, is 49 feet 11½ inches. A section of the river was taken 14 rods and 10 links long, and 5 rods 12½ links wide, average velocity of current 3 minutes and 23⅓ seconds; depth, two feet in centre. The distance from the pond to the falls named above is 514 rods.

Fifth, at the outlet of Senebec pond; saw, grist, stave and shingle mill, and carriage factory, all of which produce $1,700 annually.

Sixth, below; a tannery, $5,000; carriage factory, $5,000; Messrs. Simmons, Wingate & Co.'s carriage factory produces $20,000; a saw mill and grist mill, which produce annually $860.

The natural reservoirs of these privileges are Senebec pond in Union and Appleton, Quantabacook pond in Searsmont, Stevens' and George's ponds in Liberty, which have an area of more than 1,500 acres, none of which are used exclusively as reservoirs. The mills on Nos. Five and Six are run most of the season, and they are enabled to grind, even in the driest seasons, some portions of every day; and, if the ponds above referred to were flowed, the power might be quadrupled.

The next four powers are situated on Easton stream, the outlet of Lermond's pond, and tributary of Crawford's pond. The declivity was found to be 158 feet, and the distance 583 rods. The amount of the water judged to be about three-eighths as much as is vented by Crawford's river.

Seventh, at the outlet; saw and stave mill; $515 annually.

Eighth, grist mill and stave mill; $700 annually; also cabinet factory.

Ninth, stave mill and threshing machine.

Tenth, saw mill, $200 annually. The fall improved on No. Seven, is 9 feet; on No. Eight, is 16 feet; on No. Nine, is 8 feet; and on No. Ten, is 10 feet; leaving on Eastern stream 115 feet unoccupied. This location is known as East Union.

Eleventh, on Pettengill stream; the total descent from the dam, at the foot of the meadows to the meadows below, is 62 feet 2 inches in 70 rods. Privilege No. Eleven appropriates 9 feet only; occupied by stave and shingle mill. Took a section of the stream 25 feet long, and five and one-half feet wide, 17 inches deep in centre, velocity five seconds. This stream has no ponds as reservoirs, but a large area of meadows is flowed from fall until spring, which makes this a good privilege at the seasons specified; some business is done here even in the dry part of the season, from June until August.

Twelfth, located on Grassy-pond stream; fall 10 feet; $250.

Thirteenth, situated on Muddy-pond stream; fall 12 feet; $400.

Fourteenth, on same stream; 10 feet fall; $375.

Fifteenth, on the same stream; a fall of eight feet; $300.

The mills on Crawford's and George's rivers operate nearly all the year at present; can be made to do a vast amount of business at all seasons. Rocks suitable for building abundant at all points; one-eighth of the basin of the streams covered with woods; lay of the land about the falls excellent for improvement. Market, Rockland and Thomaston, by road.

UNION AND WASHINGTON—KNOX COUNTY.

Statements of Union and Washington.

[See also "Union," and "Washington."]

Four Powers.

All situated on Medomac stream.

First, "Luce's Saw Mill," 15 feet head.

Second, a stave mill, 15 feet head.

Third, saw and stave mills, 14 feet head.

Fourth, stave and saw mill.

UNITY—WALDO COUNTY.

Statement of A. R. Myrick, Esq.

Four Powers.

First, "Thompson Mills," grist, saw, shingle, clapboard, picket and lath mills, all on one dam. The privilege is supported by the Twenty-five-mile pond, whose area is about four and a half square miles. Mills operate all the year.

Second, "Stevens' Mills," on Sandy stream, grist, carding and cloth mills. This is a most excellent power, beautiful falls, with any quantity of flowage land.

Third, "Comer's Mill," on Sandy stream, large grist mill.

Fourth, "Small's Shingle Mill," a small but nice water power.

UNITY PLANTATION—KENNEBEC COUNTY.

Statement of the Assessors.

There is no water-power in Unity plantation large or small.

UPTON—OXFORD COUNTY.

From Selectmen's Returns and information furnished by E. S. Coe, Esq., of Bangor.

Numerous Powers.

The "Rapid River Falls," on Rapid river, which connects Umbagog lake with the great lakes above. There are a large number of mill sites; the banks are good; rock abundant; the supply of water inexhaustible, the stream being fed by about 60 square miles of lakes, all of which have dams at their outlets for husbanding water, commanding an average head of 11 feet. The dams are used, at present, only for log-driving purposes. The total descent from lake to lake, is 200 feet in five miles, and the stream may be regarded as a continuons series of mill privileges of the highest excellence from end to end.

The storage above noted will yield on a fall of 200 feet a gross power of 18,600 horse-powers for 20 hours a day, 312 days per year, or 744,000 spindles.

One power, the "Sluice," on the Dead Cambridge stream, six miles from inhabitants; fall 10 feet.

One on the Swift Cambridge stream, near the Andover road.

"Abbott's Mills," on the Main Cambridge; dam 15 feet; saw, clapboard, and shingle machinery; grist and starch mill. Saw mill operates springs and falls; grist mill all the year.

Flutter and centre-vent wheels.

Cambridge river has a pond at its head, one by one-half miles in extent; can be dammed from "The Sluice," up three miles; no damage from freshets, nor ever need be; good rock for building on all the privileges; lay of the land excellent. The water-powers were the cause of the settling of the town.

Market, Bethel, 26 miles by road. Power owned chiefly by Hezekiah Winslow, Esq., of Portland.

VAN BUREN PLANTATION—AROOSTOOK COUNTY.

From the Assessors' Returns.

Two Powers.

First, "Hammond Mill," on Violette brook; fall 10 feet; saw mill of the best construction and best machinery; saws 700,000 clapboards, 2,000,000 shingles, and 400,000 boards yearly; also laths, as many as are required; room and power for more mills; Stevens' wheel used and much liked; mill operates all the year except in winter.

Second, one-fourth mile below; 15 feet fall; grist mill; operates all the year; mill in bad repair; new one erecting; overshot wheel.

No natural lakes or ponds; artificial reservoirs can be constructed; mills perfectly safe from freshets.

It has been contemplated to cut a channel from Long lake of the Fish-river chain, to the Violette brook, and by a dam at the natural outlet of the lake to divert its waters into said brook. A very great supply of water could thus be secured.

Rocks, slate, good for building; lay of the land good; basin of the stream nearly all covered with forests.

The improvement of the power has created a thriving and a growing village out of nothing but rocks and water in ten years' time.

Market, Fredericton and St. John, N. B.; also Boston, New York, and all coastwise points, by the St. John river.

Vanceborough Township—Washington County.

From the Returns of Calais.

One Power.

The St. Croix Log-driving Company have erected a dam at the outlet of Chiputneticook lake, and hold a 15-foot head of water. The lakes, connected with this lake, are dammed so as to retain water.

A storage of four feet on 50 square miles of the lakes above would yield on a 15-foot fall, for the ordinary working hours of the year, a gross power of 825 horse, or 33,000 spindles.

Vassalborough—Kennebec County.

From the Survey and Report of Ira E. Getchell, Esq., of Winslow, and the Statement of the Selectmen.

Nineteen Powers.

Thirteen on the outlet stream of China lake, which is 201 feet above tide, has an area of 4,000 acres, a basin of 39,520 acres, and a head of six feet on its entire surface, held by a dam, giving 1,045,440,000 cubic feet of *reserve* water, which alone will supply the stream 181 days.

The stream from the lake to Sebasticook river is six and one-third miles long, falls 160 feet, has nine dams erected and sites for three or four more. The run of water is 8,703 cubic feet per minute, for 11 hours per day, at low stage.

31

First, 120 rods below outlet dam, fall 14 feet; gross power, 233 horse; owned by the Vassalboro' Mills Company, and used by them for grist and woollen mill when in operation. H. R. Butterfield uses the surplus water for saw mill and shovel handle factory.

Second, 120 rods below, fall seven and one-half feet; gross power 123 horse; H. R. Butterfield; grist mill.

Third, 200 rods below, nine and three-fourths feet fall; 160 horse. Charles Davies; shingle mill, wood and iron machine shop.

Fourth, fall of seven and one-half feet immediately below, which might be made available by a canal or a new dam. This would give in all 17 and one-quarter feet fall and 284 gross horse-power.

Fifth, 440 rods below, fall 32 feet, obtained by a dam eight feet four inches high and canal 70 rods down the stream. Occupied by the Vassalborough Mills Company in manufacturing woollen goods, 20 sets of cards with connected machinery, wood and iron machine shop, &c. Company have a capital stock of $450,000. Gross power, about 500 horse.

Sixth, there is an unoccupied stone dam in the stream along side the canal, with a fall of 17 and one-half feet, receiving all the water not used by the factory. It has been proposed to put in new machinery at this point.

Seventh, 260 rods below, fall nine feet eight inches; 159 gross horse-power. T. S. & J. A. Lang; knit goods. C. A. Priest, shoe pegs.

Eighth, 60 rods below, fall six and one-half feet; dam; 107 horse-power. T. S. & J. A. Lang. Unoccupied. Charter just procured for a company with a capital of $100,000.

Ninth and Tenth. In the next 500 rods the stream falls 32 feet 10 inches. There are sites for two or three dams with but little damage from flowage.

Eleventh, two miles below, 10 feet fall; 164 horse-powers. T. J. Hayden; saw mill, threshing machine, &c.

Twelfth, immediately below, a fall of nine feet, with precipitous banks.

Thirteenth, 125 rods below, fall 10 feet 10 inches; 178 horse-powers. Flye & Hayden, saw mill, laths, &c. Can take logs from the Sebasticook, which is but 40 rods below.

All the *dams* on this stream are within three miles of the Somerset & Kennebec Railroad. They represent 1,600 horse-power, and there are 800 more available.

Six are situated upon the outlet stream of Webber pond; each with a dam, and a head and fall of about eight feet in a running distance of 20 or 30 rods. These are now nearly all lying idle. Two of these formerly drove paper mills, and one a sash and blind factory. All the powers on this stream are within a total distance of one and a half miles.

Veazie—Penobscot County.

From the Statement of the Selectmen.

Two Powers.

First, the "Upper Veazie Water-Power," on the Penobscot river, four miles above Bangor. Upon this privilege there are located two blocks of mills. The "Upper Block," so called, contains two gangs of saws, six single saws, and a lath mill. The "Lower Block" contains one gang of saws, three single saws, one ——— saw, lath mill, clapboard and shingle mill. When all the wheels are running in the mills they vent, according to the area of the discharge of the wheel, about 13,500 square inches. The gates which let the water from the flume into the cylinders have a discharge of about three times the area of the wheels, making a total discharge of about 40,500 square inches. There are six and a half feet head of water from top of waste dam to apron of mills; under freshets there are from 10 to 15 feet head in flumes, at low water about five feet.

Second, the "Lower Veazie Water-Power," on the Penobscot river; there is a fall of about six feet in this town from the apron of the aforesaid mills to the head of tide, at Eddington Bend, so called; not at present occupied by any dam or mills.

At extreme low run the power in the 12 feet fall is about 3,300 horse-powers, gross, for the 24 hours, or 133,000 spindles.

All the above property belongs to John W. Veazie, Esq., and the mills are known as the Veazie Mills.

Verona—Hancock County.

From Selectmen's Report.

Two Powers.

First, "Bennett's Mills," on a small stream at the eastern side of the town; fall about 16 feet in six rods.

Second, two dams, one for reservoir purposes; a saw mill, with a 16-foot overshot wheel; one up-and-down saw, will cut 2,000 feet of boards in 12 hours; works about three months in the year.

Stream varies three or four-fold at different seasons of the year.

Market, Bucksport, by land or water.

VIENNA—KENNEBEC COUNTY.

From Selectmen's Statement.

Three Powers.

First, at Vienna village, on a mill stream, the outlet of two small ponds; fall six feet; a shingle mill; formerly a shoe-peg factory.

Second, above the first, on the same stream, at the village; fall five feet; saw mill and shingle machine, which operate in time of high water, and cut the lumber used in the vicinity.

Third, on the same stream, above the second; grist mill; operates nearly all the year by careful husbanding of the water; fall six feet.

Boulders and some granite ledge.

VINALHAVEN—KNOX COUNTY.

Statement of Watson H. Vinal, Esq.

Two Powers.

First, saw and grist mill, planing and shingle machine, on a salt water stream at the head of Carver's harbor. Seven feet head.

Second, saw, grist, and shingle mills, near the centre of the town, on a salt water stream. Nine feet head.

Market, Rockland, 15 miles, by daily steamboat in summer.

WAITE TOWNSHIP—WASHINGTON COUNTY.

Statement of Peol Tomah of Indian Township.

Several Powers.

On the Tomah streams, the outlets of the Tomah ponds. Long tracts of dead water alternating with rips and falls. Ponds, three in number, cover two square miles, and can all be dammed.

WALDO—WALDO COUNTY.

From Selectmen's Returns.

Seven Powers.

First, "Hawkins Saw Mill," on a brook fed by three small ponds in the northwest part of the town; saw and stave mill; saws from fall to spring.

Second, above, "Pitman Saw Mill," pond about one acre; up-and-down-saw; used from fall until spring, part of the time.

Third, on the same stream, in the southwest corner of the town, dam already built, mill burned 10 years ago.

Fourth, above, about midway the town, "Sanborn's Mill."

The Passagassawakeag at Sanborn's privilege is fed by three ponds situated in Brooks. At the "Burnt Privilege," by six more, situated in Waldo, Morrill, Knox and Brooks.

Fifth, in the northeast part of the town, "Johnson Saw Mill," runs from fall until about the first of June; fed by a pond of 60 or 70 acres; saw, stave and shingle machinery; pond is fed by the Wescott stream.

Sixth, below, "Holme Mills;" stave and saw mill; operates from fall until about June; pond of 50 or 60 acres.

Seventh, below, "Ellis Mill; saw, stave and shingle machines; runs from fall until spring.

WALDOBOROUGH—LINCOLN COUNTY.

From Selectmen's Statement.

Twelve Powers.

Eight on the Medomac river, which falls into tide water at Waldoboro' village.

First, "Sproul's," in Waldoboro' village; fall from 10 to 15 feet; saw, grist, carding, plaster, planing, and iron-foundry machinery.

Second, "Soule's," in the village; fall from eight to ten feet; oakum, carding, and clothing mills.

Third, "Achorn's," about one-third of a mile from village; fall from 30 to 40 feet; grist, stave and shingle mills.

Fourth, "Winslow's," about three miles from village; fall about 10 feet; saw, stave and grist mills.

Fifth, "Wagner's," about four miles from village; fall about six feet; unoccupied.

Sixth, "Burns'," about six miles from village; saw, grist, and three stave mills.

Seventh, "Mink's," North Waldoboro'; fall about six feet; stave and shingle mill.

Eighth, "Mink's," North Waldoboro'; fall some six or eight feet; saw mill.

Ninth, "Weaver's," on a small stream which has no name, about five miles from village; fall some eight feet; stave and shingle mill.

Tenth, "Benner's," about five miles from village; fall not reported; saw and two stave mills.

Eleventh, "Burkett & Feyler's," on "Slago Brook," about two

miles from village, and about three miles from salt water; stave and shingle mills.

Twelfth, very near salt water and navigation, formerly occupied, but not now; fall some four or five feet.

The river is fed by several square miles of ponds which could be much improved for reservoirs. See Part II, page 140.

WALES—ANDROSCOGGIN COUNTY.

Selectmen's Returns.

One Power.

On a brook, where some little sawing is done, during the spring snow meltings, and during the season of freshets.

WALLAGRASS PLANTATION—AROOSTOOK COUNTY.

Statement of William Dickey, Esq., of Fort Kent.

Two Powers.

First, on the Fish river, six miles below the outlet of Eagle lake; fall about 20 feet; ledge bottom and banks, and in all respects one of the finest water-powers imaginable.

Second, above, at the outlet of Eagle lake, a dam can be built that will raise a head of several feet, converting the great lake above into a vast reservoir, and establishing a power that with wheels operating well under variable heads, would do a vast amount of manufacturing.

For reservoirs tributary to these powers, see last Table, page 125; also top of page 126.

By the aid of the reservoirs it is evident that the first privilege, in particular, can be made constant and equal to the demands of very extensive operations.

Both unimproved.

WALTHAM—HANCOCK COUNTY.

Two Powers.

First, in the village, on Webb's stream, a saw mill.

Second, below, a saw mill.

Webb's stream is the outlet of Webb's pond, 1.75 square miles, 10 feet storage; Scammon pond, one square mile; Abram's pond, 0.80 square miles and 10 feet storage; and Molasses pond, 2.25 square miles, and 10 feet storage. A very great supply of water could be commanded for power purposes. The storage is now used for log-driving.

WARREN—KNOX COUNTY.

From the Statement of C. T. Bean, Esq.

Two Powers.

On the St. George river, at the village. First, "Factory Fall," woollen factory, 40 hands, nice grist mill, saw, shingle, and stave mills, etc.

Second, one-third of a mile above, the "Knox Falls;" fall seventeen feet four and three-fourths inches. Improvements; a nice dam, saw mill and powder mills; power is owned by Hodgman & McCallum.

The stream is connected with eight or ten ponds in the vicinity, in addition to the large number lying about its head waters These ponds empty into the river above the falls and are susceptible, at small expense, of indefinite increase or reservoirs. The facilities for artificial reservoirs, also, should these be needed, are very superior. The stream being connected with numerous lakes, is constant at all seasons.

Counting in only 16 of the larger ponds, there are over 11 square miles of reservoirs to these powers. A head of six feet on 10 square miles, would give on the Knox falls alone, a gross power of 272 horse, for 10 hours a day, 312 days a year, 11,880 spindles. This is the power due to *storage* alone, not estimating the *natural* low run of the stream. The storage could be used in three or four months, trebling the power, the natural flow sustaining the power at this figure for the remaining eight or nine months.

The rocks are suitable for building purposes, and the lay of the land excellent for the accommodation of mills.

The use of the power now constitutes the business of the place, aside from farming, and although but a fraction of the power is used.

Market, Rockland and New York. Tide waters are within half a mile, and the railroad from Bath to Rockland, now building, passes near the power.

The large volume of water, the constancy of the flow, the accessibility of the power, and the facility and cheapness with which it can be improved, render this a privilege of quite unusual excellence and value.

WASHBURN—AROOSTOOK COUNTY.

From Selectmen's Returns.

One Power.

"Salmon Brook Falls," upon Salmon brook; fall 25 feet in three-fourths of a mile.

A saw mill; the mills formerly upon it were burned in 1864. Turbine wheel employed; efficiency four to one as compared with wheels previously used.

The power, if fully used, would cut 2,000,000 feet lumber, 1,500,000 shingles, 100,000 clapboards, and grind 50,000 bushels of grain.

Stream connected with a pond 500 acres in extent, the capacity of which could be greatly increased by dams; artificial reservoirs could be inexpensively constructed. Perfectly safe from damage by freshets.

Rock, limestone, suitable for building purposes. Improvement of the power has doubled the wealth of the town. Annual product of the power as now used, but a small part, $5,000.

WASHINGTON—KNOX COUNTY.

From the Statement of J. L. Rockwell, Esq., and a Plan of the Town.

[See also "Union and Washington."]

Fifteen Powers.

Clark's pond, 350 acres, could be drained into Washington pond, 1.25 square miles, and thus abundant water for all the mills be secured for the whole year.

First, below outlet, 12 feet head; new dam and mills; various saws.

Second, below, 300,000 staves and heading per year. Eleven feet head. Power not all used.

Third, below, 14 feet head, tannery and stave mill, not used.

Fourth, below, saw and tannery, 13 feet head.

Fifth, below, new grist mill, 12 feet head.

Sixth, below, old saw mill, 13 feet head.

Seventh, below, saws.

Eighth, below, 12 feet head.

Ninth, below, saws, 13 feet head.

Tenth, below, 9 feet head, staves.

Eleventh, below, saws, 8 feet head.

Twelfth, below, 10 feet head, stave and grist mills.

Thirteenth, on Damariscotta stream, staves, water five months.

Fourteenth, below, staves, 10 feet head.

Fifteenth, below, staves, 11 feet head.

Waterborough—York County.

From Selectmen's Returns.

[See also "Limerick and Waterborough."]

Eight Powers.

First and Second, on Branch brook; run three-fourths of the year.

Third, on the outlet of the Little Ossipee pond; runs four saws and one planer.

Fourth, on Smith brook; runs two saws through the year.

Fifth, on the Colcord brook; one saw; runs half the year.

Sixth, on Down's brook; is not now occupied.

Seventh, on Johnson's brook; runs two saws half the year.

Eighth, on Roberts' brook; runs one saw half the year.

Waterford—Oxford County.

From Selectmen's Returns.

Several Powers.

The larger powers, two in number, are situated in the south part of the town, one on the outlet of Bear pond, which itself receives the discharge of Moose and Thomas ponds, and one on the stream connecting Thomas and Bear ponds.

The first mentioned is called the "Dudley Privilege;" the second the Hapgood privilege. The fall at the former is 15 feet in four rods; of the latter 17 feet in the same distance.

Only a part of the power employed at either privilege; a saw mill and grist mill on each at present; ample power for others, "or for factories."

The first power is connected with three ponds whose combined extent is 2,140 acres; the second with one pond 484 acres in area. The capacity of the ponds connected with the former could not readily be increased; with the latter, at an expense of $300.

Suitable building stone within a short distance; land level and gently sloping about the falls. Power not yet sufficiently improved to affect wealth and population materially; serves simply local uses.

Market, Norway and Bridgton, 10 miles each, by road; Portland nearest city, by railroad from South Paris, and by canal from

Harrison; South Paris 12 miles, and Harrison four miles distant. No information given respecting the smaller powers. Undershot and breast wheels.

Particular attention called to the "Dudley" privilege. This has 500 acres of reservoir; is within 50 rods of the lake, so that the delivery of water can be regulated with ease; in particular the mill pond can be dried up day or night in cold weather, and water let on in the morning, warm from the pond, and so the formation of ice is prevented; thirdly, it is within 50 rods of the county road from Fryeburg to South Paris, and only 10 miles from South Paris depot, and four miles from the head of the Cumberland and Oxford canal; fourthly, a dam can be erected at very trifling expense; fifthly, the owners desire to sell to any party who will improve. Good building stone within 30 rods.

Other privileges on the same stream further down, equally good; unimproved.

WATERVILLE—KENNEBEC COUNTY.

From the Selectmen's Returns, and from the Statement of John Ayer, Esq., for West Waterville.

[See also "Waterville and Winslow."]

Fifteen Powers.

On Messalouskee or Emerson's stream, and eight of them at West Waterville; these, with the improvements thereon, will be considered first.

The distance from Snow pond to Rice bridge, below West Waterville, is about two miles, and the total fall nearly 111 feet, divided as follows:

First dam; at the foot of the pond; fall six feet; owned by Ellis Saw Company, and others.

Second dam; fall nine feet; owned by Hubbard & Blake, and others.

Third dam; fall 13 feet.

Fourth dam; and the "Cascade falls;" fall 44 feet.

Fifth dam; fall 14 feet. The Third, Fourth and Fifth, are owned by the Dunn Edge-Tool Company; the total fall being 70 feet with the "Cascade."

Sixth, a privilege, no dam; fall 11 feet; owned by Emerson & Blaisdell.

Seventh, near Rice bridge; a privilege, no dam; fall 10 feet; owner not stated.

The Cascade, Waterville.

Eighth, falls between the dams; four feet descent; owner not stated.

The largest fall in the above series is, as appears above, the "Cascade," the total fall of which is 44 feet in eight rods. The stream is about 70 feet wide and flows over the dam about one foot deep.

About one-fourth part of the whole power is improved. The power is sufficient to saw 40,000,000 feet per annum. The improvements are five dams, saw mill, grist mill,——— manufactory, tannery, machine shop, foundry, scythe and tool shop, etc.

The Tuttle, Blake and Tub wheels used. The Blake wheel uses less water but is not as strong as the Tuttle.

The improvement of the power has doubled both the wealth and population of West Waterville. Annual production, $300,000.

Market, the United States and the Provinces, via Maine Central Railroad and connections.

The above statement applies to West Waterville only.

The following powers are found upon the same stream at Waterville village:

Ninth and Tenth, "Crommett's Mills;" two dams; on the first a saw mill, sash and door factory, and carding mill. The saw mill is owned by T. E. & L. E. Crommett; running the principal part of the time through the year. Sash and door factory owned by Furbish & Sanders, built last year, and doing quite an extensive business. The carding mill is owned by T. E. Crommett. The west end of the dam is unoccupied; owned by T. W. Herrick, Joshua Nye, John & C. K. Matthews, with about 30 acres of land; dam 12 feet high.

Eleventh, a few rods below; a dam, about eight feet high, on which is a match factory, at present unoccupied; Pearson & Lords' old tannery is situated on this dam, now owned by S. H. Ricker & Co. The head and fall of these two dams is about 23 feet.

Twelfth, some three-fourths of a mile further down, the "Paper Mill;" dam six feet high; owned by J. S. Monroe of Massachusetts. The mill is doing quite an extensive business, running day and night through the year. Nathan Stiles, Agent.

Thirteenth, some twenty rods further on, the "Iron Foundry;" dam built by the Fairbanks' establishment of Vermont; was bought out, some 25 years ago, by Webber & Haviland, the present owners, who are doing quite a large business, and might do much more. The east end of this dam is unoccupied; dam 12 feet high.

Fourteenth and Fifteenth, still further on, are two good water-powers, on one of which is a dam, 12 feet high; unoccupied; owned by W. B. S. Moore and others.

As appears from the foregoing exhibit, there are 10 dams on this stream; five at or near Waterville village, and five at West village, with good chances for three or four more.

The stream upon which these powers are situated, is remarkable for its constancy, being supplied by lakes almost exclusively. The lake chain tributary to it, is reputed to have a length of 60 miles, and covers not far from 27 square miles of surface. The lakes are very deep, some of them from 90 to an 100 feet, and constitute reservoirs of the highest excellence. The water from the lakes is so warm in winter that ice is never troublesome. The total range of water on the dams from highest to lowest, is only three feet, or thereabout.

A storage of six feet on 20 square miles of the lakes would yield on the total fall (as given) of 164 feet, a gross power of 5,576 horse, for 10 hours a day, 312 days a year, or 223,000 spindles. This is the power due to storage alone, and to it should be added the power due to the *natural* low run of the stream.

The underlying rock is slate, of quality suitable for construction purposes, but not the best. Lay of the land about the falls favorable.

Total annual production of mills in Waterville, estimated $500,-000.

WATERVILLE AND WINSLOW—KENNEBEC COUNTY.

From Materials furnished by G. A. Phillips, Esq., and Col. H. A. De Witt.

[See also "Waterville," and "Winslow."]

Two Powers.

First, the "Ticonic Falls," on the Kennebec river at Waterville village, 17 miles above the Kennebec dam at Augusta, and four miles below the Kendall's Mills dam in Fairfield.

At this point a continuous ledge of hard slate crosses the river diagonally, quite uniform in height, and presenting a well-defined crest, upon which the dam is located. The ledge is extended into the banks and along the river bed above and below the falls, and offers the best possible foundation for structures of all

Ticonic Falls, Waterville and Winslow.

descriptions. The height of the natural fall is 13 feet, in a few rods.

The dam, completed this season, 1869, is of an average height of seven feet, giving an available head and fall of 20 feet. Over 1,200,000 feet of lumber have been used in its construction; it is ballasted with stone, and is altogether unsurpassed for solidity and strength. Its length across the river is —— feet, being divided into sections by an island in the river. On the Waterville side it is extended down the bank of the river, forming a grand canal, in connection with which four raceways have already been constructed, either of which is of sufficient size to accommodate a mill of the capacity of the "Bates" at Lewiston. The total length of the dam, including the wing, is 1,700 feet; and its cost when completed will be about $40,000.

The view accompanying this statement was taken prior to the completion of the dam, at mid-summer low water, and represents the section of the river then remaining open, with a portion of the dam at the extreme left.

Second, "College Rapids," on the Kennebec river, 40 rods above the Ticonic dam. As respects favorable disposition of the river bed and banks and foundations for dams, mills, and appurtenant structures, this privilege is in no respect inferior to the above. The natural fall is 10 feet in 10 rods, upon which a head of 20 feet can be had by means of a dam, without infringing upon the rights of proprietors above. A *natural canal*, apparently in former times, and even now in freshets, one of the channels of the river, offers at insignificant cost facilities for the conveyance of water and its use, of quite remarkable character. The island formed by this channel and the main river is elevated just enough above freshets for convenience and security, and affords unsurpassed sites for mills or other structures. No part of this privilege is in use.

Volume of Water and Power.—The volume of water on the Kennebec river at this point, in the unimproved condition of the reservoirs above may be assumed to be, in a severe drouth, 30 per cent. less than at Augusta, or 119,000 cubic feet per minute for 11 hours a day. The enormous increase in the flow that can be realized from the use of the lakes and ponds above may be realized upon reference to Part II, pp. 94–98. The above, it will be understood, is the flow in an extremely dry season.

The available power at the Ticonic dam in a severe drouth is accordingly, for the ordinary manufacturing hours of the day, about 4,500 horse-powers, in gross. That of the "Rapids," upon development will be at same, a total of 9,000 horse-powers, or 594,000 spindles with preparation or print cloths, or 360,000 spindles for average work. It can be doubled or trebled, as appears from inspection of the reservoirs at command.

Proprietorship.—Both the above privileges are the property of the Ticonic Water-Power Manufacturing Company. The company own 400 acres of land contiguous to the river, with a river front of one and three-fourths miles on the east side and of three-fourths of a mile on the west side of the Kennebec, with all the water rights, buildings, and property necessary for the present development of the power, the accommodations being ample for all required mill sites, village sites, farming lands, and other appendages of manufacturing towns.

The lay of the land upon both these privileges is singularly favorable; for the most part naturally graded for the reception of mill structures, and admirably disposed upon both sides of the river for the convenient location of a large city.

Accessibility.—The tracks of the Portland & Kennebec Railroad pass directly by the side of the proposed mill sites, and the railroad company have arranged to afford all additional facilities of tracks as wanted. The depot of the Maine Central Railroad is also within convenient distance for freight and passenger use.

Construction materials of all sorts abundant, timber, brick, granite, and slate, and of the best quality.

Mills, etc.—A grist mill, plaster mill, door, sash and blind factory, saw mill, and a large wooden mill used for cutting lumber, are the only structures in occupation. These employ an insignificant fraction of the power.

It is believed by practical men, that the Waterville water-power in the Kennebec river, from the amount of constant power furnished, the facilities for increasing the power in the future by a system of reservoirs above, the economy of construction, the convenience of location as regards freight and passenger facilities, the advantage of a fine farming country around it, and of obtaining plenty of the best kind of mill help, is justly entitled to be ranked as one of the best undeveloped water-powers in New England.

Wayne—Kennebec County.

From the Statement of W. Jordan, Esq., and of the Selectmen.

Three Powers.

Two of these constitute the "North Wayne Privilege," owned by the North Wayne Tool Company.

First, "Upper Dam," head and fall 12 feet at ordinary height of water, occupied as follows:

Two hammer shops now in use; one grindstone shop, four 6-foot stones; two polishing shops; one hardening and tempering shop; one saw mill, one saw and circular saw; one grist mill, three runs stones. Equal to 16 single saw mills, or 16 trip hammers for scythes and necessary machinery.

Second, "Lower Dam," 400 feet from upper dam, head and fall five feet at ordinary height of water. Occupied by grind shop, five 6-foot stones; repair shop, with circular saws, &c. At very low water shut down.

Third, "Wayne Power," fall 12 feet in 350, owned by Johnson, Turner & Brown. Grist and saw mills, shovel-handle and sash and blind shops. Power not all used.

For reservoirs tributary to the powers, see Table 2, page 84, Part II. As will be seen a large amount of additional storage can be had when needed.

The machinery is not the best for economizing power. The wheels are similar to the Blake, Kendall and Rose patterns.

The underlying rock at North Wayne is a form of slate, with granite in limited quantities. At Wayne, granite suitable for building purposes. One-sixth of the basin of the streams is covered with woods.

Lay of the land at North Wayne, is good; at Wayne, is very superior.

Total annual product at North Wayne, $75,000; at Wayne, $35,000. The improvement of the powers has benefited the town very greatly; almost the entire village of North Wayne has been built by the Tool Company and their workmen.

Market, the whole country, by railroad.

Webster—Androscoggin County.

From Selectmen's Returns.

Four Powers.

On Sabattus stream, the outlet of Sabattus pond.

First, fall 12 feet; Second, 14 feet; Third, 12 feet; Fourth, 18 feet.

Dams and mills upon each fall. A large amount of unused power; mills operate all the year; privileges all owned in town.

Sabattus pond covers four square miles and is dammed. Its reservoir capacity could be considerably increased. Stream very safe and constant; abundant water all the year.

The power of the above falls may be inferred from the fact that at the "Factory Fall" in Lisbon below, 175 horse is secured on a 10-foot fall, with turbine wheel.

Building stone on the fourth fall only; there it is abundant and good. Land upon each of the falls level and convenient for the location of mills. One third of the basin covered with woods.

Market, Lewiston, six miles, by road or railroad.

WEBSTER PLANTATION—PENOBSCOT COUNTY.

Statement of D. Butters, Esq., of Prentiss.

One Power.

On the west branch of Mattagordus stream, where a 10-foot head would flow six or eight hundred acres; stone for dam close at hand. No improvement.

WELD—FRANKLIN COUNTY.

From Selectmen's Returns.

Fourteen Powers.

The town of Weld is almost entirely surrounded by mountains, from which seven streams, converging to the centre of the town, are received in the great Webb's pond there situated; upon six of the streams are water-powers.

First, Second, Third, Fourth and Fifth, on the Houghton brook; grist, saw, shingle, sash and door, and spool mills; another mill building. Water sufficient to run the mills for the most of the year. Fall 50 feet in 50 rods.

Sixth, about three miles above, "Holden Mills," with power sufficient to run most of the year; saw and shingle.

Seventh, on the East brook, board, shingle, clapboard, lath and clover mills. Other mills might be erected and the water used over repeatedly. The volume of water is something greater than that of the Houghton brook. This power is situated at Weld corner, near the centre of the town.

Eighth, one-fourth mile above, carriages, cabinet work, chairs, &c.; the power is only part used.

Ninth and Tenth, three miles above, small powers; saw mill, clapboard and shingle mill.

Eleventh, on West brook, volume of water sufficient to carry a number of mills through the year; fall 20 feet in 40 rods.

Twelfth, on Snowman brook, saw, clapboard and shingle mill; can operate nearly all the year.

Thirteenth and Fourteenth, on Skoefield brook, small powers; saw, threshing, clapboard and shingle machinery.

On the mountains, a large amount of spruce, hemlock, bass, rock-maple, beech, birch and white ash, which can be easily conveyed to the mills or the pond and run through the outlet. A large amount of ship timber might be obtained. Soil good for grain and potatoes; great facilities for raising stock, &c.

"The scenery of Weld is very beautiful, the town being nearly surrounded by mountains with the pond in the centre, forming a vast basin. A first-class hotel for summer tourists wanted."

Wellington—Piscataquis County.

From Selectmen's Returns.

Six Powers.

First to the Fourth, inclusive, in the westerly part of the town, on the Hegan stream.

Fifth, on a branch of the Hegan stream, near the centre of the town.

Sixth, on the Carlton stream, in the northeast corner of the town. The height of the several falls not reported.

Two of the powers would saw 300,000 feet of lumber. The powers are not all used; five are improved in mills. The mills work about one-third part of the year; one not improved would run the greater part of the year.

Breast, Stearns and Rose wheels. Basin heavily wooded. Annual products, $4,000.

Market, Bangor and Skowhegan, by road.

Wells—York County.

From the Returns of George Goodwin, Esq.

Fifteen Powers, Small.

Ten on Little river, two on Ogunquitt river, two on Webhannett river, one on Branch river.

The fall at the various privileges is from 10 to 15 feet; the

32

power capable of sawing 1,000,000 feet of lumber, less or more, yearly. It is all improved as now used, with not the best machinery. Rose, centre-vent, spile-vent wheels.

Streams not connected with lakes or ponds; artificial reservoirs not feasible. Good granite; convenient sites; but little forest. The powers give employment to about fifty men for about half of the year, and so aid them materially in the way of business. Value of lumber sawed, $75,000.

Market, mostly Boston, by water or rail.

WESLEY—WASHINGTON COUNTY.

From the Selectmen's Statement, and a Plan of the Streams.

Eleven Powers.

First, "Bacon Dam," on the Chain-lake stream; seven feet head; flows eight miles by three-fourths mile. A dam is to be built to give an eight-foot head, forming a large reservoir. There are three ponds in the series.

Second, "Groves' Dam," below; head seven feet.

Third, "Hayward Mill," below; nine feet head.

Fourth, "Joe Hill Dam;" five feet head, on Old stream.

Fifth, on New stream, "Cate's Dam;" nine feet head.

Sixth, "College Falls," on New stream; ten feet descent over solid ledge, with rock bank on each side.

Seventh, on Seavey brook, below the upper Seavey pond; dam seven feet head.

Eighth, on the same stream, below the lower Seavey pond; dam seven feet head.

The Seavey ponds are both dammed for reservoirs.

Ninth, Tenth and Eleventh, dams on Beaver-dam brook, in the northeast part of the town.

None of the power is now improved; has been in years past in saw mills; these have been burned, or otherwise disabled.

Market, Machias, twenty miles.

WEST BATH—SAGADAHOC COUNTY.

Statement of the Selectmen, and of A. W. Ring, Esq.

Numerous Powers.

"Tide privileges are numerous; if properly improved would drive sixty up-and-down saws the year round. This is our deliberate judgment, though not based upon careful survey."

Cumberland-Mills Falls, Westbrook.

The mean fall at the privileges is seven feet; mills will operate seven hours to the tide, with a common six-foot, perpendicular shaft, iron wheel.

WESTBROOK—CUMBERLAND COUNTY.

The Statement of George W. Hammond, Esq., in behalf of the Selectmen of Westbrook.

Twelve Powers.

Three of the above are situated on the Presumpscot river; one at Cumberland Mills village, five miles from Portland, on the Portland & Rochester Railroad, and two in the village of Saccarappa, six miles from Portland, also on the same railroad.

First, "Cumberland Mills Power," a fall of 20 feet, containing 14 mill-powers, or 2,013 horse-powers, of which about one-half is now in use in the manufacture of paper. The mean velocity of the stream is 1.52 feet per second, or 18¼ inches, taken from five observations; the mean depth of the stream, taken 500 feet above the falls, (an average of cross section of 682½ feet) is 3.31 feet; the width of the stream being 176 feet.

The mills are owned by S. D. Warren, Esq., and are worked the whole year. They give employment to 125 men and 100 women, and produce an annual manufacture of over $1,000,000. The improvement of the power has increased the population and wealth of the village to a very large extent, there being from 1854 to 1867 an increase of resident families from 16 to 66, and of dwelling-houses for the same period, from 16 to 48. The height of these falls above the sea is about 30 feet, and the range from high to low water is five feet. The market is chiefly Boston and New York, reached by Portland & Rochester Railroad and teams to Portland, thence by railroad and steamers.

Second and Third, the "Upper Power," at the village of Saccarappa, has a fall of 12 feet, and the "Lower Power" of 19 feet; containing, respectively, 13 and 8 mill-powers, making a total of 21 mill-powers; of which number 13 are now in use. The cross section of the upper fall is about 10 feet, and that of the lower eight feet, taken 15 feet above the falls. A small portion of the powers is improved.

The several mills are owned as follows: on the northeast side of the river, by the Westbrook Manufacturing Company and Messrs. King & Warren. Those on the southwest side, by

Messrs. Warren & Walker, the Patent Wire Company, Judge Fitch, Hon. J. Libby, and others.

The following are the productions of the mills and the names of those who now are working them, viz:

The Westbrook Manufacturing Company, in the manufacture of cotton, employing 75 men and 150 women, and producing over $300,000 annually.

Messrs. Dana & McEwan, in the manufacture of cotton yarn, employing 10 men and 10 women, and producing over $50,000 annually.

Messrs. Warren & Pennell, in the manufacture of wire, employing from 12 to 15 men, and producing about $30,000 annually.

Messrs. S. T. Raymond & Co.; grist and plaster mill; employing six men, and producing over $125,000 annually.

Messrs. Babb; iron foundry; employing 10 men and producing $12,000 annually.

Messrs. Knowlton Brothers; machine shop; employing four men and producing $4,000 annually.

Crowley's laundry, employing four men and two women, and producing $4,000 annually.

Foster's dye-house, employing four men, and producing $4,000 annually.

Messrs. Warren & Clements, in the manufacture of lumber, and grist mill, employing about 70 men, and producing about $600,000 annually.

Making the total amount of manufacture about $2,130,000.

The machinery is for the most part very good for economizing power, though not the best. The wheels used are Gates' centre-vent, Reynolds', Blake's and Tuttle's.

The reservoirs available to these powers may be seen upon reference to Part II, pages 143–4. The volume of freshets as compared with the ordinary volume of the stream, is but little more than double. There has been no destruction in past years from high water. The stream can be made uniform in its volume throughout the year. The lay of the land about these falls, with reference to the convenient location of mills and workshops, is all that can be desired for the most part. About one-eighth of the river basin is covered with forest. The height of the river at Saccarappa is about 62 feet above the sea. The out-cropping and underlying rocks, blue trap, are well adapted for rough, strong erections.

Duck Pond stream takes its rise from the pond of the same name, which pond is over three square miles in extent and over 20 feet average depth. It is supplied chiefly from small ponds and springs, and is 171 feet above the level of the sea. The stream is over 10 miles in length from "Pride's Bridge" to the pond, and is 161 feet above the river at this point. The width of the stream is pretty uniform at about 40 feet.

Fourth, the only improved power on this stream is at the outlet of the pond. The height of the falls is 17 feet, and the power is estimated at 50 horse. It is owned by the Cumberland Bone Manufacturing Company, and is employed in the manufacture of bone manure, and of pails and tubs; employing about 25 men and producing in the manufacture of bone manure about $25,000 annually, and that of pails and tubs about $20,000.

Fifth, Sixth, Seventh, Eighth and Ninth; there are five additional good mill-sites on this stream, which with the aid of dams would give a fall of from 15 to 22 feet each,, and from 50 to 75 horse-power. About one-sixth of the basin of the stream is covered with forest. The population and wealth are nearly all due to the power improvement. The market is chiefly in this State, by teams to Portland. Wheels are Tuttle's and spiral-vent. The capacity of the pond could not be increased with advantage to any great extent. There has been no injury in years past from freshets. Stream may be made perfectly uniform throughout the year. The lay of the land for mills and workshops, good. Rock, blue trap. Large quantity of granite very convenient.

Tenth, on the Stroudwater river, in the village of Stroudwater, about two and one-half miles from Portland. The falls are twelve feet high, and the grist, salt and spice mills upon them, are owned by W. H. Stevens. Three runs of stones and three Tub wheels, employ about eight men, produce about $20,000 annually; capable of grinding 40 bushels of corn per hour. The average depth of stream is about 10 feet, taken 100 feet above the falls. The falls are 12 feet above the sea. The market is chiefly Portland, reached by teams.

Eleventh and Twelfth, about three miles further up the stream, within one mile from the village of Saccarappa. The upper, known as the "Johnson Falls," is 17 feet high. The lower fall is 18.9 high, and is known as the "Babb Falls." The height specified is attained respectively in a horizontal distance of about 1,000 feet. The falls are situated about one-half mile from each other. The upper fall is rated 30, and the lower sixty-three and one-half horse-power.

There is a small threshing and saw mill owned by Rufus Johnson, but scarcely in running order yet. No other improvement on either fall. The river has only a small flow of water, but there is generally a stream of not less than one foot cube.

Lay of the land eligible for mill purposes. Trap rock; no injury to be apprehended from freshets. The dams for these two powers would require but a small outlay; the water could be taken in a penstock, and by so doing a dam one or two feet high, would be all that is required.

WEST GARDINER—KENNEBEC COUNTY.

Statement of the Selectmen.

Two Powers.

First, "Collins' Mills," on the Cobbosseecontee river; 16 feet fall; work all the year; saw, shingle, lath and picket machinery. Grist mill, two tanneries. Power sufficient for the largest manufactories; water abundant all the year. Lay of the land eligible for mill purposes.

Second, one mile above, 16 feet fall, and equally improvable with the other; no improvement.

The Cobbosseecontee being fed by great lakes which are improved for reservoirs, is free from drouths or freshets; the supply of water is copious, and can be made much more abundant. See "Reservoirs of the Cobbosseecontee," page 97, Part II, of this Report.

WESTON—AROOSTOOK COUNTY.

Statement of Selectmen.

Two Powers, Small.

First, on Cold brook, in the northwest corner of the town, with a privilege on it that has run a saw mill perhaps eight or ten weeks in a season.

Second, formerly a grist mill on Trout brook, in the southwest part of the town, that would grind a few weeks in a season.

WESTPORT—LINCOLN COUNTY.

Reported by Heal Brothers.

Three Powers.

First, a tide power, 10 acres of pond, a dam, a saw mill out of repair, will operate 12 hours per day; a turbine wheel of 20 horse-power. Not now in use.

Second, a tide power, 32 acres of pond, dam, saw mill in good repair; will run three turbines, 20 horse-power each, 12 hours per day, and cut 1,400,000 long lumber per year, and various short lumber. Owned by Heal Brothers.

Third, the "Riggs' Mill," tide power, 10 acres of pond, saw mill and grist mill, two turbine wheels, 12 hours per day, 20 horse-power each; cut 700,000 of lumber and grind 5,000 bushels of grain per year. Owned by Heal Brothers.

WHITEFIELD—LINCOLN COUNTY.

From Selectmen's Returns.

Ten Powers.

First, on the East branch of the Sheepscot river at the extreme northern limit of the town, a fine mill privilege, saw, grist, shingle and other machinery. Not occupied upon the western side.

Second, 20 rods south, a good privilege; shingle and grist mill.

Third, three miles south, on an outlet of Pleasant pond, a fine privilege within 20 rods of the main river; saw and shingle mill.

Fourth, one mile south, on the main river, a fine privilege; saw, shingle, grist, carding and clothing mills.

Fifth, on the western branch, two miles north, a good privilege; formerly a saw mill.

Sixth, south of the Fourth, about three miles on the main stream, a good privilege; formerly two saw mills.

Seventh, one mile south of the last mentioned, the best privilege on the river; formerly two saw mills, grist, box and shingle mills and blacksmith shop.

Eighth and Ninth, two and a half miles further south, a good privilege. In the southeastern part of the town, on a small stream flowing into the main river, another privilege; saw and shingle mill.

Tenth, on another small stream flowing into the *main river* near the centre of the town, half a mile north of No. Seven, a shingle mill. Other good privileges on the main river that have never been occupied.

The head and fall of each of the privileges on the main river will average 10 to 12 feet. Stream fed by various ponds, all used for reservoirs, and all capable of further improvement.

WHITING—WASHINGTON COUNTY.

Five Powers.

First, on Orange stream, the outlet of Orange, Rocky, and other ponds, covering three or four square miles; at the village, a grist mill, —— feet fall.

Second, a short distance above, a saw mill, fall —— feet.

Third, on the outlet of Roaring lake, a shingle mill.

Fourth, on the outlet stream of Rocky and several other ponds, a saw mill.

Fifth, on Holmes' stream in the southwest part of the town, a saw mill.

The powers on Orange stream are inferred to be of considerable value from the apparent facilities for storage on the lakes and ponds above.

WHITNEYVILLE—WASHINGTON COUNTY.

From the Returns of N. Bacheller, Esq.

One Power.

The "Middle Falls," or "The Mills," on Machias river. Height 10 feet in 50 rods. The dam is 15 feet high, and ponds the water back five or six miles. Improvements, three gang saw mills, five single saws, four lath mills, one shingle and one clapboard mill. Mills work about half of the year. Shingles and laths are sometimes sawed in the winter. The Stearns wheel used. Power owned by an association known as the Whitneyville Agency. The members of it reside part in Whitneyville and part in Boston.

The power with the present machinery, dams, etc., would saw 10,000,000 of long lumber, 10,000,000 of laths, 800,000 shingles, and 50,000 clapboards. In 1866 the mills cut 11,000,000 long lumber, 11,000,000 laths, 800,000 shingles, some clapboards, and a few thousand spool bolts.

With a good dam, a gang and single saw, and lath mill, could undoubtedly run through the whole summer.

If the volume of water in an ordinary summer season be assumed to be 14,500 cubic feet at this point, that at Machias being 15,000, the power on the whole fall of 25 feet is 675 horse or 27,000 spindles. With regard to the increase of the volume of water, see page 132, Part II, of this Report.

The lakes are now to a considerable extent dammed, but the water is used for only log-driving purposes, and of course is not available for manufacturing. Six hundred acres of artificial reservoirs may be had at small expense.

With the present machinery and no development of the lakes for summer storage, the power is about all used.

Market, by railroad to Machiasport, seven and a half miles distant, and thence by sea, in vessels of all sizes, to all quarters.

Williamsburg—Piscataquis County.

From Selectmen's Returns.

Three Powers.

First, on the west branch of Pleasant river, at the mouth of Roaring brook; would drive a saw mill and grist mill all the year. Unimproved.

Second, on Roaring brook, two miles from its mouth; would drive a grist mill and saw mill one-half of the year. It is unimproved. An artificial reservoir feasible.

Third, on Whetstone brook; a saw mill about going up, with shingle machine; will operate about half of the time.

First and Second are in the unbroken wilderness.

Wilton—Franklin County.

From the Statement of C. Bartlett, Esq., and the Returns of Maj. John H. Willard.

Twenty Powers.

Nine of the above are situated on Wilson's stream, the outlet of Wilson's pond, in the south part of the town, which forms the reservoir for the powers at and below the outlet.

This pond, according to the town plan, contains 390 acres; but the surface now flowed by the dam, which is five feet six inches high, is much greater. The pond is very deep; in one part no bottom can be found with a line 175 feet long. This great body of water retains the heat, so that there is no trouble from ice at the mills near the pond.

First, at the foot of the pond, head and fall of 15 feet; can be increased; saw and shingle mill, with right to draw one and a half feet below the top of the dam; will cut 3,000 feet hemlock and 7,000 shingles per day; except in drouth can saw most of the time summer and winter; also grist mill with complete equipment; uses with all gates hoisted 277 inches water; will operate six hours a day with full head and all gates hoisted, after the saw mill has to stop; also a starch factory, with right to draw water necessary, for nine months.

Second, below, about 40 rods, "Brown's Furniture Factory;" two planing machines.

Third, below, carriage shop, six feet head.

Fourth, nine feet head, "Furnel's Woollen Factory;" machinery not yet in.

Fifth, "Hobbs' Rake Factory," planing machine, etc.; seven feet fall.

Sixth, Bass' tannery; five feet head.

Seventh, fall 15 to 20 feet; F. Robbins; no improvement.

Eighth, below, Bartlett's saw mill, threshing machine, shingle machine; also a building 64 by 42 feet, flume built, ready for wheel, cotton yarn factory proposed; proprietor will let or lease; located within 40 rods of Androscoggin Railroad station; a most excellent privilege.

Ninth, 50 rods below, nine feet head can be had; J. Robbins; no improvement.

Tenth, one-half mile below, and one-third of a mile below the mouth of North Pond brook; 10 feet head can be had; W. S. Hinkley; no improvement.

Twelfth, below, and at East Wilton, Holt's scythe factory, Harper's saw mill, spade-handle factory, &c.; plenty of water year round.

Thirteenth, fall 13 feet; Wilton woollen factory; three sets machinery, 40 inch, now run. Mr. Townsend, the agent, says there is plenty water to run five sets.

Fourteenth, fall 10 feet; Swayne's estate; grist mill, shingle machine and threshing machine. In addition to the water of East Wilton, this power has the water from Pea pond, 99 acres.

North pond, the area of which is nearly equal to that of Wilson pond, (little over half its extent being represented on the county map) is now used as a reservoir by the East Wilton Woollen Manufacturing Company, who own the privilege and the right to control the water. On the outlet stream are several privileges.

Fifteenth, at the outlet, an old grist mill and saw mill, but not used.

Sixteenth, Seventeenth, Eighteenth, etc., below; small powers of not much value owing to the use now made of the pond for storage, the delivery of water being regulated by the demand at East Wilton.

Twentieth, on the main inlet of Wilson pond; small power; not occupied.

The water-power in this town is of unusual constancy owing to the land upon the tributary streams of the ponds being springy and charged with water, so that the reservoirs hold out remarkably.

It also enjoys excellent facilities of access to market, the Androscoggin Railroad passing in the immediate vicinity of the Wilson-stream powers.

Windham—Cumberland County.

From the Statement of William H. White, Esq.

[See also "Gorham and Windham," and "Standish and Windham."]

Eight Powers.

First, the "Narrows' Falls,"on Pleasant river, at the outlet of Little Sebago pond, fall 10 feet; owned by J. Pope & Co. Unimproved, the mills having been carried off by the dam giving away.

Second, "Legrows' Falls," below, on the same river, seven feet fall. Unoccupied.

Third, "Carney's Falls," below, 10 feet fall, occupied by stave mill and other machinery.

Fourth, "Andrews' Falls," below, eight feet fall. Unoccupied.

Fifth, "Pope's Falls," below, ten feet fall, woollen, saw, stave mills, &c.

Sixth, "Allen's Falls," below, seven feet fall. Unoccupied.

Seventh, "Baker's Falls," below, 10 feet fall, stave mill.

The above powers are valuable, the supply of water being constant and freshets being wholly under control. Little Sebago pond is "ten miles long and a mile wide." It is already raised seven feet by a dam, and can be raised five feet more, increasing the storage capacity nearly three-fold.

Eighth, "Kennard's Mill," on the outlet of Turtle, Mud, and other ponds; fall seven feet, stave mill.

Market, Portland, by canal, road, and part by rail.

Windsor—Kennebec County.

Four Powers.

First, on the west branch of Sheepscot river, south of the centre of the town, grist and saw mills.

Second, above, at the junction of the river and the Sevade pond stream, a saw mill; a large mill pond and two considerable ponds on the stream.

Third, on the outlet stream of Moody pond, a saw mill.

Fourth, a saw mill on a small stream in the south part of the town.

WINN—PENOBSCOT COUNTY.

From the Returns of Winn.

[See also "Chester and Winn," and "Mattawamkeag and Winn."]

Three Powers.

First, "Upper Mattakeunk Falls," on the Mattakeunk river; fall 50 feet in 100 rods; saw mill. Otherwise totally unimproved.

Second, "Lower Mattakeunk Falls;" fall 15 feet in 125 rods; not improved. About 500 square inches of water.

Third, rapids on Salmon stream; saw mill; otherwise not used; will operate half the year.

All the powers, except the last, will carry a large amount of machinery all the year. An insignificant portion of the power is now improved. Granite and slate rock abundant; sites excellent, in every case. Nine-tenths of the basins of the streams are covered with wood. Yearly product of mills, about 1,000,000 feet lumber. Stream fed by Mattakeunk pond 1,000 acres, dammed; can be made a great reservoir.

Market, Bangor, by rail and river.

WINSLOW—KENNEBEC COUNTY.

From Selectmen's Returns, including a Plan of the Water-Power.

[See also "Waterville and Winslow."]

Seven Powers, and More.

First, on the Mill brook, fed by large ponds in China. "Upper Dam;" a woollen factory, owned by J. D. Lang; turns out eighty dollars per day of manufactures when in operation. Peg factory on the other side.

Second, "Second Dam;" no machinery in operation.

Third, "Haydon's Dam;" saw mill, shingle mill, threshing machine, picket mill, and the power is but partially used.

Fourth, "Fourth Dam;" saw, shingle, picket and lath machine; power part used.

Fifth, on the outlet of Pattee's pond; grist mill and shingle mill; formerly a saw mill; power only partially used.

Sixth, on the outlet of Webber's pond; a saw mill; can operate one saw.

From Benton falls to the mouth of the Sebasticook, I. E. Getchell, Esq., reports a fall of 22 feet six inches, the whole distance being five miles. From the falls to Winslow line, three-fourths of a mile run, and eight feet six inches fall; thence to the head of dead water one and a quarter miles run, and six feet eight inches fall; thence two miles of dead water and two feet four inches fall; thence to the mouth of the river, one mile run and five feet fall; total fall as above.

Mr. Getchell judges a fine power could be developed at the mouth of the Sebasticook, the bottom and banks being favorable for dam and mills; logs can be taken from both the Sebasticook and Kennebec.

WINTERPORT—WALDO COUNTY.

Statement of the Selectmen.

Seven Powers, or More.

First, "Plummer's Mills," on the Marsh river, fall 25 feet; power sufficient to run saw, stave and shingle mills.

Second, the "Boyd Mill," on Marsh river, fall 15 feet; saw mill.

Third, "Tapley Mills," on Marsh river, 15 feet fall; power has been sufficient to carry a grist mill with two runs of stone, saw mill, and card and clothing mill. Mill was burned last fall, and has not been rebuilt.

Fourth, on Cole's brook, at North Winterport, "Baker Mill," fall 12 feet; stave and shingle mill.

Fifth, Sixth, Seventh, etc. There are several more privileges on the Marsh river, never occupied, between the above mentioned mills.

WINTHROP—KENNEBEC COUNTY.

From Selectmen's Returns.

Six Powers.

Four situated at the village, and between the two ponds called North and South.

First, a woollen factory, 15 feet head and fall; manufactures blankets, &c.; uses 400 pounds wool per day, and pays $100 per day for labor; amount of goods sold per annum, $150,000.

Second, a grist mill of about the same power, and a bark and fulling mill, on same dam. The grist mill grinds 12,000 bushels of grain of all kinds per annum; the bark and fulling mills are unemployed.

Third, a saw mill and cotton factory, same dam, about 12 feet head and fall; mill saws about 200,000 feet of lumber annually; the factory makes cotton yarn and lines; amount of goods manufactured and sold, $75,000.

Fourth, "Whitman's Agricultural Tool Manufactory," manufactures cider mills, horse and hand rake, planing, threshing and winnowing machines, &c., &c.; iron machine shop, foundry, &c., connected, and a saw mill on the same dam; about the same as the other privileges for power; the mill cuts out 500,000 lumber per year. The agricultural implements, &c., manufactured and sold, amount yearly to from $75,000 to $100,000.

Fifth, on a small stream leading from Carlton pond, in East Readfield, is used only a part of the year; occupied by Jacob Pope of Manchester, to polish and finish hay forks, &c.; formerly used for a saw mill.

Sixth, on a small stream leading from a small pond in East Winthrop, used by Parlin Brothers for grinding bark, &c., for a tannery.

WISCASSET—LINCOLN COUNTY.

From Selectmen's Returns.

Twelve Powers.

First to Eighth, inclusive, on Mt. Sweag stream; all have been, in times past, improved; only one at present, McKenney's grist mill; six or seven feet fall; grinds six months in the year; (average) about 10 bushels per hour.

The other mills, saw and grist, have all been carried away or burned; height of fall at other places before dams were carried away, five or ten feet; average six, and about the same power of the one now standing. One of the mills sawed 100,000 feet boards, etc., per year.

Ninth, in the eastern part of the town; Wright's grist and plaster mill; partly a tide mill; grinds 50 bushels of corn to a tide. Kendall wheel; finds it much better than the Partridge or Atkins wheel for tide wheel.

Tenth, Eleventh and Twelfth, tide mills, south part of the town; saw from 100,000 to 500,000 feet per year.

WOODSTOCK—OXFORD COUNTY.

From Selectmen's Returns.

Four Powers.

First, on Concord river, the outlet of Little and Great Concord ponds. The capacity of these ponds might be increased with small expense. Six miles from market, and a bad road; "Perry's Saw Mills," operate three or four months in the year. A large quantity of spruce and hemlock in the vicinity; also a small amount of pine.

Second, at the outlet of Bryant's pond, two miles from Bryant's Pond village, on the Grand Trunk Railroad. Some timber in this vicinity; privilege not improved; it offers decided advantages for manufacturing upon a small scale. The capacity of this pond could be increased without a very heavy expense; it has already been considerably increased by a company located at South Paris. Great quantity of granite in the vicinity and of good quality.

Third, on a branch of the Little Androscoggin river; convenient to market. "Andrews' Mill," boards, coffins, sash, doors, &c. Small amount of timber in this vicinity.

Fourth, at North Woodstock, on a branch of the Little Concord river, two miles from Bryant's Pond station on the Atlantic and St. Lawrence Railroad. "Crocker's Saw Mill," not used now. Considerable timber in this vicinity; the location offers advantages for manufacturing lumber on a limited scale.

The natural falls at these privileges are slight, their capacity being increased by dams. Wheels and machinery are not generally of the most approved kind. Freshets have done but slight damage in years past; streams variable.

WOOLWICH—SAGADAHOC COUNTY.

Five Powers, and More.

First, on a creek tributary to Back river, a tide power, two saw mills.

Second, a tide power in the southeast part of the town, a saw mill, quite a mill pond.

Third, at the mouth of the Monsweag river, a saw mill.

Fourth, on a tributary to the Monsweag river, a grist mill.

Fifth, on the outlet stream of Nequosset pond, a saw mill; pond covers nearly a square mile.

Various sites for tide mills.

YARMOUTH—CUMBERLAND COUNTY.

From Selectmen's Returns.

Six Powers.

They are called—one, "Gooch's;" four, "Baker's;" one, the "Factory Fall." All are situated on Royal river; combined height, 66 feet in one mile.

Power estimated sufficient to grind 75 bushels of grain per hour each; more could be done with the best machinery. Mills work all the year.

Stream connected with three small ponds. Range from lowest to highest water, six feet. Effect of the improvement of the power upon the wealth of the town, excellent.

Sabbath-day pond in New Gloucester, is now, 1869, being converted into a reservoir to Royal river; 10 feet head will be commanded upon the pond and surrounding low land, 500 acres in all.

Market, Portland, by Grand Trunk Railroad, and by sea.

YORK—YORK COUNTY.

From Selectmen's Statement.

Two Powers.

First, "Chase's Wool Factory," upon a fall of 19 feet, on the outlet stream of Chase's pond, 350 acres in extent. A pond above, of 100 acres, might easily be drained into Chase's pond.

Second, two miles below, "Webber's Mills," on a fall of 35 feet; saw, grist, and shingle mills.

None of the mills work all the year.

Z TRACT—PENOBSCOT COUNTY.

[South of Nicatou.]

One Power.

On Pattagumpus stream, a saw mill.

APPENDIX.

In his report of the water-powers in Bradley, Milford and Oldtown, S. F. Harrison, Civil Engineer, gives the following details respecting the volume of the Penobscot river:

"August 22, 1868, I measured a section of the river about half a mile below the Great Works Mills (Bradley and Oldtown) where I found a very uniform bed and uniform current, about 2,000 feet in length, and with a breadth of water at the time varying from 377 to 400 feet. Soundings were taken every 10 feet, and the surface current timed at each section by floats, for 1,000 feet. The measurements of the current were made in the afternoon, commencing at 3 o'clock, the accumulations in the mill-ponds above the dams made in the hours of partial non-use in the night time having by that hour become drawn down, and the river accordingly running at its natural minimum volume. The volume found was 243,480 cubic feet per minute."

This exceeds considerably, it will be noticed, Mr. Mills' estimate for the excessive drouths of 1864–5. See page 105.

Mr. Harrison estimates the maximum flow at this point in the spring freshet of 1869, at 4,200,000 cubic feet per minute, not including the Stillwater branch.

The range from lowest to highest water at this point is in the average of years, nine feet. In the spring of 1869 it was nine feet three inches. At other points in this general section of the river the range is greater, from 13 to 14 feet.

Bradley—Penobscot County.

Statement of S. F. Harrison, Civil Engineer, based upon his Survey in August and September, 1868.

[See also "Bradley and Oldtown," and "Bradley and Orono," in Appendix.]

Eighteen Powers.

Eleven of these are on the Great Works stream, and seven on the Blackman or Nichols stream.

First, on Great Works stream, about 40 rods from its outlet into the Penobscot, and 11 miles from Bangor; fall 11 feet; two shingle mills; owned by N. Kittredge & Co. Run nine months in the year, manufacture 2,500,000 shingles. The mills are so situated as to take stock from the Penobscot as well as from their own pond.

The erection of a 5-foot dam at the foot of the meadow one and a quarter miles up stream, would form a reservoir of about 800 acres, ponding the water back about six miles, and supply water sufficient for 15 horse-powers through three months drought, the power for the remainder of the year would be much larger.

Second, Third, Fourth, Fifth, and Sixth. Above this power and below said meadow, are four other powers of nine feet head and fall each, and one of 14 feet head and fall. The last-mentioned has been improved by mills and dam, burned a few years ago.

Seventh, seven miles above, on the north branch of said stream, "Shepley's Falls," formerly shingle mills, burned a few years ago. Sufficient water to run a shingle mill eight months in the year and do good business.

Eighth, Ninth, Tenth, Eleventh, Twelfth, above, on the same branch, and within two miles, head and fall from 11 to 14 feet each; a 6-foot dam at the upper would pond back the water about three miles, and furnish a reservoir of about 60 acres. There are no large ponds on this branch.

About nine-tenths of the basin of this stream is wooded, and large quantities of timber are cut and hauled into the stream every year.

On the Blackman or Nichols stream there are seven powers all within nine to ten miles of Bangor, and at varying distances from the outlet of the stream into the Penobscot river for one and a half miles up said stream.

Thirteenth, the first or lowest on the stream, about 10 rods from the Penobscot; 11 feet head; a single saw, shingle and lath mill, one each, run 10½ months, manufacture 500,000 feet of long lumber, 1,000,000 shingles, 500,000 laths; stock can be taken from the Penobscot river into the mill, and the lumber can be very conveniently loaded on teams or rafted down the river to Bangor. This power is perfectly safe from danger by ice or freshets, and is considered by lumbermen one of the best powers on the river. Owned by Blackman brothers, who also own all the other powers on the stream except two.

Fourteenth, about 20 rods above, at present unoccupied, grist mill going up soon.

The total fall at the foregoing two powers, is 28½ feet in a horizontal distance of 25 rods. A toll-bridge across the Penobscot near these two powers is soon to be built, giving access to Orono and the European and North American Railway, greatly enhancing the value of all the powers on the stream.

Fifteenth, Sixteenth, Seventeenth, Eighteenth, above, and within one and a half miles, unimproved; head and fall from nine to 12 feet each. One of nine feet fall is improved by two shingle mills, one set of heading machinery, which run 10½ months, and manufacture 2,000,000 shingles, 60,000 feet spool lumber, 53,000 pair heading, 50,000 staves, 40,000 broom handles.

Both of the improved powers have ample ponds for the storage of all the stock they can manufacture, and more.

Bradley and Oldtown—Penobscot County.

Statement of S. F. Harrison, Civil Engineer, based upon his Survey in August and September, 1868.

[See also "Bradley," and "Oldtown," in Appendix.]

One Power.

"Great Works Falls," on the Penobscot river, about 11 miles from Bangor; elevated 70 feet above tide-water; total descent 11 feet.

The amount of power estimated for the volume of water found by Mr. Harrison in his survey, is 5,000 horse. Estimated for the volume found by Mr. Mills near Bangor in the great drouth of 1864–5, the power is about 3,000 horse.

The natural falls are formed of two ridges of ledge extending across the river about 80 rods apart, and with a fall of about three and a half feet each. The height of the upper ridge is increased one and a half feet by a low dam and apron occupying about 200 feet of the central part of the river. This dam is made low so as not to obstruct the passage of rafts, logs, &c. Adjoining the low dam on either side are higher dams (of wood) extending down the river and nearly parallel with its axis, to the Great-Works mills in Bradley, and to the West Great-Works mills in Oldtown. Said lateral dams are about 95 rods in length. The river at this point is about 700 feet in width.

Two blocks of saw mills and one shingle and clapboard mill are in occupation of this power on the Bradley side, owned by the Great-Works Milling and Manufacturing Company.

In said blocks there are three gang saw mills, 12 single, one muley, three lath, one clapboard, and three shingle mills; which manufacture in the seven months of running, 20,000,000 feet of long lumber, 14,000,000 laths, 300,000 pickets, 5,000,000 shingles, and 300,000 clapboards.

The power on this (Bradley) side of the river might be further improved by extending a dam down the bank of the river about 80 rods from the mills aforesaid, and so as to cross the outlet of Great Works stream. An increase of two feet head and fall would be obtained in the section below the mills by this means, or a total head of 13 feet. This would greatly increase this power at lowest water, and for five and a half months of the sawing season would increase it three-fold at least. It would also augment the capacity of the mill ponds for storing logs, &c., 50 acres. The expense for damages in making the improvement would not exceed $40,000. With the improvement aforesaid this power would not be equaled on the Penobscot river.

The lay of the land about this power is favorable for the erection of mills and the location of a town. The village at this place, called Great Works, has a population of about 700 inhabitants, who are mainly dependent upon the business furnished by this power. A large extent of unimproved lands, heavily wooded, near by, can be obtained cheap; about four-fifths of the town is covered by forest.

Market, Bangor, by road or by the river. Passengers and light freight cross the river by ferry-boat, and take the cars at the West Great-Works station, on the European and North American Railway. Heavy freight by teams one and a half miles to Milford, at either the European and North American Railway or the Bangor, Oldtown and Milford Railroad.

The Legislature at its session last winter granted a charter for a toll and railroad bridge, to cross the river at this point so as to connect with the European and North American Railway, and the prospects are favorable for its erection at no very distant day.

On the west side of the river at West Great Works in Oldtown, this power is improved by one block of mills, owned by Smith & Pearson, four gang saw mills, six single, three lath, one clapboard, two shingle mills; which run seven months and manufacture

20,000,000 feet of long lumber, 14,000,000 laths, pickets, &c., 4,000,000 shingles, 500,000 clapboards.

By a short branch track the cars of the European and North American Railway are run to these mills and loaded directly from the mills.

Bradley and Orono—Penobscot County.

Statement of S. F. Harrison, Civil Engineer, based upon his Survey in August and September, 1868.

[See also "Bradley," in Appendix, and "Orono."]

Two Powers.

First, an unimproved power located on the Penobscot river, about nine and three-fourth miles from Bangor, and one and one-fourth miles below the Great-Works falls. Total descent 13 feet from the foot of Great-Works falls. The banks of the river are sufficiently elevated to admit of a dam 11 feet high. The bed of the river at this point, and the left bank (Bradley side) to above high-water mark, are ledge, the bottom being solid bare rock for one-third the distance across, and for the remainder being covered by large stones. The width of the river here is about 500 feet. Seven feet of the fall are attained in the first half mile above said ledge; there is also the same amount (seven feet) of fall from this fall to the Orono mill-pond half a mile below.

Second power, "Ayer's Falls," 37 feet above tide-water, 10 feet fall; river 600 feet wide. For further particulars see report of Orono, of this power and of the "Basin Mills."

Milford—Penobscot County.

Statement of S. F. Harrison, Civil Engineer.

[See also "Milford and Oldtown," in Appendix.]

There is no water-power in Milford except upon the boundary, on the Penobscot river, an account of which is given below.

Milford and Oldtown—Penobscot County.

Statement of S. F. Harrison, Civil Engineer, based upon his Survey in August and September, 1868.

[See also "Milford," and "Oldtown," in Appendix.]

Three Powers.

First, "Oldtown Falls," on the Penobscot river, between the villages of Oldtown and Milford, 12 miles from Bangor, the head thereof being 92 feet above tide-water at Eddington bend.

Formation.—The natural fall is formed by a ledge extending across the river at nearly right angles to its general course, which serves as the foundation for the mills and dams built on each side of the central part of the river. Said central part for about 300 feet in width is free from all obstructions. The natural fall is 13 feet in a horizontal distance of 190 feet, with an additional descent of three and a half feet in 20 rods. The river at this point is about 800 feet in width.

Power.—These falls (in the first 190 feet) will furnish a constant power, day and night, during the lowest run of water, of 6,000 horses, and with dams at the head of the fall to increase its height a much greater amount. This is estimated for the volume of water found by Mr. Harrison in his survey. See Appendix, page 513.

Lay of the land, etc.—The lay of the land on both sides of the river is favorable for the location of manufacturing establishments. Large quantities of stone suitable for foundations are procurable near by, and boulder granite is also found in considerable quantities. Any amount of good granite can be easily and cheaply obtained at the celebrated Prospect quarry, and cheaply transported by vessel and rail. Good brick clay near at hand. Lumber for building purposes either manufactured or in the log is obtainable in almost unlimited quantities. The great Penobscot booms, in which are stored nearly all the lumber cut on the river, are about two miles above.

Accessibility.—This power is accessible by the Bangor, Oldtown and Milford Railroad, which has a branch track to the mills at Oldtown; and also by the European and North American and Bangor and Piscataquis Railways, both of which have stations near by this power both in Oldtown and Milford; the Bangor, Oldtown and Milford Railroad also has a station near this power in Milford, being one of the termini of said road.

Improvements.—These are as follows:—On the Oldtown side of the river, two blocks of saw mills with short dams connected therewith, all built in a substantial manner of wood, and owned by the heirs of the late Samuel Veazie.

Said blocks contain 14 single saw mills, five gang, three shingle, two clapboard, four lath mills; which run about seven months in the year (could run all the year,) and manufacture in that time 25,000,000 feet of long lumber, 4,500,000 shingles, 1,000,000 clapboards, 13,500,000 laths, pickets, &c.

The lumber finds a market at Bangor, being run down the river in rafts, or sent by rail on either of the aforesaid roads.

On the Milford side of the river there is one block of saw mills, with short connecting dams all built of wood, and comparing favorably with the other mills on the river. Owned by the Milford Mill Company.

Said block has six single saw mills, four gang, one shingle, one clapboard, and four lath mills; which run about seven months in the year, and manufacture 15,000,000 feet of long lumber, 13,500,000 laths, pickets, &c., 1,500,000 shingles, 500,000 clapboards. Marketed at Bangor, by raft and rail.

Second. The second power is located at the southern extremity of Treat and Webster's island in Oldtown, and is known as the "Rufus Dwinel Privilege." It is supplied with water through the dams of the Veazie mills, aforesaid, about half a mile above. This power is very secure from damage by ice and freshets. Is accessible by the European and North American Railway, which has a station within a few rods of the mills; a branch track could be laid to the mills with very little expense. Owned by Rufus Dwinel. Fall seven and a half feet. Power not measured.

This power is improved by a block of mills and dam owned by said Dwinel. The block of mills consists of two single saw mills, two muley, two gang, three lath, one clapboard and two shingle mills. They run seven months, and manufacture 12,000,000 feet long lumber, 10,000,000 laths, 3,000,000 shingles, 600,000 clapboards.

Third. The third power is located at "Shad Rips," about half a mile below Oldtown Falls, and between the east side of Treat and Webster's island in Oldtown and the left bank of the main branch of the Penobscot (Milford side), which is about 250 feet in width and has a fall of about eight feet in three-eighths of a mile. Lay of the land is favorable for the erection of mills and dwellings. Is now unimproved, formerly occupied by a saw mill. Power at lowest stage of water 2,000 horses. Ownership unknown.

Oldtown—Penobscot County.

Statement of S. F. Harrison, Civil Engineer, based upon his Survey in August and September, 1868.

[See also "Bradley and Oldtown," and "Milford and Oldtown," in Appendix.]

Three Powers.

First, "Pushaw Falls," 16 miles from Bangor, and on the line between Oldtown and Alton, a part of the falls and improvements in each town. This power is on Pushaw stream, the outlet of the Pushaw lake, which has an area of some 12 square miles.

Improved as follows: one gang saw mill, one single mill, one shingle mill; owned by Richard S. Porter; one brush-handle factory, owned by O. W. Whitten; and two shingle mills, owned by C. Douglass.

Second, "Cooper's Falls," on the Stillwater branch of the Penobscot river, 13 miles from Bangor.

Improved as follows: one gang saw mill, one single saw mill, one shingle mill; owned by J. C. Gilman; runs about five months in a year.

Third, at Upper Stillwater, 10 miles from Bangor; two gang saw mills, four single, two lath, one clapboard, and two shingle mills, owned by Smith & Pearson of Bangor. Also two gang saw mills, two single, one lath, one clapboard, and two shingle mills, owned by A. B. Sutton. About six weeks in the driest season do not run. A 6-foot dam a short distance below the meadow, and above all the powers, about one and three-fourth miles up the stream, would flow the meadow and lake Chemo about two feet, making a reservoir of about 2000 acres. This together with the other natural reservoirs above on the stream, would furnish a total power of 160 horse at least, night and day, at the lowest stage of water any season. The damages would be light for flowing, and the dam could be erected at little expense.

The natural reservoirs on the stream are as follows:

	Acres.
Parker's pond, in Clifton, (estimated)	100
Holbrook's pond, in Dedham, (surveyed)	322
Davis' pond, in Eddington, "	396
Lake Chemo, in Clifton, Eddington and Bradley (estimated)	1,500
	2,318

Lake Chemo is about four miles above the upper power, and by the dam aforesaid would be flowed about two feet above its natural level. About half of the basin of this stream is covered with forest; there is sufficient timber to last the mills many years.

INDEX

TO

PARTS I, II, and the First Division of PART III.*

* The Second Division of Part III is sufficiently indexed by the *alphabetical* arrangement of the towns.

www.ingramcontent.com/pod-product-compliance
Lightning Source LLC
LaVergne TN
LVHW021231110826
845150LV00002B/297

* 9 7 8 1 4 2 5 5 6 3 1 2 7 *